Citizens in Europe

Essays on Democracy, Constitutionalism and European Integration

Claus Offe
Ulrich K. Preuß

First published by the ECPR Press in 2016

The ECPR Press is the publishing imprint of the European Consortium for Political Research (ECPR), a scholarly association, which supports and encourages the training, research and cross-national co-operation of political scientists in institutions throughout Europe and beyond.

ECPR Press
Harbour House
Hythe Quay
Colchester
CO2 8JF
United Kingdom

Typeset by Lapiz Digital Services

Printed and bound by Lightning Source

British Library Cataloguing in Publication Data

A catalogue record for this book is available from the British Library

HARDBACK ISBN: 978-1-785-522-38-3
PAPERBACK ISBN: 978-1-785-521-42-3
PDF ISBN: 978-1-785-521-73-7
EPUB ISBN: 978-1-785-521-74-4
KINDLE ISBN: 978-1-785-521-75-1

www.ecpr.eu/ecprpress

Contents

Figures

Chapter One

The Union's Course: Between a Supranational Welfare State and Creeping Decay

Claus Offe and Ulrich K. Preuß

The politics of European integration and the management of its various crises is currently (fall of 2015) in an unusually hectic mode. The difficulties of the Eurozone produce front page news in all major media where highly consequential last minute decisions (and the contested authority of EU institutions to make them) are being reported and commented upon. From the Euro crisis to monetary policy, to the crisis in Ukraine, to the issues of refugee migration, policy makers adopt bold and untested measures to sail uncharted seas, fully aware of heightened risks and dangers.

In such a context it may seem slightly frivolous to prepare the publication of a volume, many of the contributions to which revisit the basic institutional features and normative principles of the European Union, elaborating on key concepts such as citizenship, constitutionalism and democracy. Aren't there, given the culmination and interaction of various crises, more urgent intellectual challenges to address and policy proposals to submit? In response to such doubts, we would like to insist at the outset that the crisis may be exactly the right time to reconsider some of the basics, such as they are indicated by the three concepts in the subtitle of the present volume. That, at least, was also the view of colleagues, most prominently Dario Castiglione, who are familiar with the work that either of the two authors (and occasionally also both of us jointly) have written. These colleagues have encouraged us to put together this collection of essays which were written over a period of more than 30 years. The hope, to be either fulfilled or frustrated by the judgement of critical readers, is that the normative and analytical arguments presented in our earlier work may still throw light on the issues that the EU and its citizens must come to terms with if the current turbulences of the European integration process are at all to be coped with. Hectic emergency pragmatics, in other words, are not enough.

What is the problem the EU and its citizens are facing? It consists in the coincidence of dilemmas, processes, contradictions, events and conflicting demands which, taken together, pose an extraordinary challenge to the EU's political capabilities, arguably even its survival. The most important components of this challenge are, briefly, the following:

- the 'Euro crisis' – aptly named that way because of a dual reference: a crisis *caused* by the ill-considered introduction of a common currency in an area that was not adequately prepared for it in economic and institutional terms and a crisis *affecting*, as a consequence of these deficiencies, the very viability of the currency area itself. Another aspect of the 'Euro crisis' is that the currency has driven a wedge into the EU which is now *divided* by its common currency and the winners and losers it has created;

- the economic crisis with deflationary tendencies and economic stagnation prevailing in many EU Member States, causing high rates of unemployment, in particular amongst young people, and also causing, together with extreme monetary policies adopted by the ECB and austerity-obsessed fiscal policies, a forceful onslaught on European welfare states and the, by now largely obsolete, 'European Social Model';
- 'mass immigration' into the EU and failure of the latter to cope with the rising tide of refugees and asylum-seekers in ways which minimally conform with Europe's declared humanitarian standards; in addition, even the Treaty-based freedom of mobility within the EU has come to be challenged by several Member States;
- within many Member States, we see an escalating erosion of *party systems* (which is at best marginally compensated for by the halting emergence of a transnational European party system). While centre-left and centre-right parties are losing electoral support (as well as the capacity to defend lost ground in terms of their hegemonic capacities as they have largely become indistinguishable administrators of political and economic realities to which, they claim, 'there is no alternative'), all countries on the 'winner' side of the Euro-divide have seen the rise of rightist populist parties, making, together with the rise of leftist protest parties in some of the 'loser' countries, for an unprecedented political destabilisation of Member States and, by implication, the EU polity as a whole;
- the Ukraine conflict and the confrontation with Russia which is critical not just because of its threatening military implications but also because it epitomises the failure of the EU's Eastern Neighborhood Policy (ENP) as well as the ambiguities involved in the accession of Serbia and the other aspiring Member States of the Western Balkans;
- the EU's helplessness and virtual strategic irrelevance in the face of the armed conflicts in its Middle East and North African (MENA) neighborhood, including the precarious geopolitical situation of Israel and its failure to settle the conflict with the Palestinians in the Occupied Territories.

With the (partial) exception of the latter crisis, all the others are to a large extent 'European' by origin – endogenous and home-made by Europeans and their political elites. They have been caused by deficiencies inside the institutional system of the EU – be it by inadequacies of its institutional structure itself, be it by the absence of political leaders with the requisite far-sightedness and the failure to adopt adequate precautionary policies. This shorthand list of current crises affecting the EU serves us just to highlight the discrepancy between these events and developments, on the one hand, and the basic normative commitments of the EU to principles of citizenship, constitutionalism, and democracy. To simplify: if these principles had been more vigorously adhered to and implemented, the impact of those cumulative crises could either have been prevented from emerging in the first place or more effectively coped with after it has manifested itself. The resulting problem can be summarised in the question: Which principles and which institutional embodiments of them are called for in order to strengthen the EU's capacity to cope with those crises and prevent their perseverance or repetition? Unless that key question can be answered, the EU is not just caught in a context of crises, it is itself the core and ongoing generator of crises, and eventually likely to become its victim.

The crisis of the EU: two cases

Let us briefly look at two instances where the political realities of the EU stand in blatant contradiction to its core normative principles, thus entangling it in a profound crisis of consistency and credibility. First, *the Greek debt crisis*. In January 2015 the Greek people elected a new political force into government which credibly vowed to end the decades-old system of clientelism, nepotism, corruption, excessive defence spending and tax evasion which eventually had driven the country to the verge of state bankruptcy and ungovernability. The previous government had not only seen itself forced to accept harsh restrictions of its fiscal policies imposed by its private and public creditors which saved Greece from insolvency, but also to subject its government to a strict regime of monitoring and control of its economic and social policies which large parts of the Greek population – and beyond in the European Union – considered as humiliating and as being contrary to any semblance of democratic self-rule. To end this external control imposed by the 'Troika' on the Greek government, which amounted to a veritable political expropriation of its constituency, has been the main promise in the victorious campaign of *Syriza*. The new government, sworn in on January 26, 2015, entered into negotiations with the finance ministers of the Eurozone with the objective of modifying the 'reform program' which the previous government had been forced to adopt by Greece's international lenders (ECB, IMF, EU Commission [representing the lending states of the Eurozone]). While the economic effects of that programme of 'austerity', 'structural reforms' and privatisation of state held assets were to a large extent plainly counterproductive by increasing rather than reducing the debt/GDP ratio, the social suffering it produced has been positively disastrous as the 'reforms' resulted in unprecedented levels of unemployment as well as the 'internal devaluation' of wages, pensions, and public services. Yet the Eurozone finance ministers insisted upon the legal bindingness of the obligations which Greece had incurred. In the name of *pacta sunt servanda* and under the self-righteous (if evidently mistaken) presumption of supranational paternalism ('we know better what is good for you than you do yourself'), Greeks were administered a poisonous medicine to the further taking of which the majority of the electorate expressed its clear refusal.

This election result indicated the desperate attempt to replace an old regime of two entrenched and corrupt centrist parties with a fresh political force. This old regime was, after all, one that had collaborated in producing the economic and fiscal disaster of Greece and had run the country down to virtually the status of a third-world country. Yet this democratic change of government was in no way respected and appreciated as such within the EU: it did not give rise to an EU-wide reconsideration of the appropriateness and viability of the conditions which have produced the misery of large parts of the Greek population. To the contrary, the unmistakably expressed will of the people was dismissed as unworthy of respect, giving rise to the bitter comment of one of the Greek ministers 'If we cannot change economic policy through elections, then elections are irrelevant'[1]. While in the realm of international politics this democratic argument is normally overruled by the cold logic of creditor-debtor relations, the democratic nature of an electoral outcome should provide a compelling argument in the framework of the EU which proclaims 'democracy' as one of its core values. Is not the EU's commitment to democracy, more than anything else, an essential element of its political identity? Instead, since the beginning of the Euro crisis in 2008/2009, there is a growing tendency among EU Member States towards mutual distrust and nationalist-chauvinist quarrel which politicised their economic and cultural diversity and heterogeneity to an extent which is on the verge of undermining the entire European integration project. The idea of a supranational, i.e., heterogeneous democracy, while deeply underlying the philosophical idea and the institutional setup of the EU, is largely absent in the conduct of its policies.

The events of Greece's turbulent summer of 2015 provide compelling evidence of how the European 'institutions' have used their power to overrule the results of a democratic political process in one of the EU member states. Here is a brief recapitulation of the time line.[2] On June 25th, the 'Troika' (a supervisory body consisting of representatives of the ECB, the IMF and the European Commission installed after the adoption of the first Greek bailout program of 2010) specified its harsh austerity conditions for a renewed (third) Greek bailout programme. In mid-2015, the country had arrived at a truly dismal economic situation, unparalleled in any advanced country during peace time: GDP was down 25 per cent since 2010, unemployment averaged at 26 per cent (with a large part of the unemployed receiving no social insurance benefits whatsoever), wages went down by 38 per cent and pensions by 45 per cent. 32 per cent of the population live below the poverty line and the critical ratio of sovereign debt to GDP was approaching 180 per cent. The solvency of Greek banks is threatened by huge amounts of non-performing loans extended to both the public and the private sector.[3]

On June 27th, Prime Minister Tsipras called a referendum on the bailout conditions, which was held on July 5th. 62 per cent of voters rejected those conditions. On July 8th, Tsipras applied for an emergency loan of the European Stability Fund. Contrary to the vote of more than three fifths of voters, Tsipras had to accept the terms of a third bailout package during the decisive negotiations that took place in the Euro group in the night of July 12th in Brussels. This package provided for conditions which are even considerably *harsher* than those rejected by Greeks in the referendum. They stipulated further spending cuts (among other things concerning pensions), tax rises designed to achieve a primary budget surplus of 3.5 per cent of GDP by 2018, large scale privatisation of state-owned assets as well as a detailed schedule specifying which legislation must pass the Greek parliament within days or weeks, respectively.[4] Moreover, the Greek government 'commits to consult and agree with the European Commission' on every step of this legislative agenda, practically handing over Greek law-making powers to a non-elected body in Brussels. Jürgen Habermas rightly speaks of this exercise of raw power as the '*de facto* relegation of a member state to the status of a protectorate [that] openly contradicts the democratic principles of the European Union'.[5] The two components of this blackmail were (a) the Commission dictating the legislative agenda and decisions of the Greek parliament (which was given two days to pass required legislation, which it did on July 15th) by (b) forcing Prime Minister Tsipras to perform a plain U-turn[6] regarding the majority will the Greek electorate had expressed – and Tsipras had strongly advocated – just a week prior to the negotiations of July 12th. 'Ten days after 62 per cent of the voters rejected the terms of a harsh bail-out package, the country's parliament voted with clenched teeth for an even tougher set of reforms.'[7]

How could this brutal act of overpowering the will of the Greek people succeed? When submitting to *power* (as opposed to force or coercion), the less powerful party in a conflict makes a *choice* opting for the 'lesser evil' among two or more alternatives which are presented to it by the more powerful player. The latter exploits a condition of asymmetrical dependency for serving its own interests: Trivially, Greece depends more strongly on the ECB and the other Eurogroup members than these depend on Greece. The logic of the situation was the following: As Greece needed to obtain financial assistance from the EU in order to prevent an imminent meltdown of its banking sector (and, as a consequence, its entire economy), the country's population and its government were given the choice between being politically expropriated (deprived of the 'ownership' of even its legislative agenda, let alone sovereignty) and being instantaneously plunged into an economic disaster. Yet the negotiators on the other side of the bargaining table had also to worry about the consequences of the latter alternative, the disaster, being realised.

These worries were twofold. On the one side, the appearance and subsequent reputational and political damage had to be kept under control that negative economic consequences for Greece were caused by the pressure exercised by the majority of Eurozone members and of Germany[8] in particular. On the other, a 'Grexit' (or, even more so, a 'Graccident' in the form of an unregulated implosion of the Greek banking system and economy with all its unpredictable spillover effects) might have consequences that affected, through contagion or a domino effect, other members of the Eurozone, thus bringing the entire Euro system into jeopardy – an outcome and potential self-inflicted damage for which the protagonists of a tough approach to the bailout conditions imposed on the country would have had to anticipate blame. Given this dilemma, and also given the fact that the vast and deepening problems of the Greek economy could not possibly be solved, for legal reasons and because of the statutory irreversibility of the common currency,[9] by simply expelling the country from the Eurozone, the actual pressure used against the Greek negotiators had to be *disguised*.

For it is these two worries that appear to have motivated the German Minister of Finance to draft and circulate among Eurogroup negotiators (as well as leaking it to the media), one day prior to the negotiations scheduled for the evening of July 12th, the unprecedented suggestion to resolve on a procedure of a 'temporary Grexit', i.e. the creation of an option for Greece to leave the common currency zone for a period of five (or more) years with the (entirely unrealistic) option of re-entry at a later point.[10] Greece's making use of this option was actually incentivised in Schäuble's proposal so as to make it tempting and to create the appearance of a completely *voluntary* move. This was done by the promise attached to it of technical, humanitarian and other assistance, as well as other gestures of 'generosity' extended to the country once it accepted the leave offered to it.

Had the Greek government actually accepted this poisonous gift, it would have instantaneously relieved Schäuble and the other negotiators of the two above worries: It would have endorsed the appearance of German generosity, confirmed the narrative of a voluntary exit, and insulated the Euro system as a whole from the Greek crisis and the menace of spillover effects. Moreover, it would have taught a lesson to whoever might be tempted to emulate the Greek mistake of 'excessive' indebtedness. It would also have camouflaged the exercise of power, making its outcome appear as a freely adopted mutual agreement. Yet it would also have been an act, on the part of the Greek authorities, of causing near-suicidal damage to their country: For a 'voluntary' exit would have cut off the country from European structural funds (worth transfers of five billion Euros p.a.) and it would have necessitated the adoption of a heavily devalued national currency with the effect of substantially increasing the country's – Euro-denominated and hence entirely unsustainable – debt burden. Given this configuration of alternatives, the choice Greek negotiators made was understandably and rationally the option of submitting to blackmail.

In retrospect, this outcome is criticised on two counts: for being *illegitimate* as to its mode of coming into being and for being *ineffective* concerning its promise to solve the problems of the Greek economic, fiscal and debt crises in a durable fashion. As to its legitimacy (its capacity to oblige compliance on normative grounds), the following objections continue to be raised.[11] In response to its request for 'stability support' addressed to the European Stability Mechanism on July 8th, the Greek government was offered a third 'Memorandum of Understanding' (MoU) that specified, on its 32 pages, the legislative measures the Greek authorities would have to adopt by which month and year during the period of 2015 to 2017. This 'extraordinarily detailed list'[12] implied that legislative powers in the areas of fiscal policy, the financial system, economic policy, and the modernisation of all major branches of public administration and the judiciary were practically to be ceded to the Commission and agencies (such as the International Labor Office and the OECD) which the Commission has endowed in the Memorandum with advisory and supervisory roles. In general, the Greek government must 'commit to consult and agree with the European Commission ... on all actions relevant for the achievement of the objectives of the Memorandum ... before these are finalised and legally adopted'.[13]

Unsurprisingly, this wholesale usurpation of Greek law-making authorities by EU institutions met with the objection, in Greece itself and far beyond, that it amounts to a massive violation of the democratic principles on which the EU is supposedly built. Moreover, the politically non-accountable EU agencies who have authored the list of conditions that Greece must fulfill in exchange for a loan of 86 billion Euro for a period of three years vindicate themselves, by implication, with the wisdom that established two interrelated truths, the practical implications of which are to be paternistically enforced. First, the truth that the fully compliant implementation of the letter of the MoU will be compatible with *political* stability within Greece; second, that such implementation will be conducive to the *economic* recovery of Greece and its social, economic and fiscal viability. Both of these propositions, however, are heavily contested.

As to the first, it relates to the issue of legitimacy. The MoU is criticised for being in outright violation of the Greek people's sovereignty and self-determination. Given the political will expressed in the referendum of July 2nd, it is deemed 'inconceivable that any circumvention of the referendum outcome can ever be "in the interest of the Greek people"'.[14] Moreover, an implied violation of human rights (such as the right to health services) is seen by critics in the specification of the MoU concerning fees to be collected by hospitals. Legitimacy complaints have also been raised concerning the attempted blackmail stemming from members of the ECB Governing Council concerning a discontinuation of the ECB's emergency assistance as well as the threats of a 'temporary Grexit' coming from the German minister of finance. At the level of principle, the question is being raised as to why, in case a debtor turns out to be insolvent and the respective loan 'non-performing', the problem must be solved at the expense of the *debtor*, while the *creditor* (who quite arguably has entered into an evidently risky lending transaction expecting that he would be bailed out at a third party's expense) does not suffer any damage. To the extent this argument from fairness is valid, it would result in a justified demand for debt repudiation.

Finally, as to the issues of effectiveness, the assumed conduciveness of legislative measures imposed upon Greece (austerity, deregulation, reforms, privatisation of state-owned assets) to the economic recovery of the country is wide open to question. The primary budget surplus required – 3.5 per cent of GDP by 2018 – obstructs the possibility of stimulating growth by means of fiscal policy. Being the third MoU since 2010, one might have expected the Commission and its experts to have learned from the plain counter-productivity of the two previous editions of a trade of loans for austerity measures. The above-quoted indicators of the condition the Greek economy finds itself in, in 2015, should have provided ample evidence of the counterproductive effect of the previous programmes. According to Christine Lagarde, the IMF's Managing Director,

Greece's debt has become unsustainable ... Greece cannot restore debt sustainability solely through actions of its own. ... Greece's debt ... is expected to peak at close to 200 per cent of GDP in the next two years. ... Greece's debt can now only be made sustainable through debt relief measures that go far beyond what Europe has been willing to consider so far.[15]

If that is so, the very term 'debt' as a designation of the funds that have been transferred to Greece by private and public lenders must rather be seen to be nothing but a mendacious misnomer, invented and used for the purpose of demolishing the economic fates of an EU member state while buying (at most) three years worth of time before the issue will be on the table again.

Our second case of the EU's violation of its own core commitments relates to its *policies of asylum and immigration*.[16] The Arab Spring of 2010/2011 which had elicited many hopes for the liberation of the Arab societies from their authoritarian yokes – hopes which had been praised and applauded by northern neighbours on the European continent – in fact ended in a genuine political and humanitarian nightmare, not to mention the proliferation of state failure in Yemen, South Sudan, and Somalia and the long term consequences of the US-initiated interventions in Iraq and Afghanistan. Civil wars in Libya, Syria and Iraq and a harsh quasi-military dictatorship in Egypt triggered a huge flood of refugees which has already turned into a major challenge to the small neighbours of Syria, Jordan and Lebanon, and even to Turkey. But Europe was affected as well. Substantial numbers of these war refugees tried to escape to Member States of the EU.

The EU's reaction to the plight of refugees from civil wars and their desperate attempts to reach European soil is in no way consistent with its and its Member States' commitment to the protection of human rights. The competence for asylum and immigration was transferred from the Member States to the EU in 1997 through the Amsterdam Treaty. What this transfer of sovereign rights of Member States envisaged was a European policy of asylum and migration which recognized the right to asylum 'with due respect' for the rules of the Geneva Refugee Convention of 1951[17]. This Convention includes, *inter alia*, the prohibition of *refoulement*, i.e. the expulsion or return of a refugee 'to the frontiers of territories where his life or freedom would be threatened on account of his race, religion, nationality, membership of a particular social group or political opinion'.[18] But in the legal framework of the EU an important qualification applies: the EU commits itself to the protection of refugees 'in accordance' with the Treaty on European Union (TEU) and the Treaty on the Functioning of the European Union (TFEU).[19]

These treaties establish, as a key condition for the exercise of the right to apply for asylum in the EU, the physical presence of the applicant in the territory of one of the EU Member States, as now the new EU-Directive on the procedural requirement of asylum application explicitly specifies.[20] Hence, the actual chances of refugees to reach the border of an EU member state and to cross it in order to apply for asylum determine the extent of the protection of asylum-seekers' rights to which the EU has committed itself. Obviously the EU can influence those chances of refugees, either by facilitating the entry into its area of protection or by erecting obstacles to access. A cursory glance at the treaties and the implementing provisions clearly display the EU's dominant concern to prevent refugees from entering the territory of an EU member state and thus to avoid the applicability of the *refoulement* prohibition as far as possible.[21] Rights are being guaranteed on paper, but access to places where they can be claimed is barred. Refugees and asylum seekers experience the EU as 'Fortress Europe'.

But this 'Fortress Europe' is far from internally solid and cohesive. Consisting of a plurality of 28 'independent duchies', each of which is interested in minimising the costs of the humanitarian obligations which they regard primarily as a burden, it is not easy to develop a common asylum and immigration policy in the spirit of 'solidarity and fair sharing of responsibility, including its financial implications, between the Member States'.[22] In fact, the fairness of the rules and mechanisms which determine the responsibilities for taking charge of the refugees who seek protection in the EU is questionable. According to the so-called Dublin rules the Member States with external borders are charged with hosting the arriving refugees and processing their asylum claims. This principle is underpinned by two complementary elements, namely, the Member States' determination of, first, safe third countries, in which the application of the Refugee Convention is considered to be assured to the effect that anybody who enters a EU Member State from such a state does not qualify for the right to asylum, and, secondly, of safe countries of origin of an asylum applicant actuating the rebuttable presumption that an applicant from such a country is not supposed to be subject to persecution on the grounds laid down in the Refugee Convention. These rules were devised as an incentive for the border countries of the EU to efficiently protect the external borders of the Union and thus to limit the number of asylum claimants in the EU.

The implementation of these rules does neither satisfy the standards of the decent treatment of applicants for international protection laid down in a separate EU Directive, nor does it fulfill the mutual promise of solidarity among the EU Member States. Quite to the contrary, the dispute about every Member State's fair share of the burden to receive refugees gave rise to mutual resentment among the Member States of the EU.

As regards solidarity among Member States, the state responsible for the processing of the asylum applications is largely left alone. Once a refugee has entered an EU Member State, this state can never get rid of this responsibility without the consent of the other Member States (which is normally denied). If a refugee leaves this country and travels to another EU Member State, be it because his or her application has been rejected, be it that (s)he withdrew it or did not await the end of the procedure, the state that is responsible must take him or her back on the request of the Member State into which the refugee moved. As the vast majority of refugees to the EU take the route via the Eastern Mediterranean Sea, its coastal states Malta, Greece, and Italy have to bear the lion's share of taking charge of them, including the obligation to take back those who left the coastal state for another EU Member State – an obviously unfair scheme of burden sharing. True, in 2010 the EU established a European Asylum Support Office (EASO) which should provide adequate support to the relevant services of the Member States responsible for implementing first-entry principles. But it is restricted to facilitating, coordinating and strengthening practical cooperation between Member States, while relocation within the Union is only possible on an agreed basis between Member States.

The Dublin system is not only unfair to some Member States. It also affects negatively the rights of the asylum claimants. It presupposes an EU-wide common and relatively high standard of dealing with immigration; but, as the *European Council on Refugees and Exiles* (ECRE) stated in an assessment of the Dublin system, this presupposition 'is demonstrably inaccurate'.[23] The overload for the states that are responsible, merely due to their geographical location, means they cannot always provide decent accommodation, food and clothing, nor an appropriate duration in the proceedings about the outcome of the asylum seeker's application. Living conditions in the reception facilities, the quality of the application procedures and the acceptance rates diverge extremely between Member States. In several cases the European Court of Human Rights had to judge that asylum seekers in Greece – a country whose infrastructure has been on the verge of collapsing under the pressure of mass immigration for a long time – are 'likely to be subjected to a humiliating process, given the known procedural shortcomings of the asylum system'.[24] Some countries, like Germany, waived temporarily their right to send asylum seekers back to Greece on the ground that this country could not guarantee compliance with the EU standards for the reception of asylum-seekers.

Obviously, in September 2015 the Dublin system collapsed and definitively revealed the critical condition of the EU. It all started again – with Hungary, an almost ironic repetition of this country's triggering role in the great sea change of 1989. Since the beginning of 2015, Hungary, a country of less than ten million people with borders on non-EU-Members, Serbia and Ukraine, had experienced an inflow of nearly 150,000 asylum seekers at its border with Serbia which increased up to 3000 applicants per day in the first week of September – the fourfold of the numbers of 2014. The vast majority intended to migrate to Germany and hence refused to register as asylum claimants in Hungary. In June, the Hungarian government began with the construction of a border fence which did not only close its borders to Serbia, but, contrary to the Schengen Conventions, also to its fellow Member State Croatia. On the 6th September, 'after intense communication' between Budapest, Vienna and Berlin, the German Chancellor declared that Germany would respond to the humanitarian crisis in Hungary in the spirit of compassion and opened its borders for thousands of refugees that were jammed unsheltered in Budapest. However, the German government insisted that this act was a unique response to an exceptional situation of 'acute' distress which did not mean the suspension of the binding force of the Dublin rules.

Chancellor Merkel's magnanimous gesture opened the floodgate for an unmanageable mass entry of asylum claimants arriving via the 'Balkan route'. The opening of the borders of Germany, the target state of the vast majority of refugees, boosted the pressure on the borders of the upstream countries of the Balkans and triggered a considerable pull effect on the migration into the EU in general and to Germany in particular. Moreover, this flow of refugees has been self-augmenting as a conflict between EU Member States and signalled to potential refugees a 'now-or-never' condition. Largely defenceless against the upsurge of an unending flow of migrants mostly from wrecked Syria, the states on the route from Greece to Germany and Sweden – apart from Greece Macedonia, Serbia, Croatia, Slovenia – now began to act as mere transit states. They conduct the flow of refugees through their small countries and direct it to Austria, and finally Germany, which meanwhile – at the end of October 2015 – groans under the burden of more than one million refugees expected to arrive until the end of the year.

We are not able to suggest a viable solution to the European refugee crisis. But we can argue for a fairer distribution of the burdens of mass immigration among the EU Member States and a more humane and compassionate dealing with the challenge of the inflow of individuals who have lost their homes and the premises of a normal peaceful life, and who are desperately in need of protection and relief. According to the UNHCR, in 2014 almost 60 million individuals were forcibly displaced worldwide as a result of persecution, conflict, generalised violence and human rights violations. In the same year 625,000 individuals applied for asylum in the EU[25] – slightly more than 1% of the sum total of refugees. In fact, among the top ten refugee-hosting countries of the world there was not a single European state.[26] The mere proportions of these figures suggest the question of whether the EU should not fundamentally change the legal framework of its refugee policies in order to come closer to the self-proclaimed pledge to draw 'inspiration from the cultural, religious and humanist inheritance of Europe, from which have developed the universal values of the inviolable and inalienable rights of the human person, freedom, democracy, equality and the rule of law'.[27]

The defects of the collapsed Dublin system are obvious. It is all the more surprising that the search by the EU institutions for a solution to the European refugee crisis hardly yielded more than the intention to improve the efficiency of the already existing instruments of 'border management' among which the quasi-military protection of the external borders of the EU through the Frontex agency has a prominent place.[28] But apart from this issue there is reason for an even more serious concern, namely the collapse of the idea and practice of solidarity among the Member States in the face of the refugee crisis. Attempts of the EU, supported by the most-burdened Member States, to establish a system of fair distribution of refugees among all 28 Member States through quotas, has failed so far.[29] Germany strongly advocates this instrument, but this is an obviously self-interested claim, and possibly a hypocritical one at that, because allegedly it had voted against quotas when in the past Italy and Greece had demanded them on their part for obvious reasons. Aside from the quota issue, the refugee crisis has reinvigorated the guiding principle of national politics considered to be long outgrown in Europe, namely: act on your own without regard of the interests of others. One can hardly imagine a clearer signal that the inner existence of the EU is under threat. So it seems appropriate to us to turn to a more thorough analysis of the political grammar of the EU.

The EU: combining republican universalism with national particularism

The Greek case gives rise to remind us of the particularity of the EU as a political entity. Elsewhere we have termed it a 'republican empire',[30] an apparent oxymoron: the EU is a Union of different nation-states with distinct political and cultural identities, while at the same time its legal order treats the citizens of the Member States as one single citizenry. However, they have not become members of the Union due to submission and coercion (as is the case with empires); they have entered into the political entity voluntarily and even enjoy the right to withdraw from it.[31] The European Union is the first spatially extended union of a great number of clearly distinctive peoples that is governed as a republican regime: its constituents – the states – have a constitutional form of government, represent their peoples properly, secure their freedoms[32] and are joined together by a common legal framework which on its part respects and protects the freedom of its members. While both its voluntary character and its objective to end wars among its members, once and for all, exhibit features of Kant's 'pacific federation',[33] similarities with two features of empires are also evident: Empires are multinational in character and culturally heterogeneous, and they are geographically extended. Furthermore, empires, by definition embracing a multiplicity of nations and cultures, are characterised by the existence of a dominant entity (such as Prussia within the German *Reich*) that is more powerful than other national entities and successfully claims a leadership role. Kant believed that the same might also occur in a voluntary league of republics who seek perpetual peace, namely when one 'powerful and enlightened nation can form a republic ... this will provide the focal point for federal association among other states'.[34]

There is one aspect where the two opposite types of political order display a further similarity, namely their respective pretence to universality. As empires – unlike states – cannot accept other empires as equals, they tend to claim 'to be the rightful rulers of the universe as a whole'. As a consequence of such imperial ambition, other entities beyond an empire's borders are not considered to be 'other political communities with a right to an independent existence, but barbarians who at worst cause trouble and at best were not worth conquering'.[35] As regards republics, both ancient and medieval republics recognised the existence of their likes as mere facts of life, whereas modern republicanism – partly due to its close association with statehood – has acquired a slightly militant normative-universalistic slant. Its proponents regard the republic as the institutional embodiment of an idea which unites humankind as a whole, or, conversely, they regard the whole of the world as a kind of republic where universally valid norms and principles obtain. A striking example is the Draft Declaration of 17th May 1790 in which the French National Assembly

> solemnly declares 1. that it regards the entire mankind as a single and identical society whose goal is the peace and the happiness of all and every single of its members; 2. that in this great general society the peoples and the states as individuals are in possession of the same natural rights and subject to the same rules of justice ...[36]

However, even Kant, who had great sympathy for an international state which eventually would embrace all the peoples of the earth, realised that this is not the will of the nations and that 'the positive idea of a *world republic* cannot be realised'.[37]

Of course the EU as an institutional entity never claimed world domination. But the invocation of 'the cultural, religious and humanist inheritance of Europe, from which have developed the *universal values* of the inviolable and inalienable rights of the human person, freedom, democracy, equality and the rule of law'[38] attest to the claim of the EU to represent the globally valid pattern of political organisation. After all, 'universal values' are inherently expansive and cannot be limited to particular territorial spheres. Despite some quandaries about the democratic legitimacy of the EU, the republican elements of the EU have long been regarded as the key pillars of the EU's philosophical foundation and institutional setup.

It is only recently that we are witnessing indications that the republican-universalist architecture of the EU may no longer be robust enough so as to integrate its heterogeneous components in a 'European' manner, one inspired by some Europe-wide notion of a common good. John Stuart Mill once praised Europe for having 'made the European family of nations an improving instead of a stationary portion of mankind', namely its 'remarkable diversity of character and culture'[39] – a characteristic which made Europe even in the account of an author of the 21st century 'an innovative, decentralised, yet stable aberration' if compared to the rest of the world.[40] The above-mentioned incidence of right- and left-wing populist anti-European movements, of mutual distrust, nationalist-chauvinist quarrel, and the increasing tendency to frame socio-economic conflicts in terms of conflicts between nations are symptoms of the weakness of the institutional setup of the EU to cope with its national and cultural heterogeneities, the non-cooperative manifestations of which are mightily exacerbated by Europe's current crises. How can we explain this new and worrying development? After all, the political elites of the EU prided themselves to have invented an unparalleled model of an uncoerced union of states of very different characteristics, and justifiably so.

So far the EU has contented itself with stipulating its obligation to 'respect its rich cultural and linguistic diversity, and shall ensure that Europe's cultural heritage is safeguarded and enhanced', and, more specifically, to 'respect the equality of Member States before the Treaties as well as their national identities, inherent in their fundamental structures, political and constitutional ....'[41] Somehow, this language is reminiscent of Anatole France's sarcastic reference to the 'majestic equality of the law' which enjoins the rich and the poor alike from sleeping under bridges, begging in the streets and stealing bread. This cannot be the final response of the EU to the consequences of its increased heterogeneity – especially in terms of economic development and cultural traditions – if compared with the degree of similarity of the original six founding Member States more than fifty years ago. Today, the 'general' laws and policies of the Union cause highly diverse effects and impacts in the different Member States, with the result of producing the feeling of more and more people in more and more countries that they are ruled by 'others', not by themselves or the likes of them. In hindsight Joseph Weiler's observation fifteen years ago that 'civic tolerance' of the EU peoples led them to accept and to comply with the laws given by 'a people ... of others'[42] seems to have been overly optimistic. This statement reflected the founding era of what has been called the '*permissive consensus*' among the peoples of the EEC Member States which, as is now widely recognised, has eroded in the wake of the Maastricht Treaty.[43] In fact, this Treaty entailed fundamental changes of the previous method of integration which in turn has sparked a process of politicisation of European integration.

The politicisation of European integration

What exactly has changed? Let us recall that the 'permissive consensus' as a widespread popular attitude throughout the then small number of the six, relatively similar, founding members of 1958 plus the five newcomers which joined the EEC between 1973 and 1986[44] was underpinned by the economic welfare gains which resulted from a process of growing economic interdependence driven and controlled by predominantly legal market regulation. The Rome 'Treaty establishing the European Economic Community' (TEEC) was exactly that – a set of rules for the integration of the economies of the participating countries. But first and foremost it was a promise of economic and social progress which was expressed in its purposes to 'ensure the economic and social progress of their countries', of 'the constant improvement of the living and working conditions of their peoples', and of the guarantee of 'steady expansion, balanced trade and fair competition', to be achieved by means of 'establishing a common market and progressively approximating the economic policies of Member States'.[45] Integration was supposed to be the effect of the functioning of the market and of market-fostering economic policies, organised and operated by experts and elites. It was based upon the expectation that a skillful navigation of the economic process would render politics – i.e. the competition of different visions of the common good, contestation, struggle for power – altogether dispensable. At least in Germany this concept of integration nourished the hopes of the population – morally and physically exhausted from the trauma of World War II and the hardships of reconstruction – for a better future and a world in which social conflicts could be transformed into issues of technical solutions. Hence, as Joseph Weiler aptly put it, '*democracy was not part of the DNA of European Integration*'[46]; what kept integration moving forward was the promise and widely shared anticipation of converging levels of prosperity and social progress.

The Maastricht Treaties of 1992 – the Treaty on European Union (TEU) and the Treaty on Establishing the European Community (TEC) – did not change those economic purposes of European integration through the accomplishment of the internal market. Yet it is not by coincidence that the TEU now, for the first time, laid down the obligation of the Union to 'respect the national identities of its Member States, whose systems of government are founded on the principles of democracy.[47] The Maastricht Treaties entailed far-reaching changes among which the renaming of the European Economic Community (EEC) to 'European Community' (EC)[48] is only of minor importance, but at the same time indicative of the tendency to transform the Community from a purely economic special-purpose association into a political entity. In other words, the Maastricht Treaty entailed the 'politicisation' of integration. The establishment of the institution of 'citizenship of the Union' and of the 'Economic and Monetary Union' (EMU) was of paramount importance: the former created an explicitly political status of the individual whose legal standing in the Treaties was no longer restricted to the position of a mere factor of economic production; the latter produced a heterogeneous area of common monetary, economic and fiscal policies which required intensive cooperation and mutual consideration among the Member States with quite different basic conditions in terms of their economic standing and fiscal practices. Obviously the stipulations which specified the obligations of the Member States with respect to price stability, government deficits, national debt and other requirements of fiscal discipline[49] were bound to interfere, often quite painfully, with national preferences and those of the national parliaments. Thus the representatives of Member States as parties to the Treaties had good reason to insert a caveat, intended to protect the 'national identity' of their countries, into the Treaties. It sent the signal that the Union was no longer a market without a state,[50] but a polity composed of a plurality of distinct nations with historical, cultural and certainly also economic particularities. The Treaties can be read as restraining the dynamic of the internal market and the policies and measures of harmonisation in order to protect the cultural distinctiveness of the Member States.[51] The TFEU explicitly obligates both the EU and the Member States to take measures 'which take account of the diverse forms of national practices, in particular in the field of contractual relations, and the need to maintain the competitiveness of the Union economy'.[52] In this reading the national practices and particularities hamper the expansion of the market, they are negative, always defensive forces. Hence the establishment and the proper functioning of the internal market, including the goal of harmonisation of the national economies, has primacy over the restraining regulations in favour of the protection of national peculiarities against the dynamics of an equalising market in conjunction with efforts to satisfy demands, and do reduce the socio-economic inequalities within and among the Member States. In the light of these economic, legal and political imperatives, the Treaties' stipulation to respect the Member States' national distinctiveness may be likened to an act of protecting endangered species.

'National identities' and varieties of capitalism

Given the success story of the original European Community of the six contracting parties of the Treaty of Rome in 1957 and its progression to its present-day geographical extension and depth of European integration, the question arises of how to explain the degree of distrust and of anti-EU resentment which have recently run rampant in several Member States of the Union. Is it due to the unbalance between the EU's stated purpose to achieve socio-economic accomplishments such as growth, employment, stability and a high degree of economic convergence among the economies of the Member States on the one hand, and its obligation to respect their 'national identities' on the other? Is it a failure to deliver on either or both of these two opposing purposes which is the cause of alienation of considerable parts of the populations of almost all Member States from the EU and its integration project? Or is it that a lack of due respect for the particularities of some Member States has caused or at least contributed to their economic and social quandaries?

The concept of 'national identities' used in Article 4 para 2 of the TEU has a somewhat limited meaning in that they are mainly defined in terms of 'their fundamental structures, political and constitutional, inclusive of regional and local self-government'. The EU has to respect the Member States' constitutional setup and functioning, that is, the competences which they have not conferred on the Union – their *domaine réservé*. This understanding is confirmed and corroborated by the principles of conferral and of subsidiarity laid down in the ensuing Article 5 TEU. In other words, the obligation to respect the 'national identities' protects them against the usurpation of sovereign power by the Union. Defined in a broader sense, national identity represents the socio-moral infrastructure of a territorially bounded society, i.e. the pattern of its social and cultural norms, traditions, habits and practices which shape both the everyday life of individuals and the functioning of institutions. Ethically sensitive issues deeply ingrained in the world-views of large parts of the population of a country like matters of human reproduction,[53] or a country's 'culture of security' both in the international[54] and the domestic spheres,[55] may serve as examples for this broader reading of the idea of 'national identity'. These practices operate as an ever present social tissue which interweaves the formal structures of social life and constitutes their subtext. Whilst Art. 4 TEU defines the national identities of the EU Member States as 'inherent in their fundamental structures, political and constitutional, inclusive of regional and local self-government', we must add the respective subtexts of these fundamental structures in order to fully grasp the meaning and the political relevance of national identity for the spiritual architecture of the EU.[56] Consequently, just as much as 'one can assume that the public democracy and its realisation cannot be based primarily upon explicit legal norms'[57] the same applies to the implementation of convergence rules of the EU by the Member States. A closer look at the plurality of the Member States would certainly reveal quite 'different versions of adaptation to the European market' which mirror the divergences of their respective repertory of social norms.[58]

The German economic historian, Werner Abelshauser, has recently drawn attention to the tension between the EU's objective of extensive harmonisation of market conditions among the Member States and the tenacity of economic cultures in the several regions of the EU. Among the 'varieties of capitalism' in the EU he distinguishes the types of Rhenish capitalism, Anglo-American capitalism, Mediterranean capitalism, and a capitalism that is characteristic of the Balkans, each of which exhibits peculiarities regarding the social system of production (e.g. liberal market economy, corporatist market economy, subsidised market economy, archaic market economy), patterns of social action (e.g. institutions, clientelism, family relationship), or entrepreneurial time horizon (short-term v. long-term).[59] However debatable the details of his distinctions may be, the claim that the EU binds together divergent economic cultures can hardly be denied. As Abelshauser writes,

[t]he observance of the criteria laid down in the Treaty of Maastricht presupposes collective mentalities in the Euro states which enable them to organise state and society in such a way that these rules can be obeyed.

While it was clear from the start that the common currency area included very disparate collective mentalities, frequently formed over long historical periods of time, the proponents of the common currency never had any doubt that the common standards of budgetary deficits, debt levels or rate of inflation would get their way under the pressure of international capital markets. In the imaginary world of inevitable functional integration the social and political ability to comply with commonly set rules seemed to be reduced to a question of mere will and discipline.[60]

Arguably not only the advocates of European integration in the founding Member States believed in the modernising function of a capitalist market economy. It was probably also the political elites of the economically less advanced countries of Southern Europe who led their countries into the EU with the intention of embarking upon the one (*and only*) path to 'modernity', and thus to adapt their economies to the standard of modernity set by the advanced capitalist countries of the West. After all, none of them was 'coerced' (as opposed to incentivised by the prospect of market access) to join the EC or the EU. Thus the institutional framework and the principles of the economic and fiscal policies of the EU appear to represent the common denominator of all Member States, i.e., to be genuinely supranational. However, a brief glance at the rules about the economic and monetary policies of the EU including the stipulations of the Stability and Growth Pact (SGP) and its standards of strict fiscal discipline reveals that these norms breathe the spirit of the economically advanced countries of the Northern regions of the EU with which the 'newcomers' in the South (as well as those in the East) would have, predictably, difficulties in order to comply.

While all Member States transferred elements of their sovereignty voluntarily – whatever this term may mean in the political world of power and transnational market relations – on the EU, they did not and could not transfer the social and cultural patterns of their societies which, having evolved over long periods of time, are deeply ingrained in the everyday lives of their citizens and are simply beyond short-term political control and strategic change. And this transfer was certainly not explicitly required because, as mentioned, the necessary adjustment of the societies of the Member States to the imperatives of a common market was expected to follow quasi-automatically from the iron laws of the market economy, viz. capitalism. The fact that there is no such thing like capitalism *sans phrase* but only varieties of capitalism[61] was ignored in the construction of the EC and its successor, the EU. Had the authors of the Treaties been aware of the existence of different models of capitalism and levels of capitalist development, they would have been forced to find ways of how to make the divergent 'capitalisms' of the areas of the EU mutually compatible. This would have been a clear alternative to the prevailing conception to make the mute force of the market (together with some marginal assistance provided by structural funds) execute the requirement for a sweeping homogenisation of the divergent economic cultures and economic conditions bound together in the EU.

Hence there lurked a latent conflict in the socio-political edifice of the EU whose overt occurrence could be evaded for a long time, arguably not least due to the German governments' readiness to solve or mitigate conflicts among the Member States through augmented money transfers into the machinery of the EU. This worked as long as these conflicts could be defined in monetary terms (and Germany was not yet absorbed financially and psychologically by the recovery of its national unity). Without further research it cannot be determined when and where exactly the boundaries of this kind of conflict resolution were reached.[62] In any case we observe that today broad segments of the population in several EU Member States, most conspicuously in the Mediterranean countries, sense the normal working of the machinery of the EU as a hostile interference with the traditional forms and norms of their ordinary life. The common currency severely limits their scope for adjustment and exacerbates divergence rather than promoting social and economic assimilation. Thus the dynamics of 'borderless' capitalism affect the socio-cultural subtext of the formal rules and institutions of the countries, shaped by a distinct, neither Anglo-Saxon nor Rhenish economic culture. Unsurprisingly, this mismatch provokes the resistance of popular movements. In other words, the EU is sensed as not according due respect to their 'national identity'. What does this mean? This question leads us to more differentiated considerations on the concept of 'national identity' which requires a closer look at the elementary constituents of the nation – its citizens.

Citizenship – a paradigm for 'unity in diversity'?

The idea of 'national identity' suggests the existence of a unified and homogeneous multitude which – very much along the reasoning of Rousseau – is capable of forming, having and expressing a common will and thus displaying something like a 'national' character and political preference. Of course this is an assumption whose gross faultiness can already be discovered in the fact that the modern nation materialised hand in hand and with the evolution of the bourgeois society and its social divisions, the class conflict being the most significant one. Thus, the opposite is true: the modern nation is marked by disunity and social conflict. And yet, there is a grain of truth in that error which has to do with the concept of citizenship. Put succinctly: citizenship denotes the status of the individual as a member of the modern nation who has the right and the moral duty to actively participate in the nation's self-government, i.e. in the sphere of politics. The citizen is the creature of the process of pluralisation of the sphere of politics. Hence he – yes, the ancient Greek and also the modern European archetype is a 'he' – embodies the idea that the common good can and must be achieved through discourses among those who qualify for discourses, that is, how to deal discursively through deliberation with disagreements over issues of justice and the public good. In other words, citizenship is an ideal which stands for the capacity of a society to deal with its inherent conflicts in a civilised, i.e. non-violent manner. We may therefore say that it is a concept which, on the presupposition of a divided society and of the practice of politics as the mode of coping with its conflicts, symbolises the idea of 'unity in diversity' – the maxim of the Draft Constitutonal Treaty of 2004.[63] On closer inspection, however, it turns out that while the institution of citizenship is a necessary condition, it is by no means a sufficient one for 'unity in diversity' to prevail in the EU.

When we try to conceptualise citizenship, we can do so in either a 'vertical' or a 'horizontal' perspective. The vertical perspective follows the intuition that citizenship is something with which people have been endowed by a constitution and its makers, such as some founding fathers. According to this view, citizenship is a status, implying rights and obligations, that has been shaped and is being enforced and guaranteed by some superior agent, namely the established constitutional state. In this vertical perspective, the opposite of a citizen is a subject, i.e. a person whose endowment with rights and obligations is by some standard of equal freedom incomplete or deficient. The horizontal perspective, in contrast, focuses on citizenship in terms of how people relate to each other by recognising and treating other persons as fellow citizens to whom they perceive themselves more intensely connected (through bonds of solidarity, reciprocity or, for that matter, rivalry over scarce resources or political opposition) than to people seen as not belonging to the political community in question. In the horizontal perspective, the opposite of a citizen is simply an outsider, be it a foreign resident, a 'denizen', a mere tourist, or an asylum-seeking refugee to whom citizens of a particular political community relate in terms of international law and human rights, not in terms of fellow citizenship (in contrast to fellow human beings). Citizenship, both in the vertical and horizontal perspective, thus means a measure of reflective similarity. Citizens are people who consider each other as belonging to a collective entity the elements of which are thought to have significant characteristics in common which they do not share with outsiders. By virtue of these shared characteristics and the homogeneity derived therefrom, they are endowed with the capacity to act as a political community.

Homogeneity, or the awareness and recognition of having shared characteristics (a language, a legal system etc.), can thus be seen as an important resource that allows for collective action. How much of it is needed by a political community in order to be able to shape and control its collective fate? The big question here concerns the sources of 'needed' or 'requisite' homogeneity and what happens (and by implication: what remedies are available) in case the actually operative bonds of citizenship are inadequate relative to those 'needed'?

A standard sociological account of the evolutionary dynamics of societal modernisation suggests the following dilemma. On the one side, modernisation means differentiation – an ongoing and deepening pluralisation, polycentricity and growing heterogeneity of life chances and life courses, socioeconomic fates, belief systems, and value orientations and interests. On the other hand, modernisation implies an exponential growth of interdependencies with (known!) chains of causation and positive and negative externalities of action getting ever more extended. While differentiation and growing heterogeneity tend to weaken the bonds of mutual recognition, solidarity, and 'fellow feeling', promotes a syndrome of (neo)liberal atomisation of social structures and unleashes the individualistic pursuit of wealth and power, the management of often highly risky interdependencies appears to call for coordination, cooperation and the imposition of binding constraints on reckless and irresponsible modes of action with their (arguably increasing) potential for inflicting collective and/or long term damage on the entire political community. At any rate, much of contemporary social (including constitutional) theorising clearly converges on the diagnosis that the balance between 'exit' and 'voice', 'market justice' and 'social justice', the unbinding and self-binding capacities of modern societies, 'negative' and 'positive' integration, heterogeneity and homogeneity is severely tilted in favour of the first and at the expense of the second items within these pairs of concepts. The ties deriving from the reflective similarities of shared citizenship are broken by individuals' centrifugal and disintegrating pursuit of interests, values, and belief systems.

Returning to the issue of citizenship, there are, we submit, three potential sources of integration which can, in principle, be expected to serve as forces capable of bridging and coping with 'excessive' levels of heterogeneity, thus constituting a robust relationship of 'fellow-citizenship' within a political community. The first kind of cement that can make for integration is the shared attachment to a national culture and history which provides the foundations of collective identity – an answer to the question: 'Who are 'we'?' Religion, language, a self-described ethnic identity and myths and memories relating to the past, as well as widely shared hopes and ambitions relating to the future, are typical ingredients of a collective identity which is both distinctive of a political community and shared by (most or) all belonging to it. A fair summary of diagnostic findings concerning the potential of this cultural mode of integration, we believe, is the conclusion that a distinctive common culture is no longer viable as an underpinning of political community, be it at the national or, *a fortiori*, at the supranational or European level. The reason is not that the notion of a collective identity has become obsolete but that in any conceivable political community there is more than one notion of collective identity, varying according to region, social class, religious traditions, ethnic origin, generation etc., with none of them having a plausible claim to being accepted as an overarching and universally inclusive answer to the above question. If we observe a multiplicity of identities within a political community, the very notion of a cultural collective identity is bound to become divisive rather than integrating.[64] Political communities in Europe are essentially 'multi-cultural'. As a consequence, appeals to 'identity' issues are often not unifying but divisive (as communitarian political theorists have often been reluctant to admit), and the role they play in processes of (post)national integration therefore more likely to be a negative rather than positive one.

The second pillar on which shared citizenship can be built is, in the 'vertical' perspective, the legal and constitutional order (enshrining the rule of law, the limitation and division of powers, the democratic accountability and responsiveness of rulers, a bill of rights). It is an open question, addressed in several of the chapters of the present volume, what qualities constitutional orders must have and under what contexts they must come into being in order to perform their function of securing a societal synthesis by continuously transforming 'people' into ('good') citizens (as proponents of a republican version of political theory might put it). Not every constitution has the potential for inspiring the virtues of civic solidarity and 'constitutional patriotism', and a constitution that may be expected to do so in good times may fail in bad ones. Moreover, the more 'liberal' a constitution is (but who would deny the protection and promotion of individual freedom as a highly legitimate core cause of constitutionalism itself?), the more its actual operation may enhance heterogeneity by justifying and encouraging the largely unrestrained pursuit of material and other interests. Also, there is the asymmetry that the theory and practice of constitutionalism is still largely tied to the nation state, while higher levels of aggregation and the interdependencies unfolding at the supra- and international levels clearly lag behind in terms of their constitutionalisation, thus allowing the anarchic dynamics of transnational interaction and interdependency escape the reach of what can be controlled and regulated by essentially still national modes of constitutional rule.

If culture-based collective identity does not provide promising resources for responding to the challenges of differentiation and unruled interdependency, and if there is neither much reason to trust that legal and constitutional devices alone, being largely national in scope, can cope with those challenges, the question is whether there are conceivable other sources of integration, homogeneity, and a sense of 'fellow-citizenship' on which a durable kind of social order can be built as a counterweight to growing tendencies of disorganisation and heterogeneity. This heterogeneity is manifest, increasingly throughout the OECD world (and obviously far beyond) in growing disparities of income, wealth, employment opportunities, life chances, and socio-economic status rights. Whereas the ideology of market society claims that every participant enjoys a balanced mix of risk and opportunity, much current evidence demonstrates the unmixing of the two, resulting in polarised social structures with a shrinking minority enjoying 'opportunity' while a growing majority is exposed to 'risk'. As a consequence and under the impact of the Great Recession setting in during 2008 and bringing with it stagnation, long term mass unemployment and rising levels of socio-economic precariousness, the sense of frustration and deprivation, of fear, xenophobia, cynicism, hatred, despair, fatalism and aggressive impulses between states and within societies of the EU have reached levels which threaten to demolish the credibility of the very notion of 'citizenship', be it at the national or European level. Hence it seems that big and lasting measures of massive redistribution (across Member States, social classes, generations, and points in time), difficult though it is to envision in Europe given the configuration of political forces and constitutional provisions, is an essential requirement for any attempt to restore some of the political meaning of citizenship, together with its inherent implications of a commitment to 'civic solidarity' (Habermas) and 'social citizenship' (T. H. Marshall).

In sum, we claim that 'modern' societies typically suffer from excessive or misguided degrees of differentiation that jeopardise their capacity to gain and maintain control over their collective fates. We also claim that the precarious homogeneity of these societies can possibly be remedied by either (or a combination of) three resources of integration: ethnic identity, constitutionalism and rule of law, and distributive justice which is itself the outcome of public policies. Thirdly, we have suggested that the capacity of these three categories of resources for providing 'requisite' levels of social integration and homogeneity differs sharply. While notions of ethno-national, cultural, or religious foundations of collective identity and shared citizenship are often positively divisive and thus counterproductive, the constitutional and legal order is, by itself, at best ambivalent as to its integrative potential: it generates forces of both differentiation and integration. It therefore must be complemented by elements of integration that are associated with (to be sure: inherently also vastly controversial) standards of social justice and distributional fairness.

The constitutional dimension

This said, it seems to us appropriate to emphasise our above statement that our response to the question of how to cope with the European crisis does not lead us to submit concrete policy recommendations. We are looking, instead, for institutional conceptions which may offer productive methods for the handling of EU-Europe's problems. Our starting point is the hypothesis that the EU has not yet found the correct method how to cope with the phenomenon of an increasing politicisation of its policies and thus failed to avert the ugly tendency that transnational social conflicts are more and more framed in terms of nationalist, chauvinist and, to some extent, even racist patterns and practices.

As we see it, the present constitutional problems of the EU can largely be modelled as a dilemma of circularity, reminiscent of a standard hen-egg problem. On the one hand, it is the established institutional system with its allocation of decision making powers (consisting of the Treaties, the European Council, the Council of Ministers, the independent ECB presiding over the common currency, the EP and the ECJ) that prescribe what Member State governments are permitted or prohibited to do. The Euro crisis, and the financial market crisis giving rise to it, have led many observers (including, for instance, ECB president Draghi) to argue that the coordination capacity of this institutional system is deficient. This deficiency is partly due to the fact, as many experts have warned long before the adoption of the common currency, that the EU has failed to complement the common monetary system with an equally integrated system of Europeanised fiscal policy. The numerous mechanisms of negotiation, compromise-building, and the encouragement of cooperation that the Treaties provide for, may not appear strong enough to generate 'requisite' levels of cooperation which at the very least would be capable to prevent further disintegration. In order to heal this deficiency, ECB President Draghi has even called for the need for an EU finance minister who would be endowed with the authority of making taxing and spending decisions that bind all member state governments. But such a proposal, plausible though it may appear from the point of view of coordination, remains plainly a mere technocratic fantasy (as it amounts to 'taxation without representation'), as no democratic body is in place by which a European finance minister could be held accountable. As a consequence, member state governments, being accountable to their national constituencies, remain free to engage in highly non-cooperative strategies without there being a corrective force capable of inducing them to adopt more collectively beneficial policies. In a way, this pattern of member state behaviour can be seen as an artefact of an institutional order that fails to impose constraints on non-cooperative strategic actors and to incentivise the adoption of far-sighted and collectively beneficial policies.

Yet, on the other hand, the institutional order that has proven to be inadequate when it comes to coping with the fiscal and economic crises, and in averting the further deepening of the division of Europe, does not only shape the action of Member States and private sector actors. It is conversely itself, including its ongoing revision and elaboration, shaped by the degree and robustness of cooperative dispositions of members and their strategic preferences. If the alleged deficiencies of the institutional order enshrined the Treaties are to be healed, it will be a joint accomplishment of Member States' enlightened readiness to do so. In other words, the binding discipline that a constitution imposes upon members of the transnational political community of the EU is, in the final analysis, contingent on the willingness of members to bind themselves and to revise the institutional setup accordingly. Yet it seems fair to generalise that such readiness and willingness declines in direct proportion to the seriousness and divisiveness of the crisis as well as its duration.

The EU's socio-economic and socio-cultural diversity, one time so much appreciated, runs the risk of becoming the source of irreconcilable categorical conflicts[65] which undermine the EU's aim to promote solidarity among its Member States[66] and will ultimately jeopardise supranational redistributive policies in the EU altogether.

Needless to say that from the outset economic, social and cultural diversity among the Member States of the EU has been the premise of the whole undertaking of the establishment of the European Community and the European Union, respectively. The economic discrepancies between advanced industrialised countries of the North and the less developed economies of the Mediterranean rim, later also of the East and Central European post-communist newcomers, have always been in the focus of European policies. Whereas it was widely assumed that the market forces would eventually lessen the gap between economically advanced Member States and those lagging behind in terms of productivity, it must not be forgotten that the other leverage effect of socio-economic approximation and assimilation, viz. modernisation, can be expected from the redistributive policies resulting from the idea of a Social Europe.[67] It is an empirical question which effects these modernisation efforts have had on the different societies. While it is likely that they somehow influence the economic incentive schemes in a relevant manner, it is unclear whether they can fundamentally change the entrenched social patterns and cultural habits of a society in the short and medium term. To a large extent this is even true in the economic sphere where adaptation pressures of globalised market forces are particularly strong. A cursory view at – to some degree comparable – endeavours to graft modern legal structures on culturally thoroughly differing societies – such as Iraq and Afghanistan, but also in Europe (Bosnia and Herzegowina, Kosovo)[68] – attest to the persistence of age-old social patterns. If this is so, the EU will be faced with a socio-cultural diversity among its Member States for quite some time in the future even if economic inequalities should be significantly mitigated. How, then, can we conceive of an EU which lives up to the solemn motto of the aborted Constitutional Treaty of the EU of 2005: 'United in diversity'?[69]

First and foremost we must shun the idea that diversity and unity are two fixed, opposed and mutually exclusive states of social organisation whereby the former has to be transformed into the latter so that a state of order and stability will be achieved. In the context of the European Union the diversity among the Member States persists concurrently with unity as created by the implementation of the treaties which provide the instruments for the Member States' joint action. 'United in diversity' includes more than the mere recognition of the Member States' sovereignty in those areas of competence which – according to the principle of conferral – they have not transferred upon the Union in the Treaties. Moreover, the recognition of their national identity must not be misunderstood as just requiring respect of a more or less introverted social life isolated from the outside world beyond the national boundaries.

The EU is a *political* innovation which establishes a new mode of political discourse – not, of course, as an aim in itself, but as a necessary implication of the unprecedented and bold undertaking to create a deep union of sovereign states. Obviously it is not possible to capture the cooperation of the Member States through the mediation of the Union and its institutions in a fixed scheme of competences and their clear-cut delimitation. After all, as a political entity the EU needs democratic legitimation. Democracy means contestation and struggle over what is the right path to a good life for all affected. In a diverse polity, contestation and struggle necessarily mirror the discrepancies of the world views, values, interests of the involved individuals and groups – hence the democratic institutions of a diverse polity cannot be difference-blind. They must include devices which give the diverse political and cultural forces and currents a voice. It is of critical importance that these different perspectives, as such, are not reified as the subject matter of social conflicts to the effect that non-negotiable 'national identities' stand against each other. Rather, they should operate as an inherent element of the process of mutual cross-border understanding of the inherently, social, not cultural conflict and eventually contribute to its solution.

In the context of the EU this entails the institutionalisation of a dynamic interactive process among the Member States and between the Union and the several Member States. The 'national identities' of the Member States, invoked in Art. 4 TEU, radiate, as it were into the different levels on which the political struggles within the EU occur. What is more, we would miss the character of the political if we assumed that once a political process has resulted in a common decision – here: in the treaties which constitute the EU – political struggles have ended because they have been transformed into legal discourses. This assumption is particularly erroneous in the case of the EU where the involvement of the dissimilarities of the Member States is a constituent element of its political idea and institutional setup.[70] Culturally-specific views in economic, social and political matters, handled in the EU frame, form an inherent element of its political discourse, i.e. the object of contestation and struggles. In other words, the national identity of the Member States is politicised.

This is not a new observation. What, however, requires increased attention is a hitherto rarely reflected implication regarding the EU, namely: in contrast to the traditional view according to which the recognition of a political entity's identity after more or less protracted struggles is stable, constitutionally secure and hence exempt from political contestation, the involvement of the Member States' distinctiveness in transnational European social conflicts amounts to no less than the partial politicisation of its constitution (whereby we adopt the view of the ECJ that the Treaties of the EU form its constitution). As James Tully aptly states,

> the question of just and stable forms of recognition must now be reformulated for the twenty-first century as an open-ended series of questions addressed to specific struggles and experiments with institutional solutions to them within the broader horizon of the politics of recognition as a long-term activity of politics, no different in this regard from other types of political activity (such as, say, struggles over distribution).[71]

At first glance this does in no sense fit the conventional understanding of the status of a constitution. According to this perception the constitution embodies the consensus about the basic values and the institutional character of the polity which have been put beyond dispute by way of constitutionalisation. Although propositions for constitutional amendments are likely to prompt political debate, the usual requirement of a supermajority tends to direct this debate toward a new consensus. This is the more or less routine pattern of politics in entrenched constitutional states. It is rather rare in culturally diverse constitutional states such as Canada, Belgium, Spain or even the UK. Here the constitution is not the result of a unitary constituent power of one more or less homogeneous people but has the character of a treaty between heterogeneous parts whose coexistence in one polity remains always precarious. This is even more the case in an entity like the EU which is composed of different nations and/or states each of which is itself organised as a democracy. While a democratic polity may enter into a union of democratic or non-democratic polities – for the sake of the future generations it is prevented from using its democratic form of government for the relinquishment of its right to self-determination.[72] Hence, with accession to the EU, a sovereign state does not give up its people's right to self-determination including its constituent power. On the other hand, the accession to the EU Treaties entails the entry into a web of mutual obligations towards the other parties to the contracts which bind the state. But this binding force cannot overrule the people's right to argue in public discourses over the appropriateness of their political organisation including the character of the state's international and supranational obligations. Thus, the two principles of constitutionalism – the rule of law and the democratic principle of self-determination – must somehow coexist in the EU. Therefore the contestability of constitutional elements of the EU is no justification or even encouragement of a breach of contract; it is, rather, a more appropriate description of the point of departure for the understanding of the democratic element of the idea of constitutionalism for culturally diverse polities like the EU. Referring to the Canadian experience with the struggle about the status of the province of Quebec, James Tully submits that the

> democratic practices of disputation and contestation that were previously assumed to rest on permanent constitutional arrangements, to which the people were supposed to have agreed once and for all, are now seen to apply to those arrangements as well, and thus 'agonism' ... is seen to be a defining feature of democratic constitutionalism.[73]

In other words, disagreements over constitutional issues are never fully settled and must not be presumed to be finally settled if democratic freedom shall endure. Tully concludes that democratic freedom implies the necessity and the right to 'enter into agonistic negotiations over the prevailing constitutional arrangements (or some subset of them)'.[74] We agree with some hesitance because this approach may underestimate the institutional and political benefits of a relatively stable legal framework for the handling of political disputes with a cultural impact. There looms the risk that the institutional architecture of the EU might be dissolved into a series of conferences and negotiations entailing the permanence of uncertain law – admittedly an oxymoron. While it is imperative that constitutional disagreements rooted in the diversity of the constituent segments of the Union have to be processed through negotiations among the involved parties, there must be an institutional frame which models these negotiating processes. The balanced simultaneity of the rule-of-law and the democratic elements of constitutionalism requires a constitution which finds a way to establish the principle of difference before the law – the legal recognition that the treaty norms, although differently interpreted and practiced in the Member States according to their respective socio-cultural backgrounds,[75] still commit the Member States to the republican principles of the EU. First and foremost such a constitution would have to include rules about rule-making (meta-rules) in a diverse polity 'including methodologies that are adapted to the persistence of variety'.[76] Arguably the goal of European integration remains the creation of 'an ever closer union among the peoples of Europe' as laid down in the preambles of the Treaties; but integration as an end in itself has lost much of its previous persuasive power. Today it seems that the EU should harness its integration drive and focus its efforts more on conciliating the imperatives of the internal market and the requirements of economic convergence – its commitment to the 'culture of market'[77] – with the appropriate regard to the unmarketable distinctiveness of the Member States' societies.

How should that be done? The issue at stake is to find a balance between the two basic principles of the EU spelled out in Article 4 para 2 TEU: respect for the equality of Member States before the Treaties as well as for their national identities in the sense spelled out in this sketch. In other words, the task is to combine the republican element of the EU (equality) and the individuality and obstinacy of the peoples of its Member States with the aim of 'republic of others' (to paraphrase Weiler's reading of the EU as a 'community of others'[78]).

This is a matter of the EU's constitution whereby we do not necessarily imply the formal amendment of the Treaties. More productive appears an approach to something like constitutional experimentalism or, as Corkin suggests, experimental constitutionalism.[79] So, to begin with, why should one not establish a practice according to which – as a positive analogy to Art. 7 TEU, possibly also to Protocol No 2 – a Member state may voice its concern for the essentials of its people's living conditions and open the path for public discussions and negotiations about the chosen path of integration? Next to the Greek case, the outcome of the national election in the UK of May 2015 and the prospect of a referendum about its exit from the EU in 2017 provide an excellent opportunity for the EU to rediscover its spirit of constitutional innovation.

Notes

1. *International New York Times*, 28 February – 1 March, 2015, p. 1.

2. A detailed account of the dramatic – and in all likelihood game-changing – chain of events from the Greek referendum of 5th July to the signing of the bailout package and the third Memorandum of Understanding on 19th August, 2015 is in part available at 'Greek debt crisis: deal reached after marathon all-night summit – as it happened' http://www.theguardian.com/business/live/2015/jul/12/greek-debt-crisis-eu-leaders-meeting-cancelled-no-deal-live (accessed 29 January 2016).

3. 'According to some estimates, there are around 320,000 families in Greece that are not paying down their mortgages and obviously these bad loans are dead weights for the banking system.' M. Minenna, 'New Countdown For Greece: A bank bail-in is looming' http://www.socialeurope.eu/2015/11/new-countdown-for-greece-a-bank-bail-in-is-looming/ (accessed 29 January 2016).

4. Cf. 'Greece debt agreement: the Eurozone summit statement', http://www.theguardian.com/business/2015/jul/13/greece-debt-agreement-eurozone-summit-statement; subsequent negotiations resulted in a detailed 'Memorandum of Understanding between the European Commission ... and the Hellenic Republic', signed by Greek government and its European creditors on August 19, 2015: http://ec.europa.eu/economy_finance/assistance_eu_ms/greek_loan_facility/pdf/01_mou_20150811_en.pdf (accessed 29 January 2016).

5. cf. http://www.theguardian.com/commentisfree/2015/jul/16/jurgen-habermas-eu-greece-debt-deal (accessed 29 January 2016).

6. ... for the performing of which he was then widely ridiculed in the German media as an unreliable and erratic character!

7. http://www.economist.com/news/europe/21657836-chastened-nation-and-its-leader-face-more-hard-choices-rage-resignation (accessed 29 January 2016).

8. After the end of the negotiations of July 12th, Italian Prime Minister Renzi is reported by Reuters news agency to have angrily remarked about the behaviour of German negotiators: 'Enough is enough! The German government has to compromise and not humiliate Athens. Humiliating a European partner after Greece has given up on just about everything is unthinkable.' cf. http://www.reuters.com/article/2015/07/12/us-eurozone-greece-renzi-idUSKCN0PM083 20150712#rlWEidmqjQC9999z.99 (accessed 29 January 2016).

9. The Treaties do not provide for a procedure that allows a country to leave the Eurozone without leaving the EU altogether according to Art. 50 TEU. The initiative for the latter step must be taken by the country that wishes to leave, not by the countries remaining members of the EU.

10. cf. http://www.faz.net/aktuell/wirtschaft/eurokrise/griechenland/eurofinanzminister-treffen-schaeuble-bringt-grexit-auf-zeit-ins-gespraech-13697851.html (accessed 29 January 2016).

11. In the following points on this dual failure, we rely in part on the findings of a commission of experts set up by the President of the Hellenic Parliament in early 2015. These findings of the *Truth Committee on Public Debt* are contained in its *Preliminary Report* of June 2015: http://www.auditoriacidada.org.br/wp-content/uploads/2014/06/Report-Greek-Truth-Committee.pdf and its final report *Illegitimacy, Illegality, Odiousness and Unsustainability of the August 2015 MoU and Loan Agreement*, published on 4th October 2015: http://www.hellenicparliament.gr/UserFiles/8158407a-fc31-4ff2-a8d3-433701dbe6d4/7AEBEF78-DE85-4AB3-98BE-495803F85BF6Mnimonio_ENG_1.pdf (accessed 29 January 2016).

12. *The Guardian op.cit.*

13. MoU, *loc. cit.* p. 4.

14. *Illegitimacy...*, *op. cit.*, p. 7.

15. IMF statement of July 14, 2015, available at https://goo.gl/hMdL4p (accessed 29 January 2016).

16. Cf. the overview of G. Papagianni, *EU Migration Policy*, in A. Triandafyllidou and R. Gropas (eds), *European Immigration: A sourcebook* in Aldershot, Burlington, VT, Ashgate, 2014, pp. 377–388; C. Teitgen-Colly 'The European Union and asylum: an illusion of protection' *Common Market Law Review* vol. 43, no.6, 2006, pp. 1503–1566.

17. Art. 6, TEU in conjunction with Art. 18 of the Charter of Fundamental Rights of the European Union.

18. Art. 33 Geneva 'Convention Relating to the Status of Refugees' of 28 July 1951, entered into force on 22 April 1954.

19. Art. 18 Charter of Fundamental Rights.

20. Directive 2013/32/EU of the European Parliament and of the Council of 26 June 2013 on common procedures for granting and withdrawing international protection (recast), Art. 3 para 1; indirectly, yet unmistakeably, the preceding Directive 2011/95/EU.

21. See e.g. EU Council Action on Migratory Pressures – a Strategic Response (23 April 2012) [8714/1/12 REV 1].

22. Art. 78–80 [quote 80] Treaty on the Functioning of the European Union.

23. ECRE Comments on the European Commission Proposal to recast the Dublin Regulation. April 2009, p. 3 – http://www.ecre.org/component/downloads/downloads/112.html (accessed 22 October 2015). This evaluation was performed before the changes made in Dublin III of 2013. Yet this reform did neither change the first-entry principle nor its accompanying concept of safe third countries.

24. Grand Chamber case of M.S.S. v. Belgium and Greece Judgment of 21 January 2011 (*Application no. 30696/09*), p. 106–7; see also case application no. 2237/08 of 07.06.2011.

25. Source: eurostat newsrelease 53/2015 – 20 March 2015.

26. UNHCR Global Trends. Forced Displacements in 2014, at pp. 2, 12 – http://www.unhcr.org/556725e69.html (accessed 28 October 2015).

27. Treaty on European Union, Preamble.

28. See the *Leaders' Statement* of the European Leaders' Meeting on refugee flows along the Western Balkans Route in Brussels on 25 October – http://ec.europa.eu/news/2015/docs/leader_statement_final.pdf (accessed 28 October 2015).

29. i.e. end of October 2015.

30. C. Offe and U. K. Preuß, 'The Problem of Legitimacy in the European Polity: Is democratization the answer?', in this volume, Chapter Twenty.

31. Art. 50 TEU.

32. P. Pettit, 'A republican law of peoples', *European Journal of Political Theory*, 9/1 (2010): 70–94.

33. I. Kant, *Perpetual Peace: A philosophical sketch* [1795], in H. Reiss (ed.) *Political Writings*, Cambridge, New York, Cambridge University Press, 1992, pp. 93–130 [104].

34. *Ibid.*, p. 104.

35. M. v. Creveld, *The Rise and Decline of the State*, Cambridge and New York, Cambridge University Press, 2002, pp. 40–1.

36. W. Grewe (ed.), *Fontes Historiae Iuris Gentium: Sources relating to the history of the law of nations*, vol. II, Berlin and New York, Walter de Gruyter, 1988, p. 646.

37. Kant, *Perpetual Peace*, p. 105, *loc. cit.*

38. Recital 2, TEU, see also recital 4 and Art. 2, 21 TEU [emphasis added].

39. J. S. Mill, *On Liberty and Other Writings*, S. Collini (ed.), Cambridge, Cambridge University Press, 1989 [1859], p. 72.

40. E. L. Jones, *The European Miracle: Environments, economies, and geopolitics in the history of Europe and Asia*, 3rd edn, Cambridge and New York, Cambridge University Press, 2003, p. 225.

41. Art. 3 para 3, 4, para 2, see also recital 6 TEU.

42. J. H. H. Weiler, 'Federalism without Constitutionalism: Europe's *Sonderweg*', in K. Nicolaidis and R. Howse (eds) *The Federal Vision: Legitimacy and levels of governance in the United States and the European Union*, Oxford, Oxford University Press, 2001, pp. 54–70 [67–8].

43. L. Hooghe and G. Marks, 'A postfunctionalist theory of European integration: from permissive consensus to constraining dissensus', *British Journal of Political Science*, vol. 39, no 1, 2009, pp. 1–23.

44. UK, Denmark, Ireland (1973); Greece (1981), Portugal, Spain (1986).

45. Quotes from the recitals and Art. 2 of the Rome Treaty of 1957.

46. J. H. H. Weiler, 'Democracy without the people: the extinction of European legitimacy', *Schlossplatz3*, vol. 13, 8–15, 2012, [15].

47. Art. F, Maastricht Treaty.

48. Art. G sect. A, Maastricht Treaty of 7 February 1992.

49. See the Art. 109j TEC (Maastricht) and Protocol on the convergence criteria referred to in Article 109j of the Treaty establishing the European Community.

50. Cf. C. Joerges, The Market without the State? The 'Economic Constitution' of the European Community and the Rebirth of Regulatory Politics. European Integration online Papers (EIoP), vol. 1, no. 19, November 24, 1997. Available at SSRN: http://ssrn.com/abstract=302710 or http://dx.doi.org/10.2139/ssrn.302710 (accessed 29 January 2016).

51. Art. 3 para 3 subparagraph 3 TEU.

52. Art. 151 para 2 TFEU.

53. Cf. the case of abortion in Ireland, European Court of Justice (ECJ) C-159/90 of 4 October 1991; details in N. R. Koffeman, 'Legal responses to cross-border movement in reproductive matters within the European Union', IXth World Congress of the IACL, Oslo 2014., http://www. jus. uio. no/english/research/news-and-events/events/conferences/2014/wccl-cmdc/wccl/papers/workshop7. html. (accessed 28 October 2015).

54. P. J. Katzenstein, *The Culture of National Security: Norms and identity in world politics*, Columbia University Press, 1996; M. Williams, *Culture and Security: Symbolic power and the politics of international security*, London, Routledge, 2007.

55. E.g. B. J. Muller, 'Securing the political imagination: popular culture, the security dispositif and the biometric state', in *Security Dialogue* 39/2–3 (2008): 199–220; J. DeCew, 'Privacy', *The Stanford Encyclopedia of Philosophy*

(Spring 2015 Edition), Edward N. Zalta (ed.), URL = <http://plato.stanford.edu/archives/spr2015/entries/privacy/> (accessed 28 January 2016).

56. Cf. K.-H. Ladeur, '"Conflicts Law as Europe's Constitutional Form" ... and the Conflict of Social Norms as its Infrastructure' in C. Joerges and C. Glinski (eds) *The European Crisis and the Transformation of Transnational Governance: Authoritarian managerialism versus democratic governance*, Oxford, Hart Publishing, 2014, pp. 383–396.

57. Ladeur *ibid.* p. 392.

58. Ladeur *ibid.* p. 393.

59. W. Abelshauser, *Europa in Vielfalt einigen: Eine Denkschrift*, pp. 21 et seq. http://wwwhomes.uni-bielefeld.de/wabelsha/Denkschrift.pdf (accessed 28 January 2016).

60. Abelshauser, *ibid.*, p. 14 [our translation].

61. Cf. the seminal volume of P. A. Hall and D. Soskice, (eds) *Varieties of Capitalism: The institutional foundations of comparative advantage*, Oxford, Oxford University Press 2001; the contributions deal solely with the Rhenish and the Anglo-Saxon variants of capitalism; regarding Rhenish capitalism see M. Albert, 'The Future of Continental Socio-economic Models', MPIfG Working Paper 97/6 (1997) – www.mpifg.de (accessed 28 January 2016).

62. M. Höpner and A. Schäfer, 'A new phase of European integration: organised capitalisms in post-Ricardian Europe', *West European Politics*, vol. 33, no. 2, 2010, pp. 344–368, offer one plausible economic interpretation: the Commission's and the European Court of Justice's approach to interpret institutional differences such as restrictions on the market freedoms of the EU.

63. The precise wording is 'United in diversity', see Treaty establishing a Constitution for Europe, Article I-8. (OJ C 310, vol. 47, 16 Dec 2004.

64. Conservative political forces in Germany have tried for decades to define and codify a German *Leitkutur*, or lead culture; they eventually were forced to the conclusion that this amounts to a futile undertaking.

65. Cf. A. O. Hirschman, 'Social Conflicts as Pillars of Democratic Market Societies', in A. O. Hirschman (ed.) *A Propensity to Self-Subversion*, Cambridge, Mass. and London, Harvard University Press, 1995: 231–248.

66. Art. 3 para 3 TEU.

67. Art. 3 I TEU, 151 et seq., 162 et seq. TFEU; cf. C. Offe, *Europe Entrapped*, Cambridge, Polity Press, 2015, pp. 120 et seq.; see also J. Neyer, *The Justification of Europe: A political theory of supranational integration*, Oxford, Oxford University Press 2012.

68. For the theoretical concept see the contributions in G. Frankenberg (ed.) *Order from Transfer: Comparative constitutional design and legal culture*, Cheltenham, UK and Northampton, MA, USA, Edward Elgar Publishing, 2013; several case studies in C. Stahn, *The Law and Practice of International Territorial Administration: Versailles to Iraq and beyond*, Cambridge, Cambridge University Press 2008.

69. Art. I-8.

70. Cf. C. Offe and U. K. Preuß, 'The Problem of Legitimacy in the European Polity: Is democratization the answer?', in C. Crouch and W. Streeck (eds), *The Diversity of Democracy: Corporatism, social order and political conflict*, Cheltenham, Edward Elgar, pp. 175–204 [192–3] (in this volume, Chapter Twenty).

71. J. Tully, 'Introduction', in A.-G. Gagnon and J. Tully (eds) *Multinational Democracies*, Cambridge, Cambridge University Press, 2001, p. 5; in the same direction J. Shaw 'Postnational constitutionalism in the European Union', in *Journal of European Public Policy*, 1999, vol. 6, no. 4, pp. 579–597.

72. S. Holmes, 'Precommitment and the paradox of democracy', in J. Elster and R. Slagstad (eds) *Constitutionalism and Democracy*, Cambridge, Cambridge University Press, 1988, pp. 195–240.

73. J. Tully, 'The unfreedom of the moderns in comparison to their ideals of constitutional democracy', *The Modern Law Review*, 2002, vol. 65, no. 2, pp. 204–228 [207].

74. *Ibid.*, p. 209 and 218 [quote].

75. A. Wiener, *The Invisible Constitution of Politics: Contested norms and international encounters*, Cambridge, CUP, 2008, pp. 21 et seq.

76. Ladeur, 'Conflicts Law', p. 396.

77. J. H. H. Weiler 'Fin-de-Siècle Europe', in R. Dehousse (ed.) *Europe after Maastricht: An ever closer union?*, München, C. H. Beck, 1994, pp. 203–216 [215].

78. Weiler, 'Federalism without Constitutionalism...', p. 67 f.

79. J. Corkin, 'Experimental Constitutionalism in the EU: Coordinating legal difference through mutual recognition, mutual law and mutual learning, in C. Joerges and C. Glinski (eds) *The European Crisis and the Transformation of Transnational Governance: Authoritarian managerialism versus democratic governance*, Oxford, Hart Publishing, 2014, pp. 359–382 [359]; an extensive account of the status of differentness in the EU presents C. Landfried, *Das politische Europa. Differenz als Potential der Europäischen Union*, 2nd edn, Baden-Baden, Nomos, 2005.

Chapter Two

The Significance of Cognitive and Moral Learning for Democratic Institutions[*]

Ulrich K. Preuß

The idea that power is legitimate only when it is granted by the will of the ruled demonstrates the normative superiority of democracy above all other forms of governing. The basic idea that freedom and authority are reconciled with each other is constitutive only for democratic models of power and indicates their uniqueness. Other concepts of political rule may make manifold promises of salvation in order to justify the individual's subordination under the requirements of their respective pledges; only democracy is a model of self-rule of the people.

This unique quality makes democracy also, in a specific manner, vulnerable to the weaknesses of human nature. There are other forms of government, such as theocracies, monarchies, aristocracies, dictatorships, and rule through specially qualified individuals (holy persons, the Lord's anointed, warriors, the initiated and the like). In a democracy, it is the ordinary citizen who rules. That is, the functioning of democracy is founded upon the intellectual and moral ordinariness of people. It is then either by chance or because of a skillful institutional arrangement that democratic power is exercised by outstanding political leaders. The omnipresent complaints about the deficits or even failure of democracy can essentially be reduced to the basic argument according to which democracy has until now not found reliable mechanisms for the selection of the persons most able to exercise democratic rule. That is a serious problem, on which I, however, will not elaborate here, because there exists a graver problem, namely how democracy can perform its mission of both effective and legitimate rule despite the uncertainties about the appropriate qualities not only of the democratic leaders but of the people themselves, whose will in the last instance determines the course of democratic politics. In other words, does democracy dispose of equipment that protects it against the weaknesses and failures of the *demos*? This is, of course, a question about the relationship between persons and institutions in the democratic system.

In what follows, I start with a brief reminder of one classical answer to this problem in democratic theory, Rousseau's claim that the identity of the rulers and the ruled ensures the good quality of democratic decisions, and its fallacy (I). In a

---

[*] 'The Significance of Cognitive and Moral Learning for Democratic Institutions', in I. Shapiro, S. Skowronek and D. Galvin (eds), *Rethinking Political Institutions: The art of the state*, New York – London, New York University Press, 2006, pp. 303–321.

second step of the argument, I show that modern complex societies are increasingly confronted with cognitive and moral problems, which require methods of solution for which the democratic means of problem solving appear insufficient (II). I then turn to the issue of learning as a problem-solving method used not only by persons, organisations, and institutions but also by political systems (III). Thereafter, I deal with the relationship between learning and power. If, according to the famous statement of K.W. Deutsch, 'power is the ability to afford not to learn',[1] the question arises whether democracy – the form of government in which the people possess the supreme power here includes the right of the people not to learn. I make the claim that the legitimacy of democratic institutions in modern societies requires openness for generating, preserving, and enhancing both cognitive and moral knowledge (IV).

I. A democratic answer to a democratic problem, and why it fails

When we reflect on the possibilities of increasing the quality of democratic governance, we always have to take into account two discrepant elements: the moral and cognitive qualities of the people who rule themselves and the impersonal functioning of institutions – rules of action that impose themselves upon the subjectivity of the individuals and that protect the people against their inclinations toward myopia and irresponsible behaviour.[2] It is the well-known tension between *ratio* and *voluntas* that is particularly relevant in democracies. The core element of democracy – the people's will as the source of supreme authority – embodies a deep tension: the people's will in its purest and most authentic quality requires its immediate presence, and, if this is not possible, its utmost mirror-image representation.[3] However, the popular will in its quality as the source of supreme authority requires the willingness of the people to mediate their more or less spontaneous intuitions, to launder, as it were, their preferences, to reflect on the effects of their will power on others who are not present but who are affected by their decisions; that is, to assume responsibility for their actions. In other words, while the former element – outwardly more authentically democratic – is prone to foster irrational and irresponsible behaviour,[4] the latter – at first glance less democratic – is likely to be more beneficial to the people.

As we know, Rousseau and all democratic theorists who follow his line of reasoning deny this kind of tension. For them, the centuries-old question of what the ideal of a good and just government demands and by which criteria of justice the rule of one person over another should be evaluated has an amazing, simple, and suggestive solution. Since the end of the eighteenth century, democracy has been recognised as the form of just rule because it is tantamount to the self-rule of the people, that is, a political order in which those who are subject to the rule are at the same time its authors. Rousseau was the first who gave this answer of seducing simplicity: when all decide over all collectively, that is, when all give the laws to themselves, then no injustice can be done to anybody. In such a case the general will is always correct, because 'there is no one who does not take that word "each" to pertain to himself and in voting for all think of himself'.[5] What comes into being is a complete mutuality among the members of the community, which prevents any kind of preference or discrimination whatsoever. In a strictly secular understanding of justice, this means nothing other than full identity of the people with itself, which signifies perfect self-determination as the means for perfect justice; one cannot be unjust to oneself. In this situation, the people '[are] in the position of a private person making a contract with himself'.[6]

Unfortunately, this conclusion suffers from a serious flaw. It does not take into account that the formation of the general will does not mean only self-binding but also binding others and being bound by others. Those who bind themselves through agreement within a collective resolution cannot unbind themselves without the agreement of all others. Collective self-determination is much more heteronomy than autonomy. If this is so, then the idea of responsibility comes into the fore; while in a framework of self-determination responsibility is irrelevant, ruling over others requires a minimum of concern for their welfare. This in turn requires that the rulers' decisions be appropriate in terms of their problem-solving capacity, that is, they must be based on both the knowledge of the relevant information and the alternatives that are available and the consciousness of principles that serve as criteria for the choices among those alternatives. In other words, responsibility demands cognitive and moral qualities of the rulers. Rousseau offered only a theory that explained why the general will was inherently just; for this theory, the cognitive and moral truth of the general will was of no systematic importance, because even a cognitively and morally deficient decision would not impair the legitimacy of the rule of the general will. It was the authorship of the people and not the quality of the decisions of the general will that created the legitimacy of democratic rule. Moreover, and this was of utmost importance for Rousseau, it was this perfectly mutual character of the general will that safeguarded individuals' freedom even under the condition of social dependence. For Rousseau and his contemporaries, living under the despotism of a feudal-absolutist regime, the protection of individuals' freedom was certainly the essential criterion for the evaluation of the quality of the collective will of the people. Today, however, we value democracy not only because it embodies the best available conditions of individual freedom but also because it is a political system that embodies the most favourable conditions for the inducement of collective reason, wisdom, and morality.

Rousseau himself suspected that these different requirements for the quality of democratic resolutions do not always stand in harmony with one another. A just collective decision that does not violate anybody's individual autonomy may still be wrong and damaging for the community.

> How can a blind multitude, which often does not know what it wants, because it seldom knows what is good for it, undertake by itself an enterprise as vast and difficult as a system of legislation? By themselves the people always will what is good, but by themselves they do not always discern it. The general will is always rightful, but the judgement which guides it is not always enlightened. It must be brought to see things as they are, and sometimes as they should be seen; it must be shown the good path, which it is seeking, and secured against

seduction, by the desires of individuals; it must be given a sense of situation and season, so as to weigh immediate and tangible advantages against distant and hidden evils. Individuals see the good and reject it; the public desires the good but does not see it. Both equally need guidance. Individuals must be obliged to subordinate their will to their reason; the public must be taught to recognize what it desires.[7]

Rousseau speaks here about wrong collective resolutions in a twofold sense: with respect to both their cognitive weaknesses and their moral faults. A decision is wrong in a cognitive sense if the people make a decision in the absence of a more enlightened account of what would be good and just ('the public desires the good but does not see it'). On the other hand, resolutions are morally insufficient when they have been made in a situation where the people have succumbed to the temptations of passions, where, in other words, the citizens recognise what is normatively correct but reject it. In the former case, the cognitive capacity is wanting; in the latter the control of reason over pure will is lacking. As we know, Rousseau pulls from this error-prone collective will the conclusion that a people actually require a superior intelligence that could safeguard the inherent cognitive and moral quality of the law, who 'could understand the passions of men without feeling any of them, whose happiness was independent of ours, but who would nevertheless make our happiness his concern'.[8]

Had Rousseau been less preoccupied with the idea that the people had to be physically present rather than being represented (e.g., in a parliament) in order to form a collective will, he might have been able to find a solution to this problem in the concept of institution. Institutions allow the conservation and the transfer of a person's knowledge and will to future generations. Just as much as, for instance, patents can be understood as private stores of knowledge[9] that continue to exist after the death of the person who created this knowledge, the constitution is a store of public knowledge in that it objectifies the will of the constituent powers for the use of subsequent generations.[10] Given that modern law (including modern constitutions) can be amended any time according to the very rules of the constitutions thanks to its positivity, constitutions can be regarded as the stores of the knowledge and experience of the chain of generations that lived under the same, if more or less, frequently amended constitution.[11] Depending upon the anti- or pro-institutionalist character of a political system, a people is doomed to gather experience for each generation anew or it can build upon the past experiences of its predecessors. Obviously, the former method is much more resource-consuming than the latter, which may account for the relative economic lag of some societies if compared with others that are more institution-friendly in their system of government.

It is plausible to assume that this correlation between knowledge and institutions, in particular between knowledge and the constitution, escaped Rousseau's attention because, for him, the question of how political power could be justified stood clearly in the foreground of his political philosophy. Since the rise of the modern European state in the seventeenth century, coercive power of the sovereign state had become the pivotal means of societal integration,[12] and political philosophers from Hobbes through Locke to Rousseau had developed systems of reasoning that aimed at limiting and legitimising the state's sovereign power through the natural rights of its subjects. Hobbes was primarily interested in the unconditional supremacy of state power over a chaotic plurality and a conflict-ridden society; Locke aimed at restricting state power firmly to its purpose to protect the natural rights of the individuals; and Rousseau, most ambitiously, claimed to have reconciled sovereign power and individual freedom in the idea of the general will emanating from the collectivity of the ruled who had turned rulers.

Yet, beyond these stark differences among them, these three philosophers converged in one particular point: power was the essential social and political energy whose quality determined the nature of the polity. When they argued for their respective conception of a good polity, they argued for or against a particular kind of power, which in their framework was, positively or negatively, the strategic resource for the shaping of the polity. In a political community whose social integration is mainly organised through the medium of power, the limitation and legitimating of this very power is the central concern. Hobbes was concerned about its supremacy, which he deemed necessary for the sake of imposing social discipline upon the society. Rousseau aimed at its preeminence because it secured the integrity of the general will. Locke, conversely, sought to limit it for the sake of the individual's freedom.

II. Problems that cannot be solved by power

Yet, power, understood in the Weberian sense of the 'probability that one actor within a social relationship will be in a position to carry out his own will despite resistance',[13] is not a resource that is able to solve all problems of a modern society. In particular, an increase of power does not mean an upsurge of problem-solving capacity, just as a reduction of power is tantamount to the weakening ability of the polity to cope with its problems. Unlimited power undermines sovereigns' authority because they cannot make credible promises, making them unable to allocate trust and, consequently, to engage in long-term social relations,[14] while self-limited power, as the case of Ulysses and the Sirens shows, can increase the range of options of the self-bound person.[15]

Moreover, coercive power has ceased to be the major force that ensures the social discipline of the individuals and the coherence of society. The basic conflicts of advanced contemporary societies cannot be understood in the conceptual framework of 'individual freedom versus sovereign power'.[16] The functional differentiation of modern societies; the acceleration of technological innovations and socioeconomic transformation; and processes of globalisation, with its shifting patterns of production, trade, financing, migration, environmental use, cultural orientation, and political domination,[17] have changed the character of conflicts and problems with which these societies have to cope. Although the traditional conflicts around socioeconomic status and cleavages, distribution and social justice, persist (though in different modes),[18] a new class of problems has turned up that follow a different logic. These conflicts include the relationship of humans to nature and to humankind's own technology; the globalisation of risks caused by people; the relationship between living generations as well between living and future generations; and the relationship between the two sexes, between various ethnic groups, and the like.

It is difficult to recognise a common positive attribute in these conflicts, but there is a negative one: none of these relationship problems can be solved with the characteristic and successful means of the modern constitutional state, namely power, law, and money.[19] Rather, we cannot fail to see that complex societies and their constituent parts exhibit a distinct functional need for responsible and ethical mass orientations, which can neither be compensated for by an ethic of responsibility on the part of elites and experts nor satisfied by falling back on the routinised, everyday moral orientations of the 'ordinary citizen'.[20] More and more, the individuals' sociability is induced less by the coercive authority of the state and built instead upon their self-regulatory capacity, that is, their own reasonable view and judgement. Political communities, in which those capacities of citizens are valued or at least seen as important, can be denominated as primarily guided by morality and knowledge.

Of course, this does not mean that previous societies, regulated mainly through power and obedience, did not require cognitive and moral capacities of their members. No social and political system could survive without a minimum standard of intellectual and moral qualities of its members. This is why, after the establishment of the absolutist state in the seventeenth and eighteenth centuries in Europe, the princes set up compulsory education in order to safeguard elementary cognitive abilities among their subjects, whereas the moral qualities were created by the churches.[21] The objective was mainly the learning of obedience as commanded by the state and its officials. Yet after the transformation of the absolutist into the constitutional state, of the subaltern subjects of a statist power machine into the citizens of a democratic republic, and after the change of the agrarian into the industrial, urban, individualised, and interdependent modern mass society, the requirements on the moral autonomy and the intellectual judgement of the individuals had considerably increased.

In the postindustrial society, whose productivity is dependent on individuals' knowledge and their ability for methodic acquisition of knowledge and information, these demands have undergone a further transformation. The modern and knowledge-based society values the disciplined acquisition and application of knowledge about industrial machinery and processes, as well as the ability for cognitive and moral orientation in extremely expanded, specialised, and complex patterns of action. The chains of action in which the individual is involved are so long and complicated that it has become ever more difficult to evaluate the social effects of one's actions according to the logic of a linear causality. To live a responsible personal life increasingly requires an almost scientific attitude and reflection of everyday life observations and experiences and the capacity and readiness to refer complex, uncertain, and often litigious connections to one's own moral constitution and, finally, to draw practical consequences from it.[22]

I will briefly specify four life spheres in which this reflexive attitude plays a pivotal role and where regulative power is of inferior significance:

1. There are spheres of life that are significant for the society at large and whose order belongs to the field of the community's responsibilities but that are insensitive to the (legally established) power of the community. The education of the children in the family and the school belongs to this field just as much as the behaviour of the sexes and the generations toward each other or their ability to cope with strangeness. Family and school have ceased to be special and paralegal spheres of internment in which parents and state rule over the bodies of children. Parents no longer possess the power to impose their will upon children with superior physical force in order to mould them into good members of the society. In order to achieve this goal today, responsible institutions must develop the ability for communication and interaction with the individual personalities of the children and young people and, most important, evoke in them the sense of the importance of this development process, which in earlier epochs would have been implanted within them more or less by authority through force.

2. There are groups in society that have become insensitive to both the rewards and the negative sanctions of its institutions. They are not attracted by the promises of a vocational career or the temptations of a high consumer level as rewards for their adjustment to the norms of the society. Nor can they be pulled back into the centre of the society through social punishments, by the neglect and discrimination of their fellow citizens, or through the inconveniencies of their material poverty. Such alienation and partly self-inflicted marginalisation, should not leave society indifferent, because their existence demonstrates a loss of control within the community and thus a challenge to and a restriction on the validity of its social, moral, and even legal norms. In extreme cases, this kind of exclusion from the society may even challenge the universality of those norms and hence endanger the identity of the community. The civilised society cannot leave drug addicts, those who have lost out because of rapid modernisation (marginalised and self-marginalised persons such as delinquents, the long-term unemployed, alcoholics, and homeless persons), and increasingly 'ghettoised' immigrants to their fates without betraying its basic principles and, in the long run, undermining its social cohesion. Police control is no answer to this question. Should society choose a strategy of coercive integration, or should one simply tolerate the status of the marginalised at the edge of the society, or should one perhaps even recognise their status in a positive sense? Questions of this kind require reactions, for which the constitutional state with its guarantee of individual rights, separation of powers and welfare institutions is hardly prepared, because it does not dispose of the necessary instruments that could influence the moral infrastructure of both the society and the individual.

3. But there are also configurations in which not only the marginalised but also those who live in the centre of society are confronted with new challenges. The constantly accelerating scientific-technological revolution exercises a strong pressure on the individual to replace outdated knowledge with new. This develops, to a certain extent, a durable 'standby knowledge alert' so that one is

always up-to-date with the conditions of the functioning of both workplace and consumer devices and with permanently changing vocational requirements. This situation asks for an epistemological attitude of experimentation, tolerance, or even indifference in relation to fixed knowledge and epistemological certainty that has up to now been seen only among scientists. Socially relevant knowledge is being accumulated less and less through experience and from perceptible, real objects (machines, books, hard currency) and more through power over immaterial information; this again requires a certain measure of theoretical knowledge about complex connections, which are transparent for a declining number of people. This is indicative of a new stage in the abstraction of social relations and knowledge about society.

The knowledge-sensitive basic attitude, which is necessary or at least useful in the spheres of occupation and consumption, has, however, an ambivalent character. As it applies to the role of the individuals as citizens it can have damaging and destructive consequences for the institutions of the community. The fulfilment of civic obligations and the observation of certain social responsibilities are based in the long run on the acceptance of ideas of legal commitment and moral certainty, and this again does presuppose an epistemology, in which knowledge, based on everyday life experience, represents a stable and reliable basis of individual acting. This civic spirit cannot be created by authoritatively imposed rules and prohibitions. Hence, there is reason to suspect that traditional means of state regulation have become increasingly ineffective.

4. Finally, the extension and intertwining of the chains of action, mentioned earlier, require a new kind of social and moral sensitivity, which no longer can be achieved through the traditional pattern of congruence of control and accountability. Traditional social morality evaluated the moral and legal character of the individual's actions and its consequences on the basis of a concept of causality, in which each part of the chain was identifiable and attributable to the acting individual. Today we speak of 'complex causality' when assessing the quality of our social, aesthetic and natural environment. Through this term we want to express that more and more conditions of our world are the effects of a combination of many different causal factors, so that only in the rarest cases is it possible to assign clear responsibilities. Attributions may be so general and vague that no one is able to derive active guidance from his or her individual conduct. If, for example, a considerable part of the ongoing climatic change is a consequence of the Western lifestyle, then the realisation of this complex chain of causality is more likely to discharge individuals of their responsibility for this result than to lead to a call for changes in human behaviour, since no individual can reasonably be burdened with the task of changing the way of life of a whole civilisation.

And yet, a well-organised society in the present requires a social and moral attitude that is willing to accept responsibilities for uncertain and remote consequences of individuals' behaviour. What was until recently almost exclusively required of scientists working at the boundaries of knowledge will increasingly be expected of the layman: since the life sciences have made the manufactured creation of human beings possible, the actual realisation of this step depends now upon the moral maturity of the society, in the end upon the individuals. The considerations called upon in this area require a much higher level of moral reflection than those demanded from the individuals in agrarian and industrial societies.

III. Institutional learning

So far I have spoken about the requirements that modern societies impose on their members and about the powerlessness of power in creating these qualities and appropriate social conduct. Power has only a limited importance for societal integration. What is required is individuals' capacity and willingness to act responsibly. Since the relevant cognitive and moral qualities of individuals are not innate, they have to be learned. Cognitive learning is a 'process of acquiring information and knowledge'[23]; moral learning is a social practice in which the normative orientations of individuals that affect their social conduct are formed.[24] Learning is a constitutive element of human beings' development and of their capacity to cope with the challenges of human life.

But not only human beings learn. Social institutions such as markets, organisations, firms, hospitals, governments, and networks learn,[25] at least in the cognitive sense of this term. Strictly speaking, only humans can acquire knowledge and moral orientations, but institutions 'learn' when their system of incentives encourage their members to create, acquire, and disseminate knowledge and values to the benefit of the institution. Institutions store not only information but also moral convictions. Institutions create models of thinking, reasoning, and social behaviour that impose themselves upon their members and develop a social environment and an institutional culture that may further or impede cognitive innovation and moral reorientation. There is plenty of research material with respect to firms and other organisations.[26]

In the field of political science, Karl W. Deutsch was the first to stress the role of communication, information, and value development in the understanding of political institutions, political behaviour, and political ideas. Thus, power is seen not simply as the ability of persons or organisations to impose their will upon the environment but as 'the most important currency in the interchanges between political systems and other major subsystems of the society'.[27] Like monetary currency, its function depends upon the trust of the society, and its coercive dimension is only a kind of safety net for the sake of damage control in case social expectations for the normal functioning of this currency are thwarted.

In this perspective, it is not coercive capabilities that define the essence of politics but 'the dependable coordination of human efforts and expectations for the attainment of the goals of the society'.[28] This explains why, for democracy as a political system that is built upon the coordination of voluntary social interaction, learning – the response to the challenge of the given state of affairs – is of pivotal significance.[29] The institution that embodies the relevant communicative – both cognitive and moral – capacities of individuals living in a democratic system is citizenship. Despite the important role of collective representative actors, such as, parties, interest groups, and parliaments, 'the quality of policy decisions and outcomes will ultimately depend upon the quality of the citizens' thought and action'.[30] The cognitive and moral resources of (active) citizens, as distinct from (subaltern) subjects, certainly depend upon their civic education both in formal institutions and in the social practice of civil society;[31] yet, arguably the basic prerequisite of citizenship is a constitutional structure in which the coercive element of power is minimised.

However, the traditional liberal constitutional paradigm of 'limited government'[32] is hardly sufficient for the fulfilment of the requirements of citizenship outlined so far, although it remains, of course, important. 'Limited government' focuses too much on the negative or positive role of state power for the organisation of the society. This approach to the understanding of the constitutional state regards all other resources, and, above all, the cognitive and moral abilities of the citizens, as unproblematic givens. As mentioned earlier, they had to be created by the absolutist state, and modern societies must care about them no less, perhaps even more.

Citizens in modern societies are not embedded in a set of homogeneous and stable values and cognitive and moral perspectives; they are confronted with processes of accelerated transformations of their natural, social, and economic environment, with technological innovations, and cultural diversity. In order to face the resulting uncertainties, they have to understand and cope with a multiplicity of epistemological and normative perspectives; they have to acquire an attitude of cognitive and moral reflection over their own acting. Hence, the process of generating the cognitive and moral resources of the citizens requires modes of learning that take the heterogeneity and multiplicity of epistemological and normative orientations into account. The learning of learning – of generating, acquiring, and applying knowledge – becomes more important than the learning of knowledge.[33] The school – the basic institution in which the future citizens of the community are formed intellectually and morally – will then no longer be a place for the conveyance of traditional knowledge but a place for acquiring the ability to understand, to bear, and to cope with the variety and openness of knowledge and of values.

Citizenship is only one, albeit the most important institution of democracy that needs particular conditions for learning and that represents the polity's self-image of what is necessary and desirable to know and to store for future generations. There are other institutions that, albeit in different ways, reflect the necessity of the political system to learn. For instance, in all modern societies, the concept of law has undergone a considerable change. Rather than representing durability and generality (as an expression of universal truth), it has become more and more an instrument of regulating and reregulating specific situations and constellations depending upon changing circumstances. As a consequence, in Germany the procedures of legislation have been made reflexive in that the effects of the laws upon the regulated object are under permanent scrutiny by scientific institutes, work groups, and NGOs. The procedural rules of the Bundestag establish a mechanism of expert advice and of 'Inquiry Commissions' in order to provide the lawmakers with appropriate knowledge, as distinct from their everyday experience and their common sense, needed for their regulative tasks. Also, the initiators of legislative bills have to designate the existing alternatives to their particular proposals. A major institutional innovation, to mention a last example, has been the long-standing jurisprudence of the German Federal Constitutional Court, which imposes upon the legislature the obligation to correct laws if the empirical assumptions underlying their normative regulations about future developments do not materialise on review; this is a particular case of institutional coping with the problem of uncertainty. Today, experimentation laws, revision clauses in laws, and time-limited laws serve as well-known instruments of the political system for dealing with cognitive uncertainty and for producing a constant readiness to correct decisions in light of better knowledge.

IV. The evolutionary risk of voluntary ignorance and the democratic duty to learn

Not only individuals but also organisation and polities can fail to learn. The demise of great empires has time and again been explained by the failure of the imperial elites to meet the challenges imposed upon them by new developments in their environment. Gibbon's *History of the Decline and Fall of the Roman Empire,* published between 1776 and 1788, has remained the outstanding and reputable work in this field. The history of the decline and fall of the Soviet Empire remains still to be written; it will certainly add another chapter to the grand book about the decline of great empires caused by their inherent incapacity to learn. But that does not mean that democracies have good reason for self-complacency and self-righteousness. They, too, are susceptible to self-destructive tendencies. Leaving aside here the conventional Tocquevillean concerns about the destruction of democratic freedom through the egalitarianism of mass democracy and the 'tyranny of the majority', today we have to care about the danger of the elimination of democracy through democratic means[34] and about what today seems to be the more serious threat, part of the 'evolutionary risks of democracy',[35] a widespread sense of dissatisfaction and frustration with democracy among the popular masses in many democratic countries. I am afraid that we have to add to this listing the danger of unnecessary, that is, self-inflicted ignorance.

Both the political and the economic system within a society can occasionally be so resistant to learning that the society's knowledge of its own malfunctioning either disappears or remains without consequence; it fails to turn into an instrument of societal self-observation, self-regulation, and, finally, self-improvement.[36] When the political or economic power elites are able to let the knowledge about the society run dry by neglecting it, then it is not sufficient to shield the institutions of knowledge production from the effects of the noncommunicative quality of power. In such a case, mechanisms have to be found that pressure the centres of power to learn. I do not mean to suggest a political system governed according to merely technical, scientific, and objective criteria. What is at stake in a democratic polity is, rather, the principle that the public and controversial debate among the various social forces about different policy options should occur on the level of the best attainable standard of knowledge. In other words, in a democratic system, collective decisions can be considered as legitimate only if they are taken on the basis of an updated standard of the ability of the people's up-to-date awareness of both their collective problems and possible solutions to those problems.

This principle may appear simplistic, but if we put it into the framework of democratic theory, many difficulties arise. When does a social group use its power in a legitimate way in order to ignore a certain knowledge about the society or to interpret it in a sense that would benefit its interests, and when does this group go beyond the border of permissible dethematisation or even suppression of knowledge? Behind this question we can discover a deeper problem, namely why it is that in a democratic society, the suppression of knowledge about the insufficiencies of the society is illegitimate if the political elites have been empowered by popular vote. Should not democracy include the right of the people to suppress or, for that matter, the right to tolerate the suppression of unpopular knowledge? Is not, to repeat Rousseau's statement referred to earlier, 'the general will ... always rightful', although 'the judgment which guides it is not always enlightened'?

Obviously, two different legitimisation principles compete here. Those who are unwilling to know derive their legitimacy from the democratic principle of the power acquired rightfully according to democratic rules – the government is elected, and interest groups are constitutionally recognised by the constitution as factors in an open political process. But which principles are invoked by those who insist upon the 'duty to know'? The freedom of sciences protects, individually and institutionally, the process of independent, power-averse 'knowledge-production', but not the transfer of knowledge from the system of scientific research to the political system, and quite rightly so, because the absence of such a guarantee is an indispensable element of the constitutional protection of the autonomy of science. But which other source of legitimisation can be invoked to support the postulate that the modern democratic community must develop the ability and the willingness to learn?

If we understand democracy as the most advanced form of collective self-determination of a civil society, then we can derive from this starting point the postulate that individuals must be able to articulate and discuss their political will among themselves on the highest level of knowledge to which they have access. The power formed in and through democratic processes of will formation is democratically legitimised only to the degree to which the members of the society can decide freely whether they agree with the political groups that canvass for their votes; and 'freely' today means with the awareness that society is constantly changing and undergoing a permanent knowledge revolution, that is, in the full knowledge of the possible continuities and discontinuities of the society's self-transformation. In other words, a legitimate process of will formation is not possible on the basis of self-inflicted ignorance; power based upon 'willful' ignorance lacks democratic legitimacy. Therefore, the constitutional guarantee of the ability and willingness to learn is an inherent requirement of the democratic principle itself. In terms of constitutional law, this constitutional guarantee is an indispensable element of the legitimacy of the democratic public authority. If we add to the traditional rules about democratic competition for power the principle that cognitive and moral learning should be the rationale of democratic institutions, this enriches considerably the value and the functioning of the democratic principle. We could prevent political power from becoming knowledge-blind, that is, from becoming the privilege of having not to learn. This privilege, like all privileges, protects only those who hold power, to the detriment of the political community as a whole.

Yet, we have to consider the possibility that ignorance can be legitimate under certain circumstances. This proposition leads back to the problem of moral learning. Cognitive learning does not stand for the appropriation of as much new information as possible; rather, it suggests a methodical attitude of individuals, giving rise to individuals' judgement and evaluation of their own role in the process of acquiring and applying knowledge. It is a reflexive attitude, which indeed can include the moral decision to remain ignorant. For instance, I may decide not to know whether I am the bearer of a potential disease against which remedies will not be available during my normal life expectancy. This kind of ignorance has a reflexive character, which the individual has chosen on the basis of the knowledge about the significance of knowledge and of ignorance. It is, in other words, a deliberately chosen ignorance. Whether intentional ignorance can also be a morally justified decision on the collective level is a difficult question, which I will only raise, without examining it here in depth. For instance, should a democratic society forbid the cloning of human beings? I restrict myself to the suggestion that a criterion for a justifiable decision should be whether ignorance is based on the effectiveness of power or on the reflection of knowledge – admittedly an abstract criterion, but one that is susceptible to being concretised and operationalised.

V. Concluding remarks

To conclude briefly: the power concentrated in the modern state which at its starting point was the secular problem solver in that it expelled all religious and moral questions from the public agenda, turned itself into a problem, whose solution since the end of the eighteenth century has been the modern constitutional state. Yet, today, the modern constitutional state is ill prepared to solve the serious problem of mass democracy – that democratic power can be unwise, corrupt, self-damaging, myopic, and irresponsible toward future generations. It is not well prepared for the inducement of cognitively and morally enlightened decisions and policies. To be sure, Lord Acton's famous statement is still true: 'Power corrupts; absolute power corrupts absolutely'. But even more suitable would be this updating: 'Power stupefies; absolute power stupefies absolutely'. And self-inflicted stupidity is immoral.

Notes

1. K. W. Deutsch, *The Nerves of Government: Models of political communication and control*, New York and London, Free Press/Collier-Macmillan, 1963, p. 111.

2. Cf. J. Elster, *Ulysses Unbound: Studies in rationality, precommitment, and constraints*, Cambridge, Cambridge University Press, 2000; S. Holmes, 'Precommitment and the paradox of democracy', in J. Elster and R. Slagstad (eds) *Constitutionalism and Democracy*, Cambridge, Cambridge University Press, 1988, pp. 195–240.

3. For the difference between a politics of presence as distinct from a politics of representation, cf. A. Phillips, *The Politics of Presence*, New York, Clarendon Press, 1995.

4. J. A. Schumpeter, *Capitalism, Socialism and Democracy*, New York, Harper Colophon Books, 1975, pp. 256 ff.

5. J.-J. Rousseau, *The Social Contract*, London, Penguin Books, 1968 (1762), II/4.

6. *Ibid.*, I/7.

7. *Ibid.*, II/6.

8. *Ibid.*, II/7.

9. H. Albach and J. Jin, 'Learning in the Market', in H. Albach *et al.* (eds) *Organisationslernen – institutionelle und kulturelle Dimensionen*, Berlin, Edition Sigma [WZB-Jahrbuch], 1998, p. 369.

10. U. K. Preuß, *Constitutional Revolution: The link between constitutionalism and progress*, Atlantic Highlands, N.J., Humanities Press International, 1995, pp. 109 ff.

11. It is therefore not just a matter of political style that France has experienced some fifteen constitutions after the revolution of 1789, while the United States has lived under one constitution that has undergone seventeen amendments in almost the same timespan.

12. M. Mann, *The Sources of Social Power,* Vol. I., *A History of Power from the Beginning to A.D. 1760*, Cambridge, Cambridge University Press, 1986.

13. M. Weber, *Economy and Society: An outline of interpretive sociology*, G. Roth and C. Wittich (eds) Berkeley, University of California Press, 1978, p. 53.

14. Elster, *Ulysses Unbound*, pp. 146 ff.

15. J. Elster, *Ulysses and the Sirens*, rev. edn, Cambridge, Cambridge University Press, 1984, pp. 87 ff.; Preuß, *Constitutional Revolution*, p. 113.

16. Preuß, *Constitutional Revolution*, pp. 115 ff.

17. D. Held, A. McGrew, D. Goldblatt, and J. Perraton, *Global Transformations: Politics, economics and culture*, Cambridge, Polity Press, 2000.

18. A. Giddens, *The Class Structure of the Advanced Societies*, 2nd edn, London, Hutchinson, 1981.

19. Cf. A. Giddens, *The Consequences of Modernity*, Cambridge, Polity Press, 1992; A. Giddens, *Modernity and Self-Identity: Self and society in the late modern age*, Cambridge, Polity Press, 1992; U. Beck, A. Giddens, and S. Lash, *Reflexive Modernization: Politics, tradition and aesthetics in the modern social order*, Cambridge, Polity Press, 1994.

20. Cf. C. Offe, 'Micro-Aspects of Democratic Theory: What makes for the deliberative competence of citizens?', in A. Hadenius (ed.) *Democracy's Victory and Crisis*, Cambridge, Cambridge University Press, 1997, pp. 81–104.

21. R. Vierhaus, *Germany in the Age of Absolutism*, trans. J. B. Knudsen, Cambridge, Cambridge University Press, 1988, pp. 72 ff.

22. Beck *et al.*, *Reflexive Modernization*, pp. 174 ff.

23. Albach and Jin, *Learning in the Market*, p. 357.

24. L. Kohlberg, *Psychology of Moral Development*, San Francisco, Harper & Row, 1981, pp. 294 ff.; L. Kohlberg, *Psychology of Moral Development*, San Francisco, Harper & Row, 1984, pp. 170ff.

25. Albach and Jin, *Learning in the Market*; F. Leeuw *et al.* (eds) *Can Governments Learn?: Comparative perspectives on evaluation & organizational learning*, New Brunswick/London, Transaction Publishers, 1994.

26. Albach and Jin, *Learning in the Market*.

27. Deutsch, *Nerves of Government*, p. 120.

28. *Ibid.*, p. 124.

29. *Ibid.*, pp. 163 ff.

30. Offe, *Democratic Theory*, p. 81.

31. C. Offe and U. K. Preuß, 'Democratic Institutions and Moral Resources', in D. Held (ed.) *Political Theory Today*, Cambridge, Polity Press, 1991, pp. 143–171; C. A. Rimmerman, *The New Citizenship*, Boulder, Westview Press, 1997; I. Davies *et al.* (eds) *Good Citizenship and Educational Provision*, London and New York, Routledge, 1999.

32. Cf. C. J. Friedrich, *Limited Government*, Englewood Cliffs, N.J., Prentice Hall, 1974.

33. K.-H. Ladeur, 'Post-Modern Constitutional Theory: A prospect for the self-organising society', *Modern Law Review*, 1997, vol. 60, pp. 617–629.

34. K. Loewenstein, 'Militant democracy and fundamental rights', *American Political Science Review*, 1937, vol. 31, pp. 417–432, and pp. 638–658.

35. D. Zolo, *Democracy and Complexity: A realist approach*, Cambridge and Oxford, Polity Press, 1992, pp. 99 ff.

36. Cf. Deutsch, *Nerves of Government*, pp. 219 ff.

Chapter Three

Democratic Institutions and Moral Resources[*]

Claus Offe and Ulrich K. Preuß

Modes of production versus modes of participation

It has been observed that 'democracy' has become a universal formula of legitimation for a broad range of radically different societies and their respective modes of governance and political participation.[1] By the mid-1970s, there was virtually no regime between Chile and China that did not rest its claim to legitimacy upon being 'democratic' in some sense, or at least upon its being in the process of some transition to some version of democracy. Thus the term 'democracy' seemed to have lost its distinctiveness: it failed to highlight significant differences between socio-political arrangements. To be sure, one still used to add qualifiers such as 'liberal', 'authoritarian', or 'people's' democracy in order to distinguish specific types and structural particularities of governments; but these, important as they may be, were often considered to be of minor significance compared with other dimensions of comparative analysis.

It has become common in the twentieth century to characterise societies with respect to *their socio-economic system* and, particularly, to the economic and technological rank they have achieved within the world economy. It has become much more common and respectable to divide the world conceptually into the 'First', 'Second', 'Third' and sometimes 'Fourth' worlds than to divide it into its 'democratic' and its 'non-democratic' parts, as the latter categorisation basically presupposes an authoritative definition of the contested notion of 'democracy'. Differences concerning various *forms of government,* and particularly specific variants of 'democracy', seemed to belong to the superstructure of societies – and to the arsenal of ideological weapons in the worldwide conflict between 'capitalism' and 'socialism'. What tended to be considered objectively distinctive – and the most basic dimension of which political variables were merely derivatives – were socio-economic and technological characteristics, or 'modes of production'.

Evidently, or so we wish to argue, this conventional and convenient 'materialist' way of portraying societies is currently losing much of its plausibility. There are a number of reasons for this. First, the notion that national societies can be unequivocally tied as a whole to some clear-cut 'mode of production' or 'stage

---

[*]   'Democratic Institutions and Moral Resources', in D. Held (ed.), *Political Theory Today,* Cambridge, Polity, 1991, pp. 143–171.

of development' is clearly obsolete. There are as many and as diverse varieties of 'capitalism' (ranging from Austria to Singapore) as there are of 'socialism' (ranging from Norway to North Korea); as far as 'underdevelopment' as an umbrella category is concerned, the analogous point has been made by Brazilian intellectuals who refer to their country as 'Belgindia', meaning 'Belgium within India'. It appears to us to be of great and not yet fully perceived significance that it is precisely the 'socialist' (Comecon) countries, i.e. those in which Marxist-Leninist party doctrines form the basis of the official self-identification, which now are in the process of undertaking major reforms starting with fundamental changes in the *political* organisation of their societies – an approach which, in terms of the hitherto official party doctrine of these countries, amounts to putting the cart before the horse. President Gorbachev has started the reform of the Soviet economy with a substantial reform of the constitution. Poland strives for a way out of its chronic economic decay by organising a new social contract in the literal sense of this term, the most important stipulations of which aim at the establishment of democratic representation and of a more responsive government. Hungary has become the first socialist country to introduce a multi-party system, with elections free by the standards of the liberal democracies, and to abolish the 'socialist' character of the country as it is laid down in the constitution. And these changes seem indeed to be experienced by the people of these countries as decisive and liberating ones – much in the same way as the people of Greece, Portugal and Spain (to say nothing of those of Argentina, Brazil and Uruguay) perceived their respective 'transitions to democracy' as constituting profound change both more significant than even a major step towards economic development and as a sign of hope that such steps might take place in the future. Clearly, the demand for political democracy is undergoing an unexpected renaissance.

Quite at variance with most versions of Marxist doctrine, it is no longer the 'autonomous' development of the forces of production which gives rise to new institutions and new forms of popular government; on the contrary, democratic institutions and procedures are being discovered as liberating and 'productive' forces *sui generis,* considered capable, apart from their political aspects, of energising the economic system and paving the road towards social and economic progress. Now it is again the political and constitutional axis along which societies are seen – and see themselves – to differ most significantly (both from other societies and from their own past), and not primarily the axis of the forces and/or relations of production. Moreover, the latter are increasingly perceived as being derivative of the former, instead of vice versa.

All this should not be mistaken for the final triumph of the Western model of liberal democracy – whatever that may be, given the widely divergent manifestations of democratic regimes even among the Western countries. After the Second World War the European countries had a fair degree of success in mitigating and taming class conflicts by making capitalism and democratic mass politics compatible with each other through the establishment of the Keynesian welfare state. However, the paradigm by which democratic capitalism reconciles individual and collective rationalities wears thin. Within this paradigm, military strength, security achieved through bureaucratic control, 'instrumental' knowledge and economic growth are all considered essential factors in the comprehensive progress of society and in the solution of all major social problems. The rationality of action will eventually contribute to the perfection of the 'system'. This equation has evidently lost its persuasiveness. It is rightly questioned whether the more that actors – be they states, be they individuals – accomplish according to the standards of these sectoral rationalities, the more they will promote their collective well-being (whether or not the 'relations of production' happen to be socialist). What is called for under this condition is, as we shall argue, a design of adequate or 'appropriate' institutions[2] that modifies the rationality of action in ways which make it more compatible with and conducive to the requirements of collective well-being.

One might suspect that the relatively comfortable and so far generally successful experience that the West European democracies have had with the constitutional arrangements adopted after the Second World War is now tending to put them in a comparatively disadvantageous position, as the 'learning pressure' to renovate institutional arrangements in the face of new conflicts and cleavages[3] has subsided much more than has been the case with many of the 'newly democratising countries'.

As a consequence of some of the structural changes taking place within modern societies, the ideal of 'progress' – technological, economic, military, social and cultural – which was the underlying and powerfully energising force for the democratic optimism of the nineteenth and, notwithstanding the barbarous regression of fascism, also of the twentieth century, has faded away. The 'limits of growth' refer primarily to physical problems such as ecological damage, changes of climate or overpopulation; but their implication is basically a social and political one. They challenge the inherent rationale of our industrial civilisation and its political institutions, throwing their basic assumptions and their almost religious certitude into fundamental doubt. The basically 'modern' vision that the use individuals make of their rational capabilities will, if mediated through the right kind of economic and political institutions, contribute to their collective progress and well-being, is being contested. At the very least, those political institutions and procedures which supposedly serve the purpose of mediating the rationality of actors and the desirability of outcomes are increasingly open to question.

The theological foundations of modern political theory

'Democracy' is arguably the only formula in the modern world which is able to legitimise all kinds of political regimes. Theorists as different as Carl Schmitt and Joseph A. Schumpeter were probably right in pointing out that the modern creed of democracy is to be understood as a secularised version of the most elementary tenets of Christian theology.[4] According to them, the democratic omnipotence of the people and of the legislator has become the substitute for the Almighty Will of God, whose commands are the ultimate sources of order in this world, and the equal value of each and every individual in modern democracy reflects the Christian belief that 'the Redeemer died for all: He did not differentiate between individuals of different social status'.[5] In view of current political conflicts in Ireland, Poland, Latin America, Lebanon, Israel, Iran, the Soviet Union and many other countries, it is plausible to assume that the intimate connection between religion and politics is not an exclusive property of the Christian world and that the striving for political order bears many attributes of a sacred cause throughout the world.[6]

If we realise that the conception of the common good is the secularised version of the 'divine order' and hence itself a religious idea, we can understand why the political principle to which it has the closest affinity is democracy: religion is dedicated to the realisation of the plenitude of human life by linking it with the divine order, and politics in its most demanding version is committed to making man the creator of his destiny in this world. It is therefore not surprising that the sole alternative to the democratic legitimation of power is the theocratic one. Despite many deep and irreconcilable differences, both theocracy and democracy make the claim that the destiny of mankind requires justification through the will of a creator that binds humankind in a 'good' order, whether divine or secular.

This reference to the concept of political theology (or, as it were, to the idea of an 'immanent transcendence') may help us to understand the tension between the claim of the political order to be 'good' and 'just' and the omnipotence of its sovereign – a tension which can only arise where we cannot resort to the authority of any external norms and principles of justice. If we ourselves are the creator of the just order, on behalf of what principle could we conceivably oppose it? The history of Christian theology gives much evidence for manifold doubts as to whether the Will of God must be regarded as omnipotent because it is inherently just or, conversely, that it cannot but be considered inherently just, because it is omnipotent.

The Rights of Man could not really protect the individual in his or her natural nakedness; they were rather the expression of isolation than its remedy, because they did not tell individuals to which community they belonged. Nor could the people's sovereignty *per se* save them from the uncertainties of their new status as an atomistic master of him- or herself, because the individual's participation in the omnipotence of the sovereign does not tell that individual what is right. Hence from the very beginning of democratic theory, theorists had to deal with the question how to secure not only the omnipotence of the new 'mortal God' – this could be deduced from the autonomy of individuals and their natural freedom and equality – but at the same time its wisdom and justice. In other words, how can we assure that, since people are not gods, although they have replaced divine commands with their own, their commands are not only the expression of a sovereign will but also of the common good? It was a difficult task to justify popular sovereignty and self-government as the consequence of individual freedom and equality; it is far more difficult – probably impossible – to justify popular self-government if it is known to be prone to fall prey to the inherent weakness and wickedness of humans.

Interests, checks and the general will

In the history of democracy we find appeals to a variety of moral capabilities in citizens which are deemed to motivate them to fulfil their civic obligations vis-à-vis the body politic and their fellow-citizens. The most prominent among these moral capabilities are virtue, reason and self-interest.

However, the framers of the American constitution did not, in the last analysis, put the decisive weight on either virtue or reason as the solid foundation of the republic.[7] And they were positively sceptical about reason as a power to rule the common will of the people. Madison himself was suspicious about the very notion of a common will: he believed it impossible that such a will could freely emanate from within a united civil society, and that it could only be espoused by a hereditary or self-appointed government. Nor did he deplore the inability of civil society to generate a united will from within, but rather saw in that fragmented and disunited nature a guarantee of the preservation of individual freedom. In other words, he relied on the fact that

> different interests necessarily exist in different classes of citizens' and that/ whilst all authority ... will be derived from and dependent on the society, the society itself will be broken into so many parts, interests and classes of citizens, that the rights of individuals, or of the minority, will be in little danger from interested combinations of the majority.[8]

Thus the American democratic model relieved the sovereign people from the heavy burden of a nearly sacred task to define and implement the common good. Instead, the model restricted itself to the task of devising institutions (such as the natural right to private property and the division of powers) which (a) allowed the individuals to pursue their diverse interests and their particular notions of happiness, thereby at the same time (b) avoiding the danger of an omnipotent government imposing its notion of collective happiness upon the people. Instead of 'unifying' the people on the basis of some collective will, it seemed more promising to the framers to move in the opposite direction of promoting the diversity and fragmentation of interests. In a way, these *institutions* were designed to play the role of 'congealed' or 'sedimented' virtue, which thus made the *actual practice* of these virtues, such as truthfulness, wisdom, reason, virtue, justice and all kinds of exceptional moral qualities, to some extent dispensable – on the part of both the rulers and the ruled. This ingenious machinery is evidently far less demanding in moral terms than what would be required of citizens in a different type of democracy, one which comes close to aspiring to the secular redemption of the people through a more or less permanent revolutionising of those social conditions which expose the people to social and economic conditions of suffering, poverty, oppression, humiliation, dependence, ignorance and superstition.

This latter kind of aspiration was in fact what inspired the French Revolution. Above all, it was a sequence of social revolutions – successively the revolutions of the nobility, of the bourgeoisie, of the urban masses, and of the peasants[9] – in which the fate of each individual was seen to be inescapably tied to the fate and action of every other individual. It is no accident that this revolution took place in a Catholic country; the conviction that every soul is equal before God, that salvation is not earned through personal excellence and superiority but is the expression of God's mercy towards the miserable and the unfortunate, if secularised, nourishes the idea of collective liberation through *social* revolution. (The impact of a political theology which is energised by the concept of social revolution, i.e. of collective emancipation, is particularly vigorous in Catholic countries of the so-called Third World, especially in Latin America.) Hence the notion of popular sovereignty was from the very beginning associated with the indivisible will-power of a collective body, be it the nation, the republic or the united people, while institutional mediations and machineries were considered to be of minor importance. 'No matter how a nation will, it is sufficient that she will; all forms are good and her will is always the supreme law'[10] proclaimed Abbé Sieyès, a Catholic theologian, on the eve of the French Revolution.

Undoubtedly Sieyès made the implication that the will-power of the nation is inherently reasonable, because it was inconceivable – particularly in the age of Enlightenment – that an arbitrary will could become the law. No more than God could have an erroneous will could the people err; by virtue of the fact of being the will of the people, this will was 'reasonable', 'right', 'just', 'virtuous'. This equation was evidently informed by Rousseau's *Social Contract* and his construction of the general will (*volonté générale*). When Rousseau stated that 'the general will is always right and aims always at the common good'[11] he did not imply, as some commentators have argued, any inherent goodness or substantive morality in the empirical will of the people. Actually, he had a better argument, namely a more procedural one. For he radicalised – by inverting it – a prescription that Montesquieu had devised to assure the reasonableness of the law. According to Montesquieu, law-givers in a democracy should always be subjected to their own laws. Rousseau turned this principle around: instead of saying 'the author of the laws must be subjected to them' he reversed the sentence, stating that 'the people that is subject to the law must be its author'.[12] What is the implication of this inversion, and what is its significance? According to both of these rules, the law is general in that it applies to both the ruled and the ruler. But Montesquieu's rule does not preclude the possibility that a ruler who is – for instance due to idiosyncratic (masochistic) characteristics or a privileged economic position – incapable of being negatively affected by the content of the law, might impose unjust suffering upon the ruled. Although the law applies to this ruler, it does so with consequences that differ from the way in which it applies to everyone else. This problematic result could only be avoided if the economic conditions, interests, needs, feelings and preferences of the law-giver and the subjects of the law were sufficiently similar as to affect all of them in substantively equal terms. This is precisely the point of Rousseau's rule. As the subject of the law is made its author, as the subject and hence the author are the popular classes, and as each participant in the process of law-making will, in the process of deliberating the content of the law, give primary consideration to the likes of him- or herself (and hence pay little attention to economic or other kinds of 'exceptional' conditions in which the law might also apply), the social impact of the law will tend to be of a highly egalitarian nature as a result of the very procedure of law-making.[13] This, in fact, is not just the psychological inclination of ordinary law-makers, but also the normative condition of a substantively just (or 'democratic') and hence of an effectively binding law.

We have dealt with Rousseau and the American conception of popular sovereignty at some length in order to explain not only that the relationship between sovereignty and reason has quite distinct roots in the different traditions of the American and the French Revolutions but that its contemporary features are still vigorously affected by this tradition. At a first glance it is surprising that precisely that theory of democracy which presupposed the utmost equality of all citizens was to nourish the revolution in a country suffering extreme inequalities, whereas in the American colonies, where social and economic inequalities were rather limited, a theory of popular sovereignty prevailed which bluntly denied the possibility of a common will and interest which would unite the people. Yet this paradox is plausibly explained by the fundamentally different characters of the two revolutions: the French was a social revolution, whereas the American Revolution, apart from being a struggle for national independence, was a purely constitutional revolution which in socio-economic respect was explicitly conservative. A social revolution determines the fate of the people as a whole and hence ties the individual strictly to the destiny of his social category. When Rousseau stated that nobody could work for himself without working for others, he was not only presenting a secularised version of the Christian command to love one's fellow-creature as oneself, but was unconsciously foreshadowing the social dimension of reciprocity and solidarity. This notion of democracy and the concept of social revolution were mutually reinforcing, because the perception of the people as a united, corporate body underscored the collective character of their destiny and hence their genuine equality, which at the same time directed their hopes towards social emancipation, because this

> image of a 'multitude ... united in one body' and driven by one will was an exact description of what they actually were, for what urged them on was the quest for bread, and the cry for bread will always be uttered with one voice.[14]

The American and French traditions in democratic theory: balancing individual interests and the common good

The American tradition views democratic politics and popular power not as an unequivocal ideal, but as something potentially dangerous. Passions must be checked – both the passions of the people (and the irreconcilable 'factions' that will of necessity emerge within the people as a whole) and the passions of the political elites who always are tempted to exploit the powers of government for their own profit and advantage. The constitutional construct that is designed to tame the dangers of passions, despotism and factions is basically one that places strong emphasis on checks and controls. First, *interests check interests* within a market society based on legal guarantees of private property and the freedom of contract. Second, *interests check governmental powers* through a dense net of democratic rights, most importantly elections and the freedom of the press. Third, *power checks power,* i.e. the holders of democratic power check each other through complicated relations of rights and powers extending between the various political institutions such as the states, the federal government, the Presidency, the Congress, the Supreme Court and the armed forces.

As a result, a polity emerges that is built around the ideal of the free pursuit of the individual's notion of happiness. Whatever *collective* notions of happiness, salvation, or the realisation of any particular group's destiny or potential may prevail, they are neither defined nor implemented through the political process, but through associative action within civil society. The common good is no more than the secure enjoyment of his or her individual good by each and every citizen. Such a model of democratic politics does evidently not make strong or optimistic assumptions concerning the moral qualities that citizens are capable of displaying in the act of democratic participation – although it can by no means do without *any* moral requirements and presuppositions, as citizens must be considered willing and able to respect the common interest in the preservation of civilized and constitutional rules, rather than to engage in an unregulated individualistic struggle of interest. Concerning moral capabilities, the American tradition – and most liberal political thought in general – relies on a realist and empiricist (as opposed to an idealist-rationalist) assumption. This assumption is based on something like the following syllogism: if men have morally 'bad' intentions, as must be realistically assumed, the highest priority is to check the potentially dangerous impact of these intentions upon the process of democratic government. If, however, these intentions turn out to be morally desirable, ample room must be left for the manifestation of these intentions within the communities and associations of civil society; hence the political order itself can afford to be morally undemanding. Consequently, and in order to be on the safe side, it is neither tolerable nor desirable to commit democratic government to any notion of republican virtue or the common good.

In contrast, the French tradition of democratic theory is firmly tied to a collectivist notion of secular salvation through social progress, with the constitution being considered as a machinery for promoting this encompassing vision of the common good. Starting with this premise, the design problem for those engaged in *politique politisante* is the inverse one from the American case. Theirs is not the problem of how to check and neutralise the dangers of faction, but how to enable citizens to be 'good' citizens – i.e. citizens committed to the common good. Given the fallibility of the will of the popular sovereign, the task of the constitution becomes one of overcoming this fallibility, and also of securing the progress that has already been made. As shown in the previous section, Rousseau was fully aware of the extraordinary difficulty of this task. The *Social Contract* can be read as a relentless effort to specify the conditions under which the *empirical* will of the people can be approximated to the *reasonable* will of the people, the *volonté générale*. And in an almost tragic case of cyclical reasoning Rousseau seems to conclude that a reliable commitment of each and every citizen to the realisation of the common good can be expected to prevail only if the revolutionary task of realising the common good is *already* accomplished! Not only does Rousseau fail, as a result of the unavailability of any notion of class conflict and class formation, to sketch the outlines of an objective dynamic of revolutionary processes that would bring people to converge upon a shared conception of what would constitute their common good (a gap later to be filled by Marx's theory of historical materialism); he also failed, probably as a result of his romanticist and anti-intellectual inclinations, to elaborate a cognitive method by which the transformation of the 'crude' into the 'refined' version of the will of the people could possibly be accomplished (a gap that today Habermas's theory of communicative action aspires to fill).[15]

Nevertheless, Rousseau's clear notion of the fallibility of the will of the people is of great importance. As 'God', or the divine order of public life, is replaced by 'the people', and 'human reason' becomes the ultimate foundation of social order, the result was the paradox of a 'mortal god'. Hobbes was probably alone in remaining able to ignore the problem implied in this substitution, as he believed that this new secular authority could be construed *more geometrico,* i.e. by logically compelling deductive reasoning alone and without any reliance upon fallible or contested normative presuppositions. The idea of a 'bad government' would have been an oxymoron to him, as he clearly saw that the frightening alternative of society's falling back into the state of nature made *any* government better than no government, and hence the question of the moral qualities of the government utterly irrelevant. But this rationalist-contractarian confidence in the desirability of government *per se* did not last for long among his successors in the history of political ideas. The insight dawned upon them that 'peace' (such as was supposedly accomplished by the Leviathan) was not enough; the problem was to determine the just peace. With Rousseau, writing three generations later, the hiatus between the *liberal* solution (i.e. the authoritatively safeguarded co-existence of divergent interests within the multitude of individuals) and the *republican* solution (i.e. the autonomous recognition of the collective interest of all and by all) had appeared on centre stage. This alternative still exhausts the range of conceivable designs in modern political theory.

On the one hand, the proponents of the former solution rest content with the unalterable diversity of the many notions of justice that ineradicably prevail among the members of even the most civilised societies; what remained to be resolved in this case was the problem of how to organise, by the means of constitutional government and the state's authority, the peaceful co-existence of the forces and factions that made up this plurality. That, according to liberal theory, is all that can be achieved on the universalist basis of a unanimous consent of the many to refrain from the use of violence in the pursuit of their interests. The portion of the freedom they give up is meant not to serve the common good, but to secure the safe enjoyment of their private goods.

On the other hand, this conclusion of liberal democratic theory is contradicted by the 'republican' tradition (later developing in the revolutionary democratic direction) that originated in French political thought. Within this tradition, two objections, one negative, one positive, are raised against the liberal version of democratic theory. The negative objection, later to be elaborated in the classical writings of historical materialism, rests its case upon the compelling observation that, given the original and unequal endowment of individuals with means and resources to engage in their pursuit of happiness, the nominal universalism of the liberal arrangement turns into a *de facto* particular-ism. Equal rights (e.g. in property) are not paralleled by the equal distribution of the resources necessary actually to enjoy these rights. Hence the constitutional universalism must be extended into a socio-economic one within a process of revolutionary social transformation. The second, positive counter-argument posits that this is not only necessary, but also possible, as men have the 'natural' interest, desire and capability to pursue a shared vision of the common good – if only they can become masters of the economic and social conditions of their life.

As a consequence of these two objections, radical political thought had to secularise the notion of salvation as well. As God was replaced by the people as the ultimate source of order and authority, so the promise of divine justice had to be complemented or replaced by the inner-worldly project of a revolutionary transformation. This alternative seemed to involve a much greater task: the task of bringing about not just peace, but an unequivocally *just* peace. The revolutionary project requires for its redemption not just the peaceful aggregation of the will of the many, but a rational cognitive process which determines what must rationally be willed by all[16] and what course the process of human and societal perfection must take as a consequence. In this case, what is required of the citizen is not just rational consent to the ground rules of a peaceful order, but the much greater effort to purify and transcend his or her supposedly selfish and myopic preferences and opinions so as to arrive at a generalisable version of his or her will. The distance that must be travelled in order to accomplish the latter is evidently much greater than that involved in the former. In order to be a rational consenter to the ground rules of a strictly liberal version of democracy, I need to show little more than the prudent pursuit of my interest, whereas to share in some collective will I need to 'launder' my preferences much more fundamentally, as the fallibility of my judgement is always in danger not just of obstructing *my* well-considered self-interest, but of missing the *volonté générale* itself. The tension between the empirical will and the will to have a 'true and reasonable' will is clearly recognised by both Montesquieu and Rousseau.[17]

So in either case, the case of the peaceful pursuit of individual interests as well as in the case of the generalisable will, some moral effort is required – albeit, as we have just argued, a much greater one in the latter case than in the former. Perhaps it is not entirely obvious why liberal theory, too, can be said to require a minimum of moral commitment Although, according to this theory, the social contract *originates* in pure self-interest, its *duration* in time cannot be accounted for in terms of interest alone. For the longer the social contract lasts, the greater the temptation either to break it for one's own self-interest (thus free-riding upon the conformity of others) or to break it first in order to pre-empt others. Thus the validity of the axiom *pacta sunt servanda* cannot be explained in terms of self-interest alone, but only with reference to some morally founded commitment and self-restraint.

Thus both of our theories imply a difference between immediate (or interest-guided) and morally refined preferences. In neither case will my immediate and unrefined impulses and inclinations suffice. From an *ex ante* perspective, the distance between the two sorts of preferences is defined through the *active use of practical reason:* from an *ex post* perspective, through the *passive experience of regret.* In either version of our two accounts of democracy, the quality of democratic institutions depends on the extent to which they are capable of activating and cultivating the practice of the former, thus minimising the experience of the latter.

One might even claim that designing institutional arrangements that favour the refinement of political preferences is the only theoretical problem that the two democratic traditions have in common. How is the 'raw material' of the will of the people, with all its blindness, selfishness and short-sightedness, to be transformed into reasonable and non-regrettable outcomes? There are several aspects of this thorny problem. First, if we inquire into what we mean by a 'rational' or 'enlightened' political will, we will hit upon three qualitative criteria. Such a will would ideally have to be at the same time *'fact-regarding'* (as opposed to ignorant or doctrinaire), *'future-regarding'* (as opposed to myopic) and *'other-regarding'* (as opposed to selfish). To be sure, it is hard to determine when and how this ideal is to be satisfied to an optimal extent. But it suffices here to postulate that whenever 'regret' is experienced concerning an earlier expression of individual and collective will, it can be traced back to deficiencies in one or more of these three dimensions. A further dimension of the 'reasonable will' problem becomes apparent if we realise that the will of the people plays a significant role at *two* places in the democratic political process, namely at its origin (where the 'inputs' of voters or participants occur) and at its end (where laws and other acts of the democratically constituted authority are executed and compliance is required). Thus the quality of the will of the people is a problem that can be split into two sub-problems: the quality of the will that is being *actively expressed* and the quality of the will that leads people to *comply passively* with – or, alternatively, to violate or resist – the law of which they are, at the same time, the collective authors and subjects. It is of course tempting to postulate that the two aspects stand in close interrelation (in that a law deriving from a unanimously expressed preference carries strong obligatory power and perhaps also that 'input'-preferences will easily converge on collective choices that are anticipated to be easily enforceable); but none the less, the two aspects deserve to be treated as analytically distinct, namely as those of rational preference formation and rationally motivated compliance.

The rather schematic way in which we have opposed the two democratic traditions – the liberal and the revolutionary – is intended to highlight one underlying analytical dimension of political theory which was first formulated by the French and American political theorists of the second half of the eighteenth century and which still constitutes the arena of the debate at the end of the twentieth century. The polar cases of a *pure* regime of checks and balances and a *pure* regime of republican virtue are of little practical significance. But they are of the greatest theoretical significance because they delimit the space within which democratic theorists try to define synthetic solutions which in their turn are also of practical and political significance. Any such synthetic solution consists in a reasoned trade-off within the unavoidable dilemma of democratic theory and its task of designing new institutions or justifying existing ones. The dilemma is this: should democratic institutions or constitutions be built around the 'empirical' or the 'reasonable' will of the people? Should constitutional rules and procedures be seen primarily as a mechanism of checks, balances, self-binding or self-paternalist arrangements that impose *constraints* upon governing elites and citizens alike, or should they be seen as constitutive, self-founding, developmental, formative and *enabling* mechanisms which are designed to alter and 'de-nature' the empirical will of the people and to approximate it towards some notion of a reasonable will? Is it the objective of constitutions to establish a *political* order (which supposedly has its value in itself) or do they aim (and to what extent justifiably?) at instrumentally transforming the *social and economic* order so as to promote some substantive notion of justice and the common good? Is it the values of freedom and liberty or those of equality, solidarity and justice that provide the ultimate justification for a democratic polity? Is it the people as an existing multitude of individuals that forms the basis and reference-point of a democratic polity, or is it the ultimately-to-be-achieved people as a corporate body with a common history and destiny? Is it the principle of legality that endows a democratic regime with legitimacy, or must legality itself be submitted to some substantive legitimacy test? Is it the institutions (as the 'congealed' outcome of experience, reflection and deliberation) which make up a democratic regime, or is it the actual capability of the citizens, as practised by them, to pursue the common good? None of these questions – all of which upon closer inspection turn out to be just variants of the single problem originally posed by the contrast of the American and the French traditions – can be answered today in an either-or fashion. Rather, they must be answered through a laborious synthetic effort aiming at a provisionally valid reconciliation of the opposites. Let us look at some examples of how these problems have been dealt with by democratic theorists in the twentieth century.

Hybrid solutions to the problem of democratic theory

The problem of the Rousseauist version of democracy is that it inevitably presupposes highly demanding conditions for the consonance of the people's will and the common good, whereas the democratic theory which places itself in the American tradition may turn out to be too undemanding in reducing the concept of the common good to little more than an aggregation of individual preferences. But even in that less demanding case it is necessary that the way in which the individual citizen pursues his or her interests and values be 'civilised', that is, firmly tied to the rules, disciplines and procedures that permit the pursuit of interest by all to remain fair, equitable and peaceful. Thus, in either of the two traditions, though to widely varying degrees, institutions must be provided that serve the purpose of purifying and refining the 'raw' and uncivilised inclinations of actors. In its more demanding version, the aim is to condition citizens to be 'good' citizens, that is, citizens able to be active authors of the common will. In the less demanding version, the aim is to bind citizens to respect the law and the constitution in the process of their pursuit of interest. In the history of modern democracy we have seen different institutional strategies designed to achieve this aim of civilising citizens.

The actual institutions and practices of modern liberal democracies do not correspond to either the French or the American tradition. Rather than solving the problem of how to refine the empirical will of the people, the dominant strategy has been to bracket and ignore the problem and to bypass the solutions that were envisaged by either version of classical democratic theory. This, at least, is what we want to argue in the following discussion of two of the key institutional features of contemporary democracies: the franchise and the welfare state.

Voting rights and representation

It is a truism that the universal right to vote is the decisive and distinctive quality of democratic regimes. There are three different justifications of the right to vote. The most fundamental and the earliest consists in the notion that, as Rousseau argued, the force of the law is conditional upon the universal franchise. The general will must originate 'in all citizens in order to apply to all citizens'.[18] But, secondly, the influential early American theory of virtual representation claimed that the binding force of the law does not necessarily rest on every citizen's right to vote, but can be achieved through 'just' representation; on the basis of this concession, a different argument for the universalisation of the franchise is required, namely, one that highlights the value that this right confers *on the individual.* According to this theory, the right to vote constitutes full citizenship status and defines who counts in the community.[19]

Thirdly, there has always been current a more or less implicit notion in terms of which the right to vote is justified and defended by reference to the quality of the outcome of the political process. According to this version, the franchise is justified by the fact that it presumably tends to *make citizens more aware of their responsibilities towards the common good.* Rousseau contended that the general will is directed towards the common good because 'everybody necessarily submits himself to the same conditions which he imposes on others';[20] in consequence of this mutuality, nobody will be tempted to impose unfair duties and sacrifices upon others which these others then will predictably reciprocate upon him – unless such duties are strictly and intelligibly called for by the common good.

Of course, a glance at the historical reality of democratic developments shows quite clearly that the reverse assumption has prevailed in practice. Rather than relying on the risky hypothesis that the extension of the right to participate would by itself and quasi-automatically elevate the individual to the status of an enlightened and responsible citizen, nineteenth-century proponents of democracy held fast to the somewhat safer hypothesis that only those who have been demonstrated to be responsible citizens in the first place (through paying taxes, achieving high educational or professional status, etc.) should be entitled to participation. Accordingly, it was only after the First World War that the universalisation of the right to vote was deemed appropriate in most West European democracies.

Apart from these ambiguities in the justification of the right to vote, a well-known dialectic ensues from the extension of this right. The broader the entitlement to participate becomes, the more it becomes dependent upon the insertion of representative intermediaries (which were anathema to Rousseau), such as political parties and legislative bodies. This insertion has been justified in the theory of party competition and parliamentary representation not just as flowing from the necessities of coping with large quantities of participating citizens dispersed over the territory of national states, but also as assuring a higher degree of comprehensiveness and far-sightedness, or, in a word, of political rationality to be employed in the decision making process.

State intervention and the regulation of production and distribution

The secular process of the extension of the right to political participation – and at the same time of the increasing indirectness and mediation of the forms through which this right could be utilised – has been one of two cumulative structural developments in the historical practice of democracy. The other development has taken place not in the social, but in the substantive dimension: after more and more *categories of people* were admitted to active citizenship in the first of the two processes, the second consisted in subjecting more and more *aspects of the life of civil society,* particularly as it affects issues of production and distribution, to the collective political will.

The French Constitution of 1791 excluded wage workers and all other categories of dependent individuals from the suffrage because poverty and dependency were thought to be obstacles to the possession of a reasonable will, and hence to participation in the formation of the nation's reasonable collective will. Consequently, the goal of democratisation came to include the abolition of material dependency and poverty through the realisation of social and economic equality, whether by the introduction of schemes of co-determination and 'industrial democracy' or through state regulation, welfare policies and 'economic democracy'.

One assumption underlying the extension of democracy into the economic and distributional as well as the educational spheres was that this would help to improve the outcomes of the political process by fostering the rational qualities, the sense of material security, the freedom from anxieties and fears, and the self-confidence of citizens enjoying the right to participate not just in properly political but also, through social and economic state policies, in economic affairs. This second extension of democracy was held to follow a logic strictly analogous to that discussed earlier, namely the logic of using 'more democracy' for the purpose of making 'better citizens'. Unfortunately, however, 'the evidence is by no means conclusive that increased participation *per se* will trigger a new renaissance in human development' or that it 'leads to consistent and desirable political outcomes.'[21]

In fact, during the course of the development of the welfare state, distributive policies came to be less and less a means to an end – the qualification of all individuals for responsible citizenship – and came rather to be valued for themselves. The welfare state and its policies of social security and redistribution can even come into conflict with the democratic ideal of civic reason if the scheme of income redistribution is uncoupled from the universalistic principle of the promotion of the common good and if it is instead guided by group strategies to appropriate portions of the gross national product at the expense of others. Moreover, the institutions of the welfare state have been rightly criticised for their tendency to foster dependency and clientilistic attitudes on the part of citizens.

The over-optimistic hypothesis that the extended participation of citizens must somehow naturally entail an improvement in the moral and cognitive quality of their decision making capabilities might even be disputed by the opposite contention: namely that participation (and the chances of collective appropriation of material values that go with it) may actually corrupt citizens by appealing to their selfishness. From this strongly pessimistic assumption the reverse suggestion would follow: only the evidence that individuals are responsible citizens would entail and justify their extended participation. The first alternative would presume that Rousseau's doctrine is still valid: the more and the more thoroughly the interests of the individuals are politicised by transferring them to the popular sovereign, the less are they vulnerable to particularistic inclinations and the more responsible are the volitions which form the collective will.[22] The other alternative would be a Lockean one; it would claim that only the force of strong individual interests in one's own private affairs can nurture – and maintain over time – a person's sense of responsibility; and that, conversely, the more the sphere of public policies and regulations is extended, the more impoverished the individual's rational civic capacities and virtues will tend to become.[23]

As in the case of a more universal and egalitarian distribution of the legal right to participate in politics, so also in the case of a more egalitarian distribution of economic rights and resources, the question must be asked whether or not (and if so, as a result of which causal mechanisms) more equality among individual citizens will give rise to the development of their moral and rational capabilities and thus, eventually, to the improvement of the outcomes of collective decision making. Raising this question does not, of course, deny the justifiability of egalitarian social and economic policies on other grounds outside democratic theory proper, such as the abolition of misery and poverty. But from the point of view of democratic theory, careful and sober consideration should be given to the question why – and under what conditions – equality among individuals can be assumed to be a necessary precondition of collective rationality.

Problems of democratic solutions

The conundrum of generating what are assumed to be collectively rational decisions in democratic ways without first generating citizens who are inspired by the desire for promoting the common good (or the common interest in the conditions of the pursuit of private interests) can be compared to the task of generating a desired effect in the absence of its necessary cause. In the absence of 'reasonable' citizens, the aggregate outcomes of their individual acts of participation must still be justified as 'reasonable'. As we have just argued, in the development of modern liberal democracy and its theoretical interpretations, there are two major ways, consecutively adopted, in which this conundrum is presumably solved. One is representation, the other is the welfare state.

In the theory of representation, the condition is relaxed that in order for reasonable *decisions* to be made, the ultimate *authors* of the decision must themselves be reasonable,[24] and that there exists a necessary convergence between the will of the people and the common good; henceforth it suffices that the members of representative legislative bodies, if properly constituted, proclaim reason *on behalf* of the people, in the vast majority of which any degree of reasonableness cannot be assumed. A tradition in democratic theory ever more vociferous in the interwar period began to denounce the hopes, voiced by the classical tradition from Rousseau to Mill, concerning the enlightening and civilising impact of the right to vote, as void and naive. As the citizen was basically considered incapable of autonomously refining his will, some vicarious preference-refining mechanism had to be put in place. Conversely, representative mechanisms were seen as barriers serving to prevent unreasonable inputs from interfering with the quality of decision outputs. Robert Michels, Max Weber, Carl Schmitt and Joseph Schumpeter, in spite of their vastly different philosophical and political orientations, all converged upon an increasingly disillusioned and often manifestly cynical view of the potential of democratic institutions to transform the empirical will of the people into something more reasonable and enlightened, taking this will instead as something inherently irrational which at best could serve as the sounding-board of charismatic leaders, an object of 'caesaristic' manipulation, or a contentless selection mechanism for political entrepreneurs.

A parallel argument applies to the actual implementation of collectively binding decisions: as it cannot be assumed that citizens will normally feel obliged to comply with the decisions that have been made not by them but in their name, so the threat of negative sanctions must be applied in order to force them to do what the law requires them to do. Thus the empirical will of the citizens is bracketed and neutralised by means of the insertion of representative mechanisms and the state's monopoly of force, which apply, respectively, to the empirical will in its active (participatory) and its passive (compliance) versions. The stronger the independent force of these two mechanisms, the lesser the requirements that must be made upon the civic spirit, virtue and insight of citizens, while at the same time the potentially dangerous impact of their 'passions' remains under effective control.

The same perspective can be applied to the welfare state, defined as the provision of entitlement-based social security for employees and their dependents. Nowhere was the welfare state designed to produce competent citizens by improving individuals' capacity to form responsible and considered judgements and to transcend the immediacy of their social and economic interests. On the contrary, it was designed to condition workers rationally to accept existing social and economic arrangements and hence to comply, as workers and as citizens, with its daily routines; once they were given a stake in the system and its continued operation, there was within it much more for them to lose than merely their 'shackles'. In contrast to any revolutionary transformation of the social and economic order along the lines initiated by Rousseau, the welfare state aimed at generating not citizens capable of the autonomous consideration of the common good, but dependable workers. Nor do other institutional patterns aim at or contribute to the development of the moral capacities of the citizens.

The institutions and procedures of liberal democracies can be criticised for involving three cumulative mechanisms of 'political alienation'. By political alienation we mean the difference and distance that intervene between the subjectivity, motives and intentions of those who are involved in the decision making process (and in whose name the decisions' validity and legitimacy are vindicated) on the one hand, and the decision outcomes, on the other. One important consequence of political alienation is the depletion of the moral resources of citizens. Political alienation can be said to occur in the temporal, social and substantive dimensions. First, political alienation in the temporal dimension results from the tension between *elections and decisions.* The mandate that voters give to legislative bodies and governments extends over a period within which decisions on issues will be made, the nature and content of which are entirely unknown at the moment of voting, and in which for this reason voters can play no role; this problem is exacerbated through the 'loss of collective memory' that is conditioned by the media and modern PR strategies. Secondly, in the social dimension, the alienation mechanism results from the apparent paradox that as rights to political participation are extended to broader and more heterogeneous categories of the population, the political class of professional legislators, policy-makers and administrators becomes more homogeneous by training and social background, thus giving rise to a growing separation between *people and politicians.* Third, and in close connection to the other two modes of political alienation, there is a growing distance between the everyday knowledge, values and experience of ordinary citizens and the expertise of political professionals. These various forms and aspects of political alienation imply two equally probable effects: either short-sighted, myopic and opportunistic modes of action on the part of political elites who are no longer effectively called upon to comply to demanding standards of political rationality and responsibility; a moral and political 'de-skilling' of the electorate and the spread of cynical attitudes about public affairs and the notion of a public good. It is easy to see how these two effects, those affecting elites and those affecting the masses, can feed upon each other.

From our brief and critical discussion of the failures of the major institutional components of modern liberal democracy, namely representation and the welfare state, we wish to draw two conclusions which might help to throw new light upon current challenges to democratic theory and democratic practice.

1. Legislation through representative bodies plus authoritative enforcement of the law are indispensable, but at the same time insufficient mechanisms to cope with collective decision making problems: for instance, in the areas of environmental protection, resource use, gender relations, health-related behaviour, intergenerational behaviour and a large number of other public policy issues. What are needed for effective implementation of policies, in addition to legal regulation, are enlightened, principled and refined preferences on the part of citizens. Moreover, there is no built-in guarantee that the decisions of representative bodies will be superior, more responsible or more reasonable than the micro-decisions of enlightened individual actors; on the contrary, most of the new issues and problems concerning the 'common good' (ranging from questions of gender relations, the Third World and peace to the natural and the built environment) have been brought up during the 1970s and 1980s not by parties and parliaments, but by new social movements working outside the formally constituted political system, while the representative institutions have often been *more* myopic, *less* other-regarding and fact-regarding, than parts of their constituencies. Nor is there any guarantee that even the most enlightened and reasonable legislation can be brought to bear, through the authoritative means of law enforcement and legal regulation alone, upon the day-to-day action of the less enlightened citizenry. What this amounts to is the diagnosis of an increasing powerlessness of constituted political powers in both their legislative and executive capacities.[25] As a result, the role of actors within civil society, both collective and individual, assumes increasing strategic significance for the solution of societal problems. As justice is no longer something that can be implemented through legislation alone, the rule of law must be complemented at the micro-level of the principled action of conscientious citizens.[26]

2. While many critics of the practices of liberal democracy, particularly on the political left, have tended to believe that the obvious cure for unreasonable and unjust outcomes of government action is the broadening of democratic participation and co-determination, first across categories of the population (women, adolescents, foreign workers, etc.) and then across substantive areas (local governments, industrial enterprises, professional services, schools, universities, etc.), this view has lost much of its compelling power.

The difficulties with this general idea are threefold. First, the approximation of the ideal that 'all' should be entitled to participate in a collectively binding decision becomes implausible as soon as the appropriate definition of what we mean by 'all' is called into question. Take the case of an airport construction project: is the universe of those affected by the decision, and for that reason the universe of those entitled to participation in making it, 'all' inhabitants of the nearby villages, or is it 'all' airlines and their clients who qualify as potential users of the new facility? As regionalist and gender issues illustrate, the thorny problem of defining the appropriate universe cannot be resolved by broadening participation; more often, the problem is felt by political activists to be how to keep 'outsiders' out. Secondly, and in a similar way, the rationality of broadening the social range of participation becomes manifestly dubious when the issue is, as in fact it is in all questions concerning human and citizen rights, not to 'win majorities', but to protect rights from being overruled by even the strongest majorities. Thirdly, and most important in the present context, what we have to confront is the disappointing possibility that the quality of outcomes is *not* always demonstrably improved through broadening the range of rights to participation and co-determination. Such rights, far from educating actors to make well-considered decisions (which therefore would turn out to be non-regrettable from an *ex post* perspective), may well work out in the opposite direction by generating a *lower* level of reasonableness of collective outcomes than that which might be achieved on the level of individual action. In such cases, the whole appears to be less (in quality) than its parts. The reason for the emergence of such sub-optimal outcomes (as viewed by the participants themselves) might be that the temptation to use the powers of co-determination and participation for short-sighted and particularist purposes is too great to be easily resisted. Many authors seem to shy away from seriously considering this disappointing possibility, as it appears to imply a suggestion of a return to predemocratic, elitist, authoritarian or paternalist modes of making collectively binding decisions.

Such implications, however, are not the only conceivable way out of the dilemma. It is also possible, as we wish to suggest in conclusion, to respond to the realistic recognition of the fact that there is no positive linear relationship between participation and reasonableness by proposing a radicalisation of the principle of democratic participation. This radicalisation would amount to a third step to follow the two that have already been taken by previous waves of democratic movements and democratic reforms, namely (1) the generalisation of the categories of persons that are entitled to participate and (2) the generalisation of the substantive areas and institutional sectors to which the right to participate is extended. A further step along this line would consist in (3) enfranchising, as it were, the various preferences that exist within individual citizens/voters so as to organise an orderly social conflict not just between majorities and minorities (or, for that matter, between workers and managers in the case of 'economic democracy'), but, in addition, an 'inner conflict' between what the individuals themselves experience as their more desirable and their less desirable desires. Such a radicalisation of the democratic principle would aim at stimulating deliberation; it would amount to the introduction of procedures that put a premium upon the formulation of carefully considered, consistent, situationally abstract, socially validated and justifiable preferences.

'It is ... necessary to alter radically the perspective common to both liberal theories and democratic thought: the source of legitimacy is not the predetermined will of individuals, but rather the process of its formation, that is, deliberation itself.'[27] This proposal to bid farewell to the notion of fixed preferences implies a learning process that aims not at some preconceived standard of substantive rationality, but at an open-ended and continuous learning process in which the roles of both 'teacher' and 'curriculum' are missing. In other words, what is to be learned is a matter that we must settle in the process of learning itself.

It appears to be a largely novel task to think about institutional arrangements and procedures which could generate a selective pressure in favour of this type of reflective and open preference-learning, as opposed to fixed preferences that are entirely derivative from situational determinants, rigid beliefs or self-deception. According to the intuition that we have identified in Montesquieu and Rousseau, all of us prefer to have preferences that enjoy the respect of even our political opponents, which have been refined through the careful consideration of all relevant information and which are reliable and identity-supporting in the sense that they are capable of surviving the passage of time and changes in situational context. It is not well understood, however, which institutions and arrangements might help in the development of such preferable preferences, and in screening out the less preferable ones. Rawls's 'veil of ignorance' is more a thought experiment than a constitutional arrangement. Habermas's reliance upon the rationality standards that must, in principle, be redeemed in any speech act is all too easily frustrated by the presence of a situational context which relieves the speaker from the rationalising force of speech, thus letting him or her get away with less than well-considered preferences and propositions.

What positive conclusions, if any, are suggested by the two negative propositions we have just tried to defend? The way in which the *problematic* of democratic theory has shifted seems obvious. First, there is the shift from the macro-democracy of representative and authoritative political institutions to the micro-level of the formation of the collectively relevant will within the various contexts of civil society, many of which are by their very nature outside the range of operation and control of state institutions, state supervision and state intervention. Secondly, there is a shift from quantity to quality in the sense that in order to produce more reasonable outcomes it often no longer makes sense to ask for broader participation, but instead to look for a more refined, more deliberative and more reflective formation of the motives and demands that enter the process of mass participation already in place.

Neither the liberal-individualist nor the republican-collectivist version of democratic theory appears to be capable today of addressing the typical major collective decision problems of modern society. This verdict applies to liberal theory in that it takes insufficient cognisance of the independent and 'social' ('*vergesellscbafte*') nature of individual action: the individual pursuit of interest generally takes place in the form of strategic, not parametric rationality, and thus it does not permit, if it is to be successful, of abstraction from what others are doing. At the same time, the collectivist search for encompassing visions of what the common good might consist in typically does not sufficiently take into account the degree of social differentiation that modern societies have reached – a differentiation that debases notions such as the 'collective' (or even 'class') interest. Much of recent sociological research has highlighted the fragmented and 'individualised' nature of modern social structures that permits at best highly complex and abstract definitions of identity, as well as the prevalence of multiple cleavages in view of which any use of binary codes (such as labour *vs.* capital, males *vs.* females, sector *vs.* sector, domestic *vs.* foreign, 'them' *vs.* 'us' etc.) appears hopelessly inadequate and misleading if employed as a guide to political preference formation. No set of values and no particular point of view can lay claim to correctness and validity by itself, but at best only after it looks upon itself from the outside, thus relativising it through the insights that are to be gained by taking the 'point of view of the other' (or the generalised 'moral point of view').

In our view, what remains after both the individualistic and the solidaristic visions have lost much of their persuasiveness is the conclusion that the institutional designs of modern democracy must be based upon the principle of reciprocity. This principle would require that democratic theorists – as well as the everyday practitioners of democracy – place greater emphasis upon the institutional settings and procedures of preference formation and preference learning within civil society. But existing institutions and political practices impose little pressure upon us as citizens actually to engage in such effort and to adopt a multi-perspectival mode of forming, defending and thereby refining our preferences. The social and political world within which we live is much more complex than the attitudes and value-judgements that it still permits us to get away with. This imbalance amounts to our being morally 'de-skilled' in our capacity as citizens, and it conditions us into being less intelligent and responsible citizens than we might wish to be – or than the risks and dangers of a highly interdependent mode of life in advanced industrial societies do indeed objectively and urgently require us to be.

Constitutional designs that might help to balance this discrepancy are not easy to come by. It is obvious that one might wish the family, the media, the institutions of formal education and training, etc. to perform a better job than they often actually do in strengthening the under-pinnings of a civilised civic culture. It is equally obvious that the organisation of production (as well as the organisation of distribution through social policies and social services, including the spatial organisation of social life) can do a great deal either to discourage or to encourage reflexive and deliberative modes of preference learning and preference revision. On the other hand, however, the potential contribution to the formation of 'good citizens' of 'good schools' or egalitarian industrial relations within an arrangement of 'economic democracy' seems limited unless it is complemented by new constitutional procedures which will help to improve the quality of citizens' involvement in the democratic process.[28]

The design of structurally and functionally 'adequate' constitutional procedures is not the task that we have set for ourselves within the confines of this essay. A slightly easier task than describing and justifying what institutions should look like is that of defining what they ideally should be able to accomplish. They should upgrade the quality of citizenship by putting a premium on refined and reflective preferences, rather than 'spontaneous' and context-contingent ones. By reflective preferences we mean preferences that are the outcome of a conscious confrontation of one's own point of view with an opposing point of view, or of the multiplicity of viewpoints that the citizen, upon reflection, is likely to discover within his or her own self. Such reflectiveness may be facilitated by arrangements that overcome the monological seclusion of the act of voting in the voting booth by complementing this necessary mode of participation with more dialogical forms of making one's voice heard. It may also be facilitated by introducing a time structure into the practice of political participation that makes preference learning and the revision of one's own previous preferences more affordable and more visible. It may be helped by inserting elements of statistical representation into the established forms of representation mediated through party competition and party bureaucracies. Finally, it may be facilitated by the introduction of mechanisms into the practice of participation that encourage citizens to make better use of available information and theoretical knowledge, instead of relying upon *ad hoc* evidence and experience.

All of these accomplishments should be achieved within a framework of liberty, within which paternalism is replaced by autonomously adopted self-paternalism, and technocratic elitism by the competent and self-conscious judgement of citizens. To describe these demanding accomplishments as an 'ideal' is indeed justified in view of the enormous efforts that are evidently required to achieve them; on the other hand, they might as well be described as the realistic minimum requirement for the preservation of a civilized democratic polity (as well as of a more open and reflective notion of social and economic progress), as the obsolescence of 'vicarious' practices of political reason assigns a decisive role to the reason that each and every citizen is capable to develop for himself or herself.

Acknowledgements: The authors wish to thank David Held for helpful and valuable criticism and suggestions he made on the draft version of this essay.

Notes

1. D. Held, *Models of Democracy*, Stanford, Stanford University Press, 1987, p. 1.

2. J. G. March and J. P. Olsen, *Rediscovering Institutions: The organizational basis of politics*, New York, Free Press, 1989.

3. What we have in mind, but cannot elaborate here, are (a) new patterns of cleavage and conflict resulting from a growing 'individualistic fragmentation' of social structures which amounts sometimes to a large-scale defection from those collective practices and collective actions that are rooted in the social division of labour and (b) the formation of 'new' collectivities based upon 'ascriptive' or 'naturalistic' categories (such as gender, age, ethnicity, region, family or health status). The politics of 'new' social movements seem to be related to both of these structural trends.

4. C. Schmitt, *Politische Theologie: Vier Kapitel zur Lehre von der Souvranitat*, 3rd edn, Berlin, Duncker & Humblot, 1979, pp. 49ff; J. A. Schumpeter, *Capitalism, Socialism and Democracy*, 4th edn, New York, Harper & Row, 1975, p. 265; see also J. Taubes (ed.), *Der Furst dieser Welt: Carl Schmitt und*

die Folgen, 2nd edn, Miinchen-Paderborn, Wilhelm Fink/Schoningh, 1983; P. H. Merkl and N. Smart (eds), *Religion and Politics in the Modern World*, New York and London, New York University Press, 1985.

5. Schumpeter, *Capitalism, Socialism and Democracy*, p. 265.

6. R. Panikkar, 'Religion or Politics: The Western dilemma', in Merkl and Smart (eds), *Religion and Politics in the Modern World*, pp. 44–60 [p. 53].

7. See also T. Pangle, 'Civic Virtue: The founders' conception and the traditional conception', in G. C. Bryner and N. B. Reynolds (eds), *Constitutionalism and Rights*, Provo, Utah, Brigham Young University, 1987, pp. 105–140.

8. *The Federalist Papers: Hamilton, Madison, Jay*, edited and introduced by C. Rossiter, New York, New American Library, 1961, pp. 323, 324.

9. G. Lefebvre, *Quatre-vingt-neuf*, Paris, Editions sociales, 1970.

10. Abbé Sieyès, *What is the Third Estate?* in M. Forsyth *Reason and Revolution: The political thought of Abbé Sieyès*, Leicester, Leicester University Press, 1987, p. 78.

11. J.-J. Rousseau, *The Social Contract*, Harmondsworth, Penguin, 1968, bk 2, ch. 3.

12. *Ibid.*, bk 2, ch. 6.

13. Rousseau, however, as is well known, displayed no certitude as to the actual achievability of this egalitarian vision (see *Social Contract*, bk 2, chs 3, 6).

14. H. Arendt, *On Revolution*, New York, Viking, 1963, p. 89.

15. 'Rousseau considers politics to be essentially a simple matter. That is why the process of the formation of the will, individual as well as collective, does not concern him' (B. Manin, 'On legitimacy and deliberation', *Political Theory*, 1987, vol. 15, p. 347).

16. This distinction is nicely symbolised by political rituals. No parliamentary speaker in any Western democracy would ever join in the applause offered at the end of his or her own speech by those sharing the demands and opinions expressed. In contrast, it is common (or at least, it has been common until recently) for Communist Party chairmen to applaud themselves after the entire party convention has risen to deliver a standing ovation. This symbolic practice is not the act of self-congratulatory arrogance that it must appear to many Western observers; rather, its meaning rests on the assumption that what has been expressed in the speech and is now being celebrated by all is not the speaker's personal or partisan opinion, but a true insight, the achievement of which is highlighted by the ritual in which the speaker himself, being simply the mouthpiece of a collective cognitive process rather than the author of his words, is therefore entitled to join. The symmetrical opposite of this ritual, of course, is to be seen in the practices of auto-criticism and brain-washing, both of which can only be defended under the assumption that they consist in the cure to a strictly cognitive error, rather than in crippling a person's integrity and identity.

17. 'And it is fortunate for men to be in a situation in which, though their passions may prompt them to be wicked, they have nevertheless an interest in not being so' (C. L. Montesquieu, *The Spirit of Laws*, Chicago, W. Benton (ed.), 1952, bk 21, ch. 20); 'Although one wishes always one's best, one does not always recognise it' (Rousseau, *Social Contract*, bk 2, ch. 3); 'People ... are often deceived, and it is ... then that they seem to wish for what is bad' (*ibid.*); 'The common will is always right, but **the** judgement which leads it is not always enlightened)' (*ibid.*, bk 2, ch. 6). All of these quotations (which are amended translations in Rousseau's case) can be read as illustrations and examples of **the** category of 'democratic regret'.

18. Rousseau, *Social Contract*, bk 2, ch. 4.

19. T. H. Marshall, *Citizenship and Social Class*, Cambridge, Cambridge University Press, 1949, p. 92; L. H. Tribe, *Constitutional Choices*, Cambridge, Mass, and London, Harvard University Press, 1985, p. 14; R. K. Goodin, *Reasons for Welfare: The political theory of the welfare state*, Princeton, Princeton University Press, 1988, pp. 83ff.

20. Rousseau, *Social Contract*, bk 2, ch. 4.

21. Held, *Models of Democracy*, pp. 280, 281.

22. Rousseau, *Social Contract*, bk 1, ch. 6.

23. Cf. D. F. Thompson, *Political Ethics and Public Office*, Cambridge, Mass, and London, Harvard University Press, 1987, pp. 44ff.

24. This realist revision of the claims for universal suffrage and representative governments asserted itself only *after* these major democratic accomplishments were reached in most of Western Europe after the end of the First World War. Before this stage, socialists in particular held the greatest hopes concerning the civilising, mobilising and, eventually, progressive impact that the right to vote was to have – not only for the external conditions of production and distribution, but equally for the moral and political formation and the development of the consciousness of the working class.

25. To the extent our assumption is warranted, it can be said to be increasingly the case that collective decision problems of the type that cannot easily and effectively be dealt with by formal-legal methods of governance do in fact make up an increasing portion of our public agenda.

26. The booming interest, both academic and non-academic, in the field of applied ethics may be interpreted as a reflection of this shifting balance between legal and statist modes of control on the one hand, and moral and societal ones on the other.

27. Manin, 'On legitimacy and deliberation', pp. 351ff.

28. Cf., for example, B. Barber, *Strong Democracy: Participatory politics for a new age*, Berkeley, University of California Press, 1984, pp. 261–311.

Chapter Four

Crisis and Innovation of Liberal Democracy: Can Deliberation Be Institutionalised?[*]

Claus Offe

Liberal democracies, and by far not just the new ones among them, are not functioning well. While there is no realistic and normatively respectable alternative to liberal democracy in sight, the widely observed decline of democratic politics, as well as state policies under democracy, provides reasons for concern. This concern is a challenge for sociologically informed political theorists to come up with designs for remedial innovations of liberal democracy. In this essay, I am going to review some institutional designs for democratic innovation. I shall proceed as follows. The first section addresses the question of the *functions* of liberal democracy. What are the features and expected outcomes of democracy which explain why liberal democracy is widely considered today to be the most desirable form of political rule? The second section looks at the *institutional structure* and the constitutive mechanisms of democratic regimes. In each of these sections four relevant items are specified and discussed. Thirdly, I shall provide a very condensed summary of critical accounts concerning democracy's actual failures and symptoms of malfunctioning. In the final section, I distinguish two families of institutional innovations that are currently being proposed as remedies for some of the observed deficiencies of democracy, with an emphasis on 'deliberative' methods of political preference formation.

Four functional virtues of liberal democracy

The question is not often asked, as its answer appears quite obvious: What is democracy *good for*? In fact, there are several answers, corresponding to different schools of political theory. A minimalist answer is the negative one: there is simply no normatively sustainable principle available in modern societies according to which any unequal distribution of political rights (i.e., a set of aristocratic, dynastic, imperial, ethnic, religious, or party-totalitarian privileges) and, following from that, anything but the universal accountability of rulers to the entire (adult) citizenry could any longer be defended. This is the intuition that guided Tocqueville's[1] analysis of democracy in America (with its implications, as the author saw them, for Europe) as well as the cautious political egalitarianism of John S. Mill.[2]

---

[*]   'Crisis and innovation of liberal democracy: can deliberation be institutionalised', *Sociologický časopis/Czech Sociological Review*, 2011, vol. 47, no. 3, pp. 447–472.

Hence the equality of political rights of all *citizens* (as opposed to *subjects*) is the default position of democratic theory (a default position that, *nota bene*, still allows for two remaining exclusions: that of children below voting age who do 'not yet' enjoy political rights, and resident foreigners who may – or may not – be on their institutionally prescribed path to the acquisition of full citizenship ('naturalisation'). Yet beyond these two categories of outsiders (outsiders in time and outsiders in space, as it were), all 'full' members of the political community enjoy equal political rights – simply because no consensual criterion is available by which an unequal distribution of rights might be justified. Political equality is thus 'good for' forestalling any attempted relapse into a stratified system of political rights.

Yet equality of political rights and universal accountability of rulers can also be advocated on *positive* grounds. I wish to further distinguish three such grounds. The first (and the oldest) one is Immanuel Kant's[3] defence of the republican form of government (with still limited political equality and accountability, according to him) on the grounds of international peace: 'Republics' will never conduct wars against other republics – arguably one of the most robust hypotheses in the history of the social sciences. Second, a strong reason for the adoption and defence of the democratic form of government was advanced in the first wave of European democratisation after the First World War. It is, as it were, the domestic equivalent to Kant's hypothesis; it states that 'territorial' representative party democracy (together with strong elements of 'functional' representation through interest associations of major socio-economic categories such as employers, investors, trade unions, the agrarian sector, the civil service, etc.) will serve to institutionalise not just the condition of *legal* peace among individuals under the rule of law but also, thirdly, *political* peace among major kinds of collective interest; the latter is accomplished through the provision of institutional outlets for the organised expression and negotiation of class and other conflicts of interest. The mechanism through which democratic equality would lead to the peaceful and stable (rather than revolutionary and disruptive) processing of conflict, its accommodation, and change was thought (e.g. by Max Weber in his political writings from 1917 to 1919 and by Hermann Heller[4] to reside in the voting and bargaining powers with which those inferior in socio-economic power were to be compensated for their relative powerlessness through the constitutional provision of political resources – an arrangement that eventually would lead to a 'balance of class forces.'[5] The socio-economic power of investors and employers would be neutralised, at least in part, by the political power that lower classes can derive, under a democratic constitution, from their quantitative majority. If every interest were given a 'voice', nobody would have any reason to 'exit' to radical anti-systemic opposition. By virtue of its procedures, democracy is able to reconcile conflict to the extent which is necessary for the maintenance of stability, and to do so more effectively than any other form of regime.

After this hypothesis of democratic stability was brutally falsified in major parts of continental Europe in the aftermath of the economic crisis of the early 1930s, it was revived after the Second World War through an institutional arrangement and policy orientation that became known as the post-war 'Keynesian Welfare State': political democracy, or so the basic tenet of this period can be summarised, is a stable political arrangement because (and to the extent that) it is capable of organising an ongoing distributional positive-sum game in which all sides involved – capital, labour, the public sector together with its social policies and social services – will simultaneously be able to gain, provided, that is, the material foundation of such encompassing social progress, namely continuous economic expansion, can be maintained or, if need be, effectively stimulated. This hypothesis – democracy is desirable because it generates balanced distributional progress – held remarkably true in the West throughout (roughly) the third quarter of the 20th century, i.e. the so-called 'golden' post-war period. In this period, there were no permanent losers in rich democracies. It came, however, at least in Europe, to an abrupt halt in the mid-seventies. Two books, James O'Connor[6] and Crozier, Huntington and Watanuki,[7] noted and analysed in quite influential ways the 'crisis of democracy' or, respectively, of 'the state' that ensued when this hypothesis, too, turned out to be dubious. Reasons for scepticism were provided by the evidence of lasting high levels of unemployment, which had been building up in European democracies since the mid-1970s, declining growth rates, and the massive increase in income and other inequalities that most OECD economies had been experiencing since the mid-nineties. The confidence in a productivist partnership between the state and social classes that would immunise democracy against the consequences of economic crisis was soon dismissed and actively rejected by the market radical regimes of monetarist economic policies associated with the names of Reagan, Thatcher, and more generally the 'Washington consensus' and 'neo-liberalism'. However, it must also be mentioned that representative democracy and universal access to political rights have in fact played a major role in preventing or reversing severe social regressions in at least some countries of the post-colonial developing world, with Indian democracy as the outstanding example. As Amartya Sen[8] has powerfully demonstrated, there has not been a single major famine or other socio-economic disaster in a democracy, whereas such disasters were allowed to take their course in party dictatorships (such as during the 'Great Leap Forward' in Mao's China).

Throughout the Cold War, representative democracy (i.e. its defining features of the constitutionally enshrined division of powers, accountable rulers, electoral competition, and civic and political rights) has served to corroborate the claim that 'the West' is not just economically superior to state socialism owing to its far better performance in terms of economic growth and mass prosperity, but also morally superior as a regime of political freedom and equality of rights. The combined institutional arrangements of political democracy and organised capitalism performed so well (relative to the political and economic realities of Soviet-style 'really existing' socialism) that nobody in his right mind could conceivably opt for the latter. Yet after the eventual breakdown of (all European cases of) state socialism in 1989–1991, the function of liberal democracy and its 'social' market economy as a political immuniser against 'Communism' was no longer needed (which explains, for instance, the breakdown of the *Democrazia Cristiana* in Italy in the early 1990s). Instead, the thorny problem of orchestrating democratic transitions and democratising former Soviet-ruled states appeared not just on the agenda of the transition countries, but on the Western agenda as well, including the project of enlarging the EU to the East. This new and historically unprecedented problem was not just to stabilise democratic capitalism in the West, but to initiate the building of democratic capitalism from the outside in regions where state socialism had vanished. Today, as the accomplishment of the latter task is clearly far from complete, given strong symptoms of democratic deficiency in the region of even the ten new EU member states of post-communist capitalism (to say nothing about their neighbours to the East), and as the accomplishment of the former task is outright questionable after the experience of the 2008 financial market crisis and its aftermath in both old and new member states, the blessings of liberal democracy and democratic capitalism are less evident (both to the outside observer and the internal participants) than they, arguably, were at any point since the Second World War.

Before leaving the question of what democracy is 'good for' (and here entirely skipping the question of how the political and economic realities of the European Union can be reconciled with democratic principles) we should at least mention a fourth theory – namely the republican theory of democratic politics and its claim that the opportunity to participate in the collective affairs of the political community will actually have a virtuous formative impact upon citizens. This impact is thought to enable him or her to be a 'good' citizen, i.e. a citizen both *able* (through enhanced understanding of public affairs) and *willing* (through the perceived moral obligation to transcend narrow and short-sighted interests) to serve the common good of the political community as a whole. As I will try to show at the end of this essay, it is this argument in support of the democratic regime form that has powerfully re-surfaced in debates on the reasons for and the future of liberal democracy.

Four defining structural features of liberal democracy

I propose a definition of liberal democracy (LD) here that consists of four basic elements: stateness, rule of law, political competition, and accountability.

1. *Stateness* – We need to realise that LD is a regime form that (so far) is tied to *states*. Democrats may advocate supranational or even global forms of democracy, but that amounts to a project that is, for the time being, evidently far from being realised. At present only states (in their turn defined by the coincidence of a territory, a people, and an effective apparatus of political rule) can be democratic.

Democracy remains thus, for the time being, plainly parasitic on statehood. It is also the case that statehood always *precedes* democracy in historical time. For democracies appear to be always 'successor regimes', following upon non-democratic regime forms in a process of democratic transition, or democratisation, of a pre-democratic (military, authoritarian, theocratic, totalitarian, colonial etc.) regime ruling over the state's territory and population.

Another link between stateness and democracy is this: in order for a state to be democratic in any meaningful way, it must possess a minimum of what is now often referred to as 'state capacity' or 'governing capacity'. State capacity is the quality that allows a state, for instance, to protect its citizens from military or economic harm, to extract and allocate significant fiscal resources, defend the territory as well as its own monopoly on violence, establish and maintain an educational system, legislate and enforce regulatory laws, provide a measure of social and physical security and welfare, and manage succession crises – all this without being significantly obstructed by so-called factual powers, be it criminal gangs and Mafia organisations, separatist ethnic mobilisations, armed forces of civil war, networks of predatory corruption, external political forces on which governing elites are dependent, or hostile religious movements. In other words: in order for a state to be a democratic state, it must be capable of delivering collectively binding decisions and an extensive variety of (often fiscally costly) public goods. If it is unable to do so (and to do so continuously over time and territorial space!) we speak of a 'failed' or 'failing' state. The latter is defined by its deficient governing capacity relative to the kind and volume of problems that must be solved by the state to ensure social integration and the systemic stability of societies]. More specifically, governing capacity (the opposite of 'ungovernability') is deficient if the state suffers from three all-too-familiar, as well as causally tightly interrelated, 'absences': the absence of *borders* (to control the outward flow of capital and the inward flow of goods and people); the absence (owing to the often giant and generally increasing levels of public debt) of *fiscal resources* available to fund public policies that serve any version of the public good; and the absence of *jobs*, which would allow the entire working-age population to participate, under acceptable terms, in the production and distribution of economic output.

If that is right, it would be a mistake to associate only impoverished third world countries and their feeble and often corrupt governments with the condition of 'state failure'. States with industrially advanced economies that are fiscally starved or in which elites subscribe to a doctrine of economic market liberalism and the radical retreat of 'bureaucracy' and regulation also can suffer from the syndrome of state failure and ungovernability. These conditions threaten to render democracy largely pointless, particularly if, as in the EU, major parts of remaining governing capacities are being transferred to supranational agencies (such as the European Central Bank, the European Court of Justice, the European Commission) which are operating beyond the reach of effective democratic accountability mechanisms. Neoliberal states are regimes whose policy agenda is so restricted that the substantive concerns of the 'people' remain largely bracketed out from it and have no access to the making of public policies, as major areas of public interest (urban development, health, education, the environment, transportation, utilities, etc.) are taken off the agenda of political authorities in the name of privatisation, deregulation, marketisation, competitiveness, and efficiency. Here, the universalism of political rights comes to stand in stark contrast to the more and more limited uses to which citizens can actually put their rights, given the restricted nature of the collective functions states are financially able, and governing elites politically willing, to perform.

The discrepancy between the political rights non-elites enjoy and constraints imposed on political elites' agendas by the factual powers of global financial markets and other supranational wielders of economic, political, and military power can cause citizens to turn away from democracy in one of two directions: they either give up the belief that political rights can be instrumentally useful for promoting their interests and improving the well-being of the political community as a whole – the familiar and today widespread attitude of distrust, apathy, political disaffection, and cynicism;[9] or, even worse, they may come to conclude that political rights, having become a blunted sword, must be beefed up with additional and non-representative political resources, such as outbursts of populist mobilisation and violent protest directed at alleged 'enemies'. As to the former alternative, it is worth keeping in mind the apparent paradox of 'participatory inequality':[10] it is precisely the less privileged strata of the population who would most benefit from the use of their political rights if state capacity were less constrained and who are most likely to drop out of participation, given their experience of and frustration over those constraints. As to the latter, the quest for additional political resources can also lead to large segments of the population resorting to non-institutional, disruptive, and more or less violently aggressive modes of political contestation which defy the official procedural rules of making collectively binding decisions.

The two conventional criteria of the strength and stability of democratic states are *legitimacy* and *effectiveness*.[11] By legitimacy we mean the quality of the holders of state power to have their decisions complied with (without the more than marginal use of coercion) even by those who see their interests and values damaged by those decisions. By effectiveness we mean the capacity of 'getting things done', solve problems, and implement plans and projects. A democratic state is stable and resilient (or 'consolidated') if and to the extent that its legitimacy and effectiveness are continuously enacted, demonstrated, and therefore taken for granted by all relevant actors, inside and outside of the state in question. But such 'taken-for-grantedness' is never irreversible: Democratic regimes can 'de-consolidate' and reach a point of self-subversion which may end in the suicidal subversion of democracy by (apparently) democratic means. Moreover, the two are related to each other in tight interaction: a state that fails to 'get things done' (e.g. because of widespread corruption or the deficiency of fiscal resources) will lose its legitimacy, and the loss of the latter will further undermine its capacity to govern.

2. *Rule of law* – Democratic states are states with a (mostly written) constitution, which provides for (at least) two ways in which the exercise of state power is limited. One of these ways is to endow citizens with a bill of equal rights which cannot be legally infringed upon by governing authorities. These rights include personal rights (protecting the integrity of body and soul/conscience), economic rights (property and contract), political rights (of assembly, media communication, association, participation, etc.) and often also 'positive' social rights (social assistance, social insurance, regulatory intervention into markets, the

state-supervised provision of services such as health and education). Democracies are 'liberal' to the extent the substantive range of possible democratic decision making is strictly limited and governments are effectively hindered from interfering with the political and civic freedoms of citizens. For instance, the citizens' equal right to democratic participation is not itself at the disposition of those participating in the democratic process; i.e. it cannot be denied to minorities by majorities. Liberal democracies establish a precarious balance between collectively binding rules that are the outcome of democratic decision making (ordinary laws) and rules which are (at any given moment, at any rate) immune from such outcomes. The other limitation of overall state power (to which I shall return) is the division and mutual constraint of (legislative, executive, federal, juridical,) state powers, with one of the most inconspicuous (though highly consequential) constraints being the temporal limitation of government (meaning that the tenure of elected office is always *ex ante* time-limited and elections are periodic).

3. Democracies organise *political competition* and institutionalise the non-violent conduct of political conflict between contending groups (parties) aspiring to government office. Winning contested elections is the procedure through which rulers gain their governing power – which means that elections generate losers (i.e. defeated parties and their supporters) who are expected to recognise the victory of the winner as legitimate – as a binding fact, if only for the time being, namely until the next election day. The identity and configuration of contending political parties is in part an artefact of the electoral system (with majoritarian electoral systems of the 'single member plurality' (SMP) type normally leading to a two-party system), in part a reflection of social cleavages (of class, religion, regional or national identities) and their organisational representations (trade unions, faith-based organisations). Democracy is the scene of 'democratic class struggle',[12] as well as other kinds of struggle for political power – struggles the outcome of which has (unless the state's capacity and agenda is severely constrained, as just discussed, by fiscal and/or ideological limitations) significant implications for people's life chances and the distribution of their capabilities.

Yet not all political competition, as carried out in electoral campaigns, is of such a substantive sort. Political sociologists distinguish between three types of competitive struggle: First, the struggle over alternative ideological and programmatic positions and goals of political parties, with the core issue being the extent to which market forces vs interventionist regulatory and distributive policies as well as social rights can and should be relied upon. Second, the struggle over alternative answers to current issues, such as 'should we withdraw our troops from Afghanistan?' or 'should we diminish our dependency on nuclear energy by investing in renewable sources of energy?'. Third, the struggle between persons competing for the trust and electoral support of constituencies that they need for their access to leadership positions in government. Most comparative and historical research on the development of these three kinds of competitive contestation supports the generalisation that parties increasingly fail to offer (and voters fail to appreciate) distinctive and encompassing programmatic positions and instead appeal to increasingly 'volatile' voters by taking positions on (and claiming superior competence for the management of) specific issues such as tax, environmental, labour market, economic, or health policy. Another trend is the growing preponderance of the 'personality' of contending political elite figures, with the design of the image and public appearance of personalities becoming increasingly the professionalised business of media and communication experts.

The ongoing surveying and measuring of public opinion trends also allows professional political communication experts to design, on behalf of the parties and elites they serve, a promising synthesis of these dimensions of political competition. There is in many OECD countries a clear tendency, and not just in the presidentialist systems, to personalise political conflict by giving (arguably undue) emphasis to the third of the above dimensions of conflict, namely leadership personality. This shift of conflict may not only have to do with the 'end of ideology' and the secular approximation of social democratic forces to market-liberal views and programmatic outlooks, but equally to the media-based nature of the competitive struggle of politics. The archetypes of 'winners' and 'losers' in the drama of a 'fight' among concrete persons can appeal to the passions in ways that are hard to match by ideological stances and positions taken on controversial policy issues. Not only are persons, as compared to issues and programmes, more easily (and more economically) portrayed and represented by print and electronic media alike; the 'like/dislike' (or 'trust/distrust') code of personalised conflict is also the more easily and deeply engrained into citizens' memory, while loyalties, judgements, and preferences concerning policy issues and overarching programmatic ideas are more demanding to establish in any durable fashion. It often seems that the vehemence of personalistic political competition is the greater the *smaller* the actual differences between the contending parties are concerning their programs and policy platforms, as all major parties try to cater to the 'median voter' and the practice of *state* craft is degenerating, as has been said, into mere *stage* craft. As a stylised extrapolation of the trend from programme competition to issue and finally personality competition we may envision a condition in which the electorate makes collective decisions at best on *who* governs while losing control over, even a cognitive grasp concerning, *what* governing elites (will) actually do, in substantive policy terms, with the mandate to govern granted to them by their constituency.

The personalisation/presidentialisation of politics often culminates in the 'populist' confrontation of personalities combined with moralised identity issues sometimes bordering on culture wars. This confrontation is designed to pose *us*, the good, honest, decent, hard-working, and deserving people, as represented by a trustworthy leader (self-styled as 'one of us'), against *them*, the evil, suspicious, corrupt, unproductive, and undeserving if not positively dangerous opponents. Populist politics are thus both unifying and divisive. They try to unify people on the basis of simple moral truths (which are held to be self-evident and do not require much of an effort of argument and reasoning) and do so by opposing 'all of us' to categories of people that need to be stopped from inflicting further damage on 'us'. Populists and populist parties pick either of two kinds of foes. One is the ruling political elite (the 'political class') itself, together with its bureaucrats, alleged cronies, and other beneficiaries of more taxes, more centralisation, and more regulation. This libertarian, often anti-statist variety of populism defends not just free markets, but also the autonomy of local communities and regional identities. This kind of populism is currently most clearly represented by the American 'Tea Party Movement' and its vehement opposition to big/central government and big spending. The other variety of populist divisiveness frames the 'otherness' that is to be opposed not in anti-elite, but in *anti-minority* terms: the category of people that is to be opposed are foreigners and foreign powers, migrants and refugees, ethnic minorities, and people on welfare. The dynamics that are at work in either of these variants of populism often lead to the crossing of the conceptual border line between *adversaries* or opponents more or less respectfully competing under mutually recognised rules for political power and *enemies* involved in a struggle in which the confrontation is over the denial of the other side's rights and the legitimacy of its presence. It is the attempted fusion of these two kinds of 'otherness' – others at the top (the centralised taxing state) and others at the bottom (migrant minorities) – that makes up the success formula in the rhetoric and politics of populist leaders (a fusion that has gained electoral strength in Europe in countries as different as Norway and Hungary) that can eventually challenge the viability of liberal democracy as it calls into question and actively undermines the fundamental democratic principle of requisite stateness and the equality of political rights.

4. *Accountability* – My last defining criterion of the institutional structure of liberal democracy is the presence of mechanisms which serve to hold ruling elites accountable for what they do, including what they fail to do. There are three kinds of such accountability enhancing institutional devices. First, in a vertical perspective and through the mechanisms of periodic general elections, party competition, and the investigative reporting of free media, citizens have the opportunity of removing governing elites and majority parties from office if they are dissatisfied with their performance and policy decisions and, *nota bene*, if they have reasons to expect that a respective alternative governing elite is likely to deliver more desirable outcomes. In the absence of such a credible alternative, accountability mechanisms in terms of policy run idle or are limited to alternative makers of basically identical policies. Second, wrongdoings of incumbent governments can be exposed as such, through horizontal accountability mechanisms, by parliaments and parliamentary committees as well as by constitutional (or 'supreme' or 'high') courts. Third, much of correction of (putative) failures, errors, and malfunctioning of government policies takes place through the ongoing and inconspicuous influence of organised interests and their veto power (which consists in an often ambiguous mix of threats, warnings, and conditional promises). The use of such power is typically focused upon alleged negative impacts certain government policies (such as fiscal reforms) are claimed to have upon macroeconomic key variables such as growth, employment, competitiveness, and fiscal and monetary stability.

Yet governing elites can also defend themselves against and escape the consequences of being held accountable for undesired results of their policies and decisions. 'Blame avoidance' is known to be a dominant tactical motivation of incumbent governments.[13] As the opposition party often does not have more desirable policy alternatives to offer, replacing the incumbent government by one that is led by the opposition is often not a promising move from the point of view of voters. In our age of 'globalisation', frustrating policy outcomes can be blamed on forces that are allegedly beyond the control of national governments – for instance, forces such as the financial market crisis. Margaret Thatcher's famous TINA argument ('there is no alternative') is often endorsed by economic orthodoxies that unfold, with a questionable claim of scientific objectivity, in all kinds of consultative bodies and in the media. Also, in an age of 'governance' (usually understood as the multi-actor and multi-level configuration of policy actors), it is hard to see who exactly is to blame for negative results and how to locate a responsible actor. Finally, governments have numerous means (among them the subtle forms of control over the media, government-sponsored information campaigns, the tactical timing of decisions, clientelism, keeping failures secret or obstructing their public uncovering) to immunise themselves against accountability mechanisms.

Diagnostics of democratic failure and the need for democratic innovation

According to the diagnosis of prominent democratic theorists, we are in the midst of a second transformation of democracy,[14] with the first one being the transition from direct (agora, town hall) democracy to party-dominated representative mass democracy. There is now a recent and abundant literature on the 'crisis' of democracy,[15] even 'the end' of democracy,[16] the 'end of politics', or the rise of 'post-democracy'[17] and the para-statist making of public policies by transnational corporations and their in-house conversion of economic into political power.[18] One of the context conditions that triggered these perceived challenges may have been the breakdown of state socialism. As long as state socialism existed, Western democracies could content themselves with claiming (and in my view rightly so) that they performed normatively as well as economically 'better' than their authoritarian counterparts. Yet, that counterpart having become obsolete, they now have to demonstrate (and to provide compelling argument) that they are 'good', i.e. normatively sustainable, on their *own* terms. What needs to be shown in a persuasive way is that the institutional structures and mechanisms of liberal democracy (as summarised above) are actually capable of delivering the functions (as discussed in the first section) for the performance of which liberal democracy is held to be the most desirable form of political rule. This demonstration is not an easy task, to put it mildly. Causal narratives on the crisis of democracy include economic globalisation and the absence of effective supranational regulatory regimes; the exhaustion of left-of-centre political ideas and the hegemony of market-liberal public philosophies, together with their anti-statist implications; and the impact of financial and economic crises and the ensuing fiscal starvation of nation states which threatens to undermine their state capacity.

For reasons of limited space, I shall mention in a stenographical manner only some of the trends and symptoms that have led authors to speak of the 'crisis' – or creeping deconsolidation – of liberal democracy. In most liberal democracies there is a secular decline in electoral turnout.[19] Also, class-specific turnout rates in general elections are drifting apart, with the least well-to-do showing the lowest interest in voting in elections, and even more so in engaging in the more demanding participatory practices of joining (movements, political parties, associations) and *donating* (of money, expertise, time).[20]

This trend is accompanied by a sharp decline in citizens' trust in politicians. Both in new and in old democracies, apathy, cynicism, and a sense of powerlessness are on the increase. Many of the terms that have been used to describe the situation of widespread political alienation start with a 'dis': dissatisfaction, disenchantment, disappointment, the sense of the people being disempowered by elites, depoliticisation, and disaffection.[21] In sharp contrast to the decline of European democracies in the inter-war period, however, such alienation has not given rise to explicitly anti-democratic movements. People remain democrats, if 'frustrated democrats'.[22] Similar trends have been documented concerning all kinds of associations in general (again, with a class bias) and membership in political parties in particular. It has been argued that contemporary democracies are in fact 'post-liberal' in that they are populated, at the level of the inputs of demands and preferences, by two categories of citizens: first, ordinary 'natural' citizens – individuals who vote and participate in various ways – and second, a poorly legitimated class of 'secondary citizens' which consists of associations, pressure groups, lobbies, and similar agents of functional representation.[23] By employing the organisational weapons of threats, warnings, and conditional promises, the latter can gain a measure of (highly non-transparent) control over public policy that the multitude of individual citizens can hardly match.

Two families of remedies

Lipset's characterisation of democracy as 'democratic class struggle' emphasises the essential aspect of contestation in the democratic process – the struggle for power among competing representative elites. Yet democratic politics does not just consist in the drama of competition, contestation, and open political conflict (a drama that is eventually to be decided at bargaining tables and by the casting of ballots in elections and the counting of votes). It also consists in the less conspicuous and less easily dramatised process in which citizens *form* judgments, interests, opinions, and preferences about the matters that affect them and the political community as a whole. The distinction between these two stages is important for democratic political theory; it is the same distinction as that between trying to persuade my opponent in a public exchange of information and argument and outnumbering my opponent through mobilising support for 'my' party or cause more effectively than the other side is able to. Democratic politics proceeds in cycles that involve *both* of these stages; we get a one-sided and defective picture of the democratic political process if we think of it only in terms of expressing preferences through voting and elections and not also in terms of the formation and revision of those preferences.[24] The two families of democratic innovations proposals focus on each of these two stages, the expression and the formation of the political will of citizens. The conflict of political wills and preferences as it is expressed in the voting booth is thus preceded by a process of will formation, in which not numbers and the logic of aggregation, but well-informed interpretations of reality, arguments, and reasons *can* play a decisive role – but so can stereotypes, prejudice, resentments, and the unthinking acceptance of strategically designed messages sent to mass constituencies by competing political elites.

The theoretical claim here is twofold. First, people do not *have* opinions and preferences (contrary to the reifying assumptions underlying much of survey research); instead, opinions and preferences are essentially in flux and constantly being *formed*, reproduced, validated, tested, abandoned, adapted, revised, upgraded, and reflectively enriched in the light of new information and experience. On most matters and issues, most people do not have an opinion and policy preference at all most of the time – until, that is, they are challenged to form one (for instance, in spontaneous reaction to being asked a question in a survey, with the implicit expectation communicated being that one 'should' or 'normally does' have a view on the matter in question). Second, the process of opinion and preference acquisition is not exclusively an internal and monological one, but always takes place in communication and interactive dialogue with others. Opinions and preferences are thus social constructs, or the joint outcome of 'my' own capacity and willingness to observe, to learn, and to reason, and of the information and social relations, constraints, expectations, and opportunities in which such learning and reasoning is embedded. We might even argue that it is quite irrational to hold beliefs and preferences which are strictly 'individual' ones, i.e. are formed under conditions of ignorance or disregard about what others, be they opposing 'my' views or concurring with them, hold to be true and desirable. For I know my preferences only after I know the preferences of others on whose cooperation I depend (or whose preferences I need to defeat) in order to realise 'our' preferences and interests. The external context of the ongoing internal process in which opinions and preferences are formed can range from coercive, repressive, or manipulative control over the information that is accessible and the preferences that are sanctioned as permissible, to, at the other end of a theoretical scale, egalitarian, open, encouraging, and challenging situations in which individuals are free to rationally consider, knowing and pondering the points of view of others (with whom they may end up agreeing or disagreeing), which beliefs and preferences they choose to form and adopt, and why. It is this latter set of qualities which is summarily referred to, in the broad current of democratic theory that has emerged since the early 1990s, as 'deliberative'.

Coming back to the two stages of democratic inputs – the stage of the *formation* and the stage of the *expression* of policy preferences – we must note two asymmetries between them. First, before we can express an opinion or preference, it must have passed through some formative stage (whatever its 'deliberative' qualities), whereas there is no 'must' in the opposite direction: a policy preference, once formed, may well be silenced when it comes to will expression, which may be due to the fact that there is no representative actor (political party, governing elite) who can be expected to 'listen to' and to whom it would make subjective sense at all to address one's expression of will.[25] The other asymmetry is this: at the stage of the expression of political will, the institutional frameworks of the process – political parties, elections, voting procedures – are all precisely defined and formally prescribed and monitored. In contrast, and while constitutional guarantees (freedoms of opinion, the media, assembly, association, etc.) play an indispensable role as providers of possibilities and opportunities (as do civics curricula and other state-organised educational facilities), much of the actual formation of opinions and political preferences is (and must be according to liberal principles) an institutionally largely uncharted space in which powerful yet informal social processes of family life, work life, the experience within local faith-based and secular communities, neighbourhoods, voluntary associations, consumption and lifestyles, media use, etc., play a decisive role in the formation, validation, and change of political views and preferences and thus the 'social realisation' of those constitutionally guaranteed rights.

The difference between the stages of the formation and the expression of political views and preferences consists in the gap concerning their degree of legal institutionalisation. Statutory (and partly also constitutional) laws exist in all liberal democracies specifying the equal right to vote (i.e. express preferences) of all citizens, the right to stand in elections as a candidate, and the procedures according to which individual votes are aggregated in order to form operating representative institutions. These equal rights are, however, being made actual use of according to highly unequal patterns, namely according to inequalities of socio-economic and educational status, among others. In contrast, not even such nominal equality is institutionally provided for when it comes to the formation of preferences – the process in which citizens *find out* about the policy options that are available, each other's arguments and preferences, the composition of potential alliances, and what, in the light of such information, may be deemed as good (or better) for 'all of us', and the remaining disagreements pertaining to this question. Again, prevailing patterns of social inequality seem to condition the highly unequal access to such opportunities of deliberative learning and clarification, with those cut off from relevant communicative and associational resources being not even able to indicate, with any measure of inter-temporal or substantive consistency, *where they stand*. Others in secure and privileged socio-economic positions have no doubt concerning this issue, as they are less affected by cognitive uncertainties and motivational cross pressures. It would not be implausible to assume that members of the former category, being confined to a condition of structural uncertainty concerning their own interests and preferences,[26] are likely to abstain from participating in political life; only those who know what to say will raise their voices.

These are empirical questions that I cannot pursue here any further. What should have become clear in our discussion of the two stages of political will formation is that liberal democracies suffer from a condition of vast under-utilisation, both quantitative and qualitative, of the political resources that are nominally available to each citizen. By *quantitative* under-utilisation, I refer to the fact of increasing overall non-participation, increasingly patterned in line with social inequalities. By *qualitative* under-utilisation, I refer to the malfunctioning of the mechanisms (the media, the educational system, political mass parties) which supposedly can transform 'raw' and unreflective political views and impulses into 'refined' and more enlightened awareness and preferences. Current debates on democratic innovations focus upon either of them and try to devise appropriate remedies. After very briefly pointing to some proposals related to how participation and citizens' involvement can be enhanced in quantitative terms and at the stage of preference expression, the final part of the essay will address some aspects of the hotly debated issue of how the quality of democratic participation might be improved through adopting deliberative procedures and institutions to upgrade the process of preference formation.

(a) Strengthening the voice of citizens and the expression of their will: modes of aggregation of 'given' individual preferences

Apart from the basic prerequisite of *knowing* about political issues, alternatives, and institutions, individual citizens can actively participate in politics through three main channels: voting (in general elections), joining (associations, parties, or movements; participating in political discussion), donating (money, time, expertise). All three are affected in contemporary democracies by either a manifest decline of their usage or/and an increasing class bias. That is to say, the middle class and those above it vote, join, and donate more often and more extensively than those below it in terms of income, wealth, socio-economic security, and education. In order to overcome those biases, a variety of measures have been proposed to facilitate, incentivise, and equalise the expression of political preferences. These include changing the electoral system to a single transferable vote (STV); making voting mandatory (as in Australia, Belgium[27]); allowing for direct democratic and plebiscitary legislation (with the practices of Switzerland and California serving as a model); enhancing devolution and increasing the autonomy of local governments; democratising the funding of interest associations;[28] allowing for vicarious voting of parents (one extra vote for every mother per son and every father per daughter[29]); introducing gender (and perhaps other, for instance birth-cohort) quotas in the operation of parties, parliaments, and governments;[30] making the number of representatives contingent upon the turnout of constituencies (cf. participatory budgeting in Brazil[31]); opening the option for voicing dissent by introducing the NOTA option into the electoral process; making membership fees (more strongly) tax deductible; and reforming political and campaign finance according to the three principles of capping overall expenditures, making 'plutocratic' donations either more anonymous to recipients or transparent to voters (and thus supposedly self-limiting), and financing campaign and political party expenditures out of public revenues.[32]

(b) Improving will formation through deliberation

There are two premises, or philosophical starting points, of any theory of deliberative democracy: first, the pursuit of *any* preference that is consistent with the law is legitimate under liberal principles. These principles deny the holders of state power the right (as it was claimed by the holders of power under state socialism) to denounce citizens holding certain (critical) preferences as suffering from 'false consciousness', thus providing a pretext to repress allegedly hostile intentions deriving from it. At the same time, we also need to keep in mind that preferences are not given and 'natural', but *formed* and motivated through cognitive and moral considerations, which in turn can be hampered by interests and passions, as well as by communicative conditions that hinder the reflective probing of one's preferences.[33] The institutional facilitation of such probing could contribute to the partial or full neutralisation of what Steven Lukes[34] has called the 'third' – and least conspicuous – face of social power, namely the power to hinder others to find out what their interests are. Moreover, the prevalence of myth, resentment, ignorance, short-termism, the fetishisation of personality and community, and aggressive impulses against elites or minorities can, if they become driving forces behind the perception of political realities and preference formation, seriously jeopardise the viability of liberal democracy. In this sense, political views, values, and preferences are not strictly a 'private' affair of individual citizens, as their pursuit can generate negative externalities that affect the rights of others and ultimately those of 'all of us'. To the extent this is so, we may well claim a public interest in enhancing the overall quality of preferences, mediated through an improvement of the social contexts of preference formation as they demonstrably contribute to such enhancement.

A second premise is this: to repeat, the formation of political (as well as other) preferences is not just a matter of intra-personal, information-gathering, consideration and reflection alone, as in the monological process of 'preference laundering'[35] taking place in some *forum internum*. Rather (and as argued above), it is a *social* process in which people find out, preferably in the course of a non-strategic exchange of information and practical reasoning, what other people consider true and desirable and fair for 'all of us' – a process in the course of which the preferences with which people have entered the exchange may undergo revisions. (Whether or not such revisions will verge on consensus is bound to remain an open question for empirical observation.) The rule governing such deliberative exchange is something like this: You know what *you* want only after you know what *others* want, and after knowing and considering the reasons on which those others base their preferences. In practical terms, learning about other people's preferences and their reasons for holding them can encourage the formation and clarification of one's own preference on the matter under joint deliberation, provided the exchange takes place with a minimum level of respect and mutual assurance.

The institutional location in which preference formation as a social process takes place is the 'life world' of everyday interaction or, more specifically, the 'third sector'[36] as a residual sphere that is constrained yet not governed by the media of money and formal authority. The sociological distinctiveness of this 'sector' consists in the fact that its organisational forms (foundations, movements, local initiatives and associations, faith-based organisations, etc.) are at the same time non-governmental organisations (NGOs) and non-profit organisations (NPOs). That is to say, what they do is not predominantly guided by criteria of legal correctness (as in public administration) or the ambition to gain law-making powers (as in political parties); and neither is it primarily guided by an economic calculus of profitability. Instead, the activities of NGOs/NPOs are dominated by normative intentions and the values to which such intentions relate. Yet, while acting outside of the realms of market competition, political contestation, or hierarchies of authority, such organisations can have a direct impact upon both economic and political processes.[37] The question of by which methods such an impact can be institutionalised in democratic polities[38] has led to numerous experiments, institutional innovations, and the empirical observation of the nature of deliberative preference formation and change.[39]

Since the early 1990s, the philosopher James Fishkin[40] has experimented in many countries and settings with the method of 'deliberative polling'. This method is designed to generate evidence of the 'hypothetical', or counter-factual, will of the people, as opposed to empirical preferences of individuals as they are mirrored by conventional methods of survey research. It shows what people would end up believing and wanting had they had the opportunity to think about, with others and under conditions promoting 'enlightened understanding'[41] and mutual respect, what they 'really' want. The hypothesis, confirmed in many cases, is that the experience of informed deliberation enables participants to clarify, revise, and upgrade their own preferences. In order to demonstrate the amount and the direction of preference revisions, Fishkin's method measures the distribution of opinions and political preferences before and after a relatively short period of deliberation in which a randomly selected group of citizens is invited to participate. When institutionalised – for instance, in the form of 'national issues conferences' preceding national elections or even in the form of an annual 'deliberation day'[42], this would arguably have a major impact upon political elites: for as a result of deliberative polls, elites are provided with the opportunity to know what the well-considered, as opposed to the 'raw' and unreflected, 'will of the people' is.

The effects of deliberation

We can distinguish four qualitative effects that the use of deliberative procedures can have upon political life. First, the experience of deliberation can have desirable consequences at the individual level of participants.[43] These include, among others, better information on the issue at hand, including the improved awareness of oppositional arguments; an increase in political tolerance and the willingness to compromise, as well as an increase in generalised social trust; an increase in the willingness to participate through voting and civic engagement, and as a result, a greater sense of political efficacy; greater consistency of opinions.

A second effect can consist in the exercise of an informal authority (or a kind of 'soft power') that originates from deliberative procedures once they are institutionalised as part of the political process. As (and to the extent that) the media will report on the consensual results and remaining disagreements of deliberating fora and mini-publics, outside observers, elite as well as non-elite, will be provided with the opportunity to learn from the difference (if any) between the 'before' and 'after' poll results in which direction and to what extent the post-deliberation ('refined') preferences will change relative to the 'raw' pre-deliberation ones. The authority of people having passed through deliberation derives precisely (and somewhat paradoxically) from the fact that the participants of deliberative fora are randomly selected ordinary citizens who, representing only themselves rather than parties or interest groups, have neither the intention nor the organisational means to acquire political power themselves. It is the very absence of power ambitions on the part of the deliberators that can increase their 'recommending force'.[44] The effect of spreading knowledge about the policy preferences of deliberating (rather than power-seeking) ephemeral bodies will predictably make life more complex for political elites, who, after such polls and the due publication of their outcomes in the media, are then publicly *known to know* that the so-called 'will of the people' (as registered by ordinary opinion surveys to which they like to refer for legitimation purposes whenever it suits them) may in fact be a mere artefact of the prevailing non-deliberative conditions of preference formation. The public can thus learn that this 'will of the people' is highly malleable and contingent upon contexts of communication. This learning is driven by a demonstration effect: if people actually had the time, expertise, and appropriate communicative framework to think seriously and competently about issues on the political agenda, chances are that they would change their original views and preferences.

Third, there are strong indications that deliberative institutions have not just the potential for widening the range of substantive policy options by bringing to evidence what people want once they have been put in the possession of pertinent information and after having debated arguments for and against the alternative policy options. They also have the potential to widen the social inclusion of participants (and contrary to so much of the anti-intellectual polemics against the idea of deliberation being an idiosyncratic leisure time activity of the educated middle class that is en vogue among conservative academics). Such potential for greater social inclusiveness can be assumed on two grounds. First, to the extent that the principle of random selection of participants can be implemented and self-selection reduced, participants will include categories of people who normally do not vote, join, donate, or even know much about political issues.[45] But, second – and in a perspective on such forms of non-participation that was first and classically stated by Schattschneider[46] – there are theoretical arguments and empirical findings suggesting that non-participation and the associated waste of political resources is 'endogenous to the failures of democracy' and of 'normal politics'[47] rather than being caused by individual characteristics such as a person's class membership or level of education. The implication of this perspective is of course that if different and additional forms of participation were available, non-participation might well be reduced. Neblo and his co-authors produce strong evidence that deliberation is in fact such an additional, participation-widening procedural device.

> It is precisely people who are less likely to participate in traditional partisan politics who are most interested in deliberative participation. ... Younger people, racial minorities and lower-income people expressed significantly *more* willingness to deliberate. ... The kinds of people attracted to the deliberative opportunities offered are fairly distinct from those drawn to partisan politics and interest group liberalism.[48]

Finally, there are also indications that while the composition of participants in deliberative procedures is designed to approximate randomness, the actual preference change that can be observed in the before/after surveys interestingly does *not* reflect a random alteration of opinions and attitudes. Instead, deliberative procedures, if conducted under conditions of randomness of participants' characteristics and thus of maximal diversity, generate qualitative outcomes concerning attitude changes and consensual policy recommendations which are *not* evenly distributed on a conservative-progressive (or 'liberal' in the American sense) dimension of political views and preferences. This finding can be accounted for with a weak and a strong explanatory intuition. The weak one suggests that the very setting of deliberative fora – highly diverse individuals hitherto unknown to each other involved in an exchange of views and arguments on issues of public policy and trying to find solutions preferred by all participants – select against purely self-serving claims and propositions. As the statement 'I am for policy X because it serves my interest' is unlikely to carry much persuasive power (and perhaps even discredits the speaker because of his or her undisguised selfishness), there is a built-in incentive to present policy preferences, even if they are driven by self-interest, as being adopted for the sake of values or reason – a rhetorical move that can subsequently trap the speaker in a dynamic of self-destructive hypocrisy: once you have started to present your interests as being congruent with *common* interests or *shared* values, you have started to force yourself to remain consistent and continue to argue in those terms, which may well lead to actually *betraying* (in either of the two senses of the word) the interests that were motivating the operation in the first place. Yet there is also reason to consider a strong explanation of how those deliberative procedures may translate into specific, non-random substantive outcomes. As Gastil, Bacci and Dollinger[49] have shown in an analysis based on attitude changes generated in 65 deliberative polls, there is evidence supporting the presence of a conversion mechanism which translates the procedural equality of the deliberative setting 'into a general orientation toward equal social relations in policy solutions'.[50] The authors' main finding is that participants, while not re-describing themselves in overall ideological terms of 'liberal' vs 'conservative', still undergo systematic shifts in preferences and beliefs; after participating in (single and relatively short) deliberative fora, participants were 'more likely to support statements that promote cosmopolitanism [and to] oppose those that favour a more nationalist and parochial view of public affairs'. As exposure to the hypothesised causal effect of participating in deliberation was just quite ephemeral, it does not come as a surprise that deliberation was found to 'weakly' promote 'agreement with egalitarian and collectivist worldviews'.[51] Future research must provide us with more robust answers to the question of whether or not we can claim that the institutionalisation of deliberative procedures would shift policy preferences and political views in 'sustainability oriented', 'cosmopolitan', and overall egalitarian and left-liberal directions – directions that are marked by greater fact-regardingness, future-regardingness, and other-regardingness. To the extent that this intuition can be further confirmed through rigorous analysis, the institutionalisation and practical use of deliberative will formation (as a complement to the conventional channels of will expression, namely voting and bargaining) could itself become a promising political project rather than remaining a matter occupying political theorists and empirical researchers.

Structures of deliberation

Having so far discussed some possible and desirable functions that deliberation can perform, let us, again, move on to the appropriate institutional structures in which these functions might be performed. Deliberative 'mini-publics'[52] must ideally conform to three criteria: they must be democratic, both substantively and socially open and unbiased, and consequential.[53] The first of these criteria, the democratic or rights-egalitarian character, can be fulfilled in two ways. One is 'open access' to an assembly: whoever wants to be present has the right to come and to present his/ her point of view. This applies, for instance, in the case of participatory budgeting or the 'deliberation day' proposal of Ackerman and Fishkin.[54] The drawback of such self-selection is the presumably significant social selectivity that manifests itself in terms of (i) who shows up and (ii) who takes the floor and speaks and for how long. The answer to both of these questions is likely to be: overwhelmingly members of the educated middle classes plus representatives of parties and interest groups. Moreover, if the assembly is large, deliberation according to the rules of a 'mini-public' is hardly possible. Therefore, and as an alternative to 'open access', advocates of deliberative procedures have typically opted for the random selection of participants and the technique of (stratified) sampling which is intended to make the composition of the mini-public as much as possible a mirror image of the constituency. In this way, an inappropriate role of political party delegates and bearers of functional representation (i.e. interest associations) can be avoided. It must be said, however, that self-selection (and the biases contingent on it, for instance age, education, rhetorical skills) cannot be fully avoided; after all, before a random selection can take place, people must declare their readiness – or else would have to be brought under the equivalent of jury duty or mandatory military service – to actually perform their role in the deliberative body should the lot decide that they are called upon to do so. Yet if the findings of Neblo et al.,[55] referred to above, turn out to be robust, deliberation would provide incentives for self-selection of participants to whom conventional channels of participation and representation do not appeal, thus neutralising the distortions caused by middle class self-selection. Although both of these 'democratic' methods of constituting a deliberative body – open access to assemblies and random selection of participants – clearly have their problems, the variety of experience, opinion, and points of view present in either of them is arguably still greater (and less affected by strategic interests in gaining and maintaining power) than it is in the case in ordinary representative assemblies.

Secondly, deliberative structures should be substantively and socially open and unbiased. Although deliberative settings will hardly ever achieve the criteria of an 'ideal speech situation', there can be a considerable approximation to it through the role of facilitators, or moderators. Participants are asked and constantly reminded by the facilitator to speak out, to listen to others, to behave respectfully, to discipline their political passions, to declare their personal interests related to the issues under discussion, to learn about the issues and alternatives they are dealing with, to respond to the queries and arguments of others; to try to persuade others of their points of view through spelling out reasons; and to arrive at a policy recommendation which reflects, as far as possible, their shared understanding of what conforms to a notion of the common good. In that communicative process, the three virtues, referred to above, will typically be insisted upon by moderators and mutually appealed to by participants: *fact*-regardingness, *other*-regardingness, and *future*-regardingness. As to fact-regardingness, the typical question is: Do we know enough and do we make consistent and unbiased use of that knowledge, in order to develop an adequately informed recommendation on some policy question? Other-regardingness concerns the readiness to take into account the interests, values, and rights of others and issues of social justice pertaining to the way a proposed policy affects interests in favourable or unfavourable ways. And future-regardingness is the ability to look at and evaluate the long-term consequences of the solutions proposed and to deal with issues of their sustainability. In order for a group of deliberators to live up to these demanding standards (and usually under severe time constraints), the group must be small in order to allow for a full presentation of arguments and opinions of its members. Also, and in order to enforce the above rules of deliberation, the facilitator must assume the role of enforcing roughly equal participation and an adequate input of information (which is usually provided by a diverse group of experts who are made available for lectures and questioning).

Perhaps hardest to realise is the third criterion: deliberations of mini-publics must be (known by participants beforehand to have a reasonably reliable prospect to be) consequential, i.e. are guaranteed to have some measure of political impact. This impact can be entirely informal, but even that presupposes that political elites and members of legislative assemblies take mini-publics seriously, and that the media report on the process and outcome (recommendations) of deliberation. 'Planning cells'[56] and 'citizen juries'[57] are cases where the promised impact was to an extent formalised: sponsoring (local) governments made a formal commitment to provide reasons in public should they choose *not* to follow the recommendations given by deliberating mini-publics. Again the most far-reaching commitment was one that the government of British Columbia made, namely the commitment to hold a referendum on the Assembly's proposal (however one with strong super-majoritarian conditions, which ultimately caused its failure by a narrow margin). At any rate, if the participants cannot rely on the expectation that what they do and come up with has at least some chance of 'making a difference' in public policy, and that their common efforts are recognised as valuable (according to some proposals, also through the payment of a nominal fee paid to deliberators), their readiness to participate, to spend time on learning and understanding, and to properly deliberate will soon be exhausted.

Conclusion

I introduced this essay by saying that contemporary liberal democracies are 'not functioning well'. Apart from the question of normative standards concerning the characteristics and criteria of a 'well-functioning' democracy that this proposition suggests, it can also be read as an empirical generalisation: Many – and probably an increasing number and highly diverse sorts of – people converge on the belief, expressed in words and even more often in their patterns of behaviour and (in) action, that the way democracies function and the political outcomes they generate are often frustrating, disappointing, short-sighted, unfair, and thus seriously deficient. Rather than this disappointment leading to widely advocated rejection of liberal democracy and its principles, there is an ongoing and vivid democratic meta-discourse on possible improvements, extensions, and innovations of the democratic mode of organising political rule.

In this discourse, participants have focused on various stages of the overall democratic political process. One focus can be described by the question how ruling elites can be prevented from violating the limitations of their office through effective constraints that would make them act in more accountable ways. The proposal to strengthen the political role of courts and fiduciary institutions is sometimes made in response to this concern. Another focus is the institutional method by which the multitude of expressions of individual preferences of citizens is to be aggregated and condensed into a single (and time-limited) collective preference. Answers to this question emerge from debates on the pros and cons of electoral systems and the virtues and vices of direct-democratic popular legislation. These two foci have remained almost entirely outside of the present discussion. Instead, I have concentrated on a third and a fourth issue. The former is the issue of actual political participation: how many people are entitled to make use of their democratic rights, how many do actually do so, how often, and concerning what categories of substantive matters. Here belong all democratic innovations that are intended to encourage more, and more evenly distributed, participation through voting and joining and other forms of expressing preferences and choices. Finally, there is the issue of how the preferences that are to be expressed and aggregated come into being in the first place – the formative phase of beliefs and preferences concerning political life. It is at this stage where deliberative modes of forming and revising preferences can come to play a role.

I have argued that the practice of giving reasons, as well as the practice of listening to, respecting, and possibly adopting reasons that others give in an openended and disciplined face-to-face setting can be institutionalised. To that end, participation in such settings would have to be randomised and thereby changed according to egalitarian principles; time, place, and topics of deliberation organised in formal ways; the mutual recognition of dissenting voices guaranteed; the civility of discourses and the availability of relevant information assured; and the public visibility of outcomes, consensual or otherwise, provided for. Institutional forms in which this happens are not a substitute for, but a complement to all those more familiar procedures of democratic politics which regulate the expression and aggregation of preferences and the accountability of office holders. Individual beliefs and preferences are logically prior to their expression and aggregation. Yet beliefs and preferences, the ultimate 'raw material' of the political process, cannot be treated as individually 'given' but are, as social constructs, in constant flux. Also, they are highly incomplete, as most people simply do not know what to believe or which of the alternative decisions to prefer most of the time. Deliberation is the process in which they find out; if properly conducted, it can also be a process in which the three virtues of taking the facts, the well-being of others, and future developments into consideration will be cultivated.

Acknowledgements: The present version of this article has greatly benefited from comments by Marek Skovajsa and Pieter Vanhuysse

Notes

1. A. de Tocqueville, *Democracy in America*, New York, Vintage, (1835, 1840) 1988.

2. J. S. Mill, *Considerations on Representative* Government, 1861.

3. I. Kant, 'Toward Perpetual Peace', in P. Kleingeld (ed.), *Toward Perpetual Peace and Other Writings on Politics, Peace, and History: Rethinking the Western tradition*, New Haven and London, Yale University Press, (1795) 2006, pp. 67–109.

4. H. Heller, *Staatslehre*, Tübingen, Mohr, (1933) 1983.

5. O. Bauer, *Die österreichische Revolution*, Vienna, Wiener Volksbuchhandlung, 1923, p. 449.

6. J. O'Connor, *The Fiscal Crisis of the State*, New York, Saint Martin's Press, 1973.

7. M. J. Crozier, S. P. Huntington and J. Watanuki, *The Crisis of Democracy*, New York, NYU Press, 1975.

8. A. Sen, *Development as Freedom*, New York, Knopf, 1999.

9. C. Crouch, *Post-Democracy*, Cambridge, Polity, 2004; M. Torcal and J. R. Montero (eds), *Political Disaffection in Contemporary Democracies: Social capital, institutions and politics*, London, Routledge, 2006.

10. A. Lijphart, 'Unequal participation: democracy's unresolved dilemma', *American Political Science Review*, 1997, vol. 91, no. 1, pp. 1–14.

11. S. M. Lipset, *Political Man*, Baltimore, John Hopkins University Press, 1981.

12. *Ibid.*

13. P. Rosanvallon, *Counter-Democracy: Politics in an age of distrust*, Cambridge, Cambridge University Press, 2008.

14. R. A. Dahl, *On Democracy*, New Haven, Yale University Press, 2000; M. E. Warren, 'A Second Transformation of Democracy?' in B. C. Cain, R. J. Dalton and S. E. Scarrow (eds), *Democracy Transformed?*, Oxford, Oxford University Press, 2003, pp. 223–249.

15. Crozier, Huntington and Watanuki, *The Crisis of Democracy*; S. J. Pharr and R. D. Putnam (eds), *Disaffected Democracies: What's troubling the trilateral countries?*, Princeton, Princeton University Press, 2000; Rosanvallon, *Counter-Democracy*.

16. J. M. Guéhenno, *La fin de la démocratie*, Paris, Flammarion, 1993.

17. Crouch, *Post-Democracy*.

18. C. Crouch, 'What will follow the demise of privatised Keynesianism?', *The Political Quarterly*, 2008, vol. 79, no. 4, pp. 476–487.

19. R. J. Dalton, *Democratic Challenges, Democratic Choices: The erosion of political support in advanced industrial democracies*, Oxford, Oxford University Press, 2004.

20. In addition to my triplet of voting/joining/donating as modes of democratic participation (see further below), one might think of 'knowing' (i.e. having access to a reasonably correct picture of the collectively relevant situation and to methods that ensure the truth of the picture). But a discussion of the conditions of adequate – and unbiased – 'cognitive participation' would have to focus on the media and their political function, a discussion I have to skip here for reasons of space.

21. Torcal and Montero, *Political Disaffection in Contemporary Democracies*.

22. Dalton, *Democratic Challenges, Democratic Choices*.

23. P. C. Schmitter, 'The Prospects of Post-Liberal Democracy', in K. Hinrichs, H. Kitschelt and H. Wiesenthal (eds), *Kontingenz und Krise*, Frankfurt, Campus, 2000, pp. 25–40; Crouch, 'What will follow the demise of privatised Keynesianism?'.

24. R. E. Goodin, 'Input Democracy', in F. Engelstad and O. Osterud (eds), *Power and Democracy*, Aldershot, Ashgate, 2004, pp. 79–100.

25. The widely documented finding that (a) electoral participation ('turnout') is low (i.e. abstention is high), (b) further declining in many 'disaffected' liberal democracies, and (c) increasingly distorted in terms of socioeconomic and educational inequalities (which thus translate into inequalities of *political representation*) has led scholars to recommend the introduction of mandatory

voting, thus eliminating citizens' option to abstain and hiding the gap between preferences and their expression (Lijphart, 'Unequal participation: democracy's unresolved dilemma'). Yet if voting were to be made mandatory, at least some voters would find themselves coerced to cast their ballot in favour of parties of whose merits and credibility they are not persuaded. This problem could be remedied by introducing the following rule: If n parties or candidates compete, the voter is given $n+1$ choices (boxes to mark on the ballot), the additional one standing for the option of NOTA ('none of the above'). The perception of political elites' deficient responsivity, as suggested by the evidence of fiscal and institutional conditions constraining state capacity, can in turn contribute to a depoliticising sense of political alienation and powerlessness, which discourages the efforts to acquire political opinions and preferences in the first place.

26. S. Lukes, *Power: A radical view*, London, Palgrave, 2005.

27. Lijphart, 'Unequal participation'.

28. Schmitter, 'The Prospects of Post-Liberal Democracy'.

29. K. Hinrichs, 'Do the old exploit the young?: Is enfranchising children a good idea?', *Archives Européennes de Sociologie*, 2002, vol. 43, no. 1, pp. 35–58.

30. A. Phillips, *The Politics of Presence: The political representation of gender, ethnicity and race*, Oxford, Oxford University Press, 1995.

31. B. de S. Santos, 'Participatory budgeting in Porto Alegre: toward a redistributive democracy', *Politics & Society*, 1998, vol. 26, no. 4, pp. 461–510.

32. Cf. K. H. Nassmacher, *Political Finance*, Baden-Baden, Nomos, 2009; cf. B. Ackerman and I. Ayres, *Voting with Dollars: A new paradigm for campaign finance*, New Haven, Yale University Press, 2004. (For overviews of these and similar proposals for innovation, see A. Fung and E. O. Wright (eds), *Deepening Democracy: Institutional innovations in empowered participatory governance*, London, Verso, 2003; P. C. Schmitter and A. H. Trechsel (eds), *The Future of Democracy in Europe: Trends, analysis and reforms*, Strasbourg, Council of Europe, 2004; G. Smith, *Beyond the Ballot: 57 Democratic innovations from around the world*, 2005. Retrieved 1 February 2011 (http://www.powerinquiry.org/publications/documents/BeyondtheBallot_000.pdf); G. Smith, *Democratic Innovations: Designing institutions for citizen participation*, Cambridge, Cambridge University Press, 2009.

33. C. Offe, 'Bindings, Shackles, Brakes: On self-limitation strategies', in A. Honneth, T. McCarthy, C. Offe and A. Wellmer (eds), *Cultural-Political Interventions in the Unfinished Project of Enlightenment*, Cambridge, MA and London, MIT Press, 1992, pp. 63–94.

34. Lukes, *Power: A radical view*.

35. R. E. Goodin, *Political Theory and Public Policy*, Chicago, University of Chicago Press, 1982.

36. R. E. Goodin, 'Democratic accountability: the distinctiveness of the third sector', *Archives Européennes de Sociologie*, 2003, vol. 44, no. 3, pp. 359–369.

37. R. E. Goodin, and J. S. Dryzek, 'Deliberative impacts: the macro-political uptake of mini-publics', *Politics and Society*, 2006, vol. 34, no. 2, pp. 219–244.

38. C. Offe, 'Microaspects of Democratic Theory: What makes for the deliberative competence of citizens?', in A. Hadenius (ed.), *Democracy's Victory and Crisis*, Cambridge, Cambridge University Press, 1997, pp. 81–104.

39. Smith, *Democratic Innovations*; M. E. Warren and H. Pearse (eds), *Designing Deliberative Democracy*, Cambridge, Cambridge University Press, 2008.

40. J. S. Fishkin, *Democracy and Deliberation: New directions for democratic reform*, New Haven, CT and London, Yale University Press, 1991; J. S. Fishkin, *The Voice of the People: Public opinion and democracy*, New Haven, Yale University Press, 1995; J. S. Fishkin, *When the People Speak: Deliberative democracy and public consultation*, Oxford, Oxford University Press, 2009.

41. Dahl, *On Democracy*.

42. B. Ackerman and J. S. Fishkin, *Deliberation Day*, New Haven, Yale University Press, 2004.

43. Fishkin, *When the People Speak*, p. 133; D. C. Mutz, 'Is deliberative democracy a falsifiable theory?', *Annual Review of Political Science*, 2008, vol. 11, pp. 521–538 [530].

44. Fishkin, *The Voice of the People*, p. 162; Fishkin, *When the People Speak*, p. 134.

45. The random composition of deliberative fora would also increase the diversity of the points of view brought forward, which in itself can add to the informal authority claimed in the previous paragraph. The more diverse the members of a group are, the more immune the results of deliberation are to the suspicion of being biased by special interests.

46. E. E. Schattschneider, *The Semi-Sovereign People*, New York, Holt, Rinehart and Winston, 1960; cf. C. Offe, 'Political Disaffection as an Outcome of Institutional Practices?: Some post-Tocquevillean speculations', in M. Torcal and J. R. Montero (eds), *Political Disaffection in Contemporary Democracies: Social capital, institutions and politics*, London, Routledge, 2006, pp. 23–45; and F. Solt, 'Economic inequality and democratic political engagement', *American Journal of Political Science*, 2008, vol. 52. no. 1, pp. 48–60.

47. M. A. Neblo, K. M. Esterling, R. P. Kennedy, D. M. J. Lazer and A. E. Sokhey, 'Who wants to deliberate – and why?', *American Political Science Review*, 2010, vol. 104, no. 3, pp. 566–583 [566, 568].

48. Neblo *et al.*, 'Who wants to deliberate – and why?', pp. 567, 571, 574.

49. J. Gastil, C. Bacci and M. Dollinger, 'Is deliberation neutral?: Patterns of attitude change during "The Deliberative Polls"', *Journal of Public Deliberation*, 2010, vol. 6, no. 2. Retrieved 1 February 2011 (http://services. bepress.com/cgi/viewcontent.cgi?article=1128&context=jpd).

50. *Ibid.*, p. 8.

51. *Ibid.*, p. 20.

52. Goodin and Dryzek, 'Deliberative impacts'; Fung and Wright (eds), *Deepening Democracy*.

53. Two additional criteria are discussed by Smith (Smith, *Democratic Innovations*): procedures must be affordable and transferable to a variety of political issues, i.e. not limited to the most basic issues having to do with electoral systems and the problem of 'choosing how to choose', as in the famous case of electoral reform in the Canadian Province of British Columbia (cf. Warren and Pearse, *Designing Deliberative Democracy*).

54. Ackerman and Fishkin, *Deliberation Day*.

55. Neblo *et al.*, 'Who wants to deliberate – and why?'.

56. P. C. Dienel, *Die Planungszelle: Eine Alternative zur Establishment-Demokratie*, Opladen, Westdeutscher Verlag, 1997.

57. A. Coote and J. Lenaghan, *Citizens' Juries: Theory into practice*, London, Institute for Public Policy Research, 1997.

Chapter Five

Democracy Against the Welfare State? Structural Foundations of Neoconservative Political Opportunities[*]

Claus Offe

Within any modern state, citizens are structurally related to state authority in three basic ways. Citizens are collectively the sovereign *creators* of state authority, they are potentially *threatened* by state-organised force and coercion, and they are *dependent upon the services and provisions organised by the state*. The notion of citizenship within liberal-democratic welfare states involves all three aspects: citizens are (1) the ultimate source of the collective political will, in the formation of which they are called upon to participate in a variety of institutional ways; they are also (2) the 'subjects' against whom this will can be enforced and whose civil rights and liberties impose, by constituting an autonomous sphere of 'private' social, cultural, and economic action, limits upon the state's authority; and finally they are (3) clients who depend upon state-provided services, programmes, and collective goods for securing their material, social, and cultural means of survival and well-being in society. It is readily evident that these three components of the concept of citizenship have their ideological roots, respectively, in the political theories of liberalism, democracy, and the welfare state.

These theories – and the corresponding dimensions of the concept of citizenship – can clearly be located on an evolutionary axis that represents the development of the 'modern' state. In such a rough historical sequence – as suggested in a famous essay by T. H. Marshall,[1] among others – first came the 'liberal' solution of the problem of state authority as a threat to life, property, and cultural/religious identity. The institutional response to this problem has been the constitutional legal guarantee of freedom and liberty, which made certain spheres of existence and activity exempt from state control. This is the *liberal* component of the modern state, the formal limitation of its power, and the exemption of market interaction and other 'private' pursuits from state control. It is a set of institutional devices that organise a protective framework ('rule of law'). This protective arrangement is intended (and often seen) to counterbalance effectively the threatening administrative, fiscal, military, and ideological means of control that the modern state has accumulated.

[*] 'Democracy against the welfare state? Structural foundations of neoconservative political opportunities', *Political Theory*, 1987, vol. 15, no. 4, pp. 501–537.

Second, because the modern state does not have a universally recognised 'meta-social' mandate from which its legitimacy can be derived, it turns to the 'people' as its ultimate source of authority. This is the 'voice' principle, institutionally embodied in the rules and procedures of *democratic* government and representation. The most important of these are the universal right to vote, competing political parties, general elections, majority rule, and so on.

Finally, the citizens depend upon the state due to the loss *both* of feudal forms of paternalistic 'welfare' *and* of individual economic autarchy. 'Insecurity' and the structural incapacity of maintaining the necessary preconditions of the existence of civil society as a whole are no longer a purely military problem (to be taken care of by the apparatus of the 'warfare state'), but also become increasingly a recognised condition of virtually all civilian actors within the civilian life of civil society. They come to depend on a great variety of economic and social policies, the institutional framework of which is today known as the *interventionist welfare state*. Thus the three components of the modern state-citizenship relation in the West can be said to be the *rule of law*, *representative democracy*, and provisions for 'civilian security' through the *welfare state*.

The problem I want to introduce is familiar from much of the recent literature on the state in general and on the welfare state in particular. It is centred on the question of the stability and viability of a political system made up of these three institutional components. Two extreme perspectives can be distinguished. One emphasises harmony, compatibility, even evolutionary mutual reinforcement among the three, while the opposite perspective emphasises strains, stresses, contradictions, and incompatibilities. It must remain a theoretical, and ultimately an empirical, question, which of these perspectives is valid, and for what reasons, in what respects, and under what conditions.

The global problem of potential inherent tensions within this *ensemble* of three institutional components can conveniently be broken down into three subproblems. These concern the viability of *partial* syntheses, namely those of (1) the liberal and democratic components, (2) the liberal and welfare state (or, in the somewhat more specific German terminology, *Rechtsstaat* versus *Sozialstaat*), and (3) the democratic and welfare state components. As far as the first of these compatibility questions is concerned, which shall remain entirely outside the scope of the present essay, there exists a large tradition of political theorising and an equally broad body of literature that is often sceptical and critical in its findings and of which the works of Wolfe, Macpherson, and Levine[2] are well-known, if heterogeneous, examples. The second compatibility problem, that of the 'fit' of liberal and welfare state institutional elements, is a favourite of the (neo)conservative political discourse and will be briefly discussed in a moment. The third set of subproblems is relatively the most neglected one in the theoretical literature. It is this subproblem to which most of the present discussion shall address itself.

Liberalism and the welfare state

In the early 1980s, much of the dominant discourse of the problems and future developments of the welfare state focused on the alleged antagonism between the collective civilian security aspect of the state (i.e., the *welfare* state) and the *liberal* aspects of the state (i.e., its guarantee of private property, of contractual market relations, and hence of a capitalist economy). This discourse, in which the philosophical and political perspectives of the neoconservative and liberal right prevail, postulates that the welfare state has become too heavy a burden on the economy, the growth potential and competitiveness of which are consequently seen to suffer from the excessive costs and rigidities imposed upon the market by state-organised welfare and social security provisions. On the other side, these theories, predictions, and alarmist speculations are countered by arguments and programmatic views by the democratic left, unions, and West European social democratic and socialist parties and governments. The *tableau* within which this debate is framed is schematically represented by the matrix (Figure 1), which categorises supposed causal links between the liberal principle of a market economy (ME) and the welfare state (WS). The propositions of the neoconservative critique are summarised in cell 4 of the schema.

Figure 1: Conceptualisations of the interaction between market economy (ME) and the welfare state (WS)

causal link	supportive		antagonistic
ME → WS	expanding private sector economy generates tax base for "growth dividend" out of which welfare state transfers and services can be financed		labor saving technical change, capital flight, domestic demand gap etc. undermine prospects for long-term full employment on which WS is premised
		1 / 2	
		3 / 4	
WS → ME	provision of skills, health, peaceful industrial relations, "built-in" demand stabilizers etc. generate necessary input for ME and support its further expansion		excessive tax burden; crowding out effect of state budget deficit; WS as disincentive to invest, employ and work; WS as cause of labor market rigidities and "immoralist" attitudes

Controversial as all of the propositions within the four cells of this schema are, they are at least explicit components of a well-established and fairly conventional economic, legal, and political debate. The only new (or perhaps very old?) argument within a broad discourse that emphasises the long-term incompatibility between the welfare state and a liberal market society is perhaps the proposition, put forward in a number of recent publications, that the damage that the welfare state inflicts upon the liberal order is not so much of an immediately *economic* but *moral* nature. According to its proponents, the 'fiscal crisis' and 'economic inefficiency' crisis of the welfare state are mediated through a moral one. Focusing on the highly developed Dutch welfare state, one author, for instance, argues that due to its abstract formal-legal *modus operandi*, the modern welfare state has cut itself loose from the moral resources, common values, and potentialities for solidarity within civil society, thereby rendering these resources useless and the adherence to solidary commitments worthless. This critique of the welfare state condemns its destructive impact upon the moral fiber of society and, by virtue of *this* effect, also upon its economic efficiency and productivity. The author gives the following illustration of the demoralising effect and hence the 'immoralist' nature of state welfare:

> After a fund-raising event for a charitable goal, members of a voluntary organisation are able to present the money personally to the recipients of their benefaction, whereas the recipients of welfare state benefaction remain anonymous members in a bureaucratic system, receive their cheques by mail, while the money of the system has been collected by a gigantic tax system. This welfare package does not require any commitment or initiative, nor can any moral energy be invested in it. Nobody bears any responsibility, nobody is accountable, nobody needs to show loyalty ... to this abstract system [which, according to this view, is characterised by an] in-built lack of moral principles [and an elective affinity] between the welfare state and the immoralist ethos.[3]

Leaving aside its alarmist undertones, there are a number of potentially valid points on which this argument can be based. These include:

1. The self-augmenting dynamic of demands made upon the welfare state – as more and better organised groups of clients and claimants are formed, as they voice demands in competition with each other, and as new issues are included in the agenda, a self-propelling process of 'rising expectations' is set into motion that implies a shift from the prevention of poverty to the universal guarantee of status. As a consequence, the welfare state 'does no longer guarantee *minimal* standards of welfare and well-being, but is counted upon as the provider of maximum standards of welfare'.[4]

2. The liberal principle of the rule of law and, more generally, the protection and recognition of the private sphere of economic and family life prevent the welfare state from transgressing, except in marginal cases, the limits of formal-legal entitlements and thus distribute benefits according to principles of attributed need and/or demonstrable desert. This also makes it infeasible

to make the receipt of benefits conditional upon any kind of moral obligation to which recipients would have to conform. This situation involves an easily exaggerated potential for '"moral hazard" and "free-riding" that ... are typical for "common-pool-problems"'.[5]

3. As social policy makers are forced to take into account the imperatives of the capitalist economy, welfare state programmes tend to be 'reactive' rather than 'active,' or 'differentiated' rather than 'integrated'[6] except under the most favorable of institutional and economic circumstances (of which the Swedish welfare state is often considered to be the prime example). That is to say, the liberal nature of the economy prevents social policies from achieving the degree of comprehensive rationality and effective implementation that would make it immune from the corrosive impact of economic change, fiscal crises, and business cycle fluctuations.[7] The very constraints that govern the formation of social policies render them highly vulnerable to changes of economic and fiscal parameters.

To the extent that these observations are valid, they are likely to lead to the cumulative frustration with the welfare state of client and claimant groups (due to point 1), of taxpayers and voters (point 2), and eventually of political elites themselves (point 3). The conflict between liberal and welfare state principles is emphasised not only by economic liberals, but also by humanistic libertarians who have grown increasingly sensitive to the alienating, decapacitating, and depersonalising effects that the welfare state and its legal-bureaucratic or professional modes of distribution, treatment, and surveillance can have upon communities and individual 'life-worlds'.[8]

The (partial) validity of these liberal and libertarian arguments, however, does not enhance the plausibility of the solutions typically proposed to overcome the conflict between liberal and welfare state principles. For the assumption that the structural 'demoralisation' of the welfare state can be overcome by some government-sponsored strategy of 'remoralisation' is as simplistic as it is questionable in terms of its ethical plausibility. Yet it is exactly this 'remoralisation' strategy for a postliberal welfare state that has been proposed, along remarkably similar lines, by Mead[9] for the United States and by Spieker[10] for West Germany. Mead criticises the American welfare state for its 'permissiveness,' by which he means its failure to impose binding 'civic obligations' upon the recipients of its benefits and services. By *civic* obligations, he means such civic duties as accepting (hard and low-paid) work, supporting one's family, respecting the rights of others, and acquiring through formal education the basic skills that are required for literacy and employability.[11] Taken together, these civic virtues make up what Mead calls the competent or 'functioning citizen', whose creation he envisages as a function of a new style of social policy that would operate with educational means and outright punishments to shape citizens after this model. 'Government must persuade people to blame themselves'; the poor must be obligated to accept 'employment as a duty'.[12]

The 'authoritative' – or authoritarian – paternalism that forms the basis of this proposal is justified by the fact that what is demanded from the welfare clientele is nothing but one set of traditionally American virtues. Thus 'being' American justifies these state-enforced moral requirements of 'civic obligation'. A similar shift from legal entitlement to moral desert is proposed by Spieker, this time not on the basis of national culture but Catholic doctrine. According to this author, the welfare state has nurtured a 'hedonistic' and 'parasitical' conduct of life,[13] against which not only work- and family-related virtues but also an attitude of 'friendship toward the state'[14] must be restored and enforced. Such proposals 'resolve' the tension between the liberal and the welfare components by abolishing both of them, certainly the former. They proclaim a state-sanctioned and state-enforced set of moral standards and virtues, although it is evidently beyond the powers of any '*modern*' state to form a unity of moral will even on the elite level, to say nothing about imposing it 'authoritatively' on the mass level. Moreover, such proposals do not recognise the contradiction that what they theoretically (though counterfactually) claim to be a *universal*, generally recognised set of virtues would turn in practice into a specific and highly *selective* disciplinary device directed against clients and recipients of benefits; for none of these authors has ever proposed state punishment for family breakup or failures to comply with the work ethic in *middle* income social categories. Finally, proponents of plans for a 'remoralisation' of the welfare state remain silent about the obvious problem of what should happen to those who *fail* as 'functioning citizens,' that is, the 'undeserving' poor. While these unsettled questions deprive the 'remoralisation' approach of much of its intellectual interest, they do not necessarily interfere with its latent political function, which is to undermine whatever norms of trust and solidarity have remained intact, to label the poor and other welfare recipients as morally unworthy and undeserving, and thus to absolve political elites (and taxpayers in general) from *their* moral obligations toward the recipients of welfare benefits and services by blaming them for failure to live up to their presumed moral obligations.

To some extent, the left-libertarian critique of the welfare state is the inverse image of the neoconservative 'remoralisation' approach. What the latter calls for as a remedy, the former criticises as a pervasive component of already existing state practices. The alienating, depersonalising and morally destructive impact of bureaucratic and professional intervention into the life-world of clients is viewed with growing alarm and suspicion, while no reasonably realistic vision of a communal, solidary, 'convivial', and nonalienating alternative to the welfare state has yet emerged very clearly.[15] All that can be stated is the deep ambiguity of state power, which, according to Habermas, is a 'perhaps indispensable, but not truly innocent' instrument for taking care of society's welfare problem.[16]

Democracy and the welfare state

Let us now turn to relationships and tensions that exist between the democratic and the welfare components of the modern capitalist state. Consider some hypothetical links between these two structural elements.

Concerning these two structural variables, much of the conventional wisdom converges on the intuitively highly plausible assumption that capitalist democracies tend to generate political forces supporting welfare state developments (Figure 2, cell 1) *and* that, unless these forces are defeated by a combination of economic crisis and authoritarian political regime changes, welfare states will then generate positive repercussions upon democratic political institutions for the kind of reasons indicated in cell 3. These two assumptions seem to capture the essentials of the mainstream of postwar social democratic theory in Europe. The welfare state is, in the words of Richard Titmuss, a set of 'manifestations, first, of society's will to survive as an organic whole and, secondly, of the expressed wish of all the people to assist the survival of some people',[17] and political democracy is the institutional means by which this manifestation and expression of will is made possible. At the same time, political democracy is seen as a powerful means of forcing political elites and ruling-class political representatives to accept welfare state arrangements. 'Elite fear of social conflict, and ultimately revolution, was the catalyst in explaining social policy making in interwar Britain.'[18] Underlying this optimistic assumption is (1) a *model of rational collective action through democratic politics* and (2) a model of self-stabilising and *self-reinforcing institutional dynamics.* The twin assumption is that rational actors in a democracy will join a pro-welfare-state majority and that, once the welfare state institutions are established, they become increasingly immune to challenges. As it is the central

Figure 2: Conceptualisations of the interaction between political democracy (PD) and the welfare state (WS)

causal link	supportive	antagonistic
PD → WS	universal franchise strengthens political power of wage-dependent majority of citizens; collective interest of wage workers in welfare state; electoral "power of numbers" outbalances economic power of property 1	welfare backlash; individualism; authoritarian anti-welfare state populism; new particularistic tendencies (tax revolt, institutional racism etc.) 2
WS → PD	3 convergent pattern of party competition; reduction of intensity of political conflict political integration of entire electorate; "end of ideology"; structural vanishing of political radicalism, which might lead to antidemocratic challenges	4 corporatist deformation of PD; marginalization of groups, interests and cleavages not served by WS; rise of new forms of non-institutional political conflict

claim in the theoretical discussion that follows that both of these assumptions are in need of basic revision, let me elaborate each of them in more detail.

1. The key figure within the collective rational action assumption is the property-less male wage labourer, employed full-time for most of his adult life, whose material subsistence and that of his family depend on a continuous stream of contractual income. He shares these features with a large number of fellow workers who, taken together, constitute the vast majority of the economically active population. Like them, he is exposed to risks partly inherent in the dynamics of the capitalist mode of production. These wage workers also share some common cultural patterns, such as a certain productivist discipline, a sense of solidarity and the perception of being involved in some fundamental social conflict that divides labour and capital. This overarching sense of solidarity and conflict manifests itself in certain political and economic forms of participation and association, experienced as the only available means of promoting their collective interests in income maintenance and social security, in adequate working conditions, in continuous full employment and the prevention of poverty, and in the redistribution of income and economic control. This configuration of conditions and orientations can be described summarily as *labour-centred collectivist statism.*

Moreover, this policy package of social security plus full employment plus health, education, and housing, plus some poverty-related social assistance is something that could appeal to rational actors *outside* the working class as well, and eventually to all well-intentioned citizens, that is, except for a small minority of the most narrow-minded and selfish ones. This is so for three interrelated reasons suggested by Therborn,[19] all of which have to do with the nature of the welfare state as a provider of public goods. First, any rational voter is supposed, according to this line of argument, to support (and be prepared to make disposable income sacrifices for) the welfare state as it helps to *avoid* collective '*evils*', ranging from street crime to the spread of contagious diseases to economic recession to disruptive political conflict. Second, support of the welfare state can be seen as an *investment* in a positive public good, such as the development of human resources, labour productivity, and so on. Finally, support for the welfare state can be perceived as the fulfillment of altruist *social obligations* and hence of normative preconditions of legitimacy and justice. With all these class-related, interest-related, and normative considerations to rely on, why should such support fail to be forthcoming in a democratic polity?

2. The corollary assumption is one of institutional self-reproduction, inertia, and irreversibility that would immunise welfare states, once entrenched, from challenges and basic revisions. This assumption, which appears rather heroic today, can still be based on the following set of arguments. Within an established welfare state, none of the competing political parties can attempt to abandon the welfare state accord, and this is more the case the broader the range of *individual* goods (such as income) provided by the welfare state and the greater the proportion of the population that benefits from these goods. Furthermore, large-scale and complex programmes (such as the various branches of social security of West European welfare states) tend to commit political elites to their continuation,

especially if major corporate collective actors are involved in social policy formation and implementation, an arrangement that would serve as a 'muffling effect of social policy'[20] and discourage protest. Finally, centripetal elite politics and the constraining power of existing programmes, budgets, and legislations not only interact with each other, but also condition favorable developments of public opinion and mass ideological orientations.[21] Along the line of this 'institutional inertia' argument, the welfare state can be expected to breed its own sources of political support, partly via the broadening self-interest of individuals and groups who receive such benefits as inflation-proof pensions, and partly via the mechanism of ideological accommodation. What emerges from this brief elaboration of the 'institutional inertia' assumption is a reassuring picture of interlocking virtuous circles, which, taken together, amount to a giant negative feedback mechanism of the welfare state in operation. Note that all of the component arguments – concerning both the 'rational collective action' and the 'institutional inertia' assumptions – are based on the presumption of rational action by individuals, classes, parties, unions, elites, voters, and clients of the welfare state.

This overall picture, however – associated with social democratic political theory – is hopelessly antiquated if we look at West European welfare states and their foreseeable futures in the mid-1980s. In none of these states a constitutional change has taken place that even comes close to the abolition of democratic procedures and institutions. Yet both the situation itself as well as its perception and interpretation on elite and mass levels, have changed in dramatic and unanticipated ways. This new divergence between democratic politics and social policies is so pervasive that it cannot be accounted for in terms of transient deviations from a long-term trajectory. It must be understood, or so the core thesis of this essay suggests, to be reflective of structural changes and new situations in which rational political actors (individual and collective) find themselves. The mutually supportive relationship of mass democracy and welfare stateness (as depicted in cells 1 and 3 of Figure 2) no longer amounts to a convincing hypothesis. To the contrary, there are many indications, as well as meaningful theoretical assumptions and conjectures, that lead us to expect that democratic mass politics will *not* work in the direction of a reliable defence (to say nothing about the further expansion) of the welfare state.

The dependent variable that thus needs to be explained is the stagnation and partial decomposition of welfare states in Western European democracies since the mid-1970s. There can be little controversy about the phenomenon itself, although the overall picture – including national variations – is hard to capture by a few indicators, especially because economic conditions, institutional structures, and cultural traditions in these countries produce a great deal of variation. I suggest the following list of indicators that produce a fairly uniform picture of what has been happening since the mid-1970s.

(a) There has been a continuous and sometimes rather dramatic series of electoral losses and defeats of social democratic and socialist parties, that is, the traditional hegemonic forces of pro-welfare-state political interests and alliances. In fact, by 1986 social democratic-led governments have been pushed back to the northern and southern margins of Europe – in sharp contrast to the situation in the late 1970s-early 1980s. On the level of public opinion as measured by longitudinal and comparative analysis of survey data, it has been observed that 'in general, the direction of the change has been to the favour of anti-welfare state views.'[22] Differences within scholarly interpretation do not concern the direction of this change, but the extent to which it has occurred, with only a few authors finding reasons to believe that the population 'in general [is] either satisfied with provision or supports more expenditures'.[23]

(b) There has been marked and often abrupt discontinuity in the development of the *absolute* level of welfare state expenditures, leading either to stagnation or slow decline of budgets, in contrast to a continuous rise of expenditures during virtually the entire period since World War II. One careful study of these fiscal and expenditure developments finds that 'cuts are on the political agenda in a way which would have been unthinkable a generation ago'.[24] Even a country that has so far been relatively unaffected by changes in growth rates and governments, namely West Germany, shows a sharp decline in the proportion of social policy legislation that implies increases in benefits or coverage.[25]

(c) There has been an even more dramatic decline of welfare state transfers and services *relative* to the level of need that is itself caused by unemployment and demographic as well as sectoral economic changes. As a consequence, for instance, a growing rate of unemployment coincides with stagnating unemployment insurance budgets, which leads either to a deterioration of benefit entitlements and/or to increased exclusiveness of entitlements of the unemployed.

(d) The growing gap between (what used to be recognised as) need and actually provided benefits has not led to large-scale and/or militant conflict in defence of the welfare state and its continued expansion. To the contrary, patterns of political conflict have shifted in three directions. One is the mainly unpromising phenomenon of militant, sectoral, local and regional strikes, and sometimes riots, such as occurred in the British mining and printing industries, and in poverty-stricken communities. Another is the sometimes dramatic electoral defection of the core working class to liberal-conservative political forces, implying a strong sign of political support for anti-welfare-state cuts and legislation even among those who belong to the classes and social categories in whose name the ideals and ideologies of state-provided welfare have traditionally been advocated. Finally, a further shift has centred on problems (such as the rights of citizens, the environmental question, feminist and peace issues) that are absent from the welfare state's agenda and that are now being carried out by nonclass social movements.[26]

(e) Parallel to these changes of policy and politics, there are strong indications that the *egalitarian-collectivist* component of its theoretical heritage is receding in significance, while *libertarian*, *antiétatist*, and *communitarian* ideals and projects become increasingly dominant on the political Left. It is exactly at the moment of severe challenges and defeats that major forces within the political Left seem to abandon what has been the Left's central project, namely, a collectivist-étatist version of industrialism. This shift in the Left's own ideological orientation is well captured by Przeworski and Wallerstein when they write:

The predicament (of the Left) is political: historical experience indicates that governments cannot be trusted with precisely those alternatives that would make a difference, those that require large doses of state intervention. The dilemma of the Left is that the only way to improve material conditions of workers and poor people under capitalism is through rather massive state intervention, and the state does not seem to be a reliable mechanism of intervention. The patient is sick, the drugs are available, but the doctor is a hack.[27]

On a more analytical level, Habermas has raised the problem that the welfare state, after having reconciled to some extent the tension between the capitalist economy and the democratic polity, is now confronting a dual problem as a consequence of which it is deprived of the mobilising potential of its utopian vision: on the one side, it is met with distrust by core working-class and upwardly mobile social categories who defect from collectivist ideas, and on the other, by those who, while recognising the welfare state's accomplishment of a measure of social justice, are aware of its built-in contradiction between state power and life-world, or between the welfare state's method and its goal.[28] Taken together, these two sources of growing frustration and disappointment would force the defenders of the welfare state to reformulate their political vision in quite fundamental ways.

Rethinking the macro-sociology of the welfare state

Largely in line with the hypotheses contained in the left-hand columns of Figures 1 and 2, recent comparative historical research has found that the rise of the welfare state has been correlated with such variables as economic growth, democratic political mass participation and bureaucratic centralisation, and the rise of collectivist tendencies in dominant ideologies and public opinion.[29] What is missing in this analytical design is the role of individual actors and their style of rational responses. Structures do not *directly* translate into outcomes and developments; they do so by virtue of the responses, interpretations, memories and expectations, beliefs and preferences of actors who *mediate* the link between structure and outcome. The recent resurgence of methodological individualist approaches in the social sciences has helped to remind us of this missing link within much of the macro-sociological research tradition.

The *social validity* of propositions concerning the correlation of, say, the democratic form of government and the welfare-stateness of the polity stands, as its were, on *two* legs, one being the testable correspondence of the proposition with *facts* and *events* in the outside world, the other being the way in which *actors* are constituted and rationally motivated to *accept* the proposition as a cognitive premise and as a guide to a particular mode of action, so as to consider it credible in itself and to adopt it as a belief – often with the consequence that the proposition is *then* validated as an empirical truth due to the operation of a self-fulfilling-interpretation loop.

There is, of course, a third type of validity of beliefs that is diametrically opposed to the second one. Its basis is neither empirically demonstrated *truth* nor strategically selected interpretation guided by *interest*, but *trust* in the validity of such norms as reciprocity, solidarity, or justice. According to this type, belief formation follows normative conceptions of the respective segment of reality-conceptions that are, as long as they prevail, counterfactual and infallible and, therefore, immune from empirical refutation and/or strategic selection. The structural conditions that can give rise to such normative foundations of validity-attribution are probably the opposite of those underlying our second type: the firmly established collective identities, homogeneity, immobility, and continuity that Rousseau described as the precondition of a viable 'volonté générale'.

Depending on which of these criteria of 'social validity' of such propositions we concentrate on, the task of the social scientist in testing, confirming, or criticising such claims differs considerably. For instance – and most important in the present context – how do we deal with politically consequential beliefs of the second type, which are 'real in their consequences' but – at least initially – unsupported by empirical fact? Their social validity results, as we have seen, not from their cognitive adequacy but from their interest-dependent individual attractiveness as a political project under conditions of high uncertainty, and thus, from strategic considerations. In such cases, both the reference to facts (i.e., type 1 beliefs) and to norms (i.e., type 3 beliefs) fail. Strategically selected and adopted beliefs, being based on interest, defy critical assessments of their irrationality, which are based on either truth or norms.

As a way out of this dilemma, it seems to me that we must return to the level of empirical analysis – this time, however, not of the *facts* to which the propositions in question refer, but to the *actors* and their individual reasons for *accepting* these propositions as valid. In this perspective, the correspondence that would become the focus of critical attention is *not* the correspondence between facts and propositions. Neither would it be the correspondence between values and political projects. Rather it would be the correspondence between certain types of social actors and the parameters of choice given within their situation of action, on the one side, and their rational motivation to adopt certain interpretive patterns about the world, on the other. It is this latter approach to the analysis of the welfare state – an approach that could perhaps be described as a combination of structural, phenomenological, and rational choice approaches – whose contours I want to explore further.

Returning to our two matrices and the propositions that are schematically represented by them, the question is no longer 'Who is right?' but rather 'Which types of structural changes, perceptions, and specific uncertainties make it rational for various categories of actors to adopt, and to act on the basis of, either of the conflicting interpretive perspectives?'

Rationality, trust and welfare

The case of the liberal-conservative democratic attack on the welfare state is easily reconstructed in terms of rational choice theory. As we know from Olson's theory of collective action, there is no natural reason for a public good to be produced even if it could be shown to be in the interest of each individual member of a (large) collectivity. For rather than contributing to the production of the public good, the more desirable option to the rational individual is to let everyone else pay for the good while the individual takes a 'free ride' on the efforts of others without contributing her- or himself. As long as the benefits from the goods cannot be limited to those who have actually contributed to its production, free-riding is a rational strategy from the point of view of the individual utility maximiser. This is so for three reasons: first, because one's own contribution to the good would be so small as to make no real difference (in a 'large' group) for the continued production of the good. Second, because the good is in fact available as a 'public' good, that is, free of charge to its individual consumers. Third, because individual actors may have reasons, according to their perception of the propensities and inclinations of other actors, for suspecting that the latter will fail to cooperate in the relevant future, which would render the original actor's position that of the 'sucker'. As a combined consequence, and as everyone waits for the others to contribute to the good, the good, although collectively beneficial, will not be produced.

This well-known paradox serves as the backdrop for the analysis of cases where collective goods *are* actually produced. In such cases, the question must be asked: what makes the members of the group act so 'irrationally' (according to the individual calculus specified above) as to actually act *in accordance* with their collective interest? The answer that Olson – who is quite careful to avoid the use of any category such as 'norms' or 'values' – has to provide comes in either of two versions. Either the people do not, in fact, act 'irrationally', because they are rationally attracted to contributing to the collective good due to the existence of some 'selective incentives' that are made available to those who do contribute (in which case the collective good becomes a mere *by-product* of individual benefit-seeking). Or seemingly irrational behaviour occurs because someone *forces* individuals to cooperate, in which case they do not *win* an individual *benefit* from contributing but *avoid* the punishment that would result from noncooperation. With these two specifications, the main argument appears to remain valid: whenever someone contributes to the production of the collective good, she or he does not act irrationally if it can be shown that she or he does so on the basis of a rational motivation through either the gain from selective incentives or the avoidance of punishment; in all other cases, rational cooperation is not to be expected.

This type of argument, however, works only as long as the punishment for noncontributors (to concentrate on this case alone) is imposed in a strictly *authoritarian* way, that is, without the option being open to the individual in question to *avoid* the alternative of either joining or being punished for not joining. The *democratic* citizen, in contrast, would in fact *have* the option to impose *his or her* will upon the government in order to prevent it from imposing *its* will upon the citizen (i.e., compulsory contribution under the threat of punishment). Seen from this perspective, the problem of democracy is that it moves – in theory as well as in practice – beyond an account in terms of simple coercion. It does so 'by introducing a framework wherein *legitimacy* may be tested'.[30] Democracy puts citizens in a position in which they are able to coerce the coercer, and it becomes quite likely that they will use their democratic rights in this way if they have to believe that a sufficiently large number of other citizens will join this strategy to force state authorities to *refrain* from forcing citizens to contribute – unless they consider the state's authority legitimate. Among such reasons can be the following: (1) many people believe that many *other* people believe that the incidence of costs and benefits of a given programme or legislation is redistributive in nature; therefore, it appears to be in their self-interest to adopt this belief themselves even in spite of individually available factual counterevidence, and to join those acting on the false belief that their action will be profitable. Such democratic evasion from collective goods contribution may also be attractive (2) for the reason that it is channeled through voting, that is, an institutional mechanism that renders individual behaviour invisible (secret ballot) and noninteractive (simultaneous voting, which renders infeasible the emergence of an assurance game).

The paradox thus appears to be this: unless citizens consider the state's authority legitimate, they can obstruct mandatory cooperation through the democratic ballot. As far as state provision for welfare is concerned, its legitimacy is not only dependent upon the citizen's perception of the nature of the rulers or the government but also upon the perception of fellow citizens and the anticipation of their action. If thus only a legitimate authority within a solidary society (i.e., one consenting on the legitimacy of the authority) can enable the state to enforce cooperation, why is such authority necessary in the first place? Why can't it be fully replaced by voluntary collective goods production?

In other words: explaining collective goods production by reference to state authority and mandatory contributions is not really an explanation but the first step in an infinite regress that can only be halted by some axiom concerning the pregiven and unquestionable existence of state authority as the ultimate coercive power. Short of such an axiom, state authority that enforces collective goods must be considered a collective good in itself, thus suffering from the same problem that it supposedly solves. As Talcott Parsons demonstrated in a famous argument against Hobbes, no deductive link exists between the ideal selfishness of the inhabitants of the state of nature and the origin of state authority; Hobbes's suggestion that there is such a link 'is really to violate his [utilitarian] postulate [and] to posit a momentary identity of interest'.[31]

Consequently, the problem of selfish noncooperation cannot be explained away by the existence of state authority, because the latter owes its origin – and continued existence – to dispositions on the part of citizens toward cooperative action. A state that is necessary to deal with the collective problems of universal and pure selfishness is at the same time impossible (and *vice versa*) because it cannot originate from a condition of such selfishness. And neither can a state maintain itself in the context of pure selfishness, least of all a democratic state.

To be sure, the individual in a democratic polity would not be able to escape the binding force of authority as long as she or he remains the *only* one who wishes to stop the government from imposing a punishment on noncontributors. But, given a democratic polity, there is no reason to expect that she or he would *remain* the only one, given the fact that (by virtue of the bare minimum definition of democracy as the system under which dissent is not punishable) there would be a zero-cost attached to noncooperation by voting. For instance, citizens would vote into office a party that promises to do away with virtually all forced cooperation in the production of collective goods. What we would expect to see is a dynamic of actual defection, anticipated defection, anticipated anticipation, and so on, leading to a self-propelling or 'autocatalytic' chain of causal effects.

This exercise in Olsonian logic of collective action seems to demonstrate that there is at least one case in which the logic does not work: that in which the 'collective good' of *abolishing* the compulsory cooperation in the production of collective goods (or, for that matter, the 'indirect' production of collective goods through the selective incentive effect) is to be had at a zero-price, which is actually the case in a democracy. But because zero-cost dissent is a real possibility, it would affect all production of collective goods (for large collectivities), which, according to Olson, can only be explained as resulting from the selective incentives or compulsory contribution effects. Consequently, we would be back to square one in our attempt to understand why, among rational actors, collective goods production occurs at all *in a democracy*.

Unless we want to stick – against the Parsonian argument – to the now questionable assumption that pure self-interest *can* lead to the constitution of an absolute authority that henceforth is immune from citizens choosing their opting-out option, we will have to take another road. The only alternative seems to be to hypothesise that actors produce collective goods not because of the rational capacity to maximise utility and to avoid punishment, but because of their normative disposition to do so, or because of the relationship of trust, reciprocity, sympathy, and fairness that they have experienced between themselves and their fellow contributors. For what, other than such legitimising notions, motivations, and identities could lead them, in a democracy, to continue to cooperate, even though they *could* withdraw at zero-cost, thereby debasing the authority that compels them to act as rational contributors?

These theoretical considerations are less remote from the problem at hand than it might appear. The problem is to test the hypothesis in cell 2 of Figure 2. For the arguments above lead us to conclude that (1) if a polity is a democracy and (2) if the state is also (and continues to be for any length of time) a welfare state, then this coexistence of structural features of the polity in question cannot be accounted for in terms of class interests (as in cell 1), but must be explained in terms of legitimising values, attitudes, and practices that inhibit and prevent actors from behaving in ways that would effectively subvert collective goods production, but that still would be attractive from the point of view of pure rational individual utility maximisers. In other words, if a democratic state is a welfare state, this is not the case *because* of democracy, but *in spite* of democracy. It must be due to solidarities and modes of normative integration that underpin the continued production of collective goods and guarantee this production, notwithstanding the fact that democracy provides a greater and less expensive opportunity and even temptation to 'opt out' and to obstruct this production than any other form of government.

To be sure, even the most ideal-typically selfish citizen would not necessarily be disposed to obstruct *all* collective goods production by the use of the democratic ballot. Mandatory liability insurance, for instance, might be an exception to this rule because it generates a collective good for the insured. This type of insurance, however, will be supported by the rational, selfish actor only as long as the operation of the insurance is perceived to be distributionally neutral. That is to say, the condition of rational consent to *mandatory* insurance is that provisions are taken that guarantee that no one can profit by exploiting the rest of the community of the insured. But this can be taken for granted only if access to the insurance is restricted to persons who regard each other as 'our kind of people' or 'the likes of us', whereas 'cheaters' (who would be defined either as those who get away with less than their proportional contribution, or as those who extract more than their 'fair share' of benefits) must be restrained or excluded. This problem is illustrated by the constant pressure on private liability, health, and life insurance companies to organise, by the differentiation of their rates and benefits, 'homogeneous risk communities', so that no segment of the membership of the insured feels threatened by the systematic opportunity of other segments to exploit the collectivity of the insured.

Slightly more complicated cases in which rational utility maximisers will still be prepared to cooperate in the production of collective goods are those in which a redistributional game *is* being played but where the actor does have reasons to believe that, in spite of such redistribution effects, she or he will derive either (1) indirect benefits or (2) special advantages from his or her continued cooperation. They will derive *indirect benefits* if the redistribution involved helps to satisfy certain moral imperatives that she or he considers as binding for her- or himself (e.g., charity), or if such redistribution helps to serve his or her own interest. Concerning the latter point, it is known that within business and employers' associations, the smaller firms often derive more than a proportional share of benefits while paying a less-than-proportional share in membership dues, thus making them clear net winners from cooperation. However, the reason that large firms find such subsidisation of the small in their indirect interest, too, is to be found in the fact that otherwise the small firms might exit from the association, which would deprive all members, including the large ones, of the collective good of being able to speak in the name of the *entire* industry. It is thus exactly because of the redistribution component that everyone – and not just the winner – is better off. In such cases, even redistributive arrangements may be seen as being in everyone's interest – if only up to the point at which the small business sector within the association starts to make 'exploitative' and hence 'unacceptable' demands upon the collectivity. Again, the continued production of collective goods appears to be premised upon some shared notion of sameness or nonrival commonality of interest.

The other case is that of *special advantages* provided for cooperation from the outside: while the weak gain more than the strong, even the strong receive more than they would be able to under any alternative arrangement that would become available to them through noncooperation. This is – or perhaps one should say this used to be – the case with many old age pension social insurance arrangements, where expected benefits for middle-and high-income participants are higher than can be anticipated from private insurance or individual savings alternatives, due to income-graduation, wage indexation, and favourable entry conditions for higher income brackets. Such special advantages, which we could think of as a compensatory *external* subsidisation of the *internal* subsidisers, were often used, in the 1950s and 1960s, as a political 'bribe' designed to keep the better-off within the pro-welfare-state alliance, and to dissuade them from considering exit options.[32] But for this mechanism to work, it already presupposes on the part of the better-off in the cooperative game a considerable measure of trust that the promise of comparative advantage will be actually honored by any future government – a trust that in the field of old age pensions insurance is rendered notoriously shaky by current and foreseeable demographic and labour market trends. Again, there is a limiting case in which either trust in the willingness or ability of future governments to honour the deal is weakened and/or in which the price that the better-off demand for their staying within the alliance begins to be perceived as 'excessive'.

An interesting further case in which collective goods production (or abstention from the democratic option of opting out) is to be expected is weakness of will. I'll consent to being forced to contribute to some collective good (such as social security) if I think of myself as a person who is (e.g., for reasons of near-poverty) incapable of doing what his or her long-term interest would require him or her to do, namely, to save for consumption in old age. Similarly, I'll consent to mandatory insurance if the redistributive effect (e.g., in favour of those who live longer and at the expense of those who experience a below-average life span after retirement) is something that I approve of as a norm of solidarity, without, however, being sufficiently certain of my actual willingness and ability to live up to that principle in concrete cases. In both cases, the collective arrangement is accepted as a 'self-paternalist' precommitment that is meant to protect me from the consequences of my own irrational inclinations to disregard either my own future wellbeing or that of my fellow citizens to whom I feel committed. A further rational motivation to join the collective arrangement may result from the consideration that its common-pool nature makes it more cost-efficient: the more people participate, the less expensive (or qualitatively more specialised and adequate, as in public health services) the unit of output becomes.

But note that all these conditions are highly sensitive to empirical counterevidence and strategic fabrication of evidence under conditions of uncertainty. Under some conditions and perceptions, my willingness to cooperate may no longer make sense, which in turn can cause domino effects in the perceptions and attitude changes of others. For instance, if I conceive of myself as someone who is conscientiously prepared to provide for his own future needs; or if I think that others are either not deserving of a share of my income, or deserve only what I shall be willing to give on an *ad hoc* and *ad personam* basis; or if I feel that the expected economies of scale in collective services do not materialise, or are weighed by monopolistic exploitation by the supplying organisations, or must be paid for in terms of poor quality and excessive standardisation – all this will damage my rational motivation for cooperating and, therefore, the collectivist arrangement as a whole. It is only my trust that my precommitment will not work out to my disadvantage, that others are worthy of participating in the common pool of resources, and that the latter will not be exploited by provider agencies that lead me to accept this 'self-paternalist' arrangement.

In all these cases of cooperative production of public goods, the critical sociological variable is some notion of commonality of interest and fate, of 'sameness', or a sufficiently binding conception of a durable collective identity, which is the ultimate resource that keeps cooperation intact beyond its initial phase. Operationally speaking, the notion of sameness, or of collective identity, is the threshold at which actors not only rationally calculate individual and instantaneous costs and utilities, and where they act on the basis of trust. Such trust also has a social dimension – trust in other people – and a temporal dimension – trust in the continued validity and bindingness of norms and institutions. At this threshold, individual actors shift, as it were, from an economic paradigm of choice and contingency into a sociological paradigm of normative bindingness and order. It is not only the durable production of public goods that is, as I shall argue, impossible without some underlying conception of sameness and collective identity; it is even impossible to define precisely the notion of a public good without making at least implicit reference to the idea of a collective identity.

The economists' definition of a public good is based on the criterion of nonexclusiveness: if the good exists at all, it serves all, not just those who have paid for it. This is exactly why no one would be rationally and voluntarily prepared to pay. This is also why payment must be enforced (or tied to selective incentives) in order to produce the public good. But the 'publicness' of the good is not a quality of the good itself, but a reflection of the interpretive perspective under which people *view* the good. Take defence as a textbook example of a public good. Even here 'inclusiveness' is not something that is inherent in a defence apparatus, but in the perspective under which it is regarded by agents in society. Its 'publicness' is entirely dependent upon that society's trust in the nonexploitative or nonredistributive nature of the good and its functions. In order for a 'good' to be a 'public good,' there must be a collectivity, the members of which refer to themselves as 'we.' In the absence of such a collectivity (which in the case of defence is normally conceptualised as a nation or a bloc of nations), there would not be a referent to whom the good is a public good. The defence arrangement would not be seen as a benefit for 'all of us' but as the outcome of a redistributional or exploitative game that takes place between taxpayers and defence contractors, military personnel and civilians, defence and civilian sectors of the budget, internationalist and national political orientations, pacifists and militarists, and so on. It is only the self-conception of a collectivity as a nation that puts an end to this type of reasoning in terms of individual and group payoffs and replaces it by a discourse of collective benefits. This example should alert us to the fact that the 'nationhood' of a collectivity cannot be taken for granted, as little as the existence of other collective self-conceptions can, and that without such notions of 'sameness' and collective identity, public goods cannot be produced (or, if produced, commonly perceived as 'public' and as 'goods') – least of all in a democracy, where there is, by definition, no ultimate authority that would be able to order such production by the fiat of its sovereign power.

If, in the course of social change, existing notions of sameness come under strain and stress, the seemingly self-evident public good undergoes a *Gestalt*-switch and turns into the object and outcome of a distributive game. Before this switch occurs, a social policy, say the introduction of unemployment insurance, will be generally discussed and perceived in terms such as the creation of a just society, the guarantee of peaceful industrial relations, or the maintenance of aggregate demand. But *after* the switch, the very same policy will be viewed in categories of equivalence, exploitation, and redistribution, for example, in terms of inappropriate burdens being imposed on the industrious and active parts of the work force, and of undeserved benefits being granted to the unemployed. Note that, in this model example, the interpretive framework within which events are perceived has changed, *not* the policy measure itself. In education, the shift is typically from an emphasis on every person's right to the fullest development of her or his potential, or from human capital considerations, to an emphasis on violations of fiscal fairness or the autonomy of parents, on competitive distortions in the job market or on undue opportunities granted to teachers to promote their collective status interests. In each case, the underlying process is one in which dominant 'parameters of sameness' are narrowed down: from the universalist notion of human rights of all human beings to the interest of the nation to the interest of certain categories of taxpayers, professional groups, and cultural communities, and finally to the interests of the individual. In all such cases, the decisive change is not on the level of objective events and facts, but on the level of interpretive frameworks and the strategic adoption of beliefs and expectations. The calculative attitude toward individual and short-term costs and benefits is therefore nothing that is inherent in human nature or an eternal standard of rational action; to the contrary, it is the product of disintegration and decomposition of cultural and structural conditions that constrain and inhibit such utilitarian orientations.

How can such a narrowing of parameters of sameness, or the fragmentation of collective identities, sympathies, and solidarities, be accounted for? Three approaches have been suggested. First, one can explain such shifts in terms of a moral or normative political theory, pointing out that broad humanitarian conceptions of human rights and human needs must be given priority over selfish or otherwise 'narrow' interest orientations. To this group would also belong the philosophical idea of an evolutionary sequence of styles of moral orientation, be it linear along an axis of universalism (Habermas), or be it cyclical according to a model of 'shifting involvements'.[33] Second, the shift can be explained in terms of changing political elites, alliances, coalitions, conjunctures, and ideologies, as a consequence of which elites' strategies are seen to undermine and disorganise 'large' collectivities and to entice and encourage citizens and voters to adopt a socially narrow and shortsighted perspective in defining their own political preferences. Thus recent analyses of the 'right turn' in the United States[34] and the syndrome of 'authoritarian populism' in Great Britain[35] have interpreted these phenomena as the outcome of a design of reactionary political elites to invoke selfish individualist attitudes, provide it with a moral pretext, and thus to divide solidaristic alliances, and even the nation as a whole, along the nonclass divide of respectable versus morally questionable and undeserving citizens and social categories. Socialist authors have recently shown an understandable, though in my view one-sided, tendency to rely on this 'elitist' interpretation exclusively. Thus Krieger writes that

> the attack on the principles of the welfare state is only part of a broader project to reshape political community. ... Particularistic and even explicitly divisive appeals replace the integrative universalist norms of the welfare state. ... Policies ... are part of a strategy to reinforce particularism ... [and] to divide citizens in highly evaluative categories of 'us' and 'them.' ... 'They' are blacks, the unemployed, the clients of the welfare state, the strikers.[36]

The problem with this approach is that it seems to assume that political elites are able to shape and change mass attitudes, opinions, and perceptions rather than merely providing excuses and justifications for reorientations that are conditioned by nonpolitical causes. As little as a pro-welfare-state climate of opinion can be created by political elites, and anti-welfare-state orientation can be imposed through policies alone. This point is well expressed by Taylor-Gooby when he writes, referring to Habermas:

> The problem is that the social mechanisms that produce allegiance are not under the control of policy, because they originate in a different level of society. ... The basic problem is that the political system cannot itself guarantee to produce the values required to assure loyalty to its policies. Values derive from culture which is independent of the state.[37]

Without denying the potential usefulness of either of these approaches, let me suggest a third, more sociological and at the same time more structural, approach. It starts from the assumption that collective identities and parameters of 'sameness' are not chosen by individuals for morally good (or bad) reasons, nor that the scope of sameness is imposed upon social actors by either the laws of moral evolution or the manipulative efforts of political elites and ideologists. What we must look for, instead, are *structural* changes within modern societies that condition, suggest, and steer the prevailing interpretive patterns of 'sameness'. Within this perspective, it is assumed that the patterns of, for example, the division of labour, of cultural differentiation, of political organisation and representation are underlying determinants of what kind and scope of collectivity people refer to when using the word 'we'.

Destruction of collectivities

It has often been observed that the most advanced and stable welfare states exist in those European societies that are highly homogeneous. Take Sweden as the prototypical case: an economy that is small and highly export-dependent; a polity that is characterised by both long-term social democratic governance and hegemony and by a virtually unparalleled associational density of highly centralised interest associations; a society and culture that is, compared to other West European countries, not only highly egalitarian (as a consequence of past redistributive welfare state policies) but also uniquely homogeneous as far as the striking absence of ethnic, regional, linguistic, religious, or other major cultural cleavages is concerned. A further characteristic is Sweden's nonparticipation in supranational military (NATO) and economic (EEC) organisations – a trait that this country shares with Austria and (partly) with Norway, that is, with two of the other most advanced welfare states. All these features would suggest that in Swedish society the prevailing conception of 'sameness' is very broad and inclusive, and that there exist powerful structural and cultural factors that effectively prevent the majority of Swedes from shifting to a view of their welfare state that would emphasise exploitation, unfair redistributional effects, free-riding, and similar utilitarian or 'rational choice' perspectives. But even in this rather exceptional case of Sweden, new divisions, antisolidaristic strategies, symptoms of lack of trust in the welfare state's administration, and particularistic tendencies have surfaced in the early 1980s that seem to put into question major achievements of public policy and neocorporatist interest intermediation between large and centralised associational blocks.[38]

When T. H. Marshall[39] theorised the inherent tendency of parliamentary democracies to transform themselves into strong welfare states (see cell 1 of Figure 2), he took for granted the existence of large, self-conscious, and well-organised collectivities and class organisations of labour that would use the ballot for strategies of social reform and expansive social policies. Since the mid-1970s, however, we witness a fairly rapid decomposition or destructuration of such collectivities. There are many indicators suggesting that political preferences and orientations of increasing segments of the electorate are a reflection of this process of fragmentation, pluralisation, and ultimately individualisation of socioeconomic conditions and interest dispositions. Issue orientation versus party orientation in voting; the increasing significance of plant-level over sectoral regulation of industrial conflict, and of sectoral over centralised national regulation; social, economic, and cultural cleavages that crosscut the dividing lines between classes and class organisations are all frequently observed symptoms of societywide destructuration processes.

The disorganisation of broad, relatively stable, and encompassing commonalities of economic interest, associational affiliation, or cultural values and life-styles is in my view the key to an adequate understanding of the general weakening of solidaristic commitments. If it no longer 'makes sense' to refer to a broad and sharply delineated category of fellow citizens as 'our kind of people', the only remaining interpretive referent of action is the individual who refers to her- or himself in rational-calculative terms. This reorientation may be accelerated by political campaigns of the populist Right that, as it were, 'cross-code' people according to criteria of moral worthiness and unworthiness. Or it may be retarded by appeals to universalist moral standards that should not be sacrificed.

But these appear to be variables of secondary importance, while primary significance rests with new forms of structural and cultural plurality leading to the virtual evaporation of classes and other self-conscious collectivities of political will, economic interest, and cultural values whose existence must be considered, as I have argued before, a necessary condition for solidary and collectivist attitudes and ideologies. The imagery of a fluid and mobile 'patchwork' is often used to describe a newly emerging structure of society and pattern of conflict – conflicts no less severe than those represented in class-conflict modes, but that differ from them in that the new pattern is made up of a plurality of relatively small groups and categories rapidly shifting in size, influence, and internal coherence with no dominant axis of conflict.

My thesis is that the welfare state as we know it as a major accomplishment of postwar West European societies is rapidly losing its political support for these reasons of structural change, and that this development can neither be fully explained by economic and fiscal crisis arguments, nor by political arguments emphasising the rise of neoconservative elites and ideologies; nor can it be undone by moral appeals to the justice and legitimacy of existing welfare state arrangements. What this structural disintegration process leaves behind is an interpretive pattern that is deeply distrustful of social policies as 'public goods', and that tends instead to unravel such policies in terms of gains and losses, exploitation, free-riding, redistribution, and so on – that is, in individualist 'economic man' categories, the behavioural consequences of which are best captured and predicted by rational choice theory.[40]

To be sure, the destructuration process and its ideological and eventually political repercussions are not uniform across countries, social classes, income categories, gender groups, or groups defined by party affiliation, nor do they affect individual components of the welfare state, its programmes and institutions, to the same extent. But some generalisations are in place in spite of these differences. One highly consequential destructuration occurs in the longitudinal dimension: the future is seen not to be a continuation of the past as far as economic growth, fiscal policy, and employment are concerned, and this anticipation undermines the plausibility of the traditional social democratic 'solution of painless redistribution by funding welfare from expansion'.[41] Another generalisation concerns an increasing differentiation between the popularity that different components of the welfare state enjoy. Some programmes and institutions – such as old age pensions and the health sector – find a greater acceptance than others (such as unemployment insurance, family allowance, youth programmes, and social assistance), the intuitively plausible reason being that it is much easier to conceive of a broad and inclusive alliance of potential beneficiaries in the first case than in the second, where clients are much more easily marginalised and stigmatised. But given the fact that the most serious of the fiscal problems of the welfare state emerge in its old age pension and health programmes, this relatively greater support for these programmes is also qualified by the individually rational temptation to 'opt out' and shift to private forms of provision. 'There has developed during the last two decades a whole series of substitutes for publicly provided social safety nets, such as private life insurance, firm pensions ... which are even cheaper as they often pool "good risks"'.[42] One might even suspect that, under these conditions, it becomes rational for some middle-class elements to express (insincere) support for the continued public provision of some minimal health and old age pension, because that would make the conditions for private provision all the more favorable – much the way in which it is rational to express strong and effective support for public transport while then expecting to be able to use private cars on the pleasantly uncongested streets.

Let me mention some of the underlying causes for the destruction of self-conscious interest communities in advanced industrial societies, and hence of the cultural and normative underpinnings of the welfare state:

1. Within the labour force of these highly industrialised democratic societies, there are increasing disparities of life-chances among the totality of wage workers. These disparities depend on variables such as industrial sector, ethnicity, region, gender, skill level, and so on. In view of such disparities, the organisational, political, and cultural resources by which some measure of commonality of interest could be established and politically enforced become increasingly debased and powerless.

2. The prevailing patterns of economic, industrial, and technical change generate the well-known disjunction between changes in economic output and changes in employment. As a consequence of this pattern of 'jobless growth', the percentage of people who find themselves in the condition of open unemployment, hidden unemployment, or labour market marginalisation, or who are rendered unemployable or discouraged from labour market participation, is rising. These categories of people, who are most desperately dependent on the welfare state's provision of transfers and services are, however, politically most vulnerable. This is so because there is little reason, either for the propertied middle classes and capital or for the core working class, to adopt the material interests of this 'surplus class' as their own. Such a reason does not exist for the core working class because there is little empirical reason to fear that the 'surplus class' could function as an effective 'reserve army', that is, depress wages and undermine employment security in highly fragmented and stratified labour markets. Similarly, there is little reason for the middle class and employers to fear that the existence of a growing 'surplus class' could lead to disruptive forms of social unrest and conflict, the prevention of which could be 'worth' a major investment in welfare policies – or even the full maintenance of those that exist.

3. Encompassing alliances of a pro-welfare-state orientation thrive in the 'good times' of economic growth and full employment (i.e., positive-sum games) and tend to decompose under zero-sum conditions. The potential for 'public-regarding' and solidaristic political commitments appears to be exhausted in many countries, both after the experience of real wage losses in the late 1970s-early 1980s and in anticipation of moderate growth rates and persistent high levels of unemployment and insecure employment. In that sense, the economic crisis of the welfare state generates individualistic political attitudes and orientations and

thus translates, without much liberal-conservative mass mobilisation and political organisation needed, into a political crisis of the welfare state.

There seems to exist an asymmetry between the sociopolitical processes that result in the expansion of welfare states and those that lead to cuts and the eventual decay of social welfare policies. In the upward direction, what is needed are broad electoral and interest group alliances that converge on the institutionalisation of collectivist arrangements. These arrangements will then persevere due to the inertia and entrenched interests of what has been set up. In order to survive, all that is needed is the absence of strong oppositional political forces. In contrast to the expansion, the decline is normally not initiated by reactionary mass movements and political forces. It normally originates from anonymous economic imperatives, such as budgetary pressures and fiscal as well as labour market imbalances that suggest cuts in social expenditures. In the presence of such economic difficulties, the tendency toward cumulative cuts could only be halted if a strong and unified political alliance were in place to defend existing arrangements. But it is exactly the formation of such an alliance that is rendered unlikely by the fragmentation, pluralisation, and individualisation of interests. As a consequence, uncertainty in the social dimension (concerning which political forces and social categories could be relied upon as trustworthy partners in a defensive alliance) is reinforced by uncertainty in the temporal dimension (concerning how much present sacrifice is likely to be compensated for by how much future gain in growth, employment, and security). In Western Europe at least, cuts in welfare expenditures do not typically occur as the political consequences of 'tax revolts'; they simply 'suggest themselves' as a consequence of changes in macroeconomic indicators, and they can be implemented without much political cost in view of the weakness of resistance. While the rise of welfare state requires mass mobilisation and large political coalitions as a sufficient condition, its demise is mediated through economic imperatives as well as the silent and inconspicuous defection of voters, groups, and corporate actors whose heterogeneous structure, perceptions, and responses stand in the way of the formation of an effective defensive alliance. To put it somewhat simplistically, it takes politics to build a welfare state, but merely economic changes to destroy both major component parts of it and potential sources of resistance to such resistance.

4. Not only the *goals* and objectives of welfare state policies (which consist in the prevention of poverty, the guarantee of social security, and the provision of public health, education, housing, and other services) meet with decreasing political support. It is also the *means* by which the goals have been traditionally implemented, namely bureaucratic and professional intervention, that seem have lost much of their acceptance, and are increasingly seen in the corrosive light of a distributional and exploitative game. That is to say, these means are no longer universally considered as a rational instrument for the implementation of 'public goods', but increasingly as a highly effective strategy of a self-serving 'new class' to cement their positions of power and privilege, and at the same time as an ineffective or even counterproductive ('dependency-creating' and 'de-capacitating') way of responding to the needs of clients and recipients.

5. A particularly important factor that helps to understand anticollectivist and anti-welfare-state reorientations of public opinion in Western democracies is the quantitative growth of the middle class, particularly the 'new' or 'salaried' middle class. As far as the *upper* strata of this broad social category are concerned, the welfare state has distributive effects that are clearly in their favour, a fact that can be partly explained through the logic of political 'bribes' referred to above. Thus one author concludes that

> the members of the salaried middle class seem to be the main beneficiaries of the welfare state. In pension, health, housing, and education it seemed that the better off you are the more you gained from the system. In terms of service, tax allowances and occupational welfare, the managers, administrators, professionals, scientists, technologicals working for large organisations benefited considerably more than manual and routine white collar workers.[43]

However, such special advantages and upward redistributive effects have failed to buy the political support of those who not only benefit from services and income-graduated transfers, but also from the secure and continuously expanding employment the welfare state had to offer them. The greater this income and privilege, the greater becomes their inclination to look for *private* alternatives to welfare-state services, the most important of which are old age pension and health services. The higher the status and income that the welfare state provides you with, the *lesser* your rational motivation to have your privileges tied to (foreseeably precarious) collectivist arrangements, and the greater accordingly the inclination to look for – and to support parties that propose designs for – private market alternatives. The dilemma of the welfare state is clear enough: any emphasis on egalitarian 'flat rate' policies would alienate those better off whose income would be used to subsidise the transfers to the less well-to-do. But the opposite policy – that of strong income differentiation and status maintenance – also would not help to keep the recipients of higher incomes within the alliance, for this policy reinforces and creates privileges that their beneficiaries are understandably unwilling to share with the rest of the welfare state's clientele.

As far as the *lower* middle class, including some segments of the skilled core working class, is concerned, its allegiance to the welfare state is notoriously questionable. Members of this 'middle mass' have formed in various countries the political base of tax revolts and the 'welfare backlash'. Wilensky, who has conducted large-scale comparative studies of these phenomena, concludes that 'as rich countries become richer, the middle mass as a political force becomes more fluid, torn loose from traditional political identities, and more strategic, larger and more potent as a swing vote'. He sees a 'developing political rage of the middle class'.[44] This tendency described by Wilensky would reverse an old and strong positive statistical correlation between welfare collectivism and economic growth and lead to a situation in which, as more people live in prosperity, they are *less* inclined to endorse such arrangements. It seems that dissolving 'traditional political identities' are not openly replaced by pure individualism, but that such a shift to individualism is provided with a justification by the formation of identities of a moralising and/or particularistic kind. What is least popular with the 'middle mass' are programmes that benefit those supposedly *morally* inferior categories (such as unemployed youth and single parents) and ascriptively defined minorities (such as ethnic or national ones).

A final observation concerning the widespread political defection of the middle class from collectivist welfare arrangements refers to the fact that since the mid-1970s much of the political energies of this social category have been invested, as it were, into issues and campaigns and conflicts of a nonclass, nonredistributive nature, ranging from civil rights to feminist, to ecological, to peace causes and movements. The reverse side of this shift in political style and emphasis of middle-class political activism is, of course, a deemphasis of conflicts having to do with social security, distributional justice, and solidarity.

6. The disappearance of a plausible and mobilising political programme or project within the European Left that would instill an idea of a mission or vision of sociopolitical transformation in the mass constituency of socialist, social democratic, and labour parties is a further important factor in the process of destruction of collective identities based on social class (or the nation in war or under the threat of war) and distributive interest. The failure of hegemonic projects – be it of *étatist* planning, be it of economic democracy – has left the traditional protagonists of the welfare state in a highly defensive position of 'maintaining what we have' ('*Besitzstandswahrung*'), which in turn allows parts of their constituency to begin to think about evasive strategies in case this defensive position fails – a case that is predicted with considerable resonance by conservative and market liberal elites.

Three observations and perceptions tend to deprive the welfare state of the moral appeal of a just and 'progressive' sociopolitical project. One concerns the evident incapacity of governments – including social democratic ones – to apply causal and preventive therapies to those socioeconomic problems that the welfare state must then solve in an ex post and compensatory manner by throwing ever-rising amounts of money at them. For example, a generous unemployment compensation for those out of work is affordable only if an active and preventive full employment policy keeps the number of those who are entitled to such benefits relatively small – in much the same way in which, as Schumpeter observed long ago, the construction of faster automobiles does not so much depend on the invention of more powerful engines but on more effective brakes. Similarly, the idea of universal health insurance coverage of all employees and their families loses much of its moral plausibility if evidently no one is able to implement large-scale and effective preventive health programmes and to control the 'cost explosion' in health – that is, the price-setting behaviour of pharmaceutical manufacturers, doctors, and hospitals. If, as a consequence, the proportion of income that is deducted for mandatory health insurance reaches record levels (currently 13% in West Germany, without, incidentally, the general health status of the population showing any objectively measurable improvement), the *Gestalt*-switch referred to above sets in with particular force: What used to be thought of as a solidary arrangement guaranteeing the protection of the health of all irrespective of income is now seen as a giant redistributive game with widely dispersed and high costs for clients, and concentrated and even higher benefits for suppliers of services.

Second, the moral appeal of the welfare state resides in the perceived justice of its distributive effects. The more the interpretation finds a base in perceived reality that the distributive effects are much more intertemporal (i.e., self-paternalist) in nature than intergroup (i.e., redistributive), the appeal and legitimacy of the welfare state project as a secularised and modern version of Christian ideals of charity must necessarily suffer severe damage, particularly as the gap the between living conditions of those depending on social security systems and those depending on welfare, social assistance, and other means-tested and family-related programmes becomes wider.

Third, pessimistic perceptions and interpretations both of the *effectiveness* of the welfare state, that is, its capacity to intervene causally into the need- and cost-inflating socioeconomic processes, and of the *legitimacy* of the welfare state, that is, its capacity to implement moral standards of redistributive justice, develop a self-reinforcing and self-propelling dynamic. This is so for the simple 'sinking-boat' strategic reason that if one sees oneself as belonging to an alliance that is doomed to lose, one better quit it earlier than others. Doing this, however, will convince others that defecting is the only remaining option for them, too. In view of giant fiscal problems that must be anticipated for the welfare state in connection with probable demographic, labour market, health, and family developments, such interactive chains of individual rational responses are something that is not only quite likely to occur, but also something that the traditional pro-welfare-state alliance of social democratic parties and unions is ideologically and hegemonically ill-equipped to prevent in most West European countries.

As a combined effect of these structural changes, we may anticipate the rise of behavioural orientations of voters and citizens that give support to anti-welfare-state policies – not primarily for reasons of bad intentions, irrational drives, or a sudden shift to neoconservative or market-liberal values and attitudes, but because of beliefs and preferences that are rationally formed in response to perceived social realities as well as to the actual experiences with the practice of existing welfare states.

What all of this amounts to is the prediction that the neoconservative denunciations of the welfare state are likely to fall on fertile ground, thereby setting in motion a political mechanism of self-fulfilling predictions and interpretations. That does not mean, however, that the neoconservative analysis and the empirical arguments on which it claims to base its validity are 'true' in any objectively testable sense, nor that they are 'right' according to substantive criteria of political legitimacy and social justice. They are, for all the reasons specified above, simply highly effective and self-confirming as a political formula with which electoral majorities can be formed, and with which existing large solidaristic communities of interest can be further disorganised. As a formula, it can be challenged only by a democratic Left that moves beyond its traditional defensive positions and adopts new concepts, goals, and strategies whose outlines today remain largely uncertain.

Notes

1. T. H. Marshall, 'Citizenship and Social Class', in T. H. Marshall, *Class, Citizenship and Social Development*, New York, Anchor, 1965 (first published 1949), pp. 71–134.

2. A. Wolfe, *The Limits of Legitimacy: Political contradictions of contemporary capitalism*, London, Macmillan, 1977; C. Macpherson, *The Life and Times of Liberal Democracy*, Oxford, Oxford University Press, 1977; A. Levine, *Liberal Democracy: A critique of its theory*, New York, Columbia University Press, 1981.

3. A. C. Zijderfeld, 'The ethos of the welfare state', *International Sociology*, 1986, vol. 1, no. 4, pp. 443–457 [452–53].

4. Zijderfeld, 'The ethos', p. 454.

5. K. Gretschmann, 'Social security in transition: some reflections from a fiscal sociology perspective', *International Sociology*, 1986, vol. 1, no. 3, pp. 223–242 [232]; L. M. Mead, *Beyond Entitlement: The social obligations of citizenship*, New York/London, Macmillan, 1986.

6. R. Mishra, *The Welfare State in Crisis*, Brighton, Harvester Press, 1984.

7. J. Habermas, 'Die Krise des Wohlfahrtsstaates und die Erschöpfung utopischer Energien', *Die neue Unübersichtlichkeit*, Frankfurt, Suhrkamp, 1985, pp. 141–163; C. Offe, *Contradictions of the Welfare State*, John Keane (ed.), London, Hutchinson, 1984.

8. Habermas, *Die neue Unübersichtlichkeit*; C. Sachsse, 'Verrechtlichung und Sozialisation: Uber Grenzen des Wohlfahrtsstaates', *Leviathan*, 1986, vol. 14, no. 4, pp. 528–545; I. Illich *et al.*, *Disabling Professions*, London, Marion Boyars, 1977.

9. Mead, *Beyond Entitlement*.

10. M. Spieker, *Legitimitätsprobleme des Sozialstaates*, Bern/ Stuttgart, Haupt, 1986.

11. Mead, *Beyond Entitlement*.

12. *Ibid.*, pp. 12–13.

13. Spieker, *Legitimitätsprobleme*, p. 328.

14. *Ibid.*, p. 323.

15. See Sachsse, 'Verrechtlichung'.

16. Habermas, *Die neue Unübersichtlichkeit*, p. 151.

17. R. Titmuss, *Essays on the Welfare State*, 2nd edn., London, George Allen & Unwin, 1963, p. 39.

18. Gilbert as quoted in P. Whiteley, 'Public opinion and the demand for social welfare in Britain', *Journal of Social Policy*, 1981, vol. 10, no. 4, pp.453–475 [455].

19. G. Therborn, 'Challenge to the Welfare State', unpublished paper, Institute for Political Science, Catholic University Nijmegen, Netherlands, 1986.

20. E. Øeyen, 'The muffling effect of social policy: a comparison of social security systems and their conflict potential in Australia, the United States and Norway', *International Sociology*, 1986, vol. 1, no. 3, pp. 271–282.

21. See R. M. Coughlin, *Ideology, Public Opinion, and Welfare Policy*, Berkeley, Institute of International Studies, 1980.

22. S. Pöntinen and H. Uusitalo, 'The legitimacy of the welfare state: social security opinions in Finland 1975–1985', *Suormen Gallup Oy Report*, 1986, no. 15, p. 26; S. Ringen, *Does the Welfare State Work?*, Oxford, Oxford University Press, 1986.

23. P. Taylor-Gooby, 'Legitimation deficit, public opinion and the welfare state', *Sociology*, 1983, vol. 17, no. 2, pp. 165–194 [175]; J. Alber, 'Der Wohlfahrtsstaat in der Wirtschaftskrise: Eine Bilanz der Sozialpolitik in der Bundesrepublik seit den fruhen 70er Jahren', *Politische Vierteljahresschrift*, 1986, vol. 27, no. 1, pp. 28–60.

24. Whiteley, 'Public opinion', p. 460.

25. While a full 81% belonged in that expansive category during 1950–74, and only 8% of the new legislation involved cuts, the federal legislative output 1975–83 consisted of 56% of new laws implying cuts while only 27% of the laws of this period led to increases (Alber, 'Der Wohlfahrtsstaat in der Wirtschaftskrise', p. 31).

26. C. Offe, 'New social movements: challenging the boundaries of institutional politics', *Social Research*, 1985, vol. 52, no. 4, pp. 817–868.

27. A. Przeworski and M. Wallerstein, 'Why Is There No Left Economic Alternative?', unpublished manuscript, University of Chicago, 1986.

28. Habermas, *Die neue Unübersichtlichkeit*, pp. 149–152.

29. H. L. Wilensky, *The Welfare State and Equality: Structural and ideological roots of public expenditures*, Berkeley, University of California Press, 1975; J. Alber, *Vom Armenhaus zum Wohlfahrtsstaat: Analysen zur Entwicklung der Sozialversicherung in Westeuropa*, Frankfurt, Campus, 1982.

30. Taylor-Gooby, 'Legitimation deficit', p. 166 [emphasis added].

31. T. Parsons, *The Structure of Social Action*, New York, Free Press, 1968 (first edition, 1937).

32. This problem would not be altered substantially if the possibility of democratic *rule*-making (of laws and constitutions) were taken into account as a further and rather obvious complication. Such rules can in fact perform the function of (self-)binding devices that make democratic decisions *temporarily* immune from revision and obstruction. But because such binding rules are never – be it *de lege* or *de facto* – absolutely and indefinitely binding, and as it appears highly questionable from the point of view of rational actors even to attempt

to extend the bindingness of rules into the indefinite future, the 'opting-out' argument itself is not affected by such rules, but only the rapidity with which the consequences can unfold.

33. A. O. Hirschman, *Shifting Involvements, Private Interests and Public Action*, Princeton, NJ, Princeton University Press, 1982.

34. T. Ferguson and J. Rogers, *Right Turn: The decline of the democrats and the future of American politics*, New York, Hill and Wang, 1986.

35. S. Hall and M. Jacques (eds), *The Politics of Thatcherism*, London, Lawrence and Wishart, 1983; B. Jessop, K. Bonnett, S. Bromley and T. Ling, 'Authoritarian populism, two nations, and Thatcherism', *New Left Review*, 1984, vol. 147, pp. 32–60.

36. J. Krieger, 'Social policy in the age of Reagan and Thatcher', *Socialist Register*, London, Merlin Press, 1987.

37. Taylor-Gooby, 'Legitimation deficit', p. 168.

38. S. Lash, 'The end of neo-corporatism? The breakdown of centralised bargaining in Sweden', *British Journal of Industrial Relations*, 1985, vol. 23, no. 2, pp. 179–203; Pöntinen and Uusitalo, 'The Legitimacy', pp. 20 ff.

39. Marshall, 'Citizenship'.

40. ... whose time seems to have come for exactly this 'structural' reason. Its fundamental methodological assumptions are in their essence antistructural, antifunctionalist, antinormativist, and thus in a way antisociological (relying on psychological and economic paradigms instead). But it is exactly this new paradigm and the dramatic shift in the intellectual climate in much of the social sciences that lends itself to a sociology of knowledge interpretation: it corresponds to a centreless, atomised, and destructured condition of social life. Without having the space here to elaborate this interpretation further, let me just suggest that I find it fruitful not only for the understanding of the growth of rational choice theory, but also for its twin phenomena, namely the rise to prominence of 'postmodernist' approaches based on the work of Foucault and Lyotard.

41. Taylor-Gooby, 'Legitimation deficit', p. 171.

42. Gretschmann, 'Social security', p. 233.

43. A. Gould, 'The salaried middle class and the welfare state in Sweden and Japan', *Policy and Politics*, 1982, vol. 10, no. 4, pp. 417–37.

44. Wilensky, *The Welfare State*, p. 116.

Chapter Six

Toward a New Understanding of Constitutions[*]

Ulrich K. Preuß

The almost global triumph of constitutionalism in the wake of what Huntington called the 'third wave of democratisation' should not mislead us to expect constitutions to create political order which, once and for all, fulfills the desires for an ideal polity in which the diversity and antagonisms of interests, beliefs and values is perfectly transferred into social harmony and peace while at the same time safeguarding a maximum of freedom for everyone. No more than the end of the Cold War after the collapse of the Berlin wall marks the end of history does the expansion of constitutions beyond the traditional extent of the Western world indicate the definitive and worldwide solution of the problem of good governance. After all, such an expectation would be misguided anyway. Constitutionalism has never been a recipe which defines a good political order; even less can it create it. It is, rather, a methodological tool of societies in their painstaking and never-ending search for appropriate solutions for their manifold conflicts, dilemmas, and antagonisms. In other words, no constitution can work miracles with the wave of a wand.

What it can and in fortunate instances does do is create such institutional conditions as are suited to exert a beneficial pressure on society to rationalise and improve itself. And this occurs – contrary to widespread popular prejudice – not by unleashing the religious, moral, intellectual, and economic energies slumbering within the individual or by restraining political power often seen as inscrutable and demonic but, rather, by providing an operational framework or, more exactly, by creating a state or condition of 'being constituted' in the broad sense of 'being a group organised on certain principles'. A society is constituted when it must constantly confront itself in suitable institutional forms and in normatively directed processes of adjustment, resistance, and self-correction. The meaning of a constitution or 'being constituted' becomes clearest if one identifies its opposite. In the heyday of constitutional enthusiasm the state of a society without a constitution was equated with despotism, or at the very least with illegitimate and backward rule. We recall here Thomas Paine's scathing comment that in England everything

---

[*] *Constitutional Revolution: The link between constitutionalism and progress*, trans. D. Lucas Schneider, Atlantic Highlands, N.J., Humanities Press, 1995. The first paragraph of the original piece has been rewritten for this volume in order to condense the original context of the book chapter. Brackets in footnotes refer to English versions of German references which have been added subsequently.

had a constitution but the nation. 'Constitution' belongs to the category of concepts which morally disqualify their opposite and which Koselleck has characterised as 'asymmetrical opposites'.[1] Today the opposite of 'constituted' is the condition of a society which can deal only very imperfectly with its destructive tendencies, its power structure, its social inequalities – in short, its institutionally underdeveloped potential for a successful confrontation of its normative foundations with real conditions. Repression in the political and the psychoanalytic sense are the two alternative strategies that form the opposite of being constituted.

As a rule we perceive a constitution alone as the opposite of a political order of repression. If, as we have seen, progress and a constitution were always seen as necessarily belonging together in the revolutions of the eighteenth century and the constitutional movements of the nineteenth century, then it was because both were constituted through a common element: freedom.[2] Freedom was the essence of a constitution; this is why human and civil rights – rights to enjoy the equal and natural freedom of all people – had such a prominent place in French constitutions of the revolutionary era. The almost automatic linking of the rhetoric of freedom with the idea of progress resulted from the unquestioned assumption that freedom was the royal road to progress, since progress was nothing other than the elimination of unnatural obstacles erected by tyrants whose 'loyal follower was superstition'. Once again it was Condorcet who expressed most clearly the connection between progress and freedom in the sense of removing obstacles from a path. Referring to revolutionary France, he wrote:

> From that happy land where *freedom* has only recently kindled the torch of genius, the mind of man, released from the leading-strings of its infancy, advances with firm steps towards the *truth*. ... We have already seen reason lift her *chains,* shake herself free of some of them.... It remains for us to study the stage in which she finally succeeds in breaking those chains, and when. .. she frees herself from them one by one; when at last she can go forward unhindered, and the only *obstacles* in her path are those that are inevitably renewed at every fresh *advance* because they are the necessary consequence of the very constitution of our understanding of the connection, that is, between our means of discovering the *truth* and the resistance that it offers to our efforts.[3]

In America, where no feudal or absolutist obstacles to progress existed, the relationship between freedom and progress was seen differently, but it was not doubted as such. Freedom was a social fact in this case, and the Constitution had to protect this prelegal state of affairs through an elaborate system of checks and balances. The fact that the U.S. Constitution was ratified at first without a Bill of Rights does not mean that freedom was less valued. On the contrary, the lack of any mention of rights was intended to demonstrate that they were in no way affected by the establishment of a government. Hamilton, for example, asked, 'Why ... should it be said that the liberty of the press shall not be restrained when no power is given by which restrictions may be imposed?'.[4] Such a position could not be maintained for long, and so the U.S. Constitution acquired an additional

Bill of Rights that was drafted in 1789 and ratified in 1791. It is all the more notable that the sole evocation of individual freedom outside the Bill of Rights (that is, in the original Constitution) appears in express connection with the idea of progress: Article 1, Section 8 gives Congress the power 'to promote the progress of science and useful arts, by securing for limited times to authors and inventors the exclusive rights to their respective writings and discoveries'. This provision is especially interesting because the founding fathers had here clearly encountered an example of the fact that freedom and progress are not necessarily always in harmony, but can on occasion be in conflict with one another. The rhetoric of pathos always implied that the works of artists, scientists, and inventors were the property of mankind; they represent the inheritance of mankind as a whole in the way we understand the resources of the oceans today, for example, as common property. On the other hand, the no less fundamental principle of freedom, which in America includes holding sacred Locke's doctrine that every individual is entitled to exclusive enjoyment of the fruits of his own labours,[5] would justify excluding humanity from the progress made in science and the arts. This section of the Constitution thus represents a compromise between these equally fundamental but colliding principles. And it is the first hint of a development in which the 'invisible hand' is replaced by the visible and ordering hand of political power. It is therefore extremely significant that this Article expressly recognises the possibility that progress is not achieved exclusively in the medium of individual freedom but can also be promoted by governmental authority.

This development gave freedom a rival for the title of 'promoter of progress',[6] namely, political power. In America this competitor remained relatively weak, but in Europe it has continued to play a significant role, particularly under the influence of Social Democratic political theory. But here again it is Marxism that represented most strictly and consistently the alternative to the axiom of 'progress through freedom' that had reigned since the last third of the eighteenth century: 'progress through power'. Marxists argued that society must be fundamentally altered before individuals would be truly free to develop their potential and the history of scientific, artistic, and moral progress could begin. And the most effective means for a total revolution of society was to concentrate the power of the whole society in the state. It is well known that socialist states see no problem at all in strong and authoritarian government power, which they exercise with a clear conscience since it is all in the service of progress.

Liberal democrats view state power as an agent of progress with extreme suspicion, and it is for this reason that democratic constitutional theory emphasises the limits to be placed on government authority. Antiliberal critics such as Carl Schmitt concluded from this that a state that merely limits powers is unimaginable, because it would be politically without substance, and that the political quality of a liberal state therefore tacitly antecedes its constitutional limitations of power (and can overstep them in times of crisis).[7] In his view the unfathomable will of the sovereign people represented this political power, and its support of the constitutional state was only conditional; the people could and must have the final say on the political fate of the society, even if that meant going against the constitution. Marxist theory also regards the latent power of the sovereign – in this case the universal class – as an ever-present adversary of the subtle constitutional mechanisms of checks and balances. Thus many liberals share with their critics on the Right and the Left the view that constitutional limits to power represent a negative and uncreative force, because in the interest of individual freedom they place insurmountable obstacles in the path of every kind of power politics, or they fetter the unfathomable and existential political will of the people, or finally because they function as impediments to the longings of the universal class for liberation and progress. The case of the United States presents an example, however, of precisely what unexpected creative potential lies within this apparently negative aspect of limits to power. One should not forget that the primary goal of the American revolutionaries was not to defeat or limit the power of a state that already existed but, rather, to create a unified power out of thirteen independent states.[8] The powerlessness of the new republic thus represented at least as big a problem as a potential abuse of power by any of its agencies. The problem the constitution faced was, therefore, how to create a powerful federal government without endangering freedom. The solution consisted not in dividing power in order to minimise it but in creating a system of counterbalancing powers. This was an imaginative application of Montesquieu's idea that power can be limited only by a countervailing check to power.[9] If the authors of the U.S. Constitution wanted a vigorous representation of the popular will in the political institutions of the republic, then an accumulation of power in one branch or agency was the wrong path, even apart from the possible danger of opening the door to tyranny. More intuitively than analytically they recognised the powerlessness of unlimited power,[10] which can prevent and control, as Tocqueville later argued, but cannot create. 'I think,' he wrote, 'that extreme centralisation of government ultimately enervates society and thus, after a length of time, weakens the government itself'.[11] Sovereignty negates and denies itself when it systematically destroys the condition of its own existence, namely, information on the object of rule. As society becomes increasingly differentiated, the truth of this observation becomes ever more compelling. It has the implication for democratic theory that a society in the process of becoming more differentiated is capable of governing itself only if it can develop the capacity to keep its institutions informed about the variety of needs and interests present within it. The complementary modern thought – which Sieyès developed to provide support for the principle of representation, incidentally – is that the division of labour and functional differentiation produce an increased number of possibilities for human action – a concept that has been particularly successful in the economic axiom of the advantages of long-term over short-term investments. If one applies this concept to legal problems, it emerges that rules which create a separation of powers limit power only superficially; in fact the separation of powers enables a government to function better, as 'specialisation enhances sensitivity to a diversity of society problems'.[12] One can see in this a further example of how a weakness can be creatively transformed into a strength, and this all the more so as the counteractive forces of a highly specialised and therefore effective central government and economic or scientific sphere largely free of political controls is widely regarded as *the* model of a successful society. For here the goal of socialism appears to have been achieved by the very means socialists rejected, namely, the institutionalisation of progress through individual freedom and the imposition of constitutional limits on government.

This model has one decisive flaw, however: It is blind to its own dynamics of progress, because in the last analysis it is based on the principle of distribution and balance of powers (even though this principle is applied most intelligently). This creates considerable sensitivity to spheres of freedom and the modes of operation of different areas, but it provides no agency through which a society could perceive the processes by which it is 'collectively harming itself',[13] let alone control or reverse them.[14] The thought that constitutions represent a form of self-limitation – through which a society can increase its potential for dealing rationally with itself and particularly with its own self-destructive tendencies – has probably been neglected in the success story of the modern constitutional democracy because in achieving and justifying it all energies have been concentrated on the opposition between freedom and power; both parties began with the shared supposition that its own position would best serve progress – be it technical, economic, scientific, artistic, social, or even moral progress. Social scientists who study how constitutions function, on the other hand, are fond of citing the example of Ulysses, who literally bound himself (to the mast of his ship), but who was thereby freed to listen to the song of the sirens without suffering any harm.[15] By doing so he exercised a kind of paternalism toward himself which can be understood as a preliminary stage of a paradigm of reflexive rationality: Aware of his own weakness and susceptibility, the individual can overcome it by binding himself in advance. One must speak of a preliminary stage here because in this instance we have a morally simple variant of individual self-instrumentalisation which does not necessarily include a compulsion on the self to act in a principled fashion.[16]

Societies are not individuals, but they are subject to even greater constraints to reflect, since their social coherence and their form of government will depend in the long run on the moral principles which are meant to guarantee the fairness and justice of their political order. As long as freedom was a moral principle in itself, the progress it promoted was also a moral fact; furthermore the constitutional rights, procedures, and institutions protecting freedom had this moral foundation. But the restrictions and obligations imposed by the modern welfare state on economic freedom in the interest of social justice no longer tend to be regarded by the liberal-democratic legal order as an expression of the moral implications of freedom; they have the status of limitations on freedom, which have come under increasing pressure as a view of freedom largely robbed of all norms demands to know why these limitations are justified. In economic terms they are not infrequently regarded as unproductive social encumbrances on a morally neutral capitalistic production of wealth. In the meantime this process of disassociating freedom from morality has advanced so far that it can borrow its rhetoric from the clichés of popular descriptions of capitalism. 'Deregulation, liquification, and facilitation of transactions in product, finance, and labour markets, increased flexibility, tax breaks, and liberalisation'[17] are the phrases which are more or less consciously always understood as phrases of progress. However, progress is no longer driven by moral rhetoric but by the naked fear of becoming unable to compete in world markets.

The task today is thus for freedom and progress to regain their moral dimension. Without it we must live with the latent danger that constitutional democracies will be defeated by the destructive and regressive dynamics of capitalist markets. I believe that the other opposite of a constitution – repression in the psychological sense – must become the focus of our interest. The answer to it lies in a concept that I would like to call 'morally reflexive constitutionalism'. Its necessity follows from the destructive potential of capitalist constitutional states that they themselves have created, a potential which cannot be 'constituted' through either the artistic constitutional architecture of checks and balances or the arrangements of a welfare-state limitation of freedom, much less a socialist revolution with its mixture of state property, party dictatorship, and enforced ideology. When I spoke above of the 'moral connectability' of capitalist constitutional states, it should first of all be recognised that, in the welfare-state mass democracy, they have found a solution to the 'social question' that is respectable, although it is neither above all criticism[18] nor guaranteed to be permanent.[19] In the meantime, however, advanced capitalist democracies see themselves faced with challenges that will put this moral connectability to a new and possibly more difficult test.

As far as I know, all serious prognostications are in agreement that for these societies the increasingly decisive contradictions and conflicts of the future will not be sufficiently grasped either in the terms of traditional liberalism, 'the individual versus the state', or in the social and economic categories of class conflict and the social question.[20] These conflicts will include the relationship of man to nature, to his own technology, the globalisation of man-made risks, the relationship between living generations to one another as well as to coming generations, the relationship between the two sexes, between various ethnic groups, and so on. The list could no doubt be even longer. It is difficult to recognise a common positive attribute in these conflicts, but there is a negative one: None of these relationship problems can be solved with the characteristic and successful means of the modern constitutional state, namely, power, law, and money. But even apart from these 'macroproblems' – which one could assume have always preceded constitutional questions, in the form of tradition, culture, or morality – we cannot fail to see that 'complex societies and their constituent parts exhibit a distinct functional need for responsible and ethical mass orientations', which can neither be compensated for by an 'ethic of responsibility on the part of elites and experts' nor be satisfied by falling back on the routinised, everyday moral orientations of the 'ordinary citizen'.[21] The examples given by Offe – such as behaviour related to rearing children; health, consumption, and traffic; or behaviour toward foreigners or the opposite sex – certainly do not describe new types of social situation, and I am also not sure whether his rather sweeping claim is accurate that reconciling them with society is possible 'only by developing a civilised sense of community that is both insightful and prudent, both abstract and characterised by solidarity'. This might underestimate the flexibility – including the moral flexibility – of our modern and individualised society. It should be mentioned in addition that not all decisions in the areas listed need always be dictated by moral principles in order to be compatible with social life. But apart from this possible exaggeration, his theory does in fact expose a new problem, namely, that an increasing number of social conflicts and situations have acquired moral relevance to the extent that the participants can arrive at a 'reasonable' solution (that is, one that serves their own well-understood interests) only by following principles 'which rational persons concerned to advance their interests would accept in [an initial] position of equality to settle the basic terms of their association'.[22] Offe similarly declares that the only person who is acting responsibly is the one who 'methodically assumes, with regard to his own acts, the simultaneous perspective of the expert, a generalised other, and his own self in the *futurum exactum* and in this way validates the criteria for action with regard to the matter, society, and time'.[23] I, too, believe that a number of the problems of advanced capitalist constitutional states have acquired such a complicated structure that they can be productively tackled (although not always solved) only by recalling the *procedures of their treatment.*

If we take a closer look at the decision making situations and conflicts that dominate our political life, it is striking that in increasing measure they have to do with questions of knowledge, with its empirical foundation, its uncertainty, its reliability (especially as a basis for prognostications), with the methods of acquiring it, explaining it, evaluating it, and devaluing it. In many areas of politics – including government budgets, health care reform, Social Security reform, and environmental regulations, to name only a few – the opposing sides as a rule are at loggerheads not over differing political options but over the 'correct' interpretation of data, the underlying causes, and the predictable effects of a given measure. Of course traditional politics had to deal with uncertainties resulting from incomplete knowledge before, but in the past they had (as they still do in part today) the status of marginal factors, since the harmful consequences of errors were limited, at least in peacetime, and were accepted as unavoidable. To the degree that advanced industrial societies rest on a knowledge-based infrastructure and technologies founded on knowledge and information determine broad areas of social life, however, the status of knowledge is altered: It becomes a significant medium for influencing the direction in which society will move and in the near future will presumably challenge the central role traditionally played by power.[24] In contrast to power, however, scientific knowledge – which is essentially what we are talking about – is directed toward the future and the exploration of the unknown, and to this degree it is the strongest force driving social change. It sets in motion a process in which advanced societies must constantly 'react to changes within themselves and ... thereby change again'.[25] This institutionalised process of change is closely connected to the specific 'risks of modernisation' for which Beck has coined the term 'risk society'. The process of subjecting more and more of nature to man's will (which is based on an immense increase in scientific and technological knowledge) is not only straining the environment to its limits but also creating new possibilities for future damage – new risks – which must be recognised and prevented if possible by the acquisition of still more knowledge.[26]

Beck has characterised the change from the 'logic of the production of wealth' to the 'logic of the production of risks' with the phrase 'poverty is hierarchical, smog is democratic'.[27] By this he means that the experience of 'collective infliction of self-damage' so characteristic of the 'risk society' is not limited to a particular class or group, and that individuals find themselves in something like Rawls's 'initial position of equality' and behind a 'veil of ignorance', where neither their social status, their education, nor their income gives a clear indication of which principles they can consider proper and just as 'rational persons concerned to advance their interests'. The likelihood now seems about equal for everyone that his or her health and well-being will be affected by harmful additives in food, air and water pollution, ionising rays, genetically manipulated organisms, or the malfunction of complex technical installations.

When we speak of 'risk' or 'danger', however, we are speaking not of actual but only of possible damage – a risk is a *judgement* about the *probability* of damage in the future. Scientific and technological knowledge has always been problematic since research became based on the possibility and acceptability of error rather than on the certainty of truth. But its status in society was unchallenged after God was dethroned and science advanced to the position of objective *pouvoir neutre* [neutral power] and unchallengeable highest authority. Today we are experiencing the erosion of this last remaining guarantor of certainty and the sense of security it gave us.[28] Our ability to manipulate nature has created a previously unimaginable potential for destruction that would make Condorcet's optimism with regard to scientific progress look positively irresponsible today. Every new expansion of our knowledge simultaneously gives rise to new and dark zones of the unknown and a frantic desire to learn even more. Science is encountering the problem of its own responsibility, that is, the question of how much is known and how far science should go in the search for further knowledge. This question cannot be answered on the basis of scientific criteria alone. And it is equally impossible to prescribe political guidelines for scientific research, since – apart from other objections – this would inevitably lead to alliances of political, bureaucratic, and scientific elites which could develop new and highly effective forms of social control. Even if one were prepared to pay this price for scientific progress, we would still not attain a secure order based on scientific certainty, since no consensus exists among scientists themselves about the consequences to be drawn from what is known and what is still unknown. We cannot assume that epistemological uncertainty results simply from a lack of knowledge and can be overcome by acquiring more knowledge; 'more research only produces more ignorance', and above all it produces more dissension about how much more research on the unknown can still be tolerated.[29] And finally ethical appeals to individual scientists are bound to fail, since they do not take into account the fact that every scientist can fall back on the excuse that he is only a tiny cog in a vast and complex machine. The suggestion that individuals can or should 'take on responsibility for everyone and everything'[30] is naive at best and leads in the worst case to the formation of self-proclaimed moral elites.

Yet a glance at the character of political discussions in the last ten years teaches us that a new arena has opened up in which political battles are waged over scientific progress; one need only think of the controversies over nuclear energy, advances in genetic manipulation, or the constitutionality of new information-storage techniques.[31] The principles, criteria, and rules underlying the processes of acquiring, applying, and interpreting knowledge have been discussed in political and moral terms, with the goal of developing procedures by means of which society can deal with the consequences of the uncertainty of knowledge. These are processes of negotiation about

> how we wish to live as members of a certain collective .... Negotiations must be based on the exchange of arguments, and whether or not they lead to *fair* compromises will depend mainly on the procedural framework, which must be judged in moral terms.[32]

The transformation of science and scientific advances into an object of negotiation and compromise must seem strange to a political culture that has expended considerable effort on eliminating religious and political influence on the field of scientific investigation in order to protect its autonomy. This development is an inevitable consequence of the fact that the most advanced industrial societies have become knowledge-based. As I mentioned above in my short sketch of the development of scientific freedom, the shift in the orientation of modern science from fixation on established truth to fallibilism became possible only on the condition that the acquisition not of truth but of probability was isolated from the rest of social life, and from the spheres of politics and religion in particular, so that scientific errors would not plunge societies into discord and turbulence. *Within* the scientific community, errors had the legitimate status of hypotheses that had been proven false.[33] Science was experimental; it was a laboratory allowed to exist under strictly limited artificial conditions, and it found access to other social spheres only in the form of experimentally validated and therefore reliable knowledge. However, the speed with which almost all other spheres of life have been penetrated by science in recent times has broken down these barriers between the artificial world of scientific experiments and 'real' life to a considerable degree. Society itself has become a laboratory.[34] To the extent that social life has become knowledge-based, that is, dependent on 'secure' knowledge for its functioning, the reliability of such knowledge must also be tested under the real conditions in which it will be applied: 'Whether releasing genetically altered bacteria into the environment is ecologically harmful or not, for instance, will never be known until it is tried'.[35] A nuclear power plant is such a complex system, linking a large number of components, technical subsystems, processes, and interactions extending to the physical and social environment (for example, air traffic, geological conditions), that its safety can be tested only under the real conditions of its actual operation, testing which in turn gives rise to new knowledge. For large-scale technical installations, every system is in some way unique; the more complex the system, the less its operating conditions will resemble those of any other system. This erosion of the barriers between the acquisition of new scientific knowledge and real life in society means that society can no longer enjoy the blessings of experimentally proven, that is, 'reliable' knowledge alone, but is now burdened with the uncertainties, errors, and risks of science. Scientific activity thus ceases to be distinct from other forms of social activity, be they economic, political, or legal.

These also contain the possibility of error, of course, and could never be tested in a laboratory first. Is not all life an experiment, in fact, since individually and collectively we are all inevitably exposed to the consequences of our imperfections and capacity for error? Why should science have a special status, and why did it have a special status? One could provide a long answer to this question, which would have to delve extensively into the relationship between social order and its basis of knowledge. I will limit myself here to a very simple yet to my mind sufficient answer. Science could make such triumphant progress only because it was freed from the responsibility for and the need to reflect on its social consequences. One can speak of 'scientific freedom' only when a scientist's error is neither punished as a sin or crime nor otherwise penalised, such as by payment of damages. And society can permit science this luxury only as long as it is protected from the deleterious consequences of possible scientific errors by institutional boundaries between science and society. These institutional boundaries consist in the main of mechanisms within the scientific community for distinguishing between the true, probable, and false, that is, in criteria specific to the particular discipline.

All three sources of human knowledge – experience, theory, and experimentation – have given rise, in the course of their historical development, to a second order of thinking, reflexivity, which can reflect on the reliability and truth of knowledge of the first order.[36] Reflexivity is of particular importance for experiments, however, because it is only in connection with experimental thinking and activity that it has become a driving force of progress in acquiring new knowledge. Experiments place 'the future hypothetically at our disposal and [make] expectation problematic. It aims at confirming not that experiences remain constant as circumstances change, but that the area of exceptional and even monstrous events is governed by predictable laws'.[37] Experiments are 'conscious and rationally assimilated experiences about how experiences can be forced to happen'; the experience that human beings have experiences becomes the point of departure for 'strategies ... which make it possible to experience what has not been previously experienced'.[38] Thus reflexivity becomes a ceaseless driving force to understand reality as a systematically exploitable source of knowledge and a point of departure for *new* experiences. To the extent to which experiences are no longer 'forced to happen' under the artificial, controlled, and repeatable conditions of the isolated scientific laboratory but, rather, in a complex and uniquely nonrepeatable reality, reflexivity solely within the bounds of science itself is no longer sufficient to protect society from science's errors. This is not primarily because scientists are not in a position – at least theoretically – to consider the reliability of knowledge with regard to even the most complicated experiments. (Every panel of experts that confirms the operational safety of a nuclear power plant in the name of science presumes it is able to do just that.) The reason for the insufficiency of purely internal scientific reflexivity lies, rather, in the fact that experimenting in and with society poses grave moral questions, for in such experiments the subjects acquire the status of a means for acquiring information and knowledge; they become objects. The moral implications of producing knowledge through experimentation has even caught up with classic laboratory experiments, as the current discussion about the ethics of animal experiments shows. For the time being only a minority of people may feel affected. In practical terms, however, we have all become guinea pigs today wherever the reliability of the knowledge on which a new technology is based can be proven only under real-life conditions.[39]

The conditions under which this may be permitted to happen, the extent to which and in pursuit of which goals it may happen, cannot be determined according to precise and unvarying criteria. But in any event the 'experimental situation' and its interpretation no longer lie exclusively within the realm of science. 'It is the product of discussion and negotiation among participants who perceive and act according to different cognitive and evaluative criteria'.[40] The development of knowledge-based civilisation has driven the moral implications of acquiring knowledge through experiments out of itself, beyond the ability of second order thinking to keep up with it. Obviously this cannot be corrected by appeals to scientific ethics, ethics commissions, or the voluntary efforts of scientists themselves. For the problem is not a lack of ethics in the scientific community but the approaching end of the moral and political neutralisation of scientific knowledge itself, which has reigned since the seventeenth century – and thus the end of our ability to take progress for granted, progress that was understood from the beginning to be above all progress in knowledge. The interplay of political power and politically and morally neutral progress is breaking down. The idea that mankind and society are capable of improvement – one of the main stimuli for the political and moral rationalisation of political power through political public opinion – is no longer automatically confirmed by progress in knowledge, since the latter's own claim to accuracy has lost its aura of certainty. It has suffered the same fate as that which overtook political power when it had penetrated all spheres of life in the era of absolutism, had finally run up against the conscience of the individual, was subjected to its standards, and finally found its rational origin in the notion of popular sovereignty. Scientific progress is no longer a metaphysical truth either; it must be defended by arguments. We can control it only by becoming aware of its moral implications and creating conditions under which we can deal with it on morally reflexive terms, that is, judging the morality of progress by moral criteria.

This picture would be very incomplete, however, if we contented ourselves with the self-pitying attitude that society is being victimised by a science obsessed with progress and failed to see that each of us is to varying degrees an active participant in this process. The development of a technical and scientific civilisation is a particularly striking example of the experience that highly specialised division of labour, the difficulty of calculating the consequences of one's action in its interplay with many other actions, and finally the enormous increase in the geographical and temporal scope of these consequences have 'led to such a complex society that traditional forms of moral decision making have become inadequate'.[41] It is growing increasingly difficult, if not impossible, to make individuals legally responsible for the consequences of actions which as a rule appear reasonable enough from their standpoint but which in combination with many other such actions contribute to 'collective self-harm' and an increase in the sum of potential risks. The consequence is that 'organised irresponsibility' (Beck) in which calculations made for personal benefit amount to a kind of experiment on society at large. Where everyone is making a small but imperceptible contribution to collective harm, and everyone is thus in some measure responsible, no one person can be singled out as the instigator.[42] Everyone is potentially both a guinea pig and an experimenter at the same time, and it is from the perspective of both roles that the problem of how to distribute responsibility correctly should be seen.

This is a new challenge to the ideal of society's constitution, since what is at stake is nothing less than the development of institutional arrangements through which high-risk activities can be traced to certain parties who are then held responsible for them.[43] Since these activities may affect large areas over long periods of time and also form part of complex larger wholes, they are clear and straightforward in neither a cognitive nor a moral sense. The constitutionalisation of responsibility will therefore have to be increasingly limited to creating conditions under which different pragmatic, scientific, and moral perspectives can coexist with one another. A constitution of scientific and technological progress can and must allow for moral reflection on progress, but it cannot point to any universal principles which make it likely that society will reach a consensus on such questions. Human rights also become equivocal in normative terms at the moment when the moral ambiguity of progress becomes apparent. Whether manipulation of the structure of human genes is morally defensible (and should in that case also be legal), for example, can be neither affirmed nor denied with arguments based on the 'natural' dignity of man, for what is human nature in the age of gene technology? Morally respectable grounds can be found both for and against such manipulation. If we are to reach a resolution, a compromise, or just the possibility for dissension that does not lead to latent or open civil war, then the discussion of these morally relevant questions must also deal simultaneously with its own presuppositions and its political and social meaning, that is, it must reflect on the conditions of its own existence.[44]

To make this possible is the purpose of a morally reflexive constitutionalism that demystifies the idea of progress but does not deny it altogether. It is more ambitious than previous concepts of a constitution, because it opens up a space for 'nontraditional, non-transcendental politics,'[45] in which questions can be discussed and also resolved, which cannot be resolved according to the premises of liberal democratic constitutionalism and which are not in need of resolution according to those of socialism, where power and morality are one. But these are questions that *must* be resolved in our present situation, because scientific progress has forced them upon us: namely, questions of moral relevance. Many questions have this status today that would formerly have been dismissed as trivial: whether nuclear power stations should be kept in operation, whether wood from the tropics should be exported to other countries, whether animal experiments should be permitted, whether recycling of bottles should be mandatory, or whether high-speed trains should be constructed. The list could be extended with countless examples from our daily political debates, which would all have one feature in common: Today they all fall under the heading of moral judgements, at least in part.

This is why public political discussion must always reflect on its own political function; otherwise we run the risk of creating a hopeless situation similar to the religious wars of the sixteenth and seventeenth centuries, from which once more only a Leviathan could emerge. The 'institutions of public freedom' that make this discussion possible 'rest on the shaky ground of the political communication of those who by using them simultaneously interpret and defend them'.[46] And who, it should be added, thereby contribute to creating the paradoxical possibility of political unity in dissension. Such a constitution establishes no political centre in which a society could recognise its own collective identity; it sees neither the state, the people, nor the nation as potential categories for a politically united will that could then impose itself as a homogenising force on a diverse society. This is intended neither to trivialise nor to deny the problem of political power; a reflexive understanding of a constitution still requires that processes of power be organised and that parliaments, governments, and courts exist to make binding decisions. But ideally power serves not as an instrument for imposing a specific idea of the correct and progressive course of social development; rather, it should create room and institutions for society to develop its moral and intellectual resources and to use them to force experiences *with itself,* that is, to treat itself as a kind of risky experiment. A constitution that makes this possible would take the idea of progress back to its original roots, to the idea of 'the improvement of mankind', to strengthening mankind's moral competence to govern itself.

Of course understanding a constitution in such terms does not require a break with the two-hundred-year-old traditions of the modern constitutional state.[47] On the contrary, this view takes up and carries on the potential contained in the modern state and also in circles of civil society for organising learning processes.[48] Thus, as I previously mentioned, the translation of the class struggle arising from the social question of the nineteenth century into the institutional forms of the democratic welfare state represents a noteworthy collective advance in learning that has contributed significantly to making capitalism more civilised, although we should not imagine that such an advance is irreversible. However, the task facing us today has become several degrees more difficult. At stake is no longer the redistribution of power and wealth but, rather, the correct distribution of responsibility when no universal criteria exist for deciding how to do it. Thus the principle of 'majority rule' has already lost much of its integrative function for the category of conflicts based on intense moral dissension.[49] It will be replaced increasingly by procedures for negotiating moratoria, trial projects, minority rights for 'moral communities', public fora to discuss alternative philosophical and moral perspectives, and procedures for negotiating compromise similar to the Round Tables. Their success will depend on whether they can be regarded and used not only – and perhaps not even primarily – as instruments for solving specific conflicts and problems but, rather, as institutional forms of social self-enlightenment, in which differing cognitive and moral perspectives confront one another, options for action are kept open, criteria for judging the reliability of knowledge are developed, and finally – in a kind of 'procedural rationality of the second order'[50] – the conditions of this discourse itself are continually reformulated.

Such a constitution of cognitive and moral learning, in which society makes itself an experiment and thus 'hypothetically open to change',[51] will above all have to strengthen the constitution of knowledge compared with the constitution of power. Specific steps in this direction are already discernible. Paradoxically, it was the authors of the constitutional committee appointed by the Round Table of the GDR that departed from the conventional framework of a liberal democratic constitution's limits on power, although the technological level of their society is far lower than in the industrialised West. On the other hand, the omnipresence of surveillance by the *Stasi,* the state security apparatus, had rendered them sensitive to the moral implications of the distribution of knowledge. The foundation of the revolution in citizen's consciences was just as much an expression of resistance to an imposed single truth as it was a search for pluralistic forms of negotiation. It is no accident that the Preamble to this constitution contains the statement that 'the citizens of the German Democratic Republic [give] this constitution *to themselves'*. The combination of the diversity of all citizens with the reflexive pronoun can be read as a programmatic alternative to the constitution of the Federal Republic, which states: 'the German people ... has enacted this constitution ... by virtue of its constituent power'. According to the Round Table's conception, a constitution is not the expression of a homogeneous and authoritative *will – voluntas populi suprema lex* [the supreme law is the will of the people] – but, rather, a compact,[52] in which each citizen promises to recognise all his or her fellow citizens as free and equal beings. It is also no accident that the authors stress the individual and political significance of the distribution of information and knowledge: protection of the private sphere is closely connected to the right of individuals to personal data and access to files and data banks containing information on them (Article 8). The passage on freedom of opinion specifically establishes the principle of the 'diversity of opinion existing in society' as a norm (Article 15). The passage guaranteeing freedom of scientific research empowers the legislature to 'limit the permitted means and methods used in research' and to establish requirements for reporting 'research involving high degrees of risk' (Article 19). All of this represents a reaction to the monopoly on information connected to the monopoly on power, to which specific reference is made in Article 4, which states that no one 'may be made the object of medical or scientific experiments without his free and express consent'. Individuals and groups are guaranteed access to data concerning the environment in which they live (Article 33), and finally 'groups which devote themselves to public issues and thereby influence public opinion (citizens' movements) ... [must be given] access to information relevant to their concerns in the possession of government agencies' (Article 35).

Although these regulations by no means represent revolutionary breakthroughs, they do reflect the character of the 'gentle' revolution of which they are part in that they take up tendencies that are already at work everywhere in the constitutional states of the West but that are still struggling for broad recognition. Nonetheless the constitutional revolutions of 1989 were not merely adaptations to the state of political culture already achieved or soon to be achieved by the constitutional state. They were new and creative not only as revolutions, but also in their contribution to our understanding of constitutions. For they have restored to the idea of progress, which informed our modern notion of a constitution in its infancy and whose moral implications have been increasingly lost, a meaning that liberates us from the false utopia of the rule of a subject of historical progress without forcing us to become either postmodern and cynical or moralising observers as society is degraded to an appendage of technological and economic progress. Surprisingly, we discover the seeds of a reflexive constitutionalism for a society which now finds both itself and progress problematic where we would have expected only backwardness. But these revolutions can remind us that progress is first and foremost a moral idea that makes us aware that 'the capacity in human nature for improvement' lies above all in reflection on this capacity. Progress consists in giving this disposition to reflection an institutional radius of action – in the form of a modern constitution.

Notes

1. R. Koselleck, 'Zur historisch-politischen Semantik asymmetrischer Gegenbegriffe', in Koselleck (ed.), *Vergangene Zukunft: Zur Semantik geschichtlicher Zeiten*, Frankfurt/M., Suhrkamp, 1989. [R. Koselleck, 'The Historical-Political Semantics of Asymmetric Counterconcepts', in R. Koselleck (ed.), *Futures Past: On the semantics of historical time*, New York, Columbia University Press, 2004, pp. 155–191.]

2. See R. Nisbet, *History of the Idea of Progress*, London, Heinemann, 1980, pp. 179ff.

3. Marquis de Condorcet, *Sketch for a Historical Picture of the Progress of the Human Mind*, London, Weidenfeld & Nicolson, 1955, pp. 124–25.

4. B. F. Wright (ed.), *The Federalist Papers*, Cambridge, Mass., Harvard University Press, 1961, no. 84, p. 535.

5. J. Locke, *Two Treatises of Government*, edited by P. Laslett, Cambridge, Cambridge University Press, 1988, ch. 5, pars. 27 and 28, pp. 305–307.

6. For more on this and the forms it took (not always convincingly argued, in my view) see Nisbet, *History of the Idea of Progress*, pp. 237ff.

7. C. Schmitt, *Verfassungslehre*, München/Leipzig, Duncker & Humblot, 1928, pp. 200ff. [C. Schmitt, *Constitutional Theory* (trans. J. Seitzer), Durham, Duke University Press, 2008, pp. 235ff.]

8. This is correctly pointed out by both H. Arendt, *On Revolution*, New York, Viking Press, 1963, pp. 149ff., and H. Vorlander, 'Forum Arnericanum-Kontinuitat und Legitimitat der Vereinigten Staaten von Amerika 1787–1987', *Journal des Offentlichen Rechts der Gegenwart*, 36, 1987, pp.451–488 [451, 461].

9. C. L. de S. Montesquieu, *The Spirit of the Laws*, Cambridge, Cambridge University Press, 1989, bk.11, ch. 4, p. 155ff.

10. For a social science perspective on this point see J. Elster, *Sour Grapes: Studies in the subversion of rationality*, Cambridge, Cambridge University Press, 1983, pp. 86ff.

11. A. de Tocqueville, *Democracy in America*, New York, Vintage Books, 1990, Vol. 2, bk. 4, ch. 4, p. 300.

12. S. Holmes, 'Precommitment and the Paradox of Democracy', in J. Elster and R. Slagstad (eds), *Constitutionalism and Democracy*, Cambridge, Cambridge University Press, 1993, pp. 195–240 [228].

13. C. Offe, 'Bindung, Fessel, Bremse: Moralische und institutionelle Aspekte intelligenter Selbstbeschränkung', in A. Honneth *et al.* (ed.), *Zwischenbetrachtungen – Im Prozeß der Aufklärung: Jürgen Habermas zum 60. Geburtstag*, Frankfurt: Suhrkamp, pp. 739–774 [742]. [C. Offe 'Bindings, Shackles, Brakes: On self-limitation strategies', in A. Honneth *et al.* (eds), *Cultural-Political Interventions in the Unfinished Project of Enlightenment*, Cambridge, London, MIT-Press 1992, pp. 63–94.]

14. See D. Grimm, 'Die Zukunft der Verfassung', *Staatswissenschaften und Staatspraxis* 1, 1990, pp. 15ff.

15. See. J. Elster, *Ulysses and the Sirens*, Cambridge, Cambridge University Press, 1984, pp. 36ff; Holmes, 'Precommitment', pp. 227–28; Offe, 'Bindung, Fessel, Bremse', pp. 748ff.

16. This is Offe's position, 'Bindung, Fessel, Bremse', p. 750; he refers to Adorno's criticism of this model for action in T. Adorno, *Negative Dialektik*, Frankfurt/M., Suhrkamp, 1966, p. 292.

17. Offe, 'Bindung, Fessel, Bremse', pp. 748ff.

18. See U. Rödel, G. Frankenberg and H. Dubiel, *Die demokratische Frage*, Frankfurt/M., Suhrkamp, 1989, pp. 180ff.

19. J. Elster correctly points this out in 'When communism dissolves', *London Review of Books*, vol. 12, no 2, 1990, p. 6.

20. This is the basic tenor of the works by U. Beck, see *Risikogesellschaft: Auf dem Weg in eine andere Moderne*, Frankfurt/M., Suhrkamp, 1986. [U. Beck, *Risk society: Towards a new modernity*, London-Newbury Park, Sage, 1992] and *Gegengifte: Die organisierte Unverantwortlichkeit*, Frankfurt/M., Suhrkamp, 1988; see also A. Evers and H. Nowotny, *Über den Umgang mit Unsicherheit*, Frankfurt/M., Suhrkamp, 1987.

21. Offe, 'Bindung, Fessel, Bremse', p. 758; Offe gives numerous examples.

22. J. Rawls, *A Theory of Justice*, Cambridge, Mass., Harvard University Press, 1971, p. 118.

23. Offe, 'Bindung, Fessel, Bremse', p. 758.

24. See H. Willke, 'Die Steuerungsfunktionen des Staates aus system-theoretischer Sicht: Schritte zur Legitimierung einer wissensbasierten Infrastruktur', in D. Grimm (ed.), *Staatsaufgaben*, Baden-Baden, Nomos, 1994, pp. 685–711.

25. *Ibid.*

26. See U. K. Preuß, 'Risikovorsorge as Staatsaufgabe', in Grimm (ed.), *Staatsaufgaben*, pp. 523–551.

27. Beck, *Risikogesellschaft*, pp. 17, 48.

28. *Ibid.*, pp. 254ff.

29. See M. Douglas and A. Wildavsky, *Risk and Culture: An essay on the selection of technical and environmental dangers*, Berkeley, University California Press, 1982, pp. 49ff and 63–64.

30. K.-H. Ladeur, 'Ethik der Komplexitat und gesellschaftliche Institutionen', *Ethik und Sozialwissenschaften* 1, 1990, pp. 74 ff.

31. See A. Rossnagel *et al.*, *Die Verletzlichkeit der 'Informationsgesellschaft'*, Opladen, Westdeutscher Verlag, 1989, and A. Rossnagel *et al.*, *Digitalisierung der Grundrechte? Zur Verfassungsvertriiglichkeit der Informations-und Kommunikationstechnik*, Opladen, Westdeutscher Verlag, 1990.

32. J. Habermas, *Strukturwandel der Öffentlichkeit*, 18th edn, Frankfurt, Suhrkamp, 1990, Foreword. [J. Habermas, *The Structural Transformation of the Public Sphere*, Cambridge, Polity, 2005.]

33. For more on this see W. Krohn and J. Weyer, 'Die Gesellschaft als Labor: Die Erzeugung sozialer Risiken durch experimentelle Forschung', *Soziale Welt*, 1989, pp. 349ff.

34. This is the convincing theory of Krohn and Weyer, *ibid.*; see also M. S. Shapo, *A Nation of Guinea Pigs*, New York, Free Press, 1979, especially pp. 29ff.

35. Krohn and Weyer, 'Gesellschaft als Labor', pp. 349–373 [349].

36. Y. Elkana, *Anthropologie der Erkenntnis*, Frankfurt/M., Suhrkamp, 1986, pp. 344ff, and Y. Elkana, 'Das Experiment als Begriff zweiter Ordnung', *Rechtshistorisches Journal* 7, 1988, pp. 243ff.

37. H. Günther, *Freiheit, Herrschaft, und Geschichte: Semantik der historisch-politischen Welt*, Frankfurt/M., Suhrkamp, 1979, p. 40.

38. W. Krohn, 'Introduction', in E. Zilsel *et al.* (eds), *Die sozialen Ursprünge der neuzeitlichen Wissenschaft*, Frankfurt/M., 1976.

39. Shapo, *A Nation of Guinea Pigs*, pp. 30ff.

40. Krohn and Weyer, 'Die Gesellschaft als Labor', p. 369.

41. F.-X. Kaufmann, 'Leistet Verantwortung, was wir ihr zumuten?', *Ethik und Sozialwissenschaften*, 1990, vol. 1, pp. 70ff.

42. See H. Lenk and M. Maring, 'Verantwortung und soziale Fallen', *Ethik und Sozialwissenschaften*, 1990, vol. 1, pp. 49ff, and the critical discussion of this article that follows.

43. Kaufmann, 'Leistet Verantwortung, was wir ihr zumuten?', pp. 71–72.

44. See also T. R. Burns and R. Ueberhorst, *Creative Democracy: Systematic conflict resolution and policy making in a world of high science and technology*, New York, Praeger, 1988, especially pp. 89ff and 127ff.

45. See the important essay by Rödel, Frankenberg and Dubiel, *Die demokratische Frage*, pp. 99ff, 117ff, and 128ff.

46. J. Habermas, 'Ist der Herzschlag der Revolution zum Stillstand gekommen? Volkssouveränität als Verfahren. Ein normativer Begriff der Öffentlichkeit?', in Forum f. Philosophie (ed.), *Die Ideen von 1789 in der deutschen Rezeption*, Frankfurt/M., 1989, pp. 7–36 [7ff., 30].

47. As P. Häberle correctly notes, '1789 als Teil der Geschichte, Gegenwart, und Zukunft des Verfassungsstaates', in H. Krauß (ed.), *Folgen der Franzosischen Revolution*, Frankfurt/M., 1989, pp. 83ff.

48. See K. Eder, *Geschichte als Lernprozess? Zur Pathogenese politischer Modernität in Deutschland*, Frankfurt/M., Suhrkamp, 1985, pp. 357ff.

49. See B. Guggenberger and C. Offe (eds), *An den Grenzen der Mehrheitsherrschaft*, Opladen, Westdeutscher Verlag, 1987; Burns and Ueberhorst, *Creative Democracy*, pp. 127ff, 131.

50. See Ladeur, 'Ethik der Komplexitat und gesellschaftliche Institutionen', p. 76.

51. Günther, *Freiheit, Herrschaft und Geschichte*, p. 40.

52. H. Hofmann, *Gebot, Vertrag, Sitte: Die Urformen der Begründung von Rechtsverbindlichkeit*, Baden-Baden, Nomos, 1993.

Chapter Seven

The Political Meaning of Constitutionalism[*]

Ulrich K. Preuß

Constitutionalism – a thriving concept

Constitutionalism is one of the few political ideas which have apparently escaped the general suspicion cast upon most of the other prominent 'isms' in the last decade. Perhaps one may even say that constitutionalism has risen to the status of the only contemporary political idea that enjoys almost universal acceptance. In the last 20 years, a considerable number of countries in different geographical regions with extremely diverse conditions have concurrently chosen the path to constitutionalism in order to find a way out of their respective quandaries: be it Argentina, Brazil, Paraguay and Uruguay in Latin America; Portugal, Spain and Greece at the Southern rim of Europe; South Africa; or Russia and the post-communist countries of Eastern and Central Europe – all of them (and several others) have regarded constitutionalism as the basic objective which sets the framework for their further economic, social, cultural, and political development. No less important is the envisioned role of constitutionalism for the project of European integration. There is a broadening consensus among the citizens of the EU Member States that a common market and more or less remote European institutions in Bruxelles, Strasbourg and Luxembourg will no longer suffice to sustain the aspiration of a European Union. Not accidentally, the idea of a European Polity – for some people a threat, for others a promise – has been associated with the quest for a European constitution. For in Europe the concept of a polity has been intimately linked with the idea of constitutionalism since the end of the 18th century.

All this conveys strong indications of the vitality of the idea of constitutionalism. It may even be justified to credit constitutionalism with certain economic achievements. A comparative view of the present political world system reveals that constitutional democracies enjoy relatively robust economies and have been relatively successful in the domestication of class cleavages and in coping with other social conflicts. Moreover, despite the tendency of the industrial societies to overuse scarce natural resources and to pursue relentlessly the principle of efficient resource allocation, the average standard of environmental protection is higher

---

[*] 'The Political Meaning of Constitutionalism', in R. Bellamy (ed.), *Constitutionalism, Democracy, and Sovereignty: American and European perspectives*, Aldershot, Brookfield USA, Avebury Ashgate, 1996, pp. 11–27.

in traditional constitutional states than in countries with authoritarian political systems. To be sure, these are correlations, not necessarily causal explanations, and there are exceptions. On the one hand, we know of constitutional states which suffer from serious economic difficulties, great social inequalities and severe religious and ethnic cleavages and yet have firmly resisted the temptation to lapse into authoritarianism. India is certainly the most prominent example. On the other hand, countries like Taiwan, South Korea, Singapore and nowadays also China, take pride in the rapid economic development which they achieved in frameworks of government which have maintained, to say the least, large distances from the essentials of constitutionalism.

Whatever the causal linkages between the constitutional form of government and economic performance, there is one experience which merits our attention. Amartya Sen[1] has pointed to the striking fact that no substantial famine has ever occurred in a country with a democratic form of government. One of the reasons for that may be, as Sen hypothesises, the existence of a free press and its function both to publish information about impending disasters and to create and sustain a framework of public accountability of the ruling authorities. This hypothesis, however verifiable or not it may be, leads to the core problem of the concept of constitution and of constitutionalism.

When we speak of constitutionalism, we refer to the set of ideas and principles which form the common basis of the rich variety of constitutions which we find in many countries of the world. Roughly speaking, constitutionalism includes the key tenets of a polity which is based on the idea that the ruled are not merely passive objects of the rulers' willpower but have the status of active members of the political community. This relation entails certain bonds of mutuality between the rulers and the ruled which form the constitution. Thus, constitutionalism encompasses institutional devices and procedures which determine the formation, structure and orderly functioning of government, and it embodies the basic ideas, principles, and values of a polity which aspires to give its members a share in the government. This basket of ideas is fairly impressive and would certainly do the most excellent political philosophers much credit. However, it does not grasp the distinctiveness of constitutionalism. This is not to be found in certain ideas or institutional devices, ingenious as they may be, like, for example, the idea of the separation of powers, or the conception of the accountability of the rulers vis-à-vis the ruled; the essence of constitutionalism which has prompted both the admiration and the constant reasoning of the most spirited political philosophers of many centuries is the mystery of its binding force.

Several political philosophers have developed ideas about how to conceive of a good polity in which the rulers are benevolent and work for the best interests of the ruled, or in which the rulers have certain duties vis-à-vis their subjects. Moreover, long before the age of modern constitutionalism, we find many examples of compacts in which a ruler enters into binding promises and guarantees vis-à-vis his or her subjects. This is not constitutional government in the modern sense of the term. Constitutionalism in this sense is the response to two conditions of modernity: first, the emergence of a monistic sovereign state power after the downfall of the balance between secular and ecclesiastic authority characteristic of mediaeval society; and, second, the idea of the natural freedom of the individual who creates his or her obligations by virtue of his or her interests. Constitutionalism is the answer to the erosion of the inherently obligating forces of the Christian–feudal order and its transformation into an order based on the subjectivity of individuals' interests. In the evolving modern world of the 16th and 17th centuries, one torn by religious cleavages and civil wars, sovereign power became the guarantor of peace and order. At the same time, only the power which could be derived from the natural freedom of the individual was legitimate. Constitutionalism is the conception of a polity in which sovereign power and natural individual freedom coexist and create a political order which cannot resort to antecedent bonds of mutual obligation but must produce its very own mechanisms of obligations. Constitutionalism is, in other words, the answer to the horrifying experience that worldly rule has become immanent; that is, that naturally free individuals have to create a good order by their own limited means. The main problem of this difficult task is the construction of a device in which the sovereign and unlimited power of the united individuals is subjected to the restraining force of legally binding rules. In fact, the legal form of government which rejects the idea of any kind of pre-legal power is the main feature and the great achievement of modern constitutionalism.

The constitution as a law

When I speak of the quality of the constitution as a law I refer to two characteristics. The first is the positivity of modern law. Positive law is the term for that kind of law which owes its authority and binding force not to its religious, philosophical or otherwise sacred content, nor to its tradition, but to its origin from a legitimate lawgiver.[2] The law has become a function of the lawgiver's power and will, and in order to motivate the obedience of the ruled it need not refer to its immanent qualities and teleology, but relies on its formal–procedural quality as the result of a more or less arbitrary enactment. This is the essence of Thomas Hobbes'[3] famous statement that not the inherent truth, but the authority of the author provides the binding force of the law – '*auctoritas, non veritas facit legem*'. It is also the hallmark of positivity.

The second property of modern law consists in the separation of morality from legality. This means the institutionalisation of obedience without the invocation of any moral grounds on which the law may, or may not, be based. Modern law encompasses and obligates all members of society, irrespective of their moral, religious, or political convictions. This makes it possible to bind them together under a common law even if, which is likely to be the case, they do not share the same religious beliefs, philosophical values or historical traditions.

These two properties of modern law allow for the enactment and change of law on mere grounds of expediency according to changing circumstances. Since in modern societies circumstances change rapidly, it is justified to say that the positivist and demoralised character of modern law implies the institutionalisation of legal changes and, by virtue of this, the abstraction from social relations which are integrated by commonly shared values.[4] As Polanyi stated for the market, so we can speak of a high degree of disembeddedness of modern law in relation to other institutions of society.

What is the implication of the legal form of the constitution? What does it mean to say that the legitimation, limitation and regulation of political power assumes the form of legality, i.e., that the obligatory character of the rules which authorise, bind, limit and make political power accountable does not emanate from the inherent dignity of the values and principles which 'govern the governor', but instead from its enactment by a legitimate lawgiver? Does this presuppose a lawgiving authority superior to the ruler which itself has to be bound? This assumption would be self-contradictory. Constitutionalism does not cast out the devil by means of Beelzebub: it does not limit the sovereign power of the lawmaking authority by superimposing a super-sovereign power on it. Only God could rightfully claim this place, but it was the erosion of the undisputed authority of His commands that engendered the secularisation of the concept of supreme power in the first place. Obviously the idea of a super-sovereign would not be the solution of the problem, but its mere displacement.

How then to solve the problem of binding the absolutist sovereign power by means of law without relapsing into the idea of a transcendent power to which could be attributed the capacity of imposing its commands on the secular power? How could one possibly conceive of a source of authority which issued laws that were able to bind the sovereign ruler without transforming this authority into a super-sovereign ruler which now in its turn had to be bound? Does not this question lead us unfailingly into a logical impasse? The answer which shifts the problem onto a new theoretical level is the famous demand: for the 'rule of laws and not of men'. From an analytical perspective, the development proceeded in two steps.

The first developmental step towards the constitutional concept of the rule of law meant: the arbitrary and discretionary willpower of the ruling person is substituted by the requirement that the government rule *through* laws.[5] Acts of domination must acquire the form of the law. Obviously this principle makes sense only if the law has qualities which distinguish it from the mere will of the sovereign. This was the claim of the anti-absolutists. Just as the laws of nature reflected the inherent rationality, predictability and immutability of the world – laws which even the Deists' God Himself could not manipulate at will – so a law which imposed its binding force on individuals, and which they had the moral duty to obey, had to have similar qualities. A law must be a rule, i.e., it must be general (as opposed to an individual order of the sovereign), and it must be immutable in order to be immune from the arbitrariness and vacillations of the power holder. The law is the institutional expression of the continuity, calculability and predictability of the social world; it is the embodiment of reason which checks the passions of the ruler.[6]

The underlying idea of the requirement that a law be abstract and general was the claim that what was binding for all should be the embodiment of universally valid truths and at the same time reflect the spirit of the whole polity, not just of particular segments or individual persons. The form of the law domesticates the willpower of the sovereign ruler and thus forces it to exercise its power in a reasonable manner. Essentially, the law is not will, but reason; not *voluntas*, but *ratio*. This is the first step towards the conclusion that the law-giving authority must be vested in a body which is qualified for issuing general rules, i.e., which in some way represents the spirit of the whole body politic.

However, this first step did not yet mean the full attainment of constitutionalism. While the requirements of the rule *through* law forced the absolutist monarch to employ the form of the law for all acts which applied to all his or her subjects, it is not at all clear how this requirement could itself acquire the binding force of a law. The difficulty was succinctly stated by Madison:[7]

> If angels were to govern men, neither external nor internal controls on government would be necessary. In framing a government which is to be administered by men over men, the great difficulty lies in this: you must first enable the government to control the governed; and in the next place oblige it to control itself.

The full elaboration of this idea is nothing less than the invention of the concept of constitutionalism.

As I stated, the rule of law in the variant of the rule *through* law contains no inherent guarantee that the law's rationalising potential will unfold. Only if the obligation of the ruler to employ the form of the law for his or her acts of rule is itself an obligation of the law can we speak of a constitutional rule. Hence, the rule of law has a twofold meaning: rule *through* law and rule *by* law:[8] acts of domination must acquire the form of the law (government *through* law), and the government itself subjects its willpower to the constraints of the law (rule *by* law). This latter element originates in the last analysis in what the famous English mediaeval jurist Henry de Bracton had already stated in the 13th century with great clarity: the king does not make the law, the law makes the king – not '*rex facit legem, lex facit regem*'.[9] In Britain, where absolutism was defeated in its early stages, the 'law-makes-the-king' doctrine gave rise to the constitutional theory that the power to make laws rested in the polity as a whole, not in any single part of it, and that the binding force of the laws followed from the consensus of all of its parts. As Richard Hooker[10] put it, a legislative power of the king which was not authorised by the constitution but exercised in his own right was tantamount to tyranny.

From a jurist's conceptual perspective, one of the main questions of constitutionalism is how to establish a legal obligation of the lawmaker him- or herself without violating sound principles of jurisprudential reasoning. At first glance, the legalisation of lawmaking – i.e., the subjection of the lawgiver and his or her actions to the rules of the law – seems to presuppose a legal hierarchy: one is led to assume that the law which stipulates the requirements for the enactment of a law must have a higher authority than the enacted law itself. However, this would force us to surmise a hierarchy of lawgiving authorities, with the truly supreme authority of the ruler who makes the rules about lawmaking at the top, and the derived authority of the lawmaker proper who is bound by the rules of the supreme power below. This hierarchical concept of law forces us to find a source of law which is superior to the sovereign law giver, and even this 'super-sovereign' must be ruled by a super-super-sovereign because, according to this hierarchical logic, his or her right to make rules for the sovereign must in turn be based on a superior law. This drives us into an infinite regression. In fact, the creative invention of constitutionalism is different.

From a sociological perspective, the legalisation of lawmaking is but one example of a more general social practice which Luhmann[11] has termed 'reflexive mechanisms'. We speak of reflexivity when a particular process is applied to itself: the learning of learning, the research on research, the talking over talk, or the making of rules for rule making, are examples of reflexive mechanisms. (Evidently H. L. A. Hart's secondary rules – rules about the making, unmaking and the validity of legal rules – are the result of reflexive mechanisms.) Two particularities of reflexivity are of special interest for our topic: first, it increases the range of options which are available in a society in that it allows for selection from among the huge bulk of possible actions. If I learn how to learn I do not have to learn everything that might be important – I gain the freedom to select what I need to learn in the different situations of life. Likewise, if a society makes rules over rule making it increases its capacity for rule making in that it creates and maintains the – more and more professionalised – knowledge about how, when and to what degree a matter should be regulated by law, and thus enhances the power to select among several possibilities.

The second property of reflexivity in our field of law, is the surprising instance that in order to establish rules about rule making it is not necessary to establish a hierarchy of legal norms, such that, rules about how to enact rules and how to establish their validity etc. are superior to the laws which regulate substantive matters. This would finally amount to the idea of a government of angels over people, whereas the problem is the government of people over people whereby 'all men are created equal'. Rousseau[12] had analysed the problem in a manner very similar to that of the Federalists. In order to find the best rules of society,

> there would need to exist a superior intelligence, who could understand the passions of men without feeling any of them, who had no affinity with our nature but knew it to the full, whose happiness was independent of ours, but who would nevertheless make our happiness his concern... .

Rather than establishing an ultimate source of authority which controls the ruler by virtue of its superior power and authority, constitutionalism imagines a non-hierarchical order in which the single one and undivided state authority is divided into different functions which, in turn, are distributed among institutionalised branches of state authority. The separation of powers, which Article 16 of the French Declaration declared an indispensable element of any constitution, is indeed essential for constitutionalism, in that it establishes a rule which 'governs the governor' without resorting to the obvious idea of a monistic supreme authority which controls the governor and which, therefore, operates as the ultimate guarantor of an orderly political rule. The characteristic of constitutionalism is a horizontal order of state authority, in which a system of careful coordination of the functionally specified powers produces a web of mutual and almost circular dependence, whereby either one state power can only act on the antecedent action of another or it is subject to subsequent scrutiny and, if need be, censure.

Although the essential property of constitutionalism is the quality of constitutions as a law, this does not mean that the source of legal authority is alike for all constitutions. In fact, I contend that the typologies and distinctions which have been offered in the long history of constitutional reasoning originate, in the final analysis, in different conceptions about the source of the legally binding force of the respective constitutions. Be it the distinction between written and unwritten constitutions; between rigid and flexible; between those which are more fundamental than ordinary laws (whatever this may mean) and those which have the status of ordinary law; between constitutions which can be amended by the ordinary legislature and those whose revision requires an exclusive amending authority, or the distinction between juridically and politically enforceable constitutions – all these distinctions aim at the clarification of the source and legitimation of the authority of the constitution in its quality as a law. Needless to say, probably the most debated questions of constitutionalism – the questions of who are the authoritative interpreters of the constitution and which methods have to be employed[13] – lie at the core of this basic problem.

Patterns of constitutional authority

In the third part of this chapter I want to give a brief account of three patterns of constitutional authority representing different versions of constitutionalism. Incidentally, they have also proven to be the most influential concepts in the last 300 years.

The British constitutional tradition

The British concept of constitutionalism is clearly the most traditional one, and at the same time, the one whose particular solution of the problem of the authority of the constitution is least transferable to other societies. At first glance it seems paradoxical to understand the doctrine of parliamentary sovereignty as the embodiment of the British concept of constitutionalism – after all, is not the negation of an unbound sovereign power the essence of constitutionalism? Does not constitutionalism require that the sovereign power, whoever may be its holder, be subject to the constitution? The British version of constitutionalism's answer to this question is rather complex. It rearranges the vertical problem of a hierarchical order, i.e., of supremacy and subordination, into a horizontal problem of coordinating and balancing different parts of the sovereign power: the Parliament consists of three elements; it is, strictly speaking, the Queen in

Parliament, including the monarch, the House of Commons and the House of Lords. They are sovereign only through common action, and being bound to each other by mutual rights and duties, the concept of sovereignty acquires a meaning entirely inconsistent with that developed by Bodin[14] or Hobbes:[15] while they conceived of it as an absolute, undivided and unbound power, in the concept of British constitutionalism it is instituted in a web of cooperative relations of the three constituents of Parliament. They can exercise their sovereign power only in joint action, and this gives rise to the complementary element of British constitutionalism, namely the doctrine of the rule of law.

Rule of law does *not* mean the supremacy of abstract legal principles over the sovereign – this would raise the logically and practically unsolvable problem of a sovereign superior to the sovereign; as I stated earlier, it signifies that the Parliament (always to be understood in its three constituents) can exercise its sovereign power only *through* law. For British subjects the 'rule of law' means the absence of 'arbitrariness, of prerogative, or even of wide discretionary authority on the part of the government'.[16] Moreover, when the British invoke the 'rule of law' they do not think of abstract principles or of an enumeration of individual rights insured to them by some supreme power, but of the existence of remedies and courts which protect their freedoms – *ubi jus ibi remedium.*[17] The law exists, as it were, in the operation of the courts which protect the citizens against any kind of wrongdoings which he or she might suffer from the government or a private person. In other words, the authority of the law which binds the government – that is, the 'law of the constitution' – does not derive from a supreme power, least of all from the sovereignty of Parliament, but from the operation of those institutions which secure the exercise of the individuals' freedoms. Note that this idea presupposes that 'there is an area of freedom into which the law should not intervene other than to ensure that the freedom is guaranteed'.[18] The rights to individual freedom are not created by the law, i.e., derived from principles of the law, but, as Dicey put it, they are 'inherent in the ordinary law of the land' in that they flow from the remedies which the British are granted by the Courts. Thus, in Britain, 'the law of the constitution is little else than a generalisation of the rights which the Courts secure to individuals', or, put conversely, the rights of individuals are part of the constitution because they are inherent elements of the ordinary course of the law of the land.[19] From this it follows that Dicey is quite right to state that, due to the embeddedness of individual rights in the institutional web of the law of the land, 'the right is one which can hardly be destroyed without a thorough revolution in the institutions and manners of the nation'.[20] If this still holds true in our day, it would mean that in order to suspend or do away with certain rights it would seem necessary to destroy entire entrenched institutions, which in the end may do more harm to the country than the cancellation of a single right by way of a revision of a written constitution. Or, to put it in a more pointed manner, in order to change the constitution the British must make a revolution, because the binding authority of their constitution is not freely disposable to an identifiable single actor, and its alteration is not subject to legally defined procedures. Thus, the constitution of Britain is very much the result of its political culture and not the emanation of one single authoritative source. Its legal quality is derived from the ordinary course of the law of the land, quite the opposite of the continental concepts of constitutionalism which teach that the validity and authority of the law is derived from the constitution. Not surprisingly, in Britain the idea of the constitution as embodied in one written document has never gained a foothold.

The American constitutional tradition

As we know, in sharp contrast to Britain, the character of the constitution as a written text has become one of the hallmarks of the American concept of constitutionalism. Its other distinctive feature is the constitution's status as a supreme law. Of course, the written form is by no means a mere formality. In fact, it is as essential to the authority and validity of the constitution as is the textual embodiment of God's spirit and word in Holy Scripture.[21] The written text is the solemn expression of the mutual promises and obligations of the citizens who by this very act constitute a polity among themselves – it is, as Hannah Arendt[22] put it, the result of a horizontal social contract which creates mutually binding legal obligations. The written form is the almost sacred affirmation of these promises. As Thomas Paine[23] wrote about the constitutions of the states which they had enacted before forming the United States of America, in each state that constitution served, 'not only as an authority, but as a law of control to the government. It was the political bible of the state'.

Evidently the authority derived from its legally binding character and that emanating from its quasi-biblical scriptural form, merge and support the other feature of the US constitution, namely its character as a supreme law. Supreme law means that all branches of government, including the legislature itself are the creatures of the constitution. This constitution is, as Thomas Paine[24] put it, 'a thing antecedent to the government', originating from a compact 'of the people with each other, to produce and constitute a government'. More striking than the priority of the constitution over the government is its priority over the will of the people itself – the US constitution is clearly supposed to restrain and even to thwart the will of the majority. This is why time and again constitutionalism and democracy have been regarded as opposites, the term constitutional democracy verging on an oxymoron.[25]

I do not want to pursue this matter but, rather, to deal with the slightly different question of how the constitution can acquire the status of a law which is able to impose its superior authority on its own creator, the people. An obvious answer is the theory of self-binding, the so-called Ulysses strategy – the people protect themselves against their own potential myopia, passions, ignorance etc. This is a functional explanation which gives no reason how it is possible that the constitution is the supreme law and can bind not only the government, but even its own creator.

The answer is somewhat surprising. When we look for a justification of the supremacy of the constitution we are inclined to reason within a hierarchical framework, e.g., in Kelsen's theory of a hierarchy of the legal order. But despite the rhetoric of 'supreme law', which indeed suggests a hierarchical order, the supremacy of the constitution derives from neither of the sources which we have dealt with thus far, i.e., neither from an authority which claims superiority over the people – this is an obvious impossibility – nor from its 'immanent and teleological qualities',[26] nor from its merely traditional character as originating in venerable old times which might convey to the constitution its superiority over all other laws. Rather, its quasi-sacred character emanates from its feature as a mutual promise of individuals who enter into a compact with each other by which they transform themselves into a nation; which means that they pledge to each other to stay together in a common polity in good and in bad times.[27] It is the sanctity of the *founding act* by which the polity has been created which imputes to the constitution the authority of the supreme law. The supremacy of its authority over all other laws flows from the inherent significance and uniqueness of the act of nation building. The essential constitutional question which arises is how to preserve the legacy of the founding act, i.e., how to keep the polity alive. Is it more appropriate (and more loyal to the ideas of the founders) to stick to the letter of their sacred scripture in which their original intentions are best determined, or does the sanctity of the founding act require an adjustment of the founders' inspirations to the conditions of the contemporary world? The locus of this debate is the field of constitutional interpretation. Is the *text* of the constitution, the written embodiment of the founders' intentions, the supreme authority, or is it the contemporary *context* which gives the text its particular and, depending on circumstances, changing meaning, so that the constitution is the object of an ever changing struggle about its appropriate interpretation and implementation?

Whatever the right answer may be, the supremacy of the constitution is, in any case, presupposed not only over all branches of government, but also over the people themselves. This is the genuinely American spirit of constitutionalism: the making of the constitution is the act of founding the nation, and whatever purposes, aspirations, hopes, fears, achievements, disappointments, traumas and tragedies of the nation through its eventful history may have occurred or may arise in the future, it is the constitution from which the people will try to extract the right answers to their questions. That is the ultimate reason for the almost obsessive passion of American scholars, lawyers, politicians and great parts of the general public for questions of constitutional interpretation. Incidentally, the other obsession is with rights. Charles Taylor[28] has drawn our attention to the slightly aggressive character of American political life and its 'culture of rights', which underscores the 'value on energetic, direct defence of rights'.[29] Not surprisingly, in this culture the main guarantor of individuals' rights are the courts. The people living under a constitution whose Bill of Rights starts with the prohibition, 'Congress shall make no law ...', would certainly sense it as a mere perversity if they should regard the legislature as the defender of their rights rather than as the main source of their endangerment.

The French constitutional tradition

This rights-protecting and -engendering role of parliament is, in fact, one of the characteristics of the French model of constitutional authority. It is neither based on the rootedness of the law in the institutions which protect individuals against arbitrary rule nor on the sacredness of a founding act of nation building which is embodied in a written document. The French concept of constitutionalism is deeply rooted in the idea of the sovereignty of the constituent power and its logical priority over the constituted powers. This opposition explains the striking feature of French constitutional history and theory: that despite the importance which the idea of the constitution has gained during the Great French Revolution, the concept of an eternal, paramount, or supreme law never arose.

The legal authority of French constitutions has been considerably lower than that of the US since their revolutionary origination in 1789 and 1791 respectively.[30] The idea that the constitution is the supreme law to which all branches of government, including the Parliament and the President, are subordinated never gained a foothold in France. Until our day, the French concept of constitutionalism has not embraced the institution of judicial review, i.e., the control of the constitutionality of an enacted law through the judiciary.[31] The arbiter in disputes over the interpretation of the constitution between the different branches of government is neither a Court nor the Constitutional Council, but the popularly elected President of the Republic who symbolises the unity and integrity of the Nation. Most surprisingly, the constitution of the homeland of the famous, and globally influential and venerated, Declaration of the Rights of Man and Citizen does not even include an explicit bill of rights. Its pre-amble contains a solemn proclamation of 'attachment' to the Rights of Man as they were defined in the Declaration of 1789, but this does not mean its legally binding incorporation into the constitution. To the contrary, Article 34 of the constitution explicitly states that the civil rights of the citizens and the guarantees for the exercise of their political freedoms will be taken care of by *law*.

In other words, when the French look for a guardian of their rights and their political freedom, they point to the parliament, not to the courts. The parliament is not viewed, as in the US, as a potential threat to individuals' rights against which the courts must be invoked, but as the guarantor of their realisation. In the French constitutional tradition the idea of political freedom has been inherently connected with the concept of the general will, which in the last analysis refers to the idea of collective redemption and to the belief in the inherent equality of all people before God. Evidently this basically Catholic doctrine stands in stark contrast to Protestant individualism. Consequently, French constitutional doctrine has always been much more concerned with the integrity of the collective will of the nation than about the rights of the individual.

What, then, is the political meaning of constitutionalism in the French tradition? On what does the authority of the constitution rest, and how can its binding force be explained? The answers are not easily found, but a few hypotheses offer themselves. First, the genuine spirit of constitutionalism and its binding force is not encapsulated in the *constitution* but in the *constituent power* of the nation. The constituent power is the creator of all constituted powers and cannot itself be bound by the constitution. The constitution is neither the source of political freedom nor of political integration, much less of political inspiration. All these purposes are embodied in the idea of the nation rather than in the notion of constitutionalism. Unlike the United States, the creation of the constitution has not been the founding act for the French nation – rather, the constitution is one of the emanations of the nation. The nation is antecedent to the constitution. True, there is also in the French version of constitutionalism a mythical founding act, but this is the act of founding the *nation*, i.e., of creating the constituent power which subsequently produces a constitution. This constitution cannot and must not bind its creator, that is, the nation itself. In the words of Emmanuel Joseph Sieyès:[32] 'The nation is prior to everything. It is the source of everything. Its will is always legal; indeed, it is the law itself'. Therefore the nation cannot be subject to the constitution.

The essence of this concept of constitutionalism, then, is not embodied in the constitution itself; it is incarnated in the power of the nation to make and unmake a constitution at will and at any time. Constitutionalism, that is, consists of what one might call, 'constitution-creativity'; the potential of the nation to constitute and reconstitute its sovereign power and give it its appropriate institutional shape at will. This dynamic idea of constitutionalism accounts for many of the particularities which we encounter in the French tradition, for example, the comparatively large number of French constitutions in the last two centuries, or the relatively weak differentiation between ordinary laws and the constitution in terms of their legally binding force. As in the US, the idea of supremacy is there; but, unlike in the US, it is not associated with the idea of the constitution, but with the pre-constitutional notion of the constituent power of the nation. In fact, the constitution is the embodiment of an inferior rather than of a superior political and legal authority.

Some preliminary conclusions

This sketchy account of the three main traditions of constitutionalism (which are of course by no means exhaustive) shows the difficulty of conceiving a clear cut, unambiguous and undisputed idea of constitutionalism. This is, of course, not very surprising, since the concept is supposed to deliver the answer to one of the most intricate problems of political philosophy, namely the 'governance of the government'. Neither Plato's idea of the rule of the philosophers, nor premodern conceptions of the ruler as the worldly proxy of a Deity, or as the Vicar of Christ, can any longer, if they ever could, provide a solution to this problem in a world of immanence in which the normatively binding force of (moral or legal) obligations can only be established by inner-worldly mechanisms. When, in the 16th and 17th centuries, the traditional conceptions of the good and the right had been eroded and become radically pluralised, the idea of authority and governance had to be reformulated in as radical a manner.

Not only the modern monistic concept of sovereignty, but its conceptual and normative foundation in the subjectivity of the governed required, but at the same time also facilitated, the conception of a political authority with which the rulers were entrusted and hence did not possess in their own right. The legal codification of this relation between the governors and the governed, who are conceived as parts of an overarching common polity, is the basic idea of constitutionalism. The quality of constitutions as laws, i.e., as generating the *legal* obligations of the governors, is essential. Only if the bond between the governors and the governed obligates the ruler, irrespective of his or her personal qualities, religious beliefs or else normative convictions, and if it cannot be revoked unilaterally by the ruler, is it possible to form a reliable institutional structure of government in which the governed are recognised as the ultimate source of political authority.

These are the common traits of any concept of constitutionalism. However, the answers to the question of how this authority is institutionalised and rendered a permanent element of the polity so that the government is effectively bound are quite different: while the British concept relies very much on the operation of deeply entrenched institutions which permeate through the social texture (the three elements of Parliament, its rule through and by law, and the remedy-engendering operation of the Courts), both the American and the French notions presuppose one single locus in which the source of the authority of the constitution is embodied. In the case of the US it is the charisma of the founding act which is to be preserved over history in the text of the constitution and which makes this document a legacy, sometimes perhaps a burdensome legacy of the past which imposes itself on future generations. Knowing that this original compact of the Founding Fathers cannot be repeated, all its solemnity and pathos is 'invested' into the text of the constitution. Not accidentally, an American author uses the image of a 'marriage consummated through the pledging partners' positive, active consent' when speaking of the founding generation, whereas for later generations the constitution 'may operate more as an arranged marriage in which consent is passive'.[33] If we may apply this somewhat frivolous comparison to the French case it is obvious that the French, rather than passively accommodating to the routine and triteness of a long marriage, prefer to start afresh if they feel that the previous bond no longer fits their needs. The constitution is no less important for them, but their underlying idea is that it should not embody the spirit of a past venerable event which should be inscribed into the collective memory of the nation, but rather should become the historically changing incarnation of the essence of the French nation, namely its supreme power, creativity and authority to freely and independently pursue its historical mission. In other words, while the Americans find their self-assurance as a nation in the preservation of the solemn founding act as authenticated in their constitution, for the French the existence of their nation is a matter of course which is not embodied in the constitution, but in the general will of its constituent power – and this is not a sacred incident of the past, but an essential and hence eternal attribute.

Thus, in the last analysis constitutionalism involves much deeper issues than the idea of limited government, important as this undoubtedly is. At the heart of the concept of constitutionalism lies the question of how to find a way of civilising the unfathomable charisma of politics without destroying liberty. Europe was the continent where this question emerged for the first time in the history of humanity. Meanwhile, since the downfall of the bipolar world and the end of communism, the search for the right answers has become almost universal. Paradoxically, this coincides with a similarly unique step which Europe is about to make, namely the search for a constitution for a supranational political community. Will the multifaceted concept of constitutionalism as developed in the last 300 years provide us with the wisdom that is required for the solution of this new problem? Evidently this is a quite new issue which patently displays that no discussion of constitutionalism whatsoever will ever be concluded. This, then, is my provisional conclusion.

Notes

1. A. Sen, 'Freedoms and needs', *New Republic*, Vol. 31, January, 1994, pp.10–17.

2. M. Weber, *Economy and Society*, G. Roth and C. Wittich (eds), Berkeley/ Los Angeles/London, University of Berkeley Press, 1978, Ch. VIII, Sect. VII, pp.866ff.

3. T. Hobbes, *Leviathan: The Latin version, Opera philosophica quae Latine scripsit omnia*, Vol. 3, London, J. Bohn, 1841, p.202.

4. N. Luhmann, *Rechtssoziologie*, Beinbek b. Hamburg, Rowohlt, 1972, pp. 209 and see also note 11.

5. F. F. Gaus, 'Public Reason and the Rule of Law', in I. Shapiro (ed.), *The Rule of Law*, (Nomos XXXVI), New York/London, New York University Press, 1994, pp. 328–364 [329].

6. G. Jellinek, *Gesetz und Verordnung*, (v. 1887), Tübingen, Neudruck d. Ausg., 1919, pp.43ff.

7. J. Madison, *The Federalist Papers No. 51*, C. Rossiter (ed.), New York/ London, New American Library, 1961, p.322.

8. Gaus, 'Public Reason and the Rule of Law', p. 329.

9. H. de Bracton, *De Legibus et Consuetudinibus Angliae*, trans. Samuel E. Thorne, Cambridge, Mass, Harvard University Press, 1968, pp.33, 306, quoted in J. Bridge, 'The Rule of Law and the Individual in the United Kingdom and in a Federal Europe', paper presented to the conference on *Constitutional History and the Rule of Law*, Bangalore, 16–18 February 1995.

10. Jellinek, *Gesetz und Verordnung*, p. 48.

11. Luhmann, *Rechtssoziologie*, pp. 32ff, 213ff; and N. Luhmann, 'Reflexive Mechanismen', *Soziologische Aufklärung*, Vol. 4, Aufl. Opladen, 1974, pp. 92–112.

12. J.-J. Rousseau, *The Social Contract*, Bk. 2, Ch. 7, trans. M. Cranston (ed.), Harmondsworth, Penguin, 1968, p.84.

13. W. F. Murphy, 'Constitutions, Constitutionalism, and Democracy', in D. Greenberg, S. N. Katz, *et al.* (eds), *Constitutionalism and Democracy: Transitions in the Contemporary World*, New York/Oxford, Oxford University Press, 1993, pp. 3–25.

14. J. Bodin, *The Six Bookes of a Commonweale*, [1576] trans. R. Knolles, K. D. McRae (ed.), Cambridge, Mass, Harvard University Press, 1962.

15. T. Hobbes, *Leviathan*, [1651], R. Tuck, (ed.), Cambridge, Cambridge University Press, 1991.

16. A. V. Dicey, *Introduction to the Study of the Law of the Constitution*, Indianapolis, Liberty Classics, 1982 (reprint of the 8th edition of 1915), p. 120.

17. *Ibid.*, p. 118.

18. Bridge, 'The Rule of Law...', p. 1.

19. Dicey, *Introduction to the Study of the Law of the Constitution*, p. 119.

20. *Ibid.*, p. 120.

21. T. Grey, 'The Constitution as Scripture', *Stanford Law Review*, Vol. 37, 1984, pp. 1–25.

22. H. Arendt, *On Revolution*, Penguin, Harmondsworth, 1973, pp. 169–173.

23. T. Paine, *Rights of Man*, H. Collins (ed.), Harmondsworth, Penguin, 1979, p. 209.

24. *Ibid.*, pp. 210, 213.

25. See, e.g. S. Holmes, 'Precommitment and the paradox of democracy', in J. Elster and R. Slagstad (eds), *Constitutionalism and Democracy*, Cambridge/New York, Cambridge University Press, 1988, pp. 145–190.

26. Weber, *Economy and Society*, p. 867.

27. Murphy, 'Constitutions, Constitutionalism, and Democracy', p. 9.

28. C. Taylor, 'Can Canada Survive the Charter?', *Alberta Law Review*, Vol. XXX, 1992, pp. 429.

29. Cf. M. J. Lacey and K. Haakonssen (eds), *A Culture of Rights: The Bill of Rights in philosophy, politics, and law – 1791 and 1991*, Cambridge, Cambridge University Press, 1992.

30. L. Henkin, 'Revolutions and constitutions', *Louisiana Law Review*, Vol. 49, 1989, pp. 1023–1056.

31. The present constitution establishes the Constitutional Council, which is more a council of elder statespeople and experienced politicians than of jurists. It has to check the constitutionality of organic laws *before* their enactment, whereas the compatibility of ordinary laws with the constitution *can* be scrutinised *before* their promulgation upon request of the President of

the Republic, the Prime Minister, of the Presidents of the two chambers of the Parliament.

32. E. J. Sieyès, *What is the Third Estate?*, [1789], trans. and introduced by S. E. Finer and M. Blondel (eds), London, Pall Mall Press, 1963, pp.124, 126–128.

33. Murphy, 'Constitutions, Constitutionalism, and Democracy', p. 9.

Chapter Eight

Citizenship and Identity: Aspects of a Political Theory of Citizenship[*]

Ulrich K. Preuß

I.

The concept of citizenship defines an individual's legal status within a nation state. To be a citizen means to have certain rights and duties which others, non-citizens, do not have. Hence the practical relevance of citizenship is frequently seen in the rights and duties which are attached to it. Viewed from this perspective, to be a citizen means to possess the qualifications which are necessary for the eligibility and the enjoyment of certain rights which are not bestowed on individuals merely by virtue of being a member of humankind. Citizenship serves as a key of the door to valuable rights and burdensome, but mostly noble, duties. Evidently the distribution of rights among the members of humankind is extremely unequal, and it is no less obvious that citizenship has a major impact on the distributional pattern. Not surprisingly, the value of citizenship is more or less precisely defined by the value of the rights (and the burden of the duties) which follow from this particular legal status. This raises the question of whether one can justify the difference citizenship makes.

In fact, to say that citizenship means having certain rights and duties is not to fully grasp its theoretical and practical implications. In its primary meaning citizenship circumscribes an individual's role of being a member of a polity. To be a citizen has the meaning of being involved in an essentially political community. This implies some kind of mutuality of rights and duties both between the polity and the individuals and among the individuals themselves. Evidently these two meanings of citizenship are closely connected with each other and are by no means mutually exclusive. To possess particular rights and duties by virtue of being a citizen and to be a citizen by virtue of being a member of a particular political community are two sides of one and the same coin whose message is: citizenship is an exclusive status, the status of the 'we' which delimits 'the others'. This fundamental distinction explains why, until recently, citizenship was always associated with the notion of both collective and individual identity. Citizenship is the label for being the member of a polity which is not accessible to other

---

[*] 'Citizenship and Identity: Aspects of a political theory of citizenship', in R. Bellamy, V. Bufacchi and D. Castiglione (eds), *Democracy and Constitutional Culture in the Union of Europe*, London, Lothian Foundation Press, 1995, pp. 107–120.

individuals and the access to which they cannot claim on the mere ground that they are human beings.

To the best of my knowledge, all modern states draw a more or less sharp distinction between those rights and duties which pertain only to their own citizens and those which are assigned to all individuals irrespective of their citizenship status. If citizenship entails the possession of certain rights (and duties), and if these rights are attractive (and the duties not prohibitively burdensome), the question arises of how an individual can acquire citizenship, and whether she can acquire it altogether at her will. Is there a right, perhaps even a human right, to citizenship? If citizenship is a synonym for membership of a community, does this mean that only the members of an existing community can become citizens? In other words, does citizenship *presuppose* the community of which the citizen is a member, or, conversely, does citizenship *create* this very community? These questions are of the utmost importance. On the one hand, an affirmative answer to the former question, i.e., the assertion that citizenship *presupposes* the community, has the implication that those who for whatever reasons do not belong to the community cannot legitimately make the claim to citizenship. On the other hand, an affirmative answer to the latter question, i.e. the statement that it is citizenship in the first place which constitutes a political community, would considerably facilitate access to the status of citizenship. In this case, the decision about an individual's admission to citizenship would be taken according to criteria of justice, i.e., it would be based on the applicant's quality as a holder of universally valid human rights, not on his or her ascriptive attributes like descent, ethnicity and so on. For those who advocate this latter answer, the barrier of collective identity, i.e., the barrier of the exclusive 'we' as opposed to the excluded 'others', would not exist, and therefore membership of the community would not be able to serve as a criterion for admission to citizenship. Although this answer would not necessarily imply a universal human right to citizenship, much less the right to freely choose one's citizenship (including the rights and duties which are attached to it), it would detach the concept of citizenship from the widespread quest for individual and collective identity.

II.

To fully grasp the importance of citizenship it seems appropriate to demarcate this status from different positions of non-citizenship, that is, from the categories of people who are excluded from citizenship. We can differentiate stateless individuals, aliens, and nationals.

The category of stateless individuals needs no further explication: they are those persons who are not members of any state whatsoever and hence must dispense with the basic entitlements to protection and security which follow from membership of a group. As authors like Hannah Arendt, Raymond Aron or Michael Walzer rightly emphasise, 'statelessness is a condition of infinite danger'.[1]

Very frequently the nationality, alien and immigration laws of modern states include stateless people in the category of aliens in that they define as an alien, any person not a citizen or national of the respective country. Whereas stateless persons are non-members altogether, aliens in the strict sense of the term are only non-members of the particular state in whose territory they sojourn, but they are still members of a state whose territory they have left temporarily or permanently. Most migrants in the world are aliens rather than stateless people. And most people who leave their country in order to live in another are refugees who have been expelled from their country by mere force or by the immediate effects of war or civil war. But there is still a considerable number of individuals who are driven out of their country not by the physical force of war and civil war, but by economic or ecological misery and by the hope of improving their life situations in another country. Evidently nationality as such, i.e. the status of membership of any state whatsoever, is not always attractive enough to restrain people from acquiring more or less voluntarily the status of an alien, because being an alien in one country may be more appealing and promising than enjoying the status of membership in one's own state.

This observation leads us to the distinction between nationality and citizenship. Under present-day conditions this division has almost entirely lost its practical significance, whereas it is of major conceptual relevance. Today, in most countries of the world, nationality is synonymous with citizenship. But at the dawn of the modern constitutional state there was a huge discrepancy between these two categories. Whereas nationality had the meaning of being subject to the government of a particular state and thus served as a demarcation against aliens, the term citizen referred to the social status within the polity: only those who, as Kant put it, were neither minors nor women and who were their own masters, i.e., who owned possessions which enabled them to lead an independent life, qualified for the status of a citizen. Only this rather small group had a stake in the polity and was entitled to participate in its legislation.[2]

While nationality conveyed a position of passive submission, citizenship included the active status of participating in the shaping of the polity. From the very outset, the concept of citizenship was socially and politically exclusive, and it is due to the democratic development of the last two hundred years that it has become ever more inclusive in that, in a continual process, the initial property and gender qualifications have been abolished and the age requirement decreased so that today virtually all adult nationals enjoy the status of citizenship. The congruence of nationality and citizenship equalised the political status of all denizens of a country and abolished one important internal cleavage within society.

Although today nationality and citizenship coincide, this does not mean that the status of passive submission has vanished in the industrial states of Western Europe and the USA. In a way, the earlier distinction between nationals and citizens, i.e., between passive denizens and active citizens, is now being reproduced in a different form. It would be more correct to speak of a hierarchy: on the top, there is the division between (national) citizens proper and permanent alien residents. Although permanent alien residents are normally called immigrants, the status of an immigrant does not necessarily include the right to nationality and, consequently, to citizenship. While the distinction between aliens and those who are subjects of, and owe allegiance to, a particular dominion dates back to the early days of the emergence of the modern state, the existence of a relatively numerous category of permanently residing aliens in a country is a rather novel experience at least for the West European nation states. While in the three EU countries to which this problem is predominantly relevant – Germany, France, and the UK – the proportion of permanently residing aliens in the whole population barely exceeds 7 per cent, the demand for the status of fully recognised legal residence, on either a permanent or a temporary basis, is of course much higher. The reason for this is that even a legal status short of citizenship involves attractive benefits such as the, albeit limited, access to the labour market and, depending on the country, the legal right to many of those welfare state benefits which are financed by the general state budget. Apart from this category, there is still the group of temporary legal residents which in Germany comprises both the asylum applicants during the application procedure and the refugees who enjoy the protection of the Geneva convention on the status of refugees. The lowest category in this hierarchy covers the illegal migrants.

Evidently citizenship is the most privileged status, and it is exclusively restricted to nationals. In order to enjoy the full scope of citizen rights a person must be or become a national beforehand. Even the rather limited stipulation of Article 8b of the 'Treaty on European Union', which grants every citizen of the Union residing in a Member State of which he is not a national the right to vote and to stand as a candidate at municipal elections in the Member State in which he resides, required constitutional amendments in most of the Member States. For this precept has been regarded as a major exception to the rule – for some even as a hardly justifiable rupture with the unquestionable political tenet – that genuine citizen rights (which include the right to vote not only at the national and state, but also at the local level) can only be attached to nationals. Is there an intrinsic connection between citizenship and nationality, and if so, what is its rationale?

III.

In order to answer this question it seems appropriate to clarify the concept of citizenship altogether. On closer examination, we can distinguish at least five different meanings which, though not necessarily mutually exclusive, reflect more or less explicitly distinct notions of a just and legitimate polity.

1. The first and probably most comprehensive concept of citizenship regards it as the embodiment of a thoroughly novel concept of politics altogether. It conceives of the polity as a 'civil union', i.e., an association of citizens who constitute the realm of politics in the dialogical form of their communication. This paradigm rejects the idea of monological and absolute power and regards the intensity of the fellows' association rather than of their dissociation as the main property of the political. The realm of politics is, as Hannah Arendt put it, 'the organization of the people as it arises out of acting and speaking together, and its true space lies between people living together for this purpose, no matter where they happen to be'.[3] The political sphere is a domain of non-coercive public

discourse among free and equal individuals who are not 'naturally' free and equal and whose rights are not inborn, but who have these rights of equal political participation and communication by virtue of their common participation in the production of their public life. For this concept of politics, membership in the polity is not a means to an end – e.g., for the protection of one's life, liberty, and property – but a constituent element of the self and an intrinsic value in itself, so to speak. In the framework of this quasi-Aristotelian understanding of citizenship – which has, of course, manifold facets in the writings of its various authors and which is obviously rather close to contemporary communitarian reasoning[4] – to be a citizen has not only the meaning of being a member of a particular political community, but of being part of a common identity of that very community. In a permanent and circular process, the identity of the community is constituted by the particularities of its individual members and the identity of the members themselves is constituted by their embeddedness in the community.

2. Given the need of modern states for efficient instruments of government, including mass compliance and undisputed power in order to meet the challenges of a rapidly changing world, it is doubtful whether this communicative concept of politics and power is an appropriate normative model for modern politics, much less of course an empirically valid description. In the modern concept of politics as first developed by Machiavelli, the fulfillment by individuals of their duty to political obedience was not contingent upon a communicative culture of politics in which power originated from communication rather than ending communication by an authoritative *fiat*.

However, this fundamental change of the concept of politics did not weaken the ancient ideal of citizenship in the writings of most of the political theorists since Machiavelli. Machiavelli himself referred time and again to Roman history and to the works of Livius, whose authority in his writings replaced that of Holy Scripture. For Machiavelli and many political theorists after him, Roman history was a paradigm for the rise and fall of empires and, by implication, for the vigour and final decline of the virtues of a good citizen. Therefore, the idea of citizenship did not die with the fall of the ancient political entities – the Greek city state and the Roman empire – but experienced a renaissance within the thoroughly new conceptual framework of modern politics. Without going into detail, it may suffice to call to our mind the line of philosophical reasoning according to which the good quality of a political order could be attained despite the prevalence of bad qualities in the individuals who comprised it, because, due to a miraculous 'invisible hand' or the 'cunning of reason', private vices turned into public benefits. At the end of the eighteenth century, the paradigm of an eternal circle of rise and fall, growth and decay had been supplanted by the idea of a continual and permanent progress. The concept of citizenship survived this theoretical transformation of the understanding of the polity, but, not surprisingly, it itself underwent considerable changes.

The most important one is its close association with the idea of individual freedom and its polemical dissociation from tradition and community. The preoccupation of both the American and the French revolutionaries of the late eighteenth century with the virtues of citizens is not a response to but rather confirmation of this change.[5] Since in the new polity the individuals were liberated from the constraints of pre-modern associations, and hence their social behaviour was not directed by 'inborn' objective ideas of morality, they had to restrain their passions and other destructive qualities in order to safeguard the coexistence and harmony of the equal freedoms of all. Hence the recurrent invocation of civic values such as the capacity for self-sacrifice, the enthusiasm for justice and a spirit of public faith.[6]

Rousseau insisted that without the obligations of a civil religion as the expression of social conscience it was 'impossible to be either a good citizen or a loyal subject', whereby this quality encompassed the capacity to 'love law and justice, or to sacrifice, if need be, his life to his duty'.[7] As we know, in the rhetoric of the French revolution the terms 'citizen' and 'virtue' became the most prominent shibboleths of that time. However, the manifold references to the Roman empire could hardly conceal that the political order which was at stake was entirely modern. Here again Rousseau had clearly defined the modern characteristic of citizens, namely that 'they share in the sovereign power'. The citizens are the persons who unite in order to form a republic or a body politic.[8] This contractual basis of citizenship was of course incompatible with the ancient concept. In other words, the ancient word 'civis' (citizen, citoyen) incorporated an entirely new meaning within the conceptual framework of the liberal constitutional state.

Some thirty years before the revolution, Rousseau complained that almost nobody had grasped the true meaning of the term 'citizen', and that the French 'use the word to designate social status and not legal right'.[9] Indeed, what constitutes citizenship in the completely new framework of the modern constitutional state established in the last quarter of the eighteenth century, is the participation of the naturally free and equal individual in the common undertaking of forming a political body. Since *all* individuals are born free and equal, and since the polity is nothing other than the association of free and equal citizens, nobody is excluded or can be excluded from acquiring the status of a citizen. To be a 'good citizen or a loyal subject', i.e., to 'love law and justice', is not a quality which *constitutes* citizenship but rather presupposes it. To fulfill legal duties and to respect the equal freedom of one's fellow citizens is a moral obligation which arises only after the individual has entered the social contract and has become a citizen. But in order to be able to enter into such a contract, i.e., to become a citizen with the associated duties, nothing more is required than to be a bearer of human rights which includes the presumption that the individual is able to fulfill the dialogic and behavioural requirements of the liberal state.[10]

The moral meaning of being a citizen, then, is the possession of the capacity to assume the duties and responsibilities of one's freedom within civil society – which is tantamount to obeying loyally the law, because civil society is constituted and maintained by the law. This is what we would call a universalist concept of citizenship. It means, to be a member of a cooperative undertaking which does not exclude some individuals or certain categories of individuals because they do not share particular antecedent moral values which are not amenable to individual moral choice, and which allegedly bind the participants together and constitute their community before they may enter into a political association.[11] Any individual can become the citizen of any kind of nation so long as it is the bearer of human rights, and this is only possible if we define the nation in the universalist manner of the French revolution (as it was succinctly put by Sieyès): namely, as 'a body whose members live under a common law and are represented by the same legislative assembly'.[12] This conceptual understanding of the modern nation[13] would not necessarily imply that it would be morally obliged to allow free access to whoever wants to enter, to settle down and to become a citizen. But it would not allow the exclusion of applicants on the ground that they do not, and cannot share, the collective identity of the citizens of this particular state because this identity is based on pre-political properties which are essentially beyond the choices of individuals.

3. This latter contention is the implication of a concept according to which citizenship is closely connected with the individual's personal identity as a moral being. In this concept, citizenship is but a species of the general concept of membership of a community, whereby membership means the individual's quasi-existential, inescapable attachment to a community which exists prior to the individual's choices and promises, and which defines his or her self – like the family or the local community. This kind of community is not a mere association which furthers the interests or values of individuals; rather, it is a form of social life which is valuable in itself, shapes the fates of its members, and gives their lives a distinctive meaning. To be a member of such a community has the important implication that the individual assumes moral duties which are more demanding than those which are owed to human beings as such.

According to 'communitarian' authors who reject the liberal axiom of the priority of the individual and her rights, citizenship has the meaning of membership in such a 'communitarian' community, namely in the nation. Obviously the term 'nation' has a meaning different from that of Sieyès – it circumscribes a 'community of fate' and presupposes a pre-political commonness of its members. Hence membership-citizenship refers to bonds of mutuality, social solidarity, sympathy, brotherhood, shared beliefs, ultimately even moral consensus among the members of a society which defines itself as a nation in the communitarian sense. It is not the case that after the constitution of the nation through the voluntary union of free and equal individuals, feelings of commonness and social solidarity ensue; rather, the antecedent feelings of commonness and social solidarity allow for the foundation of a polity – the nation state – whose member-citizens were already members before the polity even existed altogether.

Indeed, for many authors the nation is the kind of political community by which modern societies gain and sustain their collective identity. The somewhat vague term 'collective identity' includes the following two elements: (1) a group has boundaries which delimit its scope to other groups, (2) the internal cohesion of the group is based on the more or less tacit assumption that the members of the group owe each other duties of loyalty and aid by virtue of being members.[14] Thus, 'nationality and citizenship complement one another': the nation holds individuals together, whereas citizenship gives them the means to actively shape their common future as a community.[15] In this communitarian understanding of citizenship this status is not just a bundle of rights (and duties) which can be bestowed on any person who happens to stay physically, be it temporarily or permanently, within the territorial boundaries of a society, but a status of membership which requires a particularly close relation of social solidarity with the respective community.[16] Obviously, in this framework citizenship is a rather exclusive status. It is itself a good which is assigned only to those who are already members of the community which exists prior to the polity.[17] But at the same time it may also serve as a criterion for the accession of individuals to rights and benefits which are distributed by the state. This leads to a dimension of the concept of citizenship which is closely related to the welfare state.

4. The key concept for the connection of citizenship with the welfare state is the idea of 'social citizenship'. It deals with the rights and duties of people with regard to their welfare. The roots of this concept can be found in the famous essay of T. H. Marshall concerning 'Citizenship and Social Class' (1950), in which he sketched a history of consecutive steps in the development of the concept of citizenship which became ever more complex: starting with the endowment of individuals with civil rights in the eighteenth century, which were extended to include political rights in the nineteenth century, and arrived at the institution of social rights and the concept of social citizenship in the twentieth century.[18] Marshall was mainly concerned with social inequality as a major obstacle to the individual's participation in the social, cultural, and political life of the society. While he regarded the tendency towards inequality as a property more or less inherent to capitalism, the idea of citizenship represented the opposite principle, namely the principle of equality.

In order to operate as a compensating counter-principle to the inherent tendency of capitalist societies to inequality, citizenship had to embrace the right to access to the benefits and resources of modern society. In Marshall's words, it had to include

> the right to share to the full in the social heritage and to live the life of a civilised being according to the standards prevailing in the society. The institutions most closely connected with it are the education system and the social services.[19]

What was important for Marshall (and all proponents of social rights who followed his ideas) was the proviso that the admittance to the achievements of a civilised society was an individual right and that it was part of the legal status of citizenship. Thus participation in the redistributive schemes of the modern state was not prone to damage the self-respect of individuals or to marginalise them. As with the civil and the political elements of citizenship, social citizenship, too, is essentially based on the dogma of equality. In all three of its dimensions citizenship means equal citizenship, i.e., the right of the individual to be respected and treated as an equal.

This makes citizenship in general, and social citizenship in particular, a pivotal element of social and political integration. But here, too, we cannot escape the conceptual alternative between a universalist and a communitarian understanding of citizenship, perhaps even less so than in other policy areas. The welfare state is based on the idea of sharing. To share one's assets with others requires a convincing moral justification (the stipulation of statutary legal duties alone will not do in the long run). Although every person has some basic moral duties vis-à-vis every human being, it is hardly disputable that we have stronger moral duties against persons with whom we are connected by bonds which are stronger and more specific, than the mere bond of belonging to the human race (such as the bonds of the family, of friendship and the like). With regard to the concept of social citizenship, the question is whether my obligation to share is stronger vis-à-vis a fellow member of my nation than vis-à-vis any other needy human being? To put it in a different way, is the concept of social citizenship inclusive or exclusive? (The terms 'inclusion' and 'inclusive' characterise a social system, and particularly a welfare system, in which all physical participants of a given society have equal access to, and are equally dependent upon, the goods of the functional system. In contrast, a welfare system is 'exclusive' if it dispenses its benefits selectively to those who 'deserve' them, the criterion of 'desert' ranging from economic contribution to ethnic affiliation.)

Evidently the concept of social citizenship can be justified in both an inclusive and an exclusive sense.[20] The inclusive view leads to the argument that the poor and needy are only physically part of the society. Socially they are standing outside society or, for that matter, outside the particular social and moral community on whose territory they reside because they do not have the material, moral, and intellectual means to enjoy the manifold material and moral benefits of social association. In order to include them, i.e., to transform their merely physical affiliation with society into social membership, society must allot to them the goods and services which enable them to actively take part in the full range of its opportunities and to enjoy its abundant resources. According to this argument, the assignment of social rights would cause the individual's integration in the society and create his or her status as a fully-fledged citizen. To grant individuals welfare rights means to make them citizens, that is full members of the community. Since the concept of citizenship implies equal citizenship, this line of argument necessarily requires an inclusive welfare state. The citizens' identity as citizens would be dependent on and constituted through their inclusion in the welfare scheme which, moreover, requires universalistic criteria for the distribution of its benefits. Note that this argument does not require the coincidence of nationality and citizenship. If the inclusion in the scope of welfare benefits is constitutive of citizenship, theoretically every human being would qualify. However, realistically, inclusive social policies have a much more limited reach in that they are devised according to the territorial principle. Normally they apply to individuals who reside permanently (in some rare cases, also temporarily) within the territorial boundaries of the relevant country, irrespective of their nationality. In this case the country would have more citizens than nationals, which sounds strange but is by no means inconceivable. It would mean that it is not nationality, but participation in the institutions and services of the welfare state which shapes a community.

The argument for social citizenship on the basis of exclusivity runs as follows: all citizens deserve and therefore should have welfare rights in their quality as citizens. The assignment of welfare rights does not make them citizens; on the contrary, their already existing status as citizens entails the justification for the assignment of welfare rights. This then is a justification which excludes non-citizens from welfare rights because they do not have the justifying qualities which are restricted to citizens, i.e. to members of the nation. Membership of the nation is based on qualities which precede and are independent of any kind of welfare policies and welfare rights. Rather, the nation is constituted by properties which have no relation whatsoever to a potential welfare scheme. Hence, the communitarian understanding of citizenship would rather restrict than extend the range of welfare rights, because the imperatives of social solidarity which guide welfare schemes are rooted in the special relationships of a community which distributes benefits only among its own members. Citizenship in T. H. Marshall's understanding, namely as the ideal of equal participation by every individual in the resources of a civilised society, lies outside the conceptual framework of the communitarian notion of citizenship.

5. Finally, it should be mentioned here that a concept of citizenship is emerging which tries to combine the universalist and the communitarian approach. I refer to the concept of 'earth citizenship'. Its main concern is the derivation of new moral obligations from the fact that today all human beings share a dependence on the preservation of nature and the planetary resources of atmosphere, ocean, and genetics.[21] This concept is universal in that it includes all humankind, i.e., the human species itself (some ecological theorists even include all animated nature) in the category citizen, so that there is no difference between a human being and an 'earth citizen'. On the other hand, the concept has striking similarities with the communitarian approach in that it conceives of humankind as having a 'global identity' and of sharing common purposes and actions. In this ecological perspective, 'collective identity and universal values assume a new status and significance'.[22]

But is it really possible to imagine an 'earth citizenship'? Is this not a conceptual hybrid? It is true, the world has become globalised, it has become one world: communication has become worldwide, any event in any part of the world has mostly unforeseen repercussions on other parts, the density of the net of interdependencies is leading to the effect that the globe is exposed to climatic and environmental threats which apply to humankind as a whole. Does this mean that the common exposure to global risks is constituting a world community? And would this also imply the notion of world or earth citizenship?

Citizenship means the mutual recognition of individual rights within a particular community. To recognise each other as purely human beings is a necessary, but not sufficient condition for the institutionalisation of citizens' rights such as voting or other forms of participating in the making of political decisions. The term 'citizen' implies, as I stated above, the idea of intensified duties of social solidarity and moral obligations vis-à-vis one's fellow citizens. If the moral duties are all alike, irrespective of the particular relations in which individuals are engaged, then the term 'citizen' makes no sense, because it is merely a synonym for 'human being'. Citizenship implies particular social relations and, consequently, particular rights and particular moral and legal duties. It is this particular social relation – we may call it community, although the term may make claims that are too strong – which constitutes a common understanding of the meaning of these rights and duties. Belonging to the human race does not constitute a common understanding of the meaning of rights, duties, of mutuality, promises etc., because this understanding is shaped in communities. Communities exist only as a plurality of communities, because space and time limit the scope of possible human relations. Thus, while I do not doubt that the predicament of humankind urgently requires the worldwide acknowledgement of a new kind of moral obligation, of global responsibility and universal social solidarity, I do not subscribe to the concept of 'earth citizenship' as the conceptual basis for the derivation of these rights. Much less is it possible to conceive of a 'global identity'.

IV.

This sketch of different meanings of citizenship shows that this concept is a locus of rights and duties and of identity as well. Moreover, it seems to be inseparably connected with the nation state. The very origination of the modern concept of citizenship was simultaneously the beginning of the modern nation state. Does this mean that the limits to our moral obligations and to our social solidarity are set by the physical and social boundaries of the nation state? Does our quest for identity set the boundaries to our sense of justice? This question leads back to the discussion of the relation between nationality and citizenship mentioned above.

While it is widely held that it is the very essence and the intrinsic purpose of the concept of citizenship to limit the (physical and social) scope of our moral duties, I doubt whether this assumption really exhausts the full meaning of the idea of citizenship. Historical development since the end of the eighteenth century clearly shows the prevalence of the moral element of citizenship in nurturing the individual's sense of identity. As already stated, the present-day coincidence of nationality and citizenship developed only gradually during the last two hundred years: the acquisition of nationality and the assignment of citizenship followed different criteria. Depending on the respective country, nationality has been and is being acquired either according to the '*ius sanguinis*', i.e. the principle of descent, or the '*ius soli*', i.e. the rule of territorial affiliation. While these two modes of acquiring nationality draw in different ways the physical boundaries of a group, the moral requirements of the concept of citizenship are more demanding. According to them, to be a citizen means more than mere physical affiliation; it presupposes the capacity of the individual to play a responsible role in the maintenance and development of the polity. Hence at the genesis of this concept, this status was bestowed only on those nationals (i.e. those who were physically affiliated) who were supposed to possess the capacity to fulfill this role, namely reason and property. Therefore minors, women, lunatics, and all non-propertied classes were excluded. Conceptually, nationality and citizenship could exist independently of each other. Not only was the overwhelming proportion of nationals excluded from citizenship, during the heyday of the revolution there was even a small group of citizens who were not nationals. This followed from the stipulation of the constitution of 1793, which authorised the national assembly to bestow the rights of a French citizen on aliens (such as Tom Paine) who, in the words of Article 4, 'deserve well' of humanity.

Due to the inherently egalitarian dynamics of the idea of citizenship it was finally extended to all adult nationals. However, until today not all nationals have been citizens. That only mentally healthy adult individuals enjoy the totality of citizen rights can be explained by the underlying presupposition that individuals who have the right to participate in the shaping of the collective fate of a society must be equipped with a minimum degree of reasonableness. While gender and property have been abolished as criteria by which reasonableness can be measured, age is still regarded as a viable indicator. This makes it clear that the nation state limits democratic participation for the sake of the rationality of the outcomes of the political process. The expressive role of citizenship, its 'identity-engendering' function so to speak, is set behind its role to safeguard the prevalence of reason in the political process.

If this is so, why then is citizenship restricted to nationals? Why has a permanent alien resident who has no intention of returning to his native country less rights than his fellow-men on the sole ground that he is not a national? Why does the egalitarian principle of citizenship not leap across the boundaries of nationality? (The afore-mentioned case of the French constitution of 1793 has remained a rare, perhaps even unique, exception.) The reason which is frequently given is the assertion that only nationals share the common fate of the nation which they, in contrast to aliens, cannot escape. There are convincing arguments against this assumption which I cannot go into now. Rather, I want to point to an argument which is in line with the universalist premises of the modern constitutional state without denying the limiting function of citizenship.

According to this argument, aliens do not have the full rights of citizens because it cannot be presumed that they share the understanding of rights, of legal and moral duties, of mutuality and of a multitude of symbolic actions which constitute and maintain a polity and which refer to the mostly implicit cultural heritage of a society. While this argument says that only those can acquire citizenship who are able and willing to participate in the development of a common understanding of the mutual rights and duties and of the common goals as well, it does not say that this capacity is the exclusive property of nationals. With respect to nationals there is the presumption that they are qualified to fulfill this requirement because they have been bred in this society. Undoubtedly this does not apply equally to all aliens. But if the nation state sticks to its universalist principle to grant every human being the right to have rights, then it cannot exclude aliens from the right to acquire citizenship on the mere ground that they are aliens. This would be tantamount to defining the modern nation state as a community of fate, the fate being either the commonness of blood or that of history. We know that neither descent (blood) nor history are able to constitute a modern state and to safeguard its reliable operation.

There are, of course, justifiable reasons why the existing nation states are neither legally nor morally obliged to accept everybody who wants to settle down in their territories. I do not deal here with this question. The conclusion which I draw from what I have stated so far is that citizenship is a principle which determines the creation and assignment of particular legal and moral rights and duties without serving as an entitlement to invalidate the principles of a universalist morality. It is not identity which determines citizenship; rather, it is citizenship which creates (political) identity.

Notes

1. M. Walzer, *Spheres of Justice*, New York, Basic Books, 1983, p. 32.
2. I. Kant, 'Über den Gemeinspruch...', *Werkausgabe* XI, Wiesbaden, Suhrkamp, 1977, p. 151; see also *Metaphysik der Sitten,* W. Weischedel (ed.), *Immanuel Kant: Schriften zur Ethik ... Werkausgabe VIII*, Wiesbaden, Suhrkamp, 1977, pp. 432 f.
3. H. Arendt, *The Human Condition*, Chicago, University of Chicago Press, 1958, p. 198.
4. See S. Avineri and A. de-Shalit (eds), *Communitarianism and Individualism*, Oxford, Oxford University Press, 1992.
5. For the American case see T. L. Pangle, 'Civic Virtue: The Founders' conception and the traditional conception', in G. C. Bryner and N. B. Reynolds (eds), *Constitutionalism and Rights*, Provo, Utah, Brigham Young University, 1987, pp. 105–140.
6. *Ibid.*, p. 106.
7. J.-J. Rousseau, *The Social Contract*, Book IV, in M. Cranston (trans and intro), Harmondsworth, 1968, Ch. 8, p. 186.
8. *Ibid.*, Book I, ch. 6, pp. 61–62.
9. *Ibid.*, Book I, ch. 6, p. 61 in the footnote. The French version reads as follows: "ce nom [i.e., citoyen], chez eux, exprime une vertù, et non pas un droit". This makes it clearer than the English translation that citizenship does not designate a moral, but a legal status.
10. See B. A. Ackerman, *Social Justice in the Liberal State*, New Haven, Yale University Press, 1980, pp. 70–103.
11. See M. Sandel, 'The Procedural Republic and the Unencumbered Self', in Avineri and de-Shalit (eds), *Communitarianism and Individualism*, pp. 12–28; see also idem 'The Political Theory of the Procedural Republic', in Bryner and Reynolds (eds), *Constitutionalism and Rights*, pp. 141–153.
12. E. J. Sieyès, *What is the Third Estate?*, New York, Praeger, 1963, ch. 1, p. 58.
13. It should be noted here that this concept of the modern nation implies the concept of the nation state, because it is based on the rights of the individuals whose universalising and levelling allows neither the merely local or regional

validity of rights nor their unequal application. Hence the concept of equal national citizenship, which is characteristic of French history since the revolution of 1789, is incompatible with the idea of a stateless nation, which is widely held in Central and East European political discourses.

14. See D. Miller, *Market, State, and Community*, Oxford, Oxford University Press, 1989, pp. 227–51.

15. *Ibid.*, [quoted from Avineri and de-Shalit (eds)], p. 94.

16. See particularly Walzer's *Spheres of Justice*, pp. 65 ff.

17. This is a pivotal issue in Walzer's reasoning about membership, see his *Spheres of Justice*, pp. 65 ff.

18. See T. H. Marshall, *Class, Citizenship, and Social Development*, New York, Garden City, 1964, pp. 73 ff.

19. *Ibid.*, p. 74.

20. For the different kinds of connection of welfare rights with the concept of citizenship see R. E. Goodin, *Reasons for Welfare: The political theory of the welfare state*, Princeton, Princeton University Press, 1988, pp. 70–118.

21. F. Steward, 'Citizens of Planet Earth', in G. Andrews (ed.), *Citizenship*, London, Lawrence & Wishart, 1991, pp. 65–75 [74].

22. *Ibid.*, p. 65.

Chapter Nine

Competitive Party Democracy and the Keynesian Welfare State: Factors of Stability and Disorganisation*

Claus Offe

I. Introduction

If we compare 19th century liberal political theory on the one side and classical Marxism on the other, we see that there is one major point of agreement of the two. Both Marx and his liberal contemporaries, such as J.S. Mill or de Tocqueville, are convinced that, in their contemporary societies, capitalism and full democracy (based on equal and universal suffrage) do not mix. Obviously, this analytical convergence was arrived at from diametrically opposed points of view: the classical liberal writers believed that freedom and liberty were the most valuable accomplishments of societal development which deserved to be protected, under all circumstances, from the egalitarian threats of mass society and democratic mass politics, which, in their view, would lead, by necessity, to tyranny and 'class legislation' by the propertyless as well as uneducated majority.[1] Marx, on the other side, analysed the French democratic constitution of 1848 as a political form that would exacerbate societal contradictions by withdrawing political guarantees from the holder of social power while giving political power to subordinate classes; consequently, he argued, democratic conditions could bring the proletarian class to victory and put into question the foundations of bourgeois society.[2]

From the 20th century experience of capitalist societies, there is a lot of evidence against this 19th century hypothesis concerning the incompatibility of mass democracy (defined as universal and equal suffrage plus parliamentary or presidential form of government) and bourgeois freedom (defined as production based on private property and 'free' wage labour). The coexistence of the two is known as *liberal democracy*. To be sure, the emergence of fascist regimes in some of the core capitalist countries testifies to the continued existence of tensions and contradictions that prevail between the two models of economic organisation and political organisation, and to the possibility of the outbreak of such tensions under the impact of economic crises. But it is also true that most advanced capitalist countries have also been liberal democratic states throughout

* 'Competitive party democracy and the Keynesian welfare state: factors of stability and disorganization', *Policy Sciences*, 1983, vol. 15, no. 3, pp. 225–246.

most of the 20th century and that 'all major advanced bourgeois states are today democracies'.[3] In view of this evidence and experience, ours is in some way a *problematique* that is the reverse of what the classical writers of both liberalism and Marxism concerned themselves with. While they *prognosticised* the incompatibility, we have to *explain* the *coexistence* of the two partial principles of societal organisation. More precisely, we want to know (a) which institutional arrangements and mechanisms can be held responsible for the pattern of coexistence that proved to be solid beyond all 19th century expectations and (b) what, if any, the limits of such arrangements are. These limits, or failures of the working of mediating mechanisms, would be defined analytically as those points at which either capitalist societies turn non-democratic or democratic regimes turn non-capitalist. It is these two questions with which I will be concerned in this article. To put it schematically, the course of the argument starts from the problem of how we *explain* the compatibility[4] of the structural components of 'mass polity' and 'market economy', and then goes on to focus, on the level of each of these two structures, on the factors *contributing to* as well as those putting into question such compatibility. This is done in the sequence of boxes (1)-(4) of the following schema:

	Factors maintaining stability	Factors paralysing stability
Mode of democratic mass participation	(1)	(2)
Mode of economic steering (Keynesian Welfare State)	(3)	(4)

To pose this questions at all is to presuppose, in accordance with both Marx and Mill, that there *is* some real tension between the two respective organising principles of social power and political power, market society and political democracy, a tension that must be (and possibly cannot indefinitely be) bridged, mediated and stabilised. This is by no means an undisputed assumption. For instance, Lenin and the Leninist tradition deny that there is such tension. They assume, instead, that there is a prestabilised harmony of the rule of capital and bourgeois democratic forms, the latter mainly serving as a means of deception of the masses. Consequently, it does not make sense whatsoever to ask the question of what makes democracy compatible with capitalism and what the limits of such compatibility might be, because democracy is simply seen to be the most effective and reliable arrangement of capitalist class dominance. 'What is central to Lenin's position is the claim that the very organisational form of the parliamentary democratic state is essentially inimical to the interests of the working class', as one recent commentator has succinctly stated.[5] Plausible and convincing as this view can be taken to be if based on the constitutional practice of Russia between

1905 and 1917, its generalisation to the present would have, among other and still worse political consequences, the effect of grossly distorting and obscuring the very problematique which we want to discuss.[6]

The reciprocal distortion is the one promulgated by some ideologists of pluralist-elitist democratic theory. They claim (or, more precisely, they used to claim in the fifties and early sixties) that the tension between the principles governing capitalist market society and political democratic forms had finally been eliminated in the American political system. According to this doctrine, the class struggle on the level of bourgeois society has been replaced by what Lipset calls 'the democratic class struggle' which is seen to make all social arrangements, including the mode of production and the distribution of economic resources, contingent upon the outcomes of democratic mass politics. The underlying logic of this analysis can be summarised in an argument like this: 'If people actually wanted things to be different, they simply would elect someone other into office. The fact that they don't, consequently, is proof that people are satisfied with the socio-political order as it exists'. Hence, we get something like the inverse of the Leninist doctrine: democracy is not tied to capitalism, but capitalism to democracy. Both of these perspectives deny major tensions or incompatibilities between mass democracy and the market economy.

Thus, both the Leninist and the pluralist-elitist conceptions of democracy are missing the point that interests us here. The one dogmatically postulates total *dependence* of democratic forms and procedures upon class power, while the other equally dogmatically postulates total *independence* of class and democratically constituted political power. The question that is at the same time more modest and more promising in leading to insights of both intellectual and practical significance is, however, this: which institutions and mechanism regulate the *extent* to which the two can become incongruent in a given society, and what are the *limits* of such potential incongruity, – limits, that is, which would constrain the range of potential variance of class power and democratically constituted political authority?

Marketisation of politics and politicisation of the private economy

In what follows, I will argue that the continued compatibility of capitalism and democracy that was so inconceivable to both classical liberalism and classical Marxism (including Kautsky and the Second International) has historically emerged due to the appearance and gradual developments of two mediating principles, (a) political mass parties and party competition and (b) the Keynesian welfare state (KWS). In other words, it is a *specific version* of democracy, political equality and mass participation that is compatible with the capitalist market economy. And, correspondingly, it is a *specific type* of capitalism that is able to coexist with democracy. What interests us here are those specificities of the political and economic structures, the way in which their mutual 'fit' is to be explained by the functions each of them performs, and furthermore the strains and tensions that affect those conditions of 'fit.'

Historically, each of those two structural components of 'democratic capitalism' has largely taken shape in Europe either during or in the aftermath of the two World Wars; democracy through party competition after World War I and the Keynesian welfare state after World War II. Each of these two principles follow a pattern of 'mixing' the logic of authority and the logic of the market, of 'voice' and 'exit' in Hirschman's terminology. This is quite obvious in the case of the Keynesian welfare state for which the term 'mixed economy' is often used as a synonym. But it is no less true for the political sphere of capitalist society which could well be described as a 'mixed polity' and the dynamics of which are often, and to a certain extent appropriately, described as the 'oligopolistic competition' of political elites or political 'entrepreneurs' providing public 'goods'.[7] The logic of capitalist democracy is one of mutual contamination: authority is infused into the economy by global demand management, transfers and regulations so that it loses more and more of its spontaneous and self-regulatory character; and market contingency is introduced into the state, thus compromising any notion of absolute authority or the absolute good. Neither the Smithean conception of the market nor the Rousseauan conception of politics have much of a counterpart in social reality. Thus, one of the ways in which compatibility is accomplished appears to be the infusion of some of the logic of one realm into the other, i.e., the notion of 'competition' into politics and the idea of 'authoritative allocation of values' into the economy.

Let us now consider each of the two links, or mediating mechanisms, between state and civil society in turn. Following the problematique developed before, we will ask two questions in each case. First, in what way and by virtue of which structural characteristics do political parties and the Keynesian welfare state *contribute to the compatibility of* capitalism and democratic mass politics. Second, which observable trends and changes occur within the institutional framework of both the 'mixed economy' and the 'mixed polity' that *threaten the viability* of the coexistence of capitalism and democracy?

II. Stabilisation through competitive party democracy

The widespread fear of the German bourgeoisie during the first decade of this century was that once the full and equal franchise was introduced together with parliamentary government, the class power of the working class would, due to the numerical strength of this class, directly translate into a revolutionary transformation of the state. It was the same analysis, of course, that inspired the hopes and the political strategies of the leaders of the Second International. Max Weber had nothing but sarcastic contempt for both these neurotic anxieties and naive hopes. He was (together with Rosa Luxemburg and Robert Michels who conducted the same analysis with their own specific accents) among the first social theorists who understood (and welcomed) the fact that the transformation of class politics into competitive party politics implies not only a change of form, but a decisive change of content. In 1917, he stated that 'amongst us, organisations like the trade unions, but also like the social democratic party, are a very important counterweight against the typically real and irrational power of street mobs in purely plebiscitary nations'.[8] He expected that the bureaucratised political party, together with the charismatic and demagogic political leader at its top, would form a reliable bulwark to contain what he described as 'blind mass rage' or 'syndicalist insurrectionary tendencies'.

Rosa Luxemburg's account of the dynamic of political mass organisation differs only in its inverse evaluative perspective, not its analytical content. In 1906, she observed the tendency of working class organisations (i.e., unions and the party) to follow specialised strategies according to a tacit division of labour and of the organisations' leadership to dominate rather than serve the masses of the constituency. The tendency of the organisations' bureaucratic staff consists, according to Luxemburg, in a 'great trend of rendering itself independent', 'of specialising their methods of struggle and professional activity', 'of overestimating the organisation which becomes transformed into an end in itself and the highest good', 'a need for rest', 'a loss of general view of the overall situation', while at the same time 'the mass of comrades are being degraded into a mass which is incapable of forming a judgment'.[9] Biographically, politically and intellectually, Robert Michels absorbs and integrates the ideas of both Luxemburg and Weber by formulating, in 1911, his famous 'iron law of oligarchy' in which the observation of empirical tendencies of organisations is transformed in the proclamation of an inexorable historical necessity.[10]

It is probably not too much to say that the 20th century theory of political organisation has been formed on the basis of the experience and the theoretical interpretation of these three authors who, interestingly enough, arrived at widely divergent political positions at the end of their lives: Luxemburg died in 1919 as a revolutionary democratic socialist and victim of police murder, Weber in the same year as a 'liberal in despair,' and Michels in 1936 as an ardent admirer and ideological defender of Mussolini and Italian fascism. In spite of the extreme diversity of their political views and positions, there is a strong common element in their analysis. This element can be summarised in the following way: as soon as political mass participation is organised through large scale bureaucratic organisation (a type of organisation, that is, which is presupposed and required by the model of electoral party competition and institutionalised collective bargaining), the very dynamic of this organisational form contains, perverts, and obstructs class interest and class politics in ways that are described as leading to opportunism (Luxemburg), oligarchy (Michels) and the inescapable plebiscitarian submission of the masses to the irrational impulses of the charismatic leader and his demagogic use of the bureaucratic party 'machine' (Weber).

According to the common insight underlying this analysis, as soon as the will of the people is expressed through the instrumentality of the competitive party striving for government office, what *is* expressed *ceases* to be the will of the people and is instead transformed into an artefact of the form itself and the dynamics put into motion by the imperatives of political competition.

More specifically, these dynamics have three major effects. First, the deradicalisation of the ideology of the party: to be successful in elections and in its striving for government office, the party must orient its programmatic stance towards the expediencies of the political market.[11] This means two things: first, to maximise votes by appealing to the greatest possible number of voters and consequently to minimise those programmatic elements that could create antagonistic cleavages within the electorate. Second, vis-à-vis other parties, to be prepared to enter coalitions and to restrict the range of substantive policy proposals to those demands which can be expected to be negotiable to potential coalition partners. The combined effect of these two considerations is to dissolve any coherent political concept or aim into a 'gradualist' temporal structure or sequence, giving priority to what can be implemented at any given point in time and with the presently available resources, while postponing and displacing presently unrealistic and pragmatically unfeasible demands and projects. Also, the fully developed competitive party is forced by the imperatives of competition to equip itself with a highly bureaucratised and centralised organisational structure. The objective of this organisation is to be present continuously on the political market, just as the success of a business firm depends in part upon the size and continued presence of its marketing and sales organisation. The bureaucratic organisation of the modern political party performs the tasks of (a) collecting material and human resources (membership dues, other contributions and donations, members, candidates), (b) disseminating propaganda and information concerning the party's position on a great number of diverse political issues and (c) exploring the political market, identifying new issues and monitoring public opinion and (d) managing internal conflict. All of these activities are normally executed by a professional staff of party officials who develop a corporate interest in the growth and stability of the apparatus that provides them with status and careers. This pattern of internal bureaucratisation that can be found in parties of the right and the left alike, has two important traits. First, the social composition (as measured by class background, formal education, sex, occupation, age, etc.) of the party leadership, its officials, members of parliament, and government becomes more and more at variance both with the social composition of the population in general and the party's electoral base in particular. And second, the professionalisation of party politics leads to the political dominance of professional and managerial party personnel who typically come, by their training and professional experience, from such backgrounds as business administration, public administration, education, the media, or interest organisations.

A second major consequence of this bureaucratic-professional pattern of political organisation is the deactivation of ordinary members. The more the organisation is geared toward the exploration of and adaptation to the external *environment* of the political market in what can be described as a virtually permanent electoral campaign, the less room remains for the determination of party policies by *internal* processes of democratic debate and conflict within the organisation. The appearance of internal unanimity and consensus is what any competitive party must try to cultivate in order to become or remain attractive to voters, as a consequence of which internal division, factionalism and organised conflict of opinion and strategy are not only not encouraged, but rather kept under tight control or at least kept out of sight of the public in a constant effort to streamline the party's image and, as it were, to standardise its product. (It is tempting to compare, in this respect, the *practise* of some social democratic parties to the *theory* of the Leninist party, and I suspect we would find some ironic similarities.) The highly unequal importance of external and internal environments frequently becomes evident when the results of public opinion surveys, which today are routinely commissioned by the party leadership, suggest positions and strategies which are in conflict with declared intentions of party members who then, in the interest of 'winning the next elections', are called upon to yield to political 'reality'.

The third characteristic of what Kirchheimer has called the modern 'catch-all-party' is the increasing structural and cultural heterogeneity of its supporters. This heterogeneity results from the fact that the modern political party relies on the principle of 'product diversification' in the sense that it tries to appeal to a multitude of diverse demands and concerns. This is most obvious in the case of social democratic and communist parties who have often successfully tried to expand their base beyond the working class and to attract elements of the old and new middle classes, the intelligentsia and voters with strong religious affiliations. The advantage of this strategy is quite obvious, but so is its effect of dissolving a sense of collective identity which, in the early states of both socialist and Catholic parties, was based on a cultural milieu of shared values and meaning.

It is easy to see why and how the three consequences of the organisational form of the competitive political party that I have discussed so far – ideological deradicalisation, deactivation of members, erosion of collective identity – contribute to the compatibility of capitalism and democracy. Each of these three outcomes helps to contain and limit the range of political aims and struggles, and thus provides a virtual guarantee that the structure of political power will not deviate so far from the structure of socio-economic power as to make the two distributions of power incompatible with each other. 'The party system has been the means of reconciling universal equal franchise with the maintenance of an unequal society', McPherson has remarked.[12] The inherent dynamic of the party as an organisational form which develops under and for political competition generates those constraints and imposes those 'non-decisions' upon the political process which together make democracy safe for capitalism. Such 'non-decisions' affect both the *content* of politics (i.e., what kinds of issues, claims, and demands are allowed to be put on the agenda) as well as the *means* by which political conflicts are carried out. The constraints imposed upon the possible content of politics are all the more effective since they are non-explicit, i.e., not based on formal mechanisms of exclusion (such as limitations of voting rights, or authoritarian bans on certain actors or issues), but rather constituted as artefacts and by-products of the organisational forms of universal political inclusion. This conclusion, of course, is strongly supported by the fact that no competitive party system so far has ever resulted in a distribution of political power that would have been able to alter the logic of capital and the pattern of socio-economic power it generates.

To avoid misunderstanding, I should emphasise that what I intend here is not a *normative* critique of the organisational form of the political party which would lead to the suggestion of an alternative form of political organisation. Rather than speculating about the comparative desirability of anarchist, syndicalist, council-democratic, or Leninist models of either non-party or non-competitive party organisation, let us now look at the future viability of this organisational form itself – its potential to construct and mediate, as it did in the post-war era, a type of political authority that does not interfere with the institutional premises of the capitalist economy. The question is, in other words, whether the institutional link that in most advanced capitalist countries has allowed capitalism and political democracy to coexist for most of the last 60 years is likely to continue to do so in the future. How solid and viable are the organisational forms that bring the 'iron law' to bear upon the process of politics?

One way to answer this question in the negative would be to expect political parties to emerge which would be capable of abolishing the above-mentioned restrictions and constraints, thus leading to a challenge of class power through politically constituted power. I do not think that there are, in spite of Eurocommunist doctrines and strategies that have emerged in the Latin-European countries in the mid-seventies, and in spite of the recently elected socialist communist government in France, many promising indicators of such a development. The other possibility would be a *disintegration of the political party as the dominant form of democratic mass participation* and its gradual replacement by other forms which possibly are less likely than party competition to lead to 'congruent' uses of state power. As we are concerned with the prospects of competitive party democracy in the eighties, it might be worthwhile to explore this possibility a little further.

Causes of the decline of the party system as the dominant form of mass participation

It is well possible today to argue that the form of mass participation in politics that is channelled through the party system (i.e., according to the principles of territorial representation, party competition and parliamentary representation), has exhausted much of its usefulness for reconciling capitalism and mass politics. This appears to be so because the political form of the party is increasingly bypassed and displaced by other practices and procedures of political participation and representation. It is highly doubtful, however, whether those new and additional practices that can be observed in operation in quite a number of capitalist states will exhibit the same potential of reconciling political legitimation with the imperatives of capital accumulation that has been, at least for a certain period, the accomplishment of the competitive party system. Again, three points – referring in a highly schematic fashion to new social movements, corporatism and repression as phenomena – tend to bypass, restrict, and subvert the party system and its political practices and their reconciling potential.

First, in many capitalist countries, the new social movements which have emerged during the seventies are, for a number of reasons, very hard to absorb into the practices of competitive party politics. Such movements include ethnic and regionalist movements, various urban movements, ecological movements, feminist movements, peace movements, and youth movements. To a large extent, all of them share two characteristics. First, their projects and demands are based not on a collective contractual position on either goods or labour markets, as was the case, for instance, with traditional class parties and movements. Instead, their common denominator of organisation and action is some sense of collective identity (often underlined by ascriptive and 'naturalistic' conceptions of the collective 'self' in terms of age, gender, 'nation' or 'mankind'). Closely connected with this is a second characteristic: they do not demand representation (by which their market status could be improved or protected) but, autonomy. In short, the underlying logic of these movements is the struggle for the defence of a physical and/ or moral 'territory', the integrity of which is fundamentally non-negotiable to the activists of these movements. For the purpose of this defence, political representation and parliamentary politics are often considered unnecessary (because what is requested of the state, as can be illustrated in the issues of abortion or nuclear energy, is not to 'do something' but to 'stay out'), or even dangerous, because the state is suspected of attempting to demobilise and disorganise the movement. To the extent such movements attract the attention and the political energies of people, not only individual political parties, but the traditional competitive party system as a whole will lose in function and credibility because it simply does not provide the arena within which such issues and concerns can possibly be processed. These 'new social movements' are not concerned with what is to be created or accomplished through the use of politics and state power, but what should be saved from and defended against the state, and the considerations governing the conduct of public policy. The three most obvious cases of such movements, the peace movement, the environmental movement and various movements centred on human rights (e.g., of women, of prisoners, of minorities, of tenants) all illustrate a 'negative' conception of politics trying to protect a sphere of life against the intervention of state (or state-sanctioned) policy. What dominates the thought and action of these movements is not a 'progressive' Utopia of what desirable social arrangements must be achieved, but a conservative Utopia of what non-negotiable essentials must not be threatened and sacrificed in the name of 'progress'.

Second, many observers in a number of capitalist states have analysed an ongoing process of deparliamentarisation of public policy and the concomitant displacement of territorial forms of representation through functional ones. This is most evident in 'corporatist' arrangements which combine the function of interest representation of collective actors with policy implementation vis-à-vis their respective constituencies.[13] The functional superiority of such corporatist arrangements, compared to both parliamentary-competitive forms of representation and bureaucratic methods of implementation, resides in their informal, inconspicuous, and non-public procedures and the 'voluntary' character of compliance that they are said to be able to mobilise. Although the dynamics and limits of corporatist forms of public policy making, especially in the areas of economic and social policies, are not of interest to us here, what seems to be clear is that there has been a trend toward such arrangements, most of all in countries with strong social democratic parties (such as in Europe, Sweden, the UK, Austria, and Germany) which has worked at the expense of parliament and the competitive party system. A number of Marxist and non-Marxist political scientists have even argued that 'parliamentary representation on the basis of residence no longer adequately reflects the problems of economic management in a worldwide capitalist system', and that 'a system of functional representation is more suited to securing the conditions of accumulation'.[14]

Third, a constant alternative to free party competition is political repression and the gradual transformation of democracy into some form of authoritarianism. In an analytical sense, what we mean by repression is exclusion from representation. Citizens are denied their civil liberties and freedoms, such as the right to organise, demonstrate, and express certain opinions in speech and writing. They are denied access to occupations in the public sector, and the like. The expansion of police apparatuses and the practice of virtually universal monitoring and surveillance of the activities of citizens that we observe in many countries are indications of the growing reliance of the state apparatus upon the means of preventive and corrective repression. More importantly, in our context of discussing the limits of competitive party democracy, is one other aspect of the exclusion from representation. It is the de facto and/ or formal limitation of competitiveness within the party system: be it by strengthening of intra-party discipline and the sanctions applied against dissenters; be it in the election campaigns from which substantive alternatives concerning the conduct and programmatic content of public policy often seem to be absent; be it, finally, on the level of parliament and parliamentary government where the identity of individual (and only nominally 'competing') parties more and more often disappears behind what occasionally is called the 'great coalition of the enlightened', inspired by some vague 'solidarity of all democratic forces'. Referring back to the economic metaphor used before, such phenomena and developments could well be described as the 'cartelisation' of political supply and the closure of market access.

If I am correct in assuming that the displacement of the role and political function of the competitive party system, as indicated by the emergence of new social movements, increasing reliance on corporatist arrangements, and self-limitation of the competitiveness of party systems is a real process that could be illustrated by many examples in numerous advanced (and not so advanced) capitalist states; and if I am also correct in assuming that the organisational form of the competitive political party plays a crucial role in making democratic mass participation compatible with capitalism, then the decline of the party system is likely to lead to the rise of less constrained and regulated practices of political participation and conflict, the outcomes of which may then have the potential of effectively challenging and transcending the institutional premises of the capitalist form of social and economic organisation.

I have so far focused only on those limits of the 'reconciling functions' of the organisational forms of mass democracy which consists in the weakening and, more or less, gradual displacement of the dominant role of political parties as mediators between the people and state power. But the picture remains incomplete and unbalanced as long as we concentrate exclusively on cases in which the 'channel' of political participation that consists of party competition, elections and parliamentary representation is bypassed (and reduced in its legitimacy and credibility) by the protest politics of social movements or corporatist negotiations among powerful strategic actors, or where this channel is altogether reduced in significance by 'repressive' mechanisms of exclusion.

The other alternative, alluded to before, consists not in a process of displacement and loss of relevance of the organisational form of political parties, but in the successful strategy of 'self-transcendence' of the party moving from 'political' to 'economic' democracy. All models and strategies of *economic* democratisation (beginning in the mid-twenties in Austria and Germany and continuing through the current Swedish concepts of wage earner funds and the Meidner plan[15] rely on the notion that the tension between the democratic principle of equal mass participation and the economic principle of unequal and private decision making power could be put to use by instituting, by the means of electoral success and parliamentary legislation, democratic bodies on the level of enterprises, sectors of industry, regions, cities, and so on. The central assumption that inspires such strategies is that

> democracy would explode capitalism (and) that the democratic state, because it could be made to represent the people, would compel entrepreneurs to proceed according to principles inimical to their own survival... The working class, as the spokesmen for the great, non-capitalist majority, would enforce the primacy of politics throughout the economy, as well as in politics *per se*.[16]

Although this alternative course of suspending the compatibility of democracy and capitalism is part of the programmatic objectives of almost all social democratic/socialist (and, increasingly, communist) parties in Europe (and even of some forces in North America), it has nowhere been carried out to the point where the private character of decisions concerning the volume, kind, point in time and location of investment decisions would have effectively been transformed into a matter of democratic control. In the early eighties, the European Left seems rather to be divided as to the strategic alternatives of trying to overcome the constraints of political democracy and its oligarchic organisational dynamics, either by supporting those 'new social movements' and engaging in their politics of autonomy and protest, or to stick to the older model of economic democratisation. Both tendencies, however, provide sufficient reason to expect a weakening of these organisational and political characteristics which so far have made democratic mass participation safe for capitalism. The extent, however, to which it becomes likely that competitive party democracy is either displaced by social and political movements and corporatist arrangements or is complemented by 'economic democracy', will probably depend on the stability, growth and prosperity the economy is able to provide. Let us, therefore, now turn to the question of the organisation of production and distribution and the changes that have occurred since Andrew Shonfield's classic *Modern Capitalism* came out in 1965.[17]

III. The Keynesian welfare state and its demise

Let me now try to apply the analogous argument, in an even more generalised and schematic fashion, to the second pillar upon which, according to my initial proposition, the coexistence of capitalism and democracy rests, namely the Keynesian welfare state (KWS). The bundle of state institutions and practices to which this concept refers has been developed in western capitalism since the Second World War. Until the decisive change of circumstances that occurred after the mid-seventies and that was marked by OPEC price policies, the end of *détente,* and the coming to power of Thatcher in the UK and Reagan in the US (to mention just a few indicators of this change), the KWS has been adopted as the basic conception of the state and state practice in almost all western countries, irrespective of parties in government, and with only minor modifications and time lags. Most observers agree that its effect has been (a) an unprecedented and extended economic boom favouring all advanced capitalist economies and (b) the transformation of the pattern of industrial and class conflict in ways that increasingly depart from political and even revolutionary radicalism and lead to more economistic, distribution-centred and increasingly institutionalised class conflict. Underlying this development (that constitutes a formidable change if compared to the dynamics of the capitalist world system during the twenties and thirties) is a politically instituted class compromise or 'accord' that Bowles has described as follows:

> [The accord] represented, on the part of labour, the acceptance of the logic of profitability and markets as the guiding principles of resource allocation, international exchange, technological change, product development, and industrial location, in return for an assurance that minimal living standards, trade union rights, and liberal democratic rights would be protected, massive unemployment avoided, and real incomes would rise approximately in line with labour productivity, all through the intervention of the state, if necessary.[18]

It is easy to see why and how the existence of this compact has contributed to the compatibility of capitalism and democracy. First, by accepting the terms of the accord, working class organisations (unions and political parties) reduced their demands and projects to a program that sharply differs from anything on the agenda of both the Third and the Second Internationals. After the physical, moral and organisational devastations the Second World War had left behind, and after the discredit the development of the Soviet Union had earned for communism, this change of perspective is not entirely incomprehensible. Moreover, the accord itself worked amazingly well, thus reinforcing a deeply depoliticised trust in what one leading German Social Democrat much later came arrogantly to call the 'German

Model' (*Modell Deutschland*):[19] the mutual stimulation of economic growth and peaceful class relations. What was at issue in class conflicts was no longer the mode of production, but the volume of distribution, not control but growth, and this type of conflict was particularly suited for being processed on the political plane through party competition, because it does not involve 'either/or' questions, but questions of a 'more or less' or 'sooner or later' nature. Overarching this limited type of conflict, there was a consensus concerning basic priorities, desirabilities and values of the political economy, namely economic growth and social (as well as military) security. This interclass, growth-security alliance does in fact have a theoretical basis in Keynes' economic theory. As applied to practical purposes of economic policy making, it teaches each class to 'take the role of the other'. The capitalist economy, this is the lesson to be learnt from Keynesianism, is a positive-sum game. Therefore, playing like one would in a zero-sum game is against one's own interest. That is to say, each class has to take the interests of the other class into consideration: the workers profitability, because only a sufficient level of profits and investment will secure future employment and income increases; and the capitalists wages and welfare state expenditures, because these will secure effective demand and a healthy, well-trained, and well-housed working class.

The welfare state is defined as a set of legal entitlements providing citizens with claims to transfer payments from compulsory social security schemes, as well as to state organised services (such as health and education) for a wide variety of defined cases of need and contingencies. The means by which the welfare state intervenes are thus bureaucratic rules and legal regulations, monetary transfers and the professional expertise of teachers, doctors, and social workers. Its ideological origins are highly mixed and heterogeneous, ranging from socialist to Catholic-conservative sources; its character resulting from ideological, political and economic interclass compromises is something the welfare state shares with the logic of Keynesian economic policy making. In both cases, there is no fast and easy answer to the zero-sum question of who wins and who loses. For, although the primary function of the welfare state is to cover those risks and uncertainties to which wage workers and their families are exposed in capitalist society, there are some indirect effects which serve the capitalist class, too.

This becomes evident if we look at what would be likely to happen in the absence of welfare state arrangements in a capitalist society. We would probably agree that the answer to this hypothetical question is this: first, there would be a much higher level of industrial conflict and a stronger tendency among the proletariat to avoid becoming wage workers. Thus, the welfare state can be said to partially dispel motives and reasons for social conflict and to make the existence of wage labour more acceptable by eliminating parts of the risk that result from the imposition of the commodity form upon labour.[20] Second, this conflict would be much more costly in economic terms by its disruption of the increasingly complex and capital-intensive process of industrial production. Therefore, the welfare state performs the crucial function of taking part of the needs of the working class out of the class struggle and industrial conflict arenas, of providing the means to fulfill their needs more collectively and hence more efficiently, of making production more regular and predictable by relieving it of important issues and conflicts, and of providing, in addition, a built-in stabiliser for the economy by partly uncoupling changes in effective demand from changes in employment. So, as in the case of Keynesian doctrines of economic policy, the welfare state, too, can be seen to provide a measure of mutuality of interest between classes that virtually leaves no room for fundamental issues and conflicts over the nature of the political economy.

The functional links between Keynesian economic policy, economic growth and the welfare state are fairly obvious and agreed upon by all 'partners' and parties involved. An 'active' economic policy stimulates and regularises economic growth; the 'tax dividend' resulting from that growth allows for the extension of welfare state programmes; at the same time, continued economic growth limits the extent to which welfare state provisions (such as unemployment benefits) are actually claimed. And the issues and conflicts that remain to be resolved within the realm of formal politics (party competition and parliament) are of such a fragmented, non-polarising, and non-fundamental nature (at least in the areas of economic and social policy) that they can be settled by the inconspicuous mechanisms of marginal adjustments, compromise and coalition-building.

If all of this were still true, today's ubiquitous critiques and political attacks directed at Keynesianism, the welfare state and, most of all, the combination of these two most successful political innovations of the post-war era, would be plainly incomprehensible. They are not. As in the case of competitive political parties, these innovations and their healthy effects seem to have reached their limits today. While the integrative functions of the party system have partly been displaced by alternative and less institutionalised forms of political participation, the Keynesian welfare state has come under attack by virtue of some of its less desirable side effects and its failure to correct some of the ills of an economic environment that has radically changed, compared to the conditions that prevailed prior to the mid-seventies. Let us look at some of the reasons why there are very few people remaining – be they in academia or politics, on the Left or the Right who believe that the Keynesian welfare state continues to be a viable peace formula for democratic capitalism.

My thesis, in brief, is this: while the KWS is an excellent and uniquely effective device to manage and control some socioeconomic and political problems of advanced capitalist societies, it does not solve all those problems. And the problems that can be successfully solved through the institutional means of the welfare state no longer constitute the most dominant and pressing ones. Moreover, this shift of *the socioeconomic* problematique *is in part an unintended consequence of the operation of the KWS itself.* The two types of problems to which I refer, are the production/exploitation problem and the effective demand/ realisation problem. Between the two, a trade-off exists: the more effectively one of the two is solved, the more dominant and pressing the other one becomes. The KWS has indeed been able to solve, to a remarkable extent, the problem of macroeconomic demand stabilisation. But, at the same time, it has also interfered with the ability of the capitalist economy to adapt to the production/exploitation problem as it has emerged ever more urgently since the mid-seventies. The KWS, so to speak, has operated on the basis of the false theory that the problems it *is* able to deal with are the only problems of the capitalist political economy, or at least the permanently dominant ones. This erroneous confidence is now in the politically and economically, equally painful process of being falsified and corrected.

To the extent the demand problem is being solved, the supply problem becomes wide open. The economic situation has changed in a way that lends strong support to conservative and *neo-laissez-faire* economic theory. Far from stimulating production any longer, the governmental practice of deficit spending to combat unemployment contributes to even higher rates of unemployment, by driving up interest rates and making money capital scarce and costly. Also (and possibly even worse), the welfare state amounts to a partial disincentive to work. Its compulsory insurance schemes and legal entitlements provide such a strong institutional protection to the material interest of wage workers that labour becomes less prepared and/or can be less easily forced to adjust to the contingencies of structural, technological, locational, vocational and other changes of the economy. Not only wages are 'sticky' and 'downwardly inflexible', but, in addition, the provisions of the welfare state have partly 'decommodified' the interests of workers, replacing 'status' for 'contract', or 'citizen rights' for 'property rights'. This change of industrial relations that the KWS has brought about, has not only helped to increase and stabilise effective demand (as it was intended to), but it also has made employment more costly and more rigid. Again, the central problem on the labour market is the supply problem, how to hire and fire the right people at the right place with the right skills and, most important, the right motivation and the right wage demand. Concerning this problem, the welfare state is justifiably seen by business not to be part of the solution, but part of the problem.

As capital (small as well as big) has come to depend and rely on the stimulating and regularising effects of interventionist policies executed on both the demand and supply sides, and as labour depends and relies on the welfare state, the parameters of incentives, motivations, and expectations of investors and workers alike have been affected in ways that alter and undermine the dynamics of economic growth. For capital and labour alike, pressures to adjust to changing market forces have been reduced due to the availability of state-provided resources that either help to avoid or delay adaptation, or due to the expectation that a large part of the costs of adaptation must be subsidised by the state. Growth industries such as defence, civilian aircraft, nuclear energy, and telecommunications typically depend as much on markets created by the state (and often capital provided by the state) as stagnant industries (such as steel, textiles, and, increasingly, electronics) depend on state protection and subsidised market shelters. Economic growth, where it occurs at all, has become a matter of political design rather than a matter of spontaneous market forces.

The increasing claims that are made on the state budget both by labour and capital, and both by the growing and the stagnant sectors of the economy, cannot but lead to unprecedented levels of public debt and to constant efforts of governments to terminate or reduce welfare state programmes. But economic growth does not only become more costly in terms of budgetary inputs that are required to promote it, it also becomes more costly in terms of political legitimation. The more economic growth becomes 'growth by political design', and the more it is perceived to be the result of explicit political decisions and strategies of an increasingly 'disaggregated' nature (i.e., specified by product, industry, and location), the more governments and political parties are held accountable for the physical quality of products, processes and environmental effects resulting from such industrial policies. The widespread and apparently increasing concern with the physical quality of products and production, and the various 'anti-productivist' and environmentalist political motives and demands that are spreading in many capitalist countries have, so far, mostly been interpreted in the social science literature either in objectivist terms ('environmental disruption') or in subjectivist categories ('changing values and sensitivities'). In addition, I suggest, these phenomena must be analysed in terms of the apparent political manageability of the physical shape and impact of industrial production and growth, a perceived area of political decision- and non-decision making that gives rise to a new arena of 'politics of production'. The outcomes of the conflicts in this arena, in turn, tend to cause additional impediments to industrial growth.

The strategic intention of Keynesian economic policy is to promote growth and full employment, the strategic intention of the welfare state to protect those affected by the risks and contingencies of industrial society and to create a measure of social equality. The latter strategy becomes feasible only to the extent the first is successful, thus providing the resources necessary for welfare policies and limiting the extent to which claims are made on these resources.

The combined effect of the two strategies, however, has been high rates of unemployment *and* inflation. At least, economic and social policies have not been able to check the simultaneous occurrence of unemployment and inflation. But one can safely say more than that. Plausible causal links between the KWS and today's condition of 'the worst of both worlds' are suggested not only by conservative economic policy ideologues advocating a return to some type of monetarist steering of a pure market economy. They are equally, if reluctantly, accepted by the practice and partly by the theories of the Left. The relevant arguments are:

1. The Keynesian welfare state is a victim of its success. By (partly) eliminating and smoothening crises, it has inhibited the positive function that crises used to perform in the capitalist process of 'creative destruction'.

2. The Keynesian welfare state involves the unintended but undeniable consequence of undermining both the incentives to invest and the incentives to work.

3. There is no equilibrating mechanism or 'stop-rule' that would allow us to adjust the extension of social policy so as to eliminate its self-contradictory consequences; the logic of democratic party competition and the social democratic alliance with unions remains undisciplined by 'economic reason'.

While the latter argument is probably still exclusively to be found in the writings of liberal-conservative authors,[21] the other two can hardly be contested by the Left. Let me quote just one example of an author who clearly thinks of himself as a social democratic theoretician:

> It is unfortunate that those wish to defend the welfare state... spend their energies persuading the public that the welfare state does not erode incentives, savings, authority or efficiency... What the Right has recognised much better than the Left is that the principles of the welfare state are directly incompatible with a capitalistic market system. ... The welfare state eats the very hand that feeds it. The main contradiction of the welfare state is the ... tension between the market and social policy.[22]

It must not concern us here whether such blames and charges that today are ever more frequently directed against the KWS are entirely 'true', or, in addition, partly the result of paranoic exaggerations or a conscious tactical misrepresentation of reality on the part of capital and its political organisations. For what applies in this context is a special version of a law known to sociologists as the 'Thomas theorem': what is real in the minds and perceptions of people will be real in its consequences. The structural power position of the owners and managers and associational representatives of capital in a capitalist society is exactly their power to define reality in a highly consequential way, so that what is perceived as 'real' by them is likely to have very real impacts for other classes and political actors.

Without entering too far into the professional realm of the economist, let me suggest two aspects of a potentially useful (if partial) interpretation of this change. One is the idea that the Keynesian welfare state is a 'victim of its success', as one author has put it:[23] the side-effects of its successful practice of solving one type of macro-economic problems have lead to the emergence of an entirely different problematique which is beyond the steering capacity of the KWS. The familiar arguments that favour and demand a shift of economic and social policy making toward what has been named 'supply-side economics' are these: the nonproductive public sector has become an intolerable burden upon the private sector, leading to a chronic shortage of investment capital; the work ethic is in the process of being undermined, and the independent middle class is being economically suffocated by high rates of taxation and inflation.

The other set of arguments maintains that, even in the absence of those economic side effects, the political paradigm of the KWS presently is in the process of definitive exhaustion due to inherent causes. The relevant arguments, in brief, are two. First, state intervention works only as long as it is not expected by economic actors to be applied as a matter of routine, and therefore does not enter their rational calculations. As soon as this happens, however, investors will postpone investment because they can be reasonably sure that the state, if only they wait long enough, will intervene by special tax exemptions, depreciation allowances or demand measures. The spread of such ('rational') expectations is fatal to Keynesianism, for to the extent it enters the calculations of economic actors, their strategic behaviour will increase the problem load to which the state has to respond or at least will not contribute, in the way it had been naively anticipated, to resolving the unemployment (and state budget) problem. This pathology of expectations, of course, is itself known to (and expected by) actors in the state apparatus. It forces them to react either by ever higher doses of intervention or, failing that possibility for fiscal reasons, to give up the interventionist practice that breeds those very problems that it was supposed to solve. This would lead us to conclude that state intervention is effective only to the extent it occurs as a 'surprise' and exception, rather than as a matter of routine.

A further inherent weakness of the KWS resides in the limits of the legal-bureaucratic, monetarised and professional mode of intervention. These limits become particularly clear in the areas of personal services, or 'people processing organisations', such as schools, hospitals, universities, prisons and social work agencies. Again, the mode of intervention generates the problems it is supposed to deal with. The explanation of this paradox is well-known: the clients' capacity for self-help – and, more generally, the system of knowledge and meaning generating such capacity – are subverted by the mode of intervention, and the suppliers of such services, especially professionals and higher level bureaucrats (who are in neo-conservative circles referred to as the 'new class'), take a material interest in the persistence (rather than the solution) and in the continuous expansion and redefinition of the problems with which they are supposed to deal.[24]

Thus, for reasons that have to do both with its external economic effects and the paradoxes of its internal model of operation, the KWS seems to have exhausted its potential and viability to a large extent. Moreover, this exhaustion is unlikely to turn out to be a conjunctural phenomenon that disappears with the next boom of economic growth. For this boom itself is far from certain. Why is this so? First, because it cannot be expected to occur as the spontaneous result of market forces and the dynamics of technological innovation. Second, it apparently cannot be generated and manipulated either by the traditional tools of Keynesianism nor by its 'monetarist' counterpart. Third, even to the extent it does occur either as an effect of spontaneous forces or state intervention, the question is whether it will be considered desirable and worthwhile in terms of the side-effects it inevitably will have for the 'quality of life' in general and the ecology in particular. This question of the desirability of continued economic growth is also accentuated by what Fred Hirsch has called the 'social limits to growth' and by which he means the decreasing desirability and 'satisficing potential' of industrial output, the use-value of which declines in proportion to the number of people who consume it.

IV. Conclusion

We have seen that the two institutional mechanisms on which the compatibility of the private economy and political mass participation rests – namely the mechanism of competitive party democracy and the paradigm of the Keynesian welfare state – have come under stress and strain, the order of magnitude of which is unprecedented in the post-war era. Limitations of space do not allow me to explore in any detail the interactive and possibly mutually reinforcing dynamics that take place between the two structural developments that I have sketched here.

One plausible hypothesis is that, as the political economy turns from a growth economy into a 'zero-sum society',[25] the institutional arrangements of conflict resolution will suffer from strains and tensions. These tensions are probably best described, using the conceptual paradigm of 'organised capitalism' as a referent,[26] as threats of *disorganisation*. Such threats are likely to occur on two levels: (a) on the level of interorganisational 'rules of the game' and (b) on the level of the organisation of collective actors. Under positive-sum conditions, it is not only a matter of legal obligation or traditional mutual recognition, but of the evident self-interest of each participant to stick to the established rules of interaction and negotiation. As long as one participates, one can be at least sure not to lose, to receive future rewards for present concessions, and to have one's claims respected as legitimate, since the process of growth itself provides the resources necessary for such compensation. Stagnation, and even more recession or expected no-growth conditions, destroy the basis for cooperative relations among collective actors; confidence, mutual respect, and reciprocity are put in question, and coalitions, alliances, and routinised networks of cooperation tend to be seen as problematic and in need of revision by the organisational elites involved. Crucial as these 'social contracts' – i.e., subtle 'quasi-constitutional' relations of trust, loyalty, and recognition of the mutual spheres of interest and competence are in a complex political economy[27] the interorganisational relations that are required for the management of economic growth tend to break down under the impact of continued stagnation. This is illustrated by growing strains within party coalitions, between unions and parties, employers' associations and governments, states and federal governments, all of which find the principle of *'sich auf die eigene Kraft verlassen'* (i.e., to engage in uncooperative strategies either because nothing appears to be gained from sticking to the rules and/or because relevant others are anticipated to do the same) increasingly attractive in a number of Western European political systems, including the European Community itself.

The second type of disorganisation that follows from stagnation has to do with intraorganisational relations within collective actors such as trade unions, employers associations, and parties. Such organisations depend on the assumption shared by their members that gains achieved by collective action will be achieved at the expense of *third* parties, not at the expense of groups of members and in favour of other groups of members. As soon as this solidaristic expectation is frustrated, the representativeness of the organisation is rendered questionable, and 'syndicalist', 'corporativist' or otherwise particularistic modes of collective action suggest themselves. The consequences of this internal disorganisation of collective actors include either increasing 'factionalism' of political and economic interests within the organisation and/or a shrinking of the social, temporal, and substantive range of representation the organisation is able to maintain.[28] The political and economic variants of the interclass accord that have gradually developed in all advanced capitalist states since the First World War and that have helped to make capitalism and democracy compatible with each other are clearly disintegrating under the impact of these developments and paradoxes.

Does that mean that we are back in a situation that supports the convergent views of Marx and Mill concerning the antagonism of political mass participation and (economic) freedom? Yes and no. Yes, because we have numerous reasons to expect an increase of institutionally unmediated social and political conflict, the expression of which is not channelled through parties or other devices of representation, and the sources of which are no longer dried up by effective social and economic policies of the state. But no, because there are strict limits to the analogy between the dynamics of 'late' and 'early' capitalism. One important limit derives from the fact that the forces involved in such conflicts are extremely heterogeneous, both concerning their causes and socioeconomic composition. This pattern is remarkably different from a bipolar 'class conflict' situation which involves two highly inclusive collective actors who are defined by the two sides of the labour market. But, in spite of this highly fragmented nature of modern political conflict, its outcomes may well involve fundamental changes of either the economic or the political sphere of society, changes that have, for just a limited and short period of time, been inconceivable under the unchallenged reign of competitive party democracy and the Keynesian welfare state.

Notes

1. For instance, J. S. Mill's argument on the necessary limits of the extension of *equal* voting rights as developed in Ch. 8 of his *Considerations of Representative Government*, Cambridge, Cambridge University Press, 2010.

2. This idea is stated in all three of Marx's major political writings on France, namely *Die Klassenkämpfe in Frankreich von 1848–1850* (1850), *Der achtzehnte Brumaire des Louis Bonaparte* (1852) and *Der Bürgerkrieg in Frankreich* (1871).

3. G. Therborn, 'The rule of capital and the rise of democracy', *New Left Review*, 1977, vol. 103, pp. 28.

4. This procedure is followed on the basis of the rather trivial, if not uncontroversial, idea that compatibility, stability, continuity or 'self-reproductiveness' of any social system is not sufficiently accounted for in terms of its 'inertia' or its presupposed 'adaptive capacity', but can and must be explained as *a process* of reproduction in which integrative tendencies outweigh those of change or disruption. Cf. C. S. Maier, 'The two postwar eras and the conditions for stability in twentieth century Western Europe', *The American Historical Review*, 1981, vol. 86, pp. 321–352.

5. B. Hindess, 'Marxism and parliamentary democracy', in A. Hunt (ed.), *Marxism and Democracy*, London, Lawrence and Wishart, 1980, pp. 21–54.

6. Lenin writes in *State and Revolution*: 'The democratic republic is the best possible political shell for capitalism, and therefore capital, once in possession ... of this very best shell, establishes its power so securely, so firmly, that *no* change of persons, of institutions, or of parties in the bourgeois democratic

republic can shake it.' Having in mind the Leninist tradition of thinking of the state as a mere reflection of socioeconomic power structures – and the corresponding theorem of the eventual withering away of the state after the revolution – the Italian political theorist Norberto Bobbio has rightly asked the question whether there is at all something like a 'Marxist theory of the state' which would be conceptually equipped to grasp the 'specificity of the political'. Cf. N. Bobbio's contributions to *Marxismo e lo Stato*, Roma, Mondo Operaio Edizioni Avanti, 1976; quoted after the German translation *Sozialisten, Kommunisten und der Staat*, Hamburg, VSA, 1977, pp. 15–61.

7. It is only on the basis of *real* assimilation of the practices of political parties to market behaviour that the 'economic paradigm' in democratic theory (as formulated in the famous works of Schumpeter, Downs and Olsen) could become so plausible and influential.

8. M. Weber, *Gesammelte politische Schriften*, Tubingen, Mohr, 1958, p. 392.

9. R. Luxemburg, *Massenstreik, Partei und Gewerkschaften*, Gesammelte Werke Vol. II, Berlin, Dietz, 1924, pp. 163–165.

10. Cf. R. Michels, *Soziologie des Parteiwesens*, Stuttgart, 1925; W. J. Mommsen, 'Max Weber and Robert Michels', *Arch. Eur. Soc.*, 1981, vol. 22, pp. 100–116; D. Beetham, 'From socialism to fascism: the relation between theory and practice in the work of Robert Michels', *Political Studies*, 1977, vol. 25, pp. 3–24, and pp. 161–181.

11. See the brilliant analysis of this problem by A. Przeworski, 'Social democracy as a historical phenomenon', *New Left Review*, 1980, vol. 122, pp. 27–58.

12. C. B. McPherson, *The Life and Times of Liberal Democracy*, London, Oxford University Press, 1977, p. 69.

13. The most comprehensive account of recent theorising and discussion on 'corporatism' is P. C. Schmitter and G. Lehmbruch (eds), *Trends Toward Corporalist Intermediation*, London, Sage, 1979.

14. B. Jessop, 'The transformation of the state in post-war Britain', in R. Scase (ed.), *The State in Western Europe*, London, Croom Helm, 1980, pp. 23–93.

15. Cf. for a detailed account of current Swedish debates on these plans and the debates surrounding them, U. Himmelstrand *et al.*, *Beyond Welfare Capitalism?*, London, Heinemann, 1981, esp. pp. 255–310.

16. D. Abraham, '"Economic Democracy" as a Labor Alternative to the "Growth Strategy" in the Weimar Republic', Unpublished manuscript, Princeton, 1982, pp.16 ff.

17. A. Shonfield, *Modern Capitalism: The changing balance of public and private power*, London, Oxford University Press, 1965.

18. S. Bowles, 'The Keynesian Welfare State and the Post-Keynesian Political Containment of the Working Class', Unpublished manuscript, Paris, 1981, pp. 12ff.

19. This slogan has since become a technical term, in comparative politics; c.f. A Markovits (ed.), *The Political Economy of West Germany: Modell Deutschland*, New York, Praeger, 1982.

20. For a detailed formulation of this argument see G. Lenhardt, and C. Offe, 'Staatstheorie und Sozialpolitik: politisch-soziologische Erklärungsansätze für Funktionen und Innovationsprozesse der Sozialpolitik', in C. v. Ferber and F. X. Kaufmann (eds), *Kölner Zeitschrift für Soziologie und Sozialpsychologie*, *Sonderheft 19*, Opladen: Westdeutscher Verlag, 1977, pp. 98–127.

21. See N. Luhmann, *Politische Theorie im Wohlfahrtsstaat*, München, 1981; S. Huntington, 'The United States', in M. Crozier *et al.*, *The Crisis of Democracy*, New York, NYU Press, 1975, pp. 59–118; B. Cazes, 'The welfare state: A double bind', in OECD, Paris, 1981, pp. 151–173. See also the powerful critique of *The Welfare State in Crisis*, Paris, OECD, 1981; 'economic reason *vs.* political irrationality' argument by J. Goldthorpe, 'The Current Inflation: Towards a sociological account,' in F. Hirsch, and J. Goldthorpe (eds), *The Political Economy of Inflation*, London, Martin Robertson, 1978, pp. 186–214.

22. Quoted from a paper by G. Esping-Anderson, 'The incompatibilities of the welfare state', *Working Papers for a New Society*, January, 1982.

23. See J. Logue, 'The welfare state- victim of its success', *Daedalus*, vol. 108, no. 4, 1979, pp. 69–87; also R. Klein, 'The welfare state: a self-inflicted crisis?', *Political Quarterly*, 1980, vol. 51, pp. 24–34.

24. On this problem of the new 'service class' and its (partially converging) critique from the Left and the Right, see I. Illich (ed.), *Disabling Professions*, London, Marion Boyars, 1977; a penetrating and influential economic analysis of the rise of 'unproductive' service labour is R. Bacon and W. Eltis, *Britain's Economic Problem: Too few producers*, London, Macmillan, 1976.

25. See L. Thurow, *The Zero-Sum Society: Distribution and the possibilities for economic change*, New York, Basic Books, 1980.

26. See J. Kocka, 'Organisierter Kapitalismus oder staatsmonopolistischer Kapitalismus. Begriffliche Vorbemerkungen', in H. A. Winkler (ed.), *Organisierter Kapitalismus*, Göttingen, Vandenhoek, 1974, pp.19–35.

27. Cf. E. W. Bockenforde, 'Die politische Funktion wirtschaftlich-sozialer Verbände', *Der Staat*, 1976, vol. 15, pp. 457–483.

28. See, for the case of German and Italian unions, R. G. Heinze *et al.*, 'Einheitsprobleme der Einheitsgewerkschaft (1982)', in *Soziale Welt*, 1981, vol. 32, pp. 19–38; and M. Regini, 'Repräsentationskrise und Klassenpolitik der Gewerkschaften', *Leviathan*, vol. 10, 1982.

Chapter Ten

Main Problems of Contemporary Theory of Democracy and the Uncertain Future of its Practice[*]

Claus Offe

Let me start my remarks with a brief reflection on the relationship between two concepts that everywhere play a paramount role when normative foundations of post-authoritarian societies arid polities are being discussed. These two normative standards are those of 'justice' and 'democracy'. What is their relation? I wish to draw our attention to the fact that that relation can be read in both directions. First, one might argue that democracy – or equal political rights of participation and representation within the framework of strongly protected individual liberties and division of state powers – is derivative from justice, or an embodiment of its principles. But conversely, one might also argue that justice (of which there are many conflicting versions when it comes to the concrete assignment of rights and duties) is the outcome of processes of legislative, executive, or juridical decision making that conforms to democratic procedural rules. In this sense, we must envisage the relationship between justice and democracy in terms of a circular model, according to which either of them determines, and at the same time derives from, the other.

To this, let me add another observation that turns to the concept of democracy itself. We can think of democratic forms of government in terms of a life cycle: democracies are 'born' at a certain point in time and under certain circumstances, and it would at least be naive to exclude the possibility that they can 'die', as these forms of government are evidently not automatically self-enforcing and self-perpetuating. The existence of democracies within a possibility space of a non-democratic past as well as a non-democratic future is what makes them both precious and precarious. What I want to do here is to highlight an interesting asymmetry between the two limiting points of democracy within this possibility space, its beginning and its end. While it is virtually axiomatic that democracies do not come into being in democratic ways (but rather emerge from revolutions, wars, occupation regimes, *coups d'etat,* etc.),[1] it is quite possible that they disintegrate as a consequence of individual and collective forms of action, the emergence of which can neither be theoretically nor practically excluded within a democracy. If the people cease to participate in constitutionally prescribed ways,

---

[*]   'Main problems of contemporary theory of democracy and the uncertain future of its practice', *Theoria*, 1995, vol. 86, pp. 21–33.

elites fail to cooperate according to constitutional rules, parliaments abdicate their powers, governments and courts fail to implement their decisions or implement them without regard for constitutional rights of citizens, there is nothing that the subjectless 'democratic form of government' by itself can do in order to defend and assert itself. If it can be defended, it must be due to the loyal, prudent, and principled action (or inaction) of citizens and elites who are aware of the dangers to which the democratic form of government may fall victim, as well as being determined to prevent or resist these dangers. As democracies are inherently vulnerable, they need to be intelligently protected. And the mode of protecting democracies cannot be regulated by democratic constitutions alone. Democracies, in a word, in order to survive depend upon being willed, supported, and defended.

Concerns about the future of democratic forms of government raise two questions. First, which are the (economic, social, cultural, political) preconditions and determinants that are conducive to – or must be seen as a minimum requirement of – the continued viability of democratic regimes where they exist, as well as the further spread of such regimes to places where they do not yet exist? And what can we anticipate with some degree of certainty about the socio-economic and cultural trajectories along which these, as it were, pre-constitutional determinants will develop in the future? Second, to the extent to which the prospects for democratic regimes can be shown to be favourable, the question must be asked which *variety* of democratic regime is more – or less – likely to survive the challenges and turbulences to which democratic regimes are typically exposed? The first of these two questions is framed in a yes/no logic as it addresses the rise and *sustainability* of some kind of democracy, and the second in a more-or-less logic that concerns the *kind* and quality of democracy.

These two sets of questions have acquired – somewhat paradoxically, it might appear – a new sense of urgency and uncertainty by the most momentous and consequential event in recent history, the end of the Cold War and the breakdown of the Soviet system of state socialism. What appears paradoxical is that the future of liberal democracy has become the object of melancholic conjectures and it appears problematic[2] exactly at the point when it seems to have scored a definitive victory over its only competitor in the modern world. State socialism, as long as it was a historical reality, also provided a reference point to liberal democracies in relation to which the latter could make a strong and successful claim to be 'better' – in both economic and moral terms. Could it be that the measure of self-assurance that liberal democracies enjoyed throughout the period after World War II was in fact parasitic upon the existence of state socialism – a system almost generally considered inferior in both its legitimacy and effectiveness? If so, the new legitimation problem of liberal democracy would be that it is no longer enough to be 'better'; it is now required to be 'good', as measured by a set of universally shared normative criteria. This latter standard, of course, involves much heavier burdens of argument and proof. Also, the normative theory supporting liberal democracy would have to come to terms with the apparent puzzle that, if liberal democracy is held to be the most legitimate and effective, the most civilised and morally most attractive way to organise social and political life, why is it that not all political forces in all previously non-democratic countries appear to embrace it as the uniquely desirable institutional model, and why is it that those who do so still seem to encounter severe difficulties in implementing it?

One of the central issues in contemporary political philosophy can be summarised in the following question. Given the unavoidable and irreversible 'pluralism' within and between societies in the modern world, and also given the fact that contact and rivalry cannot be avoided between the plural interests and ideas that make up this world, we must face the reality of intense and irreconcilable conflict between proponents of different interests and forms of life and the very particular notions of the 'good' life each of them pursues. Given this intensity of conflict, on the basis of which conditions and which arguments should any of these groups develop a strong and robust commitment to rules specifying the 'right' procedures according to which the conflict can be solved? If the 'right' procedures are seen to compromise prospects for the realisation of the 'good' life, why should anyone opt for the former – particularly if not 'everybody else' is trusted to do the same and/or if violation of the rules is expected to go unpunished in concrete cases? Must the democratic citizen be compartmentalised into two sub-units – one pursuing the concrete and substantive 'good', while the other remains faithful to the formal and abstract 'right' that is designed to civilise the coexistence of divergent and conflicting conceptions of the 'good'? And, if so, how do we provide for the stability and balance of the division of each citizen's dual self?

Without pursuing these philosophical questions any further, I try to approach them by specifying a number of context conditions for the viability of the democratic form of political organisation. The first five of these context conditions relate to political and other elites, and the second five to non-elites, or the mass of ordinary citizens.

1. *Internal sovereignty.* If the people should somehow 'govern' in a democracy, this principle must, first of all, be read in the negative sense: *No one else but the people* (and the representatives elected by it) ought to govern. In other words, elected officials should hold a monopoly over the making of public policy decisions[3] and ultimately over the legitimate use of force. Schmitter and Karl[4] read this condition as meaning that 'popularly elected officials must be able to exercise their constitutional powers without being subjected to overriding (albeit informal) opposition from unelected officials'. This amounts to the absence, as a condition of *internal sovereignty,* of internal strategic actors capable of exercising veto power in order to obstruct, preclude, or otherwise interfere with or control decisions of elected officials. (The obvious candidates for the source of such obstruction are military elites, business elites, criminal, terrorist, or ethnic collective actors, with any number of ingenious combinations and mixed cases among them coming to mind.)

This is clearly a very demanding condition. If we take it in a strict sense, the prospects for democratic regimes would appear to be threatened not only by military counter-elites (e.g. Spain in the late seventies), terrorist organisations, mafia type illegal economic organisations (Italy), drug cartels (Colombia), militant separatist movements (Spain, Northern Ireland), but also by strategic actors representing multinational corporations that are sufficiently powerful to effectively blackmail (among other things, through the threat of disinvestment) or corrupt democratically elected governments. As complexity and interdependency increase, and particularly as the means of violence, individual and mass communication, and transportation become more readily available to everyone (and hence their use becomes more difficult to control for government authorities), and as capital stocks become organisationally and financially 'mobile', the least we can say is that the opportunities for such obstruction tend to increase, as do the incentives to exploit these opportunities. As a consequence, democratic sovereignty becomes increasingly vulnerable to the 'power of obstruction' that is provided for by the virtually uncontrollable international flow of arms, drugs, and 'dirty' as well as 'clean' money that is facilitated by the use of modern means of communication and transportation and the institutional realities of largely open borders.

To be sure, it will always remain a matter of difficult judgement to what extent the democratically illegitimate (though perhaps perfectly legal) use of such means does in fact amount to a *strategic obstruction* of constitutional democratic government (as opposed to ordinary business, or, for that matter, ordinary crime, committed for the sake of private gain). Furthermore, the mere presence or even the fictitious assumption of such dangers and opportunities may serve as an excuse for governing elites to curtail the rights of citizens in anticipatory compliance with what are regarded as the requirements of a 'favourable investment climate' and in ways which are in conflict with the proper operation of democratic institutions.

2. *External sovereignty.* Schmitter and Karl[5] mention as a further demanding condition that 'the polity must be self-governing; it must be able to act independently of constraints imposed by some other overarching political system'. This is the condition of *external sovereignty.* Two elections that were held in the month of March 1990 may serve as an example to illustrate how difficult it is to meet this condition, given the highly porous as well as the highly stratified nature of the international system. The elections held in Nicaragua and in the post-Communist German Democratic Republic shared two features. First, they were the first fair and clean elections to be held in the respective countries in a long time. Second, every voter in these two countries was acutely aware of the fact that the government of some other country (the US and West Germany, respectively) would take an intense interest in the election's outcome and would respond to the actual outcome in terms of either strongly negative or positive sanctions that would not just affect the newly elected government, but virtually every citizen in quite direct ways. It could therefore be said that, while

the government-to-be-elected was under the control of the electorate, the electorate was to a significant extent under the effective control of some foreign government that was interfering with the electoral process through threats and promises.

The interconnectedness of national policies as well as the vast disparities of political, economic and military powers among the nation states defies the notion of democratic self-determination of nations.

> The very process of governance can escape the reach of the nation-state. National communities by no means exclusively make and determine decisions and policies for themselves, and governments by no means determine what is right or appropriate exclusively for their own citizens.[6]

Such inbound and outbound spillovers affect national sovereignty in negative ways, regardless of whether they are accounted for by formal arrangements of transnational decision making (as in the European Union with its proverbial 'democratic deficit') or, *a fortiori,* if no such institutional mechanism of transnational consultation and bargaining exists (as in the case of the central bank of one country unilaterally setting the parameters for the economic recovery of others).

3. *Oligarchic control.* A third variety of mechanism by which democratic sovereignty is curtailed by elite action occurs when domestic representative elites exercise more control over constituencies than constituents can exercise over representatives. This is the familiar phenomenon of oligarchic control over captured (e.g. 'clientelistically bribed') constituencies. Political parties, government bureaucracies, monopolistic associations, and mass media are often able to determine the rise and configuration of 'critical' issues, the range of choice of the electorate, and the actual choices made, to an extent that makes the 'will of the people' appear a virtual artefact of strategic elite action.[7] Such a reversal of the direction of control – and the concomitant escape of supposedly representative elites from meaningful accountability – is part of the inherent pathologies of democratic regimes. Citizens depend on strong representative actors, in particular political parties, for their meaningful political participation, but they are also threatened by the monopolistic power position that this dependency can provide to these corporate intermediaries.

In all three cases of curtailed popular sovereignty – non-political strategic counter-elites, foreign governments, unaccountable representative monopolies – the thorny analytical issue is to determine the point at which the condition of collective autonomy of a political community (i.e. its sovereignty) is actually being subverted. For on the one hand, it is of course part of the everyday business of democratic governments to cope with a domestic and international environment that is constituted in part by the presence of rigidities, hostilities, scarcities, dependencies, and threats. Again, the banal and ubiquitous fact of the presence of such political and economic constraints is certainly no sufficient reason to consider a democratic regime as being put into jeopardy. On the other hand, if such elites are in a position to strategically impose their interest upon democratically elected governments, to determine the domestic agenda, to prevent issues from being raised through the power of making 'non-decisions', some point can be reached at which merely 'constraining facts' turn into *poderes facticos* ('factual powers') capable of exercising a measure of control over domestic politics that would make the idea of democratic accountability rather meaningless.

It is the tipping point between these two distinct phenomena that is so hard to define in theory (and to recognise in practice). All we can safely say is that this tipping point will be reached the more readily the more penetrable national borders become, the more asymmetrical the dependencies between national political systems are, and the more effectively national representative organisations manage to insulate themselves from popular control and accountability.

4. *Elite consensus.* But not only are elites – military, administrative, foreign governments, ethnic minority, or economic – the sources of potential threats to democratic regimes. Elites are also the key actors to play an indispensable role in the formation and preservation of such regimes. As democracies are not founded and do not come into being in democratic ways, which is true by definition,[8] it is only the enlightened consensus of elites and their willingness to enter into binding pacts and constitutional agreements that makes democracy possible and operative. Moreover, as governments of democratic regimes, for the sake of their own security, have very good reasons to prefer their neighbours also adopting or maintaining a democratic political order, a dynamic of external incentives and supports may be hypothesised to contribute to the stability and spread of democracies. As a consequence, democracy may be thought of as thriving internationally according to a pattern of virtuous contagion and international – as well as intra-national – pact-making.

5. *Meaningful choice.* In addition to the negative implication of the principle of democracy (*'no one else* but the constituted citizenship should be entitled to determine the content of public authority'), there is the *positive* implication of *meaningful choice.* If the options concerning public policy are effectively reduced to one, democracy is reduced to zero. Elite cartelisation, and other tactics of political closure, are symptoms of the constraining of options that are to be observed in many democratic political systems. Inter-party convergence and the vanishing of opposition can be premised, as Otto Kirchheimer observed in the sixties, upon the experience of 'success stories' (cf. the convergence of Christian and Social Democrats in the context of West German post-War reconstruction and the Cold War during the fifties) or, in contrast, by policy failure, stalemate, or some crisis condition.

More specifically, there is a strong incentive for bipartisan convergence and elite closure if challenges are perceived to be of a non-routine order of magnitude. Severe turbulences (including conditions that are skillfully dramatised as severe turbulences) tend to bring political competition to a temporary standstill. The formation of a great coalition government in West Germany in 1966, and similar responses to the challenges of political terrorism in Germany and Italy in 1977 are cases in point.

While success-stories, however, make convergence and the smooth withering away of ideological conflict between parties and other political elite segments both likely and unproblematic, a negative kind of equilibrium will be reached if parties converge under exceptional challenges and *then fail to cope successfully.* While inter-party convergence can be due to the hegemonic force of particularly successful policy ideas, it can also be due to the manifest exhaustion of any ideas, e.g. ideas as to how to combat mass unemployment in open economies, or how to control the budget deficit, or how to end ethnic wars raging within the ruins of former states, etc. In cases of the latter sort of convergence due to inter-party helplessness, which we may also term 'crises of excessive convergence', the manifest lack of effectiveness of a governing party will not increase the political opportunities of the opposition or some alternative coalition to move into government position, as the opposition is not credited (due to its similarity with the incumbent party) with the capability for handling acute problems more successfully. If political codes such as 'left' *vs.* 'right', 'government' *vs.* 'opposition', 'conservative' *vs.* 'progressive' cease to be operationally meaningful in terms of policy proposals and promising in terms of policy effectiveness, such codes are superseded in the public political discourse with another, at least potentially anti-democratic code: the code of 'the political class' (with its connotations of both incompetence[9] and corruption) *vs.* 'everyone else' or 'the people'. If major problems (such as high levels of unemployment, inflation, budget crisis, decline of economic performance, ethnic conflict, 'civil' insecurity due to crime and violence, military failures) are experienced to persist no matter what the colour of the incumbent government happens to be, dissatisfaction with government translates into frustration with, and hence loss of legitimacy of, the democratic regime as such. The condition of perceived regime impotency (as opposed to failure of parties and other elite segments) will then activate the search for either (authoritarian, populist, secessionist etc.) *alternatives* to, or major institutional *modifications* of, the liberal democratic regime.

I now wish to turn to the requirements on the level of non-elites or 'masses'. From a top down perspective, for democracies to be viable, elites must acquire some measure of credible sovereignty and provide a meaningful choice between policy alternatives. In addition, and from a bottom up perspective, the trivial fact is that the durability of democratic regimes is contingent upon a 'mass base' of democratic citizens willing to support and defend democratic rights and institutions. The validity of democracy resides in citizens willing to validate it. While it is true that democratic institutions, once established, can have a powerful socialising effect upon citizens who gradually get 'used to' and 'take for granted' and eventually become committed to democratic practices, this is not the whole story. Democracies can fail, or fail to come into being, not only by elite subversion, but also by mass defection from (or mass rejection of) democratic principles. Five conditions are known under which such defection/rejection is likely to prevail.

6. *Theocracy* vs. *democracy*. Theocratic regimes and their religious doctrines are – and continue to be – a powerful obstacle to both the foundation and the survival of democratic regimes. Schematically speaking, such regimes *negate* one boundary that should be present in a democracy, namely the boundary between the religious and the secular (which in Christianity was established by the Reformation). If every 'secular' conflict is ultimately to be resolved according to the will of God and according to the letter of some sacred script, there is simply no legitimate space for democracy. In a theocratic society, the people feel that it is positively dangerous and sinful to let the people decide on issues, the resolution of which can only be accomplished through divine wisdom and grace, and the religious elites that lay claim to both. Conversely, there is also a boundary which should *not* be present in a democracy, namely the boundary between believers and non-believers in the respective religions. In theocratic societies, the presence of this boundary precludes the granting of equal citizenship rights of political participation, which is an obvious prerequisite of democracy.

7. *Distributional fairness and positive-sum economic games.* Low and unequally distributed per capita incomes, such as they are typically found in agrarian and developing societies, do not favour modes of political reasoning and political aspirations that are compatible with the broadly supported adoption and effective consolidation of democracy. Instead, what prevails as a cognitive frame (and eventually as self-fulfilling prophecy) is a 'theory of the limited good', or the image of the constant-sum-game. Its underlying intuition, shared by both sides of a distributional conflict, is that if 'we' are to gain, this can only come about if 'they' lose, while the idea of universal, if asymmetrical gains provided for by a growth dividend lacks any plausibility supported by experience. If democracy is thus staged as an expropriation game, it will probably be effectively resisted by the likely candidates of such expropriation. Even if it succeeds, the kind and scope of redistribution that follows will trigger a negative-sum-game that is soon to be abandoned due to this disappointing outcome. To overcome this deadlock, the presence of an established urban middle class and its experience of redistribution-cum-growth seems indispensable.

8. *National unity* vs. *primordial markers.* Strong racial and ethnic divisions within a society can preclude the mass recognition of the abstract notion of citizenship, particularly if there is a significant history of conflict across this 'ascriptive' divide and/or if strong distributional disparities prevail.

The mass resistance to full democracy under such conditions is based on the (often well-founded) fear that as soon as equal political resources are granted to all, this will exacerbate distributional conflict or enable newly enfranchised groups to retaliate for deprivations they have suffered in the past. Again, these at least partly rationally founded fears (as opposed to 'prejudices') amount in many countries to powerful roadblocks on the way to democracy which can only be overcome in the process of elite negotiations and pacts (as in South Africa), not through a democratic process – one reason being that the people cannot decide who belongs to the 'people', i.e. the democratic constituency. As a consequence, both admission of previously excluded segments of the population of a territory into a political community and secession from a political community are a-democratic occurrences that are brought about through negotiations and, often, violence preceding these negotiations (Spain, Israel, South Africa, Northern Ireland) or following failed negotiations (Yugoslavia).

9. *Trust in effective governance.* Mass defection from democratic practices and the subsequent turn to authoritarian forms of government can result from widespread dissatisfaction with the regime's (as opposed to a particular government's) effectiveness in providing what states are supposed to provide for their people, namely (as a minimum condition), military, physical, and other material security. Democratic regimes, much as any other regimes, are presumed to effectively protect the most citizens' life, liberty, and property most of the time – and only their demonstrated success in doing so can motivate citizens to grant governments the right to demand that some citizens sacrifice some of their life (in military service), property (through taxation) and liberty (through respect for the law). But always, must the balance of the values protected and the values sacrificed for the sake of protection be positive. However, while authoritarian regimes do not depend for their preservation upon much support of their citizens, but can easily survive by force, regardless of what their level of effectiveness is, democracies have ultimately no such external guarantees to rely on. They are condemned to succeed or at least to perform in ways that are perceived by critical parts of the population to be superior to any non-democratic alternative regime form. (Such a widely shared perception of relative effectiveness had obviously evaporated in the final years of the Weimar Republic.)

10. *Trust in collective actors and representatives.* Mass defection from democratic practices can also occur if democratic collective actors (parties, associations) and procedural institutions (division of powers, parliamentary legislation) are perceived as having lost their legitimating substance, even if their effectiveness remains satisfactory. Thus the perceptions that the government is corrupt and the political parties unaccountable, that associations have turned into exploitative cartels and the civil service into a wasteful and self-serving apparatus, that the military is involved in conspiracies, and that individual elite members as

well as the media in general cannot be trusted, will add up to populist-authoritarian sentiments and a widespread willingness to abandon commitments to democratic rights and rules in favour of some 'clean', 'responsive' and 'honest' form of authoritarian rule. As the feeling of being betrayed by the 'political class' gives rise to cynicism, apathy, and a sense of popular inefficacy and powerlessness, these attitudes and their spread are also likely to affect the capacity of regimes to live up to some standard of effectiveness. Such loss of faith in democratic institutions can be observed both in old and presumably rather robust democratic regimes (such as Italy) and particularly in newly established ones (such as Russia and other post-Communist countries).

To summarise these latter points, the future of democracy thus appears to be contingent upon cultural requisites in two ways. First, *'pre-modern'* dispositions and cognitive frames must be overcome in order for the highly demanding notion of democratic citizenship to become viable. This implies, first of all, the slow and however partial neutralisation of religious and ethnic markers that stand in the way of inclusion into a legal community of citizens. Second, and concerning established democratic regimes, the spread of *'post-modern'* dispositions (the erosion of solidarities, the cult of difference, political cynicism, abstention, unfettered subjective welfarism and a general disenchantment with public causes) would also have to be checked and reversed, particularly, but by no means solely, because the spread of these 'post-modern' dispositions can make democracies defenceless and vulnerable to the return of those 'pre-modern' ones. Pessimistic assumptions concerning civic self-confidence and the role that the individual citizen can possibly play in a modern system of governance are further strengthened by the experience of cognitive incompetence. This experience is that virtually every issue that arrives on the political agenda undergoes such a rapid process of 'complexification' that it escapes the comprehension, let alone the competent judgement, of the average citizen (including many non-specialist politicians) within the first two weeks or so of its life cycle. Again, the answer to this post-modern condition of reflexive ignorance may often be sought in the retreat to pre-modern markers, myths, and prejudices – rather than to suitable ways of coping with recognised cognitive deficiencies.[10]

In sum, viable democratic regimes depend upon the presence of a rather peculiar set of civic commitments and cognitive frames that are being established on the mass level. To be sure, these norms can be inculcated, and their growth cultivated, by democratic institutions, and, I might add, by some variants of democratic institutions more easily than by others. But some cultures, particularly those that do not allow for the separation of political from religious conflict or that tend to strongly emphasise racial or other primordial identities, do not seem to provide a fertile ground for democratic regimes. Moreover, established democracies can fail in that they do not cultivate the social and cultural 'capital' on which they depend; by their very mode of operation they virtually deplete (or fail to accumulate sufficient amounts of) such capital.

Notes

1. More precisely, the will of the people (or the will of whatever part of it or of any non-popular agency) to establish a democracy is expressed and enforced in ways that are different from the ways in which the will of the people (or parts thereof) are expressed or enforced in an established democracy. This difference is conventionally referred to as that between *pouvoir constituant* and *pouvoir constitué.*

2. If there is anything that theorists (as well as many of the more thoughtful practitioners of the democratic form of government) agree upon, it is the call for an institutional renewal of democratic institutions that proceeds from the insight that 'democracy as a system cannot rest where it is' (I. Budge, 'Direct Democracy: Setting appropriate terms of debate', in D. Held (ed.), *Prospects for Democracy*, Cambridge, Polity, 1993, pp. 136–155 [154]).

3. R. A. Dahl, *Dilemmas of Pluralist Democracy: Autonomy vs. control*, New Haven, Yale University Press, 1982, p. 11.

4. P. C. Schmitter and T. Lynn Karl, 'What democracy is ... and is not', *Journal of Democracy,* 1991 (Summer), vol. 3, no. 3, pp. 75–88 [81].

5. *Ibid.*

6. D. Held, 'From City-States to a Cosmopolitan Order?', in D. Held (ed.), *Prospects for Democracy,* Cambridge, Polity, 1993, pp. 13–52 [25–26].

7. Cf. N. Bobbio, *The Future of Democracy*, Cambridge, Polity, 1987; D. Zolo, *Democracy and Complexity*, Cambridge, Polity, 1992.

8. That is to say: at the beginning of any democratic regime, agents (such as military occupation regimes, constituent assemblies, the holders of emergency powers, 'round tables', elite negotiators, or the leaders of rebellious popular forces) play decisive roles that are not themselves constituted in ways described by democratic procedures. Note, however, the asymmetry that consists in the fact that, in the absence of special provisions excluding this event, democratic procedures can well result in the abolition of democratic regimes.

9. Such lack of competence for the formation of effective policies, however, does not necessarily have to be rooted in opportunism, lack of determination, or shortsightedness of policy-makers and their 'irresistible temptation for free-riding', as Sartori suggests (G. Sartori, 'Rethinking Democracy: Bad polity and bad polities', *International Social Science Journal*, 1991, 43, no. 3, pp. 435–450 [445]). It may as well – and less optimistically – be the case that the means at the disposal of even the most determined and principled democratic policy-makers and national governments are incapable of coping with the kind of problems that inescapably appear on their agenda.

10. Cf. R. Dahl, 'The problem of civic competence', *Journal of Democracy*, 1992, vol. 3, no. 4, pp. 45–60.

Chapter Eleven

Constitutionalism in Fragmented Societies: The Integrative Function of Constitutions[*]

Ulrich K. Preuß

There are rare cases where a political scientist has enriched and refined the understanding of constitutionalism and constitutional law – obviously Andrew Arato is one of them. Strongly inspired by the transformations of the formerly communist societies of Central and East Europe, of which he has a deep knowledge and subtle understanding, he has raised new questions which deal with the thorny issue of the sustainability of these countries' path towards a constitutional mode of governance which they started off only twenty years ago. After all, the state of democratic affairs in Bulgaria, Hungary, Poland, Romania, let alone Russia, gives rise to serious concerns: corruptive structures and networks which pervade many areas of society have furthered political apathy and cynicism and encouraged the renaissance of nationalist, xenophobic, and anti-Semitic tendencies which may no longer remain limited to the fringes of society and undermine citizens' trust in the capacity of democratic institutions to cope with the manifold conflicts of modern societies. As in all revolutionary changes of truly historical dimensions, the societies which underwent these changes and at the same time actively pushed them forward, simply did not have the time for reflection about the development to which at least their active parts should commit themselves. Such an undertaking requires the passion for making the world better and at the same time the capacity for intellectual objectivity and truthfulness. Obviously Andrew Arato is a prime example of this kind of political intellectual. The secular revolutions in East and Central Europe in the 1980s and 1990s lured his interest and spirited erudition in the field of social and political philosophy into the area of constitutional politics. Here he delved into what Hannah Arendt called the 'perplexities of the beginning', developing and sharpening the conceptual tools for the understanding and eventually shaping of social, cultural, and institutional change.

However, as Arato's publications show,[1] he is by no means a mere regional specialist of Central and East Europe. His expertise stretches from West, Central, and East Europe, through Latin America, to the conflict-ridden Middle East. In his involvement in practical issues of constitution-making as an adviser in Central and East Europe and in Iraq, he unites in a truly exceptional manner the highest standard of the state of the art of constitutionalism in its philosophical, legal, and political

---

[*] 'Constitutionalism in Fragmented Societies: The integrative function of constitutions', in E. Peruzzotti and M. Plot (eds), *Critical Theory and Democracy: Civil society, dictatorship, and constitutionalism in Andrew Arato's democratic theory*, New York, Routledge, 2013, pp. 41–55.

dimensions. This, then, gives rise to open a conversation with him about the force of constitutionalism and constitution-making under precarious conditions, namely in deeply divided societies. These are polities in which profound conflicts among the members of society undercut their motives to engage in durable schemes of social cooperation and thwart the genesis of trust in the beneficial effects of institutions. These conflicts may have socio-economic, religious, cultural, ethnic, or historical roots – what poses a threat to the stability of society is the underlying premise that institutions, and constitutions in particular, cannot contribute to the solution or mitigation of these conflicts. The stability and orderly functioning of institutions presuppose a minimally consolidated order of society, or so is a widely held assumption both on the right and the left side of the political spectrum. It is uncertain whether this idea fully grasps the relationship between society and constitutionalism. In the following – admittedly quite sketchy – reconstruction of this relationship we may find arguments that paint a more differentiated picture. It is, of course, not by accident that at the end of these reflections Arato's idea of a post-sovereign understanding of constitutionalism will be taken up.

I.

The most succinct definition of a constitution was laid down by the framers of the French Declaration of the Rights of Man and of the Citizen of 1789. Its legendary Article 16 reads: 'A society in which the guarantee of rights is not assured, nor the separation of powers defined, has no constitution at all'. This definition became the forefather of all minimalist concepts of the constitution according to which a constitution does not need more than a bill of rights, stipulations about the machinery of government and amendment rules. In the 1970s a distinguished US-German constitutional theorist condensed the essence of constitutionalism even more, into two words: 'Limited Government'.[2] In fact, the function of a constitution to limit state power – both through the separation of powers and the guarantee of individual spheres which were closed to any kind of state intervention – was the key concern of the forces which at the end of the eighteenth century struggled for a constitution in France and in the newly independent American states. The reason is easy to understand: in France the members of the Third Estate had suffered from the omnipresence and omnipotence of the royal bureaucracy that had suffocated the frail beginnings of civil autonomy. In the former British colonies of North America, the fear of royal despotism and of any kind of autocracy, even one based upon democratic elections, motivated them to think first and foremost of the restraining attributes of a constitution.

However, we must not misunderstand this time-dependent concept of the constitution as the definitive fixing of its inherent meaning and rationale. Rather, the concept which predominated at the end of the eighteenth century must be comprehended as the first instance of the historical experience that constitutions mirror and process the key societal and political conflicts of any particular historical epoch. Either the text or its interpretation, or both, undergo changes in which each generation tries to find an appropriate institutional solution for the most relevant societal and political problems of the time. Thus, in the dawn of modern constitutionalism, at the end of the eighteenth century, the key political issue was the struggle of the emerging bourgeois class against dynastic absolutism. Its power-sensitive agenda entailed its imprint as liberal constitutionalism. During much of the nineteenth century, after the demise of absolutism and the establishment of the constitutional state as a system of bourgeois class domination, it was the battle of broad segments of the excluded inferior classes for their recognition as citizens through the extension of suffrage.[3] In some European countries this was not achieved until after World War I, when – as a new challenge to liberal constitutionalism – the organised working class claimed their 'entry into the arena of national politics' (Bendix) and set off the epoch of mass democracy.[4] In each of these developmental stages constitutionalism changed its character, its institutions, and the legal instruments for coping with new challenges. The changing meaning of the concept of citizenship is the most significant indicator of this development.[5]

Hence, we can trace back the different dimensions of our contemporary concept of constitutionalism to the different historical constellations of social and political conflict. As we have seen, the basic and original function of constitutionalism – the *limitation of power* – must be assigned to the beginning of modern constitutionalism when it was a forceful weapon of the emerging bourgeois class in its power struggle with the old regime. In the US, where the successful struggle for independence of the former colonies had bonded the people, the main issue of the constitution was to find appropriate institutional devices for constituting the multitude of individuals – largely freedom-loving settlers – as 'we the people', i.e., as a sovereign polity in the first place. At the same time the constitution had to protect the individuals' liberty against the power of the collective will of that very sovereign polity, the unified people. Obviously this was the central theme of the Federalist Papers of the founders of the USA.[6]

The US example points to the *constitutive function* of the constitution and the need to find a balance with its freedom-protecting function. This is the starting point of what Stephen Holmes has called the Janus face of the constitution.[7] Above and beyond its originally purely negative and defensive dimension, it also plays a positive role in that it constitutes the unorganised multitude of people as a political body by establishing basic institutions of self-rule. The constitutive function plays a central role in constitutions which are primarily concerned with the creation and maintenance of the integrity of a democratic state power. In the case of the US, the framers were worried about the construction of a superior power of a centralised authority, the Union. In the continental European context of the nineteenth century where popular sovereignty had still to be gained by strenuous efforts – where, in other words, political power was effectively organised, if in an undemocratic mode – the key problem of constitutionalism was the *legitimation of the existing political authority*. Of course, since the French Revolution the only legitimising principle of modern constitutions has been the principle of popular sovereignty. But political realities were not up to this political principle. As a result, in addition to the aforementioned struggle for the extension of the suffrage, different devices of power-sharing between the traditional monarchical power and the newly emancipated social classes surfaced. Incidentally, power-sharing was also the constitutional solution of some of the social and political conflicts of the twentieth century in cases where the principle of popular sovereignty could not be realised due to the continuing power of an old regime. The Round Table agreement, which the then communist government of Poland concluded with the Solidarity movement in 1989, is an obvious illustration. The National Peace Accord of South Africa, a multiparty agreement signed in September 1991, which started the negotiations about a peaceful transition to a non-racial democratic political system, is another case in point.

II.

These examples lead us to the *integrative function* of many modern constitutions, the focus of this chapter. It deals with the question of whether constitutions do not only organise the machinery of government and establish basic rights but, beyond that, create a sense of commonness, mutuality, and civic solidarity among citizens. In other words, the question is whether a constitution has the capacity to unite a society which is riven by manifold cleavages – economic, social, cultural, religious, ideological, and political – into a nation. The German constitutional lawyer Rudolf Smend first put the idea of an integrative function of the constitution forward in 1928 with respect to the Weimar Constitution of Germany.[8] Smend argued against a purely liberal understanding of the constitution as a system of limitations and demarcations of state competences. He maintained that the Weimar Constitution, rather, embodied the national spirit of the German people and its will to live together and to form a political community, frequently labeled as a 'community of fate'. However, this claim was by no means a descriptive account of the function of the Weimar Constitution. On the contrary, it was a kind of normative cry of help and an attempt to mitigate the troubled situation of the Weimar Republic, which was strongly polarised along class divisions, confessional cleavages, and ideological schisms.

It is a matter of debate whether the appeal to the people's national feelings as such is an effective remedy against deep social divisions. But constitutions can contain elements that encourage integrative effects, especially by the invocation of aspirations, values, and basic convictions commonly held by its members and which bind them together. In this case a constitution may serve as a kind of secular catechism. The US constitution played this role at least in the first decades of its existence.[9] Today the most apparent property of constitutions which have been designed with the aim to fulfill an integrative function is their more or less detailed catalogue of state goals and the concomitant guarantee of social and economic rights (such as the rights to education, to health, to shelter, to labour). Many of the new constitutions in the post-communist countries of East and Central Europe exhibit these attributes.[10]

It is not by accident that the issue of the alleged or actual integrative force of constitutions came up in the twentieth century. It was no earlier than in the twentieth century that constitutions embraced the whole of society, which means: the complexity of a modern differentiated and cleaved society. In the early periods of constitutionalism, constitutions presupposed the unity and homogeneity of the polity because the polity consisted basically only of one social class, the taxpayers, i.e., of the members of the bourgeoisie. Women and the inferior classes were excluded and did not count as members of the polity – they were considered unable to enjoy the status of citizenship. Hence, the constitution did not have to cope with the problem of social integration and disintegration. In the nineteenth century, as mentioned, the main constitutional struggles were connected to the claim of the hitherto excluded segments of the population into the polity; the issue was how to draw the lines between those who qualified for citizenship and those who did not. The issue was not yet the capacity of the constitution to sustain a polity in which all nationals have acquired citizenship. This situation was only reached in most European countries after World War I.

Despite the triumphant procession of constitutionalism since the end of the eighteenth century it was not the only pattern of political order. There were two powerful rivals that challenged its legitimacy – socialism and nationalism. The former was based on the theories of Karl Marx and Friedrich Engels who regarded constitutionalism as a subtle means of bourgeois class domination (which was not entirely wrong for the early periods of constitutionalism). They envisioned a world in which the solidarity of the working class would provide the appropriate principles of political order beyond legal institutions and render constitutions superfluous. The latter claimed that the commonness of ethno-national belonging should be the basis of political organisation which, too, could dispense with a constitution. As constitutionalism embodies the principle of equal citizenship irrespective of ethnic affiliation, in the view of nationalists it had to be rejected offhand.

Note that each of these two contenders of constitutionalism included an implicit programme of social integration of their own: socialism in its Marxist version relied on working class solidarity (during the period of the struggle for the classless society); nationalism claimed the inherent social solidarity based upon ethnic sameness and homogeneity of all members of the society. Both ideological strands were incompatible with the universalist axioms of constitutionalism: a political system in which the collective goals of a classless society or, respectively, of ethno-national homogeneity are the highest values cannot respect a polity which is governed according to the rule of law and the recognition of each individual's dignity and freedom.

After World War I, when the entirety of the society became politically organised by constitutions, constitutionalism came under pressure from powerful and militant social movements identified with the communist and nationalist-fascist ideology respectively. Obviously most of the European constitutional states could not withstand these pressures in the inter-war period and fell prey to some kind of authoritarian or totalitarian regime. Their constitutions were simply not up to the dynamics of social conflicts propelled by those movements. The collapse of the Weimar Constitution in Germany, mentioned above, and the rise to power of Nazism, has proved the most dramatic and momentous result of this development. Must we assume that constitutions are only appropriate institutional devices for societies which are largely consolidated?

III.

There is a long and venerable history of political reasoning which claims that economic development is an important, perhaps even indispensable precondition for the sustainability of democracy. 'Democracy' in this context means 'constitutional democracy', i.e., a system of popular rule embedded in a constitutional framework.

In 1959 Seymour Martin Lipset published his seminal article in which this paradigm was elaborated for the first time. According to a statistical survey of the countries of that time he concluded that 'the factors of industrialization, urbanization, wealth, and education, are so closely interrelated as to form one common factor. And the factors subsumed under economic development carry with it the political correlate of democracy'.[11] As Lipset explicitly admitted exception to this correlation, his theory is still today widely accepted. Needless to say, modifications are necessary which, however, do not concern me here. But there is one recent analysis of particular interest for our topic of the integrative function of constitutions. Its subject is a comparison of the capacity of the democratic systems of the US, Canada, and India to cope with deep social divisions.[12] This comparison is relevant for our topic because its author selected these three countries not because they were particularly significant or typical of the division between poor and rich, but because they are marked by divisions which are 'formed by birth and are, for the most part and for most persons, inerasable: race, ethnicity, religion, and native language'.[13] In the US, it is 'the racial divide that has been so central to its history; Canada by the founding division between Francophone and Anglophone; and India by grave divisions in caste, religion, and language'.[14] Obviously India is of special interest because this country, in addition, its immense economic progress in the last decade notwithstanding is still 'a poor country, and yet it is a well-established democracy'.[15]

In fact, when we speak of a country's divisions we must distinguish between the socio-economic rift between poor and rich and the one which pertains to issues of identity, which Glazer calls 'inerasable' and which I call 'identity conflicts'. Conflicts arising from those deep divides tend to be particularly intense and uncompromising. While pursuant to a well-known liberal line of argument in the social sciences, conflicts have a positive effect upon the social coherence of societies, this can hardly be said with respect to identity conflicts.[16] The American political economist Albert O. Hirschman offers an important distinction. In his view not all conflicts further coherence in all kinds of societies; rather, he claims, social conflicts have only positive effects in democratic market societies, and even this may be true only for a certain genre of conflicts.

> Many conflicts of market society are over the distribution of the social product among different classes, sectors, or regions. Highly varied though they are, they tend to be divisible; they are conflicts over getting more or less, in contrast to conflicts of the either-or, indivisible category that are characteristic of societies split along rival ethnic, linguistic, or religious lines.[17]

These conflicts, which Hirschman labels as 'categorical' and which I call 'absolute', are disputes about the moral, legal, and political status of members of ethnic minorities or religious communities, about philosophical truths or political ideologies. By contrast, conflicts about the appropriate policies for the whole polity, including distributional conflicts, are relative conflicts characteristic of pluralist societies.

Thus, we should distinguish conflicts about how a country should be governed from disputes about who belongs to the polity and who is qualified and entitled to rule over the people. Conflicts about the former question are usually settled within the framework of liberal constitutionalism. They are disputes about the direction of political action, about the right options among alternative policies, or about what justice requires in a given situation – they are largely conflicts about the right pattern of distribution both of fundamental rights and liberties and of economic and social benefits (in the Rawlsian sense).[18] The basic institution is equal citizenship: all individuals are integrated into a polity irrespective of their sex, birth, language, ethnic and social origin, faith, religion, or political opinion, let alone socio-economic status. Obviously the concept of equal (national) citizenship is blind, if not hostile towards any claim to the recognition of a distinct identity of individuals in the public sphere. This is due to its strong commitment to the universalist principle that each individual has an equal value (dignity) as a human being and merits equal respect irrespective of his or her particular attributes. Moreover, since the inerasable properties of individuals which form their identity have, most of the time in many countries, been the reason for severe forms of discrimination, liberal constitutionalism is particularly suspicious of any kind of recognition of identity as a constituent element of the polity.

Indeed, were the constitutional state prepared to recognise the identity of individuals or of groups as a relevant parameter of the cohesion of the polity, it might open Pandora's box. While obviously it would have to make the demand upon its citizens to recognise each other as equally constituent parts of the polity, the official acknowledgement of the significance of their differences may impede rather than facilitate these demanded acts of civic recognition. What follows from the incidence of, say, a deeply rooted antipathy, disdain, and distrust of major segments of the population against certain minorities whom they deny the quality to belong to the polity? A society in which major conflicts exist about the morally justified belonging of certain classes of individuals to the political community as equal citizens, and about the question of who is morally entitled to rule, is a fragmented or deeply divided society. On this view the US society in which the moral right of the Afro-American part of the population to rule the country has long being called into question was a fragmented society for a long period of time, perhaps up until our days. In many East and Central European states ethnic and national conflicts have dominated the political discourse since their very foundation at the beginning of the twentieth century and have remained the main causal factor of their contemporary divisions. In Western Europe, where the ideal of equal national citizenship prevailed and where during the twentieth century the confessional conflicts subsided in the wake of developing secularisation, the pluralist mode of political integration prevailed after World War II and became an integral element of their stability and socio-economic success. However, there are now signs for their fragmentation as well.

Ideally, the entirety of the citizens of a polity constitute the nation – the nation is the community of citizens;[19] this is an equivalent term for the nation-state (*état-nation*). Membership in the civic nation (or in the nation-state) – which is tantamount to being a citizen – is the source of a sense of pride and self-esteem; it is the symbol of successful integration into the polity. Citizenship is a status implying recognition and esteem because the owner of this status participates actively in the rule of the polity, in contrast to individuals who are mere passive subjects. The source of a citizen's self-esteem is not his or her personal, prepolitical quality – in other words: his or her identity – but the fact that he or she has left the subaltern status of passive subjecthood and has entered into the role of somebody who rules his and her equals and is ruled by his and her equals.[20] Citizenship means to share a valuable experience with one's fellows. Thus, the ideal concept of citizenship as it was revived in the French Revolution amounted to the paradox that being one's equal is a status of distinction. Conversely, all particularities which constitute an individual's identity – race, ethnicity, origin, native language, membership in extra-political communities like religious communities and the like – are banned from the public sphere because their representation would undermine the coherence and the unity of the political body.

Consequently, when the politics of integration into the civic nation (or nation-state) is under study, people do not normally refer to the question of how to include members of ethnic groups, religious dissenters, or national minorities in the polity. In this concept of nation these identity-defined categories simply do not exist; the refusal of the French Republic to ratify the 'European Charter for Regional or Minority Languages', sponsored and promoted by the European Council and adopted by some twenty European states in 1992, is an obvious example for the inherent incompatibility of the identity-blind civic nation and the claim of individuals or groups that their particular identity be recognised as constituent elements of the polity.

IV.

Today, however, cleavages resulting from cultural and ethnic differences have acquired a new relevance. There are several reasons for that. Let me just mention one which is of special relevance for the relations between the United States and Germany. I mean the fact of mass immigration into many of the OECD – and the EU – countries. It has sharpened the sense of ethnic differences and strained the feelings of solidarity in many of the host countries. The members of immigrant communities tend to emphasise their identity as members of their ethnic or religious community for the reason that the host state denies them a status of recognition as equals. Conversely, the citizens of the host state frequently sense the alienage of the immigrants, their different habits, and cultural imprint as a threat to their traditional way of life and have a propensity to conceive of their polity as of a culturally homogeneous and exclusive community. But even if a country – e.g., traditional immigration countries like the US, Canada, or Australia – grant immigrants the status of equal national citizenship in a quite straightforward manner, this does not necessarily keep many of them from defining themselves primarily through their ethnic belonging. Even more and more indigenous citizens of the host society identify more with a particular community whose members share certain characteristics – e.g., gender, sexual orientation, age, physical handicaps, origin in a particular region and the like – than with the seemingly abstract nation-state. For many, equal citizenship has lost its distinctive quality because the price of this status has been the polity's indifference, even hostility towards his or her particular attributes, which the individual regards as identity-engendering. In the view of these citizens, the status of equal citizenship has become a symbol of the polity's disrespect for their individuality. For them this is all the more obnoxious since membership in extra-political communities – religious, political, ethnic, or social – frequently gives the individual the motives and the power to make use of his or her civic rights. Thus, the quest for recognition of one's particularity, i.e., of one's otherness, has become one of the most important challenges to the traditional constitutional state and its essential premise of equal citizenship.

Obviously this is a challenge to the difference-blindness of civic institutions. According to this principle each individual has the *right to equal treatment*; but the fulfillment of this right may not satisfy, or even violate another right of the individual, namely the *right to treatment as an equal*.[21] This latter right does not aim at 'the same distribution of some burden and benefit', e.g., obligations and rights, but at the right 'to be treated with the same respect and concern as anyone else'.[22] This points to the identity-shaping characteristics of the individual. If these characteristics are group-specific like ethnicity, race, or religion, the recognition of the respective group as an equally constituent part of the polity is an appropriate means to fulfill their members' right to be treated as equals.

This, then, suggests a modification of the traditional structure of modern constitutions and its principle of equal citizenship in the spirit of recognition of group identities. Kymlicka and Norman rightly state that,

> while difference-blind institutions purport to be neutral amongst different ethnocultural groups, they are in fact implicitly tilted towards the needs, interests, and identities of the majority group; and this creates a range of burdens, barriers, stigmatizations, and exclusions for members of minority groups.[23]

Of course, there are very diverse groups in the various countries of the world, and there is no ready-made constitutional pattern for all.[24] But first and foremost the politicians and constitutional theorists of contemporary constitutional states have to take into consideration the fact that only a very few countries do *not* have major minorities as a relevant part of the polity. Almost four decades ago Walker Connor counted, that of the total of then 132 countries only 12 (9.1 per cent) could be described as essentially homogeneous from an ethnic viewpoint.[25] Even today, after the disintegration of the Soviet Union and of Yugoslavia and the increase of the number of states to almost two hundred, this portion has hardly risen since the new states, which arose from the disintegration of the aforementioned multinational states, were by no means ethnically homogeneous.

If ethnic, cultural, and religious diversity has become a trait of contemporary states, the integration of minorities has become an inescapable objective of constitutions. After all, constitutions are supposed to embody the basic legal order of a polity, which requires the inclusion of all portions of the population as its constituent elements. Obviously the partition of a country or the secession of a minority are not options in the search for an appropriate constitutional design for a polity, and the same applies both to forced mass-population transfers and to forced assimilation.[26] From the viewpoint of constitutionalism and its inherent axiom of treating all human beings as equals as the only method of managing, not suppressing diversity can come into consideration. To give a few examples which merit reflection:[27]

- federalising a country to the effect that territorially concentrated minorities enjoy a certain degree of self-determination within a territorial subunit of the state;
- granting autonomy to territorially dispersed minorities in certain domains of special interest, like family law or religious traditions;
- special representation of groups or their members within government or other public/semipublic institutions (e.g., mass media, school boards);
- granting exceptions from the general laws of the land for members of minorities (like, e.g., the dispensation from the obligation to wear helmets of Sikh motorcyclists in Canada, or the exemption from the prohibition of ritual slaughter for Islamic butchers in mainly Christian countries); and
- facilitating the access to the labour market for members of disadvantaged minorities.

This is not to say that the realisation of these options is a guarantee of a decrease of tensions and conflicts resulting from ethnic, cultural, or religious diversity. It may well be that largely symbolic gestures of recognition of minority groups as constituent parts of a diverse polity (like, e.g., bi- or trilingual names for villages and cities of a region with considerable minorities) have a more integrative effect than for instance policies of affirmative action mentioned in the last bullet point.

In sum, the traditional constitutional pattern of the nation as the community of equal citizens has to be advanced towards a doctrine providing institutional devices for polities that more and more metamorphose into ethnically and culturally divided communities. As the example of India, the largest and most diverse constitutional democracy of the world shows,[28] cultural, religious, or ethnic diversity as such is not inherently incompatible with the idea of constitutionalism – the foundation of the polity upon the principle of equal respect and concern for all members of the society. Thus, despite new kinds of conflicts at the beginning of the twenty-first century there is no reason for defeatism. However, the viability of constitutionalism cannot be taken for granted. It requires an understanding of the political as a sphere of human life in which the libidinal and aggressive energies of human nature are domesticated and civilised through institutions which operate according to the principle of equal respect for all members of the community. While it is sometimes next to impossible that members of diverse groups which are deeply at enmity with each other are able to develop the moral capacity to recognise each other as equals, it seems easier to convince them that the integrity of institutions may neutralise their mutual hatred and afford them the opportunity to find common ground in the recognition of genuinely neutral institutions.

V.

Admittedly, we can hardly imagine cases where the question of whether an institution and its decision are neutral will not be contested. But this fact does not undermine the viability of constitutionalism in deeply divided societies. An indispensable element of constitutions are constitutional principles (as distinct from constitutional rules): vaguely specified legal standards of constitutional rank which, first, differ qualitatively from rules because their application requires balancing (as distinct from subsumption), and, second, differ from collective goals or policies because they follow a logic of appropriateness, which means: the criteria of what is right and proper for the self-esteem of the political 'We' of the polity, rather than the calculus of anticipated consequences.[29] A striking case of the political significance of constitutional principles is the process of constitution-making in South Africa in the years between 1990 and 1996. For Arato, this process was a paradigm of what he called a post-sovereign mode of constitution-making in that 'the constituent power is not embodied in a single organ or instance with the plenitude of power', and that 'all organic participating in constitutional politics are brought under legal rules'.[30] As a matter of fact, in South Africa the process of constitution-making was not guided by rules in the strict sense of the concept, but by principles. This distinction played a significant role in the peaceful management of the transition from the apartheid regime to constitutional democracy.

Obviously South Africa was a deeply divided country even after the abolition of the apartheid system. When in February 1990 the then government of the Republic of South Africa announced its willingness to engage in negotiations with the liberation movements, very soon the issue of a new constitution for the country came up. Both sides agreed that a constitution could not simply be negotiated but had to be created by an elected body mandated to do so. But they could not be certain that the final outcome of the deliberations of the elected constituent assembly would properly reflect the ideas of the negotiators and take into account the anxieties and expectations of the constituencies represented in the negotiations.[31] The South African Constitutional Court summed up the solution to this problem as follows:

Instead of an outright transmission of power from the old order to the new, there would be a programmed two-stage transition. An interim government established and functioning under an interim constitution agreed to by the negotiating parties, would govern the country on a coalition basis while a final constitution was being drafted. A national legislature, elected (directly and indirectly) by universal adult suffrage, would double as the constitution-making body and would draft the new constitution within a given time. But – and herein lies the key to the resolution of the deadlock – that text would have to comply with certain guidelines agreed upon in advance by the negotiating parties. What is more, an independent arbiter would have to ascertain and declare whether the new constitution indeed complied with the guidelines before it could come into force.

The guidelines were attached to the negotiated Interim Constitution, which referred to them in its preamble as 'a solemn pact recorded as Constitutional Principles'. The list of those Principles included thirty-four items, ranging from a common South African citizenship, a 'democratic system of government committed to achieving equality between men and women and people of all races' (No. 1) through the recognition of 'all universally accepted fundamental rights, freedoms and civil liberties, which shall be provided for and protected by entrenched and justiciable provisions in the Constitution' (No. 2), the 'separation of powers between the legislature, executive and judiciary, with appropriate checks and balances to ensure accountability, responsiveness and openness' (No. 6) to 'representative government embracing multi-party democracy, regular elections, universal adult suffrage, a common voters' roll, and, in general, proportional representation' (No. 8) and the 'determination of criteria shall be applied in the allocation of powers to the national government and the provincial governments' (No. 21).

As we know, the South African Constitutional Court served as this independent arbiter and performed the certification task in two proceedings.[32] The pre-formation of a constitution by a list of constitutional principles is a rather unique method of constitution-making. Certainly it is due to the particular situation of a profound political transformation in which new actors entered the political arena. After the collapse of the Soviet Union this happened in most East and Central European countries as well, and in most of them also Round Table talks and negotiations were conducted.[33] However, none of them chose the two-stage- and two-level method of South Africa, which, by standards of traditional constitutional theory, is a paradox. The political elites of South Africa acknowledged and stuck to the idea of a constituent power of the nation, which means the recognition of a constituent assembly as the supreme and sovereign source of political authority. At the same time they established an institutional device subjecting the constituent assembly to a monitoring procedure, thus seemingly denying its supremacy and sovereignty.

Actually, this was not the case. What happened was the setting up of a common ground of the various antagonistic political forces, which was broad enough as to allow all, or at least the politically most significant ones, to feel represented in the determinations of the thirty-four Constitutional Principles. Each of them is, of course, open to very divergent interpretations, depending not only on the situations where they apply, but also on the values, visions, and interests of the involved political forces and institutional actors. Think, for instance, of the principle of 'universally accepted fundamental rights, freedoms and civil liberties' (No. 2) or of the principle that minority political parties can participate in the legislative process in a manner consistent with democracy (No. 14). It is the particularity of principles that their invocation and application requires interpretation, i.e., a mindset of discourse, not of violence.

So two qualities of principles rendered the South African experience possible: first, due to their semantic wideness and vagueness they encouraged the involvement and commitment of very diverse political forces to participate in the process of transforming the country into a polity based on equal national citizenship; second, by agreeing on principles even the most antagonistic forces were lured into a situation where their disagreement and conflict was transformed into a discursive process about the appropriate interpretation of the principles and their translation into the constitution. In other words, the prior agreement on principles for the constitution created a situation where the realisation of the potentiality of a civil war could be avoided – and, to repeat that, only the vague character of principles made that prior agreement possible. So at least in the case of South Africa it is justified to speak of the integrative function of constitutional principles.[34]

As I said, the South African constitution-making process and the role of principles in that process are quite unique. After all, one is tempted to say that in this case principles were sort of super-constitutional. They did not embody the constitution proper simply because principles do not reach the degree of specificity and certainty which is a defining element of a legal text. Still, many constitutional texts contain principles, especially those aspiring to further a sense of common belonging and political identity among citizens that cannot presuppose it offhand. It is certainly not by accident that principles play a prominent role in constitutions of countries having to cope with the problems of the transition from authoritarian to democratic rule. An incomplete list of cases includes the French constitution of 1946, the Italian constitution of 1946, the German Basic Law of 1949, the Hungarian constitution (in its amended post-communist version of 1989), the Bulgarian constitution of 1991, and the Polish constitution of 1997. Constitutional principles embody the undisputed or least disputed values and objectives of a polity – a fact that has two paradoxical implications. First, in order to be undisputed, principles must be vague and open to very diverse, even opposite interpretations. Second, by that very openness to interpretation they open the door for dispute and political struggle. But, and this is the cunning of reason inherent in the concept of constitutional principles, these struggles are conducted in the field of constitutional interpretation. Constitutional principles are standing invitations to the actors in the polity to get involved in the process of their concretisation. They guide the political antagonists away from the brink of civil war, and transform politics by luring the involved parties into a mode of institutionalised, discursive and, consequently, civilised conflict management.

This is not to say that constitutionalism is a panacea for each and every deeply divided society. Constitution-making cannot replace politics and diplomacy. But it creates an incentive to all political actors to explain their claims and to solicit support by way of argumentation. It has the potential to trigger political dynamics which may profoundly change the character of deep political conflicts. This is no promise, just a modest hope – but sometimes conflicts are so hopelessly bogged down that even a modest hope can encourage people to seek a political compromise rather than killing each other. Perhaps this is the most significant implication of 'post-sovereign constitutionalism'.

Notes

1. See, e.g., A. Arato's works: *Civil Society, Constitution, and Legitimacy*, Lanham, Boulder, New York and Oxford, Rowman & Littlefield Publishers, 2000; 'Interim imposition', *Ethics & International Affairs*, 2004, vol. 18, no. 3, pp. 25–50; *Constitution Making Under Occupation: The politics of imposed revolution in Iraq*, New York, Columbia University Press, 2009; 'The Constitutional Reform Proposal of the Turkish government: the return of majority imposition', *Constellations*, 2010, vol. 17, no. 2, pp. 345–350.

2. C. J. Friedrich, *Limited Government: A comparison*, Englewood Cliffs, NJ, Prentice-Hall, 1974.

3. R. Bendix, *Nation-building and Citizenship: Studies of our changing social order*, New Brunswick, NJ, Transaction Publishers, 1996.

4. C. Offe, 'Competitive party democracy and the Keynesian Welfare State: factors of stability and disorganization', *Policy Sciences*, 1983, vol. 15, no. 3, pp. 225–246.

5. T. H. Marshall, *Class, Citizenship, and Social Development*, Garden City, NY, Doubleday, 1964.

6. Cf. A. Hamilton, J. Madison, and J. Jay, *The Federalist Papers*, C. Rossiter (ed.), New York and Scarborough, The New American Library, 1961 (1788).

7. S. Holmes, 'Precommitment and the Paradox of Democracy', in J. Elster and R. Slagstad (eds), *Constitutionalism and Democracy*, Cambridge, Cambridge University Press, 1988, pp. 195–240.

8. R. Smend, *Verfassung und Verfassungsrecht*, München and Leipzig, Verlag von Duncker & Humblot, 1928.

9. Cf. U. K. Preuß, *Constitutional Revolution: The link between constitutionalism and progress*, Atlantic Highlands, NJ, Humanities Press, 1995, pp. 25 ff.

10. J. Elster, C. Offe, and U. K. Preuß, *Institutional Design in Post-communist Societies: Rebuilding the ship at sea*, Cambridge, Cambridge University Press, 1998.

11. S. M. Lipset, (1959) 'Some social requisites of democracy: economic development and political legitimacy', *The American Political Science Review*, 1959, vol. 53, no. 1, pp. 69–105 [80].

12. N. Glazer, 'Democracy and deep divides', *Journal of Democracy*, 2010, vol. 21, no. 2, pp. 5–19.

13. *Ibid.* p. 5.

14. *Ibid.*, p. 8.

15. *Ibid.*

16. See the overview of the literature in A. O. Hirschman, 'Social Conflicts as Pillars of Democratic Market Societies', in A. O. Hirschman, *A Propensity to Self-Subversion*, Cambridge, MA and London, Harvard University Press, 1995, pp. 231–248 [236ff.].

17. *Ibid.*, p. 244.

18. J. Rawls, *A Theory of Justice*, Cambridge, The Belknap Press of Harvard University Press, 1978, pp. 195 ff.

19. D. Schnapper, *La communauté des citoyens: Sur l'idée moderne de nation*, Paris, Gallimard, 1994.

20. J. G. A. Pocock, (1995) 'The Ideal of Citizenship Since Classical Times', in R. Beiner (ed.), *Theorizing Citizenship*, Albany, State University of New York Press, 1995, pp. 29–52.

21. This distinction was introduced by R. Dworkin, *Taking Rights Seriously*, Cambridge, Harvard University Press, 1978, p. 227.

22. *Ibid.*

23. W. Kymlicka and W. J. Norman (eds), *Citizenship in Diverse Societies*, Oxford and New York, Oxford University Press, 2000, p. 3.

24. See the typology of groups in *ibid.*, pp. 18ff.

25. W. Connor, 'Nation-building or nation-destroying?', *World Politics: A Quarterly Journal of International Relations*, 1972, vol. 24, no. 3, pp. 319–355 [320].

26. Cf. Kymlicka and Norman, *Citizenship in Diverse Societies*, p. 12.

27. See also *ibid.*, pp. 24 ff.

28. See the account of Glazer, 'Democracy and Deep Divides' p. 14; see also H. Lerner, *Making Constitutions in Deeply Divided Societies*, Cambridge, Cambridge University Press, 2011, pp. 109 ff.

29. See the debate about the structure of constitutional principles in Dworkin, *Taking Rights Seriously*, pp. 22 ff.; R. Alexy, 'On the structure of legal principles', *Ratio Juris*, 2000, no. 3, pp. 294–304; F. Schauer, 'Balancing, subsumption, and the constraining role of legal text', *Law & Ethics of Human Rights*, 2010, vol. 4, no. 1, pp. 34–45; see also the overview of U. K. Preuß,

'Philosophical Perspectives on Principles in Constitutional Law', Paper presented at the VIIIth World Congress of the International Association of Constitutional Law, 5–10 December 2010 in Mexico City.

30. Arato, *Constitution Making Under Occupation*, pp. vii, 63 ff.

31. See Constitutional Court of South Africa, Case CCT 23/96 (Certification of the Constitution, 6 September 1996), para 12.

32. Case CCT 23/96 (1st proceeding) and Case CCT 37/96 (2nd proceeding, 4 December 1996).

33. Cf. J. Elster, *The Roundtable Talks and the Breakdown of Communism*, Chicago, University of Chicago Press, 1996.

34. A similar conclusion is drawn by A. Jakab, 'Re-Defining Principles as "Important Rules": A critique of Robert Alexy', in *On the Nature of Legal Principles. ARSP-Beiheft* 119, Baden-Baden, Franz Steiner Verlag – Nomos, 2010, pp. 145–159 [159].

Chapter Twelve

'Homogeneity' and Constitutional Democracy: Coping with Identity Conflicts through Group Rights[*]

Claus Offe

In this article I explore some ancient issues of political theory in the light of some contemporary social and cultural issues. After developing a check list of the virtues and vulnerabilities of constitutional democracy (Section I), I go on to discuss some types and symptoms of difference, conflict, fragmentation and heterogeneity (Section II). I then proceed to a critical review of a particular set of strategies and institutional solutions – political group rights – that are often thought promising devices for strengthening the virtues and overcoming the vulnerabilities of the constitutional democratic form of regime (Section III).

Much of the contemporary philosophical and political discussion of these issues is enchanted by the post-modern spirit of 'multiculturalism', 'diversity' and 'identity'. It tends to neglect issues of citizenship and social justice. It also tends to fixate on North American examples, neglecting some of the less benign West European and, in particular, Central East European varieties of identity politics.[1] The discussion here, while mostly raising questions rather than claiming to provide definitive answers, nevertheless tries to overcome some of these biases.

I. Virtues and vulnerabilities of constitutional democracy

To start with some basics, a state is the coincidence of three things. First, the concept of a state (or 'country') refers to a fixed territory. This territory is defined by borders recognised by neighbouring states, as well as by other members of the international community. Even in the special case of island states where borders are defined by (salt) water, these borders, nevertheless, also need to be recognised by other states; or, failing that, the island state must be able to defend its territorial integrity against attempted moves by other states to occupy or conquer it (as in the 1996 conflict between the People's Republic of China and Taiwan). Thus territories, in order to serve as the material foundation of statehood, must be based upon agreements and the internationally mutually binding recognition of borders.

Second, the concept of a state presupposes that the territory is inhabited by a population, the state's 'people' forming a nation. Largely empty land, such as

[*]   ''Homogeneity' and constitutional democracy: coping with identity conflicts through group rights', *Journal of Political Philosophy*, 1998, vol. 6, no. 2, pp. 113–141.

Antarctica, is not suitable for supporting a state, if only because there is nobody to defend it and nobody who is to be defended.

Third, the concept of the state presupposes a constituted government, or sovereign authority. Such authority is supposed to be superior to any other political authorities or social powers within the territory, as well as being capable of asserting itself against foreign interference. In short, a state is the coincidence of a country, a nation and a regime.

The problem with these three constituent elements of a state is that they are, in a specific sense, 'contingent'. That is to say, they are the outcome of historical events and developmental trends. They originate, among other things, from climatic and physical features of the territory that make it inhabitable and resource-rich, from migration and other demographic trends, wars, dynastic politics, military occupation, conquest, revolutions, contracts of international law and the like. In other words, states are in all three of their aspects the accumulated sediment of history. Negatively, that means that democratic politics (that is, politics determined by egalitarian mass participation and elite accountability within the framework of constitutionally fixed rights and procedures) cannot determine the constituent features of a state. All three components of a state must be in place before any specific form of regime, including the democratic one, can possibly begin to operate.

Next, constitutional democracy. There are a number of valuable accomplishments that constitutional democracies are often credited with. If we ask the (uncommon)[2] question of what democracy is good for and what makes it preferable to other regime forms, we would come up with four cumulative answers. First, there is the 'liberal' accomplishment. Rights and liberties are guaranteed and a clear line of demarcation is thereby drawn between what can be contingent upon the outcome of the political process and the conflicts of interest entering into it, and what cannot be the object of such conflict because it is constitutionally entrenched. As a consequence of both rights and procedures being thus guaranteed, democracies make for a non-violent, limited and civilised character of political conflict and incremental change. Second, there is the 'international' accomplishment. The 'democratic peace' hypothesis posits that democracies will not wage war against other democracies. Third is a 'social progress' accomplishment. Since democracies rest upon majority rule, and majorities are typically made up of those who do not share in economic privilege and social power, and since democratic state power is in fact able to affect the size and distribution of economic resources (through, for example, promoting growth, taxation and social security) in non-marginal ways, therefore democracies will normally work to serve the interests of the less fortunate segments of the population, thereby promoting 'positive' or 'social' rights and prosperity and social justice more generally. Finally, there is the 'republican' accomplishment. 'Subjects' are transformed into 'citizens' – agents committed to and capable of employing their cognitive and moral resources in deliberative and intelligent ways so as to solve political problems, according to a logic of collective learning, and eventually striving to serve the 'public good'.

There are of course a number of conditions which must be fulfilled in order for democracies to do all those good things (or at least to do them more consistently and reliably than any alternative regime-form). For instance, there must be a solid and widely shared support for the democratic regime form, emanating from a democratic political culture. There must be an actual possibility of controlling, through the means of democratic politics, parameters and conditions of social life (such as the means of production and the means of violence) which are crucial for the protection of liberty and the promotion of social progress, with no 'reserved domains' standing in the way of such political control.[3] There must be a judiciary and an administrative system that actually implements democratically legitimated laws and policies, without either violating the rights of citizens or being overly (or corruptly) 'sensitive' to some economic or military 'de facto powers' or subservient to the corporate self-interest of the state bureaucracy itself. But all that is well known and therefore need not be of any further concern in the present context.

Those are the (evidently, I submit, highly desirable) accomplishments that we have come to associate with, and expect from, the democratic form of government, at least as a realistic possibility. There are also, however, a number of democratic impossibilities: matters which, by their very logic, cannot be resolved in democratic ways. If we ask what democracies cannot do – and what hence, in case it needs to be done, must be done by methods other than democratic procedures – four things come to mind.

First, the democratic form of government cannot be brought into being by democratic means. This is almost a matter of logic. The *pouvoir constituant* is prior to and unconstrained by the democratic principles which govern in a democratic regime once it is established. The agents governing that *pouvoir constituant* may well be, and as a rule are, inspired by democratic beliefs and intentions. But the 'initial framework in which democratically legitimated power is to be created is not enacted democratically'.[4] Moreover, all democracies appear to have non-democratic roots – be it a coup d'état, a democratic popular movement, round-table talks, a regime breakdown, an occupation regime, a war of independence or whatever. This observation is less trivial than it may seem, as this feature of non-democratic origin may later be held against the democratic regime itself, as an alleged 'birth defect' or self-contradiction. It can be denounced, as by the far right under the Weimar Republic, as owing its existence not to its inherent qualities but rather to a 'stab in the back' of the old regime, or to the exploitation of its weakness or defeat, thus being a coup as much as any other imposition of a regime form. Furthermore, nascent democracies are not state-founding but merely regime-transforming, a limiting case being the transformation of a former colony into an independent democratic state. Democracies cannot establish states, but they impose new forms upon preexisting non-democratic states upon whose previous existence they are parasitic – also in the sense that the experience of authoritarian rule, with its systematic denial of liberties, may nurture the aspirations and resolve for a transition to democracy.[5] In these two senses, democracies are by necessity heirs of non-democracies: they owe their existence to an antecedent non-democratic state and, as I just pointed out, to a non-democratic process of overthrowing the regime form of this non-democratic state.

Furthermore, not only are democracies unable to bring themselves into being: they are also able to undo themselves. That is to say, democracies are ultimately defenseless against movements and anti-democratic elites that use democratic procedures to reinstall an authoritarian regime. Taken together, these considerations lead us to conclude that democracies are unable either to create or reliably to preserve themselves. Democracies are neither self-founding nor self-enforcing.[6] Both their origin and their continued existence is a matter of favourable circumstances which are beyond the reach of what can be done through democratic procedures proper.

A second democratic impossibility concerns the scope of the political community which the democratic regime governs. It is democratically impossible for the people to decide or (re)define who belongs to the people (as opposed to who is to be enfranchised within an existing people), either by excluding parts of the population from the citizenship (for example, through ethnic cleansing) or by unilaterally incorporating collectivities that are outside the 'given' political community.[7] Democratic theory or constitutionalist doctrine does not provide us with good reasons as to why the social extension of the people should be what it empirically is.[8] But neither are there good reasons to undo the 'arbitrariness' of history that has brought together a number of individuals in a certain territory under a shared regime of citizenship by claiming that 'in some cases there are two or more "peoples" in a single country', as Kymlicka puts it.[9]

Third, and closely related to the previous point, territorial borders cannot be changed in obviously democratic ways. Again, this applies to moving the borders 'inward' (creating borders where there were none before) as much as 'outward' (eliminating pre-existing borders at the expense of the territorial base of some other state). The 'inward' case is equivalent to secession or separation, while the 'outward' case is the military conquest of the territory controlled by other states. Any inward move is bound to lead to procedural deadlock. After all, which constituency is to decide on secession: the majority of the separatist part, the whole, or concurrent majorities of both constituencies? And which constituency is to decide in the highly likely event of a second-order conflict over these procedural alternatives? A democracy cannot provide a formula for this kind of conflict, and a broad popular consensus to disunite (and where exactly to draw the line)[10] is highly unlikely to emerge, though not logically to be excluded. If the constitutionally unpaved road to an accord reached through inter-group negotiations fails, the most likely outcome is secessionist ambitions and, possibly, civil war. Conversely, it is international war in the 'outward' case of territorial change, as there are no populated stateless territories in the modern world. To be sure, international law provides the instrumentalities that can lead to the fusion of two states (as in the case of German unification); but that is not a matter of democratic decision of the constituency of one state, but a matter of an international treaty between two states whereby one or both of them renounce sovereignty. Incidentally, an attempt to 'conquer' the territory of another state by unilateral 'democratic' decision would be a blatantly self-contradictory act as it would be based on the claim that the people of state A have the right to decide that the people of state B have no right to decide whether or not B-land should become an integral part of A-land. This logic would clearly amount to denying prospective fellow-citizens equal political rights.

Finally, the citizenry of a democracy cannot decide on the issues the citizens are to decide on. This is the problem of democratic agenda-setting. The role of the citizens in a democracy is to answer questions, not to formulate and ask the questions that are to be answered by the people. The latter task resides with elites (such as political parties nominating candidates and proposing alternative policy platforms) or, for that matter, with nascent counter-elites (such as the activists of social movements introducing hitherto ignored issues into the arena of politics) or elites of other institutional sectors (such as science, the arts or religion). One may consider this problem to be mitigated by the fact that (at least part of the) elites involved in agenda-setting have themselves been elected and thus given a mandate to ask questions and propose alternatives. But these elites, before being confirmed in their elite role through a democratic vote, have themselves been nominated and promoted to the role of candidacy through forces that are not democratically accountable. Note that this problem cannot be made to disappear through any dose of plebiscitary or 'direct democratic' procedural innovations, which in turn would strengthen rather than weaken the role of elite agenda-setters and issue-raisers. To be sure, a strong public sphere within civil society can impose moral pressures upon elite members which they cannot afford to ignore or escape. But even given such pressures, nominating candidates and proposing platforms is not a matter of popular (but at best a matter of intra-party) democracy. Nor can the people decide upon when the people should decide: that (often highly consequential) decision must be made through either elite initiative or a 'procedural clock' (such as the statutory periodicity of elections).

I have highlighted these four impossibilities and apparent deficiencies of the democratic regime form – the things that democracies cannot do – not in order to cast doubt upon the value and virtue of democracy but, rather, in order to derive the following thesis. The democratic regime form is a viable arrangement (and a promising vehicle for the four accomplishments stated at the beginning) only if, and only as long as, the four things that democracies cannot accomplish do not need to be accomplished. As long as democracies can live and prosper with their inherent deficiencies, these are at best of theoretical concern and without widely perceived practical significance. That is to say, we need not be concerned with the viability of the democratic regime form as long as:

- the regime form, in spite of its two non-democratic birth defects and its incapacity to effectively foreclose alternative regime forms, is widely accepted and unchallenged; and
- the people of a political community recognise each other as legitimately belonging to that political community without any relevant desire to exclude or unilaterally include anyone beyond the existing citizenship and the rights of political participation defined by it; and

- borders are accepted as given and lasting, recognised from within as well as by neighbours and the wider international community;[11] and
- the right and competence of political elites to ask the 'right' questions at institutionally determined points in time, to integrate different cleavages into reasonably coherent platforms and to respond to agenda innovations originating with counter-elites remain unchallenged.

The viability of democracy is all the more secure if, in addition, that regime form demonstrably excels in doing what it supposedly is uniquely capable of doing, namely, simultaneously promoting liberty, the non-violent resolution of conflict (both domestic and international), social justice and republican virtue.

A political community within which all of these positive conditions and none of the negative conditions are fulfilled can be called a 'stable' constitutional democracy. Its stability rests on the reflexive homogeneity of the political community.[12] It is homogeneous, or synonymously 'politically integrated', because all (or at any rate the vast majority) of the people share a commitment to the state and its democratic regime form, they are tied to their fellow citizens through an understanding of the communality of their fate and the recognition of equal liberties, and they rank these commitments and loyalties higher than the various cleavages that divide the national society.

II. Sources and symptoms of heterogeneity

Needless to say, however, there do exist such cleavages and differences, all of which can potentially undermine the coherence and integration of the political community. In fact, there are three different kinds of differences: interest-based, ideology-based and identity-based (the three 'i's). The 'valued things' that are contested in these conflicts can be categorised, respectively, in terms of three 'r's: resources, rights and recognition (or respect). These types of difference and conflict can be ranked according to the ease with which conflict can be resolved and civilised.[13] Pure interest-driven conflicts concerning the control over and distribution of resources are more traditionally known as 'class conflict', carried out among representative collective actors under the governance of mutually agreed-upon procedures. Such conflicts are most easily resolved – provided, of course, that the procedures are in fact recognised by all sides as impartial (failing that, the conflict of interest is nested within a conflict of ideology). Why should a pure conflict of interest be so easy to resolve? Because in the conduct of conflicts of interest the people involved (workers versus employers, manufacturers versus consumers, landlords versus tenant, and so on) learn that they depend upon those on the other side of the interest divide with whom they are, at the same time, in conflict. Their awareness of this interdependence provides a strong incentive to compromise and to prevent the situation from spiralling into a negative-sum game.

Ideological conflict, in contrast, is more difficult to resolve. Ideologies are comprehensive doctrines concerning the proper and desirable pattern of rights and duties pertaining to the polity, society and economy. Their proponents often insist upon rooting out the 'wrong' ideas of opposing ideologies, which are branded as hostile, dangerous or pernicious. Moreover, in an ideologically polarised field it often is next to impossible for the proponents to agree upon a method of conflict settlement and reconciliation, as any procedural rule (such as free and contested elections) will be suspected of being biased and unfair. It is exactly these procedures to which the conflict pertains, and any argument advanced by one side is denounced by the other side as being an argument not *for* a point of view but *from* a point of view. Thus people are seen to be tainted by 'bad' ideas, and these ideas must be rooted out or prevented from circulating through repression.

Finally, identity conflict poses the most difficult type of conflict, in that the bearers and proponents of one identity make the absence or isolation of the bearers of other identities the benchmark of their well-being (as in 'ethnic cleansing') or else they demand the full assimilation of (linguistic, religious, ethnic) minorities to their own identity. If the targets of such politics of identity discrimination refuse to go away, to assimilate or to hide – and in particular if they respond by using their political rights for the assertion of cultural, ethnic and linguistic difference and the struggle for its public recognition – the universe of the political community itself is put into question, without recognised procedures being easily made available to reconcile mobilised groups involved in the politics of identity and difference. Typical demands in identity conflicts are claims for collective rights attached to the bearers of certain identities that serve to express their 'distinctiveness' and secure its recognition. The holders of other identities often respond to such claims by aggressively denying the recognition, toleration and ultimately the right to exist of a group as a 'different' group. And both sides tend to insist on both the non-negotiable as well as the non-arguable (that is, the absence of the possibility of inter-group rational debates) nature of their respective claims, whereas proponents of ideological conflict try (at least in their rhetoric) to convince others and pretend to be themselves open to rational argument.[14]

The rough typology of differences (of interest, ideology, identity) that can give rise to conflict (over resources and their control, over rights, over recognition), and the suggested hierarchy of potential disruptiveness of the dynamics of conflict (increasing from interest to identity conflicts), can also help us understand the dynamics of the transformation of conflict and the energies that drive it. Let me discuss in passing three hypotheses concerning the dynamic interconnectedness of the three levels.[15] First, the satisfaction of interests through ongoing compromises within a robust positive-sum game will reduce the significance of ideological causes and identity antagonisms. Identity conflicts will be most effectively dissolved if they are superseded by economic conflict and competition, more specifically by the effects of successful industrialisation, urbanisation and secularisation, all of which tend to emphasise categories of 'having' while de-emphasising and reducing to virtual insignificance those of 'believing' or 'being'. These are the optimistic messages of the modernisation theory of the 1950s, with their visions of the 'end of ideology' and the 'melting pot'.

A second hypothesis concerns a displacement of the energies of conflict in the opposite direction. Losers move 'one level up'. The failure to acquire what is considered a fair share in the fruits of economic output gives rise, among the losers, to the resort to militant ideological mobilisation. Similarly, the breakdown of the ideological hegemony of state socialism is followed by the resurgence of violent forms of ethnic nationalism in the region where state socialism once prevailed. In other regions, the failure of industrial modernisation generates fundamentalist theocratic backlashes. Similarly, within the OECD world the failure of political elites to come up with economic and social policies that have a credible chance of accomplishing both economic efficiency and social cohesion under the new competitive conditions of the global economy leads those elites to replace political and economic issues with moral and religious ones and often leads masses to resort to xenophobic excesses. Inversely, societies in which identity conflicts have become dominant are not likely to experience the dynamism of economic and political modernisation. Instead, they lock themselves into the vicious cycle of fundamentalist backwardness.

Third, identity politics can also be strategically put in the service of winning or defending rights and resources. The drumming up of sub-nationalist secessionist threats can be a powerful device to extract subsidies from the center or to enforce – from Katanga to 'Padania' – the protection of (regional or other) economic privilege. The instrumental use of identity symbols can also be a device to protect regional political elites from post-communist purges, as the secession of Slovakia suggests. The mobilisation along lines of ethnicity, gender and 'race' can be used as an instrument to acquire access and improve group-specific protection in increasingly precarious labour markets. It can also be employed to promote the acquisition of rights and the exemption from duties.[16] In this sense, the instrumental use of identity politics can be seen as a device for the protection and promotion of the interests of latecomers or prospective losers in the race for the blessings of modernity.

Whether identity politics is the residual of failed economic and political modernisation and an expressive response to the frustrations over this failure (hypothesis 2), or whether it is (in part, unauthentically) employed as a pretext for strategies of acquisition and protection (hypothesis 3), the promises of modernisation theory and the universalist implications of modernisation (hypothesis 1) have evidently not come true. Instead, the politics of identity-based difference is an increasingly prominent feature of increasing segments of the contemporary world, developed and developing alike.

How can a democracy cope with these potentially disruptive politics of difference? To be sure, all types of conflicts, not just identity conflicts, harbour the potential for tearing up the political community. But democracies are not defenseless. Through the allocation of rights and resources they can contain the explosive potential of conflict, thereby reconciling the divided citizenship and strengthening the foundations of a liberal political community based upon individual and equal rights (recognised in spite of the vast variety of individual life plans and preferences), as well as promoting the republican self-recognition of the political community and the commitment of its members to the principles of fairness embodied in the constitution. In other words, the democratic legislative process can yield results which have the potential of homogenising and reconciling the citizenry, thus validating the conditions of democracy in a circular process of democratic self-consolidation, fostering democracy through democratic means. The basic idea here is one of equalising status rights and opportunities, so that no party involved in any of the three types of conflict is left with rational reasons to disrupt the political community or disregard the rules on which it is based.

More specifically, there are three measures by which such self-consolidation can be accomplished. While citizenship accords one single legal status of equal liberty for all, it does not effectively reconcile conflict but rather sets the stage on which socio-economic, political and identity conflicts are carried out. Three types of rights, corresponding to the three types of difference and conflict, have been suggested – and at least in part also implemented – by which these discrepancies between formal-legal equality and actual social inequality can be mitigated or reconciled in the service of democratic self-consolidation and on the basis of equal citizenship.

This task is most easily accomplished in the case of interest-based cleavages which divide socioeconomic groups. The formula that has been adopted in order to foreclose this source of political disintegration is social rights – both substantive social rights and social policies (devoted to workers' protection, social security and full employment, but also family allowances, farm subsidies and the protection of small businesses) and procedural social rights (such as co-determination and collective wage bargaining between trade unions and employers' associations). The net result of these policies is to involve the economically less privileged categories of society in a game of either a positive-sum ('we are all going to gain in the long run') or a *petite bourgeoisie* ('we have nothing to gain, but we certainly do have something to lose') variety. In either scenario, defection is rendered irrational, and hence widely shared support for and recognition of the political community and its order enhanced.

Perhaps less easily contained is ideological conflict. At any rate, the clash of Christian, libertarian, communist, nationalist, conservative and socialist views of how a well-ordered society must be run and organised can only be mitigated through the granting and meticulously fair implementation of political rights, including the freedom of expression, communication, association and participation. That may not be enough, as the very idea of procedural fairness is one that sometimes turns out to be impossible to agree upon among the ideologically conflicting parties. If, however, such agreement and its robust implementation are both feasible, the resulting game places a premium on either of two centripetal and integrative mechanisms. First, self-blame and learning: if the rules must be recognised as unobjectionably neutral, fair and unbiased, and if 'we' still do not win the elections, a revision of 'our' ideological stance may be called for. Second, accommodation: if marginal ideological concessions are called for in order to win representation or governing power, *quid pro quo* considerations speak in favour of actually making those concessions, given the opportunity costs of intransigence. In both cases, fairness renders ideological intransigence costly and promotes convergence, again to the advantage of political integration.

Finally, there are identity conflicts. These are the most intractable of all. Nevertheless, the antidote that constitutional democracies have available in order to cope with this type of conflict is group rights. These come, as far as political life is concerned, in three varieties: rights to self-government, polyethnic rights and special representation rights.[17] The logic behind the granting of such group rights to religious, linguistic, racial, ethnic, gender, regional and other categories of people is clear enough: members of these groups are to be assured, through tangible guarantees and concessions, of their full inclusion into the citizenship; and feelings of alienation, resentment and hostility are thus to be overcome or prevented from emerging in the first place. It is to these rights – political, as opposed to social and economic; group, as opposed to individual – that I now turn in order to evaluate them as an instrument to enhance the homogeneity and integration of the political community that democratic theory and its core standard of a unified citizenship must presuppose.

III. Group rights and identity conflicts

Let us consider these various political group rights in turn. Rights to limited self-government apply only to multinational societies. But their potential use is also limited. First, they are clearly applicable in case the (ethnic, linguistic, religious or so on) groups in question settle in – and also hold, by virtue of the territorial concentration of their members – regional 'structural' majorities in distinctive sub-territories. The mechanism of self-government does not work in diaspora situations, nor does it work in situations where the unity of the regional group is easily drawn into question, or where several minorities of roughly equal size settle in the same sub-territory. An attractive alternative to rights attached to settled groups is rights attached to geographical territories, with the intended effect being that people who consider this territory their 'homeland' will move in and minorities will move out. Second, there must also be mutually recognised substantive demarcation lines concerning the policy areas for which self-government is to apply. If the policy area for which autonomy is granted is 'education,' for instance, self-government should not be allowed to shade from there into research, taxation, labour-market or fiscal policies, to say nothing about border regimes or military forces. As long as these two conditions are securely satisfied (and a jurisdictional power settling likely disputes is firmly in place), the instrument of limited self-government is a potentially powerful device of democratic self-consolidation through power-sharing. The result would be a subnationally based 'bottom-up-federalism' (of the kind attempted in Spain, Belgium and Canada). Its use can, however, easily conflict with another instrument, namely social rights: for leaving 'too much' to regional self-government is bound to constrain the resources that the nation state has available for the promotion of social security-and distributional justice. Federalism can also conflict with notions of political equality, just as second chambers do not normally assign the number of seats according to the actual size of states or other regional units, but rather accord disproportionate advantages to small units.

Let me next discuss together polyethnic rights (applying to immigrant communities) and special representation rights (applying to non-territorial minorities). Both apply to groups which cannot be defined in territorial terms. Polyethnic rights are special legal, entitlements and policy programmes, including public funding, aimed at recognising and promoting ethnic, religious, linguistic and other groups and the contribution that they make to the life of the political community. Such official recognition can take the form of the promotion of minority languages, public support for particular cultural practices, representation of minority cultures in the curricula of public schools, the funding of libraries, museums, research projects and so on. Special representation rights, in contrast, relate to group identity more indirectly. Here the issue is not what substantive ideas and cultural traditions should be given special status (as in the case of polyethnic rights) but, rather, who should do the representing or whose chances of winning elected office should be selectively improved – on the assumption that the more people of category X are represented in parliament or political parties, the more forcefully the specific ideas and traditions of group X will be promoted.

The issue of group rights raises at least four normative questions.[18] First, what are normative arguments that can motivate a majority of citizens to grant such rights to groups and tolerate the exercise of these rights, even though they violate the principle of numerical equality? Second, is it actually in the best interests of members of groups to claim and use collective rights? Third, what qualifies a 'group' as a collectivity worthy and deserving of such rights? And fourth, what determines and justifies the extent of rights accorded to the group(s) in question? In what follows, I focus principally upon the latter two questions, addressing the former just in passing.

A. What is a group?

Before entering into a discussion of these normative-cum-sociological issues, we need a reasonably robust concept of the phenomenon in question. How do we recognise a group if we see it, either from within (the demanding side of group rights) or from the outside (the granting side)? The question is less easily answered than it might appear.

Group rights, as discussed here, are minority rights.[19] Note, however, that not all kinds of minorities are (nor conceivably should be) protected by collective minority rights. For instance, employers are typically a tiny minority compared to employees. Yet their interests are not protected by 'minority rights', but by individual (property and other) rights that provide them with considerable leverage in the defense of their interests. Similarly, no one would think of minority rights applying to the universe of those citizens who have voted for the party that lost the last elections. Again, the legitimate concerns and interests of this political minority is normally thought to be taken care of through individual rights of political participation, communication and association which, taken together, may be seen as providing a fair chance that the minority becomes the majority in the next elections.

What we mean as a 'minority', that is, a candidate for group rights, is instead a 'structural minority' – a minority which, by virtue of its constitutive characteristics and the shared identity resulting therefrom, is bound to remain a minority even after its members have used their individual rights to a maximum extent. But the minority, in order to make a plausible moral claim to special rights, must also be seen as an (unjustly)[20] 'oppressed' group – a group, in other words, that 'deserves' fuller recognition than it can achieve through its own structurally limited means, whether for the sake of the full self-realisation of its members or (in addition) for the sake of its potential of 'enriching' the political community as a whole with its distinctive contributions.[21]

So far the result is that group rights are rights claimed by or granted to unjustly oppressed structural minorities. But *of what* is the minority a minority? Minorities may be minorities relative to the entire population resident in a territory, or they may be minorities relative to segments of that population.[22] While women are, at least in Western society, almost nowhere minorities in the first sense, they are almost everywhere minorities in the second sense – if we focus, for instance, upon the subset of people holding political and other elite positions. Similarly, Albanians are a vast majority in Kosovo but a minority in Serbia as a whole. 'Structural' minorities are groups whose members share essential characteristics that can neither be acquired nor given up quickly and easily. Structural minorities are thus 'locked into' a set of properties which are considered significant (or constitutive of a collective 'identity') either by themselves and/or by others and which can neither be acquired nor given up. These properties of individuals are normally acquired through birth (such as identity of the parents and their ethnicity and 'race'; gender; age; location; nationality) or shortly after, during primary socialisation (language, religious affiliation; and, according to some theories, also sexual orientation, that is, heterosexual versus homosexual). Some features that people are born with, such as left-handedness, are not significantly identity-forming; some identity-shaping properties, such as religious affiliation, can be but normally are not given up and exchanged for others. Some identity-forming properties come in grades and shades (such as 'racial' phenotypes or age), others are entirely subject to an either/or logic (such as, for all practical purposes, gender). The significance of such markers does not only result from the fact that those belonging to the minority base their own sense of identity and belonging on these markers, what we might term 'internal identity bunding'. It also, and often to a greater extent, results from the attitudes of the majority of those who do not share the property in question, and the way in which they ascribe to the property and persons possessing its legitimate access to, or exclusion from, social esteem and other valued resources. The logic of this 'external' construction of social identities is of the form: Property X conditions legitimate access to good Y and/or exclusion from good Z, in the eyes of the non-holders of property X. It is an empirical matter to what extent internal and external identity building interact according to a logic of mutual intensification, but many examples demonstrate that this is a likely event. (For instance, the immigrant Turkish minority in Germany, perhaps in response to the majority's practices of ethnic labelling and discrimination, is said to identify more strongly with the religious tradition of their country of origin than they would have done had they remained in that country.)

This case indicates how the 'identity' that makes up a 'group' is not just 'structural' (in the sense that it is typically not easily acquired or abandoned), but also to varying degrees 'voluntaristic', individually chosen as a focus of identification and emphasis in self-presentation. For instance, a descendant of an Irish mother and an Italian father living in the US can identify with neither of the two ethnic origins, or with both of them, or with either of them, or alternate between these identities. Moreover, choices made from an individual's 'identity portfolio' will be conditioned by perceived (dis)advantages associated with identifications, with strong anticipations of discrimination possibly leading to an active dissimulation or 'betrayal' of a person's 'true' group identity. This voluntaristic element of 'belonging' to a group sheds further light on the complexities of the practice of looking at societies as being composed of 'groups', and of coding individuals as unequivocally 'belonging' to groups.

But highlighting such complexities is not denying the intensity of feelings of injustice, and of conflicts emerging from such feelings, which emerge from the perceived discrimination of groups and those identifying with them. Remedial action consists in providing minorities with group rights in order to compensate for the perceived injustices of exclusion and denial of recognition. Why, then, are individual rights such as are enjoyed by everyone else deemed insufficient? In what sense are group rights different from individual rights? First, they do not apply to all citizens, but just to members of targeted groups. Second, members of the target groups are categorically and authoritatively made the beneficiary in question, without being able to individually 'opt out' of the reach of the benefits attached,[23] and without being able to give up the (by definition, ascriptive and 'unchangeable') characteristics that make up group membership. Group rights involve a strong quasi-corporatist status order: individuals are locked into group membership (whether they want it or not), and the group as a collective body becomes the target of privilege.[24]

Such granting of collective privilege may appear entirely beneficial and unproblematic. Who, after all, would object to being legally entitled to partaking in group benefits?[25] Problems arise however when we consider two possible, and in fact common, implications of the granting of group rights. One implication is that groups, who then become the bearers of rights, must first be designated in an act of political decision that turns some alleged 'group in itself' into a legally-recognised and, as it were, accredited group. Such a political definition of group status may err – and subsequently become controversial – in either of two ways. First, the authoritative assignment of group quality to a collectivity may be overly encompassing, forcibly tying together into a common membership status people who had never thought of themselves as belonging to one and the same group or, for that matter, to any group at all.[26] The other way in which group incorporation can become contested is when the groups, which are made the target of privilege, are too narrowly defined.[27] This happens if some groups are granted group rights in order to compensate for their past unfair discrimination, but other groups who feel equally discriminated are left out, with the consequence that they feel discriminated against by their being excluded from the benefits of anti-discriminatory policies. Every act of recognition of a group, as the bearer of group rights, is bound to divide the world into three segments: those who do not need group rights, because they do not belong to an unjustly oppressed minority; those who do belong to such a minority and are henceforth recognised as such; and those who aspire to such recognition but fail to win it, at least for the time being.[28]

It might appear that, in order to find out whether a group 'is' in fact a group, deserving a privileged legal status which compensates its members for injustices suffered in the past, we may want to consult history books. This is not a consistently promising way out of our definitional dilemmas. First, history books are written 'now'; and even though they are based upon historical documents, these are being 'discovered' now and interpreted now. All of which is to say that groups can 'invent' and establish themselves and their claims to group rights by invoking a history that is being written and disseminated for the purpose of group formation and collective status politics. Second, even in cases where such doubts clearly do not apply, the analytical and normative issues of inter-temporal justice need to be settled. For instance, to what extent can the present level of life chances and recognition enjoyed (and experienced as unfair disadvantages) by members of group X be causally attributed to the fact that the ancestors of those members, say, four generations back were, by the standards of today, unjustly deprived of rights and resources? And even if we could make those attributions, for how long can 'we', the non-minority, be held morally responsible for compensating for the wrongdoing of our ancestors and for the irreparable damage they have inflicted upon the minority's ancestors as well as on the descendants of those ancestors? There is, after all, no such thing as the legal entity 'Afro-Americans Inc.', the accounts of which would have to be balanced. Instead, there are ties of historical causation on the one hand and ties of recollective identification on the other, both of which can be either weaker or stronger.

Another complication with the 'oppressed minority' criterion of groups claiming rights is that every group can be easily subdivided into a virtually endless number of component groups, if a tactical interest arises for doing so.[29] What is the right level of aggregation here? Why stop at the level of 'African Americans' rather than further disaggregating this 'group' into male and female, Spanish-speaking and English-speaking, Christian and Muslim African Americans? In the other direction, the contours of the 'oppressed minority' are also easily blurred, as the vast majority ('everyone but relatively well-off, relatively young, able-bodied, heterosexual white males'[30]) can arguably be included, or in good conscience include him/herself, into a giant rainbow-coalition of oppressed minorities.[31] Under the umbrella of such an alliance, and given the potential for sub-division of every group, the potential for the proliferation of group rights claimed (as well as group rights granted or group privileges attacked) becomes evident. The results of that will hardly contribute to what group rights were originally meant to achieve, which is the integration of the political community.

Note that that still leaves unanswered our initial question: 'What is a group worthy of, special substantive and/or representation rights?' One is tempted to despair about the feasibility of a normatively meaningful answer and to resort to sociological realism, with the result being something like this: A group enjoying special rights is a collectivity, the elites of which have, in spite of the minority position of its constituency, managed to mobilise a sufficient amount of political resources in order to extract from the majority special concessions and privileges collectively assigned to the group's members. If that were right, however, it would make no sense anymore to describe such groups as 'oppressed' and 'powerless'; on the contrary, the very acquisition of group rights testifies to the group's significant control of social and political power, whereas truly disadvantaged groups, such as the European Gypsies, have hardly the organisational and political resources at their disposal that are needed in order to raise the issue of their discrimination and marginalisation.

As an alternative to sociological 'realism', and in order to stem the danger of the proliferation of ever further 'groups', one might also try to establish criteria which a group must meet in order to qualify for special collective status rights. Three such criteria are conceivable, and they would probably have to apply cumulatively. First, the group must be 'relevant' in quantitative terms. For instance, groups that make up less than one per cent of the population would not qualify for any special rights. Second, the group must be 'authentic'. That is to say, there must be clear indications of a distinctive life form and the serious and lasting allegiance of most nominal members to it, without an excessive measure of fragmentation of the group into sub-groups and sub-sub-groups. Third, and perhaps most controversial, there must be a measure of 'affinity and compatibility' between the group's life form and the life form of the majority. Taken together, this set of criteria would amount to the restriction of group rights to relatively large, internally closely integrated and easily compatible minorities that share many, though certainly not all, values and cultural patterns with the majority.[32] The reader is invited to conduct a thought experiment: how many, if any, 'groups' within her/his society qualify for 'groupness' according to these criteria?

B. What are rights?

Having pinpointed a few of the problems associated with the deceptively simple issue of 'groups' and their cognitive as well as moral and legal recognition, let us now examine the analogous problems that emerge as we look at 'rights'.[33] Probably the most general thing one can say about rights is that the more rights a person has the better for him or her, as rights provide the freedom to conduct one's life in preferred ways. It is far from certain, however, that group rights actually perform this freedom-enhancing function for group members. The trouble with group rights is that the benefits involved may not be entirely unqualified, but must be paid for by (some) group members in terms of corresponding losses and sacrifices. This applies to cases where the privilege which is granted to group members is not particularly appreciated as such by individuals within the group (because, for example, their commitment to the religion, language or other bases of collective identity is not very intense), or where members see their civil liberties being violated by the group-rights regime subjecting them to regimentation by the group's authorities. Kymlicka illustrates the possible antagonism between group rights and individual rights by reference to the rather distant case of the millet system in the Ottoman empire: 'while the Muslims did not try to suppress the Jews, or vice versa, they did suppress heretics within their own community'.[34]

The mode in which group rights operate can be either (or both) of two kinds: a plus in terms of rights enjoyed by group members (relative to the individual rights of everyone else outside the group) or a minus in terms of duties. Thus, an ethnic minority may be endowed with publicly funded support for its specific cultural practices, say, a folk dance academy. Alternatively, or in addition, group rights can consist in the exemption from duties that everyone else must comply with, an example being the permission granted to members of religious groups to have their female children not participate in otherwise obligatory gym classes in high school, or exemption from military service for reasons of belonging to a religious faith. It appears that the two – legal privilege and exemption from duties – are not strictly symmetric, as they differ in the scope of the externalities they inflict upon the larger society and its cohesion. The right to be taught language X at school may be considered harmless from this point of view, as the vast majority is neither capable of speaking nor interested in learning that language. When it comes to exemption from duties, however, the situation changes, as such exemption may be polemically depicted as 'free-riding' which, if visibly permitted, undermines the general bindingness of the law and invites others to invent reasons for claiming exemption (from military service, for example) as well.

Political group rights can be intended to be a temporary measure or a permanent one. In the first case, the justification is analogous to protective tariffs: A 'weak' group must be encouraged to develop resources, competence and self-confidence in order to become capable of eventually competing on the basis of its own resources; until it is able to do so, special preferential conditions are granted to its members. For this effect to be accomplished, an expiration clause or review procedure would have to apply. In this sense, quota rules for women concerning leadership positions in political parties (as adopted so far by the Green and Social Democratic parties in Germany) could be justified as an anti-discriminatory political head-start programme that generates the conditions of its justified abolition at a later point. But expiration (or even review) clauses are typically missing in such arrangements. Group rights are granted as permanent rights. This suggests a different justification of these rights, namely, the justification of enriching the life of the community (or party, as well as enhancing its electoral prospects) by the guaranteed special representation of supposedly group-specific styles, values and concerns of women.

Another, supposedly 'liberal' argument for group rights is proposed by Kymlicka for immigrant minorities in polyethnic societies: 'If we demand that immigrants integrate into the institutions [of the country they migrate to], we must ensure that their religious holidays, dietary requirements and dress codes are respected'.[35] The argument is based on a quid pro quo logic. But the argument raises more questions than it explicitly addresses. Why 'must' we, given the fact that the immigrants, knew or could know what was awaiting them in terms of cultural adjustment requirements, and also given the fact that new (mixed, assimilated or diasporic) cultural patterns will inevitably develop in the second and third generation? How much quid for how much quo? Why not let the general freedom of religion, diet and dress that is (supposedly) guaranteed in the host country do the job of facilitating integration? Will the purposive legal engineering aiming at 'integration' actually generate 'respect'? Where is the line to be drawn between 'benign multiculturalism', based upon civic respect, and institutionalised identities protected by and frozen into group rights?[36]

We do not need to consult books on Ottoman history to encounter the antagonism between group and individual rights. Group rights granted to religious groups imply that spiritual leaders or parents are permitted to impose rules on members, monitor their compliance and constrain their civil liberties. An extreme example is the religious belief that modern medicine is evil, and the ensuing practice of denying members access to medical emergency services. Such imposition may be motivated by the group leaders' desire to prevent assimilation, with the rational fear in mind that assimilation may undermine the power and privilege of leadership. 'To prevent religious or cultural assimilation, the minority must precommit itself in ways that reduce the freedom of its individual members.'[37] The granting of group rights is often justified as a necessary condition of preserving the group's distinctive identity. This, again, raises the question why such identity cannot be preserved on the basis of the rights of equal citizenship alone, including of course the right to form associations and communities within which religious beliefs and cultural traditions can be cultivated and propagated. Even if we were to agree in a slightly paternalist perspective (reminiscent of the protection of endangered species) that the preservation of identities must be assisted by special legal provisions (rather than through generally available liberties), we would still have to come to terms with the thorny question of what exactly the 'substance' is that is to be protected and whether such benevolent protection does not interfere with spontaneous processes of cultural change. Given that there is no clear-cut measure as to what kind of rights and how many of them are required for exactly that purpose to be achieved, and given that the elites of groups (such as ethnic artists and intellectuals, movement entrepreneurs, regional politicians and religious leaders) have obvious vested interests to expand these rights, the escalation of special rights, including representation rights, is an inherent dynamic element in the situation.

This dynamic of escalation is enforced by two factors. One is inter-minority rivalry following a 'me too' logic. The more groups are endowed with group rights, the more rights they may feel they need in order to preserve their identity and make their voices heard. The other is the use of group rights for the purpose of acquiring additional rights: for example, minority language rights, once granted, are used for mobilising more far-reaching demands, such as minority language radio stations or minority-language teacher colleges. Once a minority culture is institutionalised through a set of protective rights, there is no obvious equilibrium or saturation point. On the contrary, the more rights are granted, the easier it becomes for the group's leadership to mobilise demand for even more rights.

In principle, and from a liberal and individualistic point of view, there are two normative yardsticks by which to evaluate these group rights and the built-in dynamic of their expansion. They can be formulated in the questions of: (a) whether or not group rights do actually benefit, or protect the best interest of, the members of the group; and (b) whether the non-members can be justly expected to pay the costs of group privilege. We can refer to these as an 'internal' and as an 'external' justification of group rights respectively.

As to the first, increments in the rights of minorities can well go hand-in-hand with a decrease of the rights and actual life-chances of minority members, even if such sacrifice is not imposed by the group's leaders in the interest of maintaining their power and privilege. Language acquisition is a case in point. The opportunity costs that are involved in studying a regional language at school are often equivalent to the non-acquisition of a foreign language that may be of greater practical use. Thus, students pay for the benefit of having their linguistic identity strengthened by risking forgoing labour market opportunities. Another case in point is political affirmative action, or preferential representation rights. As in ordinary quota and affirmative action practices, chances are that a vengeful majority of white males will tend to discredit and stigmatise resulting advantages as undeserved and illegitimate, thereby reversing the intended effects of 'reverse discrimination' without any enforceable rule being available to control such second-order hostile responses.[38] This raises the question of the extent to which recognition and respect can be mandated and enforced by formal law, as opposed to the insistence upon informal standards of common decency and civility which may or may not be strengthened by the law and the mechanisms of its enforcement. At any rate, group rights of minorities must be honoured and redeemed by majorities, and honoured as a recognised 'duty', not just as a statutory rule.[39]

C. Motivating recognition: group rights and majorities

Turning to the second of the above criteria – the sacrifices the majority can legitimately be expected to make in favour of minority rights – it is sometimes said that such costs are not a sacrifice but an investment that society makes to its own multiculturalism, thereby enriching, as it were, its cultural genetic pool.[40] In other words, it is not just the majority's moral duty but, at the same time, it is in its long term collective self-interest to honour group rights. Now, arguments according to which self-interest and moral duty coincide are always suspicious. At any rate, the alleged collective advantage of diversity must be balanced against the collective disadvantage of increased transaction costs of communication and of the ongoing adjudication of polyethnic rights, as well as the conflicts over the limits of those rights, which is to say, the costs of such 'investment' in diversity. Given these costs, and due to the awareness of these costs, the consequentialist argument that diversity is enriching is hard to trust in the abstract.

Proponents of this argument usually refer to some specific group or group practice (such as an art form or ethnic cuisine) which they happen to consider as enriching with typically less sanguine emphasis on the potential contribution of others. Nor can such implicit ranking be avoided. If that is true, then by implication there are also groups and cultural practices which do not enjoy the reputation of being 'enriching' but are instead considered alien, unworthy, dangerous and potentially hostile – and therefore not deserving any sacrifice or toleration on the part of the majority. Hence 'enrichment-oriented multiculturalism' may turn out not to be colour-blind but rather, in effect, strongly discriminating. On the other hand, if the argument for toleration does not start from desirable contributions and enrichment coming from the group in question, it must start from the desired consequence of enhancing democratic homogeneity by eliminating reasons for justified complaint about non-admittance to a homogeneous citizenship status. But that could also be achieved, and in collectively less costly ways, through stricter provision and enforcement of universal citizen rights and equal opportunities which, after all, include the opportunity to pursue a great diversity of values, styles and identities (but which would then have to be relegated to a 'sub-political' realm of the personal conduct of life). Consideration of consequences does not seem to yield a conclusive argument concerning costs and sacrifices the majority can be required to make.

Alternatively, one can (and, in fact, must) rely on the 'justice argument' that it is the duty, whatever the costs involved, of the majority to eliminate the minority's suffering that would result from inadequate opportunities to practice its inherited life form and cultural tradition. The Achilles heel of this argument from justice is that it is so difficult to assess the amount of such suffering in unobtrusive ways. Revealed preferences for the preservation of 'identity' values must always be suspected, in either negative or positive ways, of being tainted by strategic considerations. Moreover, some cultural life forms, including languages, have disappeared as a living cultural practice even in the absence of any trace of discrimination, and perhaps even painlessly so; they have simply fallen victim to the forces of cultural change, resistance to which can hardly be postulated to be a moral duty. At any rate, any indicator as to how strongly the minority actually values and needs, for its collective self-realisation, the protection of its life form is unlikely to be strategy-proof.

Certainly the strongest moral reason for recognising group rights is the majority's awareness of past injustices inflicted upon a group by its predecessors. Accordingly, minorities will find it easier to extract concessions from majorities if they can invoke the logic of a fair compensation for such injustices. This applies to the cases of Afro-Americans, ex-colonial populations resident in France, Britain or the Netherlands, aboriginal peoples in Canada, Australia or the US, the Basques in Spain, to say nothing about Jews and other Holocaust victims in Germany. Feminists have made analogous arguments in view of the injustices inflicted upon women by millennia of patriarchy. But even in these cases, and with the passing of the generations of both the immediate victims and the immediate perpetrators, it is an open question as to when it is appropriate to switch from a backward-looking logic of compensation to a forward-looking logic of colour-blind fairness and equal opportunity. As 'equal opportunity' involves issues of sharing and redistribution as opposed to the symbolic practice of recognition, the former is likely to be morally more, not less, demanding (as well as more honest) than the ambiguous and often backfiring practices of attaching a 'positive stigma' to groups through 'reverse discrimination'.[41]

So far we have discussed two classes of objections to group rights. First, given hostile reactions to and opportunity costs of such rights, they may not really be in the best interest of the members of the group that is seemingly favoured by such rights. This is also the case because group rights will typically empower group representatives who can use these rights in order to infringe upon individual rights or discriminate against internal heretics or others whom they consider less 'worthy' members of the group they represent. Second, the damage caused by group rights affects everyone in the political community, whether through the transaction costs caused by multilingualism or through the dynamic of demand escalation and group proliferation that is set in motion once the first group rights are adopted. It is unclear and cannot be discussed here whether, third, there is also a class of objections based upon the legitimate interests of the majority not to have their (linguistic, religious and so on) form of life disturbed and threatened by overly generous concessions to minorities, particularly if the majority fails to appreciate the legally enforced polyethnicity as an unqualified 'enrichment' of their social life and national culture (as most Estonians do not so regard the Russian minority in that country, for example).

A final objection to group rights must be mentioned. There cannot be any doubt that ascriptive groups whose members attach great value and significance to the practice and preservation of group identity exist in modern societies. Neither can there be any doubt that members of groups often suffer severe disadvantages due to the fact that they belong to and identify with the group. The denial of the right to express and practice their identity, and the attachment of negative sanctions and deprivations to bearers of the marks of ascribed identity are injustices that stand in the way of the consolidation of a homogeneous citizenship status – which is, in turn, an essential precondition for democratic stability, for if the belonging to the political community and the equal liberty it guarantees is put in question, then there arises a type of conflict with which the highly precarious regime form of liberal democracy cannot easily cope. What does not, however, follow from this set of considerations is the proposition that the integration of groups into civil society is best served by granting them group rights, as opposed to individual rights like the standard rights of religious and cultural freedom and the right to form voluntary associations, and various other social rights nowadays ordinarily ascribed to individuals.

These sceptical considerations apply all the more, as there is an obvious inter-group difference in the chances of groups to acquire group rights. The willingness of majorities to grant group rights to minorities is contingent upon both properties of the minority in question and properties, perceptions and considerations of the majority.

As far as minorities are concerned, their struggle for rights will succeed more easily the larger the group is and the more political resources it has at its disposal due to its size and visibility. If the group in question is an ethnic group, it will also benefit from the presence of nearby patron states of the same ethnicity. Similarly, in the case of religious groups, international religious organisation (such as the Roman Catholic Church or Islamic theocracies) will mobilise effective support. Moreover, international examples, policy moves and role models can both encourage minorities and discourage their opponents in the struggle for group rights, as is indicated by the advances of feminist movements that have been a distinctively international phenomenon throughout the OECD world and beyond in the 1970s and 1980s. Conversely, the acquisition of minority rights will be a vastly more difficult matter if the group is relatively small or highly dispersed, if it is poorly organised, does not enjoy the patronage of transnational forces or movements, and if it does not enjoy the moral advantage of being able to trace its plight back to previous acts of unfairness, now recognised as such, committed by the majority's state (all of which applies to the Romany in East Central Europe). Finally, it is likely that those minorities who are most similar and show the greatest affinity with the majority in terms of cultural (phenotypic, ethnic, linguistic and religious) traits will be given priority in the granting of group rights.[42]

From the point of view of the majority which is called upon to grant group rights, all depends upon how strongly it values 'diversity'. The belief that 'interaction with different cultures, belief systems and presumptions makes us smarter' is typically not shared by everyone in the majority, nor does it apply to every minority.[43] By the same logic, some groups may be branded as having no potential for 'making us smarter'. Beyond the appreciation of diversity, two additional points play a role in motivating recognition.[44] First, group rights will be conceded more easily if there is no fear of proliferation – no expectation that group rights, once granted to one group, will soon be demanded by other groups as well. That is to say, the group to which rights are conceded must be in some plausible sense singular, so as to preclude proliferation of demands for rights with its incalculable implications. Second, the majority that is to grant the rights will be more forthcoming in doing so if it has reasons to expect that, once these rights are granted, a durable balance will be reached. That is to say, demands for group rights should not be seen as potentially instrumental for the acquisition of further group rights, and thus as the initial step in a process of escalation eventually leading to the break-up of the political community.[45] Thus the hypothesis is that majorities tend to grant group rights most readily to those minorities which cause the least concern that the granting of such rights will trigger the dynamics of proliferation or escalation.

IV. Conclusion

Of the four principal strategies that democracies have available to consolidate a homogeneous *demos* and to implement the ideal of citizenship – civil, social, political and 'identity group' rights – the last one is less promising in its effects than those belonging to the previous three 'generations'. Equalising citizenship rights by granting special group rights to minorities is at best an ambiguous formula, because both the questions of what constitutes a 'group' and what is the adequate and sufficient amount of 'rights' remain contested and tend to give rise to the dynamics of proliferation and escalation. Group issues are susceptible to tribalistic political entrepreneurship precisely because the number of groups, the groups' identity, the strength of the sense of group allegiance on the part of members, the durability of such allegiance, and the alleged suffering resulting from the state's policy of 'colour-blindness' do not lend themselves to easy and unobtrusive measurement. In consequence, group rights (other than sub-territorial rights to self-government at the municipal or state level) have a strong potential for further dividing rather than unifying the encompassing political community, and of weakening civic republican loyalties and commitments. This is also the case because any recognition of political groups and their rights elevates the status of the collective recipient of these rights relative to those potential groups that are not, or not yet, considered worthy of being granted such rights, with new acts of unfairness being implied by the very method of compensating for unfairness.

Individual civic, political and social rights, including the rights to form civic as well as religious associations and to mobilise for support through fair access to the media, appear fully sufficient to voice the concerns of 'ascriptive' groups.[46] That applies, of course, with the proviso that governments are effectively hindered (if need be, through the supervisory role performed by international juridical institutions) from curtailing the individual rights of categories of their citizens for the sake of fostering 'national unity'. Moreover, social rights that can be claimed equally by all citizens will effectively compensate for categorical disadvantages suffered by groups. In fact, the implementation of social rights – to education, health, housing, labour market access and so on – that would redeem the liberal promise of equal opportunity are both a more demanding and more effective way to accommodate group conflict, compared to the symbolic politics of 'recognising' groups through the costless politics of assigning them collective rights. There is neither a demonstrable need for, nor an innocuous way to create and administer a fourth generation of rights in response to identity conflicts.

Acknowledgements: The author has received helpful comments from David Abraham, Rainer Dombois, Bob Goodin, Peter A. Kraus, Bernhard Peters, Ulrich K. Preuß and Philippe C. Schmitter. I am also grateful for comments on earlier versions presented to conferences at Max Mueller Bahwan, Bangalore, India; Columbia University, New York; Green College, University of British Columbia, Vancouver; and the European University Institute, Florence.

Notes

1. Cf. C. Offe, *Varieties of Transition: The East European and East German experience*, Oxford, Polity, 1996, ch. 4.

2. Cf. P. C. Schmitter and T. Lynn Karl, 'What democracy is…and is not', *Journal of Democracy*, 1991 (Summer), vol. 3, no. 3, pp. 75–88.

3. J. J. Linz and A. Stepan, *Problems of Democratic Transition and Consolidation: Southern Europe, South America and post-communist Europe*, Baltimore, Md., Johns Hopkins University Press, 1996.

4. J. J. Linz, *Democratization and Types of Democracies: New tasks for comparativists*, Mimeo, Yale University, 1996, p. 10.

5. 'It is important to stress that democracy is a way to govern a state and that, therefore, in countries where the existence of the state is in question... it is not possible to talk about a transition to democracy...To put it simply, no state – no democracy. Stateness [is] a requirement for political democracy' (Linz, *Democratization and Types of Democracies...*, pp. 6–7, 9). Incidentally, it is not entirely clear what this means regarding the potential democratic quality of the European Union, which lacks not only a pre-established stateness but also a fixed territorial extension.

6. At best, it might be said that the democratic regime form propagates itself via imitation – arguably in the same way as the nation state spread internationally as a political form during the 'spring of the people' throughout nineteenth century continental Europe.

7. Note that the latter case is different from the perfectly normal democratic adoption of immigration laws, because these become effective only after a 'foreign' subject has 'voluntarily' (that is, in ways other than through the discretion of some domestic authority) declared his/her intent to become part of the domestic citizenry.

8. Cf. J. Habermas, *Die Einbeziehung des Anderen. Studien zur politischen Theorie*, Frankfurt, Suhrkamp, 1996, pp. 139f.

9. W. Kymlicka, 'Interpreting group rights', *The Good Society*, 1996, vol. 6, no. 2, pp. 8–11 [11].

10. It helps if at least one of the units to be separated is an island, as in the separation of Singapore and Malaysia.

11. Or changes of borders are pursued within the procedural limitations prescribed by international law.

12. The empirical test of homogeneity is behavioural: will those defeated in the democratic political process, in particular 'structural' minorities, still prefer to stay part of that community? Or do they show tendencies of escaping or seceding from that community or of abandoning their role and obligations within it?

13. A. O. Hirschman, 'Social conflicts as pillars of democratic market societies', *Political Theory*, 1994, vol. 22, pp. 203–218.

14. For a strong feminist critique of universalist citizenship and its opposition to identity group representation, see I. M. Young, 'Polity and group difference: a critique of the ideal of universal citizenship', *Ethics*, 1989, vol. 99, pp. 250–274.

15. Cf. W. Connor, *Ethnonationalism: The quest for understanding*, Princeton, N.J., Princeton University Press, 1994; T. Gitlin, *The Twilight of Common Dreams: Why America is wracked by culture wars*, New York, Holt, 1995.

16. Much of the legal and philosophical discussion of the issue of group exemption from the duties of citizenship is of course focused on the Old Order Amish and the decision of the US Supreme Court in *Wisconsin V. Yoder*, 406 US 205 (1972). The question, again, is whether the permission granted to one group to (partially: cf. J. Spinner, *The Boundaries of Citizenship: Race, ethnicity, and nationality in the liberal state*, Baltimore, Md., John Hopkins University Press, 1994) drop out of citizenship generates second-order effects of undermining civic commitments more broadly and/or of punishing the beneficiaries of exemption with hostile (though informal) exclusionary responses.

17. I disregard here, and in the following, those social and economic group-specific rights that are designed to compensate members of specific groups for the consequences of past and present discrimination at school, in neighbourhoods, in the media, and particularly in the job market.

18. R. Bauböck, 'Liberal Justifications for Group Rights', in C. Joppke and S. Lukes (eds), *Multicultural Questions*, Oxford, Oxford University Press, 1998, pp. 133–157.

19. W. Kymlicka, *Multicultural Citizenship*, Oxford, Clarendon Press, 1995. But upon closer inspection, not even that turns out to be true. There are a number of cases in post-Communist Central East Europe where majorities of the respective titular nation assign to themselves, constitutionally and through their citizenship laws, a privileged status so as to prevent the alleged danger of 'contamination' of the majority's identity with 'alien' linguistic, ethnic and religious influences coming from internal minorities. Cases in point are Estonia, Latvia, Slovakia and Bulgaria. See further J. Elster, C. Offe, U. Preuß *et al.*, *Institutional Design in Post-Communist Societies: Rebuilding the ship at sea*, Cambridge, Cambridge University Press, 1997, ch. 7.

20. There are also structural minorities which are justly oppressed: most people would probably consider drug dealers or child molesters as cases in point.

21. Groups might also claim group rights even if they are in no way 'oppressed' or unfairly deprived of the recognition of their identity. In fact, they may be ruling minorities. But that can only happen under non-democratic regime forms, such as South Africa under apartheid. Thus, a full account of all types of beneficiaries of group rights would have to include: ruling or otherwise privileged minorities, oppressed minorities, and majorities (such as members of the 'titular' nation).

22. A dramatically extreme case is that of the Black population in South Africa. While constituting a vast majority in the general population, Blacks were until recently denied full citizen rights and, as a consequence, access to political, economic and other elite positions.

23. This collective form of the attribution of rights is not to be confused with other forms of group privileges, such as, for instance, tax privileges granted in some countries to the publishers of academic books. While in this example no publisher is able to opt out of the privilege that is categorically accorded to

the industry, s/he may well individually opt out of the industry itself – unless we deal with an authoritarian state-corporatist regime which excludes exactly this option.

24. It is worth bearing in mind the nominal nature of that 'privilege'. For, first, preferential treatment of group members can give rise to second-order effects of retaliatory discrimination and hostility from the majority or from competing groups, against which the group's members may be entirely defenceless (see below). Second, status rights for minorities can be openly double-edged, an example being provisions that used to be in force in British institutions of higher education guaranteeing, but also limiting, the percentage of Jews among the student body.

25. The question is not quite as rhetorical as it sounds. An example is the 'gendering' of the German language that was adopted as an administrative practice in a number of states and institutional sectors during the 1980s. The result is that all nominally male forms in legal texts must be complemented by the female form (like in actor/actress), for which the German language provides abundant opportunities. It is far from evident that this grammatical advancement of the status of women must naturally be desired by all women. Objections include the adverse effect this linguistic regime has on the readability of the text of legal documents and journalistic prose for both women and men, as more than half of all nouns are subject to such gendering duplication. Another objection is that the grammatical status advancement of women is just symbolic, not real.

26. The policy of German local governments of forming '*Auslanderbeiräte*' (foreigners' councils) as consultative bodies is a case in point. People represented by such councils often belong to half a dozen or more different nationalities. It would never occur to them having their identity cast in terms of being 'foreigners', an identity label that is entirely shaped by the perceptions and preferences of the domestic majority population.

27. N. Glazer, *Ethnic Dilemmas, 1964–1982*, Cambridge, Mass., Harvard University Press, 1983, pp. 254–273.

28. Y. Soysal, (in *Boundaries and Identity: Immigrants in Europe*, Mimeo, Department of Sociology, Harvard University, 1995, p. 8) provides the example of the Netherlands, where the ethnic minority policy 'officialises' a number of ethnic immigrant groups but leaves out the Chinese and the Pakistani for the reason (as she quotes one official explaining) that 'they are assumed to have no problems with their participation in Dutch society'. That obviously raises the question: whose problems? What pretends to be respect for the 'truly deserving' minorities may also be read as an arbitrary administrative coding practice driven by opportunistic considerations.

29. To illustrate, let me take an example from social and economic rights and a case in which I have been involved. German universities have instituted 'women's promotion plans' that provide special grants for which women at advanced stages of their academic career can apply. When applying for such a

grant, one female colleague was told by administrators of the programme that, although being highly qualified on the basis of her academic record, she still could not be considered as her files showed that she is, although a women, *not a mother.* This indicates how flexibly and opportunistically criteria of group membership can be handled.

30. Kymlicka, *Multicultural Citizenship*, p. 145.

31. If the group code is so widely applied, what happens to those who do not identify with any of the groups? Is there a residual 'group' of all those lacking group markers? To assume this would be following the logic of American Protestant sects who divide the universe into two major sects: their own sect of 'true Christians' and the opposing sect of 'secular humanists'. Such sectarian social ontology is also evident in some feminist writings. As all women are seen as united and self-identified *as* women, there must also be a dominant conspiracy of 'malehood'.

32. Note, however, that the relationship between (relative) group size and the ease with which the group obtains collective rights may be U-shaped. Very small ethnic minorities can be granted rights by the majority because the risk that the disruptive mechanisms of escalation or proliferation will set in as a consequence is deemed negligible by the majority.

33. An elaborate classification of the very different kinds of group rights that are to be found in practice is provided by J. T. Levy, 'Classifying Cultural Rights', in W. Kymlicka and I. Shapiro (eds), *Nomos XXXIX: Ethnicity and Group Rights*, New York, New York University Press, 1997, pp. 22–66.

34. Kymlicka, 'Interpreting group rights', p. 8.

35. *Ibid.*, p. 10.

36. C. Joppke, 'Multiculturalism and immigration: a comparison of the United States, Germany, and Great Britain', *Theory and Society*, 1996, vol. 25, pp. 449–500.

37. J. Elster, *Ulysses Unbound: Studies in rationality and precommitment*, Mimeo, New York, Columbia University, 1996, p. 53.

38. A blatant, though not singular, example of 'secondary discrimination on the grounds of reverse discrimination' is this. In German state universities, candidates for full professorships are short-listed and ranked by the university and appointed by the state Ministry of Higher Education. As universities know that Ministries are committed to increasing the (incredibly low) proportion of women in the professorate, they can be virtually certain that a single female name, should it appear on the short list, will very likely be chosen for appointment, and the preference order of the list will be overruled. As a consequence, hiring committees (irrespective of their gender composition) have a rational interest to keep any female applicant (unless she is ranked first) off the short list in order to preserve the university's 'autonomy' to express priorities and its chance to have its priorities respected. (Thanks to Gerd Grözinger for pointing out to me this mechanism.)

39. As a shorthand for 'recognised duty', we may think of the following subtraction formula: duty is the amount of operative bindingness of social norms that remains in force of its nominal bindingness after (a) all opportunities for unsanctioned violation have been eliminated, and (b) all excuses for non-compliance have been invalidated.

40. Kymlicka, *Multicultural Citizenship*, pp. 122–123.

41. Bauböck (in 'Liberal Justifications for Group Rights') argues the following with respect to ethnic groups who have been subject to past deprivation of economic and political rights and 'second class citizenship': 'These effects are so pervasive that equal individual rights are clearly insufficient. Group-differentiated programmes of community development and affirmative action are needed to overcome them'. I disagree on both counts. If individual rights (including 'positive' rights) are deemed to be 'insufficient', they need to be augmented, in courts and legislatures, rather than supplemented – particularly as group rights are unlikely to do the job except under the most favorable of circumstances (under which they appear least needed).

42. Note, however, that 'similarity' is itself a social construct that would have to be validated by both sides involved. For instance, for the outside observer Roman Catholicism and Orthodoxy may not appear a matter of significant divergence of religious identities. That, however, is not the view taken by either the Serbs or the Croats.

43. The quoted proposition comes from an Op-Ed comment in the *New York Times*, 2 April, 1996. But Bauböck ('Liberal Justifications for Group Rights') persuasively asks the question: 'What could convince a true believer that it is better for her to live in a society together with people of other faiths, agnostics and atheists rather than in a society where her religion is shared by all?' Only religiously unaffiliated actors are likely to develop a preference for institutionalised religious diversity through group rights, if only for the (slightly cynical) reason that that arrangement would maximise her/his chance to be left alone by any of them. A more respectable argument for the intrinsic value of diversity is that it affords 'the reflexivity that results from experiencing other cultures' (*ibid.*) and, supposedly, the opportunity for self-scrutinising the limitations of one's own culture; but it is not evident that this opportunity, so ubiquitous in modern society, should be contingent upon the presence of group rights.

44. In a brief filed with the US Supreme Court in August 1997, the Clinton Administration elaborated an argument as to why adherence to affirmative action does not only make 'us' smarter, but, more specifically, the police more effective. 'Local law enforcement agencies can demonstrate a compelling need for a diverse work force that justifies the carefully tailored use of race in employment decisions. For instance, if an undercover officer is needed to infiltrate a racially homogeneous gang, a law enforcement agency must have the flexibility to assign an officer of the same race to that task' (*New York Times*, 23 August, 1997). It is, however, in no way evident that such flexibility

could not equally well – or better – be achieved within a framework of equal opportunity (as opposed to preferential) hiring practices.

45. This fear of escalation explains the stubbornness with which governments in Central East Europe have resisted the demands for ethnic minority group rights, particularly so in Slovakia, Bulgaria and Romania. The anticipation on the part of the majority is that, once we grant the first step, we are bound to be sliding down a slippery slope: from cultural rights to language rights, from language rights to an autonomous educational and media regime, from there to successful mobilisation for territorial self-government, and from there to secession or fusion with some 'historically hostile' neighboring state, with either international or civil war as the necessary by-product. These seemingly obsessive fears are often not entirely irrational, as both sides to the conflict know, and know that the other side knows, that the region has a history of imperial control, with the present minority being just a remaining residue of some former imperial power – as are the Turks in Bulgaria, Hungarians in Slovakia and Rumania, or Russians in Estonia. The result is that constitutions of these post-communist countries are not only weak on minority rights, but often strongly proclaim the cultural and ethnic majority rights of the respective titular nation (U. K. Preuß, 'Patterns of Constitutional Evolution and Change in Eastern Europe', in J. J. Hesse and N. Johnson (eds), *Constitutional Change in Europe*, Oxford, Oxford University Press, 1995, pp. 95–128; Elster, Offe and Preuß *et al. Institutional Design in Post-Communist Societies*, ch. 7).

46. C. Kukathas, *The Fraternal Conceit: Liberal vs. collectivist ideas of community*, Sydney, Centre for Independent Studies, 1991; C. Kukathas, Survey Article, 'Multiculturalism as Fairness: Will Kymlicka's multicultural citizenship', *Journal of Political Philosophy*, 1997, vol. 5, pp. 406–27; Y. Tamir, *Liberal Nationalism*, Princeton, N.J., Princeton University Press, 1993.

Chapter Thirteen

Perspectives on Post-Conflict Constitutionalism: Reflections on Regime Change Through External Constitutionalisation[*]

Ulrich K. Preuß

I. Introduction: Self-determination and imposed freedom

In the relatively short history of modern constitutionalism, constitution-making has been an act of political liberation from regimes whose legitimacy had been compromised. True, there were exceptions. In 19th century Germany during the constitutional struggles between the monarchy and democratic forces, constitutions were periodically imposed by an autocratic monarch.[1] But after the universal triumph of the principle of popular sovereignty in the decades after World War II, today the normative force of constitutions rests upon the constituent power of the people.[2] Constitution-making has been tantamount to a people's aspiration to disrupt the continuity of their political system and to found a new polity.[3] Until recently, this seemed to be an axiom of political philosophy and constitutional theory. However, this view has now been placed into question by the emergence of constitutions which do not originate from, or pay little regard to, the constituent power of the people.

Two instances come to mind. The first is the transformation of the formerly communist regimes in Central and Eastern Europe through revolutions[4] involving some kind of constitution-making.[5] What strikes the student of modern constitutional history as remarkable is the 'notable absence of constitutional constituent assemblies',[6] or any other kind of constituent power. These transformations may give rise to a new variety of constitutionalism characteristic of societies in transition from authoritarian to democratic rule, which one could term 'constitutionalism of transition'.[7] The second instance is coerced regime change from outside through the imposition not just of new rulers, but of a constitution aimed at sustaining the more or less violent conversion of an autocratic regime to a democratic system. The obvious case is Iraq where the United States, after the military defeat of the Saddam Hussein regime, established an interim constitution, soon followed by a constitution drafted by Iraqi political forces under the auspices

[*]   'Perspectives on post-conflict constitutionalism: reflections on regime change through external constitutionalization', *New York Law School Law Review*, 2006–2007, vol. 51, no. 3, pp. 467–494.

of the Americans.[8] The inauguration of democratic constitutions in Germany and Japan after World War II by the Western Allies and the Americans, respectively,[9] is largely seen as the historical precedent of what one may call heteronomous constitutionalism.

This article addresses the question of whether we are currently witnessing modes of nation-building or regime change in which the connection between popular self-determination and constitution-making is dissolved or at least significantly loosened. This article will proceed in the following steps: Part II contains a brief discussion of the ambiguous relationship between constitution-making and political freedom, and addresses the question of whether heteronomous constitutions can be legitimised. Part III describes a relevant case study, the history of the German Basic Law, which was inspired by the three Western Allies after they defeated and occupied Germany. Part IV discusses which societal preconditions must be met for an imported constitution to be compatible with the receiving social structure of a particular country and become the accepted normative foundation of the polity. Amongst numerous preconditions, two will be examined more closely, the first being statehood and secularisation and the second being ethnic and religious homogeneity. In Part V, this Article will scrutinise the role of the international community as an external actor in the creation of new constitutions for conflict-ridden societies and ask whether it is justified to speak of an emerging paradigm of constitutional interventionism. Finally, Part VI will conclude with a brief summary of why regime change through the coercive transplantation of constitutions is a promising venture.

II. Heteronomous constitutions?

Heteronomous constitutions seem possible if one reconsiders the connection between constitutionalism and autonomy. In the history of modern constitutionalism, constitutions have always been considered the embodiment of a people's self-determination as expressed by its constituent power. Constitutions are the product of severe conflict in society. Even constitutions following the paradigm of constitutionalism of transition, and its inherent tendency towards legal continuity,[10] have not been created in times of political routine. Constitutions are symbols of a new political beginning after the past order has been brought to an end in a more or less violent and abrupt manner. In a socio-political perspective, constitutions can be regarded as a ceasefire agreement or a peace treaty between social forces struggling for power in a polity. Constitutions come into being after a revolution or war, but in either case the people are deeply involved. After a revolution – the most intense kind of internal social conflict – the triumphant forces lay out their principles of how society should be ordered. This is tantamount to imposing their rule upon the defeated groups who are then usually denounced as 'counter-revolutionary', 'reactionary', or sometimes even as 'enemies of the people'. Constitution-making after a war is not very different. If the war was lost, then the demoralised masses place the blame for their defeat and sufferings on the now 'old regime', which has proved itself unable to defend the essential interests of the nation. They throw their rulers out of office and the desire for a new beginning manifests with the demand for a new constitution expected to reflect their needs, hopes, and aspirations.[11] But even after a victorious war, a new distribution of power, i.e. a new constitution, is on the agenda of the nation. The people want recognition and remuneration for their sacrifices and hence demand a new distribution of the benefits of the social compact.[12]

If constitution-making is a phenomenon of citizens' activation, then the idea of imposing a constitution upon a nation appears odd and incoherent. Imposition means degrading the people to a thoroughly passive and subaltern status which is exactly what constitutionalism is supposed to overcome in the first place.[13] On the other hand, we must not forget that since its historical breakthrough at the end of the 18th century, modern constitutionalism has been characterised by its universalist imprint. The invocation of inalienable rights of men in the American and French Revolution demonstrates that the benefit of political freedom – the core of modern constitutionalism – was not thought to be limited to those peoples who had been lucky enough to liberate themselves; rather, true freedom could only be enjoyed if it was shared with all other peoples. This is unmistakably expressed in the wording of the draft for a resolution of the French National Assembly written by Deputy Volnay in May 1790:

The Assembly solemnly declares:

1. that it regards the entire mankind as a single and identical society whose goal is the peace and the happiness of all and every single of its members;

2. ...

3. ... that, consequently, no people has the right to take possession of the property of another people or to deprive it of its freedom and its natural advantages;

4. that every war fought for another motive or purpose but the defence of a just cause is an act of oppression which every great society has to stand up against because one state's invasion of another one tends to menace the freedom and security of all.[14]

This principle did not prohibit the use of force to liberate a people living under the rule of a tyrant. Freedom was considered a benefit which rightly belonged to all, and spreading liberty worldwide was considered a service to mankind. On December 15, 1792, the French Revolutionary Convention expressed this idea in a 'Proclamation to the liberated peoples' in which it solemnly declared:

Friends and Brothers, we have conquered liberty, and we shall maintain it. We offer you the enjoyment of this inestimable benefit which has always been our right, and of which our oppressors have not been able to deprive us except by crime. We have chased away your tyrants; show yourselves to be free men, and we will guarantee you from their vengeance, their projects and their return ... .[15]

What follows are the declarations of the French Revolution, using almost the same language as the preamble to the Declaration of the Rights of Man and Citizen of 26th August 1789. In other words, liberty is a universal good which must not be restricted to a particular nation, moreover, its principles and demands are everywhere the same. In view of this there is no principal difference between the self-liberation of a people and its liberation through others. Consequently, Bonaparte's crusades, which expanded French domination over almost the entire European continent and beyond, were wars of liberation through which he intended to spread the universalist message of the French Revolution over the 'backward countries'.

While the universalisation of freedom (and constitutionalism, its institutionalised paradigm) promised the liberation of mankind from the evils of oppression and tyranny, the realisation of this high-spirited project entailed a major problem: the distinction between imperialism and liberation was blurred, and this was tantamount to confusing liberty and tyranny. Can we conceive of the paradox of 'imposed freedom'? To liberate a people means to eliminate an obstacle – for example, an authoritarian ruler – which prevents them from doing what they could otherwise do. This definition refers to Isaiah Berlin's famous notion of 'negative freedom'.[16] Negative freedom presupposes that the obstacle is perceived as just that, an obstacle which stands in the way of the actions which one would otherwise perform. If people regard their rulers as a barrier to freedom, the removal of this barrier by the army of a benevolent neighbour is an act of liberation, not of imposition (which presupposes a certain degree of coercion). If the people accept their rulers and do not consider them to be illegitimate, the removal of the rulers by a benevolent third party is not liberation, but the imposition of a way of living which they did not choose. Thus, 'imposed freedom' is a contradiction in terms: Either I am liberated in that my ruler who is a blockage to my freedom is removed – whoever removes it, the result is in accordance with my will and hence not imposed. Or the ruler is removed whom I do not regard as a barrier to my freedom – the removal may open hitherto unavailable options for me, in any case these options have been created against or at least without my will; hence they are imposed upon me.

But for some this may seem an overly simplistic criterion of liberty. It is possible that somebody lives under the rule of an oppressor but does not know what it means to be free, i.e. to enjoy new options. If so, then a person can only be free if he is truly autonomous and in full possession of his human capacities, and therefore capable of distinguishing freedom from enslavement. This is basically the argument that leads to what Berlin calls 'positive freedom'. The idea of positive freedom assumes that other persons simply do not know what is good for them, and we are fully justified in coercing them to accept what we have identified as valuable, in fact indispensable, to their true Self.[17] An example of this idea is a parent's right and duty to educate his or her children. Viewed as such, imposing freedom on others is not necessarily self-contradictory.

But imposing a constitution is a different case. Constitutions are complex devices which presuppose the political majority of the people living under it. Constitutions impose restraints on the members of a polity by limiting freedom. But, it is their paradoxical quality that they limit freedom for the sake of increasing freedom, that they are mechanisms of autopaternalism through which the members of a would-be-polity create the appropriate tools for coping with challenges and future contingencies.[18] What at first glance appear to be merely limiting and disabling schemes – for instance the separation of powers, the guarantee of fundamental rights for individuals as insurmountable barriers to governmental intrusion, or the establishment of constitutional courts and their authority to review legislative acts – are devices which enable reflection, deliberation and collective learning.[19] Most importantly, a constitution can play this enabling role only to the degree that it is a self-binding mechanism. It must be self-imposed so that its restraining force is seen as a means of achieving freedom, not incapacitation and bondage. Thus, the liberation of a people cannot occur through the imposition of a constitution.

If imposing a constitution upon a people is not a reasonable option, then liberating a people from their oppressors would only make sense if the people were able to mobilise their own constitution-making capacities. One could hypothesise that an oppressed people that have not freed themselves from their oppressors do not develop the strong motives and necessary energy to preserve the bequeathed freedom through the foundational act of constitution-making. John Stuart Mill might have had this in mind when he argued against intervention for the sake of a people's liberation. He insisted upon the principle of self-determination and argued that a people can only enjoy the freedom it achieves on its own.[20] However this may be, we must not equate freedom and constitution-making. It is one thing to liberate a people by chasing away its rulers; it is quite a different thing to arrogate the responsibility to give those people a constitution.

This difference does not necessarily mean that constitutions can only come into being through the constituent power of a free people, although this is certainly the ideal case. Mill's opinion reflects the liberal view that nations, similar to individuals, are independent and autonomous actors who are responsible for themselves and should avoid interfering with the affairs of other (individual or collective) persons. This view is supported by contemporary public international law. Article 2, paragraph 2 of the Charter of the United Nations proclaims the sovereign equality of its members as its basic principle, and paragraph 4 of the same Article prohibits the 'threat or use of force against the territorial integrity or political independence of any state'. Any state interference with the internal affairs of another state is prohibited unless authorised by the U.N. Security Council or justified by the need for self-defence. Arguably this includes interventions on humanitarian grounds to protect a state's population from injustice. At least, this appears to be the prevailing opinion among public international lawyers who regard the domestic affairs of a state, including its constitution, as remaining outside the jurisdiction and evaluation of other states.[21]

But there are other voices, the most prominent being that of the former Secretary-General of the United Nations, Javier Pérez de Cuéllar, who in his annual report to the General Assembly stated:

[T]he principle of non-interference with the essential domestic jurisdiction of States cannot be regarded as a protective barrier behind which human rights could be massively or systematically violated with impunity. The fact that, in diverse situations, the United Nations has not been able to prevent atrocities cannot be cited as an argument, legal or moral, against the necessary corrective action, especially where peace is threatened... . The case for not impinging on the sovereignty, territorial integrity and political independence of States is by itself indubitably strong. But it would only be weakened if it were to carry the implication that sovereignty, even in this day and age, includes the right of mass slaughter or of launching systematic campaigns of decimation or forced exodus of civilian populations in the name of controlling civil strife or insurrection.[22]

Scholars of public international law and practitioners alike have echoed this assessment.[23] Some go a step further and re-conceptualise the idea of sovereignty. They claim that the principle of sovereignty in public international law refers to the sovereignty of the people, not of the state and its elites. According to this view, there is an 'emerging right to democratic governance' in public international law[24] which under certain conditions may justify a unilateral armed intervention into the domestic affairs of an undemocratic state; this would be an intervention against political leaders who are not entitled to the protection of the country's sovereignty if their leadership is based upon usurpation.[25] Other authors are more reluctant, not only because they are aware of the looming danger of misuse, but because of the danger in advancing this largely procedural conception of liberal democracy as the genuine model of democracy that could legitimise imposing foreign rule upon non-Western societies.[26] There is an ongoing vibrant discussion of the problem of constitutionalising public international law.[27]

This discussion reflects the undeniable fact of an increased interdependency of the states increasing the sense of mutual responsibility on a global level.[28] Its implications for constitution-making will be discussed in Part V. It seems appropriate here to discuss one paradigmatic case of importing a constitution, namely the case of West Germany's Basic Law, generated during the period of Allied occupation after World War II.

III. Post-World War II Germany – No case of imported, much less imposed, constitutionalism

President Bush used the case of post-World War II Germany, a paradigm for the successful constitutionalisation of an occupied country, to justify his administration's attempt to impose an interim constitution on Iraq after the military defeat of the Saddam regime.[29] In fact, the Basic Law[30] originated in the political will of the Western Allies of World War II who exercised their sovereign power over the country in the decade between May 1945 and May 1955. The Basic Law has become the country's most durable constitution in its admittedly short history as a political nation since 1871. Germany's sovereignty shifted to the occupying powers (United States, Soviet Union, and Great Britain, who co-opted the Gaullist France a few months later) who jointly assumed the responsibility for the country after the unconditional surrender of the military leadership of the Nazi regime on 8th May 1945. Some scholars of public international law argued that the *Reich*, i.e. Germany as a legal and political entity, had foundered as a result of the war and disappeared from the political landscape altogether.[31] However, most authors inside and outside of Germany argued that Germany as a political entity continued to exist, even though it was unable to rule itself because the Four Allies had legally undisputed supreme authority.[32] Under this state of affairs the occupying forces pursued different political goals in their respective zones which they assigned to themselves after the occupation. Ultimately, Germany's division into four occupation zones ended in the split between the 'West' and the 'Soviet bloc', which dominated world politics until the breakdown of the Berlin Wall on 9th November 1989.

It was this constellation of world politics that gave rise to the project of a separate West German state consisting of the three occupation zones of the Western Allies. To understand how the Basic Law was created, it is necessary to emphasise that despite the ultimate sovereignty of the military commanders in their respective occupation zones, they still had to involve local German forces to establish an administration to provide basic services for the population. This entailed the gradual setting up of German local authorities based upon democratic elections and finally, the formation of states (*Länder*) with full-fledged constitutions including bills of fundamental rights and rules about the machinery of government. These *Länder* constitutions were drafted and enacted by democratically elected parliaments; moreover, most of them were submitted to plebiscitary sanction. An integral part of this democratisation process had been the licensing of political parties which occasioned a multi-party system from which only the forces of the old Nazi system were excluded. All in all, in 1948, the three Western occupation zones consisted of (at that time twelve) *Länder* which were ruled by parliaments and governments that derived their authority from democratic elections and hence represented the different political forces of the German population. However, in a strictly legal sense, the peoples in the *Länder* did not exercise their constituent power when they enacted constitutions because the supreme authority, i.e. German sovereignty, was 'vested, with full effect in International Law, either jointly with the four Powers or with any one of them in respect of the part of German territory placed under its administration'.[33]

In July 1948, the three Western Allies submitted a proposal to the prime ministers of the West German *Länder,* suggesting they convene a democratically elected constituent assembly to create a constitution for a West German state consisting of the three Western occupation zones. The new state would be the product of a new constitution. This was an idea which assumed that statehood originated from constitution-making, and that there is no state beyond and prior to the constitution – an assumption which is an inherent element of American constitutional reasoning while it is totally alien to the German constitutional and state law tradition.[34] The German politicians rejected this plan, not because of this theoretical argument, but for a strong political reason founded upon that theoretical argument. They feared that the foundation of a separate West German state would petrify the division of Germany into two states – they correctly anticipated that the Soviet Union would follow suit with the establishment of a distinct state in their military zone – and sanction the final and irrevocable dissolution of the political unity of the German nation.[35]

This refusal of the prime ministers – at that time the only Germans who could claim to be the legitimate representatives not of *the* German people, but of the peoples of the West German *Länder* – created a paradoxical situation: the military commanders held the sovereign power in their military zones and could establish any kind of political regime, both individually in their respective zones and jointly for the three Western zones. The only option excluded from their range of possibilities was to create a constituent assembly of the populations of the German *Länder.* The obstacle was not erected by public international law. Although the then fresh Charter of the United Nations established the right of self-determination of peoples,[36] and arguably entailed new limits to the rights of occupying military forces of a conquering nation, Article 107 of the Charter stipulated certain exceptions at the expense of the 'enemy states' Germany and Japan.[37] Rather, the reason has to do with the very concept of constitutionalism. The Western Allies' project was essentially a command to the Germans in the three Western military zones to organise themselves as one people and secede from the German people as it still legally existed in the German Reich.[38] Here again the different conceptual premises of the Germans and, in particular, the Americans came to light. For the American understanding, the will of a multitude to unite under a common constitution is tantamount to creating a nation. Therefore the Americans found nothing wrong in their bid to those Germans who had the chance to live under conditions of freedom, to draw the political consequences, and to constitute themselves as 'we the people' who are united under a constitution of freedom. This was not so to the German heads of the *Länder* governments who, it should be emphasised, embodied the then German democratic elite, consisting largely of refugees returned from exile, former prisoners of the Nazi regime, or those who had survived the twelve barbaric years in what later was called the 'internal emigration'. Even they, whose democratic credentials were beyond any doubt, insisted on the reality of a German people prior to the constitution. For them, a constitution which did not recognise the logical priority of the people as a historical and quasi-existential entity did not fit the needs of the pre-existing German nation. In fact, it could even jeopardise the existence of the nation in that it could encourage tendencies towards the secession of some parts of the country. Thus, it is understandable that the Western Allies' offer to the West Germans to enact a constitution which would solemnly authenticate the freedom which they already enjoyed was resented by many as a severe interference with their democratic freedom. Some had the impression that they were 'forced to be free'.[39]

The Western Allies could have ordered the convocation of an assembly elected by the population in their zones and assigned it the task of drafting and enacting a constitution. But such a process would not have met the requirements of constitution-making and its power to legitimise the existence and the authority of a polity. Constitution-making demands the constituent power of a collective that defines *itself* as a political entity and disposes of the institutional means to develop and to express its own political will. In other words, constitution-making is an act of political self-determination.[40] While public international law did not prevent the Allies from imposing their rule upon the German people, they could not create the legal and political effects of a constituent power by their sovereign *fiat*.

Perhaps the Western Allies were acknowledging the limits of their sovereignty when they finally abstained from pursuing their project of an imposed German constituent assembly. In any case, a compromise was reached that established a Parliamentary Council consisting of delegates elected by the West German *Länder*. The Parliamentary Council represented the plurality of the political forces of the peoples in the *Länder* – not of 'the people' of the three Western occupation zones, nor of 'the people' of the new would-be West German state, nor much less of 'the German people' as it latently still existed in the persisting 'Germany as a whole' (a term which had replaced the German *Reich*). The Parliamentary Council (composed of political party representatives including the two deputies of the Communist Party) wanted to maintain the unity of the German nation, so they created the West German state under the name 'Federal Republic of Germany' as a transitory and intentionally short-lived political body which was to serve as a stand-in and to act for the momentarily incapacitated German nation (i.e. the people of the German *Reich*). This is also the main reason why the Parliamentary Council did not call their creation a 'constitution,' but rather 'Basic Law for the Federal Republic of Germany', which they did not submit to plebiscitary approval. Thus, the majority of its members could accept the 'stain' that the Western Allies reserved the right to veto stipulations of the draft document and to give their final authorisation. It was only after this sanction through the sovereign that the draft constitution was submitted to the parliaments of the *Länder* for approval. Only the parliament of Bavaria refused to consent, but that had no tangible consequences. Since the new entity was not devised as a federation but as a federal state,[41] the unanimous consent of all *Länder* was not required for the validation of the constitution. Having passed this complex procedure, the Basic Law was solemnly proclaimed on 23rd May 1949.

Was the Basic Law an imposed constitution? And if so, was the imposition legally justified? By today's standard of the right to self-determination[42] it was certainly imposed. Bearers of this right are not only ethnic minorities living in an ethnically different state but also peoples who live on the territory of a state [43] – this was the case with the Germans whose territory was conquered by the Allies, but not annexed. In other words, they had not become the subjects of another state. The right of self-determination includes the people's freedom to decide on its form of government without external intervention. The Allies' influence on the content of the Basic Law and their right to authorise its enactment by the Parliamentary Council restrained the Germans' freedom to decide about the particular character of their government. This is of course not to say that this restraint was illegal – as indicated above, the then valid international law did not forbid the assumption of the supreme authority of the country and, consequently, the establishment of a new political and administrative order for an entity which was not supposed to be a fully sovereign state.

Apart from this somewhat formalistic account, there is a substantive criterion to judge the role the Western Allies played in the making of the German Basic Law. Democratically elected Germans drafted the Basic Law, it had been approved by all but one *Länder* parliaments, and even the Bavarian *Landtag* which refused consent did not want a completely different structure of the constitution, merely a stronger federal setup. Moreover, the rules of the Basic Law opened a range of democratic freedoms and provided instruments of democratic self-determination which were by no means inferior to those afforded by the Weimar constitution which had been created by the constituent power of the German people.[44] Thus, the people of the Federal Republic of Germany were not forced to live under rules which they rejected. The only 'blemish' of the Basic Law was its lack of plebiscitary sanction: no constituent assembly had been elected, nor had the result of the deliberations of the Parliamentary Council been submitted to plebiscitary approval.[45]

National unity was the only issue where the political aspirations of the Germans living in the Federal Republic collided with the (original) political purposes of the Allies: had the Allies forced them to create a new state and to accept it as the final palladium of their political identity this would have been tantamount to the imposition of a foreign political will. This, however, did not occur. On the contrary, Western Allies accepted the formula of the preamble of the Basic Law in which an explicit reference was made to the 'German people' and its constituent power. Moreover, the final Article gave emphasis to the purely transitory character of the Federal Republic and its Basic Law.

When the Federal Republic became sovereign in May 1955, no political force demanded a new constitution, opting instead for national unity in one German national state as they did in 1949. But even after the fall of the Berlin Wall and the accession of the (formerly communist) German Democratic Republic to the Federal Republic in October 1990, the constituent power of the now united German people was invoked only by politically marginal groups in the two German states. As a result, Germany lives under a constitution which was initiated by occupation powers who assumed sovereign power over the German people and devised for a non-sovereign political entity. The constitution was never approved by the constituent power of the German people, but is accepted as perfectly legitimate by the great majority of the German people. In the German case, the process of constitution-making seems to have inserted less legitimacy into the Basic Law than the crucial role of the constituent power in constitutional theory presupposes.[46]

Still, there is no reason to dismiss the significance of the process of constitution-making. Had the Allies insisted on their original project and forced the (West) Germans to create a constitution through a constituent assembly and/ or plebiscitary approval in a referendum, the outcome could have been resented by the Germans as a foreign project which lacked sufficient legitimacy. This could have undermined the force of the constitution irrespective of its presumably acceptable substance. On the other hand, the proper process is only a necessary, not a sufficient condition. A polity is likely to view a constitution as illegitimate if its substantive stipulations do not fit in the context of that polity; after all, the constitution is not, as some claim, a suicide pact. Even the most appropriate and legitimacy-engendering process will ultimately not be strong enough to save a constitution if its rules and principles do not satisfy the needs of the country. The Weimar constitution is a sad example for this truth.

The reference to the Weimar constitution gives rise to an observation which will eventually lead to the reflections in the third part of this essay. In many instances the Basic Law has been drafted by its authors as an attempt to avoid the mistakes and insufficiencies of the Weimar constitution, which they attributed to be part of the cause of the collapse of the Weimar Republic. Thus, to give just a few examples, they put the bill of fundamental rights on top of the Basic Law and made it the binding normative guideline for the conduct of public authorities on the federal, state, and local levels; they avoided even the least plebiscitary elements which played a certain, if largely overestimated role in the Weimar Republic; they loosened the dependency of the executive from the political will of the parliament, making a vote of no confidence extremely difficult and thus establishing a strongly executive-biased system of government; and they eliminated the possibility of the eradication of democracy through democratic means by establishing a so-called eternity clause (Article 79, paragraph 3) which excluded certain basic principles of the constitution from any kind of constitutional amendment. More or less they established a type of 'militant democracy,' devised and strongly recommended by Karl Loewenstein in the 1930s.[47]

Regardless of the Weimar constitution's failures,[48] the relevant point is that the Basic Law was created by a long and protracted constitutional discourse over the requirements of a modern constitution that would be able to meet the challenges of a new age – the age of mass democracy dealing with the severe socioeconomic conflicts of a class-cleaved society without abandoning the basic principles of constitutionalism that had been developed at the end of the 18th century. In Germany this debate began before the end of World War I and the creation of the Weimar constitution in 1919. It mushroomed after the establishment of the Weimar Republic and was accompanied by an overall sense of deep political and cultural crisis.[49] In other words, the German constitutional discourse of the 20th century was based upon a deep and painful experience and understanding of the fragility and vulnerability of the civilising capacity of constitutions to such a degree, that the term 'imposition' for the depiction of the involvement of the three Western Allies in the creation of the Basic Law appears inappropriate in the first place. The level of reflexivity about the risks of a failed constitution and about the embeddedness of constitutions in suitable pre-constitutional contexts was so high on both sides that it seems more fitting to describe the achievement of the Basic Law as a mutual learning process.[50]

IV. Preconditions of successful constitution making

Looking at the contextual character of constitutions reveals the requisite preconditions for constitutions to function as a means of civilising the political life of a country. Of course, it is impossible to give an exhaustive account. In view of the increasing occurrence of weak and failing states, this discussion is limited to two conditions which seem particularly relevant to this topic: the first is statehood and secularisation, and the second is ethnic and religious homogeneity.

The German case was a unique historical occurrence, but also a link in a chain of events which resulted in the transition from authoritarian rule to democracy. These transitions include the wave of democratisation after World War II (Germany, Italy, Japan, Austria), followed by the regime changes in the Mediterranean area and in Latin America between 1974 to 1985 (Greece, Portugal, Spain, Brazil, Uruguay, and Argentina), and the transformation of Central and Eastern European countries from communist rule to some kind of constitutionalism.[51] These experiences caused quite different, country-specific patterns of constitutionalisation. All of them assumed that the receiving countries kept certain basic institutional and cultural conditions which somehow were attuned to constitutionalism. This assumption has become doubtful. The contemporary debates about importing or imposing constitutions deal with countries which have only a weak if any constitutional history. This applies to most of the Arabic nations. The compatibility of their political culture with constitutionalism is doubtful at best. This matter should be further researched and explored using cultural and area studies. Scholars of constitutionalism can contribute to this research by analysing the pre-constitutional conditions of constitutionalism. Is the idea of constitutionalism less universal than its essential message suggests? Two elements appear particularly problematic in this respect.

A. Statehood and secularisation

The history of modern constitutionalism is strongly connected with the development of statehood, its bureaucracy, territorial character, policing and military, diplomatic capabilities, etc.[52] After all, constitutionalism was an important tool of rationalising state power.[53] Although the modern state originates in the European history and culture,[54] it has become the universal political form of the 20th century. Its essential elements – territoriality, sovereignty, coercive control of the population living within the boundaries of the territory[55] – do not seem overly demanding and hence are conducive to every geographical and cultural environment. In an age when weak and failed states come ever more to the surface[56] this assumption is no longer certain.[57]

If we look at the post-communist societies of Eastern and Central Europe including Russia, we realise that the institutional devices of a modern constitutional state have been established. This holds true for those countries which, on 1st May 2004, acceded to the European Union; this was only possible after a difficult process of assimilating to the economic and political structures of the European Union, laid down in the 'Copenhagen Criteria' of the Treaty on the European Union.[58] However, what is prevailing in some countries, Poland for example,[59] is a deep disappointment with the new political system's capacity to cope with the economic and social problems of an order which they had passionately yearned for under communist rule. Indeed, in these countries the life situations of many ordinary people have dramatically deteriorated under the auspices of the new political order. What is even more serious is that the new political structures of the constitutional state rarely generate the degree of political stability which seems necessary for the reconstruction of the economy, particularly for attracting foreign investors. Evidently, the formal institutions of the constitutional state are a necessary but not a sufficient condition for satisfactory state functioning. If this holds true, the question arises as to which additional preconditions are required for the smooth operation of the constitutional state.

There is one requirement which is for the most part undisputed, namely the constitutional state must be a *state* in the modern sense of this term. It must be a political organisation which monopolises the authority to wield legitimate coercion, including physical force, thus placing all individuals equally under its power, outlawing any kind of self-help or self-justice and prohibiting any kind of intermediary force which could either claim loyalty from its members, or accumulate so much power that it could become a competitor to the state. Max Weber established the classical definition for the modern state as 'a compulsory organization with a territorial basis. Furthermore, today, the use of force is regarded as legitimate only so far as it is either permitted by the state or prescribed by it,'[60] and, elsewhere today, 'legal coercion by violence is the monopoly of the state'.[61]

There is good reason to highlight the state's monopoly of legal coercion. Today we experience a serious malfunction of constitutions whenever this requirement is not satisfied. The aforementioned category of failed states which has become a major problem of international politics[62] is unequivocal evidence for the renaissance of a phenomenon of the past, namely unconsolidated statehood. This results in unsettled disputes about territorial boundaries, about nationality and citizenship, and about the principles and forms of government, including the struggle about who is entitled to rule. The formation of the modern state in Western Europe – its territorial basis, its monopoly of legal coercion, its compulsory jurisdiction about all actions taking place in the boundaries of its territory, and its continuous operation – was the result of long and cruel religious and civil wars in the 16th and 17th centuries in which the different religious denominations, churches, and sects not only struggled for the right religious doctrine, but for the imposition of their respective religious truths upon all members of the society. The connection of religious truth with political authority was one of the inexhaustible sources for civil war in 16th- and 17th-centuries-Europe.

In the history of political ideas it was obviously Thomas Hobbes' concept of a political order which provided a way out of the never-ending struggle for religious truth and metaphysical certainty. For him, the inherent rationale of a good polity consisted in its capacity to preserve peace and to prevent civil war. Satisfying the basic human need for physical security and lessening fear of a violent death was more important than the concern for eternal life and salvation which had dominated political reasoning during the Christian period of European history.[63] In other words, Hobbes removed religion as a source for rules about the character of a polity and thus opened a new area of reasoning about the appropriate structure of the polity – one may call this the sociological turn in the justification of political rule.

The concept of sovereign state power and the state's monopoly of legitimate coercion, then, is the immediate result of a secular justification of the polity. It resulted from the emergence of a world that lost its common religious fundaments and the economic basis of the feudal communal life as well. The European world of the 17th century fell apart, and the universalism of the Catholic world was replaced by the plurality of subjective world views of individuals, groups, sects, new social entities, etc. How could one conceive of an order which was able to bind the individuals together, i.e. which was able to prevent civil war among them, without imposing on them a common social and cultural form of life which had lost its cohesive force?

This predicament of the European world of the 17th century was the starting point for the career of a completely new theoretical paradigm, namely the paradigm of interest. As Albert O. Hirschman has thoroughly analysed,[64] the rationality, calculability and hence predictability of the interest – as opposed to the irrationality and unpredictability of the passions – became the key concept for understanding the world and the legitimation of individuals' actions since the 17th century. To struggle for wealth, which had been disqualified as a sin by the Catholic church for centuries, now received an increasingly positive colouring, until, finally, it was praised as a virtue. The most drastic theorist of the interest as the basis of all social actions was of course Thomas Hobbes, for whom the interest of the individual in his or her self-preservation was the only valid criterion for the legitimacy of his or her actions. Consequently, he became the most radical advocate of the sovereignty of the state and its monopoly of legitimate coercion. For him the undisputed authority of the state to keep peace and order was the only means to satisfy the individuals' interest in their self-preservation. In order to fulfil this task, the sovereign even had the right to determine the religious and the epistemological truth which his subjects had to believe in because, in Hobbes' view, it was primarily the quarrel about the right religion which had led the people to argue and fight with each other, and ultimately to violate peace and order and engage in civil war.[65]

In a nutshell, the genesis of the modern state, its monopoly of legitimate coercion, and its legitimation as an order which is specialised in the maintenance of peace and order in the external world is due to a process of secularisation.[66] Perhaps it is more correct to speak of a process of continuous domestication of the religious energies of the European societies since the 17th century. In the perspective of political and constitutional theory, the relations between church and state were, of course, particularly important. There have been different answers to this problem – reaching from the concept of a state church, predominant in Germany until the 19th century and still valid in contemporary England, up to the most radical separation of church and state in the establishment clause of the First Amendment of the U.S. Constitution – all of which are anxious to safeguard the integrity of a sphere of politics, civil liberty and political obligation where the commands of the church have no legally binding character. Given the plurality of religious and value orientations in modern societies it is not surprising that the injection of particularly religious commands into the secular legal order – for example the prohibition of divorce, the unconditional prohibition of abortion, or the denial of equal rights to women – normally tends to weaken the binding character of the legal order. Its strength and legitimacy rests on the strict separation of morality and legality, and this implies that it does not make any claim on the moral or religious beliefs of its citizens.

B. Ethnic and religious homogeneity as preconditions of the constitutional state?

This last issue leads to a second condition which seems indispensable to the viability of a constitutional order. This is the capacity of a society to cope with its internal conflicts without resorting to civil war. Of course, one may say that a main feature of constitutions is that they preclude civil war and society's relapse into an uncivilised mode of existence, i.e. a Hobbesian state of nature. However, the fate of the Weimar constitution clearly displays that sometimes a constitution is not strong enough to stand firm against the power of forces which are hostile against its intellectual and moral foundations. Constitutions are about proper institutions which guarantee a sphere of free, spontaneous, and autonomous interactions among the members of what we call civil society, and about the procedures through which civil society is able to constitute itself as a polity and to develop a collective will. These two pillars of modern constitutionalism presuppose that neither civil society nor the polity are homogeneous consensus-based social entities, but rather consist of individuals pursuing a plurality of competing, mutually exclusive values and interests which have to be harmonised. In other words, constitutions are institutional devices which aim at making compatible the economic, social, and cultural plurality of a 'society of individuals'.[67] This entails that they are specialised in coping with conflicts arising among members of the society, related to various issues, ranging from the proper delineation of boundaries in the political vis-à-vis the sphere of civil society through the principles of social justice, to the definition of guidelines for collective action like the 'national interest'. They are conflicts about what it means to live together, in one polity, under a constitution.

Paradoxically it is this permanent struggle for the definition of the common good which generates a spirit of community in a society of individuals – at least this is the assumption of authors who claim that conflicts have a positive effect upon the social coherence of societies.[68] In a critical analysis of this time-honoured line of argument in the social sciences, Albert O. Hirschman offers an important qualification which is relevant to this chapter. In his view, not all conflicts further coherence in all kinds of societies; rather, he claims, social conflicts have only positive effects in democratic market societies, and even this may be true only for a certain genre of conflicts. In developing his argument he writes:

> Many conflicts of market society are over the distribution of the social product among different classes, sectors, or regions. Highly varied though they are, they tend to be divisible; they are conflicts over getting more or less, in contrast to conflicts of the either-or, nondivisible category that are characteristic of

societies split along rival ethnic, linguistic, or religious lines. Nondivisible conflicts have recently also become more prominent in the older democracies and particularly in the United States, as a result of the importance assumed by such issues as abortion and by problems arising out of multiculturalism.[69]

Hirschman's reference to the United States – the oldest constitutional state – gives rise to the question of whether any attempt to import a constitution into a conflicted country is doomed to failure. Here, again, it seems appropriate to remind us that the idea of homogeneity has frequently been invoked as a necessary element of the modern constitutional state – authors of the liberal and left spectrum tended to emphasise socio-economic homogeneity,[70] while in the more conservative field the idea of national, ethnic, or religious homogeneity prevailed.[71] Today it is the latter dimension of homogeneity which arouses concern because it refers to national, ethnic, and religious conflicts which appear irreconcilable in many regions of the world and which in several cases have assumed the character of international crisis (e.g. conflicts in Congo, Sri Lanka, or Chechnya). What comes to the fore in these conflicts is the quest for commonness, or sameness as the pre-political foundation of a polity. As stated above, in Europe the religious conflict between the several Christian confessions, denominations, and sects was domesticated by the establishment of sovereign statehood, and in the United States the separation of religion and politics has become one of the fundamentals of its constitutional system.[72] Thus, religion has never been a viable candidate as a pre-constitutional groundwork of the constitutional state.

But something like a secular religion has had an important influence at least upon the European version of the constitutional state, namely the nation. In its historical development over the last two-hundred years, nationality, or nationhood, has turned out to be the most vigorous concept of commonness. Max Weber's observations on the constitutive character of nationality and ethnicity for the self-understanding of political communities are surprisingly up-to-date. But he, too, fails to fully explain the predominant 'connotation that whatever is felt to be distinctively common must derive from common descent', although, as he notes, in reality 'persons who consider themselves members of the same nationality are often much less related by common descent than are persons belonging to different and hostile nationalities'.[73] From this point of view, nationhood or nationality constitutes an antecedant community which appears able to create that kind of commonness and pre-political social solidarity required for the functioning of a polity based upon a society of individuals.

Note, however, that since the end of the 18th century two different concepts of nation have been competing for recognition. On the one hand, there is the French concept of nation according to which, in the famous words of the Abbe Sieyès, a nation is '[a] body of associates living under *common* laws and are represented by the same *legislative assembly*'.[74] In this understanding, the nation is constituted by the entirety of the denizens of a particular territory who, by the very act of forming a political entity and of being subject to common laws, acquire the status of citizenship and constitute the *demos*.[75] This political concept of nation diverges significantly from a concept that has been prevailing in Germany and in Eastern Europe since the end of the 18th century: the nation as a pre-political community constituted by the commonness of such ascriptive properties as origin, race, language, religion, culture, history, and the like. Here the nation is not the *demos*, but the *ethnos*.[76] It is this ethnic definition of nationhood which is an almost insurmountable obstacle to the inclusion of individuals in the nation who do not meet the terms of ethnicity as defined by the group which dominates the country. Ethnic plurality is largely regarded as spoiling the integrity of the political community – the end goal being ethnic identity and authenticity. The ultimate criterion of justice is not the universalist standard of what is right for all human beings, but what is good 'for us'. Hence pluralist democracy which represents the universalist values of modern constitutionalism is barely compatible with political forces which aspire to an ethnically homogeneous polity.

A further aspect of constitutionalism seems relevant here. One of the core principles of constitutionalism is the limitation of political power.[77] This is coherent with the idea of an autonomous civil society which, due to its inherent plurality of ideas and interests, develops a high degree of creativity and innovation which is a driving force of the idea of progress associated with the idea of constitutionalism.[78] This is difficult to reconcile with ethnic identity as a pivotal idea of a polity. In fact, as Weber wrote in view of the conflicts within the multinational empire of the Hapsburgs:

> [T]he concept 'nation' directs us to political power. Hence, the concept seems to refer ... to a specific kind of pathos which is linked to the idea of a powerful political community of people who share a common language, or religion, or common customs, or political memories; such a state may already exist or it may be desired. The more power is emphasized, the closer appears to be the link between nation and state. This pathetic pride in the power of one's own community, or this longing for it, may be much more widespread in relatively small language groups such as the Hungarians, Czechs or Greeks than in a similar but much larger community such as the Germans 150 years ago ....[79]

Perhaps Weber's observation is still valid today. The Balkan Wars of the 1990s come to mind. There are indications today that the pride of the power of one's own community also feeds the idea of an ethnic understanding of the nation and vice versa. If this hypothesis holds true it would mean that implanting constitutions in divided societies, in which the groups struggling for power define their vision of a good polity in ethnic terms, appears to be a particularly difficult if not entirely fruitless undertaking. Constitutionalism requires a polity whose members are citizens, not brothers/sisters or otherwise bound together by pre-political and pre-legal 'ascriptive' attributes, who are aliens to each other and yet are able to recognise each others as equals.[80]

A final remark as to the issue of religion. As stated above, in the Western tradition of constitutionalism, religion was not a serious candidate for forming the pre-political community of the constitutional state because modern statehood rested upon the political and legal isolation of religion from politics. Here a qualification seems appropriate. Today we observe signs of a renaissance of conflicts between religion and politics on a worldwide level. Against many predictions, religious conflicts are not restricted to premodern societies;[81] they cannot be understood as pure modernisation conflicts, they are also conflicts of modern societies. Also, in the secularised world of today, religious issues create deep political tensions in many constitutional states. After all, Northern Ireland has been living on the verge of a religious civil war for over twenty-five years. There are other cases of deep politico-religious tensions which need political accommodation and constitutional solution, for instance the recent French debate (and legislation!) about the right of Muslim women to wear the scarf in public institutions (like schools or universities), a debate which in a different version has also reached Germany.[82] Other examples of political and, consequently, constitutional disputes in advanced modern societies are the well-known battles in Germany and in the United States, respectively, about school prayers, about displaying religious symbols like the crucifix in public schools, or about religious instruction.

Until the middle of the 20th century, constitutionalism was mainly a Euro-Atlantic concept and political practice, and therefore constitutionalism dealt primarily with the conflicts which resulted from the confessional splits within Christianity. Two major developments have changed this situation. First, Christianity no longer defines the framework of religious conflicts, not even in traditionally Christian European and U.S. societies. They have undergone profound transformations to multiethnic, multireligious, and multicultural societies which comprise communities of all major world religions including the increasing group of atheists. Second, constitutionalism is no longer an exclusively Euro-Atlantic concept. At the end of the 20th century constitutionalism has become a universal yardstick for civilised governance. Yet the assumption that the Euro-Atlantic experience with the role of constitutionalism in the containment of religious conflicts may serve as a model for other regions is obviously premature. As stated above, the Euro-Atlantic experience was restricted to the confessional conflicts within Christianity; it has been ignorant with respect to conflicts between different religions. There were no Muslim communities in the early modern world of Europe which engendered constitutionalism, much less other non-Christian religious communities with the exception of the Jews. But the members of this religious minority were almost everywhere victims of persecution or severe discrimination despite the principle of toleration which eventually developed into the constitutional right to religious freedom.[83] Thus, the tradition of constitutionalism – Euro-Atlantic in essence – does not provide answers for the religious conflicts of the 21st century. In view of the aforementioned difficulties of the multireligious and multicultural Western societies to cope with their present-day problems of integrating religious energies into their concept of governance, it is questionable whether they are in the position to offer convincing solutions for other regions of the world which are deeply divided on religious issues.

This does not mean, of course, that deeply divided societies cannot learn from the Euro-Atlantic constitutional experience. Nor should we dismiss projects of constitutionalising conflict-ridden societies as intrinsically futile. There are approaches to establishing post-conflict constitutionalism which seem more promising than a mere imposition of constitutions after a coerced regime change. Post-World War II Europe is an example for rising above never-ending and bloody conflicts of the past through the creation of new forms of interdependency among the former enemies. The European Union of today, having evolved from the incipient European Economic Community of 1957, has become the most advanced model of mutual interdependence of nation-states. This has generated a new type of composite constitution in which the legal orders of the supranational European Union and of the member states complement each other to the effect that none of them can claim the status of autonomy.[84] There are indications that the involvement of external actors may become a general pattern of constitution-making worldwide.

V. The influence of International Law upon the constitutionalisation of conflict-ridden societies – international 'constitutional intervention'

The international community has increased its role in the creation of constitutions, especially in fragile states. The analysis of the structures of governance in the 21st century can no longer presuppose the time-honoured distinction between inside and outside the state, that is, clear-cut boundaries between the national and the international spheres. Both the spheres of sovereign statehood and of inter-state relations have lost their distinct characteristics and have undergone a process of profound transformation. This process is, to put it succinctly, an evolution from a 'pluriverse-of-states order' into what one might call, paraphrasing Ulrich Beck, a 'transnational cooperative order'.[85] The former, formally recognised in the Peace Treaties of Westphalia, was a design of spatial differentiation of the politically relevant parts of the globe into a pluriversum of sovereign states. This new spatial order became the model for the social and political organisation of the modern world, in that it created and established new patterns of interaction and spatial ontologies.[86] The most important was, of course, the distinction between inside/outside,[87] making boundaries between territories 'meaningful dividers between social, economic, and cultural systems'.[88]

Obviously, today this spatial order no longer exists. The porosity of state boundaries, the diminished relevance of state territory, and the decreasing control of the states' authority over the life world of their population have created a global space in which the decision making power is no longer distributed along the lines of state borders. In the developing world of globalisation new modes of governance have emerged. In the international sphere they include policy-networks of state agencies, NGOs, transnational corporations, law firms, and international organisations, as well as multi-level arrangements of governance using complex methods of cooperation and consociational procedures at different geographical and functional levels.[89] The states' autonomy and their claim to monopolise the power and the authority to determine the character and the quality of public goods for their polities have greatly decreased, as they have become entangled in those tight networks of public goods production.

Unsurprisingly this has also had considerable effects upon the role of constitutions. No longer can we regard them as purely domestic instruments of government of a nation-bound population which exercises its right to national self-determination without concern of its regional or global surroundings. Even in the United States, the seemingly most self-sufficient global power, a vivid debate has developed about the question of whether the courts are allowed to refer to foreign law when they adjudicate a national case.[90] There are other states which are much more exposed to external influence than the United States. Obviously I refer to the increasing number of states which simply do not dispose of the indispensable institutional requirements of statehood, the most important being undisputed territorial boundaries, the state's monopoly of coercive power, and a minimal apparatus of law enforcement built upon basic forms of the rule of law. This sad predicament is usually the consequence of unresolved domestic conflicts frequently triggering civil war. It is this category of the above-mentioned failed states which is highly dependent upon the support of the international community. While, of course, the aid of material goods like food, health care, and basic physical infrastructure are of utmost importance, good internal governance is at least as important for the sustainable development of those countries.

The relationship between a country's commitment to the rule of law and the respect of human rights and its material welfare, has been convincingly shown by the research of economists, most prominently by Amartya Sen.[91] Similarly, the then Secretary-General of the U.N., Boutros-Ghali, in his 17th June 1992 report to the Security Council, *Agenda for Peace,* drew his audience's attention to the

obvious connection between democratic practices – such as the rule of law and transparency in decision making – and the achievement of true peace and security in any new and stable political order. These elements of good governance need to be promoted at all levels of international and national political communities.[92]

He urged the leaders of States 'to find a balance between the needs of good internal governance and the requirements of an ever more interdependent world'.[93] Although the *Agenda for Peace* does not explicitly mention the issues of state-building and constitution-making, it certainly became an important founding document for the several activities of the U.N. in this area of international politics.[94]

Thus, the concern for the constitutional character of a country has become an important element of international politics. Recently Daniel Thürer, the Swiss scholar of public international law, has explored the international influence upon national processes of constitution-making and discovered different roles of the international community which includes manifold non-state actors. These modes of involvement in the constitutional affairs of a country range from initiating through accompanying and steering, to the instatement of such processes.[95] We may call this kind of international aid 'constitutional intervention', using the analogy to the established term 'humanitarian intervention'. To be sure, while the latter includes military means, the former is thoroughly civil in character.

An embryonic form of this type of U.N. 'intervention' dates back to 1984 when the U.N. Security Council closely watched the constitutional development of South Africa and its apartheid system. In its Resolution 554 (17 Aug. 1984) it declared the 'new' constitution which the regime had enacted in 1983 'as null and void'. This resolution was a precursor of a development which, after the end of the Cold War and the emergence of thoroughly new constellations in international politics, became a pattern of international governance. Although taking account of the specific character of the conflicts and of their underlying conditions in the relevant countries, the general line of action of the U.N. is the establishment of an International Interim Authority (occasionally under the authority of Chapter VII of the U.N. Charter), the explicit recognition of the sovereignty, independence, territorial integrity and national unity of the relevant country, and the appeal to all parties involved in the conflict to cooperate with the Interim Authority with the aim to reach a reconciliatory settlement.[96]

IV. Conclusion

This article reflects some of the complexities of 'constitutional interventionism'. It tries to sharpen the awareness of how difficult it is to import constitutions into regions where constitutionalism is a minor element of the political culture at best. The main reason why the importation, much less the imposition, of constitutions in the course of coerced regime change is likely to fail is the fact that the authority of constitutions rests largely upon the legitimacy of the processes through which they are generated; substance, although of course important, plays a secondary role. The case of post–World War II Germany, which has been analysed at some length, is an example of the significance of involving the local population in the process of constitution-making, even if this population acts in the shadow of the sovereign of a conquering military power. Besides the appropriateness of the process of constitution-making in terms of a fair involvement of the people, there are demanding requirements which have to be met in order that a constitution can flourish. In this chapter two of them are addressed, namely the prerequisite of statehood, based upon a secular justification of its monopoly of coercive power, and the domestication of 'categorical conflicts',[97] ethnic and religious clashes being the most divisive ones. In view of these requirements, the project of importing constitutions by way of regime change appears quite unpromising. Still, there is the need to assist conflict-ridden and failing states in regaining civilised forms of governance. The article gives a brief account of the constitutionalisation of collapsed, or in danger of collapsing, states through international action (largely under the control of the U.N. Security Council). This international involvement in intra-state constitution-making is regarded as an emerging pattern of connecting domestic governance of states with the international and transnational space characteristic of a globalising world of overlapping jurisdictions and increasingly permeable state borders.

Notes

1. E. R. Huber, *Deutsche Verfassungsgeschichte seit 1789*, 2nd edn, 1968, vol. 2, p. 763; E. R. Huber, *Deutsche Verfassungsgeschichte Seit 1789*, vol. 3, Göttingen, Vandenhoeck & Ruprecht , pp. 11, 29, 35.

2. See M. Loughlin and N. Walker (eds), *The Paradox of Constitutionalism*, Oxford, Oxford University Press, 2007.

3. Cf. B. Ackerman, *The Future of Liberal Revolution*, New Haven and London, Yale University Press, 1992, pp. 14, 46 (discussing constitution-making as the top priority in a revolutionary situation); see also U. K. Preuß, *Constitutional Revolution: The link between constitutionalism and progress*, (trans. D. Lucas Schneider), Amherst, Prometheus Books, 1995, pp. 81–89.

4. See A. Arato, *Civil Society, Constitution, and Legitimacy*, Lanham, Rowman & Littlefield Publishers, 2000, pp. 81–129.

5. J. Elster, C. Offe and U. K. Preuß, *Institutional Design in Post-Communist Societies: Rebuilding the ship at sea*, Cambridge, Cambridge University Press, 1998, pp. 63–108.

6. R. Teitel, 'Post-communist constitutionalism: a transitional perspective', *Columbia Human Rights Law Review*, 1994, vol. 26, pp. 167–190 [172].

7. *See* R. Teitel, 'Transitional Rule of Law', in A. Czarnota *et al.* (eds), *Rethinking the Rule of Law After Communism*, Budapest, Central European University Press, 2006, p. 279.

8. See A. Arato, 'Interim imposition', *Ethics and International Affairs*, vol. 18, no. 3, pp. 25–50, [36].

9. See N. Johnson, 'Constitutionalism in Europe Since 1945: Reconstruction and reappraisal', in D. Greenberg *et al.* (eds), *Constitutionalism and Democracy: Transitions in the contemporary world*, New York, Oxford University Press, 2001, pp. 26–45; H. Otake, 'Two Contrasting Constitutions in the Postwar World: The making of the Japanese and West German constitutions', in Y. Higuchi (ed.), *Five Decades of Constitutionalism in Japanese Society*, Tokyo, University of Tokyo Press, 2001, pp. 34–71 [43]; see also P. H. Merkl, *The Origin of the West German Republic*, Oxford, Oxford University Press, 1963, (detailing the specifics of the German case).

10. See Arato, *Civil Society, Constitution, and Legitimacy*, p. 171.

11. This pattern surfaced in Germany after World War I and in France after World War II and reemerged in the post-communist countries of Central and Eastern Europe after 1989.

12. The British welfare state set up by the Labour government after World War II is an obvious example.

13. See W. F. Murphy, 'Constitutions, Constitutionalism, and Democracy', in D. Greenberg *et al.* (eds), *Constitutionalism and Democracy: Transitions in the contemporary world*, New York, Oxford University Press, 1993, pp. 3–25 [9]; see also Preuß, *Constitutional Revolution*, p. 109.

14. W. G. Grewe (ed.), *Fontes Historiae Iuris Gentium: Quellen Zur Geschichte Des Volkerrechts*, Vol. 2, Berlin, New York, Walter de Gruyter, 1995, p. 646.

15. *Ibid.*, p. 656.

16. I. Berlin, *Four Essays on Liberty*, New York, Oxford University Press, 1970, p. 122.

17. *Ibid.*, p. 132.

18. S. Holmes, 'Precommitment and the Paradox of Democracy', in J. Elster and R. Slagstad (eds), *Constitutionalism and Democracy*, Cambridge, Cambridge University Press, 1988, pp. 195, 235.

19. *Ibid.*, p. 239.

20. J. S. Mill, 'A Few Words on Non-Intervention', in J. S. Mill, *Dissertations and Discussions: Political, philosophical, and historical*, Vol. 3, Whitefish, Kessinger Publishing, 2004 (1873), p. 154.

21. See, e.g., A. Randelzhofer, 'Introduction Art. 2', 'Arts. 2 (4)', in B. Simma (ed.), *The Charter of the United Nations: A commentary*, Oxford, Oxford University Press, 2nd edn, 2002, p. 51.

22. The Secretary-General, 'Report of the Secretary-General on the Work of the Organization, 5, delivered to the General Assembly', U. N. Doc. A/46/1 (13 Sept. 1991).

23. See, e.g., International Commission on Intervention and State Sovereignty, *The Responsibility to Protect*, International Development Research Centre, 2001, http://www.idrc.ca/openebooks/960–7/.

24. See T. M. Franck, 'The Emerging Right to Democratic Governance', *American Journal of International Law*, 1992, vol. 86, no. 1, pp. 46–91 [46]; see also, W. M. Reisman, 'Sovereignty and Human Rights in Contemporary International Law', in G. H. Fox and B. R. Roth (eds), *Democratic Governance and International Law*, Cambridge, Cambridge University Press, 2000, pp. 239–258 [240].

25. Reisman, 'Sovereignty and Human Rights...', pp. 248–249.

26. See B. R. Roth, *Governmental Illegitimacy in International Law*, Oxford, Oxford University Press, 2000, pp. 420–425.

27. B. Fassbender, 'The Meaning of International Constitutional Law', in R. St. J. Macdonald and D. M. Johnston (eds), *Towards World Constitutionalism: Issues in the legal ordering of the world community*, Leiden and Boston, Martinus Nijhoff Publishers, 2005, pp. 837–851.

28. International Commission on Intervention and State Sovereignty, *The Responsibility to Protect*, p. 39.

29. For more on the imposition of the interim constitution in Iraq see Arato, 'Interim imposition'.

30. West Germany's constitution until 1990 and the united Germany's constitution since 3rd October 1990.

31. E.g., H. Kelsen, 'The legal status of Germany according to the Declaration of Berlin', *American Journal of International Law*, 1945, vol. 39, no. 3, pp. 518–526 [518–519].

32. L. F. L. Oppenheim, *International Law: A treatise,* Vol. 1, Hersch Lauterpacht (ed.), London, Longman, 1947, p. 519.

33. *Ibid.*, p. 520. For the German text see Bundesgesetzblatt [Federal Law Gazette] 1990, BGBL 1, pp. 1318.

34. Cf. A. J. Jacobson and B. Schlink, 'Introduction, Constitutional Crisis: The German and the American experience', in A. J. Jacobson and B. Schlink (eds), *Weimar: A jurisprudence of crisis 1*, Oakland, University of California Press, 2000, pp. 1–39.

35. For the details see R. Mussgnug, 'Zustandekommen des Grundgesetzes und Entstehen der Bundesrepublik Deutschland', in J. Isensee and P. Kirchhof (eds), *Handbuch Des Staatsrechts Der Bundesrepublik Deutschland*, Heidelberg, C. F. Müller, 1987, pp. 219–258; M. Stolleis, 'Besatzungsherrschaft und Wiederaufbau deutscher Staatlichkeit 1945–1949', in J. Isensee and P. Kirchhof (eds), *Hanbuch Des Staatsrechts*, pp. 173–217.

36. See K. Doehring, 'Special Section: Self-determination', in B. Simma (ed.), *The Charter of the United Nations 1*, pp. 47–63.

37. However, whether these exceptions also apply to the right of self-determination is not fully clear. Cf. G. Ress, 'Article 107', in B. Simma (ed.), *The Charter of the United Nations 2*, p. 8.

38. Which, as noted, had survived as a legal entity but was unable to form a collective will.

39. This is Rousseau's notorious and seemingly paradoxical statement from J.-J. Rousseau, *The Social Contract*, trans. M. Cranston, London, Penguin Books, 1968 (1762), p. 64. Note, however, that Rousseau's contention was not paradoxical at all. He referred to a person who had agreed to enter the social contract and committed himself to accept the burdens and the benefits of the contract, the essential benefit being the freedom of the individual. Hence to force someone to be free was just a somewhat pointed version of the truism that a contract into which I have entered voluntarily can be coercively enforced against me.

40. See Preuß, *Constitutional Revolution*; U. K. Preuß, 'Constitutional power-making for the new polity: some deliberations on the relations between constituent power and the constitution', *Cardozo L. Rev.*, 1993, vol. 14, p. 639–660.

41. See generally M. Forsyth, *Unions of States: The theory and practice of confederation*, Leicester, Leicester University Press, 1981.

42. U.N. Charter Art. 1, para. 2; U.N. International Covenant on Civil and Political Rights Art. 1, para. 1; U.N. International Covenant on Economic, Social, and Cultural Rights, Art. 1, para. 1.

43. See Doehring, 'Special Section: Self-Determination', pp. 55 56.

44. See C. Gusy, *Die Weimarer Reichsverfassung*, Tübingen, Mohr Siebeck, 1997; E. R. Huber, *Deutsche Verfassungsgeschichte*, Stuttgart, W. Kohlhammer, 1789 (1981), vol. 4.

45. See Merkl, *The Origin of the West German Republic*, pp. 55, 128–29, 176, 181.

46. Cf. M. Loughlin and N. Walker (eds), *The Paradox of Constitutionalism*, Oxford, Oxford University Press, 2007. For the German case see C. Möllers, 'We are (afraid of) the People: Constituent power in German constitutionalism', in Loughlin and Walker (eds), *The Paradox of Constitutionalism*, pp. 87–106.

47. K. Loewenstein, 'Militant democracy and fundamental rights, I', *American Political Science Review*, 1937, vol. 31, pp. 417–432; K. Loewenstein, 'Militant democracy and fundamental rights, II', *American Political Science Review*, 1937, vol. 31, pp. 638–658.

48. Cf. C. Gusy, *Weimar – Die wehrlose Republik? Verfassungsschutzrecht und Verfassungsschutz in der Weimarer Republik*, Tübingen, Mohr Siebeck, 1991; C. Gusy (ed.), *Weimars Lange Schatten – ‹Weimar› Als Argument Nach 1945*, Baden-Baden, Nomos, 2003.

49. See Jacobson and Schlink, 'Introduction, Constitutional Crisis'.

50. This dimension of constitution-making has been introduced by A. Arato, 'Constitutional Learning', *Theoria*, 2005, vol. 52, pp. 1–36; see also Preuß, *Constitutional Revolution...*

51. See Elster, Offe, and Preuß, *Institutional Design in Post-Communist Societies...*, p. 4 (describing the several waves of democratisation); R. Doorenspleet, 'Reassessing the Three Waves of Democratization', *World Politics*, 2000, vol. 52, pp. 384–406.

52. See, e.g., C. J. Friedrich, *Constitutional Government and Democracy: Theory and practice in Europe and America*, Waltham, MA, Blaisdell Publishing Co., 1968 (1937); C. Tilly (ed.), *The Formation of National States in Western Europe: Studies in political development*, Princeton, Princeton University Press, 1975; M. Van Crevald, *The Rise and Decline of the State*, Cambridge, Cambridge University Press, 1999; W. Reinhard, *Geschichte der Staatsgewalt: Eine vergleichende Verfassungsgeschichte Europas von den Anfänfen bis zur Gegenwart*, 1999.

53. D. Grimm, 'Der Verfassungsbegriff in historischer Entwicklung', in D. Grimm, *Die Zukunft der Verfassung*, Frankfurt am Main: Suhrkamp Verlag, 1994, pp.101–55.

54. G. Poggi, *The State: Its nature, development and prospects*, Cambridge, Polity Press, 1990, pp. 34.

55. *Ibid.*, p. 19. See also the famous juristic definition of G. Jellinek, *Allgemeine Staatslehre*, 3rd edn, Gentner, Darmstadt, 1960 (1900), pp. 183, 394.

56. See R. I. Rotberg, *When States Fail: Causes and consequences*, Princeton, Princeton University Press, 2004.

57. For the prospects of statehood in the extra-European world see Reinhard, *Geschichte der Staatsgewalt*, p. 480.

58. Consolidated version of the Treaty on European Union, Art. 49, O.J. C 325/5, at 31 (2002), 37 I.L.M 67, at 78 (ex Article O).

59. Let alone those which have not (yet) joined the European Union or will not be able to join it.

60. M. Weber, *Economy and Society*, G. Roth and C. Wittich (eds), Berkeley, University of California Press, 1978 (1968), p. 56.

61. *Ibid.*, p. 314.

62. See generally, M. Kaldor, *New and Old Wars: Organized violence in a global era*, Cambridge, Polity Press, 1999.

63. T. Hobbes, *Leviathan*, Indianapolis, Bobbs-Merrill Educ. Publishing, 1978 [1651], pp. 104–109.

64. See A. O. Hirschman, *The Passions and the Interests: Political arguments for capitalism before its triumph*, Princeton, Princeton University Press, 1978.

65. See Hobbes, *Leviathan*, p. 147.

66. See H. Kroger, *Allgemeine Staatslehre*, Stuttgart, W. Kohlhammer, 1964, p. 32; A. D. Lindsay, *The Modern Democratic State*, Oxford, Oxford University Press, 1947, pp. 64–65; E.-W. Böckenförde, 'Die Entstehung des Staates als Vorgang der Säkularisation', in *Staat, Gesellschaft, Freiheit*, Frankfurt, 1967, pp. 44–64.

67. See N. Elias, *The Society of Individuals*, M. Schröter (ed.), E. Jephcott (trans.), Oxford, Basil Blackwell, 1991, pp. 3–66.

68. For an overview of the literature see A. O. Hirschman, 'Social Conflicts as Pillars of Democratic Market Societies', in *A Propensity to Self-Subversion*, Cambridge Mass., Harvard University Press, 1995, pp. 231, 236.

69. *Ibid.*, p. 244.

70. See O. Kirchheimer, *Politics, Law, and Social Change: Selected essays*, New York, Columbia University Press, 1969, p. 40.

71. See, e.g., C. Schmitt, *The Crisis of Parliamentary Democracy*, Cambridge Mass., MIT, 1985, p. 9.

72. See H. J. Berman, *Faith and Order: The reconciliation of law and religion*, Grand Rapids, W. B. Eerdmans Publishing, 1993, pp. 221–235.

73. Weber, *Economy and Society*, p. 395.

74. E. J. Sieyes, *What is the Third Estate?*, S. E. Finer (ed.), M. Blondel (trans.), New York, Frederick A. Praeger, 1963 [1789].

75. See E. J. Hobsbawm, *Nations and Nationalism Since 1780: Programme, myth, reality*, Cambridge, Cambridge University Press, 1990, pp. 14–45.

76. See E. K. Francis, *Interethnic Relations: An essay in sociological theory*, Amsterdam, Elsevier, 1976, pp. 43–115.

77. See K. J. Friedrich, *Limited Government: A comparison*, Englewood Cliffs, NJ, Prentice-Hall, 1974; A. Sajo, *Limiting Government: An introduction to constitutionalism*, Budapest, Central European University Press, 1999.

78. See Preuß, *Constitutional Revolution*.

79. Weber, *Economy and Society*, p. 398.

80. See S. Benhabib, *The Rights of Others: Aliens, residents, and citizens*, Cambridge, Cambridge University Press, 2004; P. Riesenberg, *Citizenship in the Western Tradition: Plato to Rousseau*, Chapel Hill and London, The University of North Carolina Press, 1992; U. K. Preuß, 'Citizenship and Identity: Aspects of a political theory of citizenship', in R. Bellamy *et al.* (eds), *Democracy and Constitutional Culture in the Union of Europe*, London, Lothian Foundation Press, 1995, pp. 107–120.

81. See generally P. Beyer, 'Globalizing systems, global cultural models and religion(s)', *International Sociology*, 1998, vol. 13, no. 1, pp. 79–94; R. Inglehart and W. E. Baker, 'Modernization, cultural change, and the persistence of traditional values', *American Sociology Review*, 2000, vol. 65, no. 1, pp. 19–51.

82. See the decision of the Bundesverfassungsgericht [BVerfG] [Federal Constitutional Court] 24 Sept. 2003, 108 Entscheidungen des Bundesverfassungsgerichts [BVerfGE] 282 (F.R.G.), available at: http://www.bverfg.de/entscheidungen/rs20030924_2bvr143602.html(German), http://www.bverfg.de/entscheidungen/rs20030924_2bvr143602en.html (English).

83. P. Zagorin, *How the Idea of Religious Toleration Came to the West*, Princeton, Princeton University Press, 2003, pp. 7–13, 54, 293.

84. I. Pernice, 'Multi-level constitutionalism in the European Union', *European Law Review*, 2002, vol. 27, pp. 511–529; U. K. Preuß, 'Prospects of constitution for Europe', *Constellations*, 1996, vol. 3, no. 2, p. 209–224; J. H. H. Weiler, 'On the power of the word: Europe's constitutional iconography', *Int'l J. Const. L.*, 2005, vol. 3, pp. 173–190 [176].

85. U. Beck, *What is Globalization*, Cambridge, Polity Press, 2000, pp. 133, 135.

86. R. D. Sack, *Human Territoriality: Its theory and history*, Cambridge, Cambridge University Press, 1986.

87. R. B. J. Walker, *Inside/Out: International relations as political theory*, Cambridge, Cambridge University Press, 1993.

88. A. B. Murphy, 'The Sovereign State System as Political-Territorial Ideal: Historical and contemporary considerations', in T. J. Biersteker and C. Weber (eds), *State Sovereignty as Social Construct*, Cambridge, Cambridge University Press, 1996, pp. 81–120 [90].

89. See the selection of an abundant literature in D. Held and A. McGrew (eds), *The Global Transformations Reader*, Cambridge, Polity Press, 2003; E. Kofman and G. Youngs (eds), *Globalization: Theory and practice*, 2nd edn, New York, Continuum, 2003.

90. I refer to the debate following Roper v. Simmons, 543 U.S. 551 (2005).

91. See, e.g., A. Sen, *Poverty and Famines: An essay on entitlement and deprivation*, Oxford University Press, 1983 [1981].

92. The Secretary-General, 'An Agenda for Peace Preventative Diplomacy, Peacemaking and Peace-Keeping', 59, delivered to the Members of the United Nations, U.N. Doc. A/47/277, S/24111 (June 17, 1992), available at http://www.un.org/Docs/SG/agpeace.html.

93. *Ibid.*, at 17.

94. See R. Caplan, *International Governance of War-Torn Territories: Rule and reconstruction*, Oxford, Oxford University Press, 2005; S. Chesterman, *You, The People: The United Nations, transitional administration, and state-building*, Oxford, Oxford University Press, 2005.

95. D. Thürer, *Kosmopolitisches Staatsrecht: Grundidee Gerechtigkeit*, Vol. 1, Berlin, Berliner Wissenschafts-Verlag, 2005, pp. 3–39.

96. See, e.g., S.C. Res. 1589, U.N. Doc. S/RES/1589 (Mar. 24, 2005) (establishing an international interim authority in Afghanistan); S.C. Res. 1338, U.N. Doc. S/RES/1338 (Jan. 21, 2001) (establishing an international interim authority in East Timor); S.C. Res. 745, U.N. Doc. S/RES/745 (Feb. 28, 1992) (establishing an international interim authority in Cambodia). See also the particularly complex case of Kosovo, S.C. Res. 1244, U.N. Doc. S/RES/1244 (June 10, 1999). For more details see Thürer, *Kosmopolitisches Staatsrecht*. See now most recently P. Dann and Z. Al-Ali, 'The Internationalized Pouvoir Constituant: Constitution-making under external influence in Iraq, Sudan and East Timor', in A. von Bogdandy and R. Wolfrum (eds.), *Max Planck Yearbook of United Nations Law*, 10, Leiden, Martinus Nijhoff, 2006, pp. 423–463.

97. Hirschman, *The Passions and the Interests*.

Chapter Fourteen

Is There, Or Can There Be, a 'European Society'?[*]

Claus Offe

Curiously enough, it is not easy to find social scientists who seem to know – and are ready to explain – what a 'society' is. Yet it seems possible to put together a number of constituent notions that most authors, more or less implicitly, refer to when using the term. Among those notions, I submit, are the following.

1. A society consists of individual actors, the number of which is relatively large (relative to members of families, business firms or localities), yet relatively small compared to the global human population, or 'mankind'.

2. These actors are related to each other through a greater density of interaction, functional interdependence, and shared institutions than with outsiders or members of other societies.

3. The internal density or cohesion of societies is generated by institutionalised rules. These impose constraints on the individually rational pursuit of gain (of power or wealth) or the avoidance of costs. Living in a society means sacrificing some kind of (short-term, individual) advantage for the sake of collective goods and the maintenance of social order.

4. These constraining rules have the quality of trans-individual durability. They (are expected by members of a society to) last and stay valid for longer than the individual's lifetime and originate from a time that is prior to that lifetime. Some of these rules and institutions are typically still around when, after about three generations, the entire 'personnel' of a society has been exchanged.

5. Members of societies are reflexively aware of these rules as 'social facts', and they are also aware of their durability (or rootedness in some historical tradition and culture that is characteristic of their society); they are further aware of the contingency ('non-naturalness' and potential changeability) as well as distinctiveness (relative to other societies) of these rules.

6. Given the inherent antagonism between these rules and individual self-interest and the temptations resulting from this antagonism, these rules (unlike pure coordination rules) are not self-executing through consensus, spontaneous sympathy or solidarity. On the contrary, relationships of trust, cooperation and the observance of traditional patterns depend

[*] 'Is There, or Can There Be, a "European Society"?', in J. Keane (ed.), *Civil Society: Berlin perspectives*, New York and Oxford, Berghahn Books, 2006, pp. 169–188.

upon the legal status and backing that the respective institutions enjoy. In modern, above all in 'post-modern' societies, society-wide rules are not self-supporting. Therefore, the making, enforcement and adjudication of these rules presuppose an apparatus of political rule and control. Beyond very low levels of either size (as in tribes) or cohesion (as in empires), societies depend upon states and their making, adjudication and enforcement of binding rules. Societies (as opposed to tribes) have always extended beyond the number of people with whom any of their members is likely ever to enter into direct interaction. Yet, in spite of the fact that most members of 'our' society are bound to remain strangers to each of us forever, we still find relationships of trust, common attachment, toleration, understanding and solidarity, as well as a sense of obligation to our 'strange' fellow citizens. All of this is due to the recognition that 'all of us' belong to some shared political community, the extent and content of which are defined by constituted state power. Even the ideally autonomous public sphere is a network of ideas and communications that is both guaranteed by and focused upon the constituted political authority of a state and its way of dealing with what we, due to this shared focus, think of as 'our' common problems.

7. 'Princes' and other performers of these state functions have an intrinsic and private self-interest in providing and monopolising the public good of rule.

8. In order to be able to do so and to impose the rules (as well as to appropriate the benefits of rule to the rulers themselves), they have to make concessions to the ruled in order to secure their compliance/cooperation. This is what, from Hegel to Giddens, has been referred to as the 'dialectics of control'. If rulers want to impose duties upon society, they can do so only by granting rights to society, thereby binding/limiting themselves in the exercise of rule. If ruling elites want to extract support, taxes and military resources, they must grant something in return, such as the effective protection of life, liberty and property, or the credible representation of the society's 'national' identity. The perfect equilibrium of rule from above and consent from below is reached when, as in all contractarian theories, the political regime can be thought of (or can present itself) as freely chosen by the enlightened will of the ruled. Military, legal and social security, as well as concessions in terms of representative and constitutional government, comprise the kinds of 'services' and concessions that states must deliver to society in order to 'earn' and preserve both the privileges of rule and their capacity to impose duties. These duties include, most importantly, the duty to pay taxes, to put one's life at the disposition of the military defence apparatus, and the duty to comply with the curricular regime of public education. Through the use of their military, fiscal and educational powers, states shape societies to the same extent that they must concede the right to being shaped by society in their practice of governance.

9. Not only do societies depend upon states and their capacity for making and enforcing rules. In providing that service, states endow individuals and collective actors with rights and thereby engage in market making and other forms of 'society making'. Societies and states cohere in a relationship of circular mutual determination within the framework of a territorially bounded political community.

10. There are three types of cases in which the precarious equilibrium of political regime and society can break down. For all of these cases, events in recent history can be invoked as illustrations. First, the regime fails to extract the societal resources of support and economic performance on which it depends for its survival; this is the case of post-communist and other post-authoritarian regime breakdown, where the balance between the regime's claims on society and the concessions it grants to society is fatally upset, the result being the disintegration of the regime and the constitution of a *new regime* in place of the old. Secondly, a political regime fails to maintain the unity and integrity of society because 'deep' (ethnic, religious, linguistic or historical) divisions lead to the separation of parts of its territory and constituent population through secession; this amounts to an *inward* revision of the regime's scope. Thirdly, the congruence of regime and society is upset by an *outward* revision of the regime's scope, or the fusion of two or more regimes into a new and unified one. The latter case has occurred historically through military conquest and the imposition of foreign rule through occupation. In the more recent past, it has occurred through the fusion of regimes and the creation of a multilayered pattern of governance consisting of national and supranational regimes. The most interesting case in which such regime enlargement is currently taking place is (apart from German unification) the European Union (EU) and European integration. The question that I want to address is this: what are the causes, consequences and driving motives of the latter case of disarticulation between societies and political regimes?

The constitutional regimes of European nation states, of which the citizenry as a whole (the 'people') is thought of as the collective author, governs the scope and limits of the state's governance and at the same time creates and defines the society to which this governance applies. The problem of European political integration is that no such self-construction of the citizenry through an act of constitution-making exists. While the German Constitution (the *Grundgesetz*) ascribes, in its preamble, to the 'German people' the authorship of the document, nobody has ever claimed that the Treaties (of Rome, Maastricht and Amsterdam) that quasi-constitutionalise EU governance originate from some 'European people'. In these contracts, societies, not a society with its specific historical entity and distinctiveness, are subsumed under a supranational regime that applies to all of them with 'direct effects'. This regime is rightly seen to *dis*empower national political regimes and to render their autonomy increasingly nominal – often to the point, as is perceived within EU member states, of exercising a mild form of foreign rule. At the same time, 'Brussels' lacks the constitutional means and resources (as well as the mandate) to homogenise and 'Europeanise' the constituent societies of the EU in the same way as political elites were able to unify national societies in the process of nineteenth-century nation building. Short of a 'constitution-building coup', 'Brussels' lacks the capacities that have played a critical role in the formation of the societies of nation states: namely, the capacity to impose military conscription and action, to impose educational standards and curricular powers and to directly extract taxes from (what only then would be) a 'European people'.

While it is true that both economic transactions and the public sphere of communication are increasingly transnational ('globalised') in nature, each participant in these interactions is still enabled to participate in them by institutions and policies (ranging from corporate law to national educational systems) that are specific to and enforced by national state authorities. Even the most 'global' players pick their place of location or incorporation according to the most favourable conditions as provided by the respective host state and its (for example, tax) regime. This process has often and rightly been described as following a trajectory of 'negative' integration. This pattern of negative – or commercial, financial and monetary – integration of markets is designed to increase the options for economic 'exit' and to debase the governing capacity of national governments and their protectionist inclinations. But the process has not been complemented by some supranational 'positive' integration or the restoration of governing capacity at the European level. In fact, the residual elements of governing capacity that remain intact at the level of member states are used by them to obstruct – in the name of the 'national interest' and with the need to be (re-) elected by a national constituency in mind – the transfer of governance from the national to the European level. Thus negative integration both decimates national policy making capacity *and* induces national governments to cling to whatever remains of it, rather than sacrificing it for the sake of 'positive' integration.

In fact, the prospects for uniting a 'European' society, i.e. the supranational equivalent and extension of national societies, are exceedingly discouraging. People belonging to a society will typically communicate in one (or a small number of) idiom(s), and they will presuppose their mutual familiarity with aesthetic and other forms of symbolic expression, ranging from styles and pieces of music to religious and national holidays. None of this is present – or could be created in any foreseeable future – at the European level. Within national societies, people will be shaped, both cognitively and motivationally, by a common cultural tradition that is reflexively known to them as being more or less different from the traditions of other societies and which is transmitted through schools, media, religious associations and cultural institutions (such as museums). The most extensive and wide-ranging form in which social integration and cohesion has been developed is the framework of the nation state, which, from the early nineteenth century on, has cultivated this distinctive type of societal integration and thus covered populations that, before, never belonged or thought of themselves as belonging to the same 'society'. Nation states 'make' societies and build a *demos* by imposing upon some pre-existing patchwork of heterogeneous regional cultures and political units (such as kingdoms and principalities) clearly defined borders, as well as, within those borders, a relatively homogeneous military, fiscal, educational, economic, religious, and judicial regime and institutional order.

This process of state-initiated nation building (or 'society building') does not have an equivalent at the European level. It has been studied in the case of France's nineteenth-century dynamic of transforming 'peasants into Frenchmen' (Eugen Weber).[1] It has also been proclaimed as a (eventually successful) project that inspired the leaders of the Italian *risorgimento*: 'After we now have made Italy, let us proceed to make Italians', meaning people who feel and think of themselves as being tied to (and at the same time being the collective authors of) the encompassing political community of all other Italians, as defined by the scope of the Italian national state. Similarly, President Lincoln's Gettysburg address was part of an equally successful attempt to unite the population of a territorial state (that was torn by civil war) into a 'people', thereby creating the social and political unity and cohesion of a *demos* and its recognition of itself. These historical examples are instances of how representative political elites and their constitutive and unifying policies have actually helped to accomplish the project of *e pluribus unum*. But there are neither the incentives nor the resources available to accomplish a parallel process at the European level. (Note that virtually all types of collective and associative action, from the Red Cross to academic societies, from trade unions to business interest groups, are still based on an organisational domain that coincides with the territory of a state or its sub-territories. The principle that international communication is *international* also applies to organisations such as the United Nations, or, for that matter, the EU, the members of which are member *states,* the governments, corporate actors and citizens of which can then enter – by virtue of being constituted within the framework of a state – into transnational relations and activities, including the contractual formation of supranational institutions.)

The problem of creating both a European governing capacity that is capable of overruling nation states' regimes and, of thus, creating a European *demos* does not primarily reside with a prohibitive degree of diversity between the national components of such a *demos* nor with the aversion of national governments to cooperate. The core problem is, rather, the absence of a charismatic idea (*finalité*) that could drive attempts to overcome such obstacles to the building of a European *demos*. Here is one categorical 'dis-analogy' between the historical process of nation building and the hypothetical future process of building a European regime-*cum-demos*. Historically, nation states have come into being along two alternative trajectories: the fusion of small units into a bigger ones through national *unification*, or the splintering off of peripheries of empires (including colonial empires) in a process of national *liberation* and independence through separation. Unity and liberty have been the two driving forces and guiding values on the two alternative pathways to national statehood. Apart from cases of military conquest and occupation accomplished by outside forces,[2] all territorial reorganisation (or redefinition of borders) that was initiated from within has been driven by the idea of 'liberation' – be it liberation from the rule of oppressive or exploitative foreign (e.g. colonial) powers or liberation from princely particularism, arbitrariness, unjust oppression, and belligerent passions. Thus the idea of 'unification' need not be conceived of as an alternative to liberation, but as a sub-case of it, notwithstanding the fact that the appeal to 'unity' can be used as a powerful device to constrain the liberty of individuals as well as of sub-collectivities. At the same time, 'unity' can be an instrumental value that serves the maintenance of liberty in defence against some perceived external threat or enemy.[3]

The core problem of European integration and political unity is not so much the extent of ethnic, historical, cultural, linguistic and economic diversities and cleavages, in spite of the vast discrepancies in the size of member states and their level of economic development, but the total absence of an appeal of *liberation* in the service of which unity might be pursued. 'Europe' does – perhaps – yield a surplus value in terms of prosperity, but no such surplus value in terms of liberty. European states and their societies, which have already adopted, recently or otherwise, a liberal democratic form of regime (and only such states are conceivable candidates for EU membership), are, as it were, 'saturated' concerning their quest for liberty; at the very least, 'Europe', whatever else its *finalité* may be deemed to consist of in terms of prosperity and power, does not stand for an ambition of further liberation. (This is true, at least, if we pass over the calculus of various regionalist movements that 'Europe' will weaken the nation state and hence assist them in the acquisition of *sub*-state 'autonomy'.) Europe does not hold the promise of liberation, certainly not the liberation from the fear of European international war (which has been made a practical impossibility by other, for example, 'Atlantic', means of supranational security policy) or from the fear of a loss of freedom (a motivation that informed much of the *West* European integration that occurred under Cold War conditions). To be sure, European integration along the lines envisaged by the Maastricht and Amsterdam Treaties holds the great *instrumental* promise of reaping economies of scale, of global competitive advantage, of the pooling of civilian as well as of military resources, etc.; these benefits and economies of scale, however, can also be supplied within the framework of tight intergovernmental arrangements, beginning with common markets. But the promise of any kind of 'liberation' is not among the benefits a politically integrated Europe has to offer. Yet this promise is the *only* one which has historically driven (again, excepting international war, conquest, occupation, etc.) the territorial reorganisation of states.

Classical political theorists (such as Machiavelli and Rousseau) believed that states, in order to engender a strong spirit of solidarity and patriotic commitment among their citizenry, should be *small*, modelled after the Renaissance city republics. Others have argued that, in order to accumulate the critical mass of economic and military resources needed to prevail over rival states and to allow for a favourable size of internal markets, states should, on the contrary, be *large* in terms of their population and territory, and hence their overall resources, in spite of the internal diversity of populations that this may entail. There is no compelling calculus by which a compromise of these conflicting logics of political cohesion *vs.* economic diversification and military strength could possibly be devised. But there is an almost universal rule of state building in the twentieth century. All large states, or the largest states of their region or continent – be they large in terms of territory or in terms of population – are *federal* states, combining, as it were, the two virtues of smallness and largeness in an ingenious synthesis. This rule applies to North America (USA, Canada), South America (Argentina, Brazil), Australia, Europe (Germany) and Asia (Russia, India). It does most conspicuously (and perhaps ominously) not apply to the People's Republic of China, the largest of all. Given the fact that political and economic/military reasoning about the optimal size of states points in opposite directions, any compromise between the two, including the adoption and design of a federal system, will be guided by considerations of unity and liberation.

What is Europe?

Europe is not a state and hence not a society. The building of European statehood and, by implication, the emergence of a 'European society' is not a goal that societies within Europe could credibly and plausibly pursue in the name of any notion of 'liberation' (as opposed to market liberalisation – which, however, does not presuppose a common statehood). But there is certainly a *type* of European society. These national societies share, to a lesser or greater extent, numerous affinities, similarities and common features. These common features are most clearly visible in regional clusters of national societies and their historical experience and cultural (including religious) profiles. Such partly overlapping clusters include the Scandinavian countries, the Baltic states, the central European countries, the Mediterranean countries, the German-speaking countries, the Orthodox countries, and so on. But there are a number of features that are virtually shared by all of them, such as their being liberal democratic by regime type, or their being both enabled and constrained by their (anticipated) membership in the supranational regime of the European Union. But it is exactly because European societies are so similar already that their fusion into a 'unitary' socio-political arrangement of a 'European' society is unlikely to occur: little is to be gained, and much is to be lost, from such a fusion. It is simply a *non sequitur* to deduce from the similarity of European societies the desirability and/or probability of their eventually becoming 'one' society. Let me briefly review seven (an incomplete list) of those similarities.

1. The *circular* interaction of 'national' society shaping its state, with this state in turn shaping the institutional set-up of its society, is a peculiar European invention, which was, to be sure, transferred and copied to other parts of the world (such as the USA) in characteristically modified versions. Societies, as I have argued, are arrangements of state-sponsored civility, with the state in turn being shaped and reshaped by representative collective actors. In contrast, state building in most of the former colonies was accomplished, as far as the territorial shape of the new states as well as their regime form are concerned, not by local populations, but either by (former) colonial powers or autocratic/military elites, if not warlords

or big owners of land. But in Europe, too, the supranational institutions that exist are not made by, cannot be ascribed to and hence do not lead to the self-recognition of a 'European people', but are contracted by the governments of member states. As a consequence, the EU populations in total see themselves as affected by, but not the joint authors of, EU policies and programmes.

2. Before the modern nation state, there emerged another peculiar form of territorial regime in Europe, the *city*. Cities often formed the nucleus of a future state, of which many of them became, or strove to become, capital cities (in political terms) or dominant centres of regions (in economic terms). The city (*Stadt*), with its spatial coexistence and condensation of production and commerce, residence and consumption, associative life and political self-government, and religious, aesthetic, educational and intellectual institutions is a uniquely European evolutionary accomplishment. Partly due to the dense population of Europe and the European history of outward (mostly transatlantic) rather than inward migration, these cities tend to be medium sized; only two of the world's twenty biggest cities are located in Europe (Istanbul and London). The city was similar to the state in that it was the result of the desires of city-dwellers for liberty (from princely rule) and unity (of its citizenry); it differed from states in its greater openness to inward migration, as well as in its institutionalised relations with other cities and the countryside. It was also similar to the state in that it provided the seedbed of diversity (of trades and commodities, of the ethnic and religious background of its citizens, of opportunities to enter into contractual relations). Only states and cities have 'citizens', whereas tribes have members and empires have subjects and estates, as well as centres and peripheries as constituent social entities.

3. Throughout modern European history, *stateness was precarious and vulnerable*. This is so because states have been threatened by other states that were intent upon the project of empire building through the submission or occupation of other states. Such imperialist ambitions were executed, in a chronological sequence that is geographically clockwise, by the Ottoman empire, the Austro-Hungarian empire, the French empire, the imperialist ambitions of Nazi Germany, and the Soviet empire. Partly in addition to this and partly as an alternative, the imperialist temptations of European states were directed at territories overseas, as in the cases of Denmark, Britain, the Netherlands, Belgium, France, Spain and (first of all) Portugal. The nature of European states is that they are unsettled, precarious, threatened or threatening in their relation with other states. This world of threatened and threatening states has come to an end, as far as Western Europe is concerned, with the end of the Second World War, the first steps towards international cooperation and the subsequently completed process of decolonisation; as far as central and eastern Europe is concerned, with the end of the Cold War, the Iron Curtain, and the Soviet Union.

4. Since that time, however, stateness is threatened in many places, as it were, from the opposite direction. The dangerous dynamic is no longer the expansion of states at the expense of other states, but the *implosion of states* challenged by internal ethno-territorial cleavages. The most horrifying example of the dynamic of such cleavages is the disintegration of Yugoslavia. More benign forms of analogous processes have occurred, or are presently under way, in France, Belgium, Spain, Great Britain, Denmark and, arguably, Italy. The state-seeking ethnic and sub-nationalist groups that are now emerging are not, as their predecessors were in the nineteenth century, splitting off from empires but from (multinational) states. Also, an increasingly prominent cleavage occurs between national populations, on the one hand, and non-territorial (migrant) minorities of *extracommunitari* within member states.

5. European societies are specific in that they share a long history of international wars and attempts – frequently failed attempts – to neutralise the potential for international warfare. These wars, hot as well as 'cold', were, as far as the history of the twentieth century is concerned, driven by ideologies that we have come to speak of as 'totalitarian' belief systems and practices of domination. The crimes of these *totalitarian regimes* as well as their repressive, aggressive and genocidal conduct of rule, were rooted in ideas, it must be said, that were exclusively European in origin. But it can also be said that the standards by which they are to be judged and recognised *as* horrendous aberrations are also European by background. These standards derive from the intellectual legacies of Greek and Roman antiquity, Christianity, the Renaissance, the Reformation and the Enlightenment with its offshoots of both liberal and socialist ideas. The European history of ideas can be described as the coincidence in space of the worst crimes *and* the most elaborate and explicit standards of condemnation of those crimes. Throughout its history, Europe has supplied itself with objects of its self-critical scrutiny. Due to this perplexing coincidence of opposites, the *self-critical appreciation* of the wrongs that have been committed by Europeans in their own history is something specifically European. This inclination to self-revision and self-doubt has no parallel, as far as I can see, in any of the non-European civilizations, e.g. those of the United States or Japan.

6. The territorial and demographic situation of Europe did not, at the time of its breakthrough to economic and political modernisation in the nineteenth century, allow for the benefit of nearby 'empty space' into which relative surplus populations could be 'exported'. To be sure, this was partly compensated for by populations threatened by immiseration transferring to the Americas. But the strategy of 'going West' to a 'new frontier' was not available within Europe itself. Hence in Europe, at an earlier point and to a larger extent than elsewhere, *institutional arrangements of social and political conflict resolution* came to be adopted. As explosive social conflict could not be dealt with through 'exit' or expulsion, provisions were invented (partly

for the sake of preparing populations for international war, according to the 'welfare-warfare state' pattern) for the provision of 'voice', or the sharing of political power and, through it, economic resources. These arrangements of internal conflict resolution were premised upon the formation of strong intermediate and corporatist collective actors and forms of representation, the installation of which was in turn facilitated by the remnants of feudalism and a strong state apparatus.[4] Reconciliation through compromise and the gradual inclusion of social categories was the prevailing European pattern, while elsewhere the maintenance of hierarchies of domination or unmediated class, ethnic and religious conflict and disparity remained in place, leading to the pattern of 'deeply divided societies'. European societies are privileged by the absence of two types of populations that make for deep divides in New World settler societies, namely, an indigenous population and the descendants of former slaves. But it remains to be seen how well Old World societies will be able to integrate two other types of populations, migrant labour and refugees (in addition to sub-national minorities). Note, however, that the European capacity for reconciliation and institutionalised conflict resolution is not just a matter of industrial relations, co-determination and social security policies. It is also evident in the abolition of capital punishment and the virtual absence of urban ghettoisation, as well as in an effective enforcement of human and social citizenship rights.

7. To conclude this list of admittedly rather daring generalisations about European societies, let us look at the distribution of states in space. In between the two largest states, Russia and Germany, there is a strip of (mostly, with the exception of Poland) comparatively small countries, ranging from Finland to Cyprus, whose recent history is shaped by the threatening shadow or actual presence of imperial rule. These 'Central' European states are now in the process of 'returning' to Europe, whereas 'Eastern' Europe states (Russia, Ukraine, Belarus) are currently, and are likely to remain for the foreseeable future, outside the discourse of European identity and institutional belonging. With the exception of some still unsettled territorial issues of state building in former Yugoslavia (and arguably the Basque Country and Northern Ireland), *all states now have consolidated external borders*. None of them, except to an extent the regional cases just mentioned, can rightfully be described as a 'deeply divided society'. If new borders are drawn, these will be 'inward' redefinitions accomplished through peaceful means (granting autonomy rights, or 'velvet divorce', not civil war, as in the case of the Czech and Slovak Republics), not 'outward' redefinition through military aggression and imperial ambition. The possibility of both international war and intra-national civil war is effectively warded off by a set of effective supranational regimes, such as the Council of Europe, the Organization for Security and Cooperation in Europe (OSCE), the North Atlantic Treaty Organization (NATO) and the emerging framework of the EU's Common Foreign, Defence and Security Policy.

Diversities of states and their societies in Europe

Passports of EU countries identify their bearers first as EU citizens and second as citizens of a member country. Yet few (except for the residents of Luxembourg, 28 per cent of whom are non-nationals) would spontaneously respond to the question as to which political community they are citizens of in terms of 'European Union' citizenship. The predominant sense of belonging on the part of Europeans (except, perhaps, for members of the European elite who are asked this question in places like Hong Kong) is attached to countries (if not regions), not the EU.[5] The awareness of both similarities and interdependencies within the framework of the EU's supranational institutions does not erode, but if anything strengthens, national frames of thought, action and the pursuit of interest and identity. This is entirely unsurprising. Why?

Suppose that what has been said above – about the enormous achievement of Europeans living today in countries between which war (and within which civil war) is a virtual impossibility – is not only true, but also *known* to be true by those to whom it applies: this still does not make them 'Europeans'. On the contrary – and as far as the former Comecon countries are concerned – the pride and pleasure people take in a national statehood that is, for the first time in at least two generations, not threatened by the imperial ambitions of great European powers to the West or to the East adds a special emphasis to their adherence to nation-state principles. The memories, fears and sense of distrust inherited from the past are much too strong and too widely shared – and very understandably so – for people to sacrifice part of or even to abandon these principles in favour of some European identity. Also, people in EU countries (again with the exception of English-speaking elites) cannot communicate with most other Europeans. Patterns of religious affiliation and national cultures differ and are mutually *perceived* as constituting significant differences of collective identity, not as minor diversities within a cultural heritage that Europeans basically own in common. As there is no European idiom, there is no European public sphere that would have to be constituted by Europe-wide media and audiences, not just remote elite discourses and negotiations.

Furthermore, the national publics are strongly aware of political differences between their countries: different constitutions, parties, forms of government and welfare state regimes. They are further aware of the vast differences of size (the sizes of the biggest and the smallest, Germany and Luxembourg, are in a ratio of 204:1) and territorial location between countries (proximity *vs.* remoteness), as well as of the substantial differences in wealth and productivity, in spite of the fact that all member states are industrial societies with the institutions of liberal democracy in place. Most importantly, citizens of European countries form beliefs, accurate ones or otherwise, about how the interested behaviour of other European actors will affect 'our' or 'my' well-being and prospects. In this calculus, six concerns stand out. Taken together, they suggest the perception of the game of the European political economy as one of multidimensional rivalry clouded in deep uncertainties. Let us briefly remind ourselves of the nature of these concerns and fears.

1. The concern with inward migration of labour, with all its ramifications in terms of loss of jobs, decline of wages in the rich countries, ethnic conflict and political backlash.
2. The outward flow of investment to EU countries with lower costs of employment, and hence the loss of employment and prosperity on a national scale.
3. The fiscal redistribution within the EU (and, in particular, a larger EU), consisting not only in a net transfer of funds from the rich to the less prosperous countries and regions, but also in the relative deprivation that the previous net receivers (say, the Mediterranean countries) will suffer as a consequence of the accession of new and even poorer and therefore even more 'deserving' claimants amongst the new member countries in the east and south-east of Europe.
4. The competition in markets for goods and services, which is likely (and, indeed, is intended) to drive productivity laggards in their respective industries out of business, thereby adding to the persistently high level of unemployment in most current member countries.
5. The disadvantages imposed upon newly acceding countries by their being forced to adopt the entire *acquis communautaire* as a precondition of their accession; the disadvantages current member countries suffer in terms of the loss of protection as a consequence of European Court of Justice (ECJ) rulings; and the disadvantages that 'minorities' of one or more countries fear will result from majority decisions within the Council of Ministers that are contrary to their majoritarian national preferences – all of which give rise to the fear of 'Europe' becoming a new form of foreign rule.
6. Finally, the fear that the intensification of cross-national interaction on all these levels will seriously curtail the remaining capacity for national policy making, in particular in the policy area of social protection (which is nominally – in the name of a characteristically one-sided reading of the 'subsidiarity' principle – left to the national governments to design and adjust, but which may in fact be largely paralysed by the imperatives of competitiveness).

Taken together, these concerns have a corrosive impact precisely because it is so difficult to predict to what extent they will become reality and who is most likely to be negatively affected by them. These concerns are widely seen to have the potential to give rise to anti-European political forces, leading to an electoral backlash (particularly in countries providing for referenda in EU questions), thus blocking if not obstructing the further political integration of Europe. Pro-European enthusiasm is vanishing everywhere. Moreover, Eurobarometer findings on support for European integration provide a far too optimistic measure, as indicated by the actual voting behaviour of the very same constituencies: many still pay lip service to the standards of European political correctness in surveys, but behave differently in the voting booth (where concrete steps such as admitting new countries or adoption of the euro are at issue).

These six concerns apply to different current and prospective member countries to different extents. They are also controversial in terms of realism *vs.* paranoia, as well as of long-term versus short-term effects. Even if it were generally agreed (again, both by political elites *and* by national publics) that in the long run the game will turn out to be a strong positive-sum game, the usual 'valley of transition' scenario applies, with the two obvious questions: how wide will the valley turn out to be, and how deep?

The most interesting feature of these concerns is that they do not add up to a well-organised conflict that would divide current and prospective member countries along some clear-cut cleavage line. On the contrary, nobody is currently able to predict with any measure of certainty or authority who is going to win and lose, how much and for how long. It is *not* a game of small against large, rich against relatively backward, centre *vs.* periphery, old *vs.* new member countries. The conflict of interest is amorphous and poorly structured. Nor is it clear that the parties to the conflict are actually countries, as opposed to social classes, consumers versus producers, regions, sectors of industry, age groups or, in fact, time slices. Nor is the metric clear by which one would have to balance gains against losses. There are unanswerable questions, such as how much gain from international trade five years hence is worth how much increase in regional unemployment now or how much polarisation in political conflict and the subsequent potential for government instability for the next two years. This lack of structure is exactly the problem, for well-structured conflicts can be embedded in an institutional bargaining framework in which demands, threats and promises can be exchanged and the losers can force the winners to compensate them by sharing part of their gains. This is how societies cohere, and this is why Europe is not a 'society': the authoritatively imposed institutional setting is lacking that would be able to transform the diffuse precariousness of a 'state of nature' into clear-cut social conflict and the rules for compromise.

The conflicts that we experience are not those among players in a game that can be adjudicated by neutral and recognised judges, assisted by the testimony of trustworthy experts. Instead, the scenery bears more resemblance to a minefield than a courtroom or, for that matter, a government. Yet there is the opposite risk as well – the largely economic risk of individual countries '*missing*' European integration or staying behind. The logic is simple and compelling: the more countries joining the Economic and Monetary Union (EMU), the less the remaining countries, for reasons of their economic prosperity, can afford *not* to join. A country must be uniquely rich in natural resources (such as Norway with its oil) to afford outsider status, but even then it will find it prudent to follow the regime of EU standards for long-term considerations (as Norway in fact does) in order not to foreclose the option of joining at a later point. At any rate, the definitive decision not to join is seen by all parties involved as a relative loss in prosperity for the country that decides to do so. This does not imply that there may not be non-economic reasons for a negative decision on joining. But these are largely, as the campaign preceding the Danish referendum of 2000 demonstrated, of a sinister and xenophobic nature and imply the deliberate forgoing of economic gain for the sake of asserting an exclusionary version of nationhood and the national interest. Confronted with the choice between two options, both of which involve substantial risks, European member state constituencies show declining enthusiasm (to put it mildly) and partly majoritarian opposition to their respective country's EU membership. To make things worse, countries that are in the process of becoming members and trying to negotiate a relatively safe and painless mode of accession are in a structurally weak bargaining position, since they cannot credibly threaten actually to stay out for good, as this would arguably hurt themselves more than others. For substantial parts of the populations of countries in Europe, and to an extent also for their political elites, Europe is a matter of deep uncertainty, fear and distrust.

Is the European Union, then, experiencing a relapse into a state of nature? It is most certainly not, as Europe's great asset after the end of the Cold War – as a result of the supranational security structures in place – is the *effective ban on inter-state violence* that Europeans enjoy at the turn of the millennium, (*military* violence, that is, and only if we optimistically disregard for the moment the still unfinished task of completing the civilisation of the European system of states in the Balkans, which is not meant to belittle ongoing problems concerning the micro-violence of terrorism, on the one hand, and xenophobic aggressiveness on the other). But, arguably, Europe is in the somewhat oxymoronic situation of being in a 'peaceful state of nature'. If that is true, the task ahead is the building of a European regime that might eventually facilitate the rise of something that could seriously be called a 'European society'; the rationale of this society would be analogous to the logic according to which the uniquely European process of organising civility through state building has taken place historically.

To be sure, and for the reasons mentioned above that condition a strong and legitimate attachment to nation states, this cannot possibly take place in the form of *one* European state emerging from the fusion of all existing European states. Part of the historical legacy of all European states is a strong sense of the precariousness and vulnerability of their statehood – something that was, by comparison, entirely absent when the component proto-states of what became the United States decided to merge. At the time of the federation, none of the states had ever waged war against any of the other states! European states are 'too old', burdened with too much history, and endowed with their own specific accomplishments achieved in the course of that history, to be plausible candidates for some outright fusion. (The only place where a fusion of states has taken place, namely the country I come from, has not experienced this merger as an unqualified success story, the celebratory pronouncements on the tenth anniversary of German unification in October 2000 notwithstanding.) Nowhere would European societies be prepared to sacrifice their statehood as the institutional form by which they organise – and by which they have defended, if often unsuccessfully – their civility. (The only country whose political elites have occasionally gestured in this direction, namely Germany, has done so with the transparent aim of appeasing the concerns of its neighbours, which often enough has not actually put these concerns to rest, but exacerbated them by raising suspicions as to why a state should do such an 'unnatural' thing for reasons other than those of deceiving its neighbours.) Europeans have a lot in common, including a history that inspired them with a very rational reluctance to give up the stateness on which the coherence of their societies critically depends.

Nonetheless, the uncertain outcomes of the European integration of markets and countries do call for some kind of organising capacity that is able to impose rules (voluntarily and rationally adopted rules, that is!) on the partial European state of nature. Such rules are the means for alleviating fear, generating certainties and engendering mutual trust. Again, the task of organising civility is put on the agenda. This organising capacity must be capable of not just making markets (through 'negative integration') but of beginning to build the rudimentary foundations of a European society (through 'positive integration'). This organising capacity cannot be a state, as states are in place already and statehood is sacrosanct to the societies shaped by these states. National statehood is simply not seen by citizens as something they want to be 'liberated' from, but as something they depend upon for the sake of their protection and liberty. Hence this organising capacity must respect and, indeed, strengthen national statehood. It must respect it by leaving substantial scope for national policy making capacity in the hands of national (and even sub-national and regional) governments, which are and will remain accountable to and elected by national constituencies. It must strengthen and positively empower national governments so that these policy making capacities are not rendered nominal, as in much of the field of social security, or through the facts of competition, interdependence and interpenetration.

What states have historically done to the citizens of their societies, namely civilise and regularise their common life so that they can live in a 'society', a constitutionalised European governing capacity must do to the multitude of member countries. The task is state building, but one level up and without the template of the nation state. We are now living through a fascinating and unprecedented period, in which Europe applies to itself the logic of the circular creation of state and society that shaped the modern history of European countries. To reiterate: the agency that will eventually accomplish a regime of 'organised civility' governing the entire European space will not itself be a state, but a 'union'. It will have to leave existing states in place. But it will also have to conform to two criteria that all European states have now come to accept as the standards of acceptable political rule: legitimacy and effectiveness.

By 'legitimacy' I mean a fair and impartial way in which societies create their political authority (which, as legitimate, enjoys the compliance and support of members), and by 'effectiveness' I mean the capacity of political authorities actually to achieve their goals and impose their rules. There is little disagreement today that the EU in its current institutional state lacks both. This is the rational core of the sceptical attitudes displayed by citizens, media, and voters. It can be summarised in the question: 'As Europe (Brussels) evidently does not owe much of value to us, what do we owe to Europe?'

The holders of union powers must be *legitimate*. This is a simple thing that is hard to accomplish. Through the European institutions of governance, Europeans must be seen, and must be able to see themselves, as *governing themselves*. That is, no group of 'advanced' European countries (presumably consisting of countries that pride themselves on being more advanced and Europe-minded than others) should be seen as governing other European countries by devising a system of governance that is good for all. There is a disparity between 'founding members' and 'latecomers' anyway, and this should not be exacerbated by some core countries assuming pioneering roles and setting rules for the rest. Nor is some 'neutral' committee of benevolent experts, judges or commissioners good enough to decree the rules and institutions of European governance. In either of these two cases, the resulting regime would be insufficiently good due to the paternalist mode by which it had been brought into being, simply because opposition to such paternalism provides ample reason to defect or to disobey what actually would have to function as a European constitution. Only if the regime can be robustly presented as a self-governing and 'self-binding' (rather than 'other-binding') regime does it have a chance of winning the loyalty of all of its citizens.

Furthermore, the regime would have to be compatible with the major ideas and principles that are enshrined in existing constitutions of European states,[6] most notably the democratic principle that whoever wields governmental powers must be accountable to those over whom they are wielded. There is currently no convergent view, to the best of my knowledge, as to how this task of European constitution-making could be accomplished. The tendency in this situation would be to use gag rules, i.e. to start with the little that is relatively uncontroversial and leave the rest to later debates, foreclosing its discussion for the moment.

However, this 'wait-and-see' approach collides with the somewhat urgent requirement of *effectiveness*. In order to overcome the market-driven European state of nature and create Europe-wide institutions of bargaining and conflict resolution, the European governing capacity that is to be created on top of nation states must be highly potent. It must basically be able to accomplish two things. First, it must have at its disposal credible devices to reduce both the depth and width of the valley of transition. Only if European citizens have strong reason to believe the pains that the common market inflicts upon them – hopefully for a limited period of time – will be equitably compensated for and distributed fairly, will they become prepared to surrender some of their (increasingly nominal) reserved domains of national policy making. That is, Europe must be more than a framework for the military security of states; it must become the source and active promoter of the social and economic security of its citizens. And such security must come as a right attached to European citizenship, not as a set of discretionary programmes tabled (or withdrawn) by the Commission, as is the case with structural funds programmes.

Secondly, and as an obvious consequence of the above, the holders of European governing, capacity need, if they are to honour European citizenship rights, the authority to tax and to extract the resources that are needed to finance programmes of meaningful burden-sharing and compensation. To be sure, it is the undebatable virtue of markets to pose challenges for adjustment, learning and innovation. But it is equally beyond debate that some challenges are too demanding to be met without substantial assistance, by those (individuals, countries, sectors, regions, occupations, generations) who are affected by them. Other challenges resulting from the Commission and ECJ's quest for negative integration (e.g. concerning the way in which countries run their pension system, electronic media or alcohol regime) can be rejected as inappropriate and illegitimate. The question is obvious: which challenges belong to which of these three categories? Which pains can we be expected to live with, which call for pain relief to be administered, and which are simply unacceptable in the first place? We can begin to speak of the reality of a European society only after European authorities set up bargaining tables that allow these and related questions to be answered.

Notes

1. E. Weber, *Peasants into Frenchman: The modernization of rural France, 1870–1914*, Stanford, Stanford University Press, 1976.

2. Such conquest was the rationale of Nazi Germany's notion of a 'new European order' that was to be established under German hegemony by military means (see B. Kletzin, *Europa aus Rasse und Raum. Die nationalsozialistische Idee der neuen Ordnung*, Münster, LIT Verlag, 2000).

3. R. Swedberg, 'The idea of "Europe" and the origin of the European Union', *Zeitschrift für Soziologie*, 1994, vol. 23, no. 5, pp. 378–87; and H. Münkler, 'Die politische Idee Europa', in M. Delgado and M. Lutz-Bachmann (eds), *Herausforderung Europa. Wege zu einer politischen Identität*, Munich, Beck, 1995, pp. 9–27, have demonstrated that European 'unity' has always been invoked in situations when collective liberty was deemed to be in need of defence against internal or, more often, external threats and enemies.

4. C. Crouch, *Social Change in Western Europe*, Oxford, Oxford University Press, 1999.

5. M. Kohli, 'The battlegrounds of European identity', *European Societies*, 2000, vol. 2, no. 2, pp. 113–37.

6. H. Abromeit, *Democracy in Europe: Legitimising politics in a non-state polity*, New York, Berghahnn, 1998.

Chapter Fifteen

Problems of Constitution Making: Prospects of a Constitution for Europe[*]

Ulrich K. Preuß

Preliminaries: Why a debate about a European Constitution?

The Treaty on European Union, signed in Maastricht on 7th February 1992 by the heads of governments of the EC Member States and effective since November 1993, has triggered a debate about the 'If' and 'How' of a European constitution reaching far beyond the narrow circles of academia and of the leading cadres of the Community. It could become a public European issue. A number of reasons may explain the widespread interest: first, the politics of incrementalism which prevailed over the last forty years has produced a complex patchwork of rules and regulations which is already hard enough for legal experts to understand, but is almost incomprehensible to laypersons. Eurocrats and politicians are beginning to realise that in the long run the opacity of the Community's legal structure may undermine the legitimacy of the community at large. Usually, we assume that a written constitution enhances the transparency of public authority, which in turn is likely to increase its acceptance. The case of the EC, however, may be more complicated if, as some authors claim, a constitution for Europe would heighten the confusion about European governance rather than diminish it. I will return to this point.

The second reason for the deeply felt need for constitutional debate is the forthcoming enlargement of the Community by several applicants from East and Central Europe. In a few years, the Community will no longer consist of fifteen, as today, but of more than twenty Member States. You may remember that the institutional equipment of the EC (formerly: EEC) was devised for no more than six Member States. The enlarged Community will soon extend from Portugal in the West to Poland and possibly the Baltic States in the East, covering a vast heterogeneity of political systems, economic structures, and cultural legacies. This makes the reconstruction of the institutional system of the Community almost imperative.

Yet, the main reason for the public debate over a European constitution is the obvious increase of the power of the EC that many citizens in the Member States suspect is not being matched by a like increase in legitimation through their

---

[*] 'Prospects of a constitution for Europe', *Constellations: An international journal for critical and democratic theory*, 1996, vol. 3, no. 2, pp. 209–224.

consent. This belief is confirmed by the gap between fairly elaborate devices of democratic legitimation in the several national Member States and the advancing exodus of the powers of these to organs of the supranational Community. Thus, according to some estimates, up to 80 per cent of the legal regulations in the economic domains of the Member States originate from the Community and hence are beyond their control. While the national governments, subject to rigid and demanding requirements of democratic legitimation, find their public authority ever more emptied, the powers of the Community are steadily increasing without a parallel rise in the requirements for their legitimation. In other words: the loss of opportunities for democratic participation on the Member State level is not compensated by a like gain on the EC level. A Community constitution is rightly expected to cure this evil.

This expectation, however, is not shared by everyone. Some argue that the EC already *has* a constitution, embodied in the EC Treaty, the so-called primary Community Law. This is basically the opinion of the European Court of Justice. Others state the opposite. They argue that the Community neither has, nor can have or needs to have a constitution, at least not for the present and the foreseeable future.[1] They claim that a constitution requires an identity of the authors and the addressees of the constitution, which means: those who make a constitution make it for themselves, because constitution-making is an act of political self-determination. This identity however, is lacking in the European Community. The rules about wielding public authority, i.e., the legal rules about the authorisation, legitimation, and limitation of the Community's public power, are granted by third parties, namely by the Member States and their treaty-making power. Since the EC and EU Treaties do not derive their legal validity and their binding force from the political will of those who are subject to their stipulations, the citizens of Europe, they cannot embody the constitution for the Community. Closely connected with this claim is the argument that the constituent power of a modern constitution can only be a *demos*; without a *demos* there can be no democracy, and since there is no European *demos* – only the peoples of the Member States – there can be no European democracy; and without a European democracy, a European constitution appears plainly inconceivable.[2]

The broad scope of conflicting views on the possibility, necessity or desirability of a European constitution is perhaps the best justification for the attempt to clarify the concept of a European constitution. What is puzzling is the impression that all involved parties are somehow right: there *is* a need for more transparency, efficiency and legitimacy of the institutional structure of the Community, and this, according to our conventional wisdom, can best be delivered by a constitution. On the other hand, it is also true that the European Court of Justice (ECJ) held that the 'EEC Treaty, albeit concluded in the form of an international agreement, nonetheless constitutes the constitutional charter of a Community based on the rule of law'.[3] This supports the claim that Europe does not need a constitution. Does perhaps the peculiar structure of the Community repudiate our wisdom altogether as being simply too conventional to satisfy the complexity and novelty of the problem it is to solve, or at least to elucidate? If this is so, it becomes ever more urgent to rethink the basic assumptions of constitutionalism in order to get a clearer concept of what a European constitution could possibly be.

What are the objectives of such a constitution? What are its basic structures? Who will be the main actors in the process of constitution-making? Which institutions should have which competencies within the domains demarcated by the constitution? Unfortunately I am not able to give satisfying answers to all of these questions. Thus, in the following argument, I must restrict myself to attempting to offer some hints which may lead us to an answer. My approach consists of four steps: I start with the claim that modern constitutions have essentially been state constitutions, meaning they reacted to particular problems characteristic of modern statehood (I). In a second step, I shall demonstrate the non-statal character of the European Community (II). In view of the widespread belief that the so-called 'democratic deficit' of the European Community has become the main incentive for the call for a European Constitution, I raise the question of whether the institutional particularities of the European Community are compatible or incompatible with the principle of democracy. Rather than giving an unequivocal answer, I try to approach a possible solution in a more indirect manner. In the last part of the paper, I want to defend the argument that, while it makes sense to speak of a European constitution, the standards by which we assess its appropriateness and quality must considerably differ from those we apply to state constitutions (III).

I. Constitutionalism and statehood

What do we mean when we speak about a political entity's constitution? In ancient and medieval times the concept of a constitution was identified with the idea of the *politeia*. In this framework, the political is embedded in the social fabric of the ancient society; it is, as it were, the skin through which the social entity breathes. The *politeia* or constitution is the institutional embodiment of the concept of a good life. Under conditions of modernity, a different concept of the political developed which has profoundly changed the notion of the constitution. According to this modern concept, the political is embodied in the sovereign power of a ruler (who may consist of one or several persons). It is disembedded from the texture of the society and expresses itself in the actions through which the sovereign power imposes its will on the society. Hence modern political concepts, including the idea of constitutionalism, focus on the problem of the power relations between state and society.[4] The statal character of political rule is the premise underlying our contemporary understanding of a constitution as a device that subjects sovereign political power to legal rules.

When we speak of the state or of statehood, we refer to a particular political formation that emerged in Europe in the course of the 17th century and that possesses the following three characteristics: First, it is based on territoriality, i.e., its limits are territorially demarcated (unlike patrimonial formations, tribes, or purely personal international formations like the Catholic Church). Territoriality means, negatively, that no power is entitled to exercise authority within the boundaries of territories other than that of the state itself; positively, it means that all persons who find themselves in the territory of the state are subject to its power, whether or not they are its nationals. Consequently, territoriality is a constitutive element of the state's sovereign power.[5] Next to territoriality, it is the people that constitute statehood. Those who live in the territory are subject to the state power. In a long historical development, these subjects gradually transformed into the people of the state. 'The people' denotes: the nation, the political collectivity which forms an entity called peoplehood and which, at least according to the French tradition which can rightly be seen as paradigmatic of modern statehood, is created and molded by the state. In the democratic age, this 'people' transforms again and becomes the *demos*. Finally, the third element of statehood is its effective, exclusive and sovereign control over the territory and its residents, which means the supreme and independent power of the state to impose its will on all persons who find themselves on its territory.

The inherent rationale of the new order established by statehood is, internally, the creation and maintenance of the unity, compactness and superiority of the sovereign vis-à-vis the potential chaos of an individualised society susceptible to atomisation and self-destruction; externally, it serves to demarcate power vis-à-vis physically bordering states. Statehood involves important specificities in its mode of social ordering: the centralisation and hierarchical character of power; clear-cut, mostly binary physical and symbolic boundaries of exclusion and inclusion (e.g., the distinction between national alien; public-private; domestic-international); and the origination and legitimation of its power in one unitary, homogenous will. Properties like unity, hierarchy, compactness, and homogeneity are characteristic attributes of modern statehood. They are means of increasing the efficiency of sovereign power, which has no inherent limits other than those of efficiency. In other words, it has no inherent mechanism to generate limits and protect it from the inherent tendency towards self-destruction. To create and maintain these self-limiting mechanisms is essentially what the idea of constitutionalism is about.

The constitution is basically supposed to rationalise and civilise the sovereign power of the state. Hence, its objective is to authorise, to organise, to legitimise, and to limit political power.[6] This, then, creates a sphere of societal autonomy and individual freedom and integrates the individuals into the polity. A constitution turns passive subjects of the state into active citizens of a state-based polity. It shapes the relationship between the sphere of organised, unitary, homogeneous, and hierarchical sovereign power on the one hand, and the domain of individualised, heterogeneous, decentralised, and more or less spontaneously self-organising society on the other. The constitution's almost obsessive grappling with power and its appropriate organisation, legitimation and limitation patently shows that statehood has been the underlying premise of the concept of constitutionalism.

Of course this is the description of an ideal type. In real life we will not find a phenomenon which corresponds to this pure type. In particular, since World War II considerable modifications of the statal model of the polity have taken place. Evidently the idea of the territorial, legal and economic compactness and closedness of the modern state sharply contrasts with the accelerating globalisation of almost all life spheres and the ensuing transnational interdependencies in technological, military, economic, political, and cultural domains. The beginnings of this process can be traced back to the immediate post-World War II period, when, not incidentally, new concepts of international cooperation emerged (e.g., the idea of systems of mutual, collective security as opposed to traditional military alliances, or the concept of universal, internationally recognised human rights).

The most successful innovation, however, has been the Economic European Community (EEC), established by the Rome Treaties of 1957, transformed into the European Community (EC) by the Maastricht Treaty of 1992, and designated as the core element of the European Union (EU) by the very same Treaty.[7] The EC clearly goes beyond the boundaries of international cooperation without itself being a new state; it is a formation positioned somewhere between a federation of states and a federal state [*Staatenbund* and *Bundesstaat*]. The legal term for this character is supranationality. Its basic property is the possession of mechanisms of law-making which exist and operate independently of the legal orders of the Member States. Based on this premise, the European Court of Justice – one of the organs of the Community – has derived two principles of Community Law which have proved to be extremely consequential, namely the principles of direct effect and of the supremacy of Community Law. The former means that provisions of Community Law must be applied by the national courts of the Member States without prior passage into national law through the national parliaments; the latter signifies that a directly effective provision of Community Law always prevails over a conflicting provision of national law.[8]

The far-reaching implication of the principles of *direct effect* and *supremacy* is the creation of an immediate bond of affiliation between the citizens of the Member States and the Community. Viewed from another angle, these principles signify that the citizens of the Member States have direct rights vis-à-vis the Community and that, vice versa, the Community exercises direct authority over the citizens of the Member States. To put it in still another way: the citizens of the Member States enjoy rights and are subject to duties which do not originate in their respective national parliaments. There is only a quite long and weak chain of democratic legitimation through their consent, since the organs of the Community, particularly the Council, consist of members of national governments, which are elected by their respective, in turn, democratically elected, national parliaments. But in all matters where the Council makes decisions according to the majority rule, the chain of democratic consent is interrupted for those citizens whose governments were outvoted. Measured by the standards of the respective domestic constitutions, this thin legitimation of public authority would hardly pass the test of democratic rule. The citizens of the Member states are subject to legal provisions emanating from Community organs (the Council, the Commission, and the European Parliament) which articulate the will of the 'Community', or, in the case of the European Parliament, the will of 'the peoples of the States brought together in the Community' (Article 137, EC Treaty); but it is not the will of a European people or *demos*, i.e., the unity of the citizens of the Union.

II. The non-statal character of the European Community

This leads back to my point of departure, the relation of modern constitutionalism to statehood. If the concept of the constitution is inherently linked to statehood, and if the Community is not a state, then it follows, as I said before, that the call for a European constitution would be meaningless. In fact, the attributes of the European Community do not fit the aforementioned criteria of statehood, namely territoriality, people-hood, and sovereignty.

1. The Community has no territory of its own. Its territorial basis consists of the territories of the Member States; it is defined by them. In other words, it is the Member States, not the Community, which define the territorial limits of the Community's authority.

2. The European Community is not a body of citizens who as a politically organised unity form the personal substrate of the Community. In a draft constitution presented by members of the European Parliament, the Union has been defined as a community consisting of its Member States 'and their citizens'. However, according to the newly inserted Article 8 of the EC Treaty, only persons holding the nationality of a Member State shall be Union citizens. Thus, the status of citizenship is contingent upon the status of nationality in the several Member States. The European Parliament presents no evidence to the contrary. The members of the European Parliament, representatives of 'the peoples of the States brought together in the Community', are not elected according to a common European election law, but according to their respective national election laws.

3. The citizens of the Member States are only *indirectly* participating in the government of the Community – be it through the mediation of their respective Member States (Council, Commission, European Court of Justice) or, in the case of the direct elections to the European Parliament, through participation in a body whose legislative power is quite limited. Moreover, the EP does not even have the power to initiate legislation.

4. The duties and loyalties of the Community officials oscillate between their respective Member States on the one hand, and the Community on the other. There is no single polity which sets the standards of political behaviour. To give a few examples:

German members of the European Parliament 'shall not be bound by any instructions, only by their conscience', while according to the analogous German constitutional stipulation of Article 38 Basic Law 'they shall be representatives of the whole people'. It is open to question whom the German members of the European Parliament shall represent. Is it a hypothetical European people, the German people, or the Community at large?

With respect to the members of the Commission, Article 152, para. 2 of the EC Treaty contains an unequivocal answer: 'the members of the Commission shall, in the general interest of the Community, be completely independent in the performance of their duties. In the performance of these duties they shall neither seek nor take instructions from any government or from any other body'. Yet, this is in stark contrast to their mode of election; they are nominated and appointed by the governments of the Member States, not by any organ or representative body of the Community.

On the other hand, there are also clear indications of an emergent European commonwealth, for instance the stipulations about the responsibility of the Commission. According to Article 158, para. 2, subsection 3 of the EC Treaty, the Commission 'shall be subject as a body to a vote of approval by the European Parliament'. Not earlier than 'after approval by the European Parliament, the President and the other members of the Commission shall be appointed by common accord of the governments of the Member States'. This establishes the Commission's accountability to the European Parliament, which is even more visible in Article 144 of the EC Treaty, according to which a motion of censure on the activities of the Commission can be put forth by the European Parliament. This embryonic form of the Commission's responsibility to the Parliament is another mechanism of loosening the bonds of the Members of the Commission to their respective governments and pushing them towards the conception of a European '*bonum commune*'.[9]

In contrast to the Commission, the members of the Council are in a kind of double-bind situation between lobbyism for their country and responsibility for the common good of the Community, with the former clearly predominating over the latter. The Council is the body in which the Member States have to find a compromise between conflicting national interests, and there is no institutional device to force them to sacrifice any of their national interests for the sake of the common good of the Community. As a consequence, the Council, although the most powerful organ of the Community, is not subject to any kind of accountability. However, its members are accountable according to the rules of their respective national constitutions. Given the prerogatives which national governments usually possess in the fields of foreign policy – and Community affairs are still largely foreign affairs – this is evidently an unsatisfactory situation from a constitutional point of view.

A more detailed analysis of the ambiguities of the Community would produce many more examples. I restrict myself to summarising the diversity of structural elements in the institutional formation of the Community. We can find simultaneously:

- intergovernmental and federal elements (foreign and security policy, justice and domestic affairs on the one hand [Article J, K], common market on the other, and some policies like Article 128, para. 5, EC Treaty [culture] in between);
- territorial and functional representation[10] (on the one hand, lobbyism of the governments of the Member States for their respective countries in the organs of the EC; on the other hand, already something like a 'shift of loyalties, expectations and political activities'[11] of the mostly economic lobbies towards the organs of the Community, particularly to

the Commission, and in the long run perhaps also to the EP). This can be regarded as a first sign of the emergence of an original and powerful Community level;

- Member State and Community standards of political orientation and accountability (remember the aforementioned divergent standards of conduct for the members of the several organs of the Community);
- direct and indirect forms of belonging to the Community and of participating in the exercise of its authority (on the one hand, Union citizenship and the attached rights, or direct election to the EP, on the other hand, indirect participation in the authority of the council, via elections to the national parliaments);
- democratic and federal elements (on the one hand, an uninterrupted, if thin, chain of democratic legitimation of the Community's authority through [national and European] elections; on the other hand, a departure from the principle of *equal* representation of both the citizens and the peoples of the Member States on account of the federal principle of the protection and careful treatment of the smaller Member States and their populations).

III. Compatibility of the structures of the community with the democratic principle

Given the simultaneity and plurality of the institutional elements found in the structure of the EU, the question arises if at all and how this conglomerate heterogeneity can be constitutionalised. Among the many issues which require closer scrutiny, I here concentrate on the democratic principle. As I already mentioned, many constitutional lawyers in Europe make the claim that the often-invoked democracy deficit of the Community is inescapable on structural grounds, because the basis of democracy, a *demos*, does not exist on the European level (and is not likely to exist in the foreseeable future). Democracy in its modern constitutional meaning denotes the self-rule of a people that has established its political existence in a state, leading to what the French call *l'état-nation* and which we normally call the nation-state. Within this statal framework, only the authority of those institutions which originate in the will of the organised unity of the citizens is recognised as democratic. This is the famous *no-demos* thesis to which I referred earlier. According to this standard, the EP, which does not represent the will of the organised unity of European citizens – i.e., a European people, or *demos* – but rather consists, as Article 137 of the EC Treaty puts it, of 'representatives of the peoples of the States brought together in the Community', clearly lacks democratic legitimation. An enlargement of its competencies and its transformation into the primary organ of Community legislation would not strengthen the democratic power of that institution. On the contrary, it would even undermine democracy in that a surplus of public authority would be vested in an institution with no footing in a European *demos*.[12]

Does this mean that the democratic principle is inseparably connected with statehood, or is it possible to conceive of a non-statal, in the case of Europe, *supranational*, democracy? Rather than attempting to give a direct response to this question, I want to argue that the establishment of the traditional democratic principle at the EU and EC level may not be able to alleviate their undeniable legitimacy deficits.

1. The institutional particularities of the EC

Let me start with a brief description of four particularities which make many constitutional devices familiar from the two-hundred year history of nation-states appear inappropriate for the EU/EC.[13]

1.1 The dynamic character of a possible EC/EU constitution:

The most striking property of the community is its dynamic character. While the state as the political organisation of a territorially-bound population is primarily directed towards the preservation of its institutional identity and stability, the Community is, conversely, directed towards permanent self-transformation, both in terms of policy goals and its institutional setup. It has been said that the never-finished objective of integration is the 'political finality' of the Community. Contrary to state constitutions which accept change only as a necessary, reactive mechanism of adjustment to changing conditions, the Union's constitution would have to enable a permanent, active process of changing the shape of the Community; some authors speak of a 'change-constitution' [*Wandel-Verfassung*].

1.2 The complementary or incomplete character of a possible EC/EU constitution:

A constitution of the Community is essentially complementing the constitutions of the Member States. It cannot possibly be conceived as an independent and self-sufficient institution. Some authors speak of an 'osmotic' relationship between the Community and the Member States' constitutions. This relationship is different from the well-known dualism of federal and state constitutions in federal states like Germany, Austria, Switzerland or the United States. Thus, the Basic Law of Germany requires and guarantees the homogeneity of the constitutional orders of the central state and the federal units; by contrast, the relationship and consequently the degree of homogeneity or heterogeneity between the Community constitution and the constitutions of the Member States is only being fabricated in the process of integration itself. There is no pre-ordained order between them, not to speak of a hierarchical one. The Community is a process of institutionalised interaction between actors whose roles and functions are not pre-established in an overarching concept of political unity; rather, they are shaped in an open process in which a broad range of possible developments may surface and be pushed forward by agents that may only come into existence through this process itself.

1.3 The polycentric character of a possible EC/EU constitution.

There is no political centre in which the political substance of the Community is accumulated and embodied. Policy making is beyond the firm control of any single authority. True, this applies also to many current constitutional states where the indispensable separation of powers already prohibits the idea of a single political power centre. But the fragmentation and diffusion of power characteristic of the Community goes considerably beyond this experience with contemporary statehood. In the Community, the process of policy definition and implementation occurs in a largely nebulous and hardly comprehensible web of pluralist actors – the institutions of the Community, the Member States, the institutions of the Member States, the manifold interest groups, the incipient forms of political parties – which makes the processes of power-formation appear extremely diffuse.

1.4 The duality of legitimising principles of a possible EC/EU constitution.

In the institutional framework of the European Community, two different principles of legitimation co-exist. The first is the Lockean principle of consent, the second the principle of utility and efficiency widely associated with David Hume.[14] While consent of the ruled traditionally legitimates any public authority, it is much less familiar to ground the justification of government officially, so to speak, on the performance and efficiency of the ruler. To be sure, the two principles are not mutually exclusive. Thus the famous Lockean concept of tacit consent comes quite close to a principle of legitimacy through efficiency. It is also true that in the framework of modern statehood, the idea of efficiency plays an important role *de facto*, while *de jure* it is largely dismissed on grounds of democratic theory. However this may be, it is unequivocally and whole-heartedly accepted in the framework of the Community. After all, it was the presumed superiority of the Community's problem-solving capacity over those of the traditional nation-states which largely motivated the foundation of the Community in the fifties. In other words, reasons of efficiency and utility belong to the most significant founding rationales of the Community. Thus, consent and efficiency are two different, equally accepted and legitimate pillars of the European consensus.[15]

It is easily understandable that the institutional devices developed for the compactness and sharp demarcations of modern statehood do not fit the dynamic, polycentric, diffuse and intentionally incomplete and open character of the Community very well. However, this does not mean that the democratic principle is inappropriate for the Community. But we do have to adapt it to these particularities. Democracy in the Community is not so much about collective decision making as about creating a domain where the plurality and diversity of forces which have a stake in the Community find appropriate devices for articulating themselves and interacting with each other.

2. Interest representation in political multi-layer systems

The notion of democracy defined as the sovereignty of an *état-nation* is only one, if influential and significant, version of democratic rule. The idea that the unity of equal citizens form a homogenous will which they authoritatively impose on the society can only be recognised as the realisation of collective self-determination if one accepts the Rousseauian presuppositions that individuals are equal, have equal aspirations, exist as political animals only by virtue of belonging to the state, and, finally, that the laws have equal effect on them. As we know, in the framework of other democratic ideas these assumptions are plainly rejected.[16] The latter do not draw on the equality and political sameness of the citizens but, conversely, on the diversity of individuals, their affiliations with extra – and pre-statist associations, social contexts, networks, adherences to diverse life-styles, value orientations and interests, in other words: on the plurality and inequality of individuals and their social relations. Democratic self-determination based on the pluralist and heterogeneous character of society requires open political structures which are able to perceive and to process this conglomerate variety. It requires providing and operating channels through which individuals and groups can influence the processes of political decision making. Democracy would be a means for the realisation of civic liberties; by virtue of its manifold channels of formation and expression of a broad variety and diversity of societal needs, this structure would fit well the homologous structures of the pluralist and today's inescapably multi-cultural civil society.

I hypothesise that the aforementioned particularities of the EU/EC – its incomplete, dynamic, polycentric, and diffuse character, as well as the dualism of its legitimacy principles – display an affinity to the open, civil-society-proneness of the pluralist concept of democracy. I do not mean to say that the amorphous institutional structure of the Community is something which we could already call democracy. Instead, we see a quite diffuse and complex process of interest representation: states, regions, municipalities, transnationally acting organisations, movements, professional associations, firms, etc., that have initiated networks to articulate and process their respective functional and territorial interests, which they interpose into the different levels and agencies of Euro-policy making.[17] To be sure, this does not satisfy any high standard of democratic rule, since it does not provide an equal opportunity to each Union citizen to influence the process of policy making. Today manifestly corporatist and pluralist forms of interest representation predominate, and as a consequence, the outcomes are largely uneven.

This leads to the question of whether this complex web of interaction among a plurality of actors is and should be definable in terms of democratic theory. I doubt it. Instead, I suggest that we should try to understand the EC/EU in the conceptual framework of the political theory of federalism. Or, to be more direct: perhaps the legitimacy of the public authority of the Community is less dependent upon the consent of the Union citizens than on the Community's capacity to respond appropriately to the manifold demands of coordination and integration of the plurality of territorial and functional interests struggling for recognition in the European polity.[18] The theory of federalism is supposed to offer the conceptual framework for the elucidation of this problem. It deals with the question of how to create an appropriate political order for societies characterised by opposing integrative and disintegrative political forces within a particular geographical space. Federalism is expected to organise balanced arrangements of a complex cluster of centripetal and centrifugal forces, using 'territorial pluralism' as an additional element to organise a polity.

Obviously federal political systems are more complex than unitary ones in that, in addition to conflicts of functional interests (economic, social, cultural), they have to cope with two further problems: first, with territorially divergent interests, and second, with the need to coordinate relations among a plurality of territorially defined decision centres. In a federal system, the question of what has to be done cannot be separated from the question of who has to make and is entitled to make the decision.[19] This is likely to prompt further social conflict, which renders constitutional mechanisms of dispute resolution between the constituent parts of the federal system almost indispensable. This is one reason why constitutional courts are characteristic of and have especially great influence in federal states. Thus, one may make the claim that federal systems are better equipped to cope with social conflicts.[20] In federal systems, the existence of social conflicts is not necessarily an element of instability. However, it cannot be denied that there are also conflicts – Hirschman has called them categorical conflicts about non-divisible goods[21] – which surpass even the problem-solving capacity of a federal system. I have to leave this point aside here.

The same ambiguity applies to the problem of innovation. Depending on the distribution of powers, the federal structure of a polity can be conducive or obstructive to innovation. In any case, there is reason to assume that in a federal system the opportunities and forms of interest representation are more numerous than in a unitary one, and that both the desire and the opportunities for participation are likely to increase in such a system.

If this is a realistic view, then the EC would not be primarily a community of citizens who by virtue of their citizen rights develop a collective European democratic will; rather, it would be an institutional formation which enables better representation and coordination of heterogeneous interests than the institutions of the (mostly unitary) nation-states normally allow. This formation may eventually generate the status, and the not merely economic, but also cultural and political sphere of a genuinely European citizenry and their desire to form a collective political will. It may occur that, quite analogous to the history of the European nation-states, the emergence of the institutional forms of collective interest organisation and representation precede the constitutional establishment of democracy. In the history of federal nation-states we can find clear signs of such non-simultaneity in the development of democracy.[22]

Conclusion

The constituent elements of political multilayer-systems are more complex than those of unitary systems in which political rule has to be derived from a unitary, homogeneous general will in order to be regarded as legitimate. Both the concept of equal national citizenship and that of the unit of a homogeneous general will reflect the modern nation-state's quest for homogeneity in many respects: economic, social, cultural, and frequently ethnic as well. The general law which applies to all subjects-citizens equally and is supposed to have equal effects upon all of them is one expression of this ideal of a democratic *état-nation*. Evidently the EU cannot and must not satisfy, or strive to satisfy, this ideal. It cannot and must not aspire to comprehensiveness, compactness, exclusivity, and clear-cut demarcations of who is entitled to act in which domain with which competencies, etc.

The institutions of the Community are only one element in a comprehensive politico-economic structure which has succeeded in tying together a multitude of very heterogeneous, centrifugal and conflicting political, economic, and cultural forces and integrating them into a dynamic *and* stable order. Consequently, the criteria according to which we must measure the quality of that order cannot be reduced to a single one, namely to democracy. In saying this, I do not mean that the much-debated democracy deficit does not exist, nor that the invocation of federalism would be able to abolish it. But the democratic standard should not be isolated from other criteria used to measure the appropriateness and quality of the institutional forms of the EC. In other words, a democratic Europe does not require an unqualified application of the traditional principles of democracy to the institutions of the EC. Rather, it requires the development of structures in which the complexity of the numerous actors – the EC as a political formation with its several institutions, the Member States and their organs and institutions, their territorial subunits, the manifold interest organisations, political parties, social movements, and ultimately the multitude and diversity of the European peoples – is mirrored in its institutional setup. It must contain democratic elements so that this formation can be legitimate. But democratic legitimacy is only a necessary, not a sufficient condition for the legitimacy of that order. Other institutional elements must be added which will eventually entail a constitution characterised primarily by its capacity to coordinate differentiated and heterogeneous territorial and functional interests in an economically politically, socially, and culturally cleft and vast geographical space. The end result could be, then, a constitutionalised federation of citizens, civic associations, peoples, and states, each developing its own principles of internal democratic participation qualifying them to participate in the great variety of federal domains of political and civic action in the immense politico-cultural space called Europe.

Notes

1. The most prominent author is D. Grimm, cf. his Article 'Does Europe need a Constitution?', *European Law Journal*, 1995, vol. 1, no. 3, pp. 282–302, and a critical remark by J. Habermas, *ibid.*, pp. 303–307.

2. This thesis is extensively debated and criticised in the Article of J. H. H. Weiler, 'Does Europe need a Constitution? Demos, telos and the German Maastricht decision', in *European Law Journal*, 1995, vol. 1, no. 3, pp. 219–259, [224 ff].

3. Reports of Cases before the Court of Justice and the Court of First Instance 1991–9, Opinion 1/91 of the Court, 14 December 1991, I–6084–6112, 6102 [margin number 21].

4. A. Touraine, *Qu'est-ce que la Démocratie?*, Paris, Gallimard, 1994, pp. 37 ff., 42.

5. L. Duguit, *Droit Constitutionnel. Théorie générale de l'Etat-Organisation politique*, Paris, Thorin et fils, 1907, pp. 95–112.

6. Cf. U. K. Preuß, 'The Political Meaning of Constitutionalism', in R. Bellamy (ed.), *Constitutionalism, Democracy and Sovereignty: American and European perspectives*, Aldershot (England) and Brookfield (USA), Avebury, 1996, pp. 11–27.

7. Cf. T. C. Hartley, *The Foundations of European Community Law*, 3rd edn, Oxford. Clarendon Press, 1994, pp. 3–10.

8. The landmark decision is the van Gend en Loos case. Case 26/62 [1963], ECR 1–30; see also Hartley, *The Foundations*, pp. 195 ff.

9. Cf. J. T. Lang and E. Gallagher, 'Review of a proposal for a European Constitution', Published by the European Policy Forum, London, 1993. *Common Market Law Review*, 1994, vol. 31, pp. 445–450.

10. A. M. Sbragia, 'The European Community: a balancing act', *Publius; The Journal of Federalism*, 1993, vol. 23, pp. 23–38; A. Weale, 'The Single Market, European Integration and Political Legitimacy', Paper prepared for ESRC Evolution of Rules in the Single Market Programme, 'The Evolution of Rules for a Single European Market', University of Exeter 8–11 September 1994.

11. P. C. Schmitter, 'Representation and the future Euro-polity', *Staatswissenschaften und Staatspraxis*, 1992, vol. 3, pp. 379–405.

12. For a general account of the problems of democratic decisions on a non-nation-state level see R A. Dahl, 'A democratic dilemma: system effectiveness versus citizen participation', *Political Science Quarterly*, 1994, vol. 109, pp. 23–34; Craig Calhoun, 'Nationalism and civil society: democracy, diversity and self-determination', *International Sociology*, 1993, vol. 8, pp. 387–412.

13. Cf. A. V. Bogdandy, 'Supranationale Union als neuer Herrschaftstypus: Entstaatlichung und Vergemeinschaftung in staatstheoretischer Perspektive', *Integration*, 1993, pp. 210–224; G. F. Schuppert, 'Zur Staatswerdung Europas. Überlegungen zu Bedingungs-faktoren und Perspektiven der europäischen

Verfassungsentwicklung', *Staatswissenschaften und Staatspraxis*, 1994, pp. 35–76 [53 ff.]; T. Läufer, 'Zur künftigen Verfassung der Europäischen Union – Notwendigkeit einer offenen Debatte', *Integration*, 1994, pp. 204–214.

14. Here I draw on the analysis of A. Weale, 'The Single Market'.

15. See also A. Moravcsik, 'Preferences and power in the European Community: a liberal intergovernmentalist approach', *Journal of Common Market Studies*, 1993, vol. 31, pp. 473–524.

16. Cf. H. Sabine, 'The two democratic traditions', *The Philosophical Review*, 1952, vol. 61, pp. 451–474.

17. Cf. Schmitter, 'Representation and the future Euro-polity'.

18. Cf. M. Zürn, 'Über den Staat und die Demokratie im europäischen Mehrebenen-system', *Politische Vierteljahresschrift*, 1996, vol. 37, pp. 27–55.

19. S. Leibfried and P. Pierson (eds), *European Social Policy: Between fragmentation and integration*, Washington D.C., Brookings, 1995.

20. Cf. the contributions in the volume edited by J. Kramer, *Föderalismus zwischen Integration und Sezession. Chancen und Risiken bundesstaatlicher Ordnung*, Baden-Baden, Nomos, 1993; and S. Samardzic and T. Fleiner (eds), *Föderalismus und Minderheitenproblem in multiethnischen Gemeinschaften*, Fribourg, Institute of Federalism, 1995.

21. A. O. Hirschman, 'Social Conflicts as Pillars of Democratic Market Societies', in A. O. Hirschman, *A Propensity to Self-Subversion*, Cambridge/Mass. and London, Harvard University Press, 1995, pp. 231–248.

22. For the U.S., see M. Rosenfeld, 'The Failures of Federalism in the United States', in J. Kramer (ed.), *Föderalismus zwischen Integration und Sezession. Chancen und Risiken bundesstaatlicher Ordnung*, Baden-Baden, Nomos, 1993, pp. 247–265.

Chapter Sixteen

Revisiting the Rationale Behind the European Union: The Basis of European Narratives Today and Tomorrow[*]

Ulrich K. Preuß

Introduction

There is a broad accord among the political elites of Europe and their professional observers alike that Europe is in a deep crisis. Meanwhile a diffuse sense of crisis is also about to capture the spirit of broader segments of the peoples of the EU member States. It is about to cast a shadow on their formerly overall friendly attitude towards the project of European integration. Mass protests against the politics of austerity and budget consolidation of the governments of several member states tend to turn into a general resentment against the Union and even to reawaken nationalist stereotypes which, in some countries, foster anti-European attitudes. The reason for this changing tide may not only result from the sufferings which many people, especially in the Mediterranean rim of the EU, have to endure from painful cuts of their incomes and the ensuing critical changes in their daily lives. The fierceness of the protests may well be indicative of the deep disappointment about the EU's failure to fulfil its promise of solidarity among its member states. However, this expectation may rest upon a misunderstanding since the project of European integration as it was originally laid down in the Schuman Declaration of 9th May 1950[1] did not spring from magnanimous idealism which promised a world of peace and welfare among all men of good will. It was, rather, a down-to-earth programme of economic cooperation which, by its inherent logic, held out the prospect of increased interdependence among the involved states with the beneficial consequence of mutual economic advantages which in turn would foster a dynamics of solidarity based upon self-interest. However one may assess the proportion of the idealist and visionary part in this essentially economic logic of the European project,[2] it clearly included the promise of a better future. Weiler rightly notes that it prompted mobilising force especially among elites and youths.[3]

In view of the fact that in 2013 the EU-27 youth unemployment (young persons aged between 15 and 24) amounts to some 24 per cent – in Greece to almost 60 per

---

[*] 'Revisiting the Rationale Behind the European Union: The basis of European narratives today and tomorrow', in J. van der Walt and J. Ellsworth (eds), *Constitutional Sovereignty and Social Solidarity in Europe*, Baden-Baden, Nomos, 2015, pp. 193–220.

cent, in Spain to 55 per cent, in Italy to almost 40 per cent[4] – it is understandable that the promise of a better future has now lost much of its credibility, not to mention its visionary force. Yet the significance of the venture of European integration would be misconstrued if we assumed that its capacity to cope with serious crises depends upon statistical data about unemployment, productivity, growth and similar parameters. Although economic performance is crucial for the overall acceptance of the EU, it cannot adequately express the normative overspill which leads many citizens of the member states to recognise themselves as both national and European citizens. The fact that 50 per cent of the citizens of the EU 27 agree to the statement: 'I feel safer because my country is a member of the EU', against 45 per cent who disagree,[5] shows that for a considerable proportion of the Union's citizens, membership of their country in the EU has become an existential quality. Moreover, almost two thirds of the citizens of the EU member states feel they are citizens of the Union.[6] There are other statements which indicate that in the minds of a substantial number of Union citizens – admittedly a minority – the EU is not merely a functional purpose association for the improvement of their economic prospects but a political entity which conveys meaning to them.[7] Can we take hold of this meaning? Are there as many meanings as there are Union citizens, or can we identify something like a collectively shared understanding of what it means to be a citizen of the European Union?

An obvious way to find out is the analysis of European narratives – how do the Europeans tell themselves the story of their path to the European Union? This must not be confused with a historical account which claims objective scientific truth. A narrative is, rather, the social construction of a distinct history which conveys a particular meaning, perhaps even a particular morality to a community. It is frequently connected with a political vision of the future which is constructed as the continuation of a heroic past or, conversely, as a breach with a disgraceful past. But even in this latter case, the narrative aspires to the realisation of a not-yet existing state of affairs. It includes a political idea with a normative impetus to engage non-routine political action, as for instance the ideals of perpetual peace, of global distributive justice, or of cosmopolitan citizenship. In what follows I will explore whether the peoples of the member states of the EU have believed and believe in a dominant narrative, and if so, whether this story has undergone changes in the course of the sixty years since the EU's foundation.

I. After 1945: No European narrative due to political weariness

In the long and venerable history of the idea of Europe which dates back to antiquity[8] the famous speech of Winston Churchill at Zurich University on 19th September 1946 stands out as the most momentous political vision of a united Europe which appealed to the faith of the Europeans in the desirability of such a project. This is not to say that this speech devised merely an idealist dream out of touch with the conditions of the real world. The contrary is true. Churchill had a clear view of the quandaries of Europe after the end of World War II. He persuasively evoked the plight of 'a vast quivering mass of tormented, hungry, care-worn and bewildered human beings [who] gape at the ruins of their cities and their homes, and scan the dark horizons for the approach of some new peril, tyranny or terror'. And as a clear-sighted political leader he knew that the realistic description of a dark and desperate present was not enough to change that very present. Reminding his audience of Europe's glorious past as the 'origin of most of the culture, the arts, philosophy and science both of ancient and modern time', he offers a

> remedy which, if it were generally and spontaneously adopted by the great majority of people in many lands, would as if by a miracle transform the whole scene, and would in a few years make all Europe, or the greater part of it, as free and as happy as Switzerland is today.

The remedy, almost a secular version of redemption and at the same time the promise of the blessedness of a bright future, was a United States of Europe. 'If Europe were once united in the sharing of its common inheritance, there would be no limit to the happiness, to the prosperity and the glory which its three or four hundred million people would enjoy...' – this, in fact, is the 'Promised Land' which Churchill suggestively tried to invoke in the minds of the desperate Europeans and which made his speech a prominent example of what Weiler calls 'Political Messianism'. Unsurprisingly he expressly stated that 'In order that this should be accomplished there must be an act of faith in which millions of families speaking many languages must consciously take part'[9].

It is an irony of this speech that the vision of a United States of Europe was staged by the Prime Minister of a European nation who did not even consider to lead his country into such a strange political entity which he so evocatively painted as a desirable aspiration. No less symptomatic was the fact that he presented his idea at a place which was not supposed to join this undertaking either – Zurich in Switzerland. Still, Churchill's speech had definitively the potential for becoming the founding narrative of the European Union, perhaps even of a United States of Europe. After all, it told a story of the deep fall of a glorious continent and the promise of a splendid renaissance in a bright future if ... well, if the West European nations were prepared to give up their status as sovereign states and to merge in a supranational entity.

This, however, was not what they seemed ready to do. Jean Monnet, the most important collaborator and adviser of the then French foreign minister, Robert Schuman, had learnt from previous attempts to create supranational structures in post-war Europe – such as the European Economic Co-operation, set up in 1948, and the Council of Europe, established on 5th May 1949 – that 'the governments were jealous of their prerogatives. ... It was too much to expect States to consent to massive transfers of sovereignty, which would have injured national sensitivities only a few years after the end of the war'.[10] Thus, he proposed a path to supranationalism which later would be termed the 'method Monnet' and which the German political scientist Wolfgang Wessels has characterised as the 'dynamics in small steps with sustainable significance' (*Dynamik in kleinen Schritten von nachhaltiger Bedeutung*).[11] Its elements include, according to Wessels, the principle of specific and real solidarity, the limited conferral of tangible competences, a movement step by step towards a non-defined *finalité* of integration, the use of economic tools for political integration, the coupling of institutional design and policy making, decision making by elites through consensus, the basic conception of the European federation as a community of peace, and the Franco-German nucleus as the core of the integration process.[12]

Actually, the aforementioned Schuman Declaration of 9th May 1950, embodies these components almost paradigmatically. At the very beginning, it sets the dominant tenor with the succinct statement: 'Europe will not be made all at once, or according to a single plan. It will be built through concrete achievements which first create a *de facto* solidarity'. It was an operational plan whose core substance, although inspired by underlying political ideals and historical lessons, consisted in a rather pragmatic initiative, namely the proposal to pool the coal and steel production of France and Germany and to submit it under the control of a common High Authority 'within the framework of an organization open to the participation of the other countries of Europe'. This 'should immediately provide for the setting up of common foundations for economic development as a first step in the federation of Europe'. Monnet did not intend to offer a political vision which had the power to mobilise the hearts of the Europeans who were fully absorbed by their struggle with the hardships of their daily lives in a physically and morally ruined post-war situation. What he aimed for was a non-heroic, modest, i.e. gradualist journey towards a destination which was so distant and vague that it would not arouse any apprehension among the travellers.

Obviously this project and its method could have little appeal to the emotions of the European peoples. It was reasonable, rational, and circumspective. It did not impose overly demanding requirements upon them, least so regarding Europe's *finalité*. Thus the attitude of what has been called a 'permissive consensus' defined the dominant kind of relationship of the citizens of the European member states towards the idea of European supranationality.[13] But it was not the stuff from which narratives are made – to transform facts into a meaningful story which people tell each other, thus confirming their common belonging to a particular community. The permissive consensus – 'a mixture of a lack of interest in European integration and generally positive inclinations towards it'[14] – denoted passive acceptance, not an active attitude which motivates people to invest their interpretations, hopes, fears and fantasies into facts which have been told to them.

Since this gradualist 'Monnet method' of European integration prevailed until the beginning of the 1990s – the Maastricht Treaty of 1992 marking the opening of a new era – the lack of a European narrative persisted four decades. This does not mean that the process of European integration was short of reasonable and even persuasive explanations. Thus, motives which appeared both in Churchill's Zurich speech of 1946 and in the Schuman Declaration – especially the appeal to defend the freedom of the West European peoples against the Soviet-type organisation of the society, the necessity to integrate Germany into a structure of collective security which would prevent it from regaining hegemonic power on the European continent, and the aspiration to render a war in Europe impossible – played an important role in the political justification of European integration. But none of these motives lent itself to a European narrative. The first argument was a justification of the leading role of the United States in the world-wide Cold War between 'the West' and the Soviet-dominated world without having a particularly European impact. The second was more a strategic assessment than a story which the involved European peoples could tell each other ingenuously; after all, it was clearly based upon the distrust and fear of the many towards one of them. And the third, the pledge to make a war in Europe impossible, has lost much of its inspiring force for the younger generations for which a European war is something which they know only from their history books.

In sum, what for the founding generation of the European Community may have been and in fact were plausible reasons for accepting the integration process, set off in 1952 with the establishment of the 'European Coal and Steel Community (ECSC)' and carried forward with the 'European Atomic Energy Community (Euratom)' and the 'European Economic Community (EEC)' in 1957, was not inspiring enough as to produce a European story which later-born generations would tell each other and pass on to their children.

II. Europe's claim to its exceptionalism

Note that what I have said so far about a European narrative refers to Europe as a politico-legal entity, i.e. to the European Communities as economic and political actors who are involved both in the member states' policies and in international politics. We should distinguish this institutional shape of Europe from its character as an idea and an ideal. This latter Europe seems to be much more lively in the memories and imaginations of Europeans than the former. A recent qualitative survey on the European citizens' attitudes towards Europe showed a considerable difference between a more sceptical view as regards the benefits of the EU for their respective country and a much more positive assessment of the cultural and historic heritage of Europe as a source of mutual empathy among the European peoples.[15] Summarising the findings of his investigation, the author writes:

> The age and wealth of European History was underscored by the citizens interviewed, with shared roots in Ancient Greece and Rome being highly present in their mind; many (more in fact among the new entrants than among the old Member States) also recalled the adherence of European peoples to the same historic and political ensembles throughout the centuries. The Christian roots of Europe were also sometimes mentioned – but less than the ideas of the Enlightenment philosophers, of freedom, of non-submission to the precepts of religions and the non-intervention of the latter in the public sphere. Along with the age-old History was cultural wealth, considered as very characteristic of Europe – to the extent of sometimes suggesting the idea of a particular form of European refinement or intellectual superiority.[16]

Many interviewees specified their understanding and appreciation of Europeanness, mentioning Europe's commitment to peace, its devotion to freedom and to secularism as a pre-condition of freedom, its tolerance for cultural diversity as a receptacle of intellectual curiosity, open-mindedness and tolerance, a strong sense of equality and solidarity, and a distinct notion of respect for mankind and for the earth.[17] Of course this is a beautified and self-glorifying picture which the interviewees certainly did not misunderstand as a true representation of Europe's existent reality. It is more likely that this list of friendly characteristics rather reveals their imaginations about the ideal state of Europe.

What is more, this imagination led them to simply obliterate the dark sides of European history – such as the cruelties of religious fervour and self-righteousness in its pre-modern era, the arrogant and merciless colonial subjugation of the non-European world since the end of the 15th century, or the viciousness of the post-enlightenment epoch which witnessed the emergence of anti-humane ideologies, most disparaging racism, and the failure of the European peoples to prevent the single most atrocious collective crime of human history, the genocide of the European Jewry by the German state in the 1940s. While these historical stains will remain a heavy burden upon the moral status of Europe, it should not be neglected that the Europeans have made considerable efforts to face these dark sides of their history. Admittedly, it took two decades before the deep breach of the accomplishments of human civilisation through the Holocaust was fully realised in Germany. For the later-born generations, however, the reflection of this painful and shameful part of their history has become an element of their political identity. The same can be said of the peoples of many other European states with respect to the involvement of their ancestors in serious injustices of the past. Europe has become a continent with a vibrant culture of memorialisation of the disgraceful parts of its history and its 'dark legacies'.[18] The concept of transitional justice is an important moral and legal yield of this development. Although this idea has now spread almost globally, its historical roots date back to Europe.[19] Arguably, on a global scale the most intensive efforts to deal with the past of unjust and bloodstained periods of their own history have occurred in European nations.

Maybe this appraisal can be regarded as the latest and certainly most embarrassing kind of the Europeans' claim to exceptionalism in a long tradition dating back until antiquity beginning with Herodotus, the father of European historiography. He did not describe Europe as a geographical space, but defined it as a cultural entity which was demarcated against the world of the Asian peoples – for him the sphere of the barbarians, whilst Europe was the embodiment of happiness, copiousness and chosenness.[20] In the Middle Ages Europe was largely identified with Christendom which, while threatened by the Muslim conquest of Spain in the 8th century, launched in its turn crusades against the 'infidel' Muslims in Asia Minor between the end of the 11th until the end of the 13th centuries. The repeated, ultimately unsuccessful attempts of the Ottoman empire to expand into the Habsburg lands in South-East Europe, culminating in the siege of Vienna in 1683, tightened the sense of togetherness based on the common Christian belief of the subjects of the Holy Roman Empire. As John McCormick observes, these assertive actions 'not only gave it a separate identity from Islam, its critical external competitor, but also drove thinking about the principles upon which Europeans might relate to one another'.[21] However, while the Europeans were unified against the Muslim challenge in the name of Christianity, internally the Christian belief itself became a source of disunity about its correct interpretation which ultimately entailed the second schism in its history (after the division of Christianity into the Western Roman Catholic Church and the Eastern Byzantine Churches in the second half of the 11th century). The Reformation, instigated by Martin Luther in Germany in 1517 and pushed forward in other parts of Europe mainly by Calvin and Zwingli, divided Roman Christianity irreversibly and set off a series of religious wars which ultimately fostered the concept of the secular state but, at the same time, undermined the idea of a Christian identity of Europe.

Still, in its relations with the external world the identification of Europe with Christianity persisted still quite a long time.[22] In the sequel of the discoveries and conquest of overseas territories in the Americas, and later in Africa and Asia, the missionary zeal to spread Christianity all over the world associated itself with a strong feeling of European superiority over the indigenous peoples and their cultures. In the 18th century, after Europe had become a *pluriverse* of sovereign states, most of which had become imperial powers due to the appropriation of transoceanic territories, it was the idea of civilization and the faith in the European *mission civilisatrice* which became the predominant justificatory source of the Europeans' claim to superiority over other peoples and continents.

Actually neither Christianity nor the idea of civilisation are unequivocal legacies in which the Europeans can take pride as fundaments of European exceptionalism. Despite Joseph Weiler's contrary view,[23] Christianity does not qualify as a characteristic of European identity for obvious reasons: first, the Christian religion was born in a non-European place, and Jesus Christ was a non-European. Second, the Roman Catholic Church has become a universal spiritual power whose believers live mainly outside Europe; the same is true with respect to the manifold Protestant denominations. Third, apart from the final separation of the Orthodox Church at the end of the 11th century, the schism of the Reformation entailed a major split of Christianity which from now on could no longer claim to represent the spirit of the whole of Europe. And, finally, the Europeans do not have the reputation of being overly religious; to the contrary, Europe may certainly be said to be the home of the most secular way of life among all continents and regions of the world.

But what about the idea of civilisation? It is true that since the third quarter of the 18th throughout the 19th century, civilisation became 'a synonym for Europe' and that in view of different levels of civilisation 'Europe should be seen as the embodiment of the highest level of civilization'.[24] When the idea came up in the 18th century, civilisation was tantamount to enlightenment and progress and reflected the revolutionary idea which was best expressed in Kant's oft-quoted first sentence of his philosophical outline 'An Answer to the Question: "What is Enlightenment"?': Enlightenment is man's emergence from his self-incurred immaturity'.[25] In the 19th century the concept was more and more adapted to the pragmatic worldview of the industrialising European societies; it embodied, as a German scholar of international law defined it at the end of the 19th century, 'freedom of conscience, equality in law, free trade and World Postal Union, fee tariffs and obligatory quarantine regulations, international loans and permanent neutrality, equality of flags and freedom of settlement'.[26]

Meanwhile these achievements have become the standard, at least of the OECD-world, and hence have lost any European particularity. On the other hand – and this is certainly much more consequential – since the 20th century the connection of Europe with the idea of civilisation is now tainted with the inherently European incidences of two World Wars – which, as McCormick rightly remarks, 'in many ways began as European civil wars'[27] – with the emergence of modern totalitarian rule, and with gigantic state crimes culminating in the genocide of the European Jews. Moreover, the European colonial states' conduct in the process of decolonisation in the second half of the 20th century provided little reason to identify Europe with the idea of civilisation.[28] In other words, a particular affinity to a high standard of civilisation can barely be regarded as a feature which constitutes Europe's uniqueness.

Still, there has been an ongoing debate for decades about the striking puzzle of Europe's *Sonderweg*, its special and unique path, which is: its path breaking development from an agrarian society to modernity in a long historical process from about 1000 AD until the 19th century which has become a kind of global paradigm of the telos of human societies. At least this has been a widespread view among Western social scientists and historians.[29] The first scholar who raised this question and gave a much-disputed answer was Max Weber. His famous preliminary remark to the 'Collected Essays' in the *Sociology of Religion*, published shortly before his untimely death in 1920, started with the following sentence:

> A product of modern European civilization, studying any problem of universal history, is bound to ask himself to what combination of circumstances the fact should be attributed that in Western civilization, and in Western civilization only, cultural phenomena have appeared which (as we like to think) lie in a line of development having *universal* significance and value.[30]

In a breath-taking outline of the spheres of art and science, ranging from astrology, theology, philosophy, geometry, medicine, and chemistry through political science, law, history, music, architecture, and, most importantly, of the capitalist economy he, while acknowledging and appreciating the intellectual accomplishments especially of the Asiatic civilisations as highly developed in many respects, raises the question why the scientific, the artistic, the political, or the economic development in China or India did not 'enter upon that path of rationalization which is peculiar to the Occident?'[31]

As is well-known in his answer to this question, Weber claimed an inherent connection between the character of European capitalism with Puritanism, particularly with Calvinism which in Weber's argument, 'supplies the moral energy and drive of the capitalist entrepreneur' and the 'element of ascetic self-control in worldly affairs'.[32] A lively debate about Weber's hypothesis about Europe's *Sonderweg* got underway soon after its publication[33] and has by no means come to an end.[34] Apart from its scholarly feature, it had also some less innocent political ramifications in that the claim of Europe's *Sonderweg* could easily be misunderstood as the justification of a proudly cherished sense of distinctiveness and of a claim to Europe's superiority over all other civilisations. *Mitterauer*, who recently took up again the Weberian question, cautions against the danger of implicitly devaluating cultural phenomena which differ from particularly European ones. Referring to historical developments in the Byzantine, the Islamic, and the Chinese cultures he asserts: 'There are many special paths [*Sonderwege*] of civilizations, the European is only one among them'.[35]

Moreover, Europe's *Sonderweg,* especially its special capitalism: 'the rational capitalistic organization of (formally) free labor'[36] has not been predetermined by certain cultural properties of the Europeans; rather, it can be explained as 'an outcome of an historically specific conjunction of events' and circumstances.[37] These circumstances include demographic, geopolitical and economic elements. Arguably a major causal factor was the more or less accidental discovery of the Americas by the European naval powers on their search for a shorter route to the east and the ensuing shift of the centre of world gravity towards the Atlantic world, i.e. to the West.[38] In other words, the unquestionable rise of the West from the 16th century onward is hardly 'attributable exclusively to the internal characteristics of European society'[39] and to cultural phenomena in particular.[40]

This said, the assumption of a European *Sonderweg* can be defended without any Eurocentric tonguing or claim to superiority even where certain particularities of that special developmental path of Europe have gained importance in other parts of the world. The universalisation of technological inventions originating in Europe is apparent with respect to, for instance, steam engines, railroads, or the internal combustion engine. But it is existent in the field of political and legal inventions as well. When we try to grasp the political essence of the European Union and its suitability for inspiring a European narrative, we will inevitably come across Europe's paradigmatic role in the invention of political institutions.

III. A brief history of Europe's political creativity

In fact, Europe has been the birthplace of several ground-breaking political innovations.

1. To begin with, the very idea of politics as a distinct sphere of the life of a human association was invented by the ancient Greeks who, 'by developing the political, ... became the eye of the needle through which the whole of world history had to pass before it could arrive at the modern European stage'.[41] The embodiment of the political dimension of social life was the *polis* – the corporate association of *polites*, i.e. citizens. In the ancient world citizenship was an entirely new status of an individual.[42] When Aristotle in the third century B.C. gave his famous definition of citizenship in Book 3 of his *Politics* – 'The good citizen should

know and have the capacity both to rule and to be ruled, and this very thing is the virtue of a citizen' – this was the philosophical reflexion of a thoroughly new kind of politics which the ancient Greeks had practiced in their *polis* throughout several centuries from Solon [about 630–560 B.C.] through Cleisthenes [about 570–508 B.C.] and Pericles [495–429] until Aristotle's lifetime (384–322). The new kind of politics consisted in the unprecedented practice of, first, declaring the affairs of a group as a business which concerns the whole group as such and, second, transferring the handling of these affairs into the authority and responsibility of, so to speak, the 'membership as such', which means: an association, or union, or fraternity of equals – the *polis*. Membership of this community – citizenship – was not defined by the pre-political bonds of consanguinity but by the needs of the community; the *polis* dispensed rewards, benefits and privileges and assigned rights and responsibilities to individuals not according to their family status, but to their accomplishments for the community.[43] The fact that citizens 'constituted a minority of the entire *polis*' population' notwithstanding, this new pattern of organising the life of a community became the historical corner stone of what we understand as political life – 'politics in the sense of leaders, factions, votes, conflicts, goals, rewards'.[44]

This leads us to what, arguably, can be regarded as the most consequential implication of the invention of the political sphere, namely its concept of politics. As Pocock put it, 'the community of citizens is one in which speech takes the place of blood, and acts of decision take the place of acts of vengeance'.[45]

Everything else resulted from this pioneering innovation: the discussion, the public, the debate, in which the wellbeing of the *polis* as such represents the measure of proper action and decision making, i.e. the concept of the common good. *Polis*-like, i.e. political action did not mean the implementation commandments of tradition, of divine providence or of a salvation plan imposed on people. It was creative in that it drew its resources and ideas from the interactions of the *polites*; political acting was acting in an open process into an open future.

2. The idea of the polity and of citizenship had been invented by the ancient Greeks for their small scale city-states. Quite another social and political construction of what constitutes an abstract connection among otherwise alien individuals is rooted in the Roman tradition of citizenship which parted company with the Greek in many respects. The most important was the transfer of the status of belonging to the community from the political into the legal sphere. In Rome citizenship was not, as in Greece, a political, but a legal status. This has proved to be the case as another first-time political innovation which has become an essential element of the European heritage.

Originally the *civis Romanus* of the Republic was the person who belonged to the community of the people of Rome, quite similar to the Greek *polites*. But in Rome this status did not only involve the 'political' status of membership in the polity. Based upon the *ius civile* – as distinct from the *ius gentium* which applied to foreigners – it included both public and private legal capacity, such as the suffrage, the exemption from taxes and from bodily punishment, the right to a court, the right to own property, to engage in legal transactions and to be *pater familias*, i.e., to be the head of the family and to hold the concomitant exclusive right to the family's property.[46] The Romans' idea of civilisation included the recognition of the human being as a legal person, i.e. an individual to whom particular rights (and duties) are attached.

This kind of citizenship emanates from the more practical, down-to-earth relationship of the Romans to their social world. Persons belonged to the social world of the Roman community as 'possessors and administrators of things'[47] as distinct from the Greek understanding of social life where the 'citizens were persons acting on one another, so that their active life was a life immediately and heroically moral'.[48] While, as mentioned, in ancient Greece the *polis* abstracted from the social hierarchy and inequality of the society, by contrast in Rome the political and the social structures were closely interlocked.[49] Roman citizenship denoted the holding of rights to certain things which varied according to the social status of the relevant person.

The apolitical dimension of citizenship allowed the easing of its connection with the Roman polity and its political institutions. The extension of Rome's domain entailed a gradual extension of the endowment of citizenship to persons outside Rome proper: first to the dwellers of several other Latin cities, later to all cities of the entire Italian peninsula, by the end of the Republic (27 BC) to cities beyond these boundaries.[50] Obviously the transformation of Rome into an Empire and its geographical extension unceasingly curtailed the element of civic participation to near-irrelevance, while citizenship as a legal status to which both individuals and cities could make claim rose to its commanding feature. Given the considerable advantages in the economic and social sphere which were attached to this status, this is not surprising. When finally in 212 A.C. Emperor Caracalla enacted the *Constitutio Antoniana* which assigned Roman citizenship to all free subjects of the Roman Empire the distinction between *ius civile* and *ius gentium* within the Empire lost its entire relevance; the *ius civile* had become the bond which connected all free men of the Empire to a single legal community; it had become the common law of the then universe which was tantamount to the civilised world.[51]

By overstepping the narrow boundaries of a small scale political community Roman citizenship created a class of translocal, multiethnic and multilingual individuals which formed a previously unknown context, something like an international legal community. This construction of citizenship for an extremely heterogeneous empire paved the way for the conception of a polity which was no longer restricted to small cities of the ancient Greek kind. It

> moved the concept of 'citizen' from the *zoon politikon* towards the *legalis homo,* and from the *civis* or *polites* toward the bourgeois or burger. It further brought about some equation of 'citizen' with the 'subject', for in defining him as the member of a community of law, it emphasized that he was ... the subject of those laws that defined his community and of the rulers and magistrates empowered to enforce them.[52]

This international legal community downgraded the particularistic customs which regulated economic and social life in the numerous provinces of the Empire to mere local habits. By connecting citizenship with the law, the Romans established a uniform quasi-cosmopolitan standard of world civilization. A Roman citizen was a person who had emancipated himself from the parochialism of his local origin and had become, so to speak, a 'world citizen'. The etymological coincidence of citizenship and civilization is, of course, not accidental. Hence, legal citizenship is another institutional variant of the transformation of 'natural' or primordial modes of belonging into an 'artificial' 'we'.

3. The Roman invention of the status of citizenship as a legal status may have had a somewhat intricate influence on the development of two further political institutions which originated on European soil: the city and the territorial state. In Max Weber's seminal, posthumously published work *Economy and Society* the City was addressed as a case of non-legitimate domination, which means in Weber's conceptual framework: it did not fit any of the three pure types of legitimate authority which Weber had established as ideal types, namely legal, traditional, and charismatic authority.[53] In his comparison of the Oriental and the Occidental city he stated that 'a common trait of all cities in the world is that they were to a large extent settlements of people previously alien to the given location'.[54] Yet he also emphasised important differences, the most important being the dissolution of primordial ties in the Occidental medieval cities which became legally autonomous associations of citizens and in which 'the burgher joined the citizenry as an individual, and as an individual he swore the oath of citizenship'.[55] The connection with the Romans' legal concept of citizenship may be seen in the pivotal role of the law as the source of an individual's political status. After all, the typical medieval city is an 'institutionalized association, endowed with special characteristic organs, of people who as 'burghers' are subject to a *special law* exclusively applicable to them and who thus form a legally autonomous status group'.[56] Although Weber's analysis of the city needs qualifications and modifications in light of contemporary historical research,[57] the basic conclusion can hardly be disputed: 'The urban citizenry ... usurped the right to dissolve the bonds of seigneurial domination; this was the great – in fact, the *revolutionary* – innovation which differentiated the medieval Occidental cities from all others'.[58]

4. Finally, and perhaps most importantly, the concept of the state as a territorially defined entity endowed with sovereign authority and ruled by law is an essential part of the European heritage of political inventions. This is not the place to give a detailed account of European state formation out of the motley map of cities, petty despotisms, empires and their respective modes of collecting tributes from their subjects.[59] Suffice it to briefly characterise the innovative power which not only changed profoundly the map of Europe since the 16th century but gradually replaced both empires and myriads of local overlords worldwide as the predominant forms of domination over large areas and its peoples.[60] The universal success of statehood rests mainly on its territorial definition. It is a political unit

'fixed in space'[61] with the claim to the obedience of 'whoever is physically in that area'.[62] Obviously this container-like kind of societal integration[63] was much more efficient than that of the 'great, imperfectly integrated empires'.[64] As Khan observed, 'controlling people and things territorially simply saves effort and thus provides the 'territory owner' with a clear "evolutionary advantage"'.[65] But statehood proved also more successful than the medieval cities – 'small, but highly cohesive units' which played an important role in the formation of European states after 1500 A.D.[66] States specialised in the allocation of power, developed the traditional subsistence economy into a monetarised economy of surplus production, and thus created the basis for establishing systems of taxation which allowed them to finance standing armies and the bureaucratic apparatus which exercised monarchical control over the territory. In other words, medieval cities served as 'containers and distribution points for capital' that was urgently demanded by monarchs in their struggle for establishing their exclusive sovereign power, whilst states operated 'chiefly as containers and deployers of coercive means, especially armed force'.[67] Thus, cities and the newly emerging states could coexist. However, for lack of a professionalised administrative apparatus and the control of their hinterland cities, ultimately succumbed to the efficiency of the states.[68]

The territorialisation of authority (Sassen) had several important implications for the establishment and subsequent refinement of statehood as a new and paradigmatic kind of political organisation.[69] First and foremost, authoritative power became impersonal because the subordination under the will of a ruler was not based on personal relations and therefore did not have to be secured and affirmed for each individual person. It was valid for each person within the borders of the territory, irrespective of his or her social status or individual attributes (such as religious belief or ethnic belonging).[70] This opened the road to a system of legality based upon the principle of an equal legal status of each and every subject of the state's authority.

Second, the individuals' subordination no longer consists in their posture of loyalty towards their superiors of the social hierarchy but in a behavioural attitude of conformity to the requirements of the abstract order. Loyalty to persons gradually metamorphoses into obedience to law. The law is the command of the supreme authority which is binding upon everybody not due to its inherent rightfulness but because it has been enacted by that very authority – *auctoritas, non veritas facit legem*. This opened the road to the establishment of positive law as man-made law which became an important, if not *the* authoritative vehicle of social change.

Thirdly, the victory of the royal absolutist state over the feudal lordships and local corporations, i.e. the consolidation of centralised royal authority, advanced the separation of the spiritual powers of the church from the secular power of the state which had already begun in the 11th century with the so-called Papal Revolution.[71] However, while this revolution had produced a centralised administrative apparatus of the church which administered its spiritual affairs while maintaining its influence on the political affairs of the worldly kingdoms, it was not before the 16th century that the centralisation of secular, largely coercive power in separate independent states created the intellectual and moral realm in which the logic and the intrinsic value of the this-worldly life could be represented. Martin Luther's doctrine of the two reigns, published in 1523, is the theological expression of this new perspective: both the spiritual and the worldly kingdom are created and ruled by God, but in two different ways: the this-worldly sphere by the secular means of the law and the sword, the spiritual world by the Scripture and God's grace.[72] This distinction opened the road to the secular justification of political power through diverse social contract theories. Incidentally, it may also have opened the road to the amazingly fruitful advance of natural science since the emergence of absolutism.[73] The metamorphosis of God's omnipotence into the secular version of the sovereign power of the monarch paved the way for the exploration and, soon after, also the emulation of the laws of nature which God had made. Since the rationality of God, the creator of this world, 'was the guarantee of rational intelligibility in his creation', men could be confident 'that other rational personal beings would be able to spell out in their own earthly languages the divine code of laws which he had previously formulated'.[74]

Finally, statehood was to become the fruitful soil for the invention of constitutionalism. Here I do not refer to the function of constitutions to limit state power. Rather, in the age of its emergence in the 16th century the sovereign territorial state was a new type of polity in a much more fundamental sense. Sovereignty was defined as supreme power. That does not mean that it was merely relatively greater than other powers to which it was superior. What was new of Bodin's definition of sovereignty was that it was marked as 'the *absolute* and perpetual power of a *commonwealth*'[75] – sovereignty was absolute power because it combined, centralised and embodied the capabilities of the collectivity as such. Building an analogy to Gianfranco Poggi's characterisation of the state's terrritorial nature: 'The state does not *have* a territory, it *is* a territory',[76] one could say that the state does not *have* power but *is* a power (as is the common saying in international relations). What was important (and reminded of some elements of the ancient polities) was the separation of the state from both the ruler and the ruled and its establishment as a distinct political entity. Thus, the legitimation of the ruler to rule, i.e. the relationship between the ruler and the ruled, became a latent element of societal dynamics which became manifest in the claim of the ruled to judge the legitimacy of the ruler and, ultimately, in the French Revolution, to establish a political order which was based upon the consent of the ruled. In other words, the creation of the state as an abstract entity which embodied the power and capabilities of the ruler and the ruled opened the road to the constitutionalisation of the polity.

IV. The European Union – A new example of Europe's political inventiveness

The history of Europe's political creativity has not saved this continent from suffering long and agonising catastrophes (such as the Black Death, the pandemic in the middle of the 14th century which killed more than a third of Europe's whole population), from experiencing deep and violent conflicts (such as the religious wars of the 16th and 17th centuries) and from committing severe injustices and crimes (such as the colonial subjugation and even extinction of indigenous peoples in other continents). After all, it was Europe and its incapacity to cope appropriately with the inherent contradictions of its socio-political structure which caused the two world wars of the 20th century, and it was an allegedly 'civilised' member of the European family of states which committed the most repugnant and monstrous crime of human history, the Holocaust. In view of these secular catastrophes the current European crisis and the lasting difficulties of the European political leaders to cope with the challenges of a global economic and financial crisis are, of course, absolutely minuscule. Still, they may substantiate the widespread sense of Europe's comparatively poor standing in the fields of politics, economics, military and science. Obviously Europe is no longer a role model for other parts of the world. So, why should Europe take pride in its past political imagination and use the reminiscence of this past as a source for the construction of a narrative bound to legitimise a less than shining present?

The reason is certainly not the claim that Europe should be regarded as the role model for the organisation of political life in other parts of the world. But its very special path of development can be used as a source of cognition about politics as an essential field of the human condition. Despite its calamities, catastrophes, failures and crimes or, rather, due to those dark sides of its history referred to above, Europe represents the unfathomable character of its history of the political, its hopes as much as its futilities: when the ancient Greeks and the Romans weakened the role of kinship and clan and established the individual as the basic unit of the community – just as much as the Christian parish was a community of believing individuals[77] – they set the cornerstone for the gradual expulsion of natural, i.e. immutable and incontrovertible facts out of a group's social organisation. They created a space of joint reflexivity and debate about what was good for them. They realised, as Hannah Arendt rightly observed, that 'politics arises between men',[78] which means: it is inherently linked to the plurality of men. It 'organizes those who are absolutely different with a view to their *relative* equality and in contradistinction to their *relative* differences'.[79] Thus, from the very outset the differences of men and their modes of association and dissociation resulting from these differences have formed the core of the political.

As the above brief account of the main European political inventions illustrated, this fundamental element inhered in the Greek *polis*, the Roman concept of legal citizenship, and in the medieval cities. It was even prominent in the territorial state which is usually regarded as the great homogeniser of the many into one body politic of likes.[80] While there is some truth in it, we should not overlook that the concept of statehood implies the notion of the plurality of states and their mutual recognition as equals which became the conceptual foundation of modern international law.[81] Note that the plurality of states entailed another version of

European exceptionalism, namely the balance of power as an instrument of maintaining an international system of varieties of states. While in other parts of the world a plurality of states was largely a transitory phenomenon as incessant warring among them led to 'the conversion of the competitive states system into an empire either by the successes of one of the warring states of by an outside polity taking advantage of weaknesses produced by the warfare',[82] the European system of plural states became a structural element of the political order of the European continent.

Of course, the dark sides of this notion of politics must not be ignored. Obviously Aristotle, the main source of our understanding of the ancient Greek *polis*, defined the political as the common effort of the citizens to achieve the common good.[83] Yet the continuous internal conflicts, social unrest, periods of tyranny, oligarchical rule and the gradual demise of Athenian democracy in the third century B.C.[84] attest to the fact that the creation of a distinct sphere of politics also unleashed the individuals' potential of lust for power, struggle, division, subterfuge, hypocrisy, stratagem, nefariousness, violence and all the other shady human characteristics which some two thousand years later Machiavelli would describe as the necessary means for the efficient governance of a polity.[85] In fact, the foundation of Europe's political structure on the recognition of plurality and differentness of individuals, communities and nations did not save the continent from deep and intransigent conflicts and dreadful wars either. But they triggered collective learning processes, arguably the most prominent example being the constitutional establishment of religious freedom in the 17th and 18th centuries as a reaction to the religious wars which had erupted in many European countries in the age of the Reformation. Likewise, in the second half of the 19th century the first steps towards the establishment of a humanitarian law and the legal control of armed conflict, reflected and mitigated the cruel consequences of the concept of the states' absolute power and their *ius ad belllum* which dominated the Westphalian international order in the long 19th century until the First World War.[86] But it was only after the 'trauma of the Second World War' and the recognition of the definitive end of Europe's role as *the* leading power in world politics that the idea of a new kind of community of states was born.

Two achievements are pivotal: the sharing of sovereignty of a plurality of democratic nation-states and the establishment of a composite transnational constituent power of the peoples of the European Union and their respective democratic nation-states.[87] This is the first time in human history that sovereign states form a political community which not only established legal channels for their cooperation and the peaceful dealing of conflicts – this is, at least on paper, meanwhile the standard on the global level as well – but which has created an institutional realm in which different peoples form a political 'We' without giving up or pressed to give up their differentness as peoples with their respective national histories, cultural traditions and particular mentalities. They do not merely share an internal market which, as such, would neither require nor foster the constitution of a 'We'. Rather, they share a conjoint law which regulates important spheres of their everyday life and thus creates a quite peculiar 'We'.

A law which covers some 500 million people and regulates the lives of, meanwhile, 28 nations as diverse as Portugal and Sweden, Poland and Cyprus, France and Estonia, Italy and the Netherlands etc. etc., has necessarily so different and specific effects on the several member states that the reason for its binding force – namely the presupposition of equality and generality which binds the member states together into one legal community under the same law – is not convincing. The more heterogeneous and diverse the addressees of a law or any other authoritative regulation are, the more do they sense the law as imposed upon them by 'others', not by 'themselves'. Weiler rightly observes that it 'is a remarkable instance of civic tolerance to accept to be bound by precepts articulated not by "my people" but by a community composed of distinct political communities: a people, if you wish, of others'.[88]

Union citizenship constitutes the bond of solidarity among those who more or less consciously realise that they have a dual or even multiple identity: embedded in their several nation-state contexts and cultures, they know (or will eventually learn) that there is a more abstract sphere in which the connectedness of strangers opens new fields of cooperation, communication and understanding which allows them to realise their original national identity as just a portion of their political existence. Thus, European citizenship will also create only a fragmented 'we', but one which is able (and has to be further enabled through appropriate constitutional means) to act coherently in a world with an increasing need for cooperation, mutual understanding and common goals among strangers with quite heterogeneous cultural backgrounds.

To conclude: the problem of European democracy is not that there is no European *demos*. The *demos* presupposes the fusion of the many into one body whose coercive character requires homogeneity of the rulers and the ruled in order to legitimise the necessity of obedience. This is not the political vision of the European Union. The vision is, rather, the idea of solidarity grounded on the mutual recognition of otherness and the development of modes of cooperation and, yes, also of collectively binding decisions taken by 'others' whose bindingness is rooted in institutional devices which encourage civic solidarity and the tolerance for otherness. This, however, requires a reduction of social inequality among the Union citizens.

The EU may become the paradigm of a polity without a *demos*, based upon the solidarity of citizens who are able and willing to reflect their otherness. It is a polity in a world where people have become neighbours and still remain strangers which respect each other and accept mutual responsibilities. This genuine political and institutional innovation is the contribution of Europe to the solution of the problems of our world at the beginning of the 21st century. And the Europeans should proudly tell each other and their fellow men from other parts of the world that the Europeans have learnt from their dark history and can offer innovative ideas for the bettering of the human conditions in a world torn by serious injustices and conflicts.

Notes

1. Accessible at the Website of the European Union – http://europa.eu/about-eu/ basic-information/symbols/europe-day/schuman-declaration/index_en.htm (last accessed 22 March 2013).

2. For instance, Joseph Weiler regards the Schuman Declaration as a 'Manifesto of Political Messianism', cf. J. H. H. Weiler, 'Democracy without the people: the extinction of European legitimacy', *Schlossplatz3*, 2012, vol. 13, pp. 8–15 [12 ff.].

3. *Ibid.*, p. 12.

4. Cf. European Commission – eurostat Unemployment Statistics (Jan. 2013) http://epp.eurostat.ec.europa.eu/statistics_explained/index.php/ Unemployment_statistics#Youth_unemployment_trends (last accessed 20 March 2013).

5. Standard Eurobarometer 78/Autumn 2012 – European Citizenship –, Tables of Results at T78 – http://ec.europa.eu/public_opinion/archives/eb/eb78/ eb78_en.htm.

6. Standard Eurobarometer 78/Autumn 2012 – European Citizenship –, at 24 http://ec.europa.eu/public_opinion/archives/eb/eb78/eb78_en.htm.

7. See the detailed questions and answers in the Standard Eurobarometer 78 (November 2012), at 7.

8. Cf. R. H. Foerster (ed.), *Die Idee Europa 1300–1946. Quellen zur Geschichte der politischen Einigung*, München, Deutscher Taschenbuch Verlag, 1963; V. Der Dussen, *The History of the Idea of Europe*, Routledge, 1995; A. Pagden, *The Idea of Europe: From antiquity to the European Union*, Cambridge University Press, 2002.

9. The speech is accessible at the Website of the Council of Europe – http:// assembly.coe.int/Main.asp?link=/AboutUs/zurich_e.htm (last accessed 22 March 2013).

10. The Schuman Declaration of 9 May 1950 – Introduction by Pascal Fontaine (*Research and Documentation Service EPP-ED Group*) Brussels, 2000.

11. W. Wessels, 'Jean Monnet – Mensch und Methode. Überschätzt und Überholt?', in *IHS Vienna Political Science Series*, 2001, no. 74.

12. *Ibid.*, pp. 7 ff.

13. L. N. Lindberg and S. A. Scheingold, *Europe's Would-be Polity: Patterns of change in the European Community*, Englewood Cliffs, NJ, Prentice-Hall, 1970; see A. Hurrelmann (2007) 'European democracy, the 'permissive consensus' and the collapse of the EU Constitution', *European Law Journal*, 2007, vol. 13, no. 3, pp. 343–359 [352 ff.].

14. *Ibid.*, p. 352.

15. D. Debomy, 'Do the Europeans still believe in the EU? Analysis of attitudes and expectations of EU public opinions over the past quarter century', *Studies*

& *Research*, 2012, no. 91, Notre Europe – Jacques Delors Institute – *www. notre-europe.eu*

16. *Ibid.*, pp. 35 ff.

17. *Ibid.*, pp. 36 ff.

18. Cf. C. Joerges and N. S. Ghaleigh (eds), *Darker Legacies of Law in Europe: The shadow of National Socialism and Fascism over Europe and its legal traditions*, Oxford and Portland, Oregon, Hart Publishing, 2003.

19. J. Elster, *Closing the Books: Transitional justice in historical perspective*, Cambridge, UK, New York, Cambridge University Press, 2004; R. G. Teitel, 'Transitional justice genealogy', *Harvard Human Rights Journal*, 2003, vol. 16, pp. 69–94.

20. W. Sieberer, *Das Bild Europas in den Historien. Studien zu Herodots Geographie und Ethnographie Europas und seiner Schilderung der persischen Feldzüge*, Innsbruck, Verlag des Instituts für Sprachwissenschaft der Universität Innsbruck, 1995; see also R. Hellmut Foerster (ed.), *Die Idee Europa 1300–1946. Quellen zur Geschichte der politischen Einigung*, München, Deutscher Taschenbuch Verlag, 1963, p. 9; W. Schmale, *Geschichte Europas*, Wien-Köln-Weimar, 2001, p. 27ff.; J. McCormick, *Europeanism*, Oxford Online Scholarship 2010 – http://www.oxfordscholarship.com/view/10.1093/acprof:oso/9780199556212.001.0001/acprof-9780199556212

21. McCormick, *Europeanism*, chapter 2, p. 22.

22. P. den Boer, 'Europe to 1914: the making of an idea', in K. Wilson and J. van der Dussen (eds), *The History of the Idea of Europe*, London and New York, 1995, pp. 13–82 [34 ff.].

23. J. H. H. Weiler, (2004) *Ein christliches Europa: Erkundungsgänge*, Mit einem Vorwort von E.-W. Böckenförde, Salzburg, München, 2004.

24. den Boer, 'Europe to 1914', pp. 64–65.

25. I. Kant, (1992) 'An Answer to the Question: 'What is Enlightenment'?', in I. Kant, *Political Writings*, edited by H. Reiss, Cambridge, New York, Cambridge University Press, 1992, pp. 54–60.

26. F. v. Martiz, quoted from W. Grewe, *The Epochs of International Law*, Berlin-New York, Gruyter, 2000, p. 456.

27. J. McCormick, *Understanding the European Union: A concise introduction*, 4th edn, London, Palgrave Macmillan, 2008, p. 43.

28. Cf. M. Shipway, *Decolonization and its Impact: A comparative approach to the end of the colonial empires*, Oxford, Oxford University Press, 2008.

29. Cf. W. H. McNeill, *The Rise of the West: A history of the human community*, Chicago, University of Chicago Press, 1991 [1963], including his impressive self-critical assessment of the shortcomings of the book 'The rise of the West after twenty-five years', in *Journal of World History*, 1990, vol. 1, no. 1, pp. 1–21; D. C. North and R. P. Thomas, *The Rise of the Western World: A new*

economic history, Cambridge, Cambridge University Press, 1973; M. Mann, *The Sources of Social Power. Vol. I. A history of power from the beginning to A.D. 1760*, Cambridge, Cambridge University Press, 1986, pp. 373 ff.; D. Chirot, 'The rise of the West', *American Sociological Review*, 1985, vol. 50, no. 2, pp. 181–195; E. L. Jones, *The European Miracle: Environments, economies, and geopolitics in the history of Europe and Asia*, 3rd edn, Cambridge and New York, Cambridge University Press, 2003 [1987]; J. Darwin, *After Tamerlane: The rise and fall of global empires, 1400–2000*, London, Penguin, 2007; J. A. Goldstone, 'The rise of the West – or not? A revision to socio-economic history', *Sociological Theory*, 2000, vol. 18, no. 2, pp. 175–194; J. M. Bryant, 'The west and the rest revisited: debating capitalist origins, European colonialism, and the advent of modernity', *The Canadian Journal of Sociology*, 2006, vol. 31, no. 4, pp. 403–444; J. A. Goldstone, *Why Europe? The Rise of the West in World History, 1500–1850*, New York, McGraw Hill, 2009.

30. M. Weber, author's 'Introduction' [to the Collected Essays in the Sociology of Religion], *The Protestant Ethic and the Spirit of Capitalism* (trans. T. Parsons), London and New York, Routledge, 1992, pp. 13–31 [13 – italics in original]. The German version reads: 'Universalgeschichtliche Probleme wird der Sohn der modernen europäischen Kulturwelt unvermeidlicher – und berechtigterweise unter der Fragestellung behandeln: welche Verkettung von Umständen hat dazu geführt, daß gerade auf dem Boden des Okzidents, und nur hier, Kulturerscheinungen auftraten, welche doch – wie wenigstens wir uns gern vorstellen – in einer Entwicklungsrichtung von universeller Bedeutung und Gültigkeit lagen?'.

31. Weber, 'Introduction', p. 25.

32. A. Giddens, 'Introduction' to Max Weber, *The Protestant Ethic and the Spirit of Capitalism*, pp. vii-xxvi [xiv].

33. See Giddens, *ibid.*, p. xix ff.

34. See references in note 29, above; and M. Mitterauer, *Warum Europa? Mittelalterliche Grundlagen eines Sonderwegs*, München, C. H. Beck, 2004.

35. Mitterauer, *Warum Europa?*, p 9.

36. Weber, 'Introduction', p. 21.

37. Giddens, 'Introduction' to Max Weber, p. xx.

38. J. L. Abu-Lughod, *Before European Hegemony: The world system A.D. 1250–1350*, New York-Oxford, Oxford University Press, 1989, p. 363.

39. *Ibid.*, p. 361.

40. See the impressive book of J. M. Hobson, *The Eastern Origins of Western Civilization*, Cambridge, UK and New York, Cambridge University Press, 2004.

41. C. Meier, *The Greek Discovery of Politics*, Cambridge Mass., Harvard Univ. Press, 1990, p. 2; German original version: *Die Entstehung des Politischen bei den Griechen*, Frankfurt/M., 1983, p. 13.

42. See the details in P. Riesenberg, *Citizenship in the Western Tradition*, Chapel Hill and London, University of North Carolina Press, 1992, pp. 3 et seq., 20 ff.

43. *Ibid.*, p. 6.

44. *Ibid.*, pp. 4–5.

45. J. G. A. Pocock, 'The Ideal of Citizenship Since Classical Times', in R. Beiner (ed.), *Theorizing Citizenship*, Albany, State University of New York Press, 1995, pp. 29–52 [30].

46. A. N. A. Sherwin-White, *The Roman Citizenship*, 2nd edn, Oxford, Oxford University Press, 1973, pp. 264 ff.; H. Bruhns, 'Verwandtschaftsstrukturen, Geschlechterverhältnisse und Max Webers Theorie der antiken Stadt', in C. Meier (ed.), *Die okzidentale Stadt nach Max Weber*, München, Oldenbourg Wissensch.Vlg, 1994, pp. 59–94, pp. 83 ff.

47. Pocock, 'The Ideal Citizenship', p. 35.

48. *Ibid.*, p. 34.

49. Meier, *Die okzidentale Stadt*, p. 29; see also J. Martin, *Der Verlust der Stadt*, in Meier, *Die okzidentale Stadt*, pp. 95–114 [105 ff.].

50. Sherwin-White, *The Roman Citizenship*, pp. 275 ff.

51. Riesenberg, *Citizenship in the Western Tradition*, p. 83.

52. Pocock, 'The Ideal Citizenship', p. 38.

53. M. Weber, *Economy and Society* (trans. by G. Roth and C. Wittich), Berkeley, Los Angeles and London, University of California Press, 1978, pp. 215 ff.

54. *Ibid.*, p. 1244.

55. *Ibid.*, pp. 1244 ff., quote p. 1246.

56. *Ibid.*, p. 1240.

57. See the contributions in Meier, *Die okzidentale Stadt*; M. V. Creveld, *The Rise and Decline of the State*, Cambridge, Cambridge University Press, 1999, pp. 20 ff.; E. F. Isin, 'Citizenship after orientalism', in E. F. Isin and B. S. Turner (eds), *Handbook of Citizenship Studies*, London, Sage, 2002, pp. 117–128.

58. Weber, *Economy and Society*, p. 1239.

59. See the description of C. Tilly, 'Entanglements of European Cities and States', in C. Tilly and W. P. Blockmans (eds), *Cities and the Rise of States in Europe, A.D. 1000 to 1800*, San Francisco and Oxford, Westview Press, 1994, pp. 1–27 [7].

60. J. R. Strayer, *On the Medieval Origins of the Modern State*, with new forewords by C. Tilly and W. C. Jordan, Princeton, N.J., Princeton University Press, 2005 [1970], pp. 9 ff. and 105.

61. *Ibid.*, p. 9.

62. D. Miller and H. Sohail, *Boundaries and Justice: Diverse ethical perspectives*, Princeton, Princeton University Press, 2001, p. 4.

63. See P. J. Taylor, 'The state as container: territoriality in the modern world-system', *Progress in Human Geography*, 1994, vol. 18, no. 2, pp. 151–162.

64. Strayer, *On the Medieval Origins...*, p. 9.

65. D. E. Khan, 'Territory and Boundaries', in B. Fassbender and A. Peters (eds), *The Oxford Handbook of the History of International Law*, Oxford, Oxford University Press, 2012, pp. 225–249 [226].

66. Tilly, 'Entanglements of European Cities...', pp. 15 et seq.; v. Creveld, *The Rise and Decline of the State*, pp. 104 ff.

67. Tilly 'Entanglements of European Cities...', p. 8.

68. See H. Spruyt, *The Sovereign State and its Competitors: An analysis of systems change*, Princeton, N.J, Princeton University Press, 1994, pp. 153 ff., 177.

69. The following section draws a great deal on a text of mine published elsewhere, cf. U. K. Preuß, 'Disconnecting Constitutions from Statehood: Is global constitutionalism a viable concept?', in P. Dobner and M. Loughlin (eds), *The Twilight of Constitutionalism?*, Oxford, Oxford University Press, 2010, pp. 23–46.

70. Note, however, that the European states in their early developmental stage had still to learn about their potential for ethnic or religious neutrality, as the enforcement of the principle of *cuius regio, eius religio*, established in the Augsburg and the Westphalian Peace Treaties of 1555 and 1648 respectively, attest.

71. H. Berman, *Law and Revolution: The formation of the Western legal tradition*, Cambridge, Mass, Harvard University Press, 1983, pp. 85 ff., 113 ff.

72. U. K. Preuß, 'Martin Luther Von weltlicher Obrigkeit (1523)' in M. Brocker (ed.), *Geschichte des politischen Denkens: Ein Handbuch*, Frankfurt/M., Suhrkamp Verlag, 2007, pp. 137–150; D. M. Whitford, 'Luther's political encounters', in D. K. McKim (ed.), *The Cambridge Companion to Martin Luther*, Cambridge, Cambridge University Press, 2003, pp. 179–191.

73. Cf. S. Shapin and S. Schaffer, *Leviathan and the Air-Pump: Hobbes, Boyle, and the experimental life*, Princeton, Princeton University Press, 1989.

74. J. Needham, 'Human laws and laws of nature in China and the West (II)', *Journal of the History of Ideas*, 1951, vol. 12, no. 2, pp. 194–230 [227, 229].

75. J. Bodin, *On Sovereignty*, Cambridge, Cambridge University Press, 1992, Bk I, ch.8, at 1 [emphases added].

76. G. Poggi, *The State: Its nature, development and prospects*, Stanford, Stanford University Press, 1994, p. 22.

77. Meier, *Die okzidentale Stadt*, p. 9.

78. H. Arendt, *The Promise of Politics*, New York, Schocken Books, 2005, p. 95.

79. *Ibid.*, p. 96 [emphasis original].

80. Cf. A. Giddens, *The Nation-State and Violence*, Berkeley and Los Angeles, University of California Press, 1987, pp. 181 ff.

81. Cf. U. K. Preuß, 'Equality of states: its meaning in a constitutionalized global order', *Chicago Journal of International Law*, 2008, vol. 9, no. 1, pp. 17–49 [20 ff.].

82. Taylor, 'The state as container', p. 153.

83. Cf. C. Lord, 'Aristotle, 384–322 B.C.', in L. Strauss and J. Cropsey (eds), *History of Political Philosophy*, 3rd edn, Chicago and London, University of Chicago Press, 1987, pp. 118–154.

84. J. Ober, *The Athenian Revolution: Essays on ancient Greek democracy and political theory,* Princeton, NJ, Princeton University Press, 1999; W. K. Pritchett, *Essays in Greek History*, Amsterdam; JC Gieben, 1994; P. Rhodes, 'Athenian democracy after 403 BC', *The Classical Journal*, 1980, vol. 75, no. 4, pp. 305–323.

85. Niccolò Machiavelli, *The Prince*, 1513, chs 15 ff.

86. M. N. Shaw, *International Law*, 5th edn, Cambridge and New York, Cambridge University Press, 2003, pp. 26 ff.

87. Cf. J. Habermas, *Zur Verfassung Europas: Ein Essay*, Berlin, Surhkamp Verlag, 2011, pp. 39 et seq. [47]; C. Franzius and U. K. Preuß, *Die Zukunft der europäischen Demokratie*, Baden-Baden, Nomos Verlag, 2012, pp. 95 ff.

88. J. H. H. Weiler, 'Federalism and Constitutionalism: Europe's *Sonderweg*', Cambridge, Mass, Harvard Law School, 2000.

Chapter Seventeen

Citizenship in the European Union: A Paradigm for Transnational Democracy?*

Ulrich K. Preuß

In the accelerating process of globalisation of economic, political, cultural and scientific relations, the European Union is largely seen as a successful model of the institutionalisation of supranationality. Rather than contenting themselves with adding just one more to the manifold international treaties and organisations, the founding fathers of the European Economic Community (which, since Maastricht I, is on its way to a European Union) created, more or less without being aware of it, an unprecedented entity which they called 'Community'. Some analysts called this entity 'a market without a state' in order to emphasise its purely economic function. Yet, in contrast to a market, from its very beginning the Community possessed institutions which allowed it self-observation and self-evolution, and due to this institutional dowry it was able to develop, in the course of a long and protracted process, embryonic forms of a polity. The most evident and the most important achievements of that development have been the establishment of the principles of *direct effect* and of the *supremacy of Community law* over national law. *Direct effect* means that provisions of Community law must be applied by the national courts of the member states without prior transformation into national law through the national parliament; the principle of *supremacy* signifies that a directly effective provision of Community law always prevails over a conflicting provision of national law.[1]

The far-reaching implication of the principles of *direct effect* and *supremacy* is the creation of an immediate bond of affiliation between the citizens of the member states and the Community. They enjoy rights and are subject to duties which do not originate in their respective national parliaments, that is, in the political will of the citizenry of which they form a part. Rather, they are subject to legal provisions emanating from Community organs (the Council, the Commission and the European Parliament). Yet these organs do not articulate the will of a European *people* (or citizenry), but of the *peoples* (or citizenries) of the member states. This is also true for the European Parliament, which consists of 'representatives of the peoples of the States brought together in the Community' (Article 137, EC Treaty),

---

* 'Citizenship in the European Union: A paradigm for transnational democracy?', in D. Archibugi, D. Held and M. Köhler (eds), *Re-imagining Political Community: Studies in cosmopolitan democracy*, Cambridge-Oxford, Polity Press, 1998, pp. 138–151.

not of a European people or *demos*. Despite the *direct effect* and the *supremacy* principles, the European Community is (still?) a Community of states, at best of peoples, not of citizens. The member states, not the people living within the territory of the European Community, are the constituent factors of the political body of the Community.

However, in the Maastricht Treaty of February 1992, the governments of the member states made a further step towards institutional integration in that they created the institution of 'Union citizenship'. According to Article 8 of the amended EC Treaty, 'every person holding the nationality of a Member State shall be a citizen of the Union'. Union citizens shall enjoy the rights conferred by the Treaty, including the qualified right to move and reside freely within the territory of the member states, the right of Union citizens who reside in a member state of which they are not nationals to vote and to stand as candidates at municipal elections and in elections to the European Parliament in the member state in which they reside, the right to consular or diplomatic protection by any member state, and the right to petition the European Parliament (Articles 8a-8d, EC Treaty). At first glance, Union citizenship is not a very impressive status; nationals of third countries are excluded, and the list of rights associated with it is quite short. Still, to be a citizen of a supranational entity is a major innovation in the history of political membership which merits closer scrutiny. Can we understand this new European institution as a major breakthrough in the institutional mastering of the goal of transnational solidarity which could eventually even entail some kind of transnational democracy?

Given the complex character of the concept of citizenship I shall start with a brief account of the broad scope of historical meanings which have been associated with the concept of citizenship in Europe since antiquity. In a second step I shall draw some tentative conclusions from this record and approach the idea of supranational citizenship. This undertaking can readily be understood as a preliminary study for the more difficult venture, namely to develop the constituents of transnational citizenship. However, this exacting objective is not part of this paper.

The unclear meaning of 'European citizenship'

The idea of 'European citizenship' is quite opaque. Although the concept is not entirely novel,[2] it was not until the Maastricht Treaty that the concept (although not the term) was formally established in a legal text of the Community. While the newly inserted text of Articles 8 to 8e of the EC Treaty does not create excessively great obstacles to their legal interpretation, it is more difficult to predict how this new element of the EC Treaty may affect the process of European integration, Europe's political culture, and the still uncertain ideas of supranational constitutionalism and supranational democracy. The assessments of the importance of the institution 'citizenship of the Union' are vague and cautious at best. For example, Corbett speaks of a 'notable achievement' without explicating precisely what this achievement might consist of;[3] Curtin considers the insertion of the Articles about Union citizenship in the EC Treaty as 'real progress', while stating at the same time that what, *inter alia*, constitutes the 'unique *sui generis* nature of the European Community, its true world-historical significance', namely the character of the Union as a 'cohesive legal unit which confers rights on *individuals*', is endangered by the serious shortfalls of the Treaty of Maastricht.[4] For Meehan, citizenship of the Union is part of a complex development from 'national citizenship to European civil society',[5] while according to a seemingly more down-to-earth statement of a lawyer (written before the conclusion of the Treaty of Maastricht), Union citizenship will at least over the medium term be hardly more than the subsumption of the single rights and duties of the individual under the label 'Union citizenship', without changing either the continuance of the intermediary role of national citizenship or its salient role in the lives of Europeans.[6]

Should the idea of European citizenship in fact materialise, it is safe to assume that its meaning and its importance for the ongoing process of integration will largely be shaped by the concepts of citizenship which have been developed in the several national member states of the Community. This is of course not to say that Union citizenship will be a kind of conglomerate of the different national concepts, in the sense of the lowest common denominator of those of all member states; the hypothesis is, rather, that the diversity of traditions which have shaped the concepts of citizenship in their respective national contexts is likely to generate different or at least differently coloured versions of one single Union citizenship. This proposition is derived from the unique legal attributes of the European Union: although, of course, the rights and duties associated with Union citizenship are rights and duties vis-à-vis the Community, the principal addressee of the former and guarantors of the discharge of the latter are and will be the national member states, because the great bulk of Community law is implemented and enforced by them rather than by proper Community institutions and agencies.

If the national member states do indeed remain the principal actors in the areas in which citizenship is important for the daily life of the Europeans, then it seems safe to conclude that the national traditions and conceptual particularities of the several member states will have a major impact on the contours of an evolving concept of Union citizenship. It is hardly conceivable that an institution as essential for the structure of a constitutional polity as citizenship, could be constructed without a thorough borrowing of ideas from the basic constitutional ideas of the constituent member states. This makes it a rewarding undertaking to dig into the richness and variety of elements which constitute the idea of citizenship throughout the member states of the Community. In all probability this would bring to light whether, and to what degree, the different elements of the national concepts of citizenship are sufficiently akin to and consistent with each other in order to serve as the conceptual underpinnings of a European citizenship. Of course, the result of this comparative analysis could also be that the national concepts of citizenship diverge so much that this will eventually prevent the national political actors from finding a common understanding of what European citizenship essentially means or could mean (to them and to the individuals on whom this status is conferred as well).

In the long history since its first appearance in Greek antiquity and until recent times, the term 'citizenship' has covered an extremely broad scope of possible meanings. If it is at all possible to discover an invariable element in it, it is probably the notion of an individual's membership of a political community, be that the Greek city-state (*polis*), the Roman empire, the Christian medieval city or the modern territorial nation-state.[7] Evidently the implications of membership are largely determined by the character of the community to which the bonds of affiliation are tied. Given the diversity of communities which Europe has experienced in the last 2,500 years, it is not surprising to encounter a rich diversity of very disparate, if not opposite meanings.

Although the etymological roots of the term refer to the dwellers of a city, the 'city' (*polis*) signifies not so much a merely physical location but a symbolic space in which a new ethics of cooperation has emerged. In its ancient Greek origins, the city, and hence citizenship, replaces the familial and tribal bonds of the individuals and creates a mode of 'civic' cooperation. Its essence consists in the idea of the commonness of fates of individuals who are bound together by the more abstract ties of common religion[8] and, particularly, of common laws.[9] From its very origination in ancient Greece, citizenship has included a distinct status which draws symbolic boundaries not only against those who live physically outside the community, but, even more importantly, also against those who do live within the physical space of the community but who do not belong to it socially. In other words, in its original meaning the concept of citizenship is a social construction which is not only constitutive of the identity of a particular – political – community, but which at the same time defines the social identity of the individuals who in their quality as members replace their family, clan or tribal affiliation with their status in a more abstract community, the polity. Thus citizenship is a concept which is counterfactual in a twofold sense: it sharply distinguishes between the physical and the social boundaries of a society; and it transcends the boundaries of the 'natural' groups of the family, the clan and the tribe towards a *political* organisation of a social group.

In fact, a common feature of the concept of citizenship throughout different historical contexts has been its polemical usage as a counterterm against other social roles: a citizen is not only different but is, in a way, the positive counter-image of a person whose defining social characteristics is his or her quality as a consumer, a producer, a client, a subject, a family member or simply a private person. This is perhaps only the consequence of a more fundamental property of citizenship rooted in its historical origin, namely its inherent bent towards a universalist perception of the individual and the ensuing refusal to tie that individual to narrow, parochial and particularistic social roles. As analysed by Max Weber in his sociology of the city,[10] citizenship is a genuinely occidental institution. It is closely associated with the development of the Western-type city and its main characteristics, namely its foundation on the corporate unity of the city dwellers, as opposed to the oriental cities, which were religious and/

or clan associations and did not create a distinct sphere of corporate unity at the city level.

Abstracting from manifold historical and local differences, one prominent occurrence gave birth to a particular meaning of citizenship that was finally transplanted into the – equally occidental – concept of the modern state. Indeed the occidental medieval city, and with some qualifications the ancient Greek *polis* as well, was not the place of settlement of clans, families, tribes or other primordial communities (that is, of communities which existed *prior* to this locus) but rather the location of settlement for individuals who were alien to each other[11] and who were bound together through oaths of fraternisation which affirmed a secular community. The corporate unity of the city was based on acts of association of individuals, it was the corporation of the 'burghers as such' who in this quality were subject to a law to which only they had access and which was only shared by them.[12] Membership in the corporation of the city was an original state of social embeddedness: it was neither derived from membership in a prior social community, nor did it content itself with the requirement of a merely physical affiliation to a particular place of settlement; it was a status based on *political* association which had its own meaning and relevance in that it ultimately created an autonomous sphere of social interaction, the public sphere.

However, despite the origin of the concept of citizenship in the Greek *polis*, its relevance has not been restricted to the sphere of politics. Throughout ancient Greek history, citizenship was an institution which created distinctions which referred to almost all aspects of social life, not just to the area of 'politics' in the narrow sense of this term, that is, to the realm of public honour and the participation in the rule of the city. It was significant for the kind of military service and of religious worshipping that would be done by the members of the *polis*; it was of consequence for the nature of their occupation and for their legal capacity to own land; and it was relevant to sexual conduct.[13] Even less can we conceive of the *modern* concept of citizenship as a homogeneous and unvarying institution over the last three centuries and throughout the societies in which citizenship gained importance. The familiar civic-republican notion of 'active and virtuous participation' in the affairs of the community tends to be attributed to the ancient world, and its renaissance played, for instance, a prominent role in the reasoning of the founding fathers of the American constitution.[14] This notion, however, embodied only one meaning among several others which emerged in the modern age. For instance, according to recent research the British concept of citizenship never presupposed or entailed a 'deep concept of nationhood', nor did it 'embody notions of joint belonging, but was to be a purely personal and hierarchical one', namely subjecthood in the sense of mutual allegiance and protection to the Crown.[15]

Thus, both in the historical dimension and in contemporary debates, the scope of meanings covers extremely antagonistic understandings. They reach, for example, from a notion of citizenship which includes the right of the head of the family to participate in the governance within the hierarchical order of the premodern '*societas civilis sive politica*'[16] to the opposite concept according to which citizenship entails the passive status of a subject under an absolutist regime.[17] After the French Revolution, which established the principle of equal national citizenship in France,[18] this idea of an individual's status of political equality in a centralised state was challenged by the opposite claim that the idea of citizenship embodies membership in a rich diversity of predominantly local associations.[19] As a consequence, according to this latter understanding, citizenship does not primarily mean active political participation, but rather 'taking part in neighbourhood watch schemes, caring for dependents, running schools and housing estates, exercising consumer rights...'.[20] Or, to mention another contrasting couple, some, following the famous claim of T. H. Marshall, regard citizenship as an instrument for modifying the structure of class inequality,[21] while others tend to consider it a discursive instrument for a mere rhetoric of equality, without contributing to changing the reality of inequality in capitalist societies.[22] Finally, it may be mentioned that in the view of some theorists, citizenship is viewed as an instrument of political homogenization 'from above',[23] whereas others emphasise its usage as an instrument of political, social and economic struggle 'from below'.[24]

The broad scope of potential functions and meanings of the concept of citizenship reveals – very much like the notions of 'civil society' or *bürgerliche Gesellschaft* inherently connected with it[25] – that it contains at one and the same time economic, sociological, cultural and legal elements which in their entirety constitute the particular connotation of the concept. Depending on which of these dimensions is prevalent at different times and in different societies, the idea of citizenship will change considerably. A comprehensive historical account would certainly produce a plethora of meanings. Clearly the concept of citizenship is deeply rooted in the distinct political cultures of the various European countries. Yet there is an element of the concept of citizenship which must not be overshadowed by the colourful variety of meanings it has adopted during its long and wandering history. This is its inherent rationale of loosening the bonds which tie a person who becomes a citizen to the traditions and the 'parochialism' of his or her pre-political (in most cases culturally defined) community. This is why membership in the *polity* is an indispensable element of any concept of citizenship. The associates of a polity need not be tied together through pre-political bonds in order to be acknowledged as competent members of the society; if and when they are citizens they need not be 'brothers' in order that relations of trust and cooperation can prevail in the society. The political status of citizenship outshines, so to speak, the pre- and extra-political properties of individuals which may be significant in the non-political spheres of the society.

Even so, the concept of citizenship varies considerably among the various member states of the EU; this makes it difficult to develop a genuinely 'European' notion of citizenship, one that can be shared by all member states without abandoning their particular political and cultural traditions. Consequently, Turner has suggested a broad definition according to which citizenship should be understood as 'that set of practices (juridical, political, economic and cultural) which define a person as a competent member of society, and which as a consequence, shape the flow of resources to persons and to social groups'.[26] Citizenship in this sense would hardly be distinguishable from the legal status of any person who is at least physically part of the society and who, by this very reason, enjoys the basic human rights which in a democratic society are dispensed to every human being. The question is, then, whether we can identify properties of a particularly European status of citizenship?

The European character of citizenship: The abolition of the 'disabilities of alienage in the other states'

The most obvious property of a European status of citizenship is its non-national character. I use the term non-national to convey sub- and supranational, trans- and international, and a cosmopolitan universe in which the concept of citizenship may well be meaningful. After all, the etymology of cosmo*politan* points to the ancient Greek world of the *polis* and its members, the *politeis*. On the other hand, contrary to our intuition which is largely shaped by the French model of citizenship – 'equal national citizenship'[27] – there is also a rich tradition where citizenship embodies 'a mere local "municipal" standing to which various minor rights and obligations attached', while 'subjecthood it seemed was the "superior political status"'.[28] Still, the prevailing understanding tends to associate the concept of citizenship with the idea of the nation, or, for that matter, of the nation-state. In other words, citizenship is regarded as a status of membership in the polity which is conceived as a solidaristic community where the mutuality of burdens and benefits is based on the particularism of the nation. On a closer look at the manifold concepts of citizenship which surface in the various European countries, we are likely to discover that most of them more or less explicitly presuppose an exclusive community which defines its distinction between 'ins' and 'outs' in terms of citizenship.

However, it is doubtful whether the understanding of the concepts of nation and nation-state as delineating devices which create clear-cut in/out distinctions grasps their essential properties as they have developed in our times. It seems to overlook the experience that from the very beginning of political modernity there has been a political universe of states and, after the French Revolution, of nation-states; they have not 'existed in isolation as bounded geographical totalities, and they are better thought of as multiple overlapping networks of interaction'.[29] Of course, there is no denying that the institutions and the basic concepts in the field of political reasoning are still largely influenced by the robust presence of the nation-state. But the modern nation-state is no longer and has probably never been as impermeable as the ideal-type of closed statehood intimated. On the level of the member states of the EU the in/out division with respect to their nationals has largely blurred. This is due to the gradual transformation of the EU and its member states into a loosely coupled political multi-tier system. This is evidenced in the changes – not immediately noticeable – in the character of the addressees of the rights of member states' citizens.

Since most Community law is implemented by the administrative agencies of the member states rather than by distinct Union agencies, the Union citizen who exercises his or her 'European' rights is mostly confronted with agencies of (national) member states. The European character of the rights conferred by the Community is rarely visible. Individuals who live in their native country will be confronted with their national government agencies, and whether they enforce national or Community law will hardly be a matter of interest to them. It is certainly more important for the citizens of member states who live in a member state other than their home state. By conventional standards they are aliens. Hence, Union citizenship could make a difference to them. True, the rights stipulated or referred to in Articles 8 to 8e of the EC Treaty are not impressively numerous and cover only a small facet of the daily life of a person who lives in a member state other than their country of origin. Their status as an alien is likely to prevail over their alleged status as a fellow citizen of the European Community.

One objective of Union citizenship which goes beyond the merely symbolic could ultimately consist in making the citizens feel 'at home', as it were, in a foreign country. At least it should be possible to remove 'from the citizens of each state the disabilities of alienage in the other States'.[30] This judgement was made with reference to Article 4, section 2 of the US Constitution, which stipulates that 'the citizens of each State shall be entitled to all privileges and immunities of citizens in the several States'. In another opinion issued more than a hundred years later, the US Supreme Court ruled that 'the primary purpose of this clause ... was to help fuse into one nation a collection of independent sovereign states.'[31] A similar ruling could be found in Article 3 of the constitution of the newly created German Reich of 1871.

In the American case, the establishment of national citizenship served the goal to render the union the protector of individual rights which were jeopardised by the member states. The federal state had to protect the freedmen against the likely infringement of their rights particularly through the former slaveholder states; national citizenship became a harbour of safety against interferences by the states. Obviously this interpretation does not apply to the establishment of Union citizenship in the EC Treaty, because individual rights are essentially well protected within the constitutional systems of the member states. Moreover, the priority of Union law over member state law is secured by the aforementioned principle of supremacy of Community law over the law of the member states.[32] Hence the structural significance of the rights of the citizens of the Union consists basically in the creation of a sociolegal sphere of the Union which embodies the goal of the Union to diminish, perhaps even to abolish the 'disabilities of alienage in the other States'. This sociopolitical domain has two facets. It includes not only those who settle in a member state other than their own, but the resident nationals of the member state as well. They have to cope with the fact that persons who used to be aliens have become their fellow citizens in one respect – in their quality as citizens of the Union – without becoming full members, that is, citizens in all respects of the daily life of the respective member state. What seems paradoxical at first glance would articulate the very particularity of the European

Union: Union citizenship is not so much a relation of the individual vis-à-vis Community institutions, but rather a particular sociolegal status vis-à-vis national member states, which have to learn how to cope with the fact that persons who are physically and socially their citizens are acquiring a kind of legal citizenship by means of European citizenship without being their nationals.[33]

'Alienage' will probably be the hallmark of citizenship of the Union, a kind of permanent and structural cognitive and emotional dissonance which, in contrast to the American case, is not likely to be levelled in a unitary national culture in the forseeable future. Of course, the most serious obstacle is the lack of a common European language. Thus, unlike in most federal states, Community citizenship is not likely to supersede national citizenship or to make it a status of minor importance frequently verging on mere irrelevance; rather, both statuses will coexist, representing two different principles of political organisation. While national citizenship uses territoriality as the basic means of integrating individuals into the society, the concept of citizenship of the Union presupposes a more abstract polity and membership of that polity has the main goal of integrating individuals into national societies who – by all standards of the traditional nation-states and their social structures – are aliens, or, as it was expressed in the *Proposals Towards a European Citizenship* submitted by the Spanish government in September 1990, 'privileged foreigners'. The Spanish government anticipated that taking the step towards Community citizenship 'will eliminate the negative effects presently accompanying the condition of foreigner for a citizen of a Member State in another Member State'.[34]

It remains to be seen whether the 'abolition of the disabilities of alienage', which may sometimes amount to the attempt to avoid a 'clash of political cultures', can be understood in terms of the distinction between *territorial federalism* and *personal federalism*.[35] In any case it seems safe to assume that the understanding of the meaning of citizenship of the Union will be shaped to a considerable extent by the prevailing concepts and the pertinent traditions of the member states, because it is the emerging dualism of national and Community citizenship which will finally determine the legal status of the European citizens.

It is possible that out of the dissonances resulting from the dualism between the more tangible national citizenship and the more abstract Community citizenship, serious conflicts may arise which ultimately might thwart the goal of integration. The removal of 'the disabilities of alienage' requires the removal of 'alienage', and this in turn requires the mutual understanding of what the involved parties – migrating individuals originating in the various member states, and the hosting member states and their citizens themselves – assume when they make claim to or have to accept, respectively, the institution of Union citizenship.

There is a further possible effect of European citizenship. The right of the citizens of the member states to reside in any of the member states and to engage in economic, social, cultural, sporting and even, though in a limited way, political activities irrespective of the symbolic boundaries of the nation-states (the physical, that is territorial, boundaries have been abolished anyway) open the field to a multiplicity of social roles and loyalties which may lower the dominant role of national loyalty to just one among a bundle of social obligations. In the last instance this may entail the disconnection of three elements which have been considered inseparable for almost two centuries: nationality (represented by the passport), citizenship, and national identity.[36]

In this sense, European citizenship is more an amplified bundle of options within a physically broadened and functionally more differentiated space than a definitive legal status. Whereas in the traditional nation-state framework a citizen had to be a national, in the last instance European citizenship could even be conferred on individuals who do not possess the nationality of any of the member states. European citizenship would open the symbolic space for social activities which finally could lead to a European *societas civilis sive politica*, that is, a civil society beyond the physical boundaries of the nation-states. What is constitutive of this kind of citizenship is that, in contrast to national citizenship, it does not refer to a centralised and homogeneous sphere of political power. Thus European citizenship can be regarded as a step towards a new concept of politics inside and simultaneously beyond the framework of the traditional notion of politics defined by the nation-state.

Admittedly, it is a small step. It does not imply what Andrew Linklater in his chapter 6 above expected from the post-Westphalian era, namely 'forms of political community which are committed to realizing the Kantian ideal of a universal kingdom of ends'. It is true that, as Linklater states, 'various forces are loosening the grip of the nation-state so that a wider range of political identities and authorities can unfold'. But what the institution of EU citizenship has really brought about is the abolition of the nation-state's *monopoly* on individuals' affiliation to a polity, not of its predominant role in their lives as citizens of a political community. Among the three goods which are basically the object of political struggle – resources, rights and recognition – only recognition has found an institutional expression relatively independent of the nation-state. The idea of human rights embodies the idea of an individual's recognition as a bearer of human dignity and as a person worthy of some basic rights irrespective of his or her affiliation to a nation-state. Contrariwise, the just distribution of resources and the allocation of rights which are able to fulfil the basic needs of individuals are, even in the European Union, still to a large extent provided by the member states. Although the list of rights associated with the status of Union citizenship has been extended through the Maastricht Treaty, the basic needs and interests of individuals – ranging from the interest in a job to the provision of social and cultural services – are still mainly expected to be fulfilled by the nation-states. It is no accident that Union citizenship is a derivative of the status of nationality within one of the member states, not the other way round. (Here it is worth mentioning that Swiss nationality and citizenship is even derived from membership in a municipality; thus local communities decide about the distribution of a national good.)

Thus at present the duality of national and Union citizenships clearly displays the predominance of the former over the latter. But this is not a definitive state of affairs. Future political developments may enrich the status of Union citizenship such as to make it more attractive than at least some of the nation-state citizenships. The authors of the Treaty's rules about citizenship may have envisaged such a development because in Article 8d, para. 4 they devised an institutional tool which makes it possible to 'strengthen or to add to the rights' of citizenship outside the regular and burdensome amendment procedure. Moreover, it is conceivable that in the foreseeable future the adaptation of the member states' migration and asylum policies may entail the Community's competence to confer the status of Union citizenship on individuals who reside legally within its territory without possessing the nationality of any of its member states. The implication – the disconnection of citizenship from a nation-state's nationality – could be the starting-point for a general policy to grant individuals basic rights irrespective of their nationality. From different perspectives this idea has been suggested in this volume by Andrew Linklater, David Beetham and Pierre Hassner. Up to now the nation-states in the EU have only slightly loosened their grip on the definition of citizenship; but the EC has established the bold idea to disconnect nationality from citizenship, and this idea may well evolve to a general principle which ultimately transforms the ideal of cosmopolitan citizenship into a reality.

Notes

1. T. C. Hartley, *The Foundations of European Community Law*, 3rd edn, Oxford, Clarendon Press, 1994, pp. 195ff., 234ff.

2. See, e.g., E. Grabitz, *Europäisches Bürgerrecht zwischen Marktbürgerschaft und Staatsbürgerschaft*, Cologne, Europa Union Verlag, 1970; R. Plender, 'An Incipient Form of European Citizenship', in F. G. Jacobs (ed.), *European Law and the Individual*, New York, North Holland, 1976, pp. 39–53; A. Durand, 'European citizenship', *European Law Review*, 1979, vol. 4, pp. 3–14; G. van den Berghe, *Political Rights for European Citizens*, Aldershot, Gower, 1982; A. Evans, 'European citizenship: a novel concept in EEC law', *American Journal of Comparative Law*, vol. 34, no. 4, 1984, pp. 679–715; S. Magiera, 'Die Europäische Gemeinschaft auf dem Wege zu einem Europa der Bürger', *Die Öffentliche Verwaltung*, 1987, vo. 40, pp. 221–231.

3. R. Corbett, *The Treaty of Maastricht. From Conception to Ratification: A comprehensive reference guide*, Harlow, Longman, 1993, p. 52.

4. D. Curtin, 'The constitutional structure of the Union: a Europe of bits and pieces', *Common Market Law Review*, 1993, vol. 30, pp. 17–69 [67].

5. E. Meehan, *Citizenship and the European Community*, London, Sage, 1993, pp. 16ff.

6. T. Oppermann, *Europarecht*, Munich, Beck, 1991, pp. 563ff.

7. M. Koessler, '"Subject", "citizen", "national" and "permanent allegiance"', *Yale Law Journal*, 1946, vol. 56, pp. 58–76; S. Wiessner, *Die Funktion der Staatsangehörigkeit. Eine historisch-rechtsvergleichende Analyse unter besonderer Berücksichtigung der Rechtsordnung der USA, der USSR und*

der Bundesrepublik Deutschland, Tübingen, Attempo Verlag, 1989, pp. 1ff.; B. Manville, *The Origins of Citizenship in Ancient Athens*, Princeton, Princeton University Press, 1990; P. Riesenberg, *Citizenship in the Western Tradition: Plato to Rousseau*, Chapel Hill, University of North Carolina Press, 1992; H. van Gunsteren, 'Four conceptions of citizenship', in B. van Steenbergen (ed.), *The Condition of Citizenship*, London, Sage, 1994, pp. 36–48.

8. M. Weber, *Economy and Society: An outline of interpretive sociology*, Berkeley, University of California Press, 1964, p. 946.

9. Riesenberg, *Citizenship in the Western Tradition*, pp. 20ff.

10. Weber, *Economy and Society*, pp. 936ff.

11. *Ibid.*, pp. 947ff.

12. *Ibid.*, p. 944.

13. Riesenberg, *Citizenship in the Western Tradition*, pp. 28ff.

14. T. Pangle, 'Civic virtue: the Founders' conception and the traditional conception', in G. C. Bryner and N. B. Reynolds (eds), *Constitutionalism and Rights*, Provo, Utah, Brigham University Press, 1987, pp. 105–140.

15. M. Everson, 'Subjecthood, Citizenship and Allegiance: Cracks in the nation', unpublished paper, Zentrum für Europäische Rechtspolitik, Bremen, 1996, p. 7.

16. M. Riedel, 'Bürger, Staatsbürger, Bürgertum', in O. Brunner, with W. Conze and R. Koselleck (eds), *Geschichtliche Grundbegriffe. Historisches Lexikon zur politisch-sozialen Sprache in Deutschland*, vol. 1, Stuttgart, Klett-Cotta, 1972, pp. 672–725 [676ff.].

17. M. Stolleis, 'Untertan – Bürger – Staatsbürger. Bemerkungen zur juristischen Terminologie im späten 18. Jahrhundert', in R. Vierhaus (ed.), *Bürger und Bürgerlichkeit im Zeitalter der Aufklärung*, Heidelberg, Schneider, 1981, pp. 65–99; Riesenberg, *Citizenship in the Western Tradition*, pp. 203ff.

18. G. H. Sabine, 'The two democratic traditions', *Philosophical Review*, 1952, vol. 61, pp. 451–474 [462].

19. B. S. Turner, 'Outline of a Theory of Citizenship', in C. Mouffe (ed.), *Dimensions of Radical Democracy: Pluralism, citizenship, community*, London, Verso, 1992, pp. 33–62 [54].

20. Meehan, *Citizenship and the European Community*, p. 30.

21. T. H. Marshall, *Class, Citizenship, and Social Development*, New York, Doubleday, 1964; J. M. Barbalet, 'Citizenship, Class Inequality and Resentment', in B. S. Turner (ed.), *Citizenship and Social Theory*, London, Sage, 1993, pp. 36–56.

22. B. Hindess, 'Citizenship in the Modern West', in Turner, *Citizenship and Social Theory*, pp. 19–35.

23. M. Mann, 'Ruling class strategies and citizenship', *Sociology*, 1987, vol. 21, pp. 339–354.

24. Turner, 'Outline of a Theory of Citizenship', pp. 38f.

25. R. Koselleck and K. Schreiner, 'Von der alteuropäischen zur neuzeitlichen Bürgerschaft. Ihr politisch-sozialer Wandel im Medium von Begriffs-, Wirkungs- und Rezeptionsgeschichten', in R. Koselleck and K. Schreiner (eds), *Bürgerschaft. Rezeption und Innovation der Begrifflichkeit vom Hohen Mittelalter bis ins 19. Jahrhundert*, Stuttgart, Klett-Cotta, 1994, pp. 11–39 [p. 13].

26. B. S. Turner, 'Contemporary Problems in the Theory of Citizenship', in Turner, *Citizenship and Social Theory*, p. 2; for a more restricted concept of citizenship see D. Zolo, 'Democratic Citizenship in a Post-Communist Era', in D. Held (ed.), *Prospects for Democracy: North, South, East, West*, Cambridge, Polity Press, 1993, pp. 254–68.

27. Sabine, 'The two democratic traditions'.

28. Everson, 'Subjecthood, Citizenship and Allegiance', p. 10.

29. D. Held, *Democracy and the Global Order: From the modern state to cosmopolitan governance*, Cambridge, Polity Press, 1995, p. 225.

30. US Supreme Court, *Case Paul v Virginia*, 75 US 168, 180 (1869).

31. US Supreme Court, *Case Toomer v Witsell*, 334 US 385, 395 (1948); see L. H. Tribe, *American Constitutional Law*, 2nd edn, Mineola, Foundation Press, 1988, pp. 528ff., 548ff.

32. J. H. H. Weiler, 'The transformation of Europe', *Yale Law Journal*, 1991, vol. 100, pp. 2403–2483 [2424].

33. See the brief remarks in J. H. H. Weiler, 'Fin-de-siècle Europe', in R. Dehousse (ed.), *Europe after Maastricht: An ever closer union?*, Munich, Beck, 1994, pp. 203–216 [210].

34. Document in Corbett, *The Treaty of Maastricht*, pp. 156ff.

35. See T. Fleiner and L. R. Basta, 'Federalism, Federal States and Decentralization', in L. R. Basta and T. Fleiner (eds), *Federalism and Multiethnic States: The Case of Switzerland*, Fribourg, Institute of Federalism, 1996, pp. 1–40.

36. See H. Kleger, 'Transnationale Staatsbürgerschaft: Zur Arbeit an einem europäischen Bürgerstatus', in R. Erne *et al.* (eds), *Transnationale Demokratie. Impulse für ein demokratisch verfasstes Europa*, Zurich, Realotopia, 1995, pp. 34–59; U. K. Preuß, 'Problems of a concept of European citizenship', *European Law Journal*, 1995, vol. 1, pp. 267–281.

Chapter Eighteen

The Democratic Welfare State in an Integrating Europe[*]

Claus Offe

Everywhere, one reads the same thing: the European Union is a political construct *sui generis* – no (longer) a confederation, not (yet) a federal state, but a 'would-be polity'. It is an accurate but not very useful observation. If this definition 'by process of elimination' were to have real informative value, it would include a clear accounting of the structural differences that set the EU apart from the more familiar form of political rule, the nation-state. We would then have a tool with which to assess the EU's functional capabilities, and in particular, its ability to organise society's exercise of power over itself that was as legitimate and efficient as that for the nation-state.

Accordingly, the first part of this chapter, like Greven's, will be devoted to a consideration of how the internal relations of the EU contrast with those of a nation-state republic.[1] This is followed in the second part by a review of the practical, political motives that have driven the process of integration thus far, which in turn are shaped by that process. The aim here is an assessment of the EU's political efficiency. The chapter concludes with an examination of the prospects for the development of a mode of European integration that enhances the EU's democratic legitimacy. Special attention is paid to the sceptical assumption that, on the way to 'Europe', political resources (understood as society's ability to exercise control over its own quality and development through the means of governance) will be lost rather than gained.

The internal relations of a nation-state republic

Constitutional states differ from authoritarian and absolutist states in that political power in the former is not only exercised through law, but also established and limited, beforehand, by way of a special law – namely, the constitution. Thus, in a constitutional state, the body through which the state exercises its power is not just an empirical fact or a factual system of interactions, but also a formal, judicial fact vested with normative validity. Before the governing agency becomes active and expresses itself in concrete acts, it is already present as a normatively constituted

---

[*]   'The Democratic Welfare State in an Integrating Europe', in M. T. Greven, and L. W. Pauly (eds), *Democracy Beyond the State? The European dilemma and the emerging global order*, Boston Rowman and Littlefield, 2000, pp. 63–89.

fact, as something that 'should be' – as a normative description of the governing body's method of operation, its jurisdiction, and the limitations thereon.

The act of establishing a constitution not only sets the modalities and limits of the (future) use of power but also reflects upon the author of the constitution. The establishment of the constitution must be conceived as an act in which the constituent member, the 'people', forms itself and at the same time submits itself to the constitution.

> The full sense of the term constitution implies ... that it can be traced back to an act which the citizenry puts into place, or which is at least attributed to them, and in which they provide themselves with the political ability to take action.[2]

In this respect, the act of establishing a constitution implies not only that a legal, ordered, and limited authority of the state exists but also that a political community of the 'people' exists. This political community is created when a 'people' submits itself to a political order of its own invention, in the process gaining an identity both within itself and toward the outside world.

Thus, in the act of establishing a constitution, the 'people' ceases to be a mere ethnic fact – that is, a multitude of persons made distinct through their origin and common culture – and starts to become a *demos,* understood as the subject-object of a deliberately founded governing body. And yet, between '*ethnos*' (as the embodiment of an exclusive linguistic, religious, cultural community of origin) and '*demos*' (as the ethnically neutralised instance of the legitimation of state power), there is also continuity. Working as a catalyst,

> the national self-image builds the cultural context in which subjects could become politically active citizens. It is only the sense of belonging to a 'nation' that establishes an interrelation of solidarity between persons who up to that point had been strangers to one another. ... The nation or the spirit of the people ... supplies the judicially constituted state with a cultural substratum.[3]

The foundation of a political community by an act of will is not a chance occurrence. Rather, it is the product of dispositions that Max Weber has characterised as 'a belief in commonality' *(Gemeinsamkeits-glauben)* or 'feelings of belonging to a community' *(Gemeinsamkeitsge-filhle)*; these dispositions 'are nothing definite and can be fed by very different sources'.[4] Despite the vagueness with which Weber outlines this empirical anchor of an act of will imposing set duties, it seems clear that in the case of the nation-state, the things believed or felt to be in common would be of a spatial or temporal nature. In other words, the self-recognition of a people as a *demos* has an empirical frame of reference, which encompasses a (usually undivided) territory settled together and a history understood as 'concerning all of us'. It is a fund of positive and negative traditions and historical protagonists, whose appropriation makes up the factual 'particularity' of those who reciprocally recognise each other in normative terms as belonging to the same *demos*. Above all, the self-recognition of a people as a *demos* is grounded in the nation's history, which functions as a reference point for the establishment of a constitution in both positive (as a source of examples and traditions) and negative ways (as is often the case with post-totalitarian constitutions).

The historical-geographical grounding of the societal and governmental contract, which is completed *uno acto* with the establishment of the constitution, not only is a contingent condition for the formation of this contract but also may be a necessary condition for its continued existence. The importance of the historical or temporal aspect is demonstrated by settler societies such as the United States, where citizens' explicit memory of their common descent from far-flung ancestors becomes a basis for strengthening the willingness to practice interethnic tolerance, or by societies like Germany, where moral catastrophes remembered as part of a national history provide the foundation for the concretisation of a constitutional consensus based on civil rights.

The geographic or spatial dimension of the determination of a political community centres on the role that well-established (that is, recognised by both sides) borders play in delineating the state's territory. National borders help integrate the people into the state's constitutional political order by minimising conflicts over the area in which the order of law is valid as it pertains to individuals; that is, they guard against the emergence of a legal grey zone on the periphery, or a political claim to represent external ethnic minorities. Set territorial borders are also a reference point for the formation of a 'people', as the crisis in southeastern Europe demonstrates. They serve this function by limiting the authority of the state to its spatially determined 'area of validity' and preventing it from taking on a political 'obligation to care for the welfare of persons' who may be 'our' ethnic 'brothers and sisters', but are not by virtue of this also our 'cocitizens'. Territorial borders are also essential for maintaining public welfare within states. They permit the political community to ensure that scarce resources are conserved for internal use and to stave off the intrusion of unwelcome outside influences. Borders are not barriers, but rather filters or membranes, which can be selectively opened from within – for example, to stimulate exports or control the flow of migration. They are the 'decision points' at which the balance of positive and negative influx and outflux can be registered and controlled.[5]

Thus, the separate recognition of a common history and its meaning, and the shared recognition of a territory and its inhabitants, are together the indispensable catalysts for a political community coming into being. Conversely, sharp 'historical-political' polarisation is just as decisive a barrier on the way to the formation of a political community (or 'republic') as is discrimination against internal minorities or care for the welfare of people outside the borders of the political community.

Geography and history are not, however, the end of the story. The political community of a *demos* is also defined by a third dimension – a duly constituted authority of state.[6] This authority manifests itself by imposing duties on citizens within the limits of basic rights and demanding the fulfilment of these duties within the framework of the state's monopoly on the legitimate use of force. In addition to the obligation to obey the law generally, there are most commonly three such civic duties: compulsory school attendance, compulsory military service (or the duty of military personnel to accept risks to life and limb caused by politics), and the obligation to pay taxes. Civic duties entail a loss of freedom for the individual, who must yield this freedom without the certainty of earning any benefit in return. In this respect, civic duties are informed by a principle similar to that of nonaffectation from budgetary law – that is, fulfilling one's duties does not create any right to a corresponding service. Rather, it is an offering 'to all', the burden of which, under certain circumstances, is made lighter by the certainty that 'all others' are likewise disposed toward fulfilling their duties, or can be forced to do so.

The double restriction civic duties place on freedom of action is illustrated by comparing them with a simple purchase. Purchases are the result of a two-tiered decision, made freely. In the first step, the buyer decides how much money to spend (instead of, say, giving it away or saving it); in the second step, the buyer decides which to obtain for the money spent. With civic duties, both of these freedoms are annulled. For example, schoolgoers (legally represented by their parents) typically have neither the freedom to refuse to attend school nor the right to determine the curriculum. Instead, curricula – like state budgetary expenditures or military defence obligations – are decided upon politically by the institutions and officeholders of the three areas of state authority entrusted with those responsibilities. The individual citizen is thereby integrated into a compulsory association of cultural, defence, national budgetary, and legal communities. Although all citizens ultimately determine the content and purpose of this association through the processes of democratic legitimation and political accountability, they perform this function not as individuals but as constituent members of a political community.

This account of civic duties is not intended to provide fodder for neo-liberal attacks on the 'vampire state', but rather to introduce two propositions. Vertically, the efficacy of a state's actions requires that citizens fulfil their duties automatically, or at least that the state be able to secure their compliance with minimal use of its resources. That which is expected of the individual citizen is nothing less than the feat of taking part 'obediently' in an organisation of rule that compels one to be a member of a cultural, economic, and defence community at the cost of some freedom, some possessions, and, in some cases, one's life. Horizontally, the fulfilment of civic duties depends upon every 'duty-bound' citizen thinking of the collective author of normative duties (that is, the state, which is established by a democratic political process) and thus of 'all other citizens' (who participated in that process) as capable of sufficient reason and goodwill to accept these duties as legitimate and binding.

In order for a citizen to recognize a duty as legitimate and binding and thus to fulfil it 'voluntarily', rather than as a calculated avoidance of punishment or in deference to tradition, that person must hold two robust and resilient core beliefs about 'everyone else'. First, the citizen must have enough faith in the integrity of the other citizens that there is no perceived reason not to perform those civic duties; there is an assumption that all others will fulfil the same duties. Second, a citizen must believe that individual compliance is important even when it does not bring any direct personal benefit but rather redounds to the advantage of others, whose welfare is included in 'external' preferences. The first of these beliefs is passive and can be defined as *trust* (or the absence of fear). It can be strengthened through a constitutional and legal order, which, in guaranteeing basic rights, limits the power of the collective to make decisions affecting the individual, but it cannot be established this way. The second is an active belief and is called *solidarity* (or the absence of indifference); it, too, cannot be forced on people formally, but rather merely encouraged through state social services and the redistribution of wealth.[7]

The horizontal phenomena of trust and solidarity are preconditions for the 'vertical' phenomenon of the establishment and continued existence of state authority, manifested in effectively ensuring the performance of civic duties. In simple terms, this means that before citizens can recognise the authority of the state, they must first mutually recognise each other as being motivated by trust and solidarity. It is true that the process through which this mutual recognition develops has often been a confrontational and violent one, but until it occurs the authority of the state is uncertain. It is, moreover, precisely when this abstract but resilient trust in 'everyone else' as the collective coauthor of the obligating norms is undermined, or when citizens' active interest in each other's well-being is successfully discredited, that liberal notions about curtailing the scope of state authority flourish. Trust in one's fellow citizens provides the cognitive and moral foundations for *democracy,* the risks of which no one would reasonably accept otherwise.[8] The solidarity citizens feel toward one another, or to which they allow themselves to be obligated through their representative institutions, is also the moral basis of the *welfare state.* Thus, both democracy and the welfare state are fundamentally dependent upon the prior existence of binding motives, which in turn are tied to the form of political integration found in the nation-state.

The special ability to place citizens under obligation, which arises from their affiliation with a national political community, is, in itself, nothing mysterious. Belonging to a 'people' is essentially a *status* right. This right can be conferred upon someone (through naturalisation), but it cannot be obtained contractually (say, through purchase) – just as children do not become family members through contracts (except in the case of adoption). Because nationality is not contingent upon a contract, it is a remarkably 'fixed' status. Unlike companies or even states, nations are a form of societal organisation that can neither be 'founded' nor go into liquidation. Their origin loses itself in the mist of the past (which is also the birthplace of founding myths), and they are perceived to exist 'forever'.

For those who belong to the special social construct 'nation' (to which, in this respect, only the social group 'family' corresponds), the defining features of membership – affiliation as a status right and the fiction of permanence – make it relatively easy to engage in risky interactions such as a demonstration of trust or solidarity. Expressions of trust are made safer by the common national culture, the improbability of migration, and the ability to impose sanctions in cases of defection. Demonstrations of solidarity are less risky because the exchange relation is understood as temporally unlimited; the duties each citizen performs need not be repaid directly to that citizen, but rather can be passed down from one generation to the next in a never-ending chain. Following the conceptual model of the generational contract in social retirement insurance and the principle of what Kenneth Boulding calls 'serial reciprocity', no member of a nation is ever in danger of being the 'last' one (and hence the 'dumb' one), who contributes without being able to claim the right to services in return. Like the family on the microlevel, the nation on the macrolevel constitutes an unusually favourable structural and interpretive framework for 'assurance games' – those interactions with cooperative solutions that reproduce themselves and for which functional equivalents are not easily located above or below that level.

The idea of a totality of persons, integrated through relations of trust and solidarity and extending beyond family and tribal affiliations, though not to the extent of being 'limitless', appears to be a necessary condition for democracy. The universe of citizens who achieve their collective self-recognition, whether by ascription or after such coercive acts as civil war, has its outer borders in the nation and its 'people'. The people, not as an ethnic affiliation by origin and culture, but as a political community, self-constituted in reference to history and territory and made distinct by a willingness to demonstrate trust and solidarity, is an indispensable conceptual building block for political analysis.[9] It is the social substratum of the polity, which produces a legally formalised constitutional order and strengthens that order through its ability to integrate.

Motives for surmounting the limits of the nation-state in Europe, and consequent dilemmas

Although the nation-state generates the relations of trust and solidarity upon which democracy and the welfare state depend, it is structurally a suboptimal formation. The nation-state is economically suboptimal because it restricts the mobility of consumer and capital goods at its borders, making it less efficient than a common market, which in theory provides for the unlimited internal exchange of all goods and services under uniform conditions. It is politically suboptimal because it tends to prioritise narrowly defined national interests over transnational interests, even to the point of accepting the collective harm of war. The rational solution would be to transfer political responsibilities from national to transnational governmental authorities, particularly in the areas of foreign affairs, security, law, and monetary policy. However, if this argument appears compelling on the surface, attempts to put it into practice quickly run up against a fundamental fact of social life: it can be perfectly rational for actors to choose noncooperative tactical moves that manifestly violate long-term, global-optimisation criteria if these moves maximise their utility under given 'local' opportunity and incentive structures. Actors will be particularly inclined to do this when they perceive that other actors, upon whose cooperation global success is dependent, are caught in the same dilemma. Global-rational solutions are impeded even further if there is an uneven distribution in either the cost or the expected profits of cooperation. Clearly, then, what is needed is a rational method of resolving conflicts between local and global efficiencies, or short-term and long-term efficiencies.

Because of the lack of clear normative-analytical standards, political science research on Europe has largely avoided identifying 'rational' ways to create regional institutions, and instead has limited itself to offering explanatory reconstructions of dilemmas and the paths actors have followed in attempting to overcome them. These paths are characterised by antithetical idealised concepts such as 'negative' versus 'positive' integration,[10] or 'contract' versus 'constitution'.[11] National governments are typically seen as responding to the common market programme and its neutralisation of their economic sovereignty by seeking to preserve their political sovereignty, yielding it only through voluntary and revocable contractual agreements. Without any formalisation of the players, themes, and processes, and in the absence of any authorisation from a central governmental power, an involuntary process of negotiation begins. This process pushes on at random, arrested or accelerated by changing environmental conditions and shaped by a functionalistic logic of emergent problems, 'spill-over' effects, problem solving, and consensus building.[12] The idea that consistently emerges, from both 'realist' and 'functional' interpretations of transnational processes of integration, is that the inter-dependencies between relevant governmental and nongovernmental protagonists are noted and cumulatively included in cooperative arrangements. This process, however, is not itself embedded in political institutions, nor is it politically steered.

The conceptual alternatives that dominate the social science debate on Europe are clearly divided and are indicated by the conceptual pairings of intergovernmental voluntarism versus 'neofederalism' or 'supranationalism'. The two alternatives refer to different dynamics of integration. 'Intergovernmental voluntarism' describes a functionalist dynamic driven by national and sectoral interests or contractual compromise, wherein progress is made through cooperative tactical moves that cumulatively fulfil emergent functional necessities. Neofederalism and supra-nationalism both refer to a dynamic that envisages the intentional establishment of a political order for all of Europe, oriented toward the fulfilment of shared values and standards – that is, a federalist state order. This latter perspective can be described as intentionalistic.[13] The difference between 'negative' and 'positive' integration corresponds to the distinction drawn between intergovernmental voluntarism and supra-nationalism. Negative integration is understood here as the elimination of tariff and other barriers to trade and capital mobility sanctioned by decision of the European Commission, and, when necessary, the European Court. Positive integration refers to the emergence of a uniform, EU-wide system for the regulation of economic, trade and social relations, and presupposes a corresponding development of political will in the Council of Ministers.

In a system of economically interdependent but politically independent nation-states, there are two principal problems of cooperation, which give rise to mutually exclusive solutions. The first problem occurs when national governments act unilaterally or intergovernmentally in a manner that threatens other players with negative externalities. Behaviour of this sort can be eliminated only by reducing the scope of the nation-state's discretionary authority. One way of achieving this would be through a higher-ranking, Euro-federal governing capacity, based on positive integration and the principle of subsidiarity, which had the power to limit the exercise of national sovereignty to 'internal affairs' – affairs whose regulation would not create negative externalities. Another approach would be to foster an understanding that a strong, formally composed, European executive is the only entity capable of counteracting the homogenising forces of the market. In both cases, however, a marked expansion of 'positive' integration is clearly required, not just in the areas of foreign, domestic, and judicial policy, but also for labour market and social policies.

This leads to the second problem of cooperation. Consent to a 'strong' governmental form arouses the opposite fear among a significant number of member states – namely, that a potent European 'governing capacity', based on majority decisions and not hamstrung by voluntary adherence, could render individual member states defenceless against the political agendas of the dominant players. The most typical scenario is one in which the national preference of the majority in individual member states is drowned out as a minority position within Europe. At the core of this fear is a sense of the impending loss of the democratic nation-state's autonomy in shaping its own will.[14] This leads to a rational preference for a negative form of integration, which maximises the political jurisdiction of the nation-state.

In assessing the relative merits of negative and positive integration, it is important to recognise that the former can be just as damaging to the socioeconomic order as the latter is to national autonomy. In the case of purely negative integration, the threat is to the social welfare system, which nation-states are able to maintain only by virtue of having control over their own labour market, social, monetary, and economic policies. In the case of purely positive integration, it is the nation-state's well-adjusted mechanisms for democratic legitimation that are imperilled; these mechanisms cannot be reproduced at the European level because Europe lacks the inner structures of a 'nation' as described above. The choice is thus between the plague of negative externalities caused by voluntarism and the cholera of political determination by European institutions, against whose claim to sovereignty nation-states perceive no democratic remedy. Rather than confront the implications of this choice directly, each national government imagines that it lives in the best of all possible worlds – one in which all other governments are bound by the chains of a European government, but in which it is free to make policy in harmony with national majority preferences.[15]

My thesis is that every provisional solution between the two extremes of full nation-state sovereignty and European supranationalism inevitably violates *both* key reference values in the contemporary period – the protection of the social welfare system and the severing of democratic legitimation. The present approach to European integration thus would appear to represent a descent down the ladder that T. H. Marshall proposed as a model for the process of European political modernisation.[16] The three rungs of this ladder are liberal rights, democratic rights, and social welfare rights, achieved cumulatively. The question is whether in Europe today the social welfare and democratic rungs are being passed in reverse, reducing Euro-citizens to the status of mere participants in a neoliberal marketplace.

The degree of integration achieved in Europe since the signing of the Treaty of Amsterdam in June 1997 bears out this thesis. Post-treaty Europe is effectively suspended between the intergovernmental and supranational models. On economic matters, the EU functions as a confederation of states. The member states are engaged in the creation of a unified, transnational realm through a contractual transfer of jurisdictions. This confederation of states joined by treaties, however, is not so much a legally irreversible entity as a practically irreversible one. The parties to the contract perceive no serious option of terminating it, for such a move would trigger built-in economic sanctions of a compelling deterrent value. This makes it difficult to speak unambiguously of intergovernmental *voluntarism.*

On the other hand, there can also be no talk of a perfected European federal state. That would require a constitution establishing a balance of legitimation such that European citizens exercised democratic control directly (and not through their national governments) over the representatives of European sovereignty (the Council, the Commission, and the Court). Instead, the nation-state remains an indispensable intermediary in European politics. Such European civic duties as exist can be executed only indirectly, through nation-state administrations. Actions can be taken on the European stage only on the basis of nation-state empowerment of European authorities. Legal orders ('directives') of the European Commission develop binding effectiveness (if they are not already limited to the status of 'recommendations') only after their adoption by national legislative bodies. The European executive does not have the capacity to levy taxes, implement defence measures, enact effective orders of law, or take charge of public education.[17] As for the EU's legislative wing, its two representative bodies, the European Parliament and the Council of Ministers, are hamstrung in their efforts to generate legally binding European civic duties by exceptionally rigid procedural rules. Even the so-called *acquis communitaire,* the massive store of norms of secondary European law, has limited binding effect. Members already opt out of regulations in the interests of a 'variable geometry'. Although this remains rare, the special provisions that are certain to accompany the EU's expansion eastward are likely to increase the scope for discretion in the future.

In short, Europe today is in a muddle. National governments are the bearers of democratic legitimacy, but the transfer of authority that has accompanied the implementation of the Single Market programme has reduced their power to shape the prospects and safeguard the interests of their national populations. More and more, this role is being played by the European Court and the Commission. However, those organs act largely in accordance with the logic of 'negative' integration because, without their own base of political legitimacy, they lack the mandate (and the resources, for that matter) to spearhead the development of new political initiatives. The European Council cannot transfer this mandate to the Commission and the Court, because its members, who act on behalf of national electorates and are responsible to these electorates, currently lack the trust or solidarity to furnish 'positive' integration programmes with a political and fiscal basis. Thus, there is a disjunction between the ability and the mandate to act; the former is already largely in the hands of European institutions, but the latter still resides with national governments. Together, these mirror-image deficits threaten to demolish both the democratic and the social welfare achievements of the modern European nation-state.

There are two alternatives for addressing the democratic deficit in Europe: a transfer of the ability to act (governing capacity) back to the nation-state, or a transfer forward of democratically backed mandates to European representatives of governmental power. The first alternative is often expressed by a call for 'subsidiarity' – for the preservation of domains in which the nation-state remains sovereign. The evidence to date, however, suggests that this avenue offers little real hope. No matter how determinedly they endeavour to preserve their autonomy, national governments increasingly find their hand forced by the economic and fiscal imperatives of the Single Market, which seems inexorably to sweep national institutional structures for the development of programmes of interest mediation (such as those of Rhenish capitalism) into the vortex of market-driven institutional arbitrage.

The second alternative – the transfer of legitimated mandates and resources for action to supranational authorities – confronts the following question: Can the Council and the Commission acquire a positive identity in the eyes of European citizens and become the object of demands and expectations for a truly European political agenda? The initial outlook on this score is not promising. There has been a sharp rise in the negative politicisation of European institutions since the beginning of the 1990s, owing largely to the strains the Single Market has placed on the institutional and regulatory-political *acquis nationale* established in European countries during the postwar period. This *acquis nationale* has consisted not only in the installation of strong liberal democracies but also in the introduction of a wide range of policies of government intervention, which collectively make up the modern democratic welfare state. These policies vary across nations, but generally include measures to promote employment and modernisation, social insurance agencies, tariff and political codetermination arrangements, and other market-limiting ('decommodifying') agreements. Praised as a vehicle for fostering cohesion and institutionalising class conflict during the Cold War period, they are now seen as creating locational disadvantages in the new dynamic created by the Single Market. Their survival is threatened by competitive deregulation, regressive taxation, and a rollback of redistributive measures. European institutions have become 'negatively' politicised in this process because they are perceived to have allowed this progressive dismantling of the democratic welfare state to proceed unchecked. In essence, the charge is that they have subjected the structures of the welfare state to an efficiency test without ensuring that equivalent institutional alternatives exist in the event that reregulation is deemed necessary.

As fears mount about, for example, the effects of monetary union on employment, social standards, and monetary stability, European citizens continue to look to their national governments for a response. European institutions are not yet seen as having a valuable role to play in the search for a framework that will ensure equitable relations between states, regions, and social classes. Part of the reason is a lack of vertical efficiency in European politics; European institutions simply do not have the ability – for example, the political and fiscal 'governing capacity' – to pursue such ambitious goals. But there is also a more serious horizontal deficiency. Europeans still think of themselves primarily in national terms; they have not yet developed the relations of trust and solidarity on the European level that would be necessary to underpin a stronger European governing capacity. Only when a more abstract and wider frame of reference for a truly European people has been adopted will the cultural and cognitive prerequisites for a positive politicisation of European institutions exist.

Today in Europe, a *pouvoir constitué,* limited in its ability to govern and weak in its legitimation, controls the scene without a corresponding *pouvoir constituant.* The only remedy for this situation is the development of a widespread predisposition toward a European internationalism. Ideally, European institutions themselves would help foster this horizontal dimension, but they can do so only as a political and cultural by-product of an increase in the vertical efficiency of European politics. The development of relations of trust and solidarity on the European level is contingent upon good governance, and this means that Europe's first priority must be to establish a legitimate, transparent, and effective European governmental authority that cannot be 'negatively' politicised as a form of supranational foreign rule. Five means of supplying the institutional protagonists of the EU with the legitimation and recognition necessary to cultivate a common frame of political reference at the level of the citizens have been identified in the literature.[18]

The most economistic approach to surmounting Europe's democratic deficit sees the legitimation problem as eventually resolving itself. This argument is premised on the technocratic belief that, by placing limits on its own authority, demonstrating knowledgeable competence, and ensuring the impartiality of its executive decisions, the Commission could earn itself sufficient political credit with the European public to make further formal legitimation unnecessary. In light of the increasingly negative politicisation of the EU and its agencies, however, it now seems indisputable that this strategy was sufficient, at best, for an initial phase of negative integration during which the work of the Commission could still be presented as a pure coordination game – that is, as a process with utility that was universal and even.[19]

The second approach, which dates back to 1979, calls for transforming the EU into a parliamentary system through direct elections to the European Parliament (EP). This proposal is as unworkable today as it was then, for several reasons. The EP's role remains limited relative to that of the Commission, and there are no truly pan-European parties (at most, these are now coordinated elements in their programme of national parties), no coordinated system of franchise throughout Europe, and, above all, no European public opinion connected by the media to train a critical eye on the activities of the EP. In its capacity as a legislative assembly, the EP competes as a kind of second chamber not only with the Council but also with the national parliaments. Its potential for political legitimation, as set out by the Treaty on European Union, remains rudimentary (despite its right), restricted in terms of scope and time to participate in decisions of the Commission.[20]

The third path to democratic legitimation focuses on the Council of Ministers. This approach is flawed, however, because the Council's members are the executives of the member states, not the representatives of a European legislature. Although the issues dealt with by the Council can be discussed and voted upon by national parliaments, the cognitive resources of those bodies are inferior to those of the Commission. The Commission simply 'knows' more about the conditions necessary for successful transnational coordination and consensus building in the Council, and this gives it principal influence over the Council.[21] A further problem with relying on the Council is that its activities, unlike those of national parliaments, are usually scrutinised only by groups whose interests are directly affected, rather than evaluated in terms of their impact on the broader European public.

The fourth option for strengthening the democratic legitimacy of the EU is the expansion of the practice of qualified majority voting to the Council of Ministers. By cancelling the veto rights of individual (or smaller groups of) member states, goes the argument, it will no longer be possible for a minority of states to halt the decision making process outright or to manipulate it by extortionary means. It is questionable, however, whether this proposal genuinely aims to enhance the legitimacy of the decision making process, or simply to increase its speed and effectiveness. One obvious concern is that 'the citizens of countries whose governments are outvoted have no reason to consider such decisions as having democratic legitimation'.[22]

The fifth and final possibility depends on strengthening the mechanisms of territorial representation (elections, parties, parliaments, governments), as well as those of functional representation through interorganisational negotiations or the investiture of existing organs with political representational functions. This latter strategy is predicated upon the existence of a system of (quasi-corporatism, with organisations representing the interests of employees, employers, financial institutions, agriculture, and so on, and whose protagonists would have the capacity to lobby European institutions and build responsible compromises. The problem is that no such system currently exists on the European level, nor is one likely to be created in the near future. Neither the Economic nor the Social Committee approaches these criteria, and, when they exist, the social partners (especially the unions) are not organisationally or politically equipped to play the same role on the European stage that they have played in the corporative nation-state.[23] Furthermore, those organisations that are in a position to play this role (chiefly the sectoral industrial organisations) generally see Euro-corporatism as inimical to their interests, which they believe are better served by the free functioning of the market.

The constraints on these five reforms to enhance the legitimacy of European institutions reinforces the claim that the EU presently lacks the qualities that would make for a political community expressed in the form of a state. The EU is today neither a unified organ of efficient governance nor one expressing the democratic will. As for the demand voiced by some today that republicanism must manage without the support of the nation-state and learn to stand on its own two feet, it must be countered that the environment conducive to such learning is missing.[24] Vertical and horizontal efficiency can only be improved simultaneously. Strengthening the ability of European institutions to govern is not conceivable without an expansion of their formal democratic basis of legitimation. The EU will become the focus of the democratic will of an informed European public opinion only when it appears as a unified organ of governance, and this will require that national publics yield ground on the issue of subsidiarity and give up their opting-out privileges in favour of greater participation in pan-European politics.

It is my personal contention that steps taken to surmount simultaneously the European governmental and democratic deficits must not be thought of according to the logic of the vegetative process of 'ever closer' integration – that is, as the result of automatic actions based on rational interests. In Streeck's terms, it 'should be obvious that [the politics of integration are] *not* driven by a logic of "spill-over" from international market integration to supranational state formation'.[25] The logic of seeking advantage is unsuitable as a vehicle for building a political community, because steps toward integration will always appear, at least in the short term, as costs (such as a loss of protection or a reduction in security) and thus will carry with them the temptation to withdraw or block the initiatives of others. Even if economic and monetary union, moreover, were to prove a positive-sum game, the anticipation of such a blessing would not engender any motivational thrust, for as Jacques Delors used to say, 'You do not fall in love with a common market'.[26] No, progress toward a unity of European intention and action will materialise only when national publics are presented with *normatively* convincing grounds for political integration – reasons they would find sufficiently compelling to warrant their acceptance of the (temporary) disadvantages caused by the integration of states, regions, sectors, and social classes.

Normative arguments for European integration

Having determined the need for a more intentionalistic paradigm for European integration, we must now examine whether there exists an adequate supporting repertoire of European social norms. These norms must be potentially binding and they must have the motivating power to support the establishment of a federal European organ of governmental rule beyond particularistic and short-term calculations (and eventually in opposition to them).[27] Our examination must also embrace the related question of whether there is such a thing as a European 'identity', a totality of binding and obligating traditions originating in European history, and unanimously accepted as valid by present-day Europeans as orienting and legitimating political action at the regional level. The outlook is bleak on both fronts.

Münkler has convincingly demonstrated that the term 'Europe' lacks positive content and fails to provide practical convergent points for orienting activity.[28] Rather, it is outward looking and more in the nature of a 'counter term'. Historically, Europe has defined itself as a community of protection against the Ottoman, Asian, and Soviet 'East'; as an internally divided colonial community of 'mother countries' in relation to the South; and, from time to time, as a culturally chauvinistic community of traditions set against the Anglo-Saxon 'West' and its civilisation. When one attempts to formulate a normatively substantive and nonidealistic definition of Europe as an entity in and of itself, however, the term immediately falls apart into groupings of nation-states, whose common history is remembered as one that divides more than it binds.[29]

The roots of these, at times, partially overlapping aggregates of Europe run very deep and impede the development of binding notions of European citizenship and pan-European social solidarity. Greven convincingly develops this observation in his chapter in this book. The truth is that Europeans generally do not view each other as possessing the status of people 'like ourselves'.[30] Conceptions of family resemblance (historically, economically, geographically, politically, or however substantiated) are typically reserved for selected 'neighbours' and generally are not extended to all Europeans. In reality, the term 'European' is more a descriptive social-geographic category than a politically instructive category for common reflection and for political will that could become a basis for self-characterisation. This has disturbing implications for European integration. As Delanty writes, 'European integration must recreate what exists on the level of the nation-state, but this is impossible because Europe is devoid of a cultural framework independent of the nation-state'.[31]

Clearly, there is a need for principles that could transform European unification into a hegemonic idea, independent of the balance sheet of positive and negative 'payoffs', but the search for such principles has been held back by the absence of a clear conceptual starting point. If peace, human rights, democracy, and economic prosperity and its equitable distribution are the genuine European reference values, then the Maastricht and Amsterdam treaties are hardly documents that could feed a European constitutional patriotism based on these values. In any case, the Commission lacks the jurisdiction, the will, and the financial resources to turn the EU into such a bastion of social justice.[32] As for EMU, the present focus of the integration process, it certainly does not furnish the moral and political motives for a political union of Europe. Instead, widespread fears about its impact on economic stability and unemployment have prompted a backlash, which makes it seem unlikely that a plebiscite on further integration would achieve a positive result.[33] European political elites have endeavoured to combat this negative view of closer economic integration by appealing to the symbolic-expressive and moral principles of European identity, but to little avail. 'The articulation of a symbolic discourse of Europeanness has ... had little impact (and even that has often been negative, notably in the anti-Muslim overtones of the idea of a 'Christian' Europe), and the institutions designed to embody it (e.g., European citizenship as created by the Maastricht Treaty, or even direct elections to the European Parliament) have been highly marginal.'[34]

There are also practical obstacles to the formulation of a strong normative argument in favour of European integration. Given the size of the EU today and the diversity of economies and cultures it encompasses, it may be inevitable that attempts to transcend national particularities and to achieve a symbolic-moral self-characterisation of 'Europe' lapse into abstraction.[35] And as fiscal austerity measures undermine the EU's capacity for structural, regional, and agricultural subvention, and eastward expansion admits new members who will be net recipients of EU funds, it seems probable that what little goodwill the European public currently does bear the project of European integration will evaporate.[36] This constellation of European values and nation-state interests is leading to the visible decay of the symbolic *gestalt* of Europe and of the political-moral demands that can be plausibly attached to the EU.[37]

In the worst-case scenario, some observers have suggested that democracy – the quintessential European principle – will be damaged rather than strengthened by political integration. 'The principle of democracy is validated in the member states; these, however, see their decision making powers on the wane. The decision making powers accrue to the European Community, where the principle of democracy is only weakly developed.'[38] The above discussion of strategies to enhance the legitimacy of the European institutions has made clear that institutional reform by itself is an inadequate response to this problem. As Scharpf succinctly points out, 'the democratic deficit cannot be reformed away'.[39] Grimm, like Greven, contends that the EU's democratic deficit is rooted in its multilingualism and the obstacle this raises to the formation of a European general public capable of holding political parties and legislative institutions accountable in accordance with the standards of western European democracy.[40] In the absence of a European 'people', the demand for accountability will have to be addressed within the framework of the nation-state. Since any attempt by the EU to approach a federal state in its structures and functions will weaken democratic principles, the EU's legal basis must remain grounded in a contract binding under international law, not in a European constitution.[41]

The conclusion seems inescapable. A repertoire of social norms capable of supporting a more intentionalistic paradigm of contemporary European integration simply does not exist. Moreover, interdependence and the division of labour will not automatically generate this trust and solidarity any more than social integration, in the sense of the convergence of social norms and cognitive orientations, will flow naturally from the integration of national markets. The horizon of the Single Market coincides in principle with that of a European political society, conceived as an undivided community of will. If this society is to be brought into being, a differently motivated process is required. Five possible guiding images to such a process of political socialisation are considered below.

Europe as guarantor of peace

The political integration of Europe is to be desired (and the attendant economic costs and loss of national sovereignty to be accepted) because this would represent a definitive surmounting of the rivalries between European nation-states that led to this century's most catastrophic military conflicts. In particular, it would ensure the integration into Europe of the country of origin of the two World Wars – namely, Germany – which is also the largest and richest EU member state, and which directly borders potentially threatened neighbouring countries. The attempt to cast Europe as a guarantor of peace is driven by the twin impulses of European fear of German dominance and German anxiety about this fear.[42] It is doubtful however, that fear is 'enough to drive European integration forward'.[43] The experiences of World War II and the Nazi terror are becoming distant memories, and the prospect of a military confrontation between the stable democracies of the EU is now highly unlikely. International guarantees make state borders in Europe effectively inviolable, and, in any case, states increasingly recognise that gaining access to others' resources is more easily achieved through such 'peaceful' means as trade and the movement of capital than through the use of military force.

Of course, the inviolability of existing borders is no guarantee against the more likely danger that separatist civil wars will be fought over part of a nation-state's territory, possibly with a view to establishing new borders. It is difficult, however, to see how the EU and related regional institutions could respond effectively to threats of this sort. On the contrary, the spectacular failure of European governments to take decisive action in Yugoslavia after 1991, and their reliance on American military power thereafter, discredited the vision of the EU as guarantor-authority of a European order of peace. In short, the EU reinforces a peace that is not threatened, but it is powerless in the face of the more immediate danger of subnational wars within individual EU member states and on the region's periphery.

Europe as bastion of freedom

Since 1989, the antithesis of freedom and human rights against the 'totalitarian' bloc of the Warsaw Pact and Comecon has no longer functioned as a negative political motivator for Europe. Instead, the sudden liberation of the countries of central and eastern Europe has created a long waiting list of aspiring EU members, whom the existing member states can no longer demonise for their violations of human rights and their restriction of political and civic freedoms. The EU, however, cannot refer to these candidates for membership in unambiguously positive terms. Whether because of poor economic and political conditions or because of the lack of a strong civil society tradition, many of them fall far short of the European standard, particularly with respect to the treatment of minorities, human rights policies, and restrictions on media liberties. In southeastern Europe and the Baltic states in particular, it is questionable that the principle of freedom truly presents itself as a positive, normatively unifying bond.[44]

Europe as singular synthesis of political values and principles

Europe can be idealised from an historical perspective as the place where the tension among the three components of political modernisation – namely, equal rights of citizens, sovereignty of the people, and social justice – was resolved in theory and, on occasion, in practice. The institutionalisation of that achievement has, however, given rise today to a contradiction. On the one hand, the synthesis has been quite limited in Europe itself, occurring only under the favourable conditions of postwar prosperity in the third quarter of the twentieth century. On the other hand, the normative intention to bring about that synthesis is no longer an exclusively European goal; it has in fact become one of the hegemonic political ideas in the world. At the same time, in Europe itself, it has been eroded in various ways. Today, it is Australia that holds the honour of having achieved the most successful and lasting synthesis of the three principles of political modernisation, while in Europe liberals warn of the danger of a 'new authoritarianism' that threatens civic freedoms, rights of political participation, and social security.[45]

Present-day Europe can claim a monopoly on neither the idea nor the reality of freedom, democracy, and the social welfare state. If a sharp external distinction can be made between Europe and the rest of the world, it is a practical rather than a normative one, arising from the use of trade and immigration policy to construct a 'fortress Europe'. The values and principles upon which modern Europe established itself have become, through a synthesis of the legacies of the Judeo-Christian, enlightened liberal and socialist traditions, global common property. They are therefore not suitable (at least not without regression to a cultural and confessional strategy of political confrontation) as the distinguishing *proprium* of Europe. Cliches such as that of a 'common intellectual heritage' do nothing to address the problem because they are rooted in the past, when this heritage was in fact unique to Europe. Europe today is a motley collection of languages, cultures, religious denominations, historical traditions, and nation-bound understandings of sovereignty; this heterogeneity will only become more pronounced as the EU expands eastward. One looks in vain for standards and principles that would be authoritative *everywhere* in Europe and *only* in Europe.

Europe as shared cultural space and way of life

It is often assumed that the expansion of the EU will make national borders less motivationally and cognitively relevant and lead to a greater homogeneity of lifestyles and consumption patterns. Transnational tourism, media broadcasts of sporting events, an opening of national-linguistic spheres of communication through the spread of foreign language skills, the dissemination across Europe of visual and acoustic (that is, nonverbal) art and entertainment programs, and the extensive media coverage of European themes – all are seen as ways of creating a shared cultural space and way of life. Eventually, a new cognitive framework may emerge, one that protects local and regional traditions while remaining firmly grounded in a positive conception of a unified Europe.

In the meantime, the reality is that self-identification as 'European' remains a marginal phenomenon (except in tiny Luxembourg, with its 29 per cent share of EU-foreigners in the residential population). Only a small minority of the people living in Europe 'think of themselves presently as "European" in the psychological sense [and] academics think of themselves as "European" proportionally twice as often as persons with less formal education'.[46] The European frame of reference is, therefore, that of a narrow segment of elites, whereas attitudes toward work and politics, religion, family, and education still exhibit clear national and subregional patterns. As for political, educational, and cultural programmes aimed at shifting the focus of citizens' worldviews from the national to the European level, scepticism is warranted, especially given the reservations Europeans already have about the implications of economic integration.[47]

Europe as economy of scale

Combining the economic, political, technological, scientific, and military resources of the (expanded) EU would create opportunities far surpassing those available to conventional economic world powers, among which would be the formation of an unprecedented potential for solving political and social problems. Less obvious are the solutions for problems meriting a pooling of resources (as differentiated from the simple removal of barriers to the mobility of various resources) and the precise modalities for deploying this formidable problem-solving capacity. The only Europeans with a definite claim on the well-endowed European funds are the candidate countries of central and eastern Europe. For them, the speed and direction of economic and political modernisation are dependent upon whether and how soon they can partake, as full members, in the structural and agricultural funds of the EU. Acute budgetary and labour-market crises in many existing EU member states, however, have reduced western European tolerance for transnational redistribution.[48] Furthermore, the long-term contribution that central and eastern Europe could make to the EU's collective resources (new markets, possibilities for investment, military security, control over migration) is much less evident than that expected from Spain and Portugal at the time of the EU's expansion into southern Europe in 1986.

To complicate matters further, the European funds are not the only means of achieving the much-vaunted effects of synergy and economies of scale; these effects can also be realised below the level of the Commission through bilateral and multilateral economic, scientific-technical, and military forms of cooperation. If the full economies of scale of European integration are to be realised, mutually agreed-upon goals and projects will be necessary, to which EU members will have to be sufficiently committed to accept the necessary short-term distributional sacrifices. Such goals and projects are currently in short supply.

The problem would not be so serious if forms of positive integration existed, which could make the European polity into a vehicle for a Europe-wide social and employment pact. Instead, the opposite is the case, with the consequences of the present negative approach to integration – competitive deregulation of national employment and environmental protection standards and rising pressure to consolidate budgets – actively working against the development of a positive vision of integration. The sole remaining argument in favour of conceiving Europe as an economy of scale in political and economic terms is that the continent's political integration as 'fortress Europe' could ensure its protection from external competitors, chiefly in North America, Asia, and also within Europe. This is hardly a strong basis for that positive vision.

Conclusion

None of the five normative interpretations just considered offers a clear path toward political integration in Europe. Analysed together, however, they do reveal one important thing. The European public needs a normatively convincing defence of the integration project, and that need grows more pressing as the project moves forward. This is true for both internal and external reasons. At home, Europe confronts the rise of right-wing, populist-nationalist sentiment, primarily in Austria but also in Greece. This remains a localised phenomenon, but to the extent that it represents a backlash against the negative consequences of integration, it may intensify as those consequences become more apparent. Abroad, Europe faces a plethora of problems – involving ecology, economic stability, development, migration, crime, the media, security, and external affairs – that require concerted transnational action. In the face of these pressures, the functionalist approach to European integration, which suggests that the European project – at times haltingly, at times precipitously – will somehow, under the strain of existing interdependencies and emerging elite consensus, make itself complete 'on its own', is increasingly barren. Europe provides a framework not just for cooperative problem solving but also for problem diffusion. If the EU is to play its original role – if it is to mount a coherent defence against the disintegrating pressures of globalisation and rejuvenate the scope for political action – it will first have to reconstitute itself purposively as an effective and legitimate structure for governance.

I conclude by shifting the focus away from the normative motives for political integration to the social and moral consequences of integration. The optimistic view of Europe is that the European Union will steadily acquire greater legitimacy by virtue of its perceived accomplishments, growing citizen familiarity, and the occasional institutional innovation. The democratic deficit, in other words, will wither away of its own accord. A less optimistic, but perhaps more realistic alternative, can be summed up in the following proposition: the horizons of trust and solidarity, and the potential for creating a community on a civic-societal and republican-political basis, narrow as the frame of reference for relations of competition and interdependence widens. The delimitation of functional interrelations is accompanied by a deliberate decommitment on the part of individuals, groups, regions, and whole states to Europe as a collectivity. When the borders of nation-states become porous, the functional-systematic and social-moral modes of integration develop in opposite directions. Recent events in northern Italy and the Federal Republic of Germany may be adduced to support this claim. Neither the Padanisian fiscal secession efforts nor the German proposal for a regionalisation of the social security system can be explained without reference to the budgetary constraints and competitive conditions wrought by the Single Market.

What should we infer from this? Historically, as Greven analysed in the preceding chapter, the largest social body capable of supporting redistributive sacrifices has been the nation-state. We should therefore not be surprised by increasing resistance when the demands of redistribution are extended beyond that entity. Individuals begin to feel that excessive moral demands are being made of them, and they react by morally under-challenging themselves. As in Banfield's model of 'amoral familialism', they become vigilant lest someone outside their social circle profit from their contributions. This decline in the operative horizons of trust and obligation is caused by the opening of nation-state borders, and it can be expected equally from 'rich' and 'poor' – from the former because they will rationally attempt to evade national and transnational demands on their resources, from the latter because, as beneficiaries of regional and structural funds, they will have a strong incentive to emphasise their sub-national identities. These two strategies, moreover, are obviously in a relation of reciprocal intensification.

In the absence of coextensive efforts to create a political community, borderless systems often overestimate their moral and legitimate power. In the process, they become breeding grounds for postmodern and neoliberal tendencies, and they jeopardise the dispositions and institutional arrangements that encourage individuals and governments to consider the social, temporal, and practical effects of their actions (and inaction) in the long term. This suggests that the most important of these arrangements – the social welfare state and democracy, but also the corporatist system of comprehensive and far-sighted interest mediation – can be realised only 'within borders'. This implies a mode of socialisation limited to the nation-state, whose protagonists recognise each other as worthy of trust and solidarity and who perceive each other as equal participants in an enduring and authoritative community of law. By disregarding these connections and allowing the polity to be delimited with impunity, we undermine its power to impose duties and open the door to regional and particularist motives and strategies.

Notes

1. For an earlier treatment in German upon which this chapter is based, see Claus Offe, 'Demokratie und Wohlfahrtsstaat: Eine europäische Regimeform unter dem Stress der europäischen Integration', in W. Streeck (ed.), *Internationale Wirtschaft, nationale Demokratie, Herausforderung für die Demokratie Theorie*, Frankfurt am Main, Campus Verlag, 1998, pp. 99–136.

2. D. Grimm, *Braucht Europa eine Verfassung?*, München, Carl Friedrich von Siemens-Stiftung, 1995, p. 31.

3. J. Habermas, *Die Einbeziehung des Anderen: Studien zur politischen Theorie*, Frankfurt: Suhrkamp, 1996, pp. 135, 137.

4. M. Weber, *Wirtschaft und Gesellschaft: Grundriss der verstehenden Soziologie*, 4th edn, Tübingen, Mohr, 1956, pp. 237, 244.

5. A common market, for example, is nothing more than a partial sacrifice of this power to regulate matters within one's borders. Here, the sacrifice is motivated by the economic (e.g., the economies of scale) and political advantages that are expected to accrue from the suspension of internal borders. However, this does not change the fact that political communities are dependent upon territorial borders and empowered to act only in reference to them.

6. This is in accordance with Jellinek's well-known formula.

7. C. Offe, *Modernity and the State: East, West*, Cambridge, Polity, 1996, pp. 147–182.

8. If citizens regard each other as 'hostile' or 'malicious', they might, out of this 'timorousness' (Weber's *Timidität*), feel that their interests would be better served by an authoritarian regime.

9. L. Hoffmann, 'Das "Volk": Zur ideologischen Struktur eines unvermeidbaren Begriffs', *Zeitschrift für Soziologie*, 1991, vol. 20, no. 3, pp. 191–208.

10. F. W. Scharpf, 'Negative and Positive Integration in the Political Economy of European Welfare States', in G. Marks, F. W. Scharpf, P. C. Schmitter, and W. Streeck (eds), *Governance in the European Union*, London, Sage, 1996, pp. 15–39.

11. Grimm, *Braucht Europa eine Verfassung?*.

12. P. C. Schmitter, 'Examining the Present Euro-Polity with the Help of Past Theories', in Marks *et al.* (eds), *Governance in the European Union*, London, Sage, 1996, pp. 1–14.

13. The 'intentionalistic' conception of transnational processes of integration implies that the integration process could be disrupted by a lack of support from the national populations affected. This distinguishes it from the functionalistic theory of integration, [which] thinks of European unification as a process controlled by the leading elites of the countries involved, as well as by the functional elites of international organizations. As long as these [elites]... are in agreement that the current political and economic challenges demand international solutions, the opinion of the broader population is, to a large extent, without consequence for the course of further integration.
S. Immerfall and A. Sobisch, 'Europäische Integration und europaische Identität: Die Europäische Union im Bewusstsein ihrer Burger', *Politik und Zeitgeschichte*, 1997, vol. 10, pp. 25–37 [26].

14. F. W. Scharpf, 'Demokratische Politik in Europa', in D. Grimm *et al.* (eds), *Zur Neuordnung der Europaischen Union: Die Regierungskonferenz 1996/1997*, Baden-Baden, Nomos, 1996/1997, pp. 65–91 [65].

15. There are certain conditions under which it may be rational for nation-states to cede their sovereignty to supranational institutions. Marks *et al.* identify two such situations. First, an advantage of cooperation (for example, reduced transaction costs) may come into effect earlier than the disadvantage associated with relinquishing sovereignty. Second, the transfer of decision making rights to a higher level of government may enable governing elites to shift responsibility for the undesirable consequences of a decision to that level of government. In some circumstances, responsibility for a particular decision is a power to be avoided rather than sought. This is true if any decision on a particular issue brings more costs than benefits. See G. Marks, L. Hooghe, and K. Blank, 'European Integration since the 1980s: state-centric versus multi-level governance', *Journal of Common Market Studies*, 1996, vol. 34, no. 3, pp. 341–378. It is important to note, however, that both scenarios simply involve a trick, whereby problems of legitimation are deferred to a future date.

16. T. H. Marshall, *Class, Citizenship and Social Development*, Garden City, N.Y., Doubleday, 1964.

17. Nation-states show no signs of being willing to transfer this authority. While the members of a nation-state generally concede to their fellow citizens the right to impose normative duties according to jointly created constitutional and legislative procedural principles, and attribute to them the moral and cognitive competence to do so, they typically extend this recognition only to conationals.

18. S. S. Andersen and K. A. Eliassen (eds), *The European Union: How democratic is it?*, London, Sage, 1996.

19. F. W. Scharpf, 'Economic Integration, Democracy and the Welfare State,' unpublished manuscript, Max Planck Institute, 1996, pp. 154–155.

20. K. Middlemas, *Orchestrating Europe: The informal politics of European Union 1973–1995*, London, Fontana, 1995, pp. 340–364.

21. Marks *et al.*, 'European Integration since the 1980s'.

22. Scharpf, 'Negative and Positive Integration'.

23. Middlemas, *Orchestrating Europe*, pp. 386, 468, 487ff., and 598; Andersen and Eliassen, *The European Union*, pp. 40–51, 251.

24. Habermas, *Die Einbeziehung des Anderen*, p. 142. This environment would be conducive to learning when the two requirements formulated by Habermas are met: 'The citizens must also be able to experience the practical value of exercising their rights in the form of social security and reciprocal recognition of different cultural ways of life' (p. 143). However, the experience of 'social security' is predicated upon the existence of a European governmental authority that has already made itself visible through its ability to act, while that of 'reciprocal recognition' can result only from a legitimisation process that addresses the fear that European dictates will demolish national institutions and ways of life (for example, the Swedish liquor sales and distribution system or the German public broadcasting corporations).

25. W. Streeck, 'Neo-Voluntarism: A new European social policy regime?', in G. Marks *et al.* (eds), *Governance in the European Union*, London: Sage, 1996, p. 65 [emphasis in original].

26. Cited in B. Laffan, 'Legitimacy', *Encyclopedia of the EU*, Boulder, Col., Lynne Rienner, 1997.

27. It is notable that insistence upon the intrinsic normative value of European integration and related efforts to downplay points of view based on national interests are special peculiarities of the discourse of political and intellectual elites in Germany. Consequently, the objectives that inform this discourse are more 'Euro-federal' than 'intergovernmental'. Although strong arguments can be marshalled in favour of this one-dimensional vision of a Europe grounded in principles rather than interests, they remain vulnerable to two suspicions. Outside observers not unreasonably fear that this vision (1) merely expresses German uneasiness about persistent European fears of renewed German hegemony or, more seriously, (2) uses 'postnational' discourse as a smoke

screen to obscure a drive for dominance of a monetarily unified Europe by the German government (and its Bundesbank).

28. H. Münkler, 'Europa als politische Idee: Ideengeschichtliche Facetten des Europabegriffs und deren aktuelle Bedeutung', *Leviathan*, 1991, vol. 19, no. 4, pp. 521–541.

29. Think of the Latin-European Mediterranean states, the Greek-Orthodox countries, the Carolingian countries, the Hapsburg succession states, the German-speaking countries, the British and French model cases of western democracy, the British Isles, Benelux, Scandinavia, the Baltic states, the Allies of World War II, the emerging democracies of central and eastern Europe, the four neutral countries not members of NATO, or the coastal states of the three European seas and oceans.

30. Nor do they view each other as possessing an unconditional right to assistance arising from a European sense of solidarity. When Europeans are moved to altruism, they are far more likely to direct their charitable donations to Bangladesh than to the inhabitants of the Irish Northwest.

31. G. Delanty, 'Theories of Social Integration and the European Union: Rethinking Culture', unpublished paper, University of Liverpool, 1996, p. 6.

32. In the mid-1990s, EU social expenditures totalled 0.9 per cent of the welfare budgets of member states. R. Gomà, 'The social dimension of the European Union: a new type of welfare system?', *Journal of European Public Policy*, 1996, vol. 3, no. 2, pp. 209–230 [222].

33. Immerfall and Sobisch, 'Europäische Integration und europäische Identität'.

34. J. Crowley, 'European integration: sociological process or political project?', *Innovation*, 1997, vol. 9, no. 2, pp. 149–160 [156].

35. Presently, the EU is home to eleven languages, three large Christian and several non-Christian religious communities, growing geographic distance, vastly different member state experiences with Europe, and, above all, disparities in economic development and productive capacity. For example, with respect to the last dimension, the ratio of the per capita production of Luxembourg and Greece in 1995 was 3 to 1. See R. Rose, *What Is Europe? A dynamic perspective*, New York, HarperCollins, 1996, p. 278.

36. M. J. Baun, *An Imperfect Union*, Boulder, Col., Westview, 1996, p. 143.

37. The preceding discussion demonstrates that the EU cannot be thought of as a construct analogous to a normal 'state'. The reason is that the collapse of state socialism and its border with the West has raised questions about the limits of the European state and its 'people' that have yet to be definitively answered in the manner required for a normal and proper state.

38. Grimm, *Braucht Europa eine Verfassung?*, p. 34.

39. Scharpf, 'Demokratische Politik in Europa', p. 65.

40. The standard of western European democracy should be thought of here in contrast to what O'Donnell terms the simple 'electoralism' of Latin American 'delegative democracy'. See G. O'Donnell, 'Delegative Democracy', *Journal of Democracy*, 1994, vol. 5, no. 1, pp. 55–69.

41. Habermas vehemently rejects this conclusion, even if with a few bold normative insinuations, in *Die Einbeziehung des Anderen*. And he is not alone in dissenting from this pessimistic view of the prospects for European integration. Sassoon thinks it imaginable, desirable, and even imperative for the maintenance of the level of integration already achieved in Europe that the integration process be liberated from the shackles of the Common Market and informed instead by the objective of setting goals for a sociopolitically secured 'democratic union of citizens'. To this end, he proposes anchoring a normative minimum for the whole of Europe in a European *Charta*. This *Charta* would be more abstract than the *acquis,* and at the same time would democratise European legislation and strengthen the protection of basic and social rights in certain member states. Its purpose would be to make the political principles of a 'European model of social capitalism' binding on all present and future members of the Union. See D. Sassoon, *Social Democracy at the Heart of Europe*, London, Institute for Public Policy Research, 1996, p. 15. A similar call for the political-moral validity of a specifically 'European project of modernity', combining an emphasis on productivity with political and institutional checks on the operation of the market, is found in B. Bercusson *et al.*, *Soziales Europa – ein Manifest*, Hamburg, Rowohlt, 1996, p. 18.

42. EU member states are suspicious of the fact that Germany is the only EU member to express a national preference for supranational empowerment. Even when this preference is recognised as sincere, distrust can be stirred by the anomaly of a nation-state that has misgivings about its own sovereignty and therefore seeks to abolish it. See A. Markovits and S. Reich, *The German Predicament*, Ithaca, NY, Cornell University Press, 1997, on this subject.

43. I. Buruma, 'Fear and loathing in Europe', *New York Review of Books*, 1996, October 17, p. 57.

44. T. Judt, *Grosse Illusion Europa: Herausforderungen und Gefahren einer Idee*, München, Hanser, 1996, pp. 142–159.

45. R. Dahrendorf, 'Die Quadratur des Kreises – Freiheit, Solidarität und Wohlstand', *Transit*, 1996, vol. 12, pp. 5–28.

46. Immerfall and Sobisch, 'Europäische Integration und europäische Identität', p. 33.

47. W. Hornstein and G. Mutz, *Die europäische Einigung als gesellschaftlicher Prozess*, Baden-Baden, Nomos, 1993, pp. 22, 249.

48. For instance, it is clearly not feasible to extend the common agricultural policy, as it is presently conceived, to a country such as Poland, where no less than 27 per cent of all those employed are still in the agricultural sector.

Chapter Nineteen

The Constitution of a European Democracy and the Role of the Nation State[*]

Ulrich K. Preuß

The title of this paper is ambiguous: 'The Constitution of a European democracy' may point to or ask for the elements of the process of constituting European democracy; but it can also be read as the institutional end result of a process which aims at a constitution of European democracy and about which we speak in much the same manner as, for instance, about the constitution of French democracy. Of course this ambiguity is not accidental. There is a broad feeling of agreement that a European democracy does not yet exist, its creation requires a process which cannot simply be completed by the proclamation of the sovereignty of a European *demos*. Should there be a final result which can be labelled 'European Democracy' it is likely to be embodied in a multi-faceted complex constitutional structure rather than in a supranational variant of the concept of popular sovereignty.

In what follows I will deal with the process which may eventually entail a European constitution. What it can look like, how it can be structured, which elements of the present legal structure of the EU are conducive to a European democracy, what are impediments to it? When raising these questions I make the presupposition that European democracy is necessary for the survival and the proper development of the EU (I). Yet, in order to understand the requirement of democracy for the European Union it is indispensable to grasp the particular character of Euro-rule and its distinction from statal rule (II). Furthermore, I will defend the claim that Euro-democracy is possible if we do not simply apply the standards of democracy valid for closed nation-states but succeed in developing criteria which are more commensurate with the particular institutional qualities of the EC/EU (III).

I.

European democracy is *necessary* because, due to the principles of direct effect and of the supremacy of Community law over national law, the EC exercises authority over the citizens of the Member States without the prior consent of their parliaments. Although a general consent of the national parliaments to the transfer of sovereignty to the Community has been given in the past through the ratification of the EC Treaty (ECT) and its numerous amendments, this is hardly sufficient for the democratic legitimation of the huge number of regulations which

---

[*] 'The Constitution of a European democracy and the role of the nation state', *Ratio Juris: An International Journal of Jurisprudence and Philosophy of Law*, 1999, vol. 12, no. 4, pp. 417–428.

are issued by the Community's organs. To make a banal analogy with democratic theory in the framework of the nation state: no one would seriously claim that popular consent to a constitution renders the necessity to elect a parliament and a government within an appropriate time span dispensable. The same is true on the level of the EC/EU: democratic consent to the erection of the supranational entity and to its role to pool considerable parts of the Member States' sovereignties does not provide sufficient legitimacy for the several policies devised and conducted by the Community. Moreover, there is a significant shift of regulatory powers and competencies from the Member States to the institutions of the Community which are not yet paralleled by a similar development of the devices through which the Community authorities are made accountable to those affected by their regulations – affected, as I said, without the mediation of the government which they have legitimised through elections and which are accountable to them.

The argument for the necessity of European democracy does not determine the institutional properties of a democratic order on the European level. Yet, if the reason for the necessity of European democracy is the regulatory power of the EC/EU and its binding force which it imposes upon the Union citizens, the basic requirements of democracy are more or less predetermined: the rulers must be accountable to the ruled, and the ruled must have the right and the effective means to elect the rulers. This entails a standard of democracy which includes three elements: first, basic rights of the individuals subject to the rule of an established authority; second, an effective check of the exercise of rule of this authority through those who are affected by this rule; third, appropriate means of participation in the wielding of this rule for those who are affected by it. In principle, there is no difference in the character of democracy in the framework of the nation-state. Yet the institutional devices which have to realise this principle must take into account that the Community is not a state. It lacks the essential qualities which, despite considerable structural changes in statehood in the last fifty years, still define the character of political rule: exclusive jurisdiction over a closed territory and a circumscribed group of people, and the possession of undivided supreme power – the power of the 'last word' – for the maintenance of peace and order within the confines of its jurisdiction. Supreme power being the essential means of societal stability, properties like unity, hierarchy, and homogeneity of the physical and symbolic space and the subjects of its rule have been the defining characteristics of statehood. Not surprisingly, the efforts to domesticate this abysmal kind of political order have been adapted to these properties: constitutionalism has largely been understood as an institutional device to constrain the power of the state – 'limited government' being the emblem of this understanding, – and according to the understanding dominant in continental Europe, democracy means the unrestrained, undivided and supreme power of the people and its general and homogeneous will; in other words, democracy is nothing other than the substitution of the people's supreme power for the prince's and, in a later phase of historical development, for the state's sovereign power. The character of the polity as being ordered by the regulatory force of – constitutionally limited – power did not change after the substitution of popular sovereignty for the absolutist rule of the princes.

II.

In contrast to the modern state, the Community has no sovereign power, it is incomplete, i.e., in need of complementary political entities, it is permanently changing its institutional character, it is polycentric, and its legitimacy is not exclusively based on consent, but supplemented by the principle of efficiency. These characteristics necessitate some modifications of the democratic principle if compared with national democracy. Let me elaborate briefly.

1.

The power of the Community is derived from the Member States and their original sovereignty. To put it in the terminology of state theory, the Community has no competence-competence, which means: it cannot define autonomously the goals which it can legitimately pursue. There is no single unitary and homogeneous sovereign which is the author and hence has the authority to determine the objectives of the Community; rather, they are specified in a treaty concluded by its constituent parts, the member states. It is a matter of argument whether the EC Treaty and the EU Treaty can be regarded as the constitution of the Community and the Union, respectively. However the answer may be, what is essential for the political character of the Community (and the Union as well) is the fact that its powers are originally and inherently limited – not, as in the case of the state, originally unlimited and only externally restricted by posterior legal constraints– that their source consists of a plurality of heterogeneous constituent elements, the member states – not, as in the case of the state, of a unitary, monistic, homogeneous subject – and that, finally and following from the preceding characteristics, the regulatory power of the Community has an essentially legal character. It rests in the legal bonds among the Member States, that is, a horizontal social compact which establishes a legal community among the participants and establishes an authority whose regulatory force consists in the accomplishment of legal purposes, which means: in the accommodation of a diversity of interests and values within a heterogeneous community. By contrast, within a statal structure the purposes of the polity spring from the will-power of the sovereign and his definition of what the 'common good' requires, the 'common good' being a pre-legal objective which undergoes successive transmutation into law in order to become compatible with the rights and freedoms of individuals. The 'common good' of the Community is legally constituted, while the 'common good' in the framework of a statal polity is a pre-legal concept which is legally restricted. For lack of a more appropriate term, and for the sake of abbreviation, I call this quality the 'accommodative' character of Community law-making.

2.

The *complementary or incomplete* character of a possible EC/EU constitution: a constitution of the Community is essentially complementing the constitutions of the Member States. It cannot possibly be conceived as an independent and self-sufficient institution. Some authors speak of an 'osmotic' relationship between the Community and the Member States' constitutions. This relationship is different from the well-known dualism of federal and state constitutions in federal states like Germany, Austria, Switzerland or the United States. Thus, the Basic Law of Germany requires and guarantees the homogeneity of the constitutional orders of the central state and the federal units; by contrast, the relationship and consequently the degree of homogeneity or heterogeneity between the Community constitution and the constitutions of the Member States are only being fabricated in the process of integration itself. There is no preordained order between them, not to speak of a hierarchical order. The Community is a process of an institutionalised interaction between actors whose roles and functions are not pre-established in an overarching concept of political unity; rather, they are shaped in an open process in which a broad range of possible developments may surface and be pushed forward by agents who possibly will only be generated in this very process.

3.

The *polycentric* character of a possible EC/EU constitution. There is no political centre in which the political substance of the Community is accumulated and embodied. Policy making is beyond the firm control of any single authority. True, this applies also for many current constitutional states in which already the indispensable separation of powers prohibits the idea of one single power centre of the polity. But the fragmentation and diffusion of power, characteristic of the Community, goes considerably beyond this experience with contemporary statehood. In the Community the process of policy definition and implementation of the Community occurs in a largely nebulous and hardly comprehensible web of pluralist actors – the institutions of the Community, the Member States, the institutions of the Member States, the manifold interest groups, the incipient forms of political parties -which makes the processes of power-formation appear extremely spread out.

4.

The *dynamic* character of a possible EC/EU constitution. The most striking property of the community is its dynamic character. While the state as the political organisation of a territorially-bound population is primarily directed towards the preservation of its institutional identity and stability, the Community is, conversely, directed towards its permanent self-transformation, both in terms of policy goals and of its institutional setup. It has been said that the never-finished objective of integration is the 'political finality' of the Community. Contrary to state constitutions which accept change only as a necessary reactive mechanism of adjustment to changing conditions, the constitution of the Union would have to enable a permanent active process of changing the shape of the Community, some authors speak of a 'change-constitution' (*Wandel-Verfassung*).

5.

The *duality of legitimising principles* of a possible EC/EU constitution. In the institutional framework of the European Community two different principles of legitimation co-exist. The first is the Lockean principle of consent, the second the principle of utility and efficiency widely associated with David Hume. While consent of the ruled is a traditional basis of legitimation of any public authority, it is much less familiar to ground the justification of government officially, so to speak, on the performance and efficiency of the ruler. To be sure, the two principles are not mutually exclusive. Thus the famous Lockean concept of tacit consent comes quite close to a principle of legitimacy through efficiency. It is also true that in the framework of modern state-hood the idea of efficiency plays an important role *de facto*, while *de jure* it is largely dismissed on grounds of democratic theory. However this may be, it is unequivocally and full-heartedly accepted in the framework of the Community. After all, it was the presumed superiority of the Community's problem-solving capacity over the potentials of the traditional nation-states which basically motivated the foundation of the Community in the Fifties. In other words, reasons of efficiency and utility belong to the most significant founding rationales of the Community. Thus, consent and efficiency are two different, equally accepted and legitimate pillars of the European consensus.

III.

European democracy is also *possible*. This claim has two implications: first, democracy does not yet exist on the European level and has yet to be created; second, those who contend that there cannot be a European democracy because there is no European *demos* are wrong. As to the first claim, it may suffice to point to the extremely limited possibilities of the Union citizens to hold the European authorities accountable and to elect the top officials of the Community. Those who are elected by the citizens – the members of the European Parliament – have only a limited share in the power of the Community, whereas those who hold the essential part of it – the Council and the Commission – are not exposed to efficient devices of accountability and do not stand as candidates at European elections.

The second implication of my claim that European democracy is possible is more complex. Those who insist that in the absence of a European *demos* European democracy is impossible do, of course, not deny that according to Article 8 ECT the nationals of the Member State are citizens of the Union, that the entirety of citizens forms the citizenry of the Union, and that rights and institutional devices necessary for the realisation of democratic accountability of the European authorities could be bestowed upon the European citizenry. What they deny is the possibility of a European public sphere which, in their view, cannot arise in a conglomerate of peoples with no fewer than eleven languages none of which is spoken and understood by the majority of Union citizens.[1] Thus for want of the appropriate intermediary institutions like parties, associations, mass media and the like, Community-wide political debates about issues as important for democratic accountability as the accomplishments of the Community authorities, the appropriate standards of their evaluation, and the goals, values and interests of the Community cannot take place. As a consequence, it follows that without democratic accountability there is no democratic rule. More or less this argument amounts to the thesis that no democracy is possible without a *demos* – i.e., without a collectivity of individuals who share some basic properties by virtue of which they form a political wholeness and are capable of acting as a political entity.

1.

While the empirical observations are true, the underlying premises are questionable. Basically, there are two closely connected assumptions. First, democratic rule requires the formation of a unitary and homogeneous collective will of the ruled who, as a collective subject, must be seen as the author of the authoritative acts of the Community. Only if democratic rule and democratic accountability are regarded as requiring a homogeneous collective will which imposes itself upon the society, is it necessary to demand a coherent Community-wide public sphere and ultimately one people able to form one political will. The second assumption claims that the legal orders which are issued by the Community have the character of general laws which affect every single Union citizen in much the same manner and which, therefore, require the same mode of participation in the process of democratic authorisation.

1.1.

The first assumption draws on a democratic tradition which has been developed on the basis of the French model of the *état-nation*. It is based on the principle of equal national citizenship and lays emphasis on the equality of the citizens. As citizens they are deprived of their particularities and their embeddedness in particular communities, cultures, and social roles and conceived as abstract political beings whose opinions converge around a concept of the public good which is more or less shared by all because all are equals. Only equals can form a general will; although Rousseau insisted that these equal citizens must not communicate with one another because this would distort the generality of their will, today it is beyond doubt that the concept of a unitary *état-nation* requires a sense of shared properties among the citizens which is not a given but must be created through the proper functioning of a public sphere. While this concept of democracy is essentially inspired by the idea and the ideal of (political) equality, there is an alternative concept which relies upon liberty as the supreme value. According to this understanding, democracy is the most appropriate socio-political form of individual freedom. In order to accomplish this function democracy must provide institutional devices through which individuals can participate in the process of political decision making without being forced to give up beforehand the qualities which constitute their individuality. Hence, participation in the political process does not require the individuals to slip off their individual properties and diversities and to abstract from their affiliations to specific communities, life styles, interest groups, social contexts, etc. On the contrary, democracy as the collective form of individual freedom and autonomy encourages the incorporation of these particularities in the process of political decision making in order to carry the individuals as close as possible to the ideal situation in which they can take advantage of membership in a political association, while at the same time enjoying the utmost degree of individual freedom.

Democratic participation according to this philosophical pattern does not require the formation of a unitary homogeneous will that rules society. What is needed is, first, the existence of channels of participation where individuals can give voice to their interests and values and have an equal chance that their voice be heard and properly taken into consideration. Secondly, the individuals must be represented as equals. Hence there is no necessity for a homogeneous body – a *demos* – which is able to form a unitary will and which therefore requires an inclusive public sphere in which such a homogenising process would occur. Nor is there a need for the representation of the *demos* as a unitary body. 'We the people' does not mean a collective subject which acts (and possibly feels) like one person; rather, it refers to the plurality of the 'We' who do not cease to be a multitude of diverse individuals when they make collective decisions for themselves. There may be limits to the pluralisation of collective decisions in the framework of the nation-state which I do not intend to examine here. For the issue of European democracy it is quite obvious that the fragmented, incomplete, polycentric, and dynamic character of the EC/EU is much more disposed to this pluralist notion of democracy than to the homogenising concept of the Rousseauist type.

1.2.

This is corroborated if we briefly scrutinise the second assumption of the no-*demos*-no-democracy-thesis, namely the claim that the legal orders which are issued by the Community are in their turn general laws which simultaneously reflect and shape the homogeneity of the political body. This postulate is not confirmed by the facts. Article 189 ECT enumerates the legal instruments of the organs of the Community for the accomplishment of its goals: regulations, directives, decisions, recommendations and opinions. Directives are addressed to the member states and are only binding as to the result to be achieved, whereas it is left to the national authorities to choose the forms and methods. Recommendations and opinions have no legally binding force whatsoever. Only regulations have direct binding force in all Member States, while decisions are binding only for those to whom they are addressed. In other words, only regulations impose a uniform body of legal obligations (and rights) on the citizens of all Member States, and they have to be implemented by their several administrations because the Community does not dispose of law enforcement agencies of its own. Given the relatively small number of regulations in comparison with directives, 888, let alone if compared with the manifold forms of recommendations, opinions, Green Books, and White Books we may say that the legal instruments of ordering the Community are as fragmented and polycentric as the Community itself. There is hardly one legal act of the Community which touches the life spheres of all citizens of the Member States, i.e., whose content is general or universal enough to shape essential economic, social, or cultural conditions of the lives of all Europeans in much the same manner. Why, then, should democracy under these circumstances require the formation of a unitary, homogeneous, general will of a European *demos*?

2.

What, then, could democratic accountability under conditions of the 'accommodative', the incomplete, polycentric, and dynamic character of the EC/EU look like? For even if we accept the duality of legitimising principles, this does not of course mean that democracy is dispensable for the legitimation of acts of rule of the Community.

2.1.

If, as I stated earlier, the Community does not emanate from one source, or from an act of foundation through one homogeneous constituent political will, but consists of the mutual legal bonds which tie the Member States and their peoples together, their acts of rule have the purpose to carry out and to specify the Community's programme which has been preordained in the EC and the EU Treaties. It is not will-power which is required in order to complete the Community's programme, but the capacity to accommodate the plurality and diversity of interests involved in each enactment of a legal order, and to gain the acceptance of those addressed by it. The lack of law enforcement agencies makes the Community dependent upon the cooperation not only of the Member States and their administrative agencies, but of the addressees of its acts as well. In other words, power may remain the ultimate means in order to complete the objectives of the Community and to implement its programmes; but is certainly not the primary and the most important instrument of Community regulation. It is embedded and mostly fully replaced by processes of mutual information, bargaining, negotiating, the provision of diverse forms of cooperation as well as their temporary withdrawal, threats and promises; these are the elements which shape the process in which legally binding acts are devised and finally enacted. By standards of democratic rule the chances of participation of the interested parties are largely secured in these processes. By contrast, this is much less likely with respect to the interests of those who are unable to allocate the resources necessary to participate in this complex law-making process. Moreover, there may be, and frequently in fact are not represented, 'third parties' which are affected by the results of this process and at whose expense compromises and trade-offs among the participating interests will frequently occur. Thus, the 'accommodative' character of law-making is structurally akin to a pluralist concept of democracy, but it is by no means the satisfaction of all democratic standards.

2.2

'Incompleteness' of the Community means, as I stated above, that political decisions are shaped and fabricated in a cooperative process of several actors which makes it difficult to identify a clear-cut responsibility. For instance, a directive requires the cooperation of the Commission, the Council, the European Parliament, the national government, the national parliament, and the relevant administrative agency which in federal states like Germany is normally a *Länder* agency. Moreover, the principle of subsidiarity (Article 3b ECT, after Amsterdam: Article 5) is a flexible rule according to which the question of who is authorised to issue a legal act remains open to political and legal debates. Political controversies may not only arise about the contents of a decision, but no less about the question of who has the legal competence to make the decision. Thus the character of the public authority in the Community tends to be fluid and diffuse, and the whole process is less than transparent. In this field, democratic accountability requires first of all rights to information and to the unequivocal presentation of the institution which is responsible.

2.3.

The incompleteness of the EU is closely connected with its polycentric character. Polycentric polities open a broad variety of chances of participation in a multitude of arenas. Viewed from a concept of democracy which is rooted in the idea of individual autonomy, a polycentric order appears to be the most appropriate. Madison considered this to be the viable remedy against injustice and oppression of the minority through the majority. If the authority of the government is

> derived and dependent on the society, the society itself will be broken into so many parts, interests and classes of citizens, that the rights of individuals, or of the minority, will be in little danger from the interested combination of the majority.[2]

In a free society the security for civil rights consists in 'the multiplicity of interests [...]; and this may be presumed to depend on the extent of country and number of people *comprehended* under the same government'.[3] This is why, contrary to the traditional belief and to our spontaneous intuition, according to Madison 'the larger the society, provided it lies within a practicable sphere, the more duly capable it will be of self-government'.[4] Today we cannot satisfy ourselves with this ideal of fragmentation in the interest of the haves which aims at disabling the have-nots. On the other hand, the distribution of competencies on a multitude of supra-national and national agencies is to be regarded as a means to prevent a centralised and homogenising European decision-maker from emerging and to retain a certain degree of diversity, inequality, differences in terms of socio-economic development, etc. The constitutional problem of the EU lies in the inconsistency that it pursues the goal of a certain degree of economic and social homogeneity with a political structure which does not permit and is not supposed to permit a centralised agency which serves as a social homogeniser. If democratic participation and accountability must prevent the erection of a centralised agency which imposes policy goals, in particular distributive policies on the Member States, and at the same time shall not create mere socio-economic and political blockade and even stagnation, the constitution of a European Union must provide mechanisms which are favourable to the evolution of standards of just distribution and of the willingness of the haves to share with the have-nots. This is historically unprecedented, since redistributive policies were always associated with centralised political power, and vice versa: Decentralised political structures are likely to inhibit redistributive policies.

2.4.

The constitutional requirements of the dynamic character of the EU follow from its open developmental goal of an ever further integration of the peoples of the Union. Whether this includes the goal of an ever closer integration of citizens into a European citizenry which, finally, might even become the only constituent power of the Union is an open question which is answered by some affirmatively, by others passionately in the negative. According to our conventional understanding and the familiar conceptual frameworks of a modern polity, it is difficult to imagine a political entity whose '*pouvoir constituant*' is unclear. How can we conceive of a constitution if there is no clear-cut constituent power? The answer is at the same time simple and complex: it is a matter of the open-ended evolution of the Union to create its constituent parts, and it is the function of a Union constitution to give way to such an evolutionary process. The dynamic character and the openness of the European Union require a constitutional framework which does not fix boundaries to the evolution and self-transformation of the Union – boundaries of objectives and of competencies – but provides appropriate institutional schemes with the help of which the deliberations about the next step of the political transformation can be performed and the changes, if considered necessary or desirable, can be accomplished. In a way the relation between constituent power and constitution is reversed: it is the constitution of change – the *Wandel-Verfassung* – which creates the constituent powers of the Union. However, this *pouvoir constituant* has little to do with the omnipotent *creator ex nihilo* which Sieyès and, following him, Carl Schmitt had in mind; rather, it is a network of communication, deliberation and spontaneous civic action which embodies the learning capacity of a polycentric polity.

Notes

1. Cf. D. Grimm, *Braucht Europa eine Verfassung?*, Munich, Siemens Stiftung, 1995, p. 42.
2. J. Madison, A. Hamilton, and J. Jay, *The Federalist Papers*, New York, Buccaneer Books, 1992, pp. 324–325.
3. *Ibid.*
4. *Ibid.*

Chapter Twenty

The Problem of Legitimacy in the European Polity: Is Democratisation the Answer?[*]

Claus Offe and Ulrich K. Preuß

Is there a legitimacy deficit in the Euro-polity?

No problem, no solution

Even though complaints and uncertainties about the 'democratic deficit' of the EU are as widely shared as the perceived need to think about institutional solutions which would remedy this condition, agreement on the actual presence of such a deficit is by no means universal. Before we address the nature of and possible solution to the problem therefore, we need to deal briefly with views that deny either the existence of the problem or at least the availability of a solution.

Three such views can be identified. First, there is the *technocratic* view. This rightly claims that only the political choice between alternative courses of action advocated by different elite segments and mass constituencies qualifies as the substance of politics and hence, needs to be made within a framework of rights, values and democratic procedural rules. If, however, the agenda of European elites consists of matters that cannot be reasonably debated, but must be competently deduced from some compelling technical calculus, then making choices through democratic procedures is bound to diminish the efficiency of decision making and the quality of the decisions. These are better left to experts, professionals, epistemic communities and bureaucrats with their specialised knowledge in order to maximise ideological neutrality. The more reliably such technical decisions are insulated from politics and general legitimation demands, the more effective and efficient the process will be in which some 'one best way' will eventually be determined. As the purpose that rules are supposed to achieve is clear and unambiguous, namely Pareto optimality in the Single Market, the regulatory regime serving that purpose is entirely for the experts to determine. They have their tested methods of dealing with the three familiar types of public-choice problems and market failures. These are: (i) negative externalities (that is, economic actors securing advantages at the expense of third parties); (ii) the inverse case of the

---

[*] The Problem of Legitimacy in the European Polity: Is democratization the answer?', in C. Crouch and W. Streeck (eds), *The Diversity of Democracy: Corporatism, social order and political conflict*, Cheltenham, Edward Elgar, 2006, pp. 175–204.

provision of public goods (that is, economic actors having to be adequately rewarded for providing benefits to some collectivity, for otherwise they would not provide them); and (iii) common pool problems (that is, economic actors having to be prevented from inflicting damage upon their future selves through the unwise overutilisation of scarce resources, such as fish or the environment). This view of the EU as a technocratic regulatory state is often associated with the work of Majone.[1] In order for an efficient regulatory regime to be available, decisions must be kept strictly out of the politicised circuits of democratic representation and accountability.

Second, there is the *democratic saturation* view which, in contrast to the technocratic view, does not deny the need for democratic legitimation of the European policy process but rather claims that the democratic requirements of accountability and representation are already sufficiently fulfilled in the current institutional set-up of the EU. From a normative point of view it may be asked why there should be a need for distinct mechanisms of legitimation for EU policies since the member states, first, have voluntarily acceded to the EU, based upon democratic procedures according to their respective constitutional rules, and, second, are fully represented in the institutions which draft and implement EU policies. In other words, there is a solid and continuous chain of legitimation from the individual citizens in the member states up to the institutions of the EU. After all, the members of the Council are members of democratically elected governments of member states, and Commission members are nominated by their governments and have to withstand the scrutiny of the EP, the directly elected European legislature. So democracy is in place, people do not generally complain about its absence, and concerns about a 'deficit' are unwarranted. The author with whose writings these views are often associated[2] is Moravcsik.[3]

Third, there is the *unfeasibility/undesirability* argument. This argument comes in one of two versions. As far as the feasibility of a stronger democratic legitimation at the EU level is concerned, it invokes the seemingly obvious absence of a European *demos*. The citizenries of member states are simply 'too different' (by size, by historical experience, by religion, by language, by level of economic development, and so on) to be able to form a minimally coherent political community with which even losers in elections would identify. The presence of a durable self-identified and robust political community, as opposed to a multinational population, is an essential precondition for any form of democracy. Turned on its normative side and regarding the issue of desirability, the argument is that democratic legitimation procedures at the European level would inevitably lead to a deepening of European involvement in matters which properly belong to member states and thus, would interfere with the desire of the latter to maintain and increase national autonomy. Czech president Vaclav Klaus[4] is a prominent proponent of this view. The implication is that there is no democratic deficit because something that cannot or should not be changed cannot meaningfully be called a 'deficit'.

Why there is a problem and not just for the EU

So the very existence of the problem we are going to discuss in this chapter needs first to be established. In establishing it, we rely, among other things, on arguments advanced by Follesdal and Hix, Beetham and Lord, and Weiler, Haltern and Mayer.[5] Two points seem important. First, the lack of democratic accountability at the European level penetrates into the domestic arena and affects the quality and credibility of the practice of national democracy. Thus the problem is not primarily that the *EU* must *become* democratic; it is that *member states* must *remain* democratic. Second, major institutional actors at the EU level (the ECB, the ECJ and the Commission when operating as a rule enforcement agency) – have a direct impact upon the citizens of member states and therefore must be subjected to an institutionalised legitimacy test.

As to the first of these points, Schmitter has argued that the democratic deficit does not just exist at the EU level of the policy process but, partly as a consequence of this, at the member state level as well. '[T]he shift of functions to and the increase in the supranational authority of the EU have been contributing to the decline in the legitimacy of "domestic democracy"'.[6] National parliaments are losing control, the making of collectively binding decisions is being denationalised and 'executive actors can effectively ignore their parliaments when making decisions in Brussels'.[7] To a large extent this can be attributed to the fact that national governments, in particular parliaments, are no longer in the position to control the basic parameters of their national economies. The intensity of institutional interdependence between the national and the European levels of governance is bound to thwart all attempts to isolate the two levels and to protect the national political system from the effects of democratic deficiencies at the European polity. Thus there is in fact reason for concern that, if the shift of political power from the democratically legitimised national governments to the EU is not accompanied by some kind of compensation through additional channels of supranational legitimation, democracy within nation states will decay.

While this is clearly not the place to engage in a lengthy elaboration of the meaning of democracy, it still seems worthwhile to highlight one aspect of what we take to be one of its essential ingredients. A democracy is a system of political rule, with a basic division between rulers and ruled. There are two characteristics of how rulers are institutionally positioned in a democracy, one passive and one active. As to the passive mode, rulers and their activity of ruling are subject to the scrutiny and evaluation of voters, the media, organised interests, and so on, by whom they are held accountable. As a consequence, democratic rulers are defined by the institutionalised possibility that they may lose their office. Yet in order for a system of rule to qualify as a democracy, there is also an active aspect to the practice of ruling: rulers need not only find support; they must be willing and able, both *de lege* and *de facto,* to transform this support into policies, thus determining, at least to some significant extent, the conditions and developments of the political community on behalf of which rulers rule.

This 'active' characteristic of democratic rule is less often focused upon by democratic theorists than the 'passive' one. To reverse this imbalance, we might say: a democratic system of rule is one in which rulers are actually able to 'make a difference' in terms of the public goods and protection they provide through the making of public policy. A system of rule in which rulers are held perfectly accountable by the ruled yet cannot accomplish anything is as much a caricature, or an impoverished version, of democracy as a system of rule that is highly effective in shaping conditions and developments without being accountable to the ruled. Moreover, the two aspects of democratic rule hang together, as it appears unlikely that the ruled will have good reason to support a set of rulers whose capacity for significant policy making and problem-solving has evidently evaporated.

The ruled are powerless when the institutional resources to control rulers are absent. But the rulers themselves can also be powerless, and thus do not qualify according to our second criterion of what a democracy is, when they find themselves incapable of dealing effectively with problems of providing public goods or of protecting society from 'public bads'. When this is the case, the system of rule loses its policy making capacity, and democratically constituted political power is idled. Rulers can be deprived and dispossessed of (all or significant parts of) their policy making capacity by, for instance, military threats. In modern capitalist societies, however, the major cause of incapacitation of rulers is of an economic nature. Markets hold would-be policy-makers to ransom: as soon as they adopt an activist approach to the solution of social problems through policy making, they may be 'punished' by the adverse reactions of economic actors, such as investors or employers, on whose activities policy-makers depend for their tax base as well as their political support. The present configuration of the Euro-polity and its 'negative integration' is clearly such that it enables economic actors to make extensive use of this mechanism of 'punishment' and thus to disable the making of public policies.

It follows from this brief conceptual exploration that the democratisation of the Euro-polity would hinge on two conditions: not just on the institutionalisation of mechanisms by which ruling elites are made accountable and responsive to the ruled, but also on the enhancement of the rulers' capacity for action, that is their capacity to withstand and constrain the exercise of economic power if and whenever such power stands in the way of the making and implementing of public policy. This latter condition applies to the EU level of rule as much as it does to the policy making capacity of the governments of member states – a capacity that has been vastly decimated at the member state level by the process of EU integration, without being resurrected at the EU level itself.

As to our second point, the widely shared belief is that there is a growing imbalance between what the EU can do to European citizens and the role the preferences of European citizens are permitted to play in the EU. To be sure, European citizens can register their preferences in European elections. Yet the political resources of the EP remain limited in relation to what it can do in terms of both the selection of Commission members and the substantive legislative proposals of the Commission. European elections reveal even more of the malaise that is familiar from national elections, some of the symptoms of which are low turnout, decline in voters' party identification, and a very widespread ignorance about what European legislation involves and what the alternatives are. The low turnout in the EP elections is not necessarily a sign of citizens' indifference towards the EU but may rather be an expression of feelings of frustration and perceived powerlessness, which at some point might also undermine the trust in the regular working of national democratic institutions. In addition, as a consequence of voters' cognitive, as well as affective, distance from the issues and agendas before the EP, European elections are perceived to be somehow less important electoral contests within member state arenas, a misperception that is also suggested by the fact that the parties competing for votes are the national parties, according to the electoral law under which EP elections are held. 'Voters in Euro-elections are simply not offered an opportunity to choose between rival partisan elites presenting alternative programmes at *that* level of aggregation'.[8] For what is at issue in European elections is hardly what European leaders have done in the past or promise to do in the future. It is rather an expression of support or disapproval aimed at national parties and governments. To be sure, members of the main legislative body of the EU, the Council, obtain their mandate as the result of a democratic process. But this mandate, again, is typically both sought and won in terms of an executive role at the national level, not a legislative role at the European level. This is almost inevitable, since the Council's negotiations take place behind closed doors, typically concern policy packages and involve mechanisms such as log-rolling and variable coalition-building that remain highly opaque to the national public. Rule-making within the EU is based upon 'highly secretive and technically obscure decision making practices'.[9] The result is an extremely thin kind of accountability, leading to the condition that 'the EU adopts policies that are not supported by a majority of citizens in many or even most member states'.[10] Moreover, the main actors in the field of European economic and monetary policy (the Commission, the ECJ and the ECB) remain to a large extent unaccountable[11] to any representative body, pursue policies that privilege market-making 'negative integration', and are informed by 'a neo-liberal regulatory framework and a monetarist framework for EMU'. As a result, these policies are consistently to the right of the policy preferences of the median European voter. As the Commission, in its role as agenda setter and rule enforcer, is unaccountable to both the Council and the EP, it is all the more open to pressures and influences from organised interests that are present in Brussels.

If actors involuntarily suffer losses or disadvantages inflicted by other specifiable actors (rather than anonymous market forces), and if the infliction of such losses is not stipulated by national law (such as tax law or civil law), then such losses require justification and, failing that, compensation. While it doubtlessly provides for gains and opportunities, the EU routinely inflicts such losses. First, and due to the principle of the direct effect of EU law on member states, citizens have to comply with or are exposed to the effects of European rules even if they have not been decided upon unanimously, but by qualified majority decision in the Council. These can be described as political losses, sometimes dramatised as bordering on 'foreign rule'. Second, the EU rules and orders which the citizens of member states have to comply with, beginning with the four market freedoms, have virtually always, and in spite of the pretension of a distributionally neutral enhancement of technical efficiency ('Pareto optimality'), (re)distributive side effects, which benefit some category of economic actors and hurt others. These are equivalent to losses of economic opportunity. Third, as EU-level actors impose constraints and conditions which limit the policy making capacity of member states in such crucial policy areas as fiscal, monetary and competition policy, states and their democratically accountable governments suffer losses in terms of their political autonomy – losses which can be perceived by national constituencies as plain cases of uncompensated 'political expropriation'. These three types of losses can be sufficiently severe to require justification.

Standard justifications and their weaknesses

The two standard justifications that Europe offers its member states and citizens are: (i) the backward-looking justification that member states have, after all, voluntarily given up some of their sovereignty at the point of joining the Union; and (ii) the forward-looking, or functionalist, justification in terms of 'output legitimacy'. The latter is claimed on the grounds that general observance of European constraints and universal compliance with European regulations will eventually turn out to be for the better, in terms of prosperity, equitable burden-sharing and security from negative externalities, for all sides involved. Losses, Europeans are assured, are of a transitory nature, and corresponding gains of a long-term nature. However, because of the long time that has elapsed since the EU-6 member states originally decided to form the Community, and because of the fact that the Union was a *fait accompli* to the new members of EU-25 when they joined in 2004, justification (i) appears weak. So does justification (ii) in view of the debatable question of whether the promises and hopes for universal gains in prosperity have actually realised or, for that matter, will be redeemed at some (indeterminate) point in the future. It is in view of these two weaknesses that it seems desirable that, in addition to the backward-looking and the forward-looking justification, a third more presentist justification mechanism should be developed.

It also seems consistent to argue that the more harm and loss an institutional actor is capable of inflicting, the more strictly it should be supervised and held accountable. As Scharpf[12] has pointed out, the institutional structure of the European policy process consists of two constituent arenas. On the one hand, we find the arena of institutional actors (Commission, ECJ, ECB), who control highly concentrated power resources with a major impact upon European member states and citizens; yet these actors and the ways their resources are employed are not accountable to anybody. On the other hand, there is the arena of the Commission in its agenda-setting role, of the Council and of the EP; this is a set of institutions in which power is extremely dispersed and the number of veto points is arguably greater than it is within any national democracy. Given the highly consensual and consociational nature of this latter arena, it seems effectively prevented from doing much harm. Taken together, the proportionality rule stated in the first sentence of this paragraph is stood on its head: the more power, the less accountability, and vice versa.

As far as the second arena (Commission as agenda setter, Council, EP) is concerned, one of the most striking differences between the domestic democracies at the member state level and the EU polity is that the latter does not have an institutionalised opposition. One might say that, lacking hierarchical enforcement capacities and taxing powers of its own, the EU cannot afford an opposition, as the policy process is utterly dependent upon consensus and is extremely vulnerable to non-cooperative moves on the part of member state governments. As a consequence, legislative outcomes emerge from bargaining behind closed doors in the Council and are adopted under decision rules based on either unanimity or 'oversized majority'. In its legislative activities, the EU rules by elite consensus and compromise, and it cannot rule where these are not forthcoming. This style of ruling without an opposition is what is meant by governance – a concept whose rise to amazing popularity in academia and beyond is itself symptomatic of the scarcity of power resources that are both legitimate and effective. 'Governance' means coping with conflicts and policy problems through negotiation, compromise, deliberation, voluntary cooperation, and non-coercive ('soft') modes of persuasion and policy coordination. The Commission's White Paper on 'European Governance'[13] urges the 'use of non-legislative instruments', 'co-regulatory mechanisms' such as the 'open method of coordination', 'involving civil society' and strengthening a 'culture of consultation and dialogue'. 'Good' governance can thus be described as an activity that tries to create and maintain order in a complex world of highly interdependent elements with a blurred line between state and non-state (that is, economic and 'civil society') as well as national and supranational actors, and with multiple veto points and a severe scarcity of sovereign power resources. In this world, the activity of 'ruling' loses much of its vertical dimension of bindingness and 'giving orders'; it transforms itself into horizontal acts of winning support through partnership and a highly inclusive participation of all pluralist collective actors to the extent that they muster any capacities at all for vetoing or obstructing policy results or for contributing to desired outcomes.

Both of these institutional subsets, however, share the feature of deficient accountability. They lack what we have termed 'presentist' legitimacy. In spite of the normative appeal of some of the catchwords (such as 'openness', 'participation', 'accountability') employed in the document on European governance, we must note that the type of governance the document outlines is an elite-sponsored executive strategy to win support and cooperation in a supranational context. This strategy is driven by the necessities of scarce political resources rather than by normative principles, and it is advertised, with an evident technocratic ambition, as 'good' governance rather than normatively 'right' governance, which would be based upon and answerable to the preferences of European citizens. The legislative process is all-inclusive and non-partisan rather than based upon a set of (essentially contested) political values and programmatic priorities. The European style of governance is strongly non-adversarial and consociational, often slow, erratic and opaque as to who is responsible for which policy, its conceivable alternatives and the outcome of its implementation. Lacking an opposition and, as a consequence, an ongoing contest between governing and opposition forces, European governance at the elite level and beyond is deprived of the creative 'learning pressure' that democratic political competition can instil.

Instead of a political opposition, it is individual countries or groups of countries that are perceived to act as contestants in European policy debates within the Council. But member states and coalitions of member states are not equivalent to an opposition proper. Citizens have no choice between being, say, Spanish or Irish, while they do have a choice between supporting, say, social democratic or market-liberal policy proposals, provided such a choice were offered to them. The absence of an equivalent to an opposition (or a counter-elite to the governing elite, preparing for taking office after the next elections) has, we argue, three implications, all of which are relevant for issues of legitimacy:

First, a regime of European governance that has no opposition does not allow for institutionalised dissent. It thus tends to leave dissenters with the only option of populist, nationalist, xenophobic and protectionist anti-EU mobilisation. Such of these fundamental opposition movements, located partly on the political left but mostly on the right, have been gaining momentum in virtually all member states and even have achieved a not insignificant minority of seats in the EP itself. The elite consensus reached in the Council and the Commission remains vulnerable, and increasingly so, to what Beetham and Lord refer to as 'direct popular counter-mobilization'.[14]

Second, the highly consensual and opaque style of legislation within the Council, as well as the uncontested agenda-setting role of the Commission, leave most European citizens in a state of semi-illiteracy concerning European matters and issues. As Follesdal and Hix convincingly argue,[15] the lack of knowledge and interest that citizens show in these affairs and policy issues does not have to be genuine, but may well be an artefact of the lack of public debate and controversy at the elite level. Voters form and, as it were, 'discover' their preferences endogenously in the policy process itself, that is by following the contest between alternative policy packages and political programmes. Both the lack of such contests and the technical complexity of many of the issues make it exceedingly difficult for citizens to gain and apply what citizenship requires, namely an 'adequate understanding'[16] (Dahl) of issues, agendas and their own 'rightly understood' interests and preferences. Perceiving very well that European legislation is in some way consequential for them and their interests and values, but at the same time being deprived of the wholesome 'learning opportunity' that comes with the public debates on democratic politics and the contest of clearly distinguishable parties and programmes, citizens observe the EU policy process with a sense of apathetic fatalism and sceptical non-involvement.

Third, the legitimacy of the domestic democratic policy process itself is bound to suffer if the citizens of member states perceive that elected national governments are embarrassed by having to submit to 'Brussels-based' policy decisions which contradict the expressed preferences and evident interests of the member state government and its constituency. These citizens have reason to feel politically dispossessed if national legislatures are being by-passed[17] by the Council and the EP as institutions authorising laws that apply to the national citizenry. Inversely, and to mitigate voters' frustration with this inconsistency, member state governments have strong incentives to delay and obstruct unpopular Council decisions whenever national elections are forthcoming and the governing parties must fear losses due to the impact of EU policies upon critical parts of the national electorate.

We conclude from this discussion, to repeat, that stronger and more 'presentist' forms of legitimating EU-level decisions and policies are called for – not just for the sake of building European democracy, but equally to preserve the credibility of democratic arrangements within member states. Technocratic, or what Beetham and Lord call 'performance-based', justifications are no longer good enough. For one thing, and as the 'European Employment Strategy' (as adopted by the Lisbon European Council in 2000 and significantly watered down in its ambitions by the Brussels European Council of 2005) serves to demonstrate, indicators of actual performance are not as compelling as they would have to be if the burden of justification of EU policies were to be borne by them alone. For another, there is no such thing as exclusively 'technical' policy making that follows a 'one best way' charted by experts or, for that matter, the ECB. Any presumably expert decision has (re)distributive effects and can be politically challenged in terms of their fairness and appropriateness. Moreover, virtually all students of the politics of European integration agree that the 'permissive consensus' that used to generate passive and detached acceptance of EU decisions is wearing thin with the European citizenry, and that the EU has turned from a generator into a net consumer of generalised support.

Another reason that leads us to conclude that a more robust procedural framework of legitimation is needed derives from the dual fact that: (i) the redistributive impact of European policies is making itself felt ever more acutely by citizens (an example being the Commission's abortive Services Directive), and (ii) the tolerance for redistributive effects appears to decline with enlargement. For as long as there is a sense of shared identity, solidarity and familiarity with 'our neighbours' (say, within the EU-6), we do not object to them profiting from some redistributive effects. It is an entirely different matter if beneficiaries can be framed as 'those other people' or 'those poor newcomers' who gain (major, permanent and perhaps even seemingly 'undeserved') advantages 'at our expense'.

A final reason that adds to the urgency of legitimation issues is the fact that the EU is a moving object that is still in motion, and will remain in motion for the foreseeable future, continuing to be involved in a dynamic process of maturation, evolution and further expansion. These dynamics concern both the (mutually conflicting) objectives of territorial expansion ('widening') and of the (re)allocation of policy competences within the Union ('deepening'). We further conclude that if legitimation of EU policies can neither derive from unquestioning trust in the technical correctness of expert decisions (aptly described as 'Pareto authoritarianism' by Follesdal and Hix)[18] nor develop from the reliance on sentiments of widely shared sympathy, identity and solidarity with our fellow European neighbours, and if neither the chain of justification of domestic member state democracy that extends from national elections to the Council and the Commission is strong enough nor opposition-free consociationalist European governance is an adequate answer, then there is ample reason to explore additional options for the legitimation of European rule.

Democratic legitimacy in the absence of a *demos*?

Legitimation is a set of procedural norms from the application of which legitimacy emerges. Legitimacy must first of all be distinguished from 'acceptance', as one is the opposite of the other. The latter terms comprises favourable habitual attitudes, opinions, calculations of interests, and sentiments which, taken together, condition the empirical agreement of parts of a population with political decisions and regimes. Legitimacy, in contrast, is the effect of the compliance of actors with 'pre-established norms'[19] that generate the 'rational' motivation (which is open to argument and insight) of all members of a political community, the *demos*, to comply with acts of political rule, even if these acts (laws, executive and court decisions) are in conflict with the habits, opinions, sentiments and interests of those who still comply. These pre-established norms generate motivational force because they are believed to be intrinsically and demonstrably just and valid. They stipulate the (limited) right of rulers to rule and the (equally limited) obligation of the ruled to obey.

The source of validity of the constitutive norms can vary widely: it can be divine revelation, national tradition, the universally shared belief in the exceptional qualities of a ('charismatic') leader, or the belief that these norms, in addition to being intrinsically valid, will also have desirable consequences (such as domestic and international peace). As far as the EU and its member states are concerned, this source of validity cannot be anything other than democratic in nature, meaning, at a minimum, the equal political rights of citizens, the free exercise of these rights under a regime of civil liberties, and procedures that hold rulers accountable for what they do while ruling. These rights and obligations are always thought to be embedded in a constituted political community whose members, due to the longitudinal stability of a shared past and a hoped-for shared future, encounter each other with greater expectations of trust, reciprocity and solidarity than the expectations they have of people who do not belong to that constituted community or *demos*.

The problem, however, is that the European political community for which both the right of rulers to rule and the obligation of non-rulers to obey must be designed is different from the *demos* as we know it from consolidated national democracies. The notion of a national *demos*, because it invokes a shared past and the commonality of a common future fate, provides a powerful and pervasive reminder of the collectivity in whose collective interest rule must be conducted and in whose favour (namely that of 'our' fellow citizens and, as such, the democratic co-authors of the law) compliance is called for (from all fellow citizens).[20] There is clearly no equivalent of the national *demos* at the transnational European level. Moreover, there is hardly a prospect of the national populations of current and future EU member states undergoing a fusion that will make them into a *demos*. Even if the Treaty on the Constitution of Europe (TCE) had been adopted, the capacity of such a unifying document to integrate its subject-citizens into something remotely resembling a *demos* would remain in doubt.[21] As a rule of thumb, a durable and solidly self-recognising political community – that is, a *demos* – is created by constitutional design only under two rather exceptional context conditions: either a historical rupture associated with a liberating revolutionary experience (France, the USA) or a similarly deep discontinuity after historical defeat and breakdown, with widely shared resolve to make a new beginning (France, Germany, Italy after World War II). As neither of these conditions applies to today's Europe, the energies of passion that are released by the shared awareness of a dark past of dictatorial rule or a shining future of liberty are not generally available to drive the process of European integration. Such passions may play a limited role in the Central East European states that after 1989 escaped from the supranational regime of authoritarian state socialism. Yet in spite of all the rhetoric of 'returning to Europe', what these countries are eager to return to is the condition of their own nationhood, with joining the EU being largely perceived as a tribute to economic expediency, not to political aspiration.

If anything, the process of European integration, the substance of which has largely been 'negative' integration into the Single Market, has tended to release considerable centrifugal in addition to integrative energies. While the proverbial saying that 'good fences make good neighbours', if applied to European state borders, has been at best of limited truth in the history of the twentieth century, the opposite does make some sense in the recent experience of the Single Market: the absence of 'fences' may create tensions between neighbours. While the small North West European economies (Ireland, Denmark, Benelux) as well as the Baltic countries have every reason to appreciate the added opportunities that market integration has offered them, such is not necessarily the case with the large continental economies of France, Italy and, in particular, Germany (with its persistent burden of integrating the new *Lander* and its liability of a still basically Bismarckian social security system). In this latter group of countries, and given the new mobility in the context of vastly diverging labour costs, there are increasingly vocal groups of 'integration losers' (which come by country, by region, by sector of industry, by trade, by occupation, by size of enterprise) who relate to their more fortunate foreign neighbours with a sense of economic fear, intense rivalry, resentment, distrust and jealousy. These sentiments are bound to lead to demands for better protection and more lenient constraints for 'us' and fewer European subsidies for 'them'. It also leads to the spread of the strategic pattern of the 'competition state' that is constantly searching for ways to make conditions more attractive to foreign and domestic investors by lowering taxes and the costs of employing labour relative to conditions that prevail in neighbouring countries.

The tensions that are generated by the Single Market do not just affect integration at the international (that is, European) level; they also impact on national integration and the cohesion of national societies and economies. Political parties and movements within the wealthier regions of member states (in the South West of Germany, the North and East of Spain, the North of Italy, the North of Belgium and elsewhere) have obvious interest-related reasons to turn to their national governments, as well as to their regional constituencies, with pleas backed by powerful regional interests to relieve them from the burdens of interregional fiscal redistribution within their nation states, so that they can compete more effectively within an environment of denationalised markets.

Both European political elites and academic Europeanists have for a long time been aware of Europe's Achilles' heel of lacking a *demos* that is remotely equivalent in its internal coherence and its compliance-generating potential to the various national *demoi*. Numerous efforts have been made by European elites to alleviate this perceived defect, to build and promote through symbols the awareness of a European identity, and to stimulate the public's imagination of a Europe-wide political community. Eight types of approaches to strengthening an all-European sense of identity, belonging and common interest will be briefly mentioned here.

First, many EU documents and legal texts try to provide assurances that thinking of oneself as a 'European' need not interfere with, let alone overrule, narrower identities of a national or regional kind, as Europe is supposed to be committed to the recognition of cultural (linguistic, religious, ethnic, historical) diversity and legitimate pluralism.

Second, there are philosophical and educational initiatives that probe into the common heritage of traditions and values that may potentially overarch diversity. These include Greek antiquity, Christianity and Judaism, the Enlightenment, and the lessons from the disasters of totalitarianisms and international warfare which marked Europe's 'short twentieth century'. These references, together with the visionary assertion that European states and peoples aspire 'to build a common future' (TCE I – 1) and the reference to the distinctiveness of European values and visions, may help establish an affective dimension for European identification.

Third, a common European cultural space has been created to bridge cognitive distances between European citizens. It includes well-funded programmes for transnational scientific collaboration and student exchange programmes, including the emergence of a European scene in the 'high' as well as popular arts, entertainment and sports.

Fourth, there are the major economic programmes of structural, regional, agricultural and cohesion subsidies designed to boost the competitiveness of member states and regions and to facilitate the process of their upward harmonisation.

Fifth, there is the legal framework of secondary European law with its emphasis on creating a Europe-wide 'level playing field' of fair competition, through the protection of labour, consumers, and the environment that is made binding on all producers or employers. For the euro zone, the EMU is the main framework of denationalised monetary policy. Sixth, there is the promise of prosperity through integration. The Treaty of Rome already lists among the fundamental objectives of the European Community the constant improvement of the living and working conditions of the European peoples. Seventh, there is a dimension of integration that is abstractly referred to as 'the European social model' (ESM), comprising the combined objectives of prosperity, dialogue and inclusion in matters of social policy. The latter, however, remains firmly under the control of member states and has increasingly become a factor in member states' strategies to bolster national competitiveness. Eighth and finally, we come to the TCE, whose intended ratification by 2006 looks highly unlikely in mid-2005. As commented upon above, the TCE's integrative potential is limited, and its content undertakes to 'Europeanise' democratic principles and values, rather than creating new rights beyond what is presently constitutional law within member states. It would serve, inter alia, to specify and expand the stipulations of the Maastricht Treaty on the European Union (TEU Art. 17–22) concerning the rights attached to the status of European citizenship.

Let us briefly turn to an assessment of the empirical outcome of these various initiatives to integrate the populations of member states into something that approximates an equivalent of a European citizenry or *demos*. In doing so, we use the summary and analysis of Eurobarometer surveys provided by Nissen.[22] When EU-15 citizens are asked whether or not they think EU membership of their country is a 'good thing', the answers are roughly 50 per cent 'Yes' and 50 per cent 'No' for 2003. This is the same distribution that was found in 1983, while in the early nineties it was 70 per cent 'Yes' against 30 per cent 'No'. Support for and identification with the EU can be either of an affective or of an instrumental (or functional) kind. The latter is based on an assessment of the perceived costs and benefits of membership whereas the former values EU membership as part of one's own identity. As far as the 'sense of European identity' is concerned, one robust finding stands out: identification becomes stronger with the duration of membership, with the EU-6 countries leading the field. However, as far as utilitarian motivations ('membership is advantageous for the country') are concerned, it is equally evident that much depends upon whether one's country is a net recipient of EU funds or a net contributor to them. All the major net contributors (Germany, Austria, Sweden, the UK) are to be found at the lower end of the scale of utilitarian supporters (close to or in the cases of Sweden and the UK, substantially below 40 per cent), whereas all the 'cohesion countries' (Greece, Ireland, Portugal, Spain), with the substantial net benefits they are enjoying, turn out to be utility enthusiasts with positive answers of above 60 per cent.

The policy implications of these findings are rather clear, as stated by Nissen.[23] First, the sustained efforts of the EU to cultivate a sense of European identity by cultural, symbolic and educational strategies have not been significantly successful. Countries still differ according to their identification with Europe, and the variable that explains these differences is duration of membership, or habituation. Obviously European elites cannot administer identity any more than anyone else. Second, utilitarian support for the EU is fluctuating and is largely contingent on the perceived distributional impact of EU policies and finances. As a rule of thumb, the EU has to buy support through its allocation of costs and benefits, rather than being able to rely on robustly entrenched normative orientations. What holds European citizens together is the systemic integration of interests, interdependence and exchange, and much less so – and in markedly asymmetrical ways – the social integration of shared norms, identities and solidarities.[24] This imbalance of the two kinds of integration is widely expected to increase in the aftermath of the transition from EU-15 to EU-25.

What makes the incomplete and unsystematic list of the integration approaches and initiatives so far undertaken in the EU interesting, is what is not included in it. First, Europe does not have a foreign policy capacity, the ambitious proclamations of a 'Common Foreign and Security Policy' and the debates on a 'European security identity' notwithstanding. As the war in Kosovo of 1999 and the other post-Yugoslav conflicts have amply demonstrated, Europe has neither the military resources nor the resolve to conduct an autonomous and coherent foreign and security campaign of its own. The EU is often, in our view, wrongly credited[25] with being an institutionalised guarantor of international peace between its member states. That peace is guaranteed in Europe is surely no small accomplishment, but it is an accomplishment not of the EU, but of NATO (under its US leadership), to which the majority of member states belong. Also, a lacuna in the security capacities of the EU is its failure to address open or latent separatist civil wars within member states (Northern Ireland and the Basque country respectively), as these are left to the exclusive authority of the latter. Any attempt by the EU leadership to unify Europe by the conduct of an autonomous foreign policy would immediately backfire by deepening the divide between the 'old European' West of the continent and much of the 'new European' East that was so effectively invoked by the US administration on the eve of the American attack on Iraq.

Second, Europe does not have a consistent and reasonably promising policy on employment and social security, in spite of the increasing ESM rhetoric and the European Employment Strategy (EES) inaugurated at the Luxembourg (1997) and Lisbon (2000) summits. While these problems are themselves partly caused by the competitive conditions of the single market and negative integration, the EU largely leaves it, in the name of 'subsidiarity', to member state governments to cope with unemployment and social security finance. The policy choices for dealing with these problems in effective ways, however, are severely constrained by the monetary and fiscal regime governing the euro zone. To be sure, a rich variety of innovative and promising policy proposals for coming to terms with ever more pressing problems of poverty, exclusion and marginalisation (proposals such as basic income schemes designed to raise all European citizens beyond the poverty line by entitling them to an unconditional and tax-financed minimum income, or Schmitter's proposal for a 'Euro-stipendium'[26] have been advocated. Yet it is in the nature of open economies that member states that adopt such policy innovations unilaterally will immediately find themselves in the 'sucker' position, that is of an actor who provides uncompensated advantages to others. Meanwhile the political costs of forming a policy consensus across all or a significant number of member states appear prohibitive. If the EES, to date hardly a success story, can be taken as an indicator, it signals the growing awareness of European policy elites that issues of employment, social security and poverty will either be resolved at the supranational European level – and by policies of 'positive integration' that would have to trump or bypass existing 'subsidiarity' reservations – or they will not be resolved at all.

Europe – un objet politique non identifié

What can these and similar efforts to integrate European societies transnationally and to create some approximate equivalent to the *demos* within the nation state conceivably result in? The answer cannot possibly be that the European Union will assimilate itself to the familiar pattern of the European nation state – which, as we have argued before, is the necessary precondition for political democracy and the legitimacy that flows from it. We know that the EU is a 'non-state and non-nation'.[27] This negative classification does not tell us what kind of legitimation is both appropriate and feasible for this fabulous entity which Jacques Delors allegedly once called *un objet politique non identifié*. In fact, its combination of territorial and functional elements is puzzling and defies unequivocal classification. As an 'ever closer union among the peoples of Europe' that develops 'a single institutional framework which shall ensure the consistency and the continuity' of its activities and that has established the status of citizenship for the nationals of its member states, the EU is equipped with some of the basic features of a territorially defined polity. At the same time, the EU is hardly more than a bundle of partial regimes with varying participants, such as the internal market pursuant to Articles 3, 14 and 95 TEC, the currency union pursuant to Articles 105ff., or the common defence policy of those EU member states which are also members of the WEU (Article 17 paragraph 2 TEU).

One of the most creative attempts at a classification of the institutional particularities of the EU so far, is Philippe Schmitter's distinction between *stato/federatio, confederatio, condominio* and *consortio*.[28] These types represent different combinations of territorial and functional dimensions of political entities. The *condominio* is the one which comes closest to the EU in that it combines the same variants of functions and of territorial units. If we try to translate Schmitter's typology into the conceptual framework and the terminology of state and constitutional theory, the *stato/federatio* is the federal state (*Bundesstaat*), the *confederatio* is a confederation (*Staatenbund*), arguably the *consortio* can be understood as a pattern of intensified intergovernmental cooperation (like the EU's common defence and security policy), and a *condominio* is an entity which unites elements of a federal state (*Bundesstaat*) and of a confederation (*Staatenbund*) without strictly conforming to either of them. According to the conventional legal distinction, federal states are based upon a constitution and have a direct legal relationship to the citizens of the federal units (states, cantons, provinces, *Lander*). In contrast, confederations come into being through the conclusion of international treaties, and a legal relationship exists only between the federal entity and its member states and does not extend to the citizens of the latters. The EU combines both of these elements: it is based upon a multilateral international treaty (which does not lose this character even if its most recent version [29 October 2004] is to serve as a 'Constitutional Treaty' after its hoped-for ratification in all of the 25 member states by November 2006). At the same time, because of the principle of direct effect as well as the institution of union citizenship, there is also a direct legal relationship between the EU and the citizens of the member states. To underline the hybrid nature of this political entity, the German Federal Constitutional Court has invented the untranslatable German term *Staatenverbund*.[29]

Unfortunately, the new term does not necessarily help us to understand the genuinely political character of the EU, nor does it provide us with a new concept. Without a minimal degree of conceptual clarity about the EU, the criteria by which we can determine the requirements for the legitimation of this polity and its policies remain vague at best. In what follows, we suggest an understanding of the EU as a political entity for which a wide variety of names would fit, ranging from union, federal union or confederacy through confederation, community and system of states to perpetual league, *republique federative* and *Bund*.[30] Whatever the appropriate term, what constitutes the particular character of the EU is its origination in a treaty which not only creates a distinct political entity – the union or the *Bund* – but which at the same time transforms the political status of the parties to this treaty, the member states. In the following we will elaborate on this.

There are three basic forms of relationship between sovereign states, namely hegemony, balance of power, and those composite entities, the potential terms for which we just mentioned and which we prefer to call union or, in German, *Bund*.[31] Unions originate from treaties between sovereign states. In order to understand their particular character it is helpful to distinguish between three general classes of contracts. When actors have complementary interests and enter into a voluntary legal relationship under which they exchange valued items (goods, services, ideas and so on) this legal bond is what we call an exchange contract. When actors have identical interests and enter into a voluntary legal relationship, the contract which they conclude is what we call a purposive contract (*Zweckvertrag*). Finally there is a third kind of contract which is intended to transform, confirm or nullify the status of at least one of the parties (one dramatic example being the German Unity Contract, which stipulated that at the moment it became effective one of the two contracting parties, the GDR, would cease to exist). The marriage contract between two people is typical of what some authors call a status contract.[32] For those familiar with Henry Sumner Maine's famous statement in his 'Ancient Law' that 'the movement of the progressive societies has hitherto been a movement *from Status to Contract*',[33] the notion of a 'status contract' must appear oxymoronic. In fact, an act by which the existential conditions of a person are changed is normally not an act of the same character as a contract affecting a thing which he or she can forfeit or contribute. A status contract differs from the two other types of contract in that it is an existential contract in which a person with a particular identity enters into a new legal relationship with another person or persons, for the purpose of changing this identity in a new way. The ensuing union does not absorb the partners; but it mutually obliges them in an ongoing relationship that is basically intended to be indefinite. Note that this kind of contract is often the legal confirmation of a pre-legal relationship, such as the relationship of love in the case of a marriage contract. Such a pre-legal relationship consists in a relationship of trust between the partners and requires diffuse mutual duties of loyalty and the shared expectation of irreversibility.

The EU as a 'Republican Empire'

Status contracts are also concluded between states,[34] the relevant category for our discussion being treaties that constitute a union (or a *Bund*) between them. A union is different from a mere alliance between independent states that pool certain resources but retain their independence and identity. What is required for the creation of a union is the readiness of the parties to the status treaty to enter into mutual ties of solidarity. Tocqueville, analysing the conditions of durable confederations, emphasised 'a uniformity of interests' and the 'same stage of civilization, which almost always renders a union feasible'[35]. Similarly, John Stuart Mill claimed that federal unions between foreigners are workable only if, among other requirements, there is 'a sufficient amount of mutual sympathy among the populations'.[36] Others have referred to this requirement as that of homogeneity.[37] But such similarity does not necessarily lead states to enter into a union. Similarity is not even sufficient to hold an existing union together. The dissolution of the union of Norway and Sweden in 1905 is a striking example, the dissociation of Libya and Egypt in the seventies of the past century another one. Even more unlikely is the formation of a union between foreign nations. But it is precisely this that is constitutive of the EU. We do not deny that the majority of the European nations which are members of the EU share a cultural heritage (as based upon the cultural tradition of Greek and Roman antiquity, the Christian-Jewish religious sources of their culture, and the ideas of the Enlightenment). However, there are strong empirical indications that their populations perceive themselves mutually as foreigners, because they do not speak the same language, have different national histories and myths, have developed different concepts for understanding their political identity and, last but not least, harbour strong national prejudices, sometimes even resentments, against each other.

It is against this historical background of perceived mutual foreignness that the peculiarity of the EU must be assessed. Having been established for the purpose of 'an ever closer union among the peoples of Europe' (Article 1, para 2 TEU), the European Union is the first – by definition voluntary – federation in the history of mankind that recognises the dissimilarity of its constituent parties. The EU is a political body which is committed to respecting the distinctive national identities of its member states and citizens, yet at the same time subjects them in many significant areas to the jurisdiction of a common government. In the history of political formations, most cases in which distinct peoples have been subsumed under a common regime are those in which integration is accomplished through the hegemonic prevalence of an imperial centre and the coercive power originating from that centre.

Due to their coercive mode of integration, empires can extend themselves, depending upon the military resources at their disposal, over huge geographical areas. By doing so, they come to incorporate an increasing number and variety of peoples, tribes and nationalities. In contrast, and up to the end of the eighteenth century, republics – polities based upon the voluntary participation and the active involvement of their citizens in common affairs – had existed only at the local level of relatively small city states, and their citizenries were usually highly homogeneous in terms of their origin, language, religion and culture. Both the Federalists and Tocqueville observed that the federal system of the USA had overcome the small-scale character of the traditional republic and, for the first time in history, established a republic that resembled an empire in its spatial extension. This became possible because what Tocqueville speculated upon in his prophetic last two pages of the first volume of *Democracy in America* did come to pass:

> A time will come when one hundred fifty millions of men will be living in North America, equal in condition, the progeny of one race, owing their origin to the same cause, preserving the same civilization, the same language, the same religion, the same habits, the same manners, ... imbued with the same opinions.[38]

The first spatially extended republic in history was built upon, as Tocqueville foresaw (and considered the indispensable precondition for a durable federation), the ethnic, linguistic and cultural uniformity, or at least similarity, of citizens. If anything, this melting-pot vision of a homogeneous empire-sized republic is being trumped today by the EU polity, in that the latter has not only achieved the territorial expansion of an empire, but also allows for and consistently encourages the maintenance of national and regional diversity. The massive presence of entrenched, ineradicable, sub-territorially based and legally recognised diversities makes up the most significant difference between the EU of the twenty-first century and the USA of the eighteenth and nineteenth centuries. Even though the 'melting pot' of US society has turned into a proverbial 'mosaic' in the twentieth century, the latter refers to individual and group differences, not territorially entrenched and localised ones.[39] The European Union is the first spatially extended union of a great number of highly distinctive peoples that is governed as a republican regime. It reconciles the main attribute of an empire – multinationality – with an essential quality of a republic, political freedom, the latter resulting from the voluntary character of the former. To put it oxymoronically: the EU is a republican empire.

Legitimacy in a 'Republican Empire' with redistributive policies

But that oxymoron makes the question of legitimacy even more puzzling. What is conceivably the normative basis of rule (and as such the equivalent to either the force of imperial coercion or the bond of Tocquevillean 'similarity') that might keep the Union together? Can the absence of coercion quasi-automatically produce feelings of 'mutual sympathy among the populations' which Mill claimed is an indispensable condition of durable federations, or is the voluntary decision to join the federation in itself a sufficient warranty for its durability? Is it the republican form of government – political freedom – which is strong enough to bind a union of foreigners together, as suggested by Habermas' vision of a rise of supranational 'constitutional patriotism'?

Note that there is a European tradition for dealing with a situation in which groups are alien to or even have hostile feelings towards each other. Europeans have found a way of coping with their mutual distinctiveness within the relatively narrow and densely populated geographical boundaries of the European continent. Here we refer, of course, to the principle of toleration, which developed in Europe during the second half of the seventeenth century as a first step towards religious peace. After the disasters that plagued the first half of the twentieth century and as a consequence thereof, nationalist collective feelings of grudge and hatred have largely faded away, although national stereotypes, prejudices and a certain degree of distrust between the populations of the EU member states clearly remain. Still, this has not prevented the EU from becoming a closer union of European peoples, if perhaps only in terms of its system of governance. This is aptly grasped in Joseph Weiler's statement:

> In political terms, this Principle of Tolerance finds a remarkable expression in the political organization of the Community which defies the normal premise of constitutionalism. ... A majority demanding obedience from a minority which does not regard itself as belonging to the same people is usually regarded as subjugation ... And yet, in the Community, we subject the European peoples to constitutional discipline even though the European polity is composed of distinct peoples. It is a remarkable instance of civic tolerance to accept to be bound by precepts articulated not by 'my people' but by a community composed of distinct political communities: a people, if you wish, of others.[40]

The – admittedly sometimes disgruntled – acceptance of EU policies of gender equality and anti-discrimination, which impose severe constraints upon some member states and their political cultures, shows that the idea of constitutional tolerance is a real European phenomenon and not the offspring of constitutional idealism. We should not overlook the fact that tolerance is not an inherently democratic argument for legitimising public policies;[41] in the political history of Europe it evolved as a pre-democratic disposition of the absolutist state towards religious diversity. Modern democracies, under the impact of a 'politics of difference', have become increasingly responsive to their citizens' demand for recognition of their identity and respectful coexistence of their mutual otherness. Thus the respect for 'otherness' has become an inherent element of the democratic cultures of (most of the) current EU member states and can be extended relatively easily, across national boundaries, which in many respects have lost their exclusionary function. Although there is always some danger of backlash, the values of toleration and respectful coexistence seem to be firmly rooted in contemporary European political culture. In that sense, Europe can be described as a political community of ethnic, religious, linguistic, historical and other communities.[42]

What interests us here is the fact that this achievement is not primarily one that can be attributed to the regime quality of liberal democracy. Apart from the value of toleration being older than democracy, the latter, at least in its majoritarian variants, does not inherently foster toleration. Liberal democracy, on the other hand, has always been advocated and defended in terms of historical projects that were related to other emancipatory values, namely individual freedom *vs.* authoritarianism, national unity and self-determination *vs.* princely prerogatives and imperial rule, social progress *vs.* the rule of capital, or international peace *vs.* belligerent dictatorship. In terms of these and similar oppositions, there has always been in the history of democratic thought and practice a compellingly plausible answer to the question: What is democracy good for? This plausibility, we submit, has to some extent faded away in Europe, partly because its opposites (imperial rule, authoritarianism, the denial of national self-determination) have disappeared from the scene, and partly also because we see that large and persistent problems of social justice defy the democratic method of rule, as the ubiquitous and, it would seem, democratically irremediable crisis and decline of welfare states indicate. Democracy is being separated from the social project, the national project and (after the demise of state socialism) the anti-totalitarian project as well. Also the verb 'to democratise' has lost some of its normative appeal as it has turned from a reflexive verb ('doing something to yourself') into a transitive verb ('doing something to others'), meaning that foreign states and their populations are made, in the name of their 'democratisation', objects of wars, such as in the current American war in Iraq. Others have argued that democracy is essentially a domestic national regime form that loses much of its appeal and potential under the prevailing conditions of globalisation and denationalisation.[43]

Thus, in response to the question raised in the sub-title of the present essay, democracy does not appear to be the answer to many, and arguably the most pressing, of our contemporary problems. For the basic notion inherent in any concept of democracy is a 'vertical' one: we, the people, want to make sure that our rulers 'up there' do the right thing (the social democratic version) or at least make sure that they do not do the wrong thing (that is, interfere with our liberty – the ever more popular libertarian version); and for this we need the political resources afforded by democratic institutions. We are certainly far from a situation in which these two versions of the failure of rule have become irrelevant, and democratic antidotes obsolete. But there are other categories of problems which are, so to speak, outside the reach of national forms and scales of democracy.

What is the nature of these other problems? We think that they are located in a horizontal dimension and thus do not affect the relation between the ruled and their rulers, but instead involve border-crossing relations between the ruled plus the rulers 'here' and 'there'. While constitutional toleration is a norm that encourages difference-bridging and coexistence-enhancing practices 'here', what is called for in border-crossing relations is solidarity, perhaps best defined as an attitude of practical non-indifference towards the needs and rights of others who do not belong to 'our' national citizenry. While national citizenship has been defined as the 'right to have rights', solidarity within the 'republican empire' of the

EU can only mean the denationalisation of rights. While democracy, as we have demonstrated, is inevitably tied to the *demos* of a nation state, solidarity as the endowment of others with rights and claims is an achievement that supranational agencies specialise in and derive their legitimacy from. To the extent that the EU (as a special case of a supranational agency) is able to free rights, including social and economic rights, from their national containers and make them available to all Union citizens, it gains access to the same kind of legitimacy.

Border-transcending solidarity based upon the recognition of the rights of others is no doubt a demanding and risky policy. Its proponents must have institutional means at their disposal with which they can condition the willingness of Union citizens to share not just 'respect' but also resources with others, who are foreigners. It is one thing to recognise 'the other' as an equal, but it is much harder to share with him or her parts of one's income. For instance, a Belgian steel worker must be prepared to accept income losses in favour of, say, a Greek olive grower and the EU must be able to control political resources that induce him to do so. Democratising Europe after the model of the nation state will not increase but undermine the capacity of the Euro-polity to allocate rights and claims in a 'nation-blind' manner. Even the most robust national democracy (or, rather, precisely the most robust national democracy) does not help here, as it will function as an obstacle to, rather than a promoter of, such an institutionalised form of solidarity.

So far European citizens have been called upon to believe that negative integration through market creation will trigger an ongoing positive-sum game of Pareto optimality. As many Europeans, including entire European countries and regions, are still awaiting the onset of this game, an equivalent effect can be achieved through the carefully designed endowment of all Europeans with social and economic rights. After the most recent enlargement by the ten predominantly post-communist countries of Eastern and Central Europe, the number of recipients of EU subsidies has considerably increased; hence the sacrifices required by the populations of the relatively wealthy few net contributors to EU funds may become so painful that their national governments are likely to limit their share, lest they fall victim to anti-European popular movements. Thus constitutional tolerance is a necessary but in all likelihood insufficient condition of the domestic legitimation of transnational redistributive EU policies. The EU, in order to gain legitimacy through a 'nation-blind' and rights-based policy of solidarity among all Europeans needs to acquire the political resources that emancipate it from the transnational repercussions of national democracy.

Embryonic structural and institutional elements are visible within the present set-up of the EU which hold out some hope for the project of a solidarity-based type of legitimacy. As Karl W. Deutsch pointed out a generation ago, there are constellations among political units which may be conducive to transnational solidarity, namely mutual interdependence and mutual responsiveness.[44] In both cases, political units interact: in the former case due to a particular division of labour, in the latter as a consequence of the capacity to 'perceive one another's sensitive spots or "vital interests", and to make prompt and adequate responses to each other's critical needs'.[45] Mutual responsiveness is largely experienced through transactions, that is, the exchange of information, ideas, capital, goods, services and people. According to Deutsch, not only states but also individuals and populations can be integrated through transactions and this also applies to the European Community.[46] While transactions do not necessarily create solidarity and the willingness to share one's income with one's partners, a high volume and frequency of economic, cultural or political transactions may have 'an assimilatory impact upon people'[47] and eventually create trust among them. Whether this causality has materialised already within the EU is far from clear, though. It is a matter of further empirical research to explore the correlation of these data with the transactions among the populations of the member states.

There are also embryonic institutional patterns that might be able to develop into a culture of 'mutual responsiveness',[48] both among the citizens and member states. These would have to cultivate the capacity for role-taking and self-distantiation, both based upon the demanding insight that 'your' interests and values are as strange to me as inversely 'my' interests and values are to you, while there is no standard by which one trumps the other. We will conclude with a brief discussion of the nature and potential of Union citizenship.

If the citizens of the Union, rather than member states, can advance to the status of a constituent factor of the Union, this may be a step towards a kind of democracy without a *demos*. This seemingly oxymoronic phenomenon would mean that people who do not form one particular body of associates on the basis of their (national and other) similarities, but rather share the characteristic of being alien to each other, are still able to make collectively binding decisions. We consider the formation of a post-national collective agency as the core problem of European democracy.

While the component elements of the EU are: (i) member states, and (ii) citizens, under the present rules there is no corporate body which represents the 'citizenry of the Union' per se. The European Parliament is the representative body of the peoples of the member states,[49] that is, national subcollectivities of European citizens. However, the right of the citizens of the member states to stand as candidates in elections to the European Parliament and in municipal elections in their state of residence under the same conditions as nationals of that state is indicative of the fact that the voters in the member states do not have be represented by their fellow nationals; non-nationals, too, may run and win in national elections to the EP. In other words, democratic representation in the European Parliament and in the municipalities of the member states has already marginally overcome the 'nationality principle' and tends to allow for the representation of diversity. A French citizen who has been elected to the EP on a German party list represents neither German nor French citizens; his status is explicitly detached from his national origin as the necessary condition of his taking the role of a representative. What he represents, in a way, is the multinational character of the Union, and citizens voting for him or her would thereby express their commitment to the trans- or supranational character of European politics. On the other hand, and for the time being, the dominant interpretation (and reality) is of course that nationals of member states, not European citizens, are represented in the EP.

However, an increased significance of the nationally 'de-coloured' EU citizen might be implied by the TCE coming into effect. It envisages that the citizens of the Union 'are directly represented at Union level in the European Parliament'.[50] The qualification 'directly' suggests that they are so far only indirectly represented through their affiliation to a member state. So far, the national coding of representation stands in the way of the formation and strengthening of forces that can act independently of national affiliation. The unique trait of the notion of Union citizenship is the dissociation of nationality and citizenship. This status connects people who are strangers by conventional legal, political and cultural standards to an abstract and overarching community of citizens. The recognition of the 'foreigner' as a fellow citizen, and the solidarity out of which 'foreign' representational needs are catered to, is clearly a fundamental challenge to the Europeans' entrenched tradition of regarding only co-nationals as fellow citizens.

It is this embryonic form of non-nation-based citizenship which suggests an entirely new construction of the 'we' in the field of political action. This construction would only be a further step in the long and multifaceted history of the idea of citizenship.[51] Might Union citizenship define a new political identity, a new 'we' which is able to shape the fates of people in a new manner?

To conclude, the problem of European democracy is not that there is no European *demos*. The *demos* presupposes the fusion of the many into one body whose coercive character requires homogeneity of the rulers and the ruled in order to legitimise the necessity of obedience. This is not the political vision of the European Union. The vision is, rather, the idea of solidarity grounded in the mutual recognition of otherness. This vision, it appears to us, derives its legitimacy from being appropriate to a world where people have become neighbours and still remain strangers to each other. This genuine political and institutional innovation is the contribution of Europe to the problems of our world at the beginning of the twenty-first century.

Notes

1. G. Majone, 'From the positive to the regulatory state: causes and consequences of change in the mode of government', *Journal of Public Policy*, 1997, vol. 17, no. 2, pp. 139–169.

2. As found in A. Follesdal and S. Hix, 'Why There is a Democratic Deficit in the EU: A response to Majone and Moravcsik', *European Governance Papers* (EURO-GOV), 2005, No. C-05-02, http://www.connex~network.org/eurogov/pdf/egp-connex-C-05-02.pdf (accessed 19 September 2005).

3. A. Moravcsik, *The Choice for Europe: Social purpose and state power from Messina to Maastricht*, Ithaca, NY, Cornell University Press, 1998.

4. V. Klaus, 'Eine Gefahr für Demokratie und Freiheit in Europa', an interview with the President of the Czech Republic Václav Klaus about the EU

constitution, the government crisis in Prague and relations with Germany, *Frankfurter Allgemeine Zeitung*, 15 March 2005.

5. Follesdal and Hix, 'Why There is a Democratic Deficit in the EU'; D. Beetham and C. Lord, *Legitimacy and the European Union*, Harlow, Longman, 1998; J. H. H. Weiler, U. R. Haltern and F. C. Mayer, 'European Democracy and its Critique', in J. Hayward (ed.), *The Crisis of Representation in Europe*, London, Frank Cass, 1995, pp. 4–39.

6. P. C. Schmitter, *How to Democratize the European Union . . . And Why Bother?*, London, Boulder, New York and Oxford, Rowman & Littlefield Publishers, 2000, p. 116.

7. Follesdal and Hix, 'Why There is a Democratic Deficit in the EU', p. 5.

8. P. C. Schmitter, 'Designing a Democracy for the Euro-polity and Revising Democratic Theory in the Process', in I. Shapiro and S. Macedo (eds), *Designing Democratic Institutions*, nomos XLII, New York, New York University Press, 2000, pp. 224–250 [230], [emphasis added].

9. *Ibid.*, p. 227.

10. Follesdal and Hix, 'Why There is a Democratic Deficit in the EU', p. 6.

11. Pursuant to Article 201 TEC, however, the European Parliament can introduce a motion of censure on the activities of the Commission. If it is carried by a two-thirds majority of the votes cast, representing a majority of the Members of the European Parliament, the Commission has to resign as a body. The same rule is stipulated in Articles 1–26 paragraph 8 and III-340 of the 'Treaty Establishing a Constitution for Europe' (TCE), signed in Rome on 29 October 2004 and due to enter into force by 1 November 2006, provided that all signatory states have ratified the treaty by then (Article IV-447). Given the fact that the EP is not organised along the government-opposition divide, this high quorum for the motion of censure can hardly be fulfilled. In fact, no motion of censure against the Commission has ever been successful. Even the Santer Commission, which resigned on 15 March 1999 after an investigation into allegations of corruption, had easily survived a vote of no confidence on 17 December 1998.

12. F. W. Scharpf, 'Legitimationskonzepte jenseits des Nationalstaats', Max Planck Institute for the Study of Societies working paper 04/6, Cologne, 2004, accessed at http://www.mpi-fg-koeln.mpg.de/pu/workpap/wp04-6/wp04-6. html. add access date

13. European Commission (ed.), *European Governance: A White Paper*, COM (2001) 428 final, Brussels, 2001, accessed at http://europa.eu.int/eurlex/en/com/cnc/2001/com200L0428en01.pdf. add access date

14. Beetham and Lord, *Legitimacy and the European Union*, p. 14.

15. Follesdal and Hix, 'Why There is a Democratic Deficit in the EU', pp. 13–17.

16. R. A. Dahl, *Democracy and its Critics*, New Haven and London, Yale University Press, p. 60.

17. In this respect a major change is envisaged by the TCE in that the national parliaments will be empowered to enter into the political arena of the EU and to play an important role there. Protocol No. 1 to the TCE (which will be no less binding than the Treaty itself after ratification) recognises the significance of national parliaments for the particular constitutional organisation and practice of each member state and encourages their greater involvement in the activities of the EU. For instance, parliaments are entitled to be provided with more thorough information from the Commission. All relevant documents and draft legislative acts of the EU are therefore to be forwarded to them, and they may send to the President of the European Parliament, the Council and the Commission reasoned opinions on whether a draft legislative act complies with the principle of subsidiarity laid down in Article I-11 para 3 TCE. Second, pursuant to Protocol No. 2 they are involved in the supervision of the application of the principles of subsidiarity and proportionality (the latter being laid down in Article 1–11 para 4). Any draft legislative act must contain a detailed statement as to its implications for the principles of subsidiarity and proportionality. If the aforementioned reasoned opinions are put forward by one-third of the national parliaments, that act must be reviewed. Moreover, each national parliament has the right to appeal to the European Court of Justice on grounds of infringement of the principle of subsidiarity. These rules, although purely procedural, force the Commission to take the political particularities and problems of member states into account and to respect the need of their parliaments and governments to legitimise their policies. Admittedly, this falls short of the stimulating proposal of uniting the national parliaments of Europe and assigning them an active role as a European political actor suggests (see G. Grözinger, 'Die "Vereinigten Parlamente von Europa" und weitere tiberlegungen zur subsidiären Demokratie', in C. Offe (ed.), *Demokratisierung der Demokratie. Diagnosen und Reformvorschlage*, Frankfurt am Main, Campus, 2003, pp. 211–231).

18. Follesdal and Hix, 'Why There is a Democratic Deficit in the EU', p. 6.

19. P. C. Schmitter, *What is There to Legitimize in the European Union. . . And How Might This Be Accomplished?*, Florence, European University Institute, 2001, p. 2.

20. In order to become, say, a legitimate member of parliament in the nation state X, a person must not only win a mandate on the basis of fair, clean and contested elections, but must also hold the national citizenship of X. How could it be otherwise? The virtual self-evidence of this norm shows how deeply legitimation is rooted in the notion of *demos* and demotic identity. This demotic principle applies also to the members of the EP, who are elected by the citizens of their country of citizenship, and whose number of seats corresponds (in somewhat modified ways) to the size of population of their country of citizenship.

21. D. Grimm, 'Integration durch Verfassung. Absichten und Aussichten im europäischen Konstitutionalisierungsprozess', *Leviathan*, 2004, vol. 32, no. 4, pp. 448–463. Although, admittedly, it does not even aspire to this goal.

22. S. Nissen, 'Europäische Identität und die Zukunft Europas', *Aus Politik und Zeitgeschichte*, 2004, B38, pp. 21–9.

23. *Ibid.*, p. 29.

24. J. Delhey, 'Nationales und transnationales Vertrauen in der Europäischen Union', *Leviathan*, 2004, vol. 32, no. 1, pp. 15–45.

25. Cf. Beetham and Lord, *Legitimacy and the European Union*, p. 102.

26. Schmitter, *How to Democratize the European Union...*, pp. 44–46.

27. H. Abromeit, *Democracy in Europe: Legitimising politics in a nonstate polity*, New York, Berghahn, 1998; Schmitter, *How to Democratize the European Union...*.

28. P. C. Schmitter, 'Representation and the future Euro-polity', *Staatswissenschaften und Staatspraxis*, 1992, vol. 3, no. 1, pp. 379–405; P. C. Schmitter, 'Imagining the future of the Euro-polity with the help of new concepts', in G. Marks, F. W. Scharpf, P. C. Schmitter and W. Streeck (eds), *Governance in the European Union*, London, Sage, 1996, pp. 121–168.

29. This conceptual ambiguity was already captured by Toqueville when he anticipated a polity (actually, quite similar to the EU) which would be a 'form of society ... in which several states are fused into one with regard to certain common interests, although they remain distinct, or only confederate, with regard to all other concerns. In this case the central power acts directly upon the governed, but in a more limited circle'. Short of using the *sui generis* formula, he adds that 'the new word which ought to express this novel thing does not yet exist' (A. de Tocqueville, *Democracy in America*, vol. 1, New York, Vintage, 1990 [1835], pp. 158f.).

30. M. Forsyth, *Union of States: The theory and practice of confederation*, New York, Leicester University Press/Holmes & Meier Publishers, 1981, p.1.

31. *Ibid.*, p. 204.

32. A. Greber, *Die vorpositiven Grundlagen des Bundesstaates*, Basel, Geneva and Munich, Helbing & Lichtenhahn, 2000, p. 175.

33. H. S. Maine, *Ancient Law: Its connection with the early history of society, and its relation to modern ideas*, Tucson, AZ, University of Arizona Press, 1986 [1864], p. 165, [emphasis in original].

34. The status treaty is a well-known institution of public international law. Such a treaty is present if 'a group of Great powers, or a large number of States ... assume a power to create by a multipartite treaty some new international regime or status, which soon acquires a degree of acceptance and durability extending beyond the limits of the actual contracting parties, and giving it an objective existence' (Int. Court of Justice, Reports of Judgments, Advisory

Opinions and Orders, Int. Status of South-West Africa, Separate Opinion of Judge McNair, pp. 146–163 [153f.]; see also G. Dahm, *Volkerrecht*, volume 1, Stuttgart, W. Kohlhammer Verlag, 1958, pp. 23ff.; E. Klein, *Statusvertrtige im Volkerrecht. Rechtsfragen territorialer Sonderregime*, Berlin, Heidelberg and New York, Springer-Verlag, 1980).

35. Tocqueville, *Democracy in America*, ch. VIII, pp. 169f.

36. J. S. Mill, *Considerations on Representative Government*, reprinted 1991, Buffalo and New York, Prometheus Books, 1991 [1861], ch. XVII, p. 320.

37. C. Schmitt, *Verfassungslehre*, Berlin, Duncker & Humblot, 1965 [1928], pp. 375ff.; Forsyth, *Union of States...*, pp. 116, 207.

38. Tocqueville, *Democracy in America*, p. 521.

39. It is not by accident that the Afro-Americans as 'beings of an inferior order' (as the Supreme Court decreed in the Dred Scott case of 1857) were legally excluded from the polity until the 14th Amendment (1867) and socially until the Supreme Court's decision in Brown v. Board of Education (1954).

40. J. H. H. Weiler, 'Federalism without constitutionalism: Europe's Sonderweg', in K. Nicolaidis and R. Howse (eds), *The Federal Vision: Legitimacy and levels of governance in the United States and the European Union*, Oxford, Oxford University Press, 2001, pp. 54–72 [67f.].

41. Cf. R. Forst, *Toleranz im Konflikt: Geschichte, Gehalt und Gegenwart eines umstrittenen Begriffs*, Frankfurt am Main, Suhrkamp, 2003.

42. P. A. Kraus, *A Union of Diversity? Law, identity and political communication in Europe*, Cambridge, Cambridge University Press, 2008.

43. M. Zürn, 'The challenge of globalization and individualization: a view from Europe', in H.-H. Holm and G. Sörensen (eds), *Whose World Order? Uneven globalization and the end of the Cold War*, Boulder CO., Westview Press, 1995, pp. 137–63; S. Leibfried, and M. Zürn (eds), *Transformations of the State?*, Cambridge, Cambridge University Press, 2005.

44. K. W. Deutsch, *Political Community at the International Level*, New York, Anchor Books, 1970 (first published Garden City, NY, Doubleday, 1954), pp. 34ff.; cf. J. Delhey, 'European Social Integration: From convergence of countries to transnational relations between peoples', Wissenschaftszentrum fur Sozialforschung discussion papers SPI 2004–201, Berlin.

45. Deutsch, *Political Community at the International Level*, p. 37.

46. K. W. Deutsch, *Nationenbildung – Nationalstaat – Integration*, Düsseldorf, Bertelsmann Universitätsverlag, 1972, pp. 133ff., 185ff.

47. Delhey, 'European Social Integration...', p. 12.

48. K. W Deutsch, *International Political Communities,* New York, Anchor Books, 1996.

49. Articles 189, 190 TEC [Treaty of Nice]; pursuant to Article 1–20 TCE, the EP shall be composed of representatives of the Union's citizens. Since the

number of seats is apportioned according to the population size of the member states, the representatives remain essentially representatives of their peoples.

50. Article 1–46, para 2.

51. Cf. P. Riesenberg, *Citizenship in the Western Tradition: Plato to Rousseau*, Chapel Hill, NC, and London, University of North Carolina Press, 1992.

Chapter Twenty-One

The European Model of 'Social' Capitalism: Can It Survive European Integration?*

Claus Offe

The three sets of questions I want to discuss here are as follow:

- Is there such a thing as 'European capitalism'? Are there institutional and structural features that apply more or less to *all* European political economies and *only* to European political economies? How do European political economies and societies contrast if compared to their liberal counterparts of the Anglo-Saxon world?
- If they exist, how can these distinctive similarities, or family affinities of European capitalisms, be explained in historical terms and justified in normative or functional terms?
- What can we expect and predict concerning the impact of European integration upon the distinctive features of European 'social capitalism'? Is it likely that European societies will converge in the process of integration on the distinctive European 'social model', as represented by and inherited from European nation-states, or is there evidence of trends to the opposite? If so, European integration would undermine the 'Europeanness' of the emerging political economy of the European Union (EU).

I. 'European' capitalism?

As to the first of these sets of questions, much of the historical and social science literature is preoccupied with an approach that has been labeled 'methodological nationalism'.[1] The national state and society, not 'Europe' as a whole, is the standard unit of analysis, and for good reasons. On the one hand, the nation-state, at least in modern history, must be conceived of as a self-contained and self-governing entity with distinctive centres of legitimate political rule and the enforcement capacity which has effectively enabled it to shape the institutional structure of its society and economy. Also, until recently, most of the data which are available for social scientific analysis are gathered by national agencies, such as national statistical offices, according to national standards and definitions. Virtually all cross-sectional comparative literature compares countries, and to

---

* 'The European Model of 'Social' Capitalism: Can it survive European Integration?', *Journal of Political Philosophy*, vol. 11, no. 4, 2003, pp. 437–469.

a much lesser extent sub-national units (such as regions) or supranational units (such as 'families of nations'[2]).

There are, however, a number of features that European societies are thought to have in common. Some of these features have remained distinctively European, while others have spread from Europe and its pioneering role to other parts of the globe. Instances of such historically rooted and distinctive features of 'Europeanness' are Christianity, the legacies of the absolutist state,[3] the modes in which this form of political rule has been overcome, a history of vast interstate warfare, colonialism, doctrines and precepts of revolutionary liberation, the nation-state, the sciences, and capitalism itself. This list does, however, invite the objection that there are as many dissimilarities among European states and groups of states: Christianity is divided into Roman Catholicism and Orthodoxy in the fourteenth century and then again into the former and Protestantism in the sixteenth. Revolutionary liberation and nation-state building occurred in some countries, but not (or with much delay) in others. Some states acquired vast colonial empires, others not. Some countries in Europe were capitalist pioneers, others latecomers. And so on. Nevertheless, historians and sociologists have elaborated structural similarities which supposedly govern all (or, at any rate, most) European societies.[4]

These similarities are either of a substantive or a procedural nature, manifesting themselves in distinctive structures or in ways of 'getting things done'. As to the former, religious life, the family, the city, political parties and party cleavages, economic institutions, and artistic forms are cited as instances of shared features of all European societies. As to 'procedural' similarities (and as an offshoot of the Weberian problem of 'occidental rationalism', or 'modernization', with its dialectic of liberating gain of control and the concomitant loss of freedom within 'iron cages'), 'Europe' has been associated with the idea and practice of limiting, balancing, and managing diversity and conflict, and buffering the consequences of change, through the use of state power.[5]

The social, economic, and political contours of Europe are not easy to determine. Even if it comes to defining a sub-set of its features, such as the welfare state, we are bound to conclude that 'the idea of a European welfare state model does not leap automatically from the data'.[6] The rhetoric of the 'European Social Model', as it was inaugurated by Jacques Delors in the early 1990s, may be criticised for representing more of a normative vision than a consolidated reality. Much of the academic literature points to the wide range of variation that can be observed among European welfare states, economic institutions and forms of democracy. Perhaps a reasonably clear and meaningful identity of 'the' European model emerges only if Europe is contrasted with non-European global regions, such as East Asia, the underdeveloped South, or North America.[7] Moreover, (West) European history of the second half of the twentieth century is to a large extent shaped by the US and its military, political, intellectual, economic, and esthetic hegemony. What ties social actors together are links (such as mass air travel, global markets, the Internet) of a global, not a European scope. Arguably, 'Europeanness' is nothing that can be found in the shared histories of European societies but, to the contrary, something that is in the still elusive state of 'becoming', an artifact of European integration and its homogenising impact. Also, in speaking of 'European' society, authors often have in mind some features that characterise core West European societies and which (partly) serve as a pole of attraction or a model for imitation to societies located in Europe's eastern and southern peripheries.

Yet in spite of these various caveats concerning the risks of reifying 'Europeanness', modern European history is arguably shaped, I submit, by what one might call a 'logic of discontinuity'. This discontinuity applies in time and space. It is a 'logic' in that discontinuity poses challenges and calls for types of responses that exhibit some European elective affinity. Spatial discontinuity results from the contest over land borders and the need of all states to define and defend their contested territorial base against neighbouring states, which historically usually happened in the form of international war, conquest, and separation.[8] By discontinuity in time, I mean the relative frequency of regime changes in European history. There is hardly any European country that matches the United States in both the stability of its territorial shape and the longevity of its constitution.[9] In view of these two distinctive European features of discontinuity, every political elite of every state at virtually every moment of its modern history has to fear three kinds of enemies: 'reactionary' classes and elites representing the past who challenge the current regime; 'progressive', or 'rising' social classes threatening the current regime from, as it were, the opposite direction and in the name of some splendid future; and foreign rival states. A third kind of discontinuity within European societies has to do with an overlap of religious divisions and those of social class, with both of them being well crystallised in terms of both formal representative organisations (such as political parties, churches, associations) as well as distinct universes of social intercourse. Without taking the time here to look at the interaction of temporal (or domestic) and spatial (or international) discontinuities and sources of conflict, and without illustrating this vast and somewhat schematic generalisation on the basis of the rich evidence available, I believe, in its support by historical sociologists and social historians, let me jump to one conclusion. This conclusion is that in an environment of spatial and temporal discontinuities as well as class and religious divisions and the pervasive threats and challenges resulting from them, any 'winner-takes-all strategy' does not lead to stable and viable solutions.

People can flee unbearable threats and conflicts, and they have done so in the history of nineteenth and twentieth century Europe by the tens of millions, with most of them turning to the Americas. But entire societies and states cannot escape by relocating into insular situations or virgin lands. They are trapped in an environment of discontinuity and contest. Nor can they hope to cope with this environment of discontinuities (the most important of which come in terms of nations, social classes, and religious belief systems) by imposing upon it a lasting ('millenarian') and spatially all-inclusive ('imperial') order. The two 'totalitarian' regimes that European history has seen in the twentieth century have served to demonstrate, through the disasters they have caused and the eventual defeat they have suffered, the validity of this impossibility theorem. If discontinuities, conflicts, and diversities (of interests, of identities, of ideas) can neither be escaped from through 'exit' nor repressed through state terror, the only remaining option is to institutionalise some viable form of coexistence of classes, states, and identities. This is the lesson on the learning of which both the history and the territorial situation of Europe have put a high premium since the Westphalian peace settlement – the lesson of bridging, regulating, and constraining domestic and international conflict while at the same time recognising the legitimacy and inescapability of diversity. There is a European way in which 'diversity itself is handled' and institutionally transformed into 'ordered, limited, and structured diversity'.[10]

European states to the west of the Iron Curtain have, in the course of the second half of the twentieth century, accomplished a great deal in institutionalising a viable balance between these conflicting challenges. Not only have they created a security regime that makes international war among European states a virtual impossibility.[11] They have also, each in their specific national and path-dependent version, managed to reconcile the dilemmas of social order, thereby sharpening a distinctive profile of European political economies. The horns of these dilemmas (seventeen of them in my counting, but we can probably think of more) are well known: equality versus efficiency, collective bargaining versus individual contracting, cooperation versus conflict, rights versus resources, wage moderation versus distributive conflict, supranationalism versus intergovernmentalism, social partnership versus class conflict, proportional representation versus majoritarianism, constitutionalised basic rights versus parliamentary sovereignty, associational collectivism versus individualism, social security versus competitiveness, politics versus markets, modernism versus postmodernism, citizenship versus communitarian politics of difference, consensus versus conflict, corporatism versus pluralism, and status versus contract.

II. Status, standards, protection

There is a wealth of research which was conducted in the 1990s on comparative capitalism. In fact, the designation of a political economy as 'capitalist' (essentially meaning the dominant role of private firms whose activities are steered by market prices and based on property rights as the institutional locus of production, and the presence of labour markets and the labour contract as the key mechanisms of income distribution) has come to be seen as a universally applicable and hence rather uninformative label. After all, and after the demise of state socialism, what else, other than 'capitalism,' can we expect to find as the organising principles of economic life in 'modern', as well as in modernizing, economies? The emphasis has shifted to the plural: capitalisms instead of capitalism, and the distinguishing historical contexts, institutional features, and record of productive and distributive performance of those varieties of capitalism.

'Capitalism', once viewed as a single species of social and economic organisation, is now being rather conceptualised as a zoo full of different species. Of *how many* species, and different *in what respects*? The most fine-grained classifications come by sector of industry, country, and decade, that is, combine cross-sectional and longitudinal comparative perspectives. Here, the focus is on, say, US railway capitalism in the second half of the nineteenth century, or French biotech capitalism in the last decade of the twentieth. At the other end of the continuum, you have the coarsest distinction of liberal versus 'nonliberal' capitalisms, meaning the Anglo-American versus the European (*and* Japanese) cases of technologically advanced capitalism.[12] Intermediate classifications follow the convention of 'methodological nationalism' by focusing upon national economic regimes and their pervasive path dependencies, or they subdivide the various capitalisms by regional groups of (for example, Scandinavian) countries or political regime types (democratic versus authoritarian). I wish to stick here as closely as possible to the distinction of global regions or continents, looking at 'the' European model in contrast to the Anglo-American and (only marginally) the Japanese ones.

One defining feature of (Continental) European capitalism and the social order resulting from it is the prominence of state-defined and state-protected status categories. In each of the above seventeen pairs of concepts, Continental European capitalism (CEC) tends much more toward the first alternative than does Anglo-Saxon capitalism. By 'status' I mean a positive and statutory (as opposed to merely tradition-based) bundle of rights and duties, standards, licenses, mandates, legally prescribed procedures, entitlements, subsidies, and privileges which are attached to virtually every participant in contractual economic transactions and the collective actors representing and governing these participants. The status regime tells you where you stand in relation to others, what to do, what not to do, and how to do it. As a consequence of these status-based constraints, some economic transactions which might otherwise be voluntarily entered into are ruled out in the name not just of non-economic concerns of moral order (such as the ban on child labour or on trading illegal drugs), but in the name of long-term and collective economic interest itself. The measure of the strength of the status component of a capitalist economic system is the degree to which partners to contracts are endowed with non-negotiable entitlements and duties, as well as the degree to which obligations to third parties not immediately involved in economic transaction are stipulated and enforced by law.

This rule of voluntary transactions being constrained by status categories applies to the entire range of economically relevant institutions, including banks and financial markets; trade unions, employers' associations, and the practices of wage determination and income distribution; the regulation and protection of the commercial sector and small enterprise; agriculture; the networks of transportation, energy, and communication; vocational training and tertiary education; the role and mission of central banks; the professions; corporate governance; international trade, tariffs, and migration; the tax system; state controlled and state-subsidised patterns of housing and the real estate market, as well as urban and regional development, including the conservation of physical resources; social security and other welfare state institutions; public sector employment; company level labour relations; property rights, both in things and in ideas, and their adjudication; and the governance of research, development, and innovation.[13]

For instance, and as a rule of thumb, in the US you get paid for what you *actually* do, while in Europe you get paid for what you *can* do according to some certificate obtained through formal training. Similarly, in the US your level of pay will most often be determined by individual or company-level contractual agreements, while in most European systems trade unions and employers' associations are assigned the collective status right of determining an entire industry-wide pay regime through collective bargaining. In the latter case, the level and kind of rewards are tied to regulatory rules of training and licensing which logically precede the market and are relatively immune from market forces. The individual pursuit of economic gain is 'embedded' (this being one of the key terms of the comparative capitalism literature, a term dating back to Polanyi[14]) in a set of formal (that is, legislated) and informal (moral and culture-bound) institutional patterns which constrain the permissible range of economic transactions, as well as types of participants in contractual interaction. The degree of embeddedness is the greater the more specific and constraining the rules are that limit the pursuit of individual gain in markets (beyond, that is, what general legal rules of criminal and civil law prohibit anyway). Embeddedness refers to the degree to which contractual relations are premised upon a non-negotiable status order governing economic activity, akin to what has been termed 'decommodification' by Esping-Andersen and others.[15]

While constraining and distorting the short-term economic outcomes that would result from 'free' markets, that is, markets exclusively driven by short-term and individual cost and price considerations and voluntary contracts, embeddedness is designed, or at any rate invariably defended and justified, in terms of three standards of collective rationality. These supra-individual rationality standards are temporal, social and functional; they emphasise future-and-past-regardingness, other-regardingness, and the attention to collectively beneficial, though often non-obvious, functions and side effects they perform.

To illustrate, using the case of trade unionism. If trade unions are strong due to a strong status in wage determination assigned to them by law (or even constitutionally, as in Article 9 of the German Basic Law), and if they represent the work force of entire sectors of industry rather than that of individual companies, chances are comparatively greater that they will develop some awareness of and consideration for the consequences their demands and strategies entail for the employment prospects of workers in general, as well as for the rate of inflation and their industry's competitiveness. As a consequence of this organisational set-up, they become more readily '*other-regarding*' than company unions, due to their narrow concern for the maximisation of nominal wages of a small percentage of the industry's or nation's overall work force, could ever afford to be. Similarly, and in the *temporal dimension*, the institutionalisation of a 'skill rent' as a wage component which is being paid regardless of actual job requirements will encourage the acquisition and continuous upgrading of skills, thus creating, unlike the conditions prevailing in highly mobile 'hire-and-fire' labour markets, a reservoir of skills which will economise on transactions costs and increase the duration of job tenure due to workers' enhanced flexibility. Thirdly, high wages and high skills will provide, as a desirable *functional side effect*, a powerful incentive to employers to utilise possibilities for labour-saving technical change, thus increasing the efficiency and competitiveness of production.

Taken together, economic status rights will not only *protect* economic actors (employees, farmers, artisans, small and medium-sized business, banks, the professions etc.) from adverse market impacts; they can also *contribute* to overall and long-term (economic as well as non-economic) outcomes that are superior to pure market transaction with its blindness to the interests of others, to externalities, and to the past or future. If there is anything distinctive about the 'European' model of capitalism, it is the insight, congealed in a myriad of economic institutions and regulatory arrangements, that the interest of 'all of us' will be served well if the pursuit of the interest of 'each of us' is to some extent constrained by categorical status rights. This antithesis has been captured by conceptual pairs such as 'share holding' versus 'stakeholding', or 'efficiency' versus 'X-efficiency',[16] or 'the productivity of rules', which, although constraining market forces, will eventually and counter-intuitively (to some) be rewarded by the market outcomes.

However, it must be noted that the relationship between a market-constraining, state-sponsored order of status and standards, on the one hand, and measures of economic performance (growth, employment, productivity, competitiveness, stability) is at best a curvilinear one. 'Too little' regulation will turn out to be as counterproductive in its consequences as 'too much'. There is no valid presumption of 'the more the better'. It has been said, as a general characterisation of institutions, that they are like the force of gravity in that they prevent us from flying, but allow us to walk upright. Institutionalised status arrangements, in other words, open up valued options and at the same time preclude others. This suggests the notion of an optimum level of non-market ingredients and status rights, with further increases of these ingredients beyond the optimum leading to sclerosis and rigidity.

But this notion of rationally optimising an institutional arrangement by defining the best mix of state-sponsored status components and contractual voluntarism is clearly a 'hyper-rationalist', and ultimately a meaningless project. This is so for three reasons. First, it is not self-evident who should be authorised to *define* that point of equilibrium, as conflicting values (for example, security versus efficiency) are involved and trade-offs are essentially contested. Who, after all, is competent to determine how much allocative inefficiency is 'worth' how much gain in dynamic efficiency, with a compelling answer becoming even harder to find if the choice is not just between short-term and long-term efficiency, but between either of these and values such as security, equity, or social justice.[17] Moreover, any 'optimal' mix may be short-lived, as optimality is contingent upon changing conditions and competitive relations within the global economy. Second, even if such equilibrium could be authoritatively defined, it is not clear how the blueprint could be *implemented* against the well-entrenched political resistance of those who stand to lose from even incremental change. Third, the mode in which institutions *do change* is not so much the intentional action of designers as it is the combined and interactive effect of external shocks, contingencies, and challenges, on the one hand, and shifts in the configuration of hegemonic ideas, on the other.[18]

Philosophies of how best to organise economic life and its institutional framework come in many national, as well as ideological variants. They differ concerning the agents which are envisaged as the bearers and guardians of status rights (collective actors, as in 'societal corporatism' versus the benevolent developmental state versus the paternalistic company) and the ideological values associated with a socially controlled market economy (with social democratic proponents emphasising inclusion, security and empowerment of workers versus anti-individualistic values of conservatives and Christian socialists). Countries with European-style embedded capitalism also differ in their economic performance. The underlying claim that embedded and constrained versions of capitalism work 'better' than their liberal and 'pure' counterparts holds true in some cases and periods, but not in others. Sometimes (as in the 1980s), continental European capitalisms perform better than liberal ones; at other times (such as the latter part of the 1990s) the reverse applies. Rather than pursuing the question of comparative performance any further at this point, I wish to address the question of the robustness of the European model and potential causes of its decay.

III. Challenges to the European model

There are basically two modes in which economic institutions can change. They can lose intrinsic support or they can fail in their instrumental role of achieving desired outcomes.[19] First, according to a model of *institutional decay*, institutions change if they fail to generate the widely shared support and universal recognition on which they depend. Institutions lose their moral grip on actors, the capacity to orient their preferences and expectations. Relevant actors defect, as it were, from the congruent behavioural routines and habits that institutions require for their viability. Or rival alternative institutions emerge that pose a challenge to existing ones, and compatibility problems result which necessitate compromise and dilution. As a result of either defection or confrontation, institutions cease to 'make sense', or are perceived to become 'too costly' and their maintenance 'not worth the effort'. They are seen to become incompatible with new contexts, and thus become vulnerable to path-departure, dismantling, and innovation. The other model of institutional change follows a *natural selection* model. Institutions change or are abandoned because they are seen to fail in generating expected or promised outcomes. While both of these explanatory models can coincide – actors withdraw their loyalty and support *because* of perceived failure – such coincidence is by no means axiomatic. For as much as actors can stay loyal (for example, by adjusting their outcome expectations downwards) even in the face of manifest failure, the inverse case can also be observed: actors defect not because outcomes are seriously and consistently disappointing, but because institutions have depleted the kind of plausibility and bindingness that makes them something to be 'taken for granted'.

A second intuition and (perhaps debatable) generalisation is this. The two styles of capitalism, embedded European and 'pure', (or 'market liberal'), Anglo-Saxon, are tied to each other in an asymmetrical relation of entropy. That is to say: it is much more likely that a European-style capitalism transforms itself into a liberal model than that the Anglo-Saxon model becomes 'Europeanised' (in much the same way as, to quote Walensa, it is easier to make a fish soup out of an aquarium than the other way round). 'Embeddedness' is a condition that is more easily lost than gained, due to its dependency upon supportive dispositions of a cognitive as well as moral kind.

IV. The challenge of European integration

As noted above, the distinctive feature of European capitalisms has evolved under the impact of the 'logic of discontinuity'. This logic has necessitated the adoption of some state-sponsored status order that protects, according to precepts of a 'social' market economy and 'organised', 'embedded' and 'regulated' capitalism, economic agents from some of the impact of the 'anarchy of the market', while (ideally) at the same time improving market outcomes. The various institutional patterns I have mentioned before are designed for (or can be justified in terms of) the accommodation of conflicting interests, cooperation, bargaining, consensus, the limitation of conflict, and sustainability.

European integration is a project and partial accomplishment which, in the light of these considerations, allows for two interpretations which are radically contradicting each other. On the one hand, it can be seen as (and was certainly envisioned by its early protagonists to eventually become) a framework of cooperation and regulation that completes at the transnational plane what had been accomplished at the level of member states, namely, a regime of fair and peaceful competition that rules out not only international war in Europe, but also hostile economic rivalries, thus establishing, through 'positive' integration, a supranationally embedded political economy which serves the interests of all parties involved evenly. But on the other hand, it can also be seen as a strategy of institution building and extensive as well as intensive market enlargement that involves not the transposition of the more benign aspects of European capitalisms to the transnational level, but, to the contrary and through 'negative' integration, its demolition *at* the national level, and thus as a device that paves the way for the ultimate triumph of market liberalism on the European Continent by enforcing upon member states the adoption of regimes of privatisation, deregulation, and fiscal austerity. According to this pessimistic reading of the impact of the new Europeanised political economy (as defined by the parameters of the Single Market, EMU, and eventually Eastern Enlargement), member states will be deprived of their capacity to maintain the kind of protective arrangements and status order that each of them had built up in the course of their national history. According to this latter reading of the integration process, the Europeanised political economy will significantly deviate from the type of European capitalism that prospered under the protection of national regimes.[20]

It is too early to pass definitive judgement on which of these diametrically opposed interpretations/predictions will come closer to the truth. According to the first and optimistic reading, we would have to expect an effective supranational regime of social protection and status rights to be established at the European level. According to the pessimistic reading, we would expect social and economic insecurity to become more intense; the difference between integration winners and integration losers to widen across social classes, sectors of industry, and regions; social exclusion to become more common; the capacity of national governments to maintain their protective status arrangements to become more limited and precarious, as intensified tax competition dries up fiscal resources and the strict stability regime of the European Central Bank (ECB) penalises budget deficits; nationalist and xenophobic anti-European reactions to play an increasing role in electoral politics; and the horizons of solidarity and cooperation to shrink to relatively small sub-national (that is, regional, sectoral, and corporate) units[21] rather than expand to the inclusive level of an all-European polity and regime of social protection. In sum, and as Michael Dauderstädt, a leading expert of the Friedrich Ebert Foundation, the German Social Democratic think tank, has recently put it in an unpublished memorandum: 'Will European integration protect or destroy the 'European social model"? And if the latter, he goes on to speculate, 'it could ... turn out to be political dynamite when important social groups perceive that their interests are endangered by European policies or rules'. Similar concerns about the 'social quality' of Europe, even more so than related ones about the EU's 'democratic deficit', rank very high on the research agenda of Europeanists as well as in the normative debates on the future of the integration process.[22] After market integration has largely been accomplished, 'social' integration is becoming the key issue.

V. Social protection in a liberal market society

A liberal society consisting of contract-making individuals presupposes a rudimentary institutional framework that endows the prospective players with requisite universal status rights of 'citizenship', or the meta-right to have rights. In most elementary terms, every ten-year-old must be a fourth-grader, and every citizen has access to a court. It also presupposes means-tested income support for the worst-off, as well as incentives that supposedly will help them to help themselves. The source of these universal status rights of citizenship is a law-making and law-enforcing liberal state, in the absence of which the very notion of a 'contract' becomes insubstantial, or the mere equivalent of private promise-making. Law enforcing and contract enforcing mechanisms are needed as exogenous prerequisites to get the liberal game *started*.

But once it has started, a second type of problem emerges, that of enabling people to *stay* in the game. This is the perspective of the social democratic critique of market liberalism. The critique starts with the observation that the game of free contract-making is not self-sustaining, but inherently precarious and potentially self-subversive. This precariousness is due to the ambiguities inherent in the concept of freedom itself. Elaborating on the insights of German labour lawyers and legal sociologists writing in the Weimar Republic – most notably Hugo Sinzheimer and Franz L. Neumann[23] – four meanings of the concept of freedom, as applied to a liberal market economy, can be distinguished:

1. The right (including the possession of the legal prerequisites just mentioned) to *enter into* contractual agreements;

2. the right to *use* the tool of free contract-making for the purpose of achieving distributive outcomes according to one's assets, skills, and preferences; but also

3. the right to adopt strategies which are designed to *dispossess others* of their freedom to stay in the market and enter into contracts; an example would be the formation of cartels designed to drive competitors out of the market; a sub-case of this use of freedom for the dispossession of others of their freedom applies in labour markets, where investors' or managers' prerogative of adopting labour-saving technical, organisational and locational change can involve a corresponding loss of market opportunities for workers;

4. the right to enter into a special kind of contracts, namely labour contracts, which by their nature constrain the long-term freedom of further contract-making of those entering into the contract as wage workers.

The latter argument needs elaboration. It runs, briefly, as follows. What workers sell to employers for a wage is not just their present labour power, but more or less significant parts of their freedom to sell anything to anyone in the future, or *their long-term earning capacity*. Wage earners deplete their earning capacity without being able, like capital, to accumulate in compensation for this loss: depletion without accumulation. To be sure, the outcome of losing one's ability to sell anything is involved, as an *ex post contingency*, in any contractual economic activity in reasonably competitive markets. Who knows, after all, whether I, the self-employed businessman, can sell what I have to offer in the market, or can sell at a profitable price, X years from now? It is only in the case of labour power, however, that the gradual loss of market options, and hence of the economic freedom of the worker, is an *ex ante certainty*. For 'employability' is a perishable asset, regardless of the ups and downs of demand. In the course of the wage worker's working life, the options of acquiring new skills or of finding alternative employment options are typically diminishing. What the worker gives up in exchange for the wage is not just labour power (as well as a substantial part of the civil liberties s/he routinely enjoys outside the factory or office); s/he also enters into a contractual relation that involves the certainty of depletion of earning capacity and alternative sales options – and hence of the actual option to enjoy the freedoms of type (1) and (2) in the future. This depletion is caused by the conditions that labour power is not a 'thing', but an inseparable part of human beings and their life course. Labour power is unique among all economic resources in that it cannot be inherited by others. Labour power, unlike capital, cannot, by it own means, offset depletion through reinvestment of profits and accumulation. It cannot, as capital can, rejuvenate itself by continuously starting, as it were, a new life cycle, thereby perpetuating its own earning capacity – unless, that is, wages reach a level that allows savings and investment which in turn yield a significant and continuous stream of non-wage income, in which case the worker would gradually cease to be a wage worker.

The conclusion seemed obvious to the Weimar social democratic political theorists: If freedom (1) and (2) are to be maintained as the organising principle of a liberal social order, then the freedom-demolishing freedom of type (3) must be checked (either through anti-trust legislation and supervisory authorities or through the state's selective granting of cartel and monopoly privileges according to some notion of the public interest). Perhaps most importantly, freedom (4) must be compensated for by arrangements that control and partly neutralise the depletion of earning capacity of workers. Once labour power is 'commodified', that is, becomes subject to contractual exchange in the same way as other commodities, it must also to some extent be 'decommodified', that is, compensated for the depletion of its wage-earning capacity in terms of status rights and entitlements that flow from other sources than market transaction and sale.

The *liberal* state invests in schools, courthouses, and welfare/social assistance programmes to set up the *preconditions* of the liberal game. To *sustain* the game, the *welfare state* (in any of its many versions and normative political origins) is an arrangement of compensatory decommodification. It is designed to offset the 'depletion-without-accumulation' effect to which only wage labour is exposed through the labour market and labour contract. The liberal state and the (social democratic) welfare state stand in a relationship of uneasy coexistence and do not form a smooth synthesis. But contrary to a widely shared misunderstanding, neither the liberal nor the social democratic state has much to do with 'equality of outcomes', neither normatively nor positively. The guiding principle of the welfare state is the security and protection of workers, not equality. Or more precisely, *longitudinal* equality with inter*temporal* redistribution of income, as opposed to *cross-sectional equality* with *inter-class redistribution*. The rights and entitlements that the welfare state provides to workers are exogenously established and enforced on the basis of statutory or even constitutional status rights, that is, rights not resulting from contractual agreements between parties and not negotiable by either of them.

The welfare state is an accumulation of status rights that must not be earned, but come as an original endowment of 'social' citizenship. It can be visualised as an edifice that was erected over a period of more than one and a half centuries in what is now the OECD world. Very schematically speaking, this structure of security has three floors and a roof. Each of the floors is – and has always been since its inception – the scene of a dynamic process of ongoing remodeling, expansion, partial demolition, reconstruction, and innovation. As a result of these activities, welfare states differ widely across time and space. But the structure and function, as well as (almost) the historical sequence in which the floors were built, stay the same across welfare states, although the size and interior structure of the building and its floors differ across national welfare states. Each floor is designed to deal with a particular security concern of wage labour.

The ground floor[24] contains provisions regulating access to labour markets and to jobs and issues of health and safety *at work*. Time-related measures are probably the oldest components, namely, the limitation of the work day and the prohibition of child labour. The regulation of unhealthy work environments and the hazard of accidents were further steps. The procedural regulation of working conditions, such as the speed of assembly lines, work schedules and overtime, through works councils and other forms of codetermination were later added to the structure of the first floor, as were on-the-job training programmes and organisational innovations such as job rotation. Preventive health measures were also an important component of the work-related regime of safety and security, as were seniority rules and job tenure. All these measures were implemented through statutory law and a public machinery of factory inspectorates and labour courts, on the one hand, and legally mandated forms of codetermination and joint decision making between management and workers, on the other. The common denominator of the myriad of regulations to be found here is the intention, shared to some extent by workers and their organisations, policymakers, and employers, to protect workers from some of the disutility and hazards of the labour process, thereby enhancing not just work motivation and productivity, but also the long-term viability of the worker as a productive agent. This agent must be protected from conditions that would lead to the premature exhaustion and obsolescence of labour power, its physical condition, its loyalty and motivation, and its skills.

The second floor is the scene of provisions pertaining to the ('social') security of the wage worker *outside* of work. They consist in either transfer payments replacing wages or in social services, such as day care services. They apply to workers who are temporarily or permanently unable to sell their labour power and thus to earn income. There are two classical standard conditions which cause the non-marketability of labour: recognised *disability* (either due to chronic health conditions or to old age, whichever comes first) and *sickness* (including physical conditions resulting from work accidents). These are covered by social security arrangements, pioneered by the Bismarckian social reforms of the 1880s. They basically consist in a state-mandated and typically also state-subsidised arrangement of forced savings that generates funds out of which wages of the disabled/pensioners can be partially replaced and health/ability to work can be restored through medical treatment. Alternatively, social security can be financed out of general taxes, with less immediate implications of changing employment and demographic conditions upon the (non-wage) cost of labour. After health insurance and pension insurance, and usually much later, comes the recognition of a third risk for which wage-replacement is granted, if only for a limited period of time and after a minimum time of preceding employment, namely *unemployment* (though not failure to obtain a job in the first place!). A fourth 'risk' pertains not to the inability to earn, but to the insufficiency of the income earned due to the presence in the worker's household of dependent children, the additional expenses incurred in their upbringing, and the resulting loss of the household's earning capacity. *Family subsidies* are partly designed (in the form of tax allowances) as compensation for relative income loss (relative to households with no or fewer children and hence greater earning capacity), partly as a flat rate reward for parent-citizens and the service to the wider community it is assumed they perform through the raising of their offspring.

On the third floor, the institutional devices are located which are intended to deal with the decline of workers' capacity to *defend their income*, both in absolute terms of real income (to be defended against inflation) and in terms of relative income (to be defended against productivity increases, which shift the ratio of wages to profits in favour of the latter). The institutional pattern that serves these two purposes is trade unionism and the making of collective wage agreements, including its ultimate weapon of strike action. In order for unionism to become an 'institutional' pattern (rather than a mere fact of labour walkouts and shop floor revolts), trade unions must be recognised by employers, as well as by the legal order in general, as legitimate representatives of employees' income interests. In order to gain such recognition, which typically occurs under conditions of either international war or severe economic crisis, two obstacles must be effectively overcome. As trade unions are, from an economic point of view, nothing but supply-side cartels, recognising them as legitimate representatives means exempting them from 'anti-trust' measures and the general ban of 'combinations' that a liberal market economy is premised upon. Furthermore, and in order to enable them to wield the strike weapon, workers and unions must be exempt from the liability for the harm they inflict by using that weapon against employers. Also, the stronger trade unions are and the more they operate at the multi-company level, the more they will be inclined to fight, apart from higher wages, for a more compressed wage-scale in order to strengthen a sense of solidarity and commitment among their (potential) members and to boost union density. This effect of collective bargaining, which can be seen as the unions' complement to management's efficiency wage strategies, is today widely believed to interfere with the employment prospects of less productive workers.

Continental European labour and industrial relations systems differ from country to country in the complex ways that have been developed of endowing trade unions with these licences, collective status rights, and employment externalities, in return for which unions are more or less strictly regulated concerning the procedures that must be observed in raising and settling industrial disputes on wages and conditions.

Finally, the roof of the building. As it is in the nature and purpose of roofs, they protect the integrity of the entire building and prevent its lower parts from being damaged. The roof metaphor serves me here to summarise a set of policies that are designed to protect and safeguard the various status-conferring and security arrangements just described. These policies, epitomised by what used to be called the 'Keynesian welfare state' model, include labour market and employment policies, together with the monetary, fiscal, trade, and economic policies which are designed to promote and maintain 'full' employment on which the security of those three security arrangements critically depends. This is so because in the absence of a condition of reasonably 'full' employment, none of the three categories of status rights of workers – rights in the labour process, rights outside of work, and rights to defend distributive status through collective action of workers through unions – can be effectively maintained. In a severe and protracted labour market imbalance with an excess supply of labour, the market will be flooded by employment-seeking workers willing, for lack of a better choice, to forgo the protection at work; social security systems will break down under the imbalance of 'too few' contributors and 'too many' claimants; and trade unions will lack the organisational resources and bargaining power to raise real wages in proportion to productivity gains and redistributive goals or even defend current levels of real income.

So much seems uncontroversial among European social and economic policymakers. What is controversial, however, is the logic by which security and (full) employment are tied to each other. The majority of European *social democrats* argues that in order to *preserve* the core components of the welfare state, full employment must be restored. As a corollary to this argument, it is claimed that all three components of the welfare state arrangement, at least if appropriately revised and 'modernised', will serve as effective *instruments* for the achievement of the goal of full employment through growth. Social protection and economic performance are tied by a loop of circular causation. Status rights, safety nets, and a strong role for trade unions are held to be necessary preconditions for labour market recovery as these security arrangements facilitate flexibility and the capacity, as well as the willingness, of workers to adjust to changing economic conditions and productivity requirements. Peaceful industrial relations and stable political institutions were positively seen as guaranteed by the arrangement of social security, as it stabilises domestic consumer demand and imposes a constant pressure upon investors and employers to increase productivity, thus providing an overall boost to the global competitiveness of national economies. Also, it is assumed that the institutional shell of the welfare state structure will keep class conflict from spilling over into the political arena, thus providing for the requisite measure of 'business confidence'.

Market liberals take the opposite view by claiming that in order to restore 'full' (or rather, to generate 'more') employment, most of the structure of protective and status-conferring institutional patterns of labour regulation, social security provisions and unions' bargaining power are obstacles to full employment which must first be *largely demolished*, thereby forcing workers to adjust to market incentives and the imperatives of efficiency and competitiveness. Market liberals do not usually believe that welfare state institutions do greatly contribute to the efficiency of production any longer after the 'Fordist' pattern of mass production in relatively closed economies has largely become a matter of the past. Nor is there any reason, in their view, to fear political instability to emerge as a result of the demolition of major parts of the welfare state, at least after leftist political radicalism has also become a matter of the past.

Also, a third voice, luckily with much less resonance, is making itself increasingly heard in European politics, a voice which claims that the social security of workers (as well as the protection of citizens from violent crime), on the one hand, and efficiency of production and competitiveness, on the other, can only be reconciled if national borders are sealed to the influx of foreign people, foreign workers, foreign goods, and those praying to 'foreign' gods. Since the mid-1990s, integrating Europe has seen the sometimes sudden and spectacular rise to electoral success of figures such as Pia Kjaersgaard (Denmark), Umberto

Bossi and Gianfranco Fini (Italy), Pim Fortuyn (Netherlands), with Jean Marie Le Pen (France), Jörg Haider (Austria) and Carl Hagen (Norway) being among the pioneers of this new field of populist political entrepreneurship. Le Pen has described himself in the 2002 French electoral campaign as being a leftist in social affairs, a rightist in economic affairs, and a nationalist for everything else. This formula, which is designed to resolve the tension between liberal market freedom and welfare state status rights by ethno-nationalist, xenophobic, and anti-European appeals, is applied by his rightist populist colleagues as well. As to the welfare ingredients of this formula, the protection offered is not the one accomplished through strengthening the status, security, and bargaining power of the weaker participants in labour contracts, as in the social democratic tradition. It is through granting benefits and offering paternalistic redistribution to needy members of the national community, such as single mothers, low-income tenants, and family farmers. The emphasis is on the protection of life and property against crime, and particularly crime committed by non-nationals or facilitated by open borders (such as mandated by the Schengen Agreement). What rightist populist social policies invoke are the two quintessentially non-contractual, or 'communal', forms of collective life: the family (as opposed to marriage) and the ethnic nation (as opposed to the republic or, for that matter, the nascent Euro-polity). In recent years, the electoral fortune of the populist right has been growing in inverse proportion to that of the social democratic left. In some places, it has been able to accomplish the unlikely success of attracting both the support of prosperous libertarian middle class 'yuppies' (with their opposition to high taxes and social spending and a taste for tightening other people's belts) and frustrated working-class elements who have lost faith in leftist policies and promises.

It is the triangle of reluctant social democrats, aggressive market liberals, and more or less militant rightist populists that forms the ideological space of political contestation and policy debates in today's EU-15.

VI. Welfare states as nation-states

Fully developed European welfare states, with all four of their floors in place, were historically premised upon these states being nation-states. Nation-statehood is being superseded and challenged by the bundle of phenomena referred to as 'globalisation', of which European integration (including Eastern Enlargement) is a regional and arguably still a rather benign instance. If nation-statehood is challenged by Europeanisation, as it undoubtedly is, the question is what happens in the process to the four arrangements of security.

Before addressing that question, let us clarify in structural and functional terms what we mean by a nation-state. As far as stateness is concerned, its three classical components are a (coherent) territory, a people, and an effective regime. The latter must be able to control the entire territory and population and, in order to do so, must rely on a reasonably centralised apparatus of military, fiscal, educational, administrative and legal institutions. These institutions allow for the sovereign exercise of rule, meaning both external sovereignty (or the capacity to defend borders and to monopolise control in relation to other states) and internal sovereignty (the capacity to enforce the regime's rules and to overcome any resistance to its rule). The capacity to defend its borders in a durable fashion and to control the inward and outward flows of people and economic resources across its borders is the hallmark of stateness. As far as, in addition, the 'nation'-state is concerned, some source of cohesion is present that unites the population into a collectivity with a shared sense of its identity, its historical origin and fate, constitutive political principles, a common language and culture, and some widely recognised norm of national solidarity. Both the state's capacity to impose a system of protective status rights *and* the nation's sense of homogeneity and solidarity that supports such imposition and tolerates its redistributive outcomes, are necessary conditions for a fully developed welfare state. The security arrangement of welfare states has in turn been used to maintain and strengthen national solidarity when it was threatened by economic crisis, non-institutional forms of class conflict, or international war. Major breakthroughs in welfare state development have been by-products of wars and their consequences. 'Welfare-warfare states' have triggered social security and service programmes for veterans, workers, and the entire citizenry being prepared for, being involved in, or suffering in the aftermath of international wars.

If, as a consequence of 'globalisation', that is, the increase of international flows of investment, goods, information and people, the nation-state's sovereign governing capacity is declining, what happens to the welfare state and its components which were historically premised upon robust nation-states? Three familiar alternative trajectories can be envisaged, corresponding to the three types of political forces mentioned above. First, the architecture of security is gradually demolished, giving way to an (impoverished) version of the liberal equality of rights. According to proponents of this perspective, states must, due to their definitive loss of 'border control' and in the face of increased factor mobility, lower the ambitions invested in the social security arrangement and retreat into a regime of market freedom which leaves the third and, in particular, the fourth of the above kinds of freedom increasingly unconstrained. Or, secondly, a populist backlash will be triggered by the repercussions of internationalisation, resulting in potentially most illiberal forms of paternalistic protectionism. Thirdly, some functional equivalent of security-enhancing status rights will be transferred from the nation-state level to supranational forms of organisation.

The latter is the perspective that most European integration policymakers would subscribe to. According to this perspective, Europe is currently in need of, as well as in search of, policies and patterns of political decision making that would allow the diverse welfare state arrangements that have evolved over many decades at the national levels to be transferred to the European level. The goal is being envisaged in terms of what to avoid, not what to achieve. What is to be avoided is either of the (mutually invigorating) extremes of a mere market-liberal *'negative' integration* and rightist-populist reactions which would amount to a backlash of *positive disintegration*. Yet the road 'in between', that of 'positive integration', leads through largely uncharted territory. 'Social dumping', 'race to the bottom', 'beggar my neighbor' and the rise of the 'competition state', a fiscally starved state that is reduced to the status of a strategically impotent price-taker facing the uncontrollable dynamics of capital mobility, are some of the catchwords representing the fears that people associate with the 'negative', mere market-making instead of market-regulating form of integration of EU-15, with additional threats of heightened factor mobility, that is, massive inflows of labour and outflows of capital, being associated with the prospect of Eastern Enlargement towards E-25.

It is also widely felt by political elites that in order to maintain popular support for both the deepening of ('ever closer') European integration and the widening of its scope ('Eastern Enlargement'), Europe must present itself to its citizens as a credible project of social security and protection, and certainly not as a threat to established social status rights. At the very least, and after the EU is still evidently deficient (relative to the member state polities) in terms of its democratic legitimacy, pro-European consensus and identification among non-elites is likely to dwindle, strengthening the forces of populist re-nationalisation, in case a loss is perceived to take place not just in terms of democratic legitimation, but also of social protection and security. Thus, and in order to hold together the component parts of integrating Europe and to pave the road towards wider and deeper future integration, European elites have every political reason to go beyond the negative integration of markets and proceed, visibly and credibly, towards a positive integration of a 'social' Europe. The question is: does Europe have the resources and institutional devices to actually do so?

Yet the transition from market-*making* negative integration through the abolition of tariffs and other hindrances and distortions of competition to market-*constraining* positive integration through the adoption of a Europe-wide regime of social protection and security is a process that, if anything, will take decades rather than years to conclude.[25] This is so because of the extraordinary complexities involved. These can be summarised in seven points:

1. The scope and *level* of generosity of social protection as well as the status rights of collective actors (trade unions, employers' associations) differ from member state to member state. This implies that any European social policy regime that represents an 'average' between the high performers and the low performers would be vehemently opposed by either of them. It would be opposed by (for example, the Scandinavian) high performers because the *political* objection would apply that some of 'our' social achievements are being sacrificed on the altar of European integration. But it would also be opposed by the low social protection achievers (for example, Portugal) for the *economic* reason that 'Europe' forces 'us' to become more generous, thus undercutting the competitive advantage 'we' enjoy due to our lower costs of labour. The only conceivable way out of this conflict was seen to be in preventing it to emerge at the European level, a preventive measure known under the euphemism of 'subsidiarity' (Article 5, TEC). Yet the actual possibility of member states designing and

implementing autonomous policies of social protection has been severely constrained by an EU inaugurated EMU and Single Market regime with its effective ban on autonomous policies of setting exchange rates, interest rates, and fiscal debt, as well as controlling capital movements and movements of goods and services across their borders.

2. The actual growth and employment performance of European economies, as well as their overall level of economic development, varies by country and, in particular, by region within countries, with the better-off countries being typically the small and medium-sized ones in the West and North of the EU territory. According to the Eurostat data base, official unemployment rates range from 2 and 3 per cent in Luxemburg and the Netherlands in 2001 to between 10 and 13 per cent in Greece and Spain. GDP per person slightly exceeds the OECD average in Belgium and Denmark, while it lags as far behind as 60 per cent (Portugal) or even 58 per cent (Greece). This implies a corresponding difference in the urgency by which national governments will be prepared to make efforts to improve their employment situation as a means to maintain their level of social protection.

3. The *institutional structure* of both social security arrangements and industrial/labour relations systems differs widely among EU member states and their social policy regimes. Benefit levels vary as considerably as the modes of financing these benefits. The same applies to the institutional arrangements of wage determination. It is because each of the member states has a highly developed institutional system in place on the second and third floors of our welfare state structure, and because each of these systems has generated its entrenched interests and peculiar expectations that harmonisation or convergence is so difficult to achieve as a political project and jointly adopted institutional design. Even those who agree that a 'positively' integrated 'Social Europe' must be created in order to compensate for the Common Market's corrosive effects upon national welfare states, are unlikely to find it as easy to agree on any particular institutional blueprint according to which 'Social Europe' is to be built. This difficulty does not preclude various kinds of 'spontaneous', as opposed to agreed-upon, ones at the European level, adjustments and convergences that are necessitated by capital mobility and competitive pressures. A case in point is the corrosion of systems of multi-employer collective bargaining, which is being replaced by the practice of company level concession bargaining and government-sponsored emergency measures ('social pacts').[26] Such phenomena of de-institutionalised ad hoc crisis responses are often summarily, and in an alarmist tone, referred to as 'race to the bottom'.

4. At the same time, quantitative and qualitative regime divergences constitute not only robust obstacles to harmonisation and 'positive' integration, but also considerable *distortions of market competition*. For instance, the Bismarckian countries which finance their social security

systems largely through fixed contributions of employers and employees suffer competitive disadvantages in comparison to countries where social security expenditures are largely financed through general taxes. The presence of these distortions suggests the need for achieving a more unified welfare state regime in the interest of market integration itself, and not just in terms of some model of 'Social Europe'.

5. Such harmonisation is also called for as severe fiscal imbalances within national systems of social security, which are all the more likely to occur as a result of persistent high levels of unemployment prevailing in some of the member states, will force national governments to adopt fiscal measures (that is, budgetary deficits) which are in manifest violation of the Growth and Stability Pact, the fiscal and monetary regime adopted as a disciplinary device to sustain the EMU. If labour market and social protection policies are left to the member states in the name of 'subsidiarity', national policy actors are likely to resort to measures (such as subsidies or budget deficits) that imply severe negative externalities (such as interest rate hikes, decline of the external value of the Euro) for other member states or for the EMU as a whole.

6. Thus what appears impossible for reasons (1) to (3) is widely seen as desirable and even necessary for reasons (4) and (5), as well as a further one which derives from the consideration that some convergence and harmonisation is also called for in terms of political integration. In order to maintain the permissive consensus supportive of 'ever closer integration' and to prevent the further spread of anti-European mobilisation of the nationalist and populist-protectionist sort, national social security and collective status arrangements must be protected against the perception of being jeopardised by European market integration and threatened by 'social dumping' and a 'race to the bottom'.

7. While everything that belongs to the ground floor of the welfare state structure (the non-discriminatory regulation of access to labour markets and jobs, the rules governing health and safety at work) is firmly established and equalised across the EU by European law, it is also well understood by now that the affordability of the various national arrangements at the second and third floors (social security and wage determination) is entirely contingent upon the solidity of the 'roof', that is, the labour market performance of member states. But lacking any governing capacity and fiscal authority of its own, Commission and Council do not enjoy the authority to boost overall European labour market performance, while member state governments maintain the responsibility for labour market and employment policy in the name of 'subsidiarity' – a responsibility, however, that is largely rendered nominal by the unfettered mobility of both labour and capital, on the one hand, and the constraining EMU ('Maastricht') criteria, on the other. Thus member states have the nominal authority, yet not the effective means, at their disposal to do something about the employment situation which in its

turn determines the sustainability of the welfare state edifice. Could it be, then, that European institutions could avail themselves, even in the absence of the formal authority to do so, of the means to shape European level labour market and employment policies, in the pursuit of which some 'harmonisation through the back door' would incrementally be introduced?

I am not concerned here with the substantive developments and accomplishments that the EU has achieved so far. Rather, I will focus for the rest of this paper on new methods of 'coordinating' policy making by which European policymakers have tried to accomplish what 'cannot' be done (due to (1), (2), and (3)) yet still 'must' be done (due to (4) to (6) and under the challenges of (7)), even if without the machinery of 'direct effect' rulings and other means of authoritative making and implementing of supranational policy.

VII. 'Stateless policy making'?

There is by now a ten-year history of the EU's attempts to cope with this configuration of constraints and challenges. It starts with Jacques Delors' White Book on *Growth, Competitiveness, and Employment* which reflects the member states' great difficulties in addressing unemployment and setting the stage for addressing the issue at a European level.[27] It calls for greater coordination and convergence of employment policy. At the 1994 Essen Council, the first contours of a European Employment Strategy (EES) were worked out. These were then incorporated in the 'employment chapter' (Articles 125–130) of the Amsterdam Treaty on the European Communities (TEC), signed in October 1997 and coming into force in May 1999. The policy instruments provided for in this chapter are of a characteristically 'soft' nature: annual review of the EU employment situation at the Council level, formulation of 'guidelines' to be taken into account by member states, annual reports to be submitted by member states on their employment policies, policy recommendations addressed to member states, exchange of information on 'best practices' among member states, creation of an 'employment committee' advising the Council of Ministers. Immediately following the Amsterdam conference, the Luxemburg 'job summit' of 1997 worked out these policy instruments in more detail and included the obligation of member states to submit 'national action plans' which are subject to 'multilateral surveillance'. The development of this set of policy devices was continued at the Council meetings of Cardiff (1998), Cologne (1999) and, most significantly, Lisbon (2000), where the 'Open Method of Coordination' (OMC) that comprises these procedures was defined for the first time.[28] As a result, the scope of policy areas to which OMC was to be applied was significantly broadened so as to include issues of 'social inclusion', research policy, the formation of an 'information society', 'entrepreneurial policy', health and pension policy (Stockholm Council 2001), education, eastern enlargement, immigration policy, and 'sustainable development'. However, procedures for all these policy areas are still considerably less elaborate and specific than those applying to EES.[29]

The EU has no direct way to address issues of wage determination and the distribution of incomes. In the name of 'subsidiarity', the determination of wages and the determination of levels of social security benefits (that is, developments on floors two and three of our welfare state structure), remain entirely a matter of national politics and institutions. But there are indirect methods of getting hold of these two strategic variables, and these have recently been explored and developed, beginning with the Lisbon summit of 2000. In model terms, wage levels and the wage structure interact with (a) the quantity of *labour supply*, that is, the activity rate, and, in particular, the employment rate, within the population aged 15–64, and (b) the *skills of labour*, with upgrading skills having a positive effect upon both individual income and employment security of workers and the overall volume of employable labour.

The European priorities, as promulgated above all at the Luxemburg, Lisbon, and Stockholm summits, concentrate on these two dimensions of labour supply, quantity and skills. They do so in the name of a new normative concept (or rhetoric), that of 'cohesion', the promotion of 'inclusion' and of fighting 'discrimination'.[30] The analysis behind this strategy is roughly this. If labour market participation lags behind that actually achieved in other advanced societies, parts of Europe's growth potential will be wasted, as well as transfer budgets strained. Non-participation must be due to either of two causes: people are *prevented* from participation, which amounts to 'discrimination', or they are not motivated or *capable* to participate, in which case 'unemployability' is taken to be the cause. Both of them add up to the pathology of economic and social 'exclusion', which must be fought by strategies of 'inclusion', strengthening social 'cohesion'. Inclusion refers to fighting discrimination by race, ethnicity, and nationality, as well as physical handicaps, but most importantly by gender (Article 3 (2) ECT) and by age. Integrating the underutilised supply of female labour and 55+ labour into gainful activity is therefore a key component of all EU policy documents issued by the Commissions' Directorate-General for Employment and Social Affairs and various Council directives (such as 2000/43 and 2000/78). This antidiscrimination agenda has the dual attractiveness of (a) being 'egalitarian' in terms of rights and opportunities, without redistributive strings attached, and (b) being instrumental, if implemented, for the viability and sustainability of member states' public pension systems (as emphasised by the Stockholm summit, March 2001) as well as, less explicitly, inducing wage restraint and a downward stretching of the wage-scale through the mobilisation of additional labour supply at the lower range of it.

Nothing, however, is mandatory, binding, or authoritative in this iterative process of formulating supranational guidelines and monitoring their implementation. Hence compliance on the part of member states is entirely voluntary, concerning both the kind of their policy priorities and the degree of effort with which they are being pursued. While it is too early to assess the effects of this mode of policy making and to causally attribute any success to the OMC, two underlying assumptions of this method of policy making are fairly clear. One of them is cognitive, the other motivational.

VIII. Cognition and policy learning

One of the key mechanisms on which the OMC is assumed to operate is cognitive.[31] The key phrases are 'best practice', 'benchmarking', and 'management by objectives', 'peer control', and 'temporal standardisation and disciplining'. The background intuition is that 'we' can benefit from learning from how others have managed to succeed. For the purpose of facilitating cross-national policy learning, a substantial fund of €100 million has been set up to conduct research on discriminatory practices and to promote the exchange among member states on how to fight them (Council decision 2000/750). But it is far from obvious which practices are actually 'best', given the multitude of evaluative criteria and the trade-offs that apply to them. Extensive use of part-time employment may be the best way to create jobs and reduce unemployment, as the Dutch example suggests. But it may be far from best in stabilising household income over the life course. And even if some standard of success is unequivocal, chances are that success is not easily attributed to individual measures and programmes which are always embedded into – and whose effectiveness is contingent upon – the entire ensemble of institutions of a member state and its policy regime with its built-in priorities and constraints. For instance, some member states have a statutory minimum wage, some do not; some have a big tax component in their pension system, some rely almost exclusively on contributory schemes. Should the latter be required to imitate the 'best practice' of the former? If so, successful policy learning would not just require them to adopt new 'practices', but also to 'unlearn' and partially demolish entrenched institutional patterns (such as the trade unions', as opposed to the legislature's, jurisdiction over wage determination in the case of minimum wages or working time).

Such 'unlearning' may in fact be the main purpose of the OMC, or its hidden curriculum. The main purpose of this method of policy making seems to be that of bringing home to member states' political elites and constituencies the need for 'modernisation' and 'recalibration' of their hitherto adopted arrangements of social security, industrial relations, and labour market policies. The negative message that 'nothing can stay as it is' does not imply, however, that what is going to replace present arrangements will be a consistent and consolidated Europeanised welfare state.

Thus OMC increases the pressure to view existing arrangements as potentially obsolete, to experiment, revise, and innovate for the sake of 'more employment', on which the sustainability of both national social security and industrial relations systems depends in an increasingly competitive environment. This functionalist and productivist view of these institutional arrangements also implies that what used to be, within the framework of welfare states as relatively self-contained nation-states, *exogenously* established and enforced social policy institutions is now *endogenised* into the game itself: status, security, and solidarity does itself become contingent upon contractual voluntarism.[32] Accordingly, the game is no longer a game *under* rules, but increasingly one *about* rules. The national welfare state can no longer constrain the market and impose a regime of decommodification upon the market. To the contrary, now it is being left to the market to decide which arrangements are in fact affordable and employment-enhancing, and which ones must be dropped as a competitive liability.

Needless to say, there is nothing wrong with learning, experimentation, innovation, and institutional change – in principle, that is, and as long as learning yields demonstrably superior and fairly distributed collective outcomes, as opposed to being a euphemism for a power relation in which one side is in a position to dictate to others what to learn and unlearn. How do we tell the difference between desirable and perfectly innocent 'learning', on the one hand, and the imposition of new rules mediated by the exercise of social and economic power? Let me suggest two criteria by which this distinction might be substantiated.

First, institutional innovation is driven by social and economic power relations if it is *not formally legislated* into being, but brought about through de facto deviations from previously observed institutional practices which, while nominally remaining intact, are hollowed out by individuals' adjustments and moves of opting-out. The mode in which welfare state institutions change can be explicit reform and retrenchment. But it can also be inconspicuous and gradual decay. For instance, people may defect from public health and pension systems, trade unions see themselves forced into single-employer concessions bargaining, workers resort to unprotected forms of pseudo self-employment in order to avoid social security dues, if not to illegal ('black') forms of employment. Institutions change at the factual level; they cease to govern actual social and economic interaction, and unofficial, informal, as well as highly power-sensitive practices creep in instead. For instance, new patterns of 'productivity pacts' and 'social pacts', which expand the bargaining agenda by making both levels of pay *and* volume of employment conditional upon productivity and profitability targets being met, have been introduced by employers into collective bargaining. Such concessions can be extracted from unions because multinational corporations in which such bargaining patterns have been introduced can practice wage- and productivity-related 'regime shopping', as they enjoy the option of shifting the location of production between countries.

A second indicator of the role of social power in processes of institutional innovation is the degree to which collective actors are being disorganised or weakened through *decentralisation*. As a general rule, we observe that the wider the scope of economic interaction becomes concerning trade, investment, and migration, the *narrower* and the *less* encompassing and more disaggregated become the units covered by and involved in the making of contracts and regulations. For instance, much of the focus of German labour market policies has been moved down from federal to regional to local to 'civil society' to individual levels of intervention. A similar pattern applies to wage bargaining, much of which is currently in the process of being transferred from the sectoral and multi-company level to that of individual companies, if not to departments of companies and eventually productivity measures applied to individual workers. Similarly, changes are under way in many EU member states that are advocated under the innocent label of 'devolution' while actually resulting in the transfer of rule-making competencies from the national to the regional level, as in the transition from 'cooperative' to a more 'competitive' form of federalism, as currently suggested by the more prosperous German states.

The vision of promoting policy convergence at the European level by very 'soft' means is highly ambitious indeed, given the very 'hard' facts of national differences and priorities. The European Commission itself, in its White Paper on 'European Governance', relativises the role to be played by OMC in that 'it adds value at a European level where there is little scope for legislative solutions'. Neither can it equal in its bindingness formal European law nor change the *acquis* of European law. In order to enhance its steering capacity and its potential for promoting convergence, the OMC would have to be complemented and 'hardened' by legislative devices, now commonly referred to as 'framework directives'.[33] In the presence of authoritative framework directives, 'national policy makers could no longer afford to ignore the policy discourses of Open Coordination'[34] which in the absence of such directives they are perfectly free to do. Thus Scharpf urges the 'search for solutions [in the social policy field] which must have the character of European law in order to establish constitutional parity with the rules of European economic integration'.[35] Yet it is exactly the lack of feasibility of such directive policies that gave rise to the semi-formal and para-legislative OMC approach in the first place.

Thus the thought of endowing OMC-generated rules with quasi-governmental force clearly amounts to a bootstrapping act of presupposing as given something that, if everything goes well, will be only the outcome of the dynamics of OMC, namely, some European authority of coordination. For the time being, OMC outcomes are neither formally binding (as they cannot be enforced against the will of member states' governments) nor can they replace or alter existing *acquis* regulations. The basic question for political theorists, the answer to which is at the same time of immense practical significance, is this: How can voluntary horizontal cooperation generate outcomes that are equivalent in their substantive effect to vertical control through constituted political power? How can 'soft law' be hardened so as to achieve the same degree of bindingness as formal directives?

The answer envisaged by OMC proponents is this. Multilateral information exchange as orchestrated and supervised by the Commission will lead to 'policy learning' on the part of member states' governments. This convergent learning process will be propelled by mechanisms such as the definition of 'best practices', the call for national action plans, specific recommendations, benchmarking, peer review, blaming and shaming, and the use of agreed-upon indicators of performance.

Yet as long as compliance on the part of national governments remains voluntary, the question remains what incentives and *motives* they have to cooperate. For instance, the mechanism of 'shaming' will be viable only to the extent that national constituencies and audiences will actually adopt the standard of the Commission's guidelines etc. as a yardstick for evaluating their governments' performance. The rather heroic assumption is that national political constituencies will actually hold their governments accountable for complying with the guidelines of the Commission and the summit. That presupposes that European standards, recommendations, and benchmarks are not only known to national electorates, but, beyond that, adopted as yardsticks of good policy. Why should 'blame avoidance', the desire to escape being exposed as a poor performer or a laggard in 'policy learning', become an overriding objective of national policymakers, given the perceived (economic as well as political) costliness of compliance? As long as 'benchmarks' and standards of 'good practice' are being perceived within national public spheres as little more than cloudy and ceremonial exhortations of remote Eurocrats, their role as operative yardsticks of 'good policy' remains dubious. This objection applies all the more as national governments usually have a rich supply of reasons and excuses ('subterfuge') to invoke as to why conditions beyond their control have hindered them in doing better, in terms of labour market performance or social security finance, than they actually have. Often enough, their scope for action is constrained by national policy networks, configurations of veto players, entrenched interests, as well as the perceived national competitive advantage of non-cooperation. Thus it is that only if the goal of overcoming social exclusion, social protection, and employment problems at the *European* level were firmly adopted by electorates, collective actors, and political elites at the *national* level that the 'policy learning' dynamic and its motivational underpinnings envisaged by OMC would be likely to bear fruit.

Of course national governments, in trying to achieve the convergence of their policies with those of others through OMC, can try to escape and bypass the potential obstacles located in their national policy arena and electoral politics. Such escape would clearly exacerbate the notorious 'democratic deficit' of the EU, at least as far as 'input legitimation' through public debate and political representation is concerned. Yet it would arguably increase the effectiveness of policy decisions, or what Scharpf[36] has termed 'output legitimation'. However, in the last analysis, any trade-off between democratic legitimation *versus* policy effectiveness, or between the 'by the people' *versus* the 'for the people' principle, will itself be subject to the (electoral) test of 'input legitimation' – a test which an overly executive-centered method of reaching European convergence is unlikely to pass. This is particularly the case if the standards of 'effectiveness' are themselves open to considerable controversy, as is clearly the case in all policy areas to which OMC is intended to apply.

In order for national policies to converge in terms of policy instruments and outcomes, conditions within member states must be fairly similar in the first place. However, there can be little doubt that there is a still increasing divergence of labour market outcomes by country and, in particular, by region throughout Europe, a condition that will be exacerbated by the round of Eastern Enlargement scheduled for 2004. The peculiarities and path dependencies of national labour market and employment policies, as well as structural and institutional conditions within member countries, have generated vast differences across countries and regions in terms of their labour market performance (for example, in terms of labour market participation rates, levels of unemployment, and average individual duration of unemployment). Dissimilarities are evident not only if we compare countries and regions within EU-15, but even more so if we compare policy areas. The supranational EU regime has been amazingly successful in homogenising across the EU monetary and fiscal conditions, but not so the conditions of employment and social protection. The homogenisation of the latter has been lagging way behind, in spite of the vast expenditures invested for many years in structural and regional subsidies. As Fritz Scharpf observes: 'Efforts to promote employment and social policy at the level of the European Community have come ... late and seem feeble in comparison to the success stories of the Single Market and the Monetary Union'.[37] This difference is to be attributed to the fact that the former policies (monetary and fiscal) are of a *regulatory* nature and can be effectively enforced by the Commission and the ECB within the framework of the Treaty, whereas the latter policies are *redistributive* and thus depend for their success on the preparedness of member state governments to sacrifice not just much of the national autonomy they enjoy according to the 'subsidiarity' rule, but also, at least on the part of the better employment performers, to pay with national resources for costly European employment programmes and to forgo potential competitive advantages of their national economies. Evidently and unsurprisingly, there is neither the willingness of member states to do so nor the institutional capacity of European authorities to force them to do so.

It is for this diversity of national policy priorities that, technically, the term 'coordination' in OMC is a misnomer anyway. What the method is intended to lead to is *cooperation*, which is much harder to achieve than coordination among actors with divergent interests. In the (rare) *tabula rasa* case of pure coordination, all participants are interested in having a rule ('convention') in place, whatever the rule may be. The typical case of cooperation, however, is one in which preferences differ as to what the rule should be, and also the costs and efforts required for complying with that rule are not the same for all players involved, as some may have to make more painful adjustments than others.

The making of the internal market through competition law, monetary union, and fiscal constraints triumphs over the 'embedding' of this market in European policies of social protection and the promotion of employment. Nor is this disparity coincidental. For it is the rapid success of 'negative' integration that has caused both the still growing discrepancy of national and regional labour market outcomes and the incapacity of national governments to cope with them. To make market integration socially compatible, the voluntary adoption of policies according to OMC is not enough. '"Social Europe" would stand on safer legal grounds if the Court and the Commission could be required to apply a ... balancing test to potential conflicts between European internal-market and competition law and national policies promoting employment and social protection.'[38] Yet the 'could' in this sentence is logically as compelling as it is still purely a counterfactual.[39]

Acknowledgements: The author has received helpful comments from Robert E. Goodin and Göran Therborn; particularly helpful was the research assistance of Milena Buechs

Notes

1. A. D. Smith, *Nationalism in the Twentieth Century*, Oxford, Martin Robertson, 1979.

2. Cf. F. Castles, *Families of Nations: Patterns of public policy in Western democracies*, Aldershot, Dartmouth, 1993.

3. T. Ertman, *Birth of the Leviathan*, Cambridge, Harvard University Press, 1997; P. Anderson, *Lineages of the Absolutist State*, London, Verso, 1993.

4. H. Kaelble, *Auf dem Weg zu einer europäischen Gesellschaft: eine Sozialgeschichte Westeuropas 1880–1980*, München, Beck, 1987; C. Crouch, *Social Change in Western Europe*, Oxford, Oxford University Press, 1999; G. Therborn, *European Modernity and Beyond: The trajectory of European societies, 1945–2000*, London, Sage, 1995.

5. Cf. Crouch, *Social Change in Western Europe*, ch. 14.

6. P. Baldwin, 'Can we define a European welfare state model?', in B. Greve (ed.), *Comparative Welfare Systems*, London: Macmillan, 1996, pp. 29–44 [35].

7. H. Münkler, 'Die politische Idee Europa', in M. Delgado and M. Lutz-Bachmann (eds), *Herausforderung Europa. Wege zu einer politischen Identität*, München, Beck, 1995, pp. 9–27.

8. Just a rather trivial reminder: There is a minority of countries in Europe, as well as a small minority of spaces within these countries, where the following rule does *not* apply: you cannot travel 200 miles (half a day of travel, by modern standards) in any direction without ending up in a different country (with its different history, language etc.), or, for that matter, in saltwater. Exceptions to this rule are only to be found, within EU-27 Europe, in France, Germany, and a tiny fraction of Spain.

9. Symptomatically, Switzerland, the least Europeanised of European polities, seems to come closest to the US in these respects among all European countries; this applies also to being among the few European countries having escaped a land war on its own territory in the nineteenth and twentieth centuries.

10. Crouch, *Social Change in Western Europe*, p. 404.

11. Again symptomatically, the only exception to this rule occurs at the margin of Europe, namely the tension over territorial issues that exists – though, it seems, solidly under international control – between the two NATO members Greece and Turkey.

12. M. Albert, *Capitalisme contre capitalisme*, Paris, Éditions du Seuil, 1991; W. Streeck and K. Yamamura (eds), *The Origins of Nonliberal Capitalism*, Ithaca, N.Y., Cornell University Press, 2001.

13. A linguistic reflection of the pervasive role of status categories in Continental European capitalism is the ubiquitous presence of collectivist and organicist nouns that usually do not have an equivalent in the English language. They

refer to collectivities that are endowed with status rights and the members of which recognise themselves and each other as partaking in these rights and socioeconomic identities. Examples from the French and other Roman languages include the terms with the suffix '-*at*' (or Spanish '-*ado*,' as in *salariat, artisanat*, and *patronat*, not to forget *proletariat*). In German there is the suffix '-*schaft*' (etymologically akin to the suffix in citizen*ship*) which is widely and frequently attached to virtually every socioeconomic role and collective unit. Examples include *Studentenschaft* (student body), *Wirtschaft* (the collectivity of employers/investors), *Ortschaft* (municipality), *Bauernschaft* (the farming community), *Belegschaft* (the work force of a company), *Beamtenschaft* (the civil service), *Gewerkschaft* (trade union), and numerous others, most famously *Gesellschaft* and *Gemeinschaft*. The use of this suffix suggests the internal coherence and external recognition of pre-given, supra-individual, and non-contractual properties of all members of the group as a corporate unit, comparable to the suggestion evoked by the ending of brother*hood* (as used in the early North American trade union movement). While the German , '-*schaft*' always denotes a collectivity of the bearers of some status, the English equivalent '-ship' denotes individual instances of belonging or sharing in group properties, as in citizenship, scholarship, craftsmanship, or membership. To be sure, there is another 'collectivising' suffix in the English language, namely '-ry' (as in citizenry, yeomanry, soldiery, judiciary etc.). But it connotes just the belonging of individuals to a social category, without implying some recognition as a collective body with ascribed status rights.

14. K. Polanyi, *The Great Transformation: The political and economic origins of our time,* Boston Mass., The Beacon Press, 1944.

15. G. Esping-Andersen, *The Three Worlds of Welfare Capitalism*, Cambridge, Polity, 1990.

16. H. Leibenstein, *Beyond Economic Man: A new foundation for microeconomics*, Cambridge, Mass., Harvard University Press, 1976.

17. Cf. Streeck and Yamamura, *The Origins of Nonliberal Capitalism*, p. 4.

18. C. Offe, 'Institutional design', in P. B. Clarke and J. Foweraker (eds), *Encyclopedia of Democratic Thought*, London, Routledge, 2001, pp. 364–369.

19. J. March and J. P. Olsen, *Rediscovering Institutions: The organizational basis of politics*, New York, Free Press, 1989.

20. Cf. C. Offe, 'The Democratic Welfare State in an Integrating Europe', in M. T. Greven and L. W. Pauly (eds), *Democracy Beyond the State? The European dilemma and the emerging global order*, Boston, Rowman and Littlefield, 2000, pp. 63–89.

21. W. Streeck, 'Competitive Solidarity: Rethinking the 'European Social Model'', in K. Hinrichs, H. Kitschelt and H. Wiesenthal (eds), *Kontingenz und Krise*, Frankfurt, Campus, 2000, pp. 245–261.

22. Cf. F. W. Scharpf, *The European Social Model: Coping with the challenges of diversity*, MPIfG Working Paper 02/8, Köln, Max-Planck-Institut für Gesellschaftsforschung, 2002.

23. On Sinzheimer see O. Kahn-Freund, *Labour Law and Politics in the Weimar Republic*, Oxford, Blackwell, 1981; F. L. Neumann, 'The Concept of Political Freedom', in F. L. Neumann, *The Democratic and the Authoritarian State*, London, Free Press, 1957, pp. 160–200.

24. Underneath the ground floor, there is also a 'basement' where the non-working poor are dealt with through programmes of welfare and poverty relief; this part of the building can be ignored for the purpose of the current discussion.

25. Any speculation as to whether the conclusion of this process will still come soon enough to provide European citizens with reasons to support rather than to fear and oppose further integration, and thus the Union as a whole, with a measure of political legitimacy, is beyond the scope of the present essay.

26. A. Hassel, 'Soziale Pakte', *Europa Gewerkschaftliche Monatshefte*, 1998, vol. 10, pp. 626–637.

27. J. Delors, 'White Paper on Growth, Competitiveness and Employment', *Commission of the European Communities, 1993*.

28. The OMC mode of policy making proceeds as follows, according to the Luxemburg process and based upon Art. 128. First, the summit (European Council) adopts guidelines for employment policy to be observed by member states. These guidelines focus upon the prevention of exclusion, the activation of the unemployed, the promotion of 'entrepreneurial spirit' and start-up enterprises, flexibility, and non-discrimination. Second, each member state adopts an annual national action plan (NAP) specifying the overall guidelines for the particular context of national policy. Third, an annual report on employment, jointly authorised by Council and Commission, is submitted to the summit of the subsequent year as a feedback, eventually leading to the revision of guidelines and NAPs and potentially including specific recommendations concerning the policies and performance of individual countries.

29. For the current analysis and debate on these policy methods see: C. de la Porte and P. Pochet (eds), *Building Social Europe Through the Open Method of Coordination*, Brussels, Peter Lang, 2002; J. Goetschy, 'The European employment strategy from Amsterdam to Stockholm: has it reached its cruising speed?', *Industrial Relations Journal*, 2001, vol. 32, no. 5, pp. 401–418; D. Hodson and I. Maher, 'The Open Method as a new mode of governance: the case of soft economic policy co-ordination', *Journal of Common Market Studies*, 2001, vol. 39, no. 4, pp. 719–746; and D. M. Trubek and J. S. Mosher, 'New Governance, EU Employment Policy, and the European Social Model', in C. Joerges, Y. Mény and J. H. H. Weiler (eds), *Mountain or Molehill?: A critical appraisal of the Commission White Paper on Governance*, Jean Monnet Working Paper No. 6/01, Florence, EUI, 2001, pp. 95–117.

30. In quantitative terms, the goals set at the Lisbon summit for the year 2010 is to mobilise labour supply so that an overall employment rate of 70 per cent of the population aged 15–64 for the entire EU is reached, up from the present average of 62 per cent (1999). In order to achieve this goal, female employment rates are to be increased from 52 to 60 per cent and those of the elderly workers (aged 55–64) from 37 to 50 per cent. This ambitious set of goals is argued for in terms of securing the sustainability of national social insurance systems, that is, of breaking the vicious circle (made worse by the demographic composition of aging societies) of increasing unemployment, leading to generous allowances for early retirement as a policy response, leading to an increase of non-wage social security contributions for pension funds, leading to an increase in total labour costs, leading to increasing unemployment.

31. Cf. K. Jacobson, 'Soft regulation and the subtle transformation of states: the case of EU employment strategy, *Journal of European Social Policy*, 2004, vol. 15, pp. 355–370.

32. Streeck, 'Competitive Solidarity'.

33. Commission of the European Communities, *European Governance: A White Paper*, Brussels, European Union, 2001.

34. Scharpf, *The European Social Model*, pp. 16–17.

35. *Ibid.*, 18.

36. F. W. Scharpf, *Governing in Europe: Effective and democratic?*, Oxford, Oxford University Press, 1999.

37. *Ibid.*, p. 2.

38. *Ibid.*, p. 13.

39. The text was finalised in October 2002 and takes no account of subsequent events.

Chapter Twenty-Two

Two Challenges to European Citizenship[*]

Ulrich K. Preuß

Introduction

One of the major steps in the transformation of the European Community into the European Union by means of the Maastricht Treaty, has been the establishment of the citizenship of the Union in Articles 8 to 8e of the EC Treaty. Although the rights which have been added to those which EC nationals already enjoyed are not nearly as extensive as their respective national rights, the governments of the Member States regard the creation of European citizenship as a successful attempt to further the goal of 'creating an ever closer union among the peoples of Europe' (Article A of the Treaty). Yet, academic assessments of the importance of the institution of Union citizenship are vague and cautious at best. For example, Corbett speaks of a 'notable achievement' without explaining what this achievement might consist of,[1] Curtin considers the insertion of Part Two of the EC Treaty a 'real progress', while stating at the same time that what, inter alia, constitutes the 'unique sui generis nature of the European Community, its true world-historical significance', namely the character of the Union as a 'cohesive legal unit which confers rights on individuals', is endangered by the serious shortfalls of the Maastricht Treaty.[2] For Meehan, Union citizenship is part of a complex development from 'national citizenship to European civil society',[3] while according to the seemingly more practical and realistic statement of a lawyer (written before the conclusion of the Maastricht Treaty, but anticipating the idea of Union citizenship), it will, at least over the medium term, be hardly more than the subsumption of the single rights and duties of the individual under the label 'Union citizenship', without challenging either the intermediary role of national citizenship or its salience in the lives of Europeans.[4] Finally, an even more critical assessment denounces European citizenship as a betrayal of the 'deepest symbols of statehood' and 'the rhetoric of a superstate'.[5]

Whatever the real importance of Union citizenship for the future development of the EU may be, the concept seems to embody a symbolic meaning which the authors of the Treaty obviously considered significant for understanding the Union's political character. After all, given the intrinsic connection between the

---

[*] 'Two challenges to European citizenship', *Political Studies*, 1996 (special issue), vol. 44, no. 3, pp. 534–552.

concept of citizenship and the nation state during the last two hundred years, the idea of supra-national citizenship requires theoretical explanation and a new political legitimation.

In the rest of this chapter I shall briefly sketch the inherent rationale of citizenship, relating it to the idea of modern statehood, and to the emergence of both democracy and the nation state. I shall then discuss two challenges to the concept of citizenship traditionally associated with the idea of the nation state, returning to the concept of citizenship within the European Union in the conclusion.

The rationale of citizenship

The modern notion of citizenship gained universal prominence with the idea of equal national citizenship developed and established by the French Revolution. Yet, its connotations and semantics refer to traditions that date back to premodern times. The etymological roots of the term refer to the dwellers of a city. The significance of the ancient Greek 'city' (*polis*) consisted less in its quality as a physical location than in its character as a symbolic space. Citizenship replaced the familial and tribal bonds of individuals and entailed a new city-like, i.e. civic, ethics of cooperation. Its essence lay in the new idea of a commonness of individuals based on the abstract ties of common religion[6] and, above all, of common laws.[7] From its origins in ancient Greece, citizenship has included a distinct status which draws symbolic boundaries not only against those who live physically outside the community, but, what is even more important, also against those who live within the physical space of the community but who do not belong to it socially. In other words, in its original meaning citizenship was a social construction which was not only constitutive of the identity of a particular political community, but which, at the same time, defined the social identity of the individuals who, in their quality as members, replaced their family, clan, or tribal affiliations with their status in a more abstract community, the polity. Thus, citizenship not only sharply distinguished between the physical and the social boundaries of a society, it also transcended the boundaries of the 'natural' groups of the family, the clan, and the tribe by establishing a political organisation of a social group. Citizenship was the central element of the Greeks' invention of the political, i.e. of an autonomous sphere of social life dealing with the aspirations of the community as such.[8]

In fact, a common feature of the concept of citizenship throughout different historical contexts has been its polemical usage as a counter-term to other social roles: a citizen is not only different but is, in a way, the positive counter-image of a person whose defining social characteristics are his or her qualities as a consumer, a producer, a client, a subject, a family member, or simply a private person. This is perhaps the consequence of a more fundamental historical property of citizenship: namely, its inherent bent towards a universalist perception of the individual and the ensuing refusal to tie him or her to narrow, parochial, and particularistic social roles.

As Max Weber remarked in his sociology of the city,[9] citizenship is a genuinely Western institution. Unlike oriental cities, the occidental medieval city, and with some qualifications the ancient Greek *polis* as well, was not the place of settlement of clans, families, tribes, or other primordial communities (i.e., of communities which existed prior to this locus). Rather, it consisted of individuals who were alien to each other and who were bound together through oaths of fraternisation which affirmed a secular community.[10] The corporate unity of the city was based on acts of association between individuals, it was the corporation of the 'burghers as such' who were subject to a law to which only they had access and which was only shared by them.[11] Membership of the corporation of the city was an original state of social embeddedness, it was neither derived from membership of a prior social community, nor did it imply a purely physical association to a particular place of settlement. It was an exclusive social-political status which had a distinct symbolic meaning and relevance. Hence the conditions of access were highly selective because this status was of great importance both for the would-be member and for the host community.

This conception of an abstract 'civic' community is embodied in the idea of the republic. Essentially, citizenship means membership of the republic. Republicanism incarnates the Aristotelian idea of a body politic whose public authority is rooted in the association of free men possessing a shared understanding of the common good and who govern themselves through law. The city is a symbolic space in which individuals, who are strangers to each other, are linked together through the visibility of the institutions to which they adhere: the agora, the court house, the palace of the head of the republic, etc.

Citizenship is a status of equality, but only among equals. Hence, in its premodern meaning it was fully compatible with social hierarchy. Citizenship was a status of eminence by which a distinguished class of individuals were recognised as having a particular stake (i.e., particular rights, duties and burdens, frequently coupled with a particular status of honour) in the polity. In the republican polity citizenship denoted the legitimate and permissible status of aristocracy. Thus, the centuries-old idea that those who are subject to the laws must be their authors does not apply to the premodern republic. Both in the ancient and in the medieval city republics, the rulers – the citizens – were a small minority which ruled over the majority of non-citizens.[12] Still, the idea of a political community based on the commitment of its members to their common affairs and the creation of institutions which symbolise this separate *res publica* has not been destroyed or devalued through its social exclusivity. Admittedly, at the beginning of political modernity, i.e. in the era of the emergence of the modern state, republicanism was outdated and rejected by the theorists of statehood.[13] But ultimately these two seemingly incompatible ideas were connected and assimilated within the ideal of national citizenship – based on the modern nation's statehood.

Citizenship and modern statehood

Whilst the republic symbolised the idea of political freedom through the association of citizens, statehood reflects the emergence of an individualistic society which becomes the object of a centralised sovereign power within a demarcated territory.[14] Modern states are anxious to define sharply the physical boundaries of the territorial and the personal substrate of their authority and responsibility in the international system of states. Hence territoriality and nationality are essentials of modern statehood.

Ideally, the boundaries of the state define at the same time its territory and its subjects: all individuals residing within the confines of a given state are subject to its rule and hence by virtue of their physical affiliation are its nationals. Permanent residence within the territory of a state may be regarded as providing the most visible evidence for the less tangible 'genuine link' and 'true bond of attachment' and 'reciprocity of rights and duties' between an individual and a state which the International Court of Justice has stated are requirements of international law for the acknowledgement of the status of 'nationality', i.e. an individual's membership of a given state.[15] However, on an ideal understanding of the principle of territoriality, the mere physical attachment of an individual to the territory of a particular state would already be a sufficient condition for belonging to it. Note, that I avoid the term 'membership' because this is clearly an inappropriate understanding of the relation between the state and those who are subject to its authority.

Of course, political rule has always had a spatial dimension. Geographical boundaries have been drawn in Europe since the fourteenth century. But the sharp territorial demarcation characteristic of the modern state and its specific kind of rule is entirely recent; it did not exist prior to the end of the eighteenth century.[16] The European medieval system was structured by 'a nonexclusive form of territoriality' in which different political units like cities 'viewed themselves as municipal embodiments of a universal moral community'.[17]

In contrast, the modern state delimits its authority and sovereignty along physical boundaries, and its claim to obedience is (with a few exceptions) based on physical control over its territory. Thus, the well-known *ius soli* appears to be the appropriate and congenial principle for the determination of state membership which consequently is acquired by everybody born within its territorial boundaries. In early times, the *ius soli* was the obvious institution of settled agricultural societies and served to define the community. Conversely, the *ius sanguinis* primarily maintained the symbolic boundaries and the coherence of migrating nomadic societies. Wherever there is no physical locus, the symbolic bonds of common blood, descent, history, fate, culture, religion or language evolve into the primary source of commonness and of communal life. The *ius sanguinis* is the most important legal expression of this claim. When Marx, analysing pre-capitalist economic formations, compared the Greek and Roman ancient cities (*poleis*) with the ancient Germanic communities he discovered a significant difference: the city, although a symbolic community, was represented in the physical demarcation of the urban space; it was the materialisation of the permanence of the citizens' permanent community. By contrast, the Germanics lived separated in the forests and existed as a community only by virtue of 'every act of reunion of its members'.[18] In order to exist as a community beyond those reunions the Germanics constituted themselves as a community based on their common descent, language etc., i.e. as a 'Volk'.[19]

Modern statehood did not entirely abolish the difference between the two approaches to linking individuals to the community, even if territoriality seems to have made the *ius sanguinis* dispensable. At first glance this fact is somewhat surprising. On closer scrutiny, however, it becomes clear that the territorial character of the modern state does not eliminate the need for criteria of membership which are more demanding than the mere *ius soli*. A patent expression of this need is the obvious distinction between nationality and citizenship. Nationality denotes an individual's legal belonging to a particular state.[20] In the pluriversum of contending sovereign states each of them is interested in a sharp and unequivocal demarcation of the territorial and personal reach of their authority in order to avoid an overlap with the similar claims of other sovereign states. This interest is satisfied, among other things, by the concept of nationality. 'Nationality' defines the category of persons who sovereign states mutually recognise as the legitimate objects of their respective sovereign power; consequently, it is a term and a concept which is of primary importance in the realm of international law.

In the sphere of domestic law the corresponding concept is subjecthood. Subjects are the individuals whom the sovereign state power defines as the personal substrate of its rule.[21] Hence, nationality and subjecthood define an identical multitude of individuals, viewed from different legal perspectives – the former from the international, the latter from the domestic point of view. By contrast, citizenship and nationality do not necessarily coincide: even today in some states, not all nationals are citizens, and not all citizens are necessarily nationals.[22]

Statehood established, claimed and enforced public authority solely on account of effective and sovereign power over a physically demarcated territory, irrespective of the capacity or willingness of its residents to understand, to accept or even to participate in the exercise of that authority. This is why subjecthood is the appropriate concept for this kind of rule. Subjecthood and citizenship – or, to refer to the basic structures of political rule to which they are attached, statehood and republicanism – are different, even opposed to each other. They embody different principles of political rule: citizenship and republicanism include activity, social exclusivity and public mindedness; subjecthood and statehood require and presuppose passivity and submissiveness, they are socially inclusive because they encompass all individuals within certain territorial boundaries, and they restrict individuals to their private spheres like the family, business, leisure etc. This does not mean that statehood and republicanism, subjecthood and citizenship cannot occur at the same time in the same polity. Unlike democracy, republicanism does not require political equality, and consequently equal subjecthood – the requirement of statehood – and unequal citizenship – the requirement of republicanism – could coexist and in fact did coexist in the French republican constitutions of 1791, 1795, 1799 and 1848. Even Kant, the 'German Rousseau', did not argue for universal equal citizenship. Similarly, the 'Declaration of the Rights of Man and Citizen' celebrates the distinction between those who, in spite of their capacity as bearers of universal human rights, are merely subjects of the laws of the republic and those who are simultaneously the law-makers, i.e. its citizens.

Bridging the gap between statehood and republicanism: Democracy

The principle which attempts to bridge the gap between citizenship and subjecthood or, more generally, between republicanism and statehood, and to reconcile the social exclusivity of the former with the physical inclusiveness of the latter is, of course, democracy. Democracy stands for the Rousseauian ideal that all subjects of the laws should be their authors by virtue of their subjecthood alone, not by virtue of some particular personal aptitude which qualifies them for the noble task of law-making. The ideal result of this universalisation of an exclusive political status is the democratic republic.

However, even in this ideal institutional framework the reconciliation of republicanism and statehood via the bridge of democratic egalitarianism can only be achieved approximately; a tension between the original concept of citizenship based on republicanism and the new concept based on the idea of democratic equality remains. Note that the republican citizen is entitled to participate in the act of law-making because he – indeed, only he – is personally qualified to do so; he must have a stake in the polity and hence be committed to the public good in order to be competent to make laws. In the republican framework citizenship entails law-making. This is why it was a matter of course even for the most committed and radical republicans that only male property owners qualified for citizenship.

By contrast, the democratic citizen is a citizen by virtue of the fact that he (and some decades later also she) is granted the right to take part in the process of law-making. In the democratic framework the equal right to participate in law-making entails citizenship. No prior social qualification is required, and hence a person who is only committed to his (or her) private business and affairs is also a citizen. In other words, democratic citizens are the passive and submissive subjects who have been collectively emancipated by the democratic revolution and whose commitment to the common good has still to be brought about. Rousseau's distinction between the *volonté générale* and the *volonté de tous* is as much a reflection of the split between the republican and the democratic character of a collective will as the distinction between *citoyen* and *homme* in the 'Declaration of the Rights of Man and Citizen' of 26 August 1789. While the *volonté générale* represents the social, public and common good orientation of the citizen who exercises his political freedom, the *volonté de tous* embodies the will of the private and isolated, pre-social man, who is primarily the subject of state power and is defended by no more than mere *droits de l'homme*.[23] Thus, the social diffusion of the status of citizenship has undermined its republican spirit.[24] To draw an obvious analogy to the economic sphere: the inflation of the republican status of citizenship caused by democracy has entailed its devaluation. Yet, this is the price which democrats have been ready to pay for the principle of self-government: everyone who is subject to political authority shall be its co-author.

So far I have discussed the structural tensions between the republican concept of citizenship and both statehood and democracy. In contrast, statehood and democracy seem to be thoroughly compatible and even mutually reinforcing. The physical inclusivity of statehood (arising from the principle of territoriality) and the symbolic inclusivity of democracy (arising from its egalitarian-universalist character) formed an efficient coalition which was able to reform the social exclusivity of the republican principle and to create the congruity of subjecthood and citizenship, i.e. the identity of rulers and ruled. Every resident of the state is, by virtue of the very fact of his or her residence, subject to its public authority, and the democratic principle requires that the subject of public authority must be its author. Ideally the physical boundaries of statehood and the symbolic boundaries of belonging to the category of persons who matter in the democracy coincide.

As a matter of fact, experience tells us that this is not the case. Despite its close connection with modern statehood, the democratic principle does not simply overlap with the latter's territorial boundaries. It draws symbolic boundaries of personal relevance which are narrower than the physical ones. Given the universalist tenets of democratic theory – every person has the same stakes in the democratic polity, enjoys the same rights and benefits and has to bear the same duties and burdens – this is somewhat surprising. Instead, a different concept provides the criteria for an individual's belonging to the democratic community: the concept of the nation.[25]

Statehood, nationhood and the nation state

Membership of a society, be it based on the *ius soli* or on the *ius sanguinis*, presupposes some kind of community among the individuals who form it. We cannot conceive of a purely physical belonging of an individual to a group, much less of course of a merely physically defined group; a group is a social, not a physical entity. For that reason the modern state's territoriality as such is not able to create a social entity out of the multitude of individuals who form the personal substrate of its sovereign power. In its incipient manifestation statehood produced the commonness of subjection of individuals under its power, but it was unable (and unwilling) to create the two main institutions which later became the indispensable preconditions for the success story of West European states: markets and an active community amongst their subjects.[26] The latter idea is embodied in the concept of the nation, which did not emerge before the end of the eighteenth century.[27] In many European nation states it was inherently linked with the idea of the constitutional state.[28]

Since the end of the eighteenth century, in Europe statehood and nationhood have engaged in a close relationship whose complexity is mostly due to the ambiguity of the concept of the nation.[29] The modern state is a nation state, but this statement embraces two extremely different meanings. Their ideal types are best represented by France and Germany. According to the French concept, the nation is a purely political community, '*la communauté des citoyens*' who form an association under common laws. Their unity and coherence as a political community is incarnated in the state. Statehood is an essential element of this concept of nationhood. The nation consists of the active citizenry, and since the only political community of modernity is the state, French nationhood is inconceivable without statehood. Consequently, no individual can be a member of the nation, i.e. nobody can be a citizen without being by the same token simultaneously a subject of the state. Ideally, the reverse should apply as well: every subject of the state should be a member of the nation, i.e. a citizen. However, physical and social inclusion in the society are necessary, but not sufficient preconditions for becoming a full member, i.e. a citizen of the polity. To form an association under common laws requires the will and the capacity to participate in a common undertaking, i.e. to cooperate and to communicate with the other members, to recognise them as equals, and to be recognised by them as an equal. The *droits de l'homme* protect the individual against the violation of his or her basic rights as isolated persons; they do not include a person's right to be recognised as a fellow-citizen by the others. Conversely, the *droits de citoyen* protect the rights of individuals in their capacity as active members of the nation, but they do not include the right of every individual living within the boundaries of the state to be and to become a citizen. Subjecthood per se does not qualify one for citizenship. Yet, once the subjects are recognised as free and equal persons their demand to become active members of the nation could only be delayed for a limited time; it could not be rejected permanently, because the political definition of the nation state coupled with the idea of human rights was incompatible with the exclusion of major parts of the population from citizenship.

Still, it is undeniable that even in the most inclusive French concept of nationhood, subjecthood in the state and citizenship in the nation do not fully coincide. The ideal of the identity of rulers and ruled is doomed to remain an ideal.

In the German (and, following its tradition, the East European) model, this ideal does not exist at all. This conception conceives the nation as a prepolitical community of individuals who are bound to each other by the commonness of either their 'nature' (their blood) or their culture (their language, literature, religion, and history). Perhaps this is still the heritage of the Germanic dispersion in the forests, which made them form a community according to non-physical criteria like common blood, language etc. The nation exists prior to the state, and occasionally without the state, like the Polish nation between 1795 and 1918, or Germany before 1871. It is the nation which creates the state, not vice versa. However, statehood is still important, even though in a different sense to the French model. The state does not generate the nation. Rather, it provides the nation with the power necessary for the satisfaction of its quest for glory and recognition. Members of the nation belong to the community because they share its 'natural' or cultural particularities. Membership in the community is not a matter of choice but of 'fate'. The *ius sanguinis* is the most appropriate criterion for the definition of the symbolic and social boundaries dividing the community from non-members. In this model neither residence within the boundaries of the state, nor the capacity and the willingness to participate as an equal in the association of equals under common laws, are sufficient conditions for citizenship. Obviously the gap between subjecthood and citizenship within this conceptual framework of the nation state is wider than in the French model.

Why do statehood and nationhood encompass both quantitatively and qualitatively different categories of individuals? Essentially, the modern state is a political organisation, and so is the nation.[30] Territoriality is essential for the state; it defines its boundaries and the object of its power. We can assume that the sharp physical demarcation of political power and its historically unprecedented efficiency are mutually reinforcing, and this in turn explains the superiority of the modern state over all preceding political orders. Statehood includes, as Max Weber put it,

> coercion through jeopardy and destruction of life and freedom of movement applying to outsiders as to the members themselves. The individual is expected ultimately to face death in the group interest [which] gives to the political community its particular pathos and raises its enduring emotional foundations.[31]

Only political, not economic or other merely instrumentally rational (in the Weberian sense of *Zweckrational*) communities can legitimately ask their members to lay down their own lives.

From this it follows that membership of the political community requires a deeper, more existential and emotional kind of commonness than common residence within the boundaries of a given territory; common subjecthood under the sovereign power of the state does not constitute the kind of community capable of demanding individuals to sacrifice their lives for it. A society able to procure its members' willingness to assume duties of human solidarity vis-à-vis their fellow creatures, even of a less dramatic kind, requires bonds of commonness among them which are more specific and tighter than the commonness of subjection under a centralised sovereign power. This community is the nation. However broadly this is defined – whether in the political sense of the French model or in the ethno-cultural terms of the German tradition – it is not identical with the multitude of individuals who reside within the territorial boundaries of the state. The principles of territoriality and personality do not produce the same degree of individual belonging. That is why, despite recognition of the universal rights of man, not only the republican, but also the democratic polity establishes criteria of personal qualification which individuals have to meet in order to obtain its more moderate, though still eminent, status of citizenship. The boundaries of the state tend to be broader than those of the nation, and citizenship is associated with the latter, not with the former.

If, even in French political doctrine, the nation is the political concept which ultimately defines the individual's relationship with his or her fellows – what is the role of statehood in the democratic polity? Why not realise the identity of rulers and ruled, i.e. the identity of citizens and subjects, by defining the state and the nation by the very same boundaries? The answer is that the state's claim to sovereign power over a territory and the claim of a multitude of individuals to rule themselves have different subjects. The state's claim to the monopoly of the means of violence is based on the claim to comprehensive control over the whole social life in that territory. By contrast, democracy aims at the self-rule of a collectivity of persons. The democratic claim to collective self-determination aspires to the ideal situation which Rousseau proclaimed for the first time, namely the identity of rulers and ruled. He or she who does not rule cannot and must not be the object of the commands of the ruler. This condition places an inherent limitation on the rulers' sovereignty which prevents it from becoming despotic,[32] while the sovereign power of the state is inherently unlimited and for that reason susceptible to perversion into oppression and tyranny. The democratic nation state links the two claims in that the people become the heir of the unlimited, pervasive and comprehensive state power. When democracy goes statist and adopts the power structure of statehood, it is no longer a device of self-determination for a multitude of individuals who associate themselves under common laws. It also embraces the territorial dimension of sovereignty and oversteps the intrinsic boundaries set by the self-rule of the association of citizens. Hence the discrepancy between citizenship and subjecthood is the result of the combination of statehood with democracy, or, in the conceptual framework of modern statehood, of the principles of territoriality and personality.

This combination is embodied in the idea of the nation state. Irrespective of the conception of the nation – be it the prepolitical ethno-cultural German or the universalist political French conception – the idea of the nation state contains a tension between national principles of group solidarity and the claims to sovereign power of the modern state. This tension is expressed in the duality of the physical boundaries of the state and the symbolic boundaries of the political community, the nation. While the state boundaries impose merely external restrictions on the sovereign power, community boundaries guarantee, by virtue of the identity of rulers and ruled, inherent limitations on the sovereign power of the nation. As Rousseau argued, no associate is interested in imposing more severe limitations on the freedoms of his or her fellow citizens than he or she would be ready to accept.[33] Only in an ideal hypothetical case do the physical and the symbolic boundaries come together. This may occur in a country where a pure and unqualified *ius soli* applies and where the political community is exclusively based on universalist principles, i.e. is accessible to everybody. Yet, even in this ideal case the analytical distinction between the physical and the symbolic character of a boundary would remain necessary in order to understand their different functions. Thus, the complementarity and the incongruity of physical and symbolic boundaries is the defining feature of citizenship in the democratic nation state. The physical boundaries of an individual's belonging to the state take shape in the *ius soli* or the *ius sanguinis*; they define the multitude of individuals who are merely subjects in the first place and who have still to be transformed into a political community, i.e. into the nation. The symbolic boundaries are embodied in the rights and duties of the members of the political community which are simultaneously the source and the result of their mutual solidarity. Like every boundary, this one is exclusive in that it defines the *demos*, i.e. the persons who matter in the democracy and who constitute the nation. Yet democratic principles require that this symbolic boundary be fixed according to universalist principles. This means that the criteria of exclusion of the non-members must not discriminate according to criteria which ultimately deny a person's human dignity as an equal, like race or ethnicity.[34]

Challenges to the nation-state centred concept of citizenship

In the last decade we have been faced with two serious challenges to this ideal-typical inner balance of the nation state. The first refers to the occurrence of a new wave of international migration which is about to reach Western Europe. The second is the emergence of the European Union.

The challenge of international migration

Although today nomadic societies exist at best marginally, migration has never ceased to be a major element in human history.[35] Therefore the modern state's principle of territoriality may not be sufficient. In a situation where there is no migration, the *ius soli* and the *ius sanguinis* yield the same outcome with respect to the acquisition of citizenship. Of course, this ideal situation has hardly ever existed in human history and does not exist in the contemporary world. Migration is a basic fact of human life which reflects the quest of individuals and collectivities to improve their life conditions. Individuals and groups are either pushed to leave their homeland by war, civil war, famine, exhaustion of resources and the like, or they are pulled by the prospects of a better life in other parts of the world. Very frequently the push and the pull effect occur simultaneously.

The relation between migration and statehood is ambivalent.[36] On the one hand, statehood encourages migration in that it liberates the individual from the bonds of belonging to feudal estates and parochial communities based on inborn and ascriptive qualities which tie the individual to a particular place and to particular forms of working and living. In the earliest ages of modern state-hood, the state's principle of founding affiliation on mere physical residence was a strong incentive for free movement because it lowered the barriers to the access to new life conditions and life chances. The principle of territoriality gave rise to the expectation and the hope of many oppressed individuals that the demarcation of the state was not just physical but also symbolic, in that it served as a constitutive force for the creation of a genuinely statist society based on the exchange of obedience for protection.

On the other hand, statehood and migration do not go well with each other. Statehood requires a sharp demarcation both of the territory and the people that are subject to the state's control. Moreover, the state claims to be the only and exclusive embodiment of the political community of the individuals settling within its physical territory. Only in the second half of the twentieth century was the state able to overcome its inherent individualism and to integrate political, economic, social and cultural communities into the structure of its constitutions. Yet its social coherence and political stability is fragile. There is a widespread awareness that the modern state depends upon economic, social, and cultural preconditions which provide the indispensable forces of social cohesion. While at the dawn of modern statehood religious homogeneity was considered to embody this essential condition, the relevant candidates have changed several times, including alternatively or cumulatively national, ethnic, racial, economic, social and cultural homogeneity.[37]

However convincing and exhaustive this list may be, it reflects the modern state's demand for non-physical qualities of sameness amongst its subjects. They are regarded as imperative for the maintenance of a peaceful and cooperative society within its territorial boundaries since collective subjecthood per se does not constitute the scheme of social cooperation which produces the resources necessary for the state's operation. As argued above, the modern state's principle of physical affiliation is incomplete and needs a complementary principle of belonging which delivers the symbolic forces for the creation and maintenance of a community which generates the resources of social solidarity necessary for social cohesion.

The inherent complementarity of the physical and the symbolic criteria of belonging to the modern state makes migration a particularly difficult problem.[38] Migration involves the loosening of the two ties which link individuals to the state, since they leave the territory and evade the control of the power of their home state. Obviously, there cannot be a smooth transition from one political community to another, because the host state may be prepared to accept the physical presence of the newcomers, but normally it is either unwilling or unable to accept them immediately as full members and to integrate them into its social, economic, and cultural life, and to make them full members of the nation. Thus, the modern state's promise that the enjoyment of its protection, as well as other benefits following from one's affiliation to it, are not dependent upon inborn and unchangeable qualities of a person but solely upon a physical affiliation to its territory, is reneged by its character as a nation and hence remains unfulfilled.

This experience gives rise to two parallel developments. On the one hand, the distinction between subjecthood and citizenship is established in order to make sure that the newcomers are subject to the host state's power without having the same claims as its citizens to those benefits and assets to whose production they did not contribute. On the other hand, the newcomers have good reason to form communities within the host society in order to improve the chances of survival and advancement of their members, and to provide them with the moral and psychic support which they need in order to cope with the difficulties of their new environment. Not surprisingly, they draw the symbolic boundaries which delineate them from 'the others' in terms of commonness, which is independent of the state's criteria of belonging: ethnicity.[39]

When physical affiliation to a territory does not provide a sufficient criterion of an individual's belonging to a particular community, non-physical boundaries are created. Individuals who are exposed to the common fate of exclusion from basic benefits of the society, and at the same time share the commonness of descent, history, language and the like, will form sub-political communities within the physical realm of the modern state. Thus, the modern state's conceptual structure is self-contradictory: whereas its principle of territorial rule offers an incentive to physical and social mobility in that it neglects the individuals' particular ascriptive qualities, community affiliations and loyalties, it discourages migration in that the principle of physical affiliation needs the underpinning of a coherent, perhaps even homogeneous society, which cannot be provided by mere physical belonging. Since the symbolic boundaries of the modern nation state are much narrower than the physical boundaries of its territory, migration actuates the duality of the principles and the potential tension between them in that it spurs both the natives and the immigrant newcomers to mobilise their respective prepolitical properties in order to draw sharp symbolic boundaries between each other. Mass migration has rendered the physical boundaries of statehood almost completely insignificant as a means of demarcating the distinctiveness of societies.[40] Consequently, the importance of symbolic boundaries and their exclusionary potential has enormously increased. This may give rise to a separation of citizenship from its modern affiliation to statehood and even entail a return to the ethos of the predemocratic age, when it was the privilege of a minority. This is one potential path of development which may finally destroy the inherent rationale of the concept of citizenship as the incarnation of the idea of the republic. Once democracy has been established, the republic can no longer be conceived in an aristocratic sense.

However, the separation of citizenship from statehood does not necessarily mean the disappearance of the universalist-egalitarian qualities which it had acquired through its affiliation with modern statehood. This alternative leads to the second challenge to citizenship: the emergence of a supranational political community, the European Union.[41]

The challenge of supranationality: The European Union

The gradual evolution of the European Union indicates a profound change in the role and the significance of the nation state. It may affect not only the criteria of membership in the nation state itself but also create new forms of supra-national belonging. Although the idea of European citizenship is not entirely novel,[42] it was not until the Treaty on European Union that 'citizenship of the union' was formally established in a legal text of the Community.

For the time being these Articles embody the last step of a development of the European Economic Community which started with the purely economic aspiration of the Treaty of Rome of 1957 to mobilise the 'factors of production' in the Member States. The (political-pathetic) term 'citizen' was not in the wording of the original Treaty and probably thoroughly alien to its spirit. When the treaty dealt with persons, they were addressed in their roles as economic actors, i.e. as employers, employees, or self-employed persons. The main goal of the Community was the integration of the economies of the Member States, and consequently the rights of individuals – primarily the right to equal treatment of all participants in the market irrespective of their nationality – were tailored according to the functional requirements of economic integration. In the meantime, the development of the Community has clearly gone beyond the 'functional integration' of the economies of the Member States. The narrow conception of individuals as workers or self-employed persons has been loosened. In particular, the basic freedoms of movement and residence are no longer restricted to economic actors.[43]

The list of rights which Articles 8 to 8e associate with the status of Union citizenship is not very impressive; it includes, beyond the already existing rights to free movement and residence within the territory of the Member States, the right to vote and to stand as a candidate in elections to the European Parliament and in municipal elections at the place of one's residence on the same terms as nationals of that state, the rights to diplomatic and consular protection by any Member State, and the right to petition to the European Parliament and to an Ombudsman. Yet, the creation of an immediate legal bond between the nationals of the Member States and the European Community, and the continual dissociation of their legal protection 'from their functional status as workers'[44] signify a major step towards European citizenship. Nonetheless, because Union citizenship presupposes national citizenship of one of the Member States, supranational citizenship seems to be no challenge or even threat to the entrenched status of national citizenship. Thus, depending on one's political values, neither hopes nor fears appear justified that national citizenship might disappear in the course of European integration.

However, in the long run European citizenship may become more important and eclipse national citizenship. Two sorts of development are conceivable. We may imagine the emergence of a common European criterion which defines a class of persons who enjoy some consequential rights or privileges.[45] A common European criterion which would render an individual a 'citizen of the Community' could be, for instance, her legal residence for at least five years within the territorial boundaries of the Community. For the sake of analytical clarity, we may even make the unrealistic assumption that residence within the physical boundaries of the Community is entirely independent of the – existent or non-existent – quality of a person being a national of a Member State. Thus, it would be possible to be a Union citizen without being the national of any of the Member States because the Member States do not serve as an intermediary between the individuals and the Community. The possession of this status would be the indispensable link to the enjoyment of rights and benefits granted by the Community. This path to European citizenship may be called the status path, because the acquisition of the status of citizenship takes logical precedence over the consequential rights attached to it. Rights are derived from the status.

An alternative developmental path could pursue an approach according to which the Community would confer rights on the citizens of all Member States. Individuals would enjoy these rights irrespective of their particular nationality. Three different classes of Community rights have to be distinguished:[46] (1) rights against institutions and agents of the Community – e.g. against the Commission or the Council; (2) rights against institutions of the individual's own nation state applying Community law; (3) rights against the institutions of a Member State other than the individual's own nation state applying Community law. All three classes of Community rights drop the otherwise important criterion of Member State nationality. If the number of this 'supranational' class of rights gradually increases, then the resulting bundle of Community rights would (or at least could) eventually create a bond of commonness among individuals who enjoy the same rights and who are protected by the same law, and this common bond of mutual loyalty may finally constitute the status of Community citizenship.[47]

The Treaty on European Union has pursued the latter path, if only reluctantly. A further development in this direction, and even more so a development according to the status path, may weaken the bonds of Europeans to their respective nation states provided that a European constitution furnishes them with the appropriate institutional means for an active participation in the supranational polity. Yet, Union citizenship should not be misunderstood as a mere expansion of the traditional concept of citizenship of nation states. There is a broad consensus among experts that there are obvious dissimilarities between supranational citizenship and the traditional notion.[48] European citizenship is a particular kind of membership in the Community which is only partially comparable with citizenship based on nationality. Neither the *ius soli* nor the *ius sanguinis* are appropriate criteria for the acquisition of Union citizenship. They are related to modern statehood and its comprehensive, homogeneous, penetrating and exclusive sovereign authority, which claims to maintain a coherent social and political order within the very physical boundaries of the state territory. Although there is a territorial element in the structure of the European Union – its space consists of the territories of its Member States – its public authority is not defined in spatial terms, nor does it claim to be as monolithic, homogeneous, hierarchical, and effective as the traditional state power. Thus, clear-cut demarcations in terms of territory and persons do not fit into the conceptual framework of the European Union. Citizenship of the European Union is as novel, unprecedented, imperfect, and evolving as the European Union itself. This is why it can be defined only tentatively and in rather vague and speculative terms.

The potential meaning of European citizenship

While it is easy to give a negative definition of the European Union – it is not a state, not even a federal state, it is not a traditional alliance of states, it is not a confederacy – it is impossible, at least up until now, to define it positively. Several characteristics can be enumerated:

(i) The EU is a dynamic polity.[49] In contrast to the modern state's objective to maintain and reproduce the given order, the Community is directed at change, namely an ever further integration of the Member States. This is an open-ended process of the Community's continual self-transformation which requires institutional devices of permanent learning, self-observation and self-adaptation. This inherently changing character of the Community is in striking contrast to the structural characteristics of modern statehood.

(ii) The constitution of the Union – its basic politico-institutional structure – is meant to be complementary to the constitutions of the Member States. It is parasitic upon the political orders of the Member States not on the ground of its imperfection, but intentionally and on conceptual grounds. In contrast to federal states, the dualism of constitutions which is characteristic of the European Community does not presuppose a basic homogeneity and hierarchical relationship between the central and the federal units and a clear-cut fixed demarcation of competencies between them. Rather, the interactions between the several units are determined by the dynamics of an open process of different kinds of cooperation in which various institutional and policy solutions for a concrete problem can be generated.

(iii) Finally, unlike traditional states the European Community is characterised by its polycentric character. Although the Community is vested with power for the realisation of its policy goals, there is no single political centre in which the political substance of the Community is incarnated. Rather, the processes of policy generation and implementation take place within a web of a plurality of actors and interactions which leaves the impression of a quite diffuse concept of politics.

In sum, dynamism, openness and polycentricity are basic properties of the European Community, and they are likely to shape the future concept of a no longer mono-statist polity. Consequently, citizenship of that polity will differ considerably from our traditional, state-centred notion. Borrowing a phrase from a quite different historical and political context, we may understand European citizenship as an instrument which serves to remove 'from the citizens of each state the disabilities of alienage in the other States'.[50] This judgement was made with reference to Article 4 section 2 of the US Constitution, which stipulates that 'the citizens of each State shall be entitled to all privileges and immunities of citizens in the several States'. In another opinion, issued almost a century later, the Supreme Court made the assessment[51] that 'the primary purpose of this clause ... was to help fuse into one nation a collection of independent sovereign states'.[52]

In the American case the establishment of national citizenship served to render the Union the protector of individual rights which were jeopardised by the Member States. The Federal State had to protect freedmen against the likely infringement of their rights – particularly by the former slaveholder states. National citizenship became a safe harbour against interferences by the states. Obviously this interpretation does not apply to the establishment of Union citizenship in Part Two of the EC Treaty, because individual rights are well protected within the constitutional systems of the Member States. Rather, the structural significance of the rights of the citizens of the Union consists in the creation of a socio-legal sphere of the Union which embodies the goal of the Union to diminish, perhaps even to abolish, the 'disabilities of alienage in the other States'. This includes not only those who settle in a Member State other than their own, but those who live in their own Member State as well. They have to cope with the fact that persons who used to be aliens have become their fellow-citizens in one respect – in their quality of citizens of the Union – without becoming full members, i.e. citizens in all respects of the daily life of their own Member State. What seems paradoxical at first glance, expresses the very specificity of the European Union. Union citizenship is not so much a relation of the individual vis-à-vis Community institutions but rather a particular socio-legal status vis-à-vis national Member States which have to learn how to cope with the fact that persons, who are physically and socially their citizens, are acquiring a kind of legal citizenship by means of European citizenship without being their nationals.

'Alienage' will probably be the hallmark of Union citizenship, a kind of permanent and structural cognitive and emotional dissonance which, in contrast to the American case, is not likely to disappear in a unitary national culture in the foreseeable future. In contrast to most federal states, Union citizenship is not likely to supersede national citizenship or to make it a status of minor importance frequently verging on mere irrelevance; rather, both statuses will co-exist, representing two different principles of political organisation. National citizenship uses territoriality as the basic means for integrating individuals within society. Union citizenship presupposes a more abstract polity, whose membership serves mainly to integrate individuals who, by all traditional standards, are aliens, or, as the 'Proposals Towards a European Citizenship' submitted by the Spanish Government in September 1990 put it, 'privileged foreigners'. The Spanish Government expected that making the step towards Union Citizenship 'will eliminate the negative effects presently accompanying the condition of foreigner for a citizen of a Member State in another Member State'.[53] It remains to be seen whether the 'abolition of the disabilities of alienage', which sometimes amounts to the attempt to avoid a 'clash of political cultures', can be understood in terms of the distinction between territorial federalism and personal federalism.[54] In any case, it seems safe to assume that the meaning of Union citizenship will be shaped to a considerable extent by the prevailing concepts and traditions of the Member States, because it is the emerging dualism of national and Union citizenship which will finally determine the legal status of European citizens.

It is possible that out of the dissonances resulting from the dualism between the more concrete national citizenship and the more abstract Union citizenship serious conflicts may arise which ultimately may thwart the goal of integration. The removal of 'the disabilities of alienage' requires the removal of 'alienage', and this in turn requires the mutual understanding of what the involved parties – migrating individuals originating in the several Member States, and the hosting Member States and their citizens themselves – understand when they claim or have to accept, respectively, the institution of Union citizenship. Therefore, the future of a concept of European citizenship depends very much on the learning capacities of the would-be citizens of Europe itself, namely on their capability and willingness to accept and cope with alienage in their daily lives.

Notes

1. R. Corbett, *The Treaty of Maastricht: From conception to ratification: A Comprehensive Reference Guide*, Harlow, Longman, 1993, p. 52.

2. D. Curtin, 'The constitutional structure of the Union: a Europe of bits and pieces', *Common Market Law Review*, 1993, vol. 30, pp. 17–69 [67].

3. E. Meehan, *Citizenship and the European Community*, London, Sage, 1993, pp.16ff.

4. T. Oppermann, *Europarecht*, München, Beck, 1982, pp. 563ff.

5. J. H. H. Weiler, 'Fin-de-siècle Europe', in R. Dehousse (ed.), *Europe after Maastricht: An ever closer Union?*, München, Beck, 1994, pp. 203–216 [213].

6. M. Weber, *Economy and Society: An outline of interpretive sociology*, Berkeley, Los Angeles, and London, University of California Press, 1964, pp. 1226ff.

7. P. Riesenberg, *Citizenship in the Western Tradition: Plato to Rousseau*, Chapel Hill and London, University of North Carolina Press, 1992, pp. 20ff.

8. D. Schnapper, *La Communauté des Citoyens. L'idée moderne de nation*, Paris, Gallimard, 1994, pp. 83–88.

9. Weber, *Economy and Society*, part 2, ch. XVI, pp. 1212–1372.

10. *Ibid.*, 1244–1248.

11. *Ibid.*, pp. 1228–1229.

12. Riesenberg, *Citizenship in the Western Tradition*, pp. 203–234.

13. Cf. the historical account of the concept of republic from antiquity to the present by W. Mager, 'Republik', in O. Brunner, W. Conze and R. Koselleck (eds), *Geschichtliche Grundbegriffe. Historisches Lexikon zur politisch-sozialen Sprache in Deutschland*, vol. 5, Stuttgart, Klett, 1984, pp. 549–651.

14. For a more detailed analysis of modern statehood cf. D. Held, *Democracy and the Global Order: From modern state to cosmopolitan governance*, Cambridge, Polity, 1995, pp. 48–72.

15. See the opinion of the International Court of Justice in the famous Nottebohm Case, ICJ Reports 1955, pp. 4ff. [23].

16. W. Conze, 'Staat und Souveränität I – II', in O. Brunner *et al.* (eds), *Geschichtliche Grundbegriffe...*, vol. 6, Stuttgart, Klett-Cotta, 1990, pp. 1–25.

17. J. G. Ruggie, 'Territoriality and beyond: problematizing modernity in international relations', *International Organization*, 1993, vol. 47, pp. 139–74 [150].

18. K. Marx, *Pre-Capitalistic Economic Formations*, E. J. Hobsbawm (ed.), London, Lawrence and Wishart, 1964, p. 78.

19. C. Gamberale, 'National Identities and Citizenship in the European Union and in the US', unpublished paper, Florence, EUI, 1995, p. 11.

20. D. Gosewinkel, 'Die Staatsangehörigkeit als Institution des Nationalstaats', in R. Grawert (ed.), *Offene Staatlichkeit. Festschrift für Ernst-Wolfgang Bökenförde*, Berlin, Duncker und Humblot, 1995, pp. 359–378.

21. D. Gosewinkel, 'Citizenship, Subjecthood, Nationality: Concepts of Belonging in the Age of Modern Nation-states: Notes on the History of Concepts', unpublished paper, European Forum 1995–96 Project on Citizenship, Florence, EUI, 1995.

22. However, empirically this is a rare case. The most eminent case is Article 4 of the French constitution of 1793 according to which the legislature could bestow the rights of a French citizen on an alien who 'had done humanity great service'. Yet, this constitution was never put into force.

23. The reasons for downplaying the practical value of *droits de l'homme* as opposed to the *droits du citoyen* have been impressively analysed by H. Arendt, *The Origins of Totalitarian Rule*, New York and London, Harcourt Brace Jovanovich, 1973 [1951], pp. 290–302.

24. This is a challenge to the idea of citizenship which has been analysed by D. Schnapper, *La Communauté des Citoyens*, pp. 185–202.

25. Of course nationhood plays this selecting role also in the framework of non-democratic regimes as in ethnicist or racist political systems. But this is unsurprising and requires no theoretical explanation.

26. C. Tilly (ed.), *The Formation of National States in Western Europe*, Princeton NJ, Princeton University Press, 1975.

27. Cf. S. N. Eisenstadt and S. Rokkan (eds), *Building States and Nations*, Beverly Hills and London, Sage, 1973; P. Flora *et al.*, *State, Economy, and Society in Western Europe 1815–1975: The growth of mass democracies and welfare states*, vol. I, Frankfurt, Campus, 1983.

28. Schnapper, *La Communauté des Citoyens...*, pp. 83–101; U. K. Preuß, 'Problems of a concept of European citizenship', *European Law Journal*, 1995, vol. 1, pp. 263–277; Held, *Democracy and the Global Order*, pp. 50–52.

29. Cf. the most recent accounts of D. Schnapper, *La France de l'integration. Sociologie de la nation en 1990*, Paris, Gallimard, 1991; D. Schnapper, *La Communauté des Citoyens*; R. Brubaker, *Citizenship and Nationhood in France and Germany*, Cambridge MA, Harvard University Press, 1992; H. Schulze, *Staat und Nation in der Europäischen Geschichte*, München, Beck, 1995.

30. Weber, *Economy and Society*, pp. 901–940.

31. *Ibid.*, 903.

32. J.-J. Rousseau *The Social Contract*, trans. and intro. M. Cranston, London, Penguin, 1968, book 2, ch. 4, pp. 74–78.

33. *Ibid.*, book 1, ch. 7, pp. 75–7; see also pp. 62–4.

34. Cf. M. Walzer, *Spheres of Justice*, New York, Basic Books, 1983, pp. 61–63; B. Ackerman, *Social Justice in the Liberal State*, New Haven and London, Yale University Press, 1980, pp. 69–103.

35. Cf. W. H. McNeil and R. S. Adams (eds), *Human Migration: Patterns and policies*, Bloomington, Indiana University Press, 1978; M. Kritz, C. Keely and S. Tomasi (eds), *Global Trends in Migration*, Staten Island, Center for Migration Studies, 1981; S. Castles and M. J. Miller (eds), *The Age of Migration: International population movements in the modern world*, London, MacMillan, 1993; D. S. Massey *et al.*, 'An evaluation of international migration theory: the North American case', *Population and Development Review*, 1993, vol. 19, pp. 431–466.

36. R. Bauböck, *Transnational Citizenship. Membership and Rights in International Migration*, Brookfield, Edward Elgar, 1994.

37. For the most recent discussion about the integrating or disintegrating role of social conflict see A. O. Hirschman, 'Social conflicts as pillars of democratic market societies', in A. O. Hirschman, *A Propensity to Self-subversion*, Cambridge MA and London, Harvard University Press, 1995, pp. 231–248.

38. See also S. Spencer (ed.), *Strangers & Citizens. A Positive Approach to Migrants and Refugees*, London, Rivers Oram, 1994; P. Close, *Citizenship, Europe and Change*, Houndmills and London, MacMillan, 1995, pp. 55–137.

39. W. Kymlicka, *Multicultural Citizenship*, Oxford, Oxford University Press, 1995, pp. 10–33; D. Schnapper, *La France de l'intégration. Sociologie de la nation en 1990*, Paris, Gallimard, 1991, pp. 33–51.

40. J. G. Ruggie, 'Territoriality and beyond: problematizing modernity in international relations', *International Organization*, 1993, vol. 47, pp. 139–174.

41. From a legal point of view we must distinguish between 'European Community' and 'European Union'. In fact, the 'European Union' is a strange and legally opaque combination of the European Communities proper (European Community, formerly: European Economic Community, the European Coal and Steel Community, and the European Atomic Energy Community) and certain modes of intergovernmental cooperation (see Articles A para. 3, J and K of the Treaty on European Union, signed in Maastricht on 7 February 1992). Hence, the European Union is not a legal entity which could be the subject of rights and duties in the framework of international law.

42. See, e.g., E. Grabitz, *Europäisches Bürgerrecht zwischen Marktbürgerschaft und Staatsbürgerschaft*, Köln, Europa Union, 1970; R. Plender, 'An incipient form of European citizenship', in F. G. Jacobs (ed.), *European Law and the Individual*, Amsterdam, New York, Oxford, 1976, pp. 39–53; A. Durand 'European citizenship', *European Law Review*, 1979, vol. 4, pp. 3–14; G. v. d. Berghe, *Political Rights for European Citizens*, Aldershot, Gower, 1982; A. Evans, 'European citizenship: a novel concept in EEC law', *American Journal of Comparative Law*, 1984, pp. 679–715.

43. See Council directives No. 364/90 of June 28, 1990, in OJ 1990, L 180, p. 26 (right of residence); No. 365/90 of June 28, 1990, in OJ 1990, L 180, p. 28 (right of residence for employees and self-employed persons who have ceased their occupational activity); No. 366/90 of June 28, 1990, in OJ 1990, L 180, p. 30 (right of residence for students).

44. G. F. Mancini, 'The making of a constitution for Europe', in R. O. Keohane and S. Hoffmann (eds), *The New European Community, Decision making and Institutional Change*, Boulder CO and Oxford, Westview, 1991, pp. 177–194 [185].

45. Plender, 'An incipient form of European citizenship', p. 40.

46. Cf. A. Clapham, *Human Rights and the European Community: A Critical Overview, European Union – The Human Rights Challenge*, vol. 1, Baden-Baden, Nomos, 1991, pp. 31 ff.

47. T. H. Marshall, *Citizenship and Social Class – and other Essays*, Cambridge, Cambridge University Press, 1992; R. E. Goodin, *Reasons for Welfare. The Political Theory of the Welfare State*, Princeton NJ, Princeton University Press, 1988, pp. 83ff.

48. v. d. Berghe, *Political Rights for European Citizens*, p. 3; T. Oppermann, *Europarecht*, München, Beck, 1982, pp. 565ff.

49. J. H. H. Weiler, 'The transformation of Europe', *Yale Law Journal*, 1991, vol. 100, pp. 2403–2483.

50. US Supreme Court Case Paul v. Virginia, 75 U.S. 168, 180 (1869).

51. L. Tribe, *American Constitutional Law*, Mineola, NY, Foundation, 1988, pp. 548–553.

52. US Supreme Court Case Toomer v. Witsell, 334 U.S. 385, 395 (1948).

53. See the document in the book of R. Corbett, *The Treaty of Maastricht. From Conception to Ratification: a Comprehensive Reference Guide*, Essex, Longman, 1993, pp. 156–158.

54. T. Fleiner-Gerster and L. R. Basta-Posavec, 'Federalism, Federal States and Decentralization', unpublished paper, Institute of Federalism, Fribourg, 1993.

Chapter Twenty-Three

Europe Entrapped: Does the EU Have the Political Capacity to Overcome its Current Crisis?[*]

Claus Offe

I. The road forward blocked

The seriousness of the crisis is due to one core contradiction. In a nutshell: what is urgently *needed* to be done is also extremely unpopular and therefore democratically virtually *impossible* to do. What must be done, and everyone agrees on it 'in principle' (namely large-scale and long-term debt mutualisation resulting in massive redistributive measures both between member states and social classes), cannot be 'sold' to the voting public of the core member states which so far have been less affected by the crisis than those of the periphery. Analogously, a rapid and sustained boost of the competitiveness of the peripheral countries, an adjustment of *their unit cost of labour* (defined as the ratio of real wages and labour productivity) leading at some point to their approximation to a balanced trade and sustainable levels of budget deficits – all of this is deemed to be 'needed' yet is evidently impossible to implement without thoroughly wrecking their democratic political systems. Moreover, the incongruence between what is needed in economic terms and what is politically feasible, or the now symptomatically frequently invoked condition of 'ungovernability', applies to both sides of the current and deepening European divide of core and periphery. Yet, if the Eurozone falls apart as a consequence of the failure to square this circle, the EU is very likely to follow suit. I believe that Chancellor Merkel is right in saying so – although she forgot to add what by now is also evident: it is the untamed and institutionally unembedded dynamics of the European Monetary Union and the Euro that threatens to disintegrate the EU.

The chasm between what is 'needed' as a set of promising policy responses to the crisis and what is 'feasible' in terms of Member State politics and available as political support applies to *both* sides of that new European divide. Northern 'populists' (as well as centrist political parties fearing the success of populist competitors) reject further tax-funded transfers and credit guarantees, while their Southern friends (or, rather, enemies) reject measures being imposed upon

---

[*] 'Europe entrapped: does the EU have the political capacity to overcome its current crisis?', *European Law Journal*, 2013, vol. 19, no. 5, pp. 595–611.

them that can be denounced as being part of a counter-productive austerity conditionality. Both profit from the crisis in widening their political support. The neo-Nazi party Golden Dawn in Greece has now grown to be the third largest party, as has the rejectionist and anti-political Grillo party in Italy. The moment such a party, together with other rejectionist forces, comes to be part of a governing coalition; the Euro would be a matter of the past due to immediate responses of the European Central Bank (ECB), International Monetary Fund (IMF) and the financial markets.

II. No return to square one

On the other hand, if a cooperative way forward appears to be blocked, why not simply go back to pre-Euro conditions? I do not think that is an option, which it why I speak of a trap where one cannot move in either direction. Even if it were widely agreed by Member States that the introduction of the Euro into a fundamentally flawed currency zone was a huge mistake, the same applies by now to simply *undoing* that mistake. Legally, part of the commitments the new Member States made at the point of their accession was a promise to transform their economies in ways that made them viable, as prescribed by the Maastricht criteria, as members of the Eurozone. In return, they were endowed with the entitlement to financial aid from EU funds which supposedly (yet so far widely unrealistically) would help them to boost productivity and competitiveness of their national economies along a trajectory of 'cohesion' and 'convergence'. If these mutual commitments were to be suspended, an avalanche of adverse economic consequences would be triggered: the re-nationalisation of monetary policy would allow periphery countries to devalue their currency yet leave them all the more deeply in trouble with the challenge of servicing the Euro-denominated debt they have accumulated. Also, private sector financial lenders would immediately increase their pressure ('spreads') on Member States that have not yet left the Euro, thus causing the incalculable costs of a domino effect that eventually would also threaten the economy of the trade surplus countries because they would lose substantial parts of their export markets. Moreover, leaving the Euro would force leavers to also leave the regulatory regime of European law, as compliance with its rules would instantaneously become unaffordable to them. The dissolution of the Eurozone and, as an inescapable medium term consequence, the EU, would be equivalent to a tsunami of economic as well as political regression.

The EU has served so far, apart from being a machinery of economic liberalisation, as a monitoring and regulatory device through which major deviations from standards of human rights and liberal democracy can be kept under control, and be it, in addition to judicial devices, by the 'soft' mechanisms of naming, blaming and shaming of violators (such as the Orban government in Hungary). The EU is also the only institutional location where binding rules governing the economic and fiscal interaction between Member States can be decided upon and implemented, if so far evidently to an insufficient extent. As a supranational authority, it is a common political resource that can be used, if properly designed and further developed, for bringing order and control to not just the political economy of Europe but also for defending peace and democratic civility on the continent. It could even be argued that the distinctiveness of cultural legacies and identities of European nations can be preserved and protected against homogenising market forces *only* through the help of supranational agency. In view of these precious capacities of the EU of being a catalyst of supervisory control and cooperation, it appears frivolous to even consider the dissolution of the EU through a dynamic of re-nationalisation as an acceptable way out of the crisis. Such re-nationalisation would neither benefit individual Member States nor the EU as a whole. Instead, it would cement European divisions.

III. An unsustainable status quo

At the same time, there is no denying that the Euro was a mistake from the beginning. If one puts Greece and Germany, just to mention the two extreme cases, into one and the same currency zone, one unleashes pressures and economic constraints on the poorer, less productive participant, the one with higher unit costs of labour and hence lesser competitiveness in international trade, and deprives them of the possibility of *external* adjustment of their national currencies. True, in that regard the Euro ties everybody's hands. Yet the inclusion of the less competitive periphery into the Eurozone was one of those vicious mistakes which, once having been made, preclude the option of undoing them by returning to the status quo ante.

Currency exchange rate flexibility means that less productive national economies remain free (within limits) to devalue their currency in order to make their exports cheaper and imports more expensive, thus imposing an implicit extra tax on domestic consumers of, say, German luxury cars and Scottish whisky. Once one has adopted the Euro, the devilish implication which people start now to feel is that you cannot devalue your currency any more. Instead, countries must now engage in some kind of *internal* adjustment in order to compensate for large trade deficits, with 'internal adjustment' being a euphemism for vast cuts applying to both the state sector and labour – unless, that is, they manage somehow to increase tax revenues from high incomes and wealth, which most political forces, including all social democrats, consider hardly feasible today. Why? Because, as borders are open, wealth can escape to national regimes with lower taxes and has done so since the financial market crisis began by the hundreds of billions (the 'Depardieu effect'), depriving countries from which they escape of much of available capital for investment. And why is that? Because an EU-wide tax harmonisation has not (yet) been accomplished.

So after the option of external monetary adjustment is taken out of the game for Euro members, the only remaining options for adjustment are labour and the public sector. The trade and budget deficits must be compensated for through pressures on wages, pensions, labour market regulations and public services such as health and education. In addition, deeply indebted states are mandated by supra-national authorities (the 'Troika' of ECB, the Commission and the

IMF) to privatise state-owned assets, their political 'family silver', in exchange for financial relief (that mostly serves to recapitalise troubled national as well as international banks anyway). Everything that is financed, provided and regulated by the state needs now to be 'liberalised'. Hence, the new and already ubiquitous semantics of 'reform'. It used to be the case that by the term 'reform', we meant something proactive and 'progressive', a step towards more distributional justice. Now, we see that the opposite is meant by reform: budgetary emergency measures with regressive distributional implications. Virtually the entire political elite of Europe and of Member States proclaim that reforms (in the new sense) are necessary, urgently called for and unavoidable as a *quid pro quo* for financial aid. Besides: whatever the economic virtues of any reform proposal may be held to be, such proposals are most unlikely to be adopted if they are promoted not by a democratic political process of legislation but by foreign imposition and perceived blackmail. Little wonder that this causes a social uproar and huge protest movements. Unions fight with their back to the wall; at times, we saw explosions of these leftist populist mass movements almost every Sunday in the capitals and provincial towns of Greece, Portugal, and Spain. Italy is a little better off (but perhaps not so anymore, after the outcome of the February 2013 elections), then comes France, where Hollande is trying to assume the position of a mediator. At the same time, the twin motivators of greed and fear lead financial wealth to flee to presumably safe and profitable places, be it within Europe or off its shores.

To provide some statistics, which I found quite telling concerning what measures of 'internal adjustment' are aiming at: for the Greek balance of external trade to become even, that country needs to become no less than 40 per cent less expensive in Euro terms. On the other side, German exports would have to be 20 per cent more expensive in order to reduce that country's export surplus to zero.[1] (Incidentally, German export surplus for 2011 has been, relative to GDP, *twice* that of China.) Yet a balancing of international trade seems quite inconceivable to happen, as neither Greek workers, pensioners, and political parties trying to defend their interests, would allow this to happen nor German employers or any conceivable minister of finance. What makes things worse: even *if* the Greek state budget were to be shrunk nearly as much in response to dictates of the EU, the ECB and the IMF by some authoritarian technocrat at the top of the country's government, the net effect on the debt-to-GDP ratio would not be favourable but strongly *negative*.[2] As the debt is made to shrink, the GDP would shrink even more rapidly, thus driving the ratio of the two *up* due to the negative multiplier effect of austerity measures. And as financial investors know that only positive growth prospects (a 'credible business plan' of a country, as in Japan) will generate the future tax base out of the taxation of which their claims can be serviced, they are likely to respond to the worsening debt/GDP situation by either punitively denying credit or increasing the spread to even less sustainable levels to the extent such growth prospects are quite plausibly deemed to be missing, an assessment which in turn triggers a self-fulfilling prophecy of economic decline.

IV. Solidarity?

So the overall question is: How might such a huge and persistent trade imbalance be remedied *within* the framework of the Euro? Or can it at all be remedied? Or should Europeans better give up trying? The main ideas are: a European clearing union, fiscal union or debt mutualisation, most practically in the form of Euro bonds, a mechanism that is currently disallowed by the Treaties and would amount to export surplus countries sharing with net importers the substantial (interest rate, tax revenues, as well as external exchange rate) benefits that they derive from their comparatively good standing with the financial and export markets. And something of the sort is being tried now, if with extreme suspicions on the part of public opinion, especially in the northern countries. The EU is, after all, not a federal state with the normal mechanisms of fiscal federalism and a central government which is constitutionally committed to take care of some permanent form of interstate redistribution. Publics in core countries such as Germany have so far failed to appreciate – and political parties have to a disastrous extent failed to enlighten the public about – the (uncontroversial, behind closed doors) fact that measures such as debt mutualisation are not a matter of 'transfers' or 'altruistic donations' but a matter of *solidarity* in the proper sense. That is to say: solidarity means to do *not* what 'is good for you', but what 'is good for *all of us*'. Instead, the ruling misunderstanding that mistakes acts of solidarity (in the sense just specified) for altruistic charitable donations invites the frame of asking: 'Why should "*we*" pay for "*them*"?'

This frame is something right-wing populist parties (as well as many forces in centrist parties) are taking advantage of and use for their campaign purposes, thus preventing national and European elites from pursuing a democratically broadly supported strategy mandated by 'self-interest, rightly understood' (as Tocqueville famously put it in a different context), i.e. solidarity. In the EU, the notion of a 'we' that defines the scope of solidarity is, however, poorly established as a reference of a shared identity. The contours of the entity called 'all of us' for whose benefit solidarity is to be practised are, only 'objectively' clear (namely 'all EU Member States', the number of which is also involved in an ongoing process of expansion and thus remains a moving target) while they are blurred and contested in the subjective perceptions of Member State elites and masses alike. The horizon of the solidarity that is called for is not a state, least of all a 'family', and not an association that members are aware of having voluntarily joined and therefore obliged to practise with solidarity. It is rather an extensive community that is *still under construction* and hence weak (and getting weaker under the impact of the crisis with its winners and losers) as a source of solidarity obligations.

On the other hand: what a (currently shrinking) minority of EU enthusiasts among elites and non-elites would dream of for many years in terms of deepening the integration process, has suddenly, under the impact of the crisis, turned into the road map for an urgent rescue operation that makes the empowerment of fiscal and economic governing capacities at the EU level a plain imperative. Yet as this rescue operation lacks support of political parties (and hence voters) both in the still prosperous and the declining countries of the EU, the rescue operation is still unlikely to succeed, particularly as it is being conducted in an undemocratic, depoliticised and technocratic mode that violates standards of democratic accountability which publics in European Member States have (fortunately) learned to consider non-negotiable essentials of political life. Even in case the urgent fusion of supranational powers does succeed, it can thus easily be denounced by democrats as what it actually (and at best) is likely to be: a technocratically imposed, incompletely considered, judicially vulnerable, belated emergency operation with a dubious potential for putting the financial markets to rest and under control. To the contrary: as Member States undergo a metamorphosis from classical 'tax states' to debt states,[3] they become ever more vulnerable to the vagaries of the financial markets.

V. The financialisation of states and their inadequate governing capacity

Both proponents of the political left and the centre-right have recently called for referenda as an institutional device to bolster the democratic legitimacy of rescue operations initiated by 'Brussels', with the left reluctantly betting on a 'pro' outcome and the right on the opposite due to the prevalence of notions of 'national' interests and growing mutual resentments between supposed winners and losers of the rescue operation. But, again: before preferences of voters can be *counted*, they must first be *formed*, and formed in the light of consensual normative reasons and the 'enlightened understanding'[4] of the nature of the situation and the alternative escape routes and their consequences. In the absence of a Europe-wide party system with some hegemonic potential that could provide such enlightening orientation, and given the power of national blinders in the formation of voters' preferences, it is not easy to be confident about the 'emergency legitimation' referenda's capacity to provide support for strong interventions at the European level.

The supreme policy making body of the EU is the non-partisan intergovernmental (as opposed to supranational) European Council (EC, not to be confused with the Council of the EU, a quasi-federal chamber that plays a major role in European lawmaking). It consists of the heads of state or heads of government of Member States. It meets four or more times per year and defines the directions and priorities of the EU and gives 'impulses' for EU policies; it is not involved in European lawmaking. (After its sessions, almost always in Brussels, a subtotal of the members, those belonging to the Eurozone, stay on for separate consultations.) The mode of decision making of this body (that meets behind closed doors) is peculiar: no votes are taken, but the president of the Council draws a 'conclusion' which is considered adopted as a consensual policy document once none of the members registers a formal disagreement. It also reflects power relations that serve to silence potential opponents to the (normally) prevailing French–German consensus. This unanimity rule represents the smallest common denominator that national top politicians of Member States are able to strike a compromise on. If it were otherwise and some kind of qualified majority rule were to apply, the national constituency of presidents or prime ministers who find themselves in the minority could (and certainly would) protest that they have been made subject to some kind of 'foreign rule', the rule of the majority countries. This arrangement severely limits the potential *effectiveness* of (the non-legislative, but 'impulse giving') governance by the EC. Its democratic *legitimacy* is limited by the fact that members, while certainly being elected into their offices of prime minister etc., are thereby mandated to serve the good of the *country* in which they have been elected, not that of the *EU*; in contrast, members of the European Parliament are expressly elected to represent the European citizenry in EU legislation.

How did we get into this situation of urgently needed yet woefully deficient European and Eurozone governing capacity? What is the pre-history of the chain effects of financial market, debt and integration crisis? One element of the answer is the inexplicable (as it seems from today's perspective) failure of national and European authorities to regulate the financial industry in ways which might have prevented the chains of banks defaulting and governments stepping in to bail them out – a notable *attention deficit*[5] that has afflicted policy elites not just on Europe's side of the North Atlantic. Let me just allude to some of the deeper mechanisms that seem to have played a role in this extremely complex field. Part of the explanation of the story is that the states are so badly indebted and thus so vulnerable to the vagaries of financial markets because they had to bail out their banks, at least those which are proverbially 'too big to fail'. The public costs of saving private banks at the taxpayers' expense has added to the fiscal crisis which then in turn allows the banks to profit from crediting states – a manifestation of the banks' 'second strike capability' that is an obscenity in itself.

If one were to put oneself in the shoes of a financial investor, he wants one of two things (and there is a trade-off between these two things): *security* for the financial investment (a positive assessment of the probability that the loan will be serviced and paid off) and a high *yield* in terms of interest (as a partial compensation for the remaining risk that the debtor defaults). *States* used to be preferred debtors because they have two advantages, as seen by lenders, compared to private debtors. First, they have the political authority to *impose* taxes on citizens to service their debt. Second, they can *print* money and thus devalue their debt in real terms through inflation. The latter attraction is no longer valid if the debtor state is a Euro state, thereby being prohibited from printing its own money. The former attraction has also been rendered questionable, from the point of view of financial investors, as states are rightly perceived by them to relate to each other, as EU Member States with open borders, as rivals in a game of *tax competition*. Raising taxes in order to provide assurance to creditors is not an option either if that came to be seen by investors to undercut the state's international economic competitiveness, hence its future tax base, hence the ability to service its debt. In an open economy, states must be cautious with imposing taxes on corporations and the earners of high income; if they cannot rely, instead, on imposing them upon ordinary workers and consumers, and to the extent they cannot cut their expenditures, there remains no alternative other than relying on loans from private creditors – loans which become less readily available (or more expensive) due to the two points just made.

Throughout the period of global liberalisation, i.e. since the early 1980s of the 20th century, the total debt of OECD states has thus been continuously growing. (Incidentally, the gradual transition from the taxing state to the borrowing state has some interesting distributional implications: the *taxing* state *diminishes* the disposable income of the well-to-do through (progressive) taxation, while the *borrowing* state *increases* that income by paying interest on what the well-to-do can well afford to lend the state.) Throughout the same period, the volume of the financial sector as a whole and the portion of the revenues it derives from the financing of public debt has been growing, while the portion of income that financial investors derive from borrowers in the 'real' economy has been shrinking.

It has been argued by the German sociologist Christoph Deutschmann[6] that the shift of the financial industry from financing investments in the 'real' economy to financing sovereign debt and speculative trading in debt is due to a relative shortage of 'classical' debtors – debtors who take out loans in order to finance investment in productive activities, the returns from which allow them to service their debt. This shortage of demand for credit in the 'real' economy can arguably be attributed to the combined effect of the demographic change of aging societies (wealthy pensioners acting as *rentiers* rather than entrepreneurs) plus a secular decline of economic growth rates throughout the OECD world (as Robert J. Gordon has argued in an influential paper on US long-term growth prospects).[7] To the extent it does take place, *growth depends on credit* that is granted to states, firms and households. (As Streeck has shown in his recent book,[8] the total indebtedness (or degree of 'financialisation' of the economy and polity) has increased to a factor of *eight* times the annual GDP in Germany and of *nine* times that of the United States, roughly doubling since the 1970s in the United States and since the early 1990s in Germany, in the latter country mostly due to debt-financed unification.)

Yet, it is also true that *credit depends on growth* for its sustainability. Moreover, the stability of a capitalist society critically depends upon growth. The one thing that capitalist societies, even the most prosperous of them, cannot afford is to *stagnate* (contrary to the hopes and predictions of J. S. Mill who foresaw a liberal steady state economy).[9] For if growth were not anticipated for at least the medium term future, investors would have no reason to invest and workers no opportunity to work and earn an income from being employed. To deepen the dilemma even further, let me just point to the currently widely shared doubts whether we in the advanced societies can at all *afford* growth ('as we know it') for environmental and, in particular, climate change considerations. Taking these considerations together, we get three propositions, each of which is as plausible as they are mutually incompatible: (1) growth is indispensible, (2) growth rates are approximating zero in advanced economies, (3) growth becomes unaffordable in view of its negative externalities.

I lack both the space and the competence to do more here than just raise these questions rather than outlining answers concerning what happens in a zero growth condition. Instead, let me return to the configuration of forces and strategies in the current debt and Euro crisis. Bailing out Greece (and now Cyprus), to say nothing about Spain and Portugal and Italy, through debt mutualisation, Eurobonds, and other mechanisms of burden sharing among Member States is likely to turn out to be an extremely expensive transfer that would have to be paid through inflation or/ and increased budget deficits in the North. That is to say, it is extremely unpopular in countries which would be seen and see themselves as net contributors to the rescue operation. The only argument to possibly convince 'northern' voting publics that burden sharing (of course, with harsh conditionalist strings attached) is still an acceptable idea is the argument that *failing* to do so might be even *more* expensive. This is an entirely prudential argument, not one from solidarity obligations. Nobody can know for sure what is going to happen if *nothing* happens, i.e. if some form of debt mutualisation does *not* materialise. The most recent prognostics from a Bertelsmann study[10] suggest a disaster: a domino effect throughout the northern Mediterranean, including France and perhaps Belgium would be hugely destructive for the global economy, and in particular the entire European economy. Germany, as well as Finland and the Netherlands, would be very badly affected, too. So, as a matter of prudence rather than solidarity, it is better to bail out Greece (if need be, through another 'hair cut' at tax-payers' expense) in order to stop the predators of the financial industry from imposing ever higher 'spreads' on one after the other of the countries in question. To be sure, the financial institutions will warmly welcome such acts of anxiety-driven supra-national 'solidarity', as these acts assure them that their risk will eventually be covered, at least to an extent that allows them to stay in business. Yet more than temporary transfers are needed in order to restore the trust in the debtor countries' ability to pay and to service their debt: in order to fully assure long-term investors, what Greece would need is not just the (at any rate limited, in both time and financial volume) willingness of vicarious debtors to step in by paying for Greek debt but a recovery of the tax base of the Greek economy so that, at some point in the fairly distant future, Greece can cover its financial obligations from its own production (plus from permanent transfers from EU funds, such as an economically backward province would be entitled to receive from the central government of an ordinary federal state). That is to say, in order to prevent the banks from anticipating (and thereby causing in a self-fulfilling loop) the risk of default of Greek and other Mediterranean states, the EU, instead of urging counter-productive austerity and 'reforms', thereby further undercutting growth prospects and stirring up disruptive social conflict, would have to become instrumental in rebuilding the ailing and largely uncompetitive economies of the Southern Eurozone. But no one, argues Streeck,[11] pointing to the (presumably 'easier') intra-state examples of the post-German Democratic Republic (GDR) *Länder* and the Italian *Mezzogiorno*, knows how to accomplish that in an effective and robust manner. Besides, the sobering fact is that the EU in its present shape (lacking its own taxing power and with its medium-term budget just having been significantly decimated, in early 2013, by Member States' governments) is neither institutionally nor economically nor politically willing and able to take the initiative towards any of those things. A minimally promising 'Marshall Plan for Greece' is not forthcoming from 'Brussels'. Besides, if it were, it would not fall on the fertile ground of a post-war reconstruction boom, as did its predecessor. As long as nothing of the kind is likely to happen, the banks are bound to have the final say on what happens to the populations and economies of the South.

In an economic space where national borders are perforated so that people, investments, goods and services can freely move from member state to member state, a web of causalities and interdependencies emerges, the scope of which vastly exceeds the scope of control, or governing capacity. What 'all of us' are passively affected by cannot be actively shaped and managed by any agency that is endowed with legitimate power by 'all of us'. This gap between the horizon of causation and the horizon of control applies with particular force to members of the Eurozone: they are disempowered to manage their national currencies (as there is none anymore) yet unable to collectively establish the governing capacity that would allow them to manage their interdependency in ways that are tolerable for all and capable to curb the power of the financial sector. The ECB, being the supreme fiduciary institution of the Eurozone and remote from any political accountability has neither the mandate nor nearly the capacity to fill this control gap.

Sociologically speaking: the scope of functional integration is much wider than the scope of social integration, or what we are passively *affected by* is beyond our collective capacity to *act upon*. The European political economy is (at best) experienced by its citizens as a community of *fate* but not as one of fate *control*. Markets and the currency are international, while democratic politics remains essentially national and framed in the code of what has been called 'methodological nationalism'. The twist, however, is that some participants of this game, such as Germany, have no urgent reason nor incentive to remedy this imbalance because they can live with it or are even favoured by its outcomes, while others are on the receiving side of massive and uncontrolled negative externalities, i.e. the beggar-my-neighbour effects originating from Member States which have managed to combine high productivity with wage restraint, together yielding low unit costs of labour and high export surpluses. Yet with the EU having no taxing authority of its own, any permanent and appropriately large-scale international redistribution initiated by the Commission would meet with the complaint of 'taxation without representation'. But this imbalance can be taken care of in either of two ways: either by further cutting the budget of the EU or by endowing the EU with a democratically accountable taxing and spending authority of its own (which, to be sure, would require not only amending the Treaties, but also national constitutions, such as the German *Grundgesetz*).

It used to be the case that, in order for one country or a group of countries to take full control of the economy and polity of another country, the former must *occupy* the latter by military means. This is no longer needed. Today one can have perfectly peaceful relations with a particular country and still literally own it – simply by appropriating its economy through a permanent trade surplus and by destroying its sovereignty by depriving the country (in an *ad hoc* fashion of rescue conditionality, if not through European law) of its budgetary and other legislative autonomy. Just an example: 40 per cent of the manufacturing sector of Hungary is estimated to be owned or jointly owned by German companies. And these are only German (co-)owners – if you add France, Austria, Great Britain, this must amount to the majority of all assets of that country. Given this constellation of economic and political power, it does not come as a surprise that within those countries the situation is perceived as a new version of imperialism and dependency – a view the anti-European mobilisational potential of which yields very gloomy prospects for the future of European integration.

VI. Whose responsibility?

Coming back to the question of who can or must be 'blamed' for such international power imbalances deepening within the European political economy and the Eurozone, the only 'agent' we can point at is the institutional setup of the EU and the 'attention deficit' of its designers. Their design of the Eurozone was a giant mistake from the beginning because of the (further deepening) heterogeneity of the economies it comprises, as was the failure of the Maastricht treaty to provide effective sanctioning mechanisms for the violation of its criteria as well as the failure of the Lisbon treaty to establish an adequately capable regime at the European level for the implementation of supra-national economic, fiscal and social policies. Nor can any 'automatic' adjustment of socio-economic imbalances be expected to take place, be it through the lowering of wages and prices in the less prosperous parts of the system or through outward migration of labour to the more prosperous ones; the latter adjustment through labour mobility is largely hindered, within the EU, by the multilingual nature of the EU with its no less than 23 official languages. On top of this all, there was the mistaken political decision to engage in the competitive liberalisation of the financial industry, in Germany (under the Red-Green Schröder administration) and elsewhere. So it seems that 'all of us' have made great, serious and highly consequential mistakes.

Yet this insight, though widely and occasionally even ruefully shared by today's political elites in Europe, does not really help to redesign policy. What would help, in my view, is not to allocate *blame* retrospectively but what I would call forward-looking *remedial responsibility.* The moral principle underlying this move is simple. It postulates that the *less* an agent (member state and its economy) has suffered as a consequence of the mistakes collectively made or the *more* it even has benefitted from them having been made (through interest rates which are lower than they otherwise would be, and external exchange rates of the Euro more favourable), the *greater* the share of the burdens the agent must shoulder in compensating others for adverse consequences resulting from the original mistake. This moral calculus can even be read in a deontic and a consequentialist perspective – the latter because the beneficiary will have a long-term interest in preserving an arrangement that has yielded it so many benefits at comparatively low costs and sacrifices. Yet, however one is to read it, the answer to the question, who that agent might be that bears the greatest remedial responsibility in today's Europe is compelling: Germany. Yet, German political elites and publics are far from *appreciating* this answer as compelling and from acting accordingly – quite the contrary and certainly not at a time when incumbent parties and governments are facing national elections.

What we have here is one of the rare cases where the demands of moral duty *coincide* with those of well-considered long-term interest. Yet still, its practical implications are virtually universally being rejected. Needless to say, a proposition to

- partially sacrifice national sovereignty and substantial economic resources, for the sake of
- creating an enhanced European-level governing capacity, for the sake of
- bailing out Member States and subsidising their economic recovery as well as alleviating the misery of their social conditions, for the sake of
- appeasing the financial industry and restraining its charges of interest, in order to
- consolidate the Eurozone and eventually the EU

- such a complex chain of strategic moves is a non-starter in terms of national politics, and not just due to its complexity and the uncertainties involved. Whoever would advocate this line of action has to face fears, resentments and nationalistic backlash on a massive scale coming from all over the spectrum of political forces.

VII. The poverty of party politics

To repeat, we face the abysmal gap between policy and politics. Political parties – preferably supra-national political parties addressing a Europe-wide constituency – would have to be able to bridge this gap by shaping and educating public opinion. Instead, we see parties desperately clinging to national frames and short-term cost calculations as they are afraid to provoke the worst resentments of the voters and of losing votes to populist competitors as a consequence. What their leaders say and decide behind closed doors in Brussels is often risky to state openly and defend at home in the national media because of the omnipresent suspicion of betrayal of 'national' interests. Political parties as power-seeking organisations are corrupted by the positivistic opportunism of responding to voters' '*given*' preferences, while shying away from the challenge of *shaping* these preferences in the first place – which is arguably the supreme mission of democratic political parties.

If that mission were to be fulfilled, parties would have to accomplish a switch from the dominant code of 'nation versus nation' to an at least supplementary code of 'social class versus social class'. That is to say: two Germans, one of whom is threatened by long-term unemployment, have probably *less* in common, as far as their socio-economic interests are concerned, than two Europeans being threatened by unemployment (or, for that matter, deriving income from financial investments), one of whom happens to be a German.

As a rule of thumb, politicians can afford more consistency the more remote they are from a direct involvement in national policy making. Populist leaders, both on the left and the right, are often quite exactly consistent as they cannot hope for government office anyway. As long as governing responsibilities are out of reach, they can be denounced as 'sour grapes', and office holders denounced as self-serving, incompetent and corrupt. Populists are obsessed with what Max

Weber called 'negative politics': politics of obstruction and anti-politics. Populists such as the Italian *Cinque Stelle* movement float mobilising demands for the benefit of their campaign that they rightly do not expect to have to implement as the makers of public policy. Another current example is Horst Seehofer, the Bavarian prime minister. As his role in EU crisis policy is at best a very limited one, he can well afford to 'be tough on the Greeks' – a position on which he has to retract though when it comes to demonstrating support for Merkel's coalition government of which his party is a junior partner. On the other hand, I am less optimistic than, for instance, Habermas[12] regarding the question whether political parties *are* in fact able and willing to shape public opinion through argument and persuasion in order to generate support for far-sighted and inclusive policies. What would be needed for political parties to shape preferences through persuasion and argument is the capacity to overcome widespread fears, sentiments of distrust, short-sightedness and suspicion.

One of those popular attitudes that parties are typically not capable of coming to terms with is the suspicion that if 'we' make sacrifices in favour of 'them', 'they' will use 'our' generosity as an opportunity to take unfair advantage of 'us'. In short, 'they' are portrayed as engaging in the frivolously self-serving behaviour that economists call 'moral hazard'. The cognitive bias of mass constituencies that parties fail to overcome is the understanding that a problem is 'their' problem, not a problem of 'all of us'. This weakness could perhaps be remedied if parties were able to switch from their dominant 'nation versus nation' code to the 'class versus class' code.

Yet the primary problem is the widely shared *perception* of such threat of moral hazard and its anticipated turn into a negative-sum game. If 'we' are generous to 'them', 'they' will respond by exploiting the situation by stopping to perform 'their' obligations, thus spiralling 'all of us' into a bottomless pit. If that were so, 'we' would do better to stop making mindless sacrifices on our part, which is a politically popular conclusion which drives the whole scenario. It stands in the way of the acceptance of socially inclusive and far-sighted policies. Yet the negative-sum scenario is not just driven by the interest of potential donors in finding an excuse for not donating, but it is often also provided plausibility by observations on how recipients actually *do* behave and are induced by their institutions and traditions to behave. In several of the Mediterranean Euro countries, there is in fact credible evidence of tax authorities and entire political elites being corrupt, tax evasion being considered a mark of cleverness, special interest being institutionally privileged and tax-exempt, organised crime playing a big role in the making (or at least sabotaging) of public policy and agents in public administration and the judiciary deviating far from what in other parts of Europe is considered an appropriate ethos of public service. It is the evidence of these deficiencies (which are hardly to be overcome by foreign pressures, threats and moralising accusations) that nourishes negative perceptions and resentments on the part of those in the north of Europe who have an interest in excusing themselves from duties of solidarity, if not even a plain propensity to victim blaming. If neither the Greek state nor European legislation finds means to prevent rich citizens of

Greece to reportedly transfer every year an estimated 40 billion Euros out of the country into their Swiss bank accounts or elsewhere, this fact, as processed by media reporting, is quite unlikely to stimulate other Europeans' sense of obligation and responsibility. While Greece is probably the most ethno-nationalistic country in the EU, its economic culture is arguably also the least patriotic.

We know from surveys that in none of the countries that suffer from great trade and budget deficits majorities favour the idea of leaving the Euro – quite to the contrary. The economic and political reasons are obvious. First, by exiting from the Euro they would lose their 'nuisance value' – the capacity to pressure the EU to rescue their banks, budgets and economies. Second, they still would have to service their Euro-denominated debt on the basis of a heavily devalued new national currency. Also, no reasonably responsible politician in the rest of Europe would urge them to leave, as chain reactions affecting other countries would be likely (and at least highly incalculable as to their costs) as a consequence.

The EU and its Member States suffer from three deficits that are by now almost proverbial: The deepening *trade* deficits of the poorer economies, the ubiquitous (except for Sweden) *budget* deficits and the glaring *democratic* deficit at the level of EU governance. To briefly illustrate: GDP per capita relates from the (admittedly: outlier of) Luxemburg at the peak to Bulgaria at the bottom as 17 relates to 1, with 10 of the 12 new Member States together making up the lower end of the distribution. There is not a single Euro country where public debt levels comply with the Maastricht limit of 60 per cent of GDP. And the European institutions, in spite of the direct and deep impact they have upon the life of citizens, operate in stratospheric distance from democratic mechanisms of accountability and representation. The most supranational and most democratic of the EU institutions, the European Parliament, suffers from the anomaly that it does not meet (and will hardly ever obtain) the standard of a 'peoples chamber', or a normal legislature; for that, it would have to comply with the 'one man one vote' rule and the principle of *equal weight* of each vote. As, for instance, the populations of Germany and Luxemburg relate to each other in quantitative terms as 204:1, the constituency of Luxemburg (or Malta or one day Iceland) would hardly ever agree to be massively downgraded in its representational weight in the EP through an abolition of the rule of 'degressive proportionality' currently in force; yet that rule has already been declared 'undemocratic' for lower houses by the German Constitutional Court.[13]

These three deficits are tightly interrelated, with the last one, the democratic deficit, being the strategic leverage point for any promising attempt to deal with the other two. In order to have a steep increase in terms of integration, fiscal pact, permanent oversight of the Commission, in order to make a regime controlling banks and budgets a stable regime (rather than an ad hoc emergency measure adopted behind closed doors), most of all: in order to implement the large-scale redistribution (both interstate and inter-class) that such a regime would entail, one certainly cannot do without the political support of the European citizenry that expresses its will, as shaped and guided by political parties, in general elections and referenda. And, as democratic procedures go, the outcome can be yes, or it can be no; democratic processes are open-ended choices. Their outcomes depend upon the capacity of political parties to persuade and enlighten citizens. If we were to leave choices concerning policy, but also those concerning institutions, to the technocrats to decide upon, then chances are that everything they decide will be worthless the day after tomorrow, i.e. after the day national constitutional courts or the ECJ have passed their judgements. In order to create solidity, permanence, calculability and continuity of the terms of integration, we need democratic legitimation. This is a functional argument: if we want to be effective, we cannot do without democratic legitimacy in the first place in order to endow policies and institutions with the authority and validity that the (alleged) expertise of technocrats cannot possibly substitute for through 'output legitimacy'.

At any rate, the way forward cannot be charted by Thatcher's (and Merkel's) TINA maxim that 'there is no alternative' to what incumbent elites declare the only way out. Invoking TINA is just tantamount to admitting that previous policies have failed their mandate to *keep* choices open, thereby trapping all of us in an allegedly alternative-less situation.

No doubt, there is a problem here. Liberal democracy has been suspected to be both procedurally slow in recognising and addressing societal problems and myopic (inadequately 'future-regarding') in setting agendas as elites are fixated on what can be achieved by the date of the next election. (Either of these defects can be easily illustrated using current climate change politics and policies as an example.) On the one hand, it is in the very nature of democratic processes, including appropriate information gathering, will formation through public debate and deliberation, coalition building, campaigning etc., that it is highly time consuming, compared to decision making in de-politicised technocratic committees. This applies *a fortiori* to democratic institution building: the time needed to accomplish a major overhaul of the Treaties governing the EU can safely be estimated as ranging between five and 10 years. Yet in order to produce a viable response to emergency situations in financial markets, one often has a day or two. Sometimes it is a matter of hours to: Brussels' decisions on how to appease financial markets must be out at 2 am Sunday night, i.e. before the Tokyo stock exchange opens. Yet still: those making such decisions must be capable of being held democratically accountable or at least be able to claim legitimacy on the basis of a fiduciary mission democratically granted to them. The solution of this problem might be that policies become more proactive, anticipating and paying attention to seemingly remote possibilities (remote both in time and in probability) in order to be prepared – the opposite of what was the case in the financial market crisis of September 2008.

Besides, the absence of choice is often a false claim of politicians and their ideological preoccupations and ways of framing political and economic realities. Take the familiar case of a gaping budget deficit. The technocratic answer is the call for austerity. Yet instead of cutting expenditures, the gap can also be closed by raising taxes. Yet that would antagonise investors, whose resistance would have to be neutralised by, among other things, harmonising the system of direct taxes throughout the EU. But trying to do so would provoke objections in the new Member States which feel compelled to compete for investment through low (and often flat rate) corporate income tax rates; and so on. Claiming 'no alternatives' is often just a cover for surrendering to perceived (and no doubt: accurately perceived) power relations, the powers that defend the status quo of the free movement of financial capital.

Europe consists of nation states, citizens and social classes; there are plenty of alternatives concerning how we want to engage all these various forces and actors into the democratic process. Generally speaking: *input* legitimation is indispensable, particularly at present when *output* legitimacy – the legitimacy claimed for the making of effective decisions – is in such a miserable state. If one thinks of the so-called 'permissive consensus' in favour of Europe that prevailed until a decade ago, virtually nothing is left of it. Mass constituencies are up in arms against 'Brussels', 'Berlin', 'Europe' – thus we need to rebuild Europe on the basis of democratic mechanisms of representation and accountability.

There is no shortage of policy proposals which serve as proof that there *are* 'alternatives'. An EU-wide tax harmonisation applying to direct taxes would help to disincentivise 'regime shopping' practices and transnational capital mobility – a mobility with which labour cannot cope, partly because labour speaks in 23 languages, while capital is 'speechless'. Budget deficits can be addressed not just by austerity measures and 'internal' devaluation; they can also be solved by increasing taxes on high income and wealth, and be it by forcing the wealthy to buy government bonds. Indirect taxes have the great advantage that their tax base cannot flee the country and the well-known downside that their incidence is regressive: the relatively poor spend greater parts of their income and thus shoulder a greater proportion of the burden of indirect taxes. Why not applying a progressive schedule on Y-S = C per tax year, i.e. annual income per person minus documented savings/investment, as the basis of progressive taxation instead of a flat sales tax, thus combining the advantages, in terms of distributional fairness, of direct and indirect taxation? Furthermore, proposals have been made to Europeanise the systems of unemployment insurance[14] and social assistance/ poverty relief,[15] the realisation of which may well boost, as a side effect, the mass identification with Europe as a political entity. Moreover, without violating the 'subsidiarity' principle enshrined in the Treaties, a European legislation could be launched that specifies maximum permissible Gini-coefficients for member state societies, with the level inversely tied to their current GDP per capita values. Also, commercial banks can be prohibited to accept deposits from financial investors who can be identified as fleeing from debt-troubled countries. All of this *can* be done, but it hasn't been done. These and other policy proposals can largely be implemented through European legislation. The problem is that before that can happen, a basic 'mental reframing' of the situation is called for in that the prevailing 'methodological nationalism' code of 'nation versus nation' must be partly substituted and supplemented by a code of 'losers versus winners' of the crisis, if not socio-economic 'class versus class'.

Institutionally, and in order for any of those proposals to win favourable prospects, the European Parliament needs to be strengthened and the Commission needs to be transformed into something like a parliamentary government. It is precisely those EU institutions which have the *greatest* impact on daily life of people which are so far the *farthest remote* from democratic accountability: the European Central Bank, the ECJ and the European Commission. They are completely depoliticised and thus can act in majestic independence of whatever citizens, parties and parliaments prefer or reject. Again, we face a deep divorce between politics and policy: on the one hand, there is often populist mass politics (including identity-related 'culture wars') that has no perceptible implication for policy making on citizens' core interests and bread-and-butter issues. On the other, there is elitist policy making that has no roots in, no links to, nor legitimation through politics. This is the deepening bifurcation of those two spheres within the European polity. Political elites are increasingly unable to achieve outcomes that voters desire and to convince voters that their interests are in their, the elites', trustworthy and competent hands. What voters need and want is beyond the capacity of the political system to deliver, without the latter being able to explain to the former what the hindrances are, and how they might be removed. It is as if one has mail ordered a shirt and is supplied a pair of socks. The promises and appeals by which political power is *acquired* (i.e. *politics*) are disjointed, under the dictate of financial markets, from the purposes to the achievement of which power resources mandated to governments are *effectively employed* and used for the making of *policies*.

To this situation, elites (as well as commentators and academic observers) respond by diagnosing and complaining about an emerging condition of 'ungovernability'. Non-elites feel cheated and follow the appeals of ever shriller and ever more anti-political forms of fundamental opposition campaigns, such as that of Grillo in Italy who, right after winning a spectacular quarter of the popular vote in the February 2013 national elections, gleefully predicted the Italian Republic's disintegration and exit from the Eurozone within a matter of six month, due to its manifest fiscal starvation.

What if the Euro fails and the losers of the Euro game are forced to leave the common currency area? I suppose there are lots of drawers in lots of government offices that are filled with emergency plans for the hour when all the rescue plans have turned out futile. I have not seen these plans, nor has anyone I know. If the EU disintegrates, in 'controlled' ways or otherwise, we'll stand at the beginning of a giant negative-sum game in which everyone is going to lose. That much is well understood, and widely. As I have pointed out, one core problem for the saving of the Euro is that the banking crisis has spilled over into a debt crisis, and the debt crisis in an EU integration crisis. The latter crisis consists in the re-nationalisation of horizons of solidarity and rich countries of Europe dictating to the poorer ones the austerity cure in order for them to regain the trust of the financial industry. They do so in spite of all the evidence that austerity is a highly poisonous medicine, an overdose of which will kill the patient (rather than stimulate growth and expand the tax base), in which case the weakest Eurozone members (and eventually all of them) become ever more dependent on lenders and allow them to charge ever higher and ever more unsustainable rates. It is becoming ever more difficult to envisage the bootstrapping act by which European political elites might escape from this vicious circle. I think it will eventually need the protest and resistance of those suffering most from the crisis to push those elites on a more promising path. But nobody, as of today, can claim the possession of valid knowledge on what that path may be, nor who may assume a leadership role in guiding us there.

Notes

1. W. Schäfer, 'Die Eurozone leidet unter intern verzerrten Wechselkursen', *Frankfurter Allgemeine Zeitung*, 27 August 2013, available at http://www.faz.net/aktuell/wirtschaft/gastbeitrag-die-eurozone-leidet-unter-intern-verzerrten-wechselkursen-11868775.html. (accessed 15 February 2014).

2. O. Blanchard and D. Leigh, 'Growth Forecast Errors and Fiscal Multipliers', IMF Working Paper 2013/01, available at http://www.imf.org/external/pubs/ft/wp/2013/wp1301.pdf (accessed 15 February 2014).

3. W. Streeck, *Gekaufte Zeit: Die vertagte Krise des demokratischen Kapitalismus*, Berlin Suhrkamp, 2013.

4. See R. Dahl, *Democracy and its Critics*, New Haven, Yale University Press, 1989.

5. R. Posner, *The Crisis of Capitalist Democracy*, Cambridge, Mass., Harvard University Press, 2010.

6. C. Deutschmann, 'Limits to financialization: sociological analyses of the financial crisis', *Archives Européennes de Sociologie*, 2011, vol. 52, pp. 347–389.

7. R. J. Gordon, 'Is US economic growth over? Faltering innovation confronts the six headwinds', Centre for Economic Policy Research, Policy Insight, No. 63/2012, available at http://www.cepr.org/pubs/PolicyInsights/PolicyInsight63.pdf (accessed 15 February 2016).

8. Streeck, *Gekaufte Zeit...*, p. 233.

9. J. S. Mill, *Principles of Political Economy*, Oxford, Oxford University Press, 2008 [1848].

10. Bertelsmann-Stiftung, 'Wirtschaftliche Folgen eines Euro-Austritts der südeuropäischen Mitgliedsstaate', *Policy Brief*, 2012/06, available at http://www.bertelsmann-stiftung.de/cps/rde/xbcr/SID-267920F9-4673CEFF/bst/xcms_bst_dms_36638_36639_2.pdf (accessed 15 February 2014).

11. Streeck, *Gekaufte Zeit...*,

12. See P. Bofinger, J. Habermas and J. Nida-Rümelin, 'Einspruch gegen die Fassadendemokratie', *Frankfurter Allgemeine Zeitung*, 3rd August 2012, available at http://www.faz.net/aktuell/feuilleton/debatten/europas-zukunft/kurswechsel-fuer-europa-einspruch-gegen-die-fassadendemokratie-11842820.html (accessed 15 February 2014).

13. Judgment of the German Federal Constitutional Court on the Treaty of Lisbon, of 30 June 2009, available at http://www.bverfg.de/entscheidungen/es20090630_2bve000208.html, especially par. 274–295. (accessed 29 January 2016).

14. S. Dullien, 'Eine Arbeitslosenversicherung für die Euro-Zone', SWP-Studie, 1/2008, available at http://mercury.ethz.ch/serviceengine/Files/ISN/117151/ipublicationdocument_singledocument/5c00a007-19ac-494c-aa45-2b53189f701a/de/2008_Unemployment_Insurance_D.pdf (accessed 29 January 2016).

15. See P. Van Parijs, 'No Eurozone without Euro-dividend', Unpublished manuscript, 2012, on file with the author.

Index

Lightning Source UK Ltd.
Milton Keynes UK
UKOW04f1208160816

280806UK00001B/9/P